■ Calvin and His Influence, 1509–2009

D1477085

Calvin and His Influence, 1509–2009

Irena Backus and
Philip Benedict

OXFORD
UNIVERSITY PRESS

OXFORD
UNIVERSITY PRESS

Oxford University Press, Inc., publishes works that further
Oxford University's objective of excellence
in research, scholarship, and education.

Oxford   New York
Auckland   Cape Town   Dar es Salaam   Hong Kong   Karachi
Kuala Lumpur   Madrid   Melbourne   Mexico City   Nairobi
New Delhi   Shanghai   Taipei   Toronto

With offices in
Argentina   Austria   Brazil   Chile   Czech Republic   France   Greece
Guatemala   Hungary   Italy   Japan   Poland   Portugal   Singapore
South Korea   Switzerland   Thailand   Turkey   Ukraine   Vietnam

Copyright © 2011 by Oxford University Press, Inc.

Published by Oxford University Press, Inc.
198 Madison Avenue, New York, New York 10016

www.oup.com

Oxford is a registered trademark of Oxford University Press

Library of Congress Cataloging-in-Publication Data
Calvin and his influence : 1509–2009 / [edited by] Irena Backus
and Philip Benedict.
p.   cm.
Includes bibliographical references and index.
ISBN 978-0-19-975184-6; 978-0-19-975185-3 (pbk.)
1. Calvin, Jean, 1509–1564—Influence.   I. Backus, Irena Dorota, 1950–
II. Benedict, Philip.
BX9418.C3615 2011
284'.2092—dc22   2010054110

9 8 7 6 5 4 3 2 1

Printed in the United States of America
on acid-free paper

CONTENTS

■ ACKNOWLEDGMENTS

The essays collected in this volume were originally prepared as plenary addresses to the international conference "Calvin and His Influence, 1509–2009," held in Geneva from May 24 to 27, 2009. This gathering was organized primarily by the University of Geneva's Institute for Reformation History, in close collaboration with the university's Faculty of Protestant Theology, the Association Calvin 2009, and the Musée Historique de la Réformation et Bibliothèque Calvinienne. Generous funding by the Hans Wilsdorf Foundation, the Schweizerische Reformationsstiftung, the Loterie Romande, the Fonds National Suisse de la Recherche Scientifique, the Société Académique de Genève, and the Commission Administrative of the University of Geneva ensured that the conference and its associated public events constituted a memorable occasion.

The members of the *comité scientifique* that developed the program and selected the speakers for the conference were fundamental to the conceptualization of this volume. In addition to the editors, this committee included Emidio Campi, François Dermange, André Encrevé, Olivier Labarthe, Bernard Lescaze, Maria-Cristina Pitassi, Herman Selderhuis, and Christoph Strohm. We thank them all, as we do the authors of the individual contributions for their engagement in the project and their alacrity in responding to our occasional queries and suggestions for revision.

The essays by Friedrich Wilhelm Graf, Olivier Millet, Heinz Schilling, and Herman Selderhuis were translated by Susanna Gebhardt and Irena Backus. Calvin Tams provided valuable editorial assistance in the preparation of the manuscript and translated the essays of André Encrevé and Max Engammare. Much appreciated financial support for this work came from the Schweizerische Reformationsstiftung.

Special thanks are due to Marianne Henchoz, Bernard Lescaze, and Maria-Cristina Pitassi for their exceptional engagement, wise counsel, and invaluable assistance at so many stages along the route from the initial discussions about the conference to the final completion of this volume.

■ CONTRIBUTORS

Irena Backus is professor at the Institute for Reformation History of the University of Geneva. Her many publications include *The Reformed Roots of the English New Testament: The Influence of Theodore Beza on the English New Testament* (1980), *Reformation Readings of the Apocalypse: Geneva, Zurich, and Wittenberg* (2000), *Historical Method and Confessional Identity in the Era of the Reformation (1378–1615)* (2003) and *Life Writing in Reformation Europe*: Lives *of Reformers by Friends, Disciples, and Foes* (2008).

David Bebbington, professor of history at the University of Stirling and past president of the Ecclesiastical History Society, has written widely about modern British religious history. Among his books are *Evangelicalism in Modern Britain: A History from the 1730s to the 1980s* (1989), *William Ewart Gladstone: Faith and Politics in Victorian Britain* (1993), and *The Mind of Gladstone: Religion, Homer, and Politics* (2004).

Philip Benedict is professor at the Institute for Reformation History of the University of Geneva. His publications include *Rouen during the Wars of Religion* (1981), *The Faith and Fortunes of France's Huguenots 1600–85* (2001), and *Christ's Churches Purely Reformed: A Social History of Calvinism* (2002).

Emidio Campi, director emeritus of the Institute for Swiss Reformation History of the University of Zurich, has written widely on Peter Martyr Vermigli, the Zurich Reformation, and the wider dissemination of the Reformed tradition. His most recent book is *Consensus Tigurinus: Die Einigung zwischen Heinrich Bullinger und Johannes Calvin über das Abendmahl. Werden, Wertung, Bedeutung* (2009).

John de Gruchy, theologian and historian, is professor emeritus of Christian Studies at the University of Cape Town and extraordinary professor at the University of Stellenbosch. In addition to major studies of Dietrich Bonhoeffer and the influential *Liberating Reformed Theology* (1991), he is the author of historical studies that at once reported on and contributed to the movement against apartheid in South Africa, notably *The Church Struggle in South Africa* (1979; 25th anniversary ed. 2004).

André Encrevé, emeritus professor of contemporary history at the Université de Paris XII, is one of the world's leading authorities on modern French Protestantism. His numerous books include *Les protestants en France de 1800 à nos jours* (1986), *L'expérience et la foi: Pensée et vie religieuse des huguenots au XIXe siècle* (2001), and *Le Second Empire* (2004).

Max Engammare, publisher and scholar, is the director of the Librairie Droz, editor of Calvin's sermons on Genesis and Isaiah, and author of *On Time: Punctuality and Discipline in Early Modern Calvinism* (orig. ed. 2004; English tr. 2009), as well as of important articles on Calvin's working methods and on his knowledge of the Bible.

Friedrich Wilhelm Graf, professor of theology at Ludwig-Maximilians-Universität, Munich, has written some fifteen books on Ernst Troeltsch, German theology in the nineteenth and twentieth centuries, and the history of recent Protestantism, including most recently *Der Protestantismus: Geschichte und Gegenwart* (2006; 2nd ed., 2010) and *Wiederkehr der Götter: Religion in der modernen Kultur* (2007).

Harro M. Höpfl, research professor in the Essex Business School, University of Essex, is the author of *The Christian Polity of John Calvin* (1982) and *Jesuit Political Thought* (2004).

Cornelis van der Kooi is professor of systematic theology and director of the Center for Evangelical and Reformation Theology at the Free University of Amsterdam. His books include *Anfängliche Theologie: Der Denkweg des jungen Karl Barth (1909–1927)* (1987), *Kuyper Reconsidered: Aspects of His Life and Work* (1999), and *As in a Mirror. John Calvin and Karl Barth on Knowing God* (2005).

Diarmaid MacCulloch is professor of ecclesiastical history at the University of Oxford. His publications have progressively widened in scope from *Suffolk and the Tudors: Politics and Religion in an English County* (1986) and *Thomas Cranmer: A Life* (1996) to *Reformation: Europe's House Divided 1490–1700* (2004) and *A History of Christianity: The First Three Thousand Years* (2010).

Olivier Millet, professor of French literature at the University of Paris IV-Sorbonne, has edited many works of Calvin and written the pioneering *Calvin et la dynamique de la parole: Etude de rhétorique réformée* (1992).

Richard A. Muller is professor of historical theology at Calvin Theological Seminary in Grand Rapids, Michigan and the author of numerous studies of Reformed theology from Calvin to Arminius, including *Post-Reformation Reformed Dogmatics* (4 vols., 1987–2003), *The Unaccomodated Calvin: Studies in the Foundation of a Theological Tradition* (2000), and *After Calvin: Studies in the Development of a Theological Tradition* (2003).

William Naphy is professor of history at the University of Aberdeen. Among his books are *Calvin and the Consolidation of the Genevan Reformation* (1994), *Plagues, Poisons and Potions: Plague Spreading Conspiracies in the Western Alps, c. 1530–1640* (2002) and *Born to be Gay: A History of Homosexuality* (2004).

Heinz Schilling is emeritus professor of modern history at the Humboldt University of Berlin. His many books include *Konfessionskonflikt und Staatsbildung:*

Eine Fallstudie über das Verhältnis von religiösem und sozialem Wandel in der Frühneuzeit am Beispiel der Grafschaft Lippe (1981), *Civic Calvinism in Northwestern Germany and the Netherlands* (1991), and *Konfessionalisierung und Staatsinteressen: Internationale Beziehungen 1559–1660* (2007). His essays and edited volumes on the theme of confessionalization have shaped much of the recent agenda of international Reformation research.

Herman Selderhuis is professor of church history at the Theological University of Appeldoorn and general secretary of the International Calvin Congress. He is the author of *Calvin's Theology of the Psalms* (2007) and editor of the *Calvin Handbook* (2009).

Ernestine van der Wall is professor of church history at the University of Leiden. Her interests focus on millenarianism, on the relationship between religion and the Enlightenment as well as on global religious liberalism and modernism. Her books include: *De mystieke chiliast Petrus Serrarius (1600–1669) en zijn wereld (1987)* and *Socrates in de hemel?* (2000). She has edited volumes on *Jewish-Christian Relations in the 17th Century* (1988) and *Religie en Verlichting in Nederland 1650–1850* (2007).

ABBREVIATIONS

AEG	Archives d'État de Genève
ARG	*Archiv für Reformationsgeschichte*
BC	*Bibliotheca calviniana*, 3 vols., ed. Rodolphe Peter and Jean-François Gilmont (Geneva: Droz, 1991–2000)
BHR	*Bibliothèque d'Humanisme et Renaissance*
BSHAG	*Bulletin de la Société d'Histoire et d'Archéologie de Genève*
BSHPF	*Bulletin de la Société de l'Histoire du Protestantisme Français*
Calv. Opp.	*Ioannis Calvini opera omnia*, 59 vols, ed. G. Baum, E. Cunitz, and E. Reuss (Braunschweig: C. A. Schwetschke, 1863–1900)
Calv. Opp. R, series 2	Thomas H. L. Parker, David C. Parker, eds., *Iohannis Calvini Opera Omnia : Denuo recognita Series 2* (Geneva: Droz, 1992–)
CTJ	*Calvin Theological Journal*
HBBibl	Heinrich Bullinger, *Werke, 1. Abt.: Bibliographie*, 3 vols., ed. Joachim Staedtke et al. (Zurich: Theologischer Verlag, 1972–2004)
HBThS	Heinrich Bullinger, *Werke, 3. Abt. : Theologische Schriften*, ed. Hans-Georg vom Berg et al. vol . 1- (Zurich: Theologischer Verlag, 1983–)
HThR	*Harvard Theological Review*
Inst.	*Institutio christianae religionis/Institutes of Christian Religion*
LB	*Opera Omnia Desiderii Erasmi Roterodami* (Leiden: Peter vander Aa, 1703–1706)
NAKG	*Nederlands Archief voor Kerkgeschiedenis*
OS	*Ioannis Calvini Opera selecta.* 5 vols., ed. P. Barth and G. Niesel (Munich: Kaiser, 1926–36)
P&T	*Peace and Truth*
RGG⁴	*Religion in Geschichte und Gegenwart*, 4th ed., 8 vols., ed. Hans Dieter et al. (Tübingen: Mohr Siebeck, 1998–2007)
RHPhR	*Revue d'Histoire et de Philosophie Religieuse*
SCJ	*Sixteenth Century Journal*
ThLZ	*Theologische Literaturzeitung*
WA.	*Martin Luthers Werke, kritische Gesamtausgabe* (Weimar: Hermann Böhlau's Nachfolger, 1883–)

■ Calvin and His Influence, 1509–2009

Introduction

IRENA BACKUS and PHILIP BENEDICT

As the numerous congresses, commemorations, and publications of 2009 will have reminded many, John Calvin was born just over five hundred years ago, in 1509. Before attaining the age of thirty, he published the first version of his *Institutes of the Christian Religion*, the cornerstone of a theological oeuvre that he would enlarge for the rest of his life and that would be read for centuries to come. From 1536 to 1538 and then again from 1541 to his death in 1564, he was the driving force of a determined effort to mold Geneva into a model Christian community, an effort that many pious contemporaries judged to be exceptionally successful, and that he always understood as a part of a larger mission to make the city a lamp unto nations lighting the way to a reform of all Christendom. If his efforts did not reform all Christendom, churches that incorporated elements of his theology or of the liturgy and church institutions that he molded in Geneva soon took shape in France, the Low Countries, Scotland, England, Poland, Hungary, and parts of Germany, sometimes with his direct guidance and encouragement, in other instances through indirect chains of influence. Over the next four centuries, these Reformed churches and their offshoots would spread around the globe.

This collection of essays seeks to illuminate the nature and extent of Calvin's influence across the half millennium since his birth, chiefly within Europe, although with attention as well to the highly revealing South African case.[1] The story of Calvin's changing influence and image across the centuries constitutes an important chapter in the history of post-Reformation Protantism—indeed in the history of modern Western and, in the twentieth century, global culture. Despite its importance, the intellectual, cultural, and religious dimensions of this story have been badly neglected, even while Calvin's influence, or supposed influence, on modern politics and modern capitalism has been studied to the point of exhaustion. Recent work suggests that this is beginning to change and that interest in the cultural and intellectual aspects of this story is increasing.[2]

To trace Calvin's influence, one must obviously start with the man himself and with his writings. That is what the essays in the first half of this volume do. All seek to identify features of his personality, work, thought, and writings that explain their exceptional influence both in his lifetime and across the ages. The essays in the second half of the book then look at how Calvin's theology has been appropriated, modified, or ignored in a number of different times and places from the generations following his death to the present. These essays pay attention not only to the manner in which Calvin was perceived within different churches of the Reformed family, to the availability of his works, and to the ways in which these were understood and appropriated. Several essays explore important aspects of the history of the concept of Calvinism, thus permitting a better understanding of the relationship between

Calvin himself and later movements identified as Calvinist. Consideration is also given to the political outlook of those who can be called Calvinist, enabling an assessment of how far later Calvinism diverged from Calvin in this domain. This volume devotes little attention to Calvin's supposed contributions to modern capitalism or to modernity more generally. That is because, as we will explain at greater length later in the introduction, we are convinced that the past several generations of research have rendered implausible the grand theories that once confidently ascribed a starring role to the man or the tradition here. To have devoted too much attention to these themes would have been to take readers down blind alleys.

This introduction aims to highlight some of the central problems involved in assessing Calvin's influence across the centuries, to provide necessary background to the aspects of this subject covered in the following essays, and to suggest further approaches that we think might be helpful in addressing this topic. The story of Calvin's influence, readers will discover, is not the same thing as the history of Calvinism. All who claimed to be Calvinists were not necessarily strict followers of Calvin's own views, and some who were dedicated to keeping alive his ideas and practices sought to avoid the label "Calvinist." We first offer a brief history of the terms "Calvinist" and "Calvinism" as a way of addressing some of the fundamental semantic issues pertinent to our problem. After next exploring features of Calvin's thought and action that complement the information found in the subsequent chapters and that constitute necessary background for understanding both his influence in his lifetime and his image in subsequent centuries, we then look at the shifts involved in the transmission of Calvin's ideas to the immediately subsequent generations, both taking up once again a classic problem in Calvin studies and calling attention to a suggested new approach that we believe may be more fruitful. A final section then briefly traces the rise and fall of the grand theories of Calvinism's modernizing consequences both to illustrate the complexities of the issue of Calvin's longer-term influence and so that readers will understand why these themes are not more extensively discussed in the following chapters.

Neither the introduction nor the volume as a whole claims to exhaust the vast topic of Calvin's changing image and influence across the centuries. Our goal throughout has simply been to identify and to explore some central aspects of Calvin and his *Nachleben* and to draw readers' attention to future possibilities of studying the reformer and his legacies in an interdisciplinary, nonconfessional framework. Curiously, the nonpartisan and nonhostile study of Calvin is a recent development, and the problems of bridging the gap between theologically oriented Calvin specialists on the one hand and political, social, intellectual, legal, and literary historians on the other hand still haunt much of Calvin research nowadays. Why that should be is yet another interesting chapter of the larger story that merits more attention than we have been able to offer here.

■ "CALVINISM": THE HISTORY OF A CONCEPT AND WHY IT MATTERS

Tracing the influence of a charismatic religious leader of global significance is never simple. In the case of John Calvin, the enterprise is particularly complicated because his name soon came to be associated with an eponymous "ism" that has meant different things in different contexts and whose exact debt to its putative founder has been much debated. The problem of Calvin's influence cannot be clearly addressed without some preliminary attention to the history and multiple meanings of the word "Calvinism" and its cognates.

If Calvin's birth can be dated with confidence to July 10, 1509, it appears that the terms "Calvinism" and "Calvinist" were first used during the late 1540s and early 1550s, a sign that it was at this moment that Calvin first began to be perceived as having articulated and won a significant number of people over to a distinctive point of view. Tellingly, the two words emerged within a few years of one another amid different polemics, and in each context they denoted something different. Friedrich Wilhelm Graf's chapter in this volume, an important reflection about the term "Calvinism" and its history, identifies what appears to be its earliest recorded appearance. In a letter of 1548 that Calvin wrote to Heinrich Bullinger, he informed his Zurich counterpart that after dispute had broken out in Lausanne between supporters of his distinctive mediating theology of the Eucharist and those defending Zwingli's symbolic understanding of the rite, the leaders of the former group had been admonished by the Bernese authorities to "be done with their Calvinism and their Bucerianism."[3] Here, Calvinism designated a distinctive Eucharistic theology that made room for Christ's spiritual presence in the Lord's Supper. "Calvinist" seems first to have been used in 1553–1554, in the context of the Servetus affair, by David Joris and Sebastian Castellio, two independent-minded evangelicals who opposed the use of force to punish false belief. In some of their uses of the word it simply designated one religious party among several: Calvinists stood in contrast to papists, Lutherans, Anabaptists, and Zwinglians. On one occasion Castellio used the word to designate the Calvinists as strenuous persecutors of those who disagreed with them. On another he equated Calvinists with partisans of the doctrine of predestination, a usage that recalled Calvin's recent dispute with Jerome Bolsec over that question.[4]

Still further meanings came to be attached to the term as its use proliferated in subsequent decades. German Lutherans used "Calvinist" to designate those who denied Christ's physical presence in the Eucharistic elements. As the German Reformed theologians did not make a sharp distinction at the time between Zwingli's and Calvin's doctrine of the Eucharist, this increased the ambiguity of the term. French Catholics pinned the label on all of the institutions, practices, and members of the Reformed churches, or "secte calvinique." After the disputes over predestination that would lead to the Arminian controversy heated up within Reformed Protestantism, Calvinism became synonymous in many circles with the doctrine of the absolute decree of God preordaining some to salvation and others to damnation for all eternity in stronger terms than those used in the Canons of the Synod of Dort. This association has endured to the present in the English-speaking world. The *Oxford English Dictionary* currently defines "Calvinism" as "the doctrines of John Calvin the Protestant Reformer (1509–1564), particularly his theological doctrines on grace, in which Calvinism is opposed to Arminianism." *Webster's New Twentieth Century Dictionary* adopts a virtually identical definition: "the religious system of John Calvin (1509–1564), French Protestant reformer. The distinguishing doctrines of this system are predestination, particular redemption, total depravity, irresistible grace, and the certain perseverance of the saints."

The first two centuries of the history of the words "Calvinism" and "Calvinist" thus already show us three reasons why historians who wish to trace Calvin's influence across the centuries face a difficult task and must avoid simply conflating Calvin and Calvinism. First, Calvin was not a man of a single idea, even if one definition of the term Calvinism that subsequently came to be widely adopted might suggest otherwise. Second, what was designated or understood to be Calvinism in different times and places changed. Third, one of the most debated questions in recent Calvin studies, and one to which we return later in the introduction, concerns whether the form of Calvinism encapsulated in the modern English-language dictionary definitions that oppose it to Arminianism and summarize it in five points was true or not to Calvin's own thinking.

Complicating the issue still further is the fact that for several centuries after Calvin's death, those who were his most direct theological and institutional heirs resisted the label of Calvinist, just as virtually all sixteenth- and seventeenth-century Christians rejected any name associating their views with the legacy of a single, fallible individual. "Innovation" in theology is a disparaging term implying a heretical departure from the age-old religion. To identify any point of view with the outlook of a single individual was to suggest that it was such a departure. Hence, terms such as "Mennonite," "Calvinist," "Arminian," or "Jansenist," in this era, were almost always deployed by enemies of the groups or currents so designated. To trace Calvin's actual influence in the first centuries after his death, one cannot look for those who quote him most ostentatiously or claim his mantle. One must track echoes of his distinctive doctrinal formulations through weighty volumes of academic theology and determine the place of his works in private libraries and theological curricula. Historians have just begun to do this, as Richard Muller's contribution to this volume shows.

From the sixteenth century through the eighteenth century, the label of choice for those who today are often called Calvinists was "Reformed," but here we encounter still more complications in the matter of tracing Calvin's influence. Not only was he not a man of a single idea; his theology, like all religious teaching that has claims to orthodoxy, was anything but totally original. To "reform" the church meant to Calvin and other reformers to restitute it to its origins and to purify it of what they saw as later deviations from and corruptions of the apostolic teaching. As Diarmaid MacCulloch writes in his chapter, "The cool, measured Latin and French prose of the *Institutes,* the commentaries, and the surviving sermons are a precise, careful distillation of the Western Christian tradition as it had emerged in the fifth century on the back of Chalcedon and the teachings of Augustine." If Lutheran hostility to Calvin's Eucharistic teachings prevented this distillation from becoming the common beverage of all of magisterial Protestantism, and if Calvin's own aggressive hostility to the doctrines of Rome guaranteed its rejection by the defenders and clarifiers of Roman Catholic orthodoxy, just among the Reformed Protestants Calvin's influence is hard to titrate out, for he was not the founder of the Reformed tradition—that honor belongs, of course, to Ulrich Zwingli—and he was just one of several important theologians of the second generation that subsequent expositors regarded with respect and admiration, the most influential but still just one of several, alongside Heinrich Bullinger, Peter Martyr Vermigli, and Wolfgang Musculus. They too played an honorable role in disseminating and defending the Reformed tradition during Calvin's lifetime and after. In fact, although Calvin was the object of many portraits from the sixteenth century to the twentieth century, the Calvinist Reformation was most commonly depicted as a collective phenomenon. One frequently reproduced and often modified seventeenth-century image showed a dozen reformers including Philipp Melanchthon, Calvin, Guillaume Farel, Bullinger, and occasionally even Martin Luther sitting around a table, explicating scripture. The 1909 Genevan International Reformation Monument set Farel, John Knox, and Theodore Beza alongside Calvin in the center of the monument while relegating Luther and all traces of the Zurich Reformation to the margins.

From some point around 1800 onward, individuals or groups began to self-identify as Calvinists, but this does not simplify the problem of tracing Calvin's influence, since these self-styled Calvinists may not actually have been following Calvin's ideas. The first organized group to embrace this label of which the contributors to this volume have found a trace is the Calvinist Society founded in the first decade of the nineteenth century in the Cape Colony. This was an association of Scottish soldiers from the Highland regiments sent to South Africa that met for prayer and Bible worship. Composed of both Presbyterians and Congregationalists, it was bound together by its members' shared dislike of the ideas on grace preached by the Methodist chaplains who accompanied the troops. In other words, "Calvinist" here signaled the men's allegiance to the predestinarian wing of the British Protestant tradition, which brings one back to the debated issue of the fidelity of this tradition to Calvin's own thought. As for the most important movement of the late nineteenth century and early twentieth century to embrace the Calvinist designation, that which took shape in the Netherlands around Abraham Kuyper, Cornelis van der Kooi explains that Kuyper explicitly understood Calvinism as a steadily maturing set of principles that had only revealed its full implications over the course of the centuries after Calvin's death. Genuine Calvinism was not to be deduced chiefly from Calvin's writings. In both of these cases, then, the open embrace of the label "Calvinist" meant at most a partial rededication to Calvin's own ideas.

If self-identification as Calvinist did not necessarily imply intense, direct engagement with Calvin's own writings or rigid fidelity to his ideas, the fact that groups now began to speak actively of themselves as Calvinists was nonetheless an important turning point in the history of the reception and influence of Calvin's own ideas, for it raised his profile relative to other early Reformed theologians, encouraged the republication of his works, and promoted their canonization in theological curricula. Furthermore, by extolling the virtues of Calvinism while constructing a distinctive historicist version of the "ism," Kuyper's neo-Calvinism opened itself to challenge by others who appealed directly to the full range of Calvin's writings to articulate rival visions of true Calvinism, as John de Gruchy's essay on the later twentieth-century disputes about apartheid within South Africa's Reformed churches shows. The ultimate effect of the embrace of the Calvinist label may thus have been to give Calvin's writings more authority within some Reformed churches in the twentieth century, or at least a different kind of authority, than they had in any previous century.

Still more investigation of what those who actively called themselves Calvinists meant when they did so and of how the terms "Calvinist" and "Calvinism" evolved over the centuries needs to be a priority for further research. From this brief sketch of the history of these concepts, it should nonetheless be evident that the *Begriffsgechichte* of "Calvinism" is an essential component of the story of Calvin's image and influence, but that this story cannot simply be conflated with the history of Calvinism, and that careful attention has to be paid to how this last term is used in all discussions of this subject.

■ CALVIN IN HIS LIFETIME

One of the best of the many biographies published to coincide with Calvin's five hundredth birthday—one that is generally sympathetic to him—begins:

> John Calvin was the greatest Protestant reformer of the sixteenth century, brilliant, visionary and iconic. The superior force of his mind was evident in all that he did. He was also ruthless, and an outstanding hater. Among those things he hated were the Roman Church, Anabaptists and those people who, he believed, only faint-heartedly embraced the Gospel and tainted themselves with idolatry. He saw himself as an instrument of God, and as a prophet of the church he brooked no rivals. He never felt he had encountered an intellectual equal and he was probably correct. To achieve what he believed to be right, he would do virtually anything. Although not physically imposing, he dominated others and knew how to manipulate relationships. He intimidated, bullied and humiliated, saving some of his worst conduct for his friends. Yet as he lay dying they gathered around the bed distraught with grief. There would be no other like him.[5]

The portrait captures the paradoxes of both Calvin's personality and his influence. During his lifetime, he was an inspirational, even mythic, figure to many, especially to those who first encountered him through his limpid, inspiring words. A Catholic controversialist who had seen many of his schoolmates at Toulouse drawn to the Reformed faith in their youth recalled how they dropped everything and set forth for Geneva to hear Calvin; as they approached Geneva, they felt all of the enthusiasm that the crusaders had felt on reaching the Holy Land.[6] This is all the more intriguing as Calvin had no formal theological credentials, in contrast with other reformers such as Luther or Zwingli. He had studied law. Such theology as he had was self-taught, which is what may account to some extent for his massive blunder over the doctrine of the Trinity in 1537–1538, emphasized in the essay of Diarmaid MacCulloch, on which his opponents were quick to seize and which explains his clinging to the Nicene terminology thereafter.[7] Even though Melanchthon declared him a fully fledged theologian after his participation in the Colloquy of Worms in 1539, he remained vulnerable all his life to accusations of imposture and self-aggrandizement.[8] Despite this—or perhaps in part because of it—he managed to produce an original synthesis of Western Christian tradition of such universal appeal that it is legitimate to ask ourselves, as McCulloch does, whether he can be viewed as the fifth Doctor of the Church.

While his writings proved extremely attractive both to contemporaries and to subsequent generations of readers, face-to-face Calvin was a difficult, tightly wound individual. The negative image of him that took shape during his lifetime and that has endured ever since was created principally not by distant Catholic adversaries, but by erstwhile evangelical allies who dared to disagree with him and fell afoul of his wrath. Yet the same features that made him a difficult individual—his drive, his irascibility, his anxiety that the least concession to his opponents would open the door to rampant disorder, his awesome confidence that he was serving God's will in all he did—made him a formidable figure in the close quarters of a sixteenth-century city.

The contributions to this volume of Herman Selderhuis, Diarmaid MacCulloch, Harro Höpfl, Max Engammare, and Olivier Millet all explore aspects of Calvin the man, the author, and the theologian that exerted a crucial impact on his influence and reception. To the features of his personality and writings that they highlight, we might add another: his brevity. Calvin said relatively little about many issues. He merely pointed the reader in the general direction of his thinking. Although his pointers are generally very clear—no one would consider Calvin an apostle of free will or toleration—his brevity made his thought endlessly adaptable to all sorts of positions in continuity with his own minimalist programmatic statements. On certain topics, moreover, he was torn between two points of view. This is the case most notably with regard to civil authority. On the one hand, eager to establish that the true evangelical religion was not naturally seditious as its enemies charged, he insisted strongly that Christian believers were duty bound to obey the duly constituted authorities. On the other hand, he allowed for the possibility of resistance to unjust orders where lesser magistrates were constitutionally empowered to do this. Since he also insisted that believers should withdraw from the polluted worship of the Church of Rome, and since, through his ecclesiology, he provided a road map for setting up properly evangelical churches, his writings could both appeal to princes yet also inspire the foundation of churches in defiance of hostile authorities and even legitimize under certain circumstances the armed resistance of their members to maintain the form of worship that God had commanded. Churches inspired by his ideas would spread both through princely reformations and revolutionary reformations.

Calvin's influence flowed as much from his work as a civic reformer in Geneva and from his sense of mission as a prophet to all nations as it did from his published writings. One of the skills that he brought to Geneva was his lawyer's training. Because lawyers were scarce in the city after those around the bishop's court had been driven out at the Reformation, he was regularly consulted for advice about the drafting of laws.[9] William Naphy's contribution to this volume examines the intersection of the civil and ecclesiastical institutions forged during his stay there. This was an aspect of his work that later citizens of Geneva would not forget. "Those who think of Calvin only as a theologian underestimate the extent of genius. The drafting of our wise edicts, to which he significantly contributed, does him as much honor as his *Institutes*," Rousseau wrote in the chapter of *The Social Contract* dedicated to "the legislator."[10]

Calvin's signal achievement as an urban reformer was to secure the establishment of the largely independent system of church discipline with full powers of excommunication that other reformers such as Johannes Oecolampadius and Bucer had previously sought elsewhere with less success, and to use this along with the other means of persuasion at his disposal to cajole, shame, and browbeat Geneva into a "godly city." This required more than two decades of struggle against powerful opposition. Calvin's first stay in Geneva lasted just two years and ended when he and his fellow ministers were banished for their insistence that they, not the magistrates, had the authority to determine all questions of worship. After he returned to the city in 1541, he showed himself suppler about recognizing the ultimate authority of the civic officials, notably in the ordination of ministers. He also let himself be courted for months before consenting to come back, and he used the period of negotiations to ensure the prompt acceptance (after the Council had added some amendments) of the new ecclesiastical ordinances that he drafted. These incorporated the four-fold ministry and consistorial discipline, two features that he had come to see as essential elements of any properly ordered church during his stay alongside Martin Bucer in Strasbourg. The document was diplomatically vague about who had the ultimate say about excommunication.[11] "Les enfants de Genève" (children of Geneva), a local party hostile to Calvin and his fellow ministers, soon riposted with Ami Perrin, captain of the city's militia, at their head. This upsurge was sparked off by backlash at ministerial and consistorial intervention in personal and family affairs and by resentment of the growing numbers of religious refugees, who drove up the price of bread and acted as if they were morally and socially superior to the Genevans. As complaints, insults, and street demonstrations multiplied, the situation appeared so alarming to Calvin that he did not dare leave town for a few days to attend a friend's wedding in January 1553. The note of apology that he wrote reveals a great deal about how he viewed his opponents and what he thought was at stake:

> I would gladly have been present at your marriage, had I not been detained at home by the wickedness of those whose madness does not cease to bring destruction upon themselves and the community.... They have never exhibited more unbridled licentiousness. I shall say nothing of their mischievous plots for the destruction of the faith, of their gross contempt of God, of their impious conspiracies for the scattering of the Church, of the foul Epicurianism of their whole life.... The entire republic is at present in disorder, and they are striving to root up the established order of things.[12]

The crisis reached a boiling point a month later with the election of three of "Geneva's children" to the City's small Council and of Perrin himself to one of the posts of syndic. At this low point for the reformer, another "child of Geneva," Philibert Berthelier, who had been repeatedly barred from communion by the Consistory for a variety of forms of misbehavior including belching in front of Calvin, appealed to the Council for reinstatement to the Lord's Supper. After Calvin threatened to leave if the right of the church to control access to the Supper was disregarded, Berthelier was formally readmitted but told not to show up for the Lord's Supper "so as not to cause offense," advice he followed. Calvin stayed, and the victory of his partisans in the city elections of 1555 soon reinforced his power. Several members of the "children of Geneva" party were removed from the Council of Two Hundred and large numbers of recent French refugees were granted bourgeois status, entitling them to vote. The "children of Geneva" protested and caused a miniriot in the city in May 1555, whereupon Calvin backed merciless repression of those implicated, who were accused of a conspiracy to "overturn ecclesiastical discipline and the holy Reformation." Twelve rival leaders were arrested and interrogated under torture. The charge of conspiracy was confirmed, and twelve death sentences were passed. Four were carried out, while the remaining eight men (Perrin among them) took refuge in Bernese territory. In the years that followed, the intensity of consistorial surveillance intensified, those suspended from communion were required by the magistrates to show themselves repentant and seek reconciliation with the church within a given period of time or face banishment, and the civic morals ordinances were reinforced. Everybody went to the sermons now, even the hypocrites, one chronicler recorded.[13]

While many aspects of this struggle are narrated in the nineteenth-century history of Amédée Roget and the more recent work of William Naphy, we still lack a convincing analysis of which of the tools that Calvin used to sway public opinion and bring pressure to bear on the civic magistrates were particularly important to his success as a political actor in a city in which he had no formal power, although a great deal of moral authority. Among these tools were his sermons, in which he did not hesitate to criticize misbehavior and urge citizens to choose God-fearing magistrates; his ample correspondence with his pastoral counterparts elsewhere that enabled him to rally their support in times of crisis; and well-timed threats of resignation, which would have left the city without the most able defender of its ecclesiastical order. Whatever the causes of his triumph, the consequences are undoubted. By Calvin's death, Geneva was a very different city from what it had been when he first arrived. Herman Selderhuis's chapter recapitulates many of the key transformations of its demography and economy: the population that more than doubled; the new industries introduced by the many immigrants; the growth of a printing trade that became a fundamental instrument for the diffusion of Calvin's writings; the foundation in 1559 of the Academy, which attracted students preparing for the ministry from a wide area. Most often commented upon by contemporaries was the transformation of manners and morals achieved by the Consistory in increasingly close collaboration with the secular magistrates.[14] Central to the international dissemination of Calvin's influence would be both the city's new role as a place from which books and men went out into Europe carrying his ideas, and the prestige bestowed on its institutions by its image as a godly city.

If Calvin devoted so much of his energy to the struggle to remake Geneva, it was not because of any particular attachment to the city, which he considered until his death a "perverse and unhappy nation" of which he only became a legal citizen in 1559. His horizons were international. His primary identification was with his native France. During his years in Strasbourg from 1538 to 1541, he took part alongside Bucer and Melanchthon in the colloquies of Frankfurt, Hagenau, Worms, and Regensburg, where he was confronted by the high Roman clergy such as the cardinals Antoine Perrenot de Granvelle and Gasparo Contarini. After holding his own in the debates, he considered himself capable of speaking out on the largest ecclesiastical questions of the day and of addressing treatises to the continent's most powerful crowned heads. Among his later occasional works were an exhortation to Charles V on the necessity of reforming the church, a reply to the decisions of the Council of Trent, and a critique of the Interim imposed on the Holy Roman Empire after the first phase of the Schmalkaldic War. He wrote letters to rulers and leading aristocrats from Ferrara to England to Poland and, from 1555 onward, encouraged and partially directed the foundation of clandestine Reformed churches in France, Savoy, and the Low Countries.

A question that has divided those who have written about Calvin is that of just how flexible he was in seeking theological allies or approving a range of doctrines or practices within the churches that looked to him for guidance. A powerful negative image depicts him as rigid and narrowly intolerant. Reacting against this image, a number of historians in the past generations have emphasized his openness to different views and practices.[15] The truth lies somewhere in the middle. In his dealings with the Swiss cities that each had their own theological traditions and whose ecclesiastical and military alliance was essential for Geneva, especially in his dealings with the Zurich theologians, he was able to swallow his disappointment over their differences of opinion from him and their apparent disrespect for Luther, whom he always admired and whose views he felt should be taken into account, and hammer out a compromise position on the Eucharist, the *Consensus Tigurinus*, that created a firm alliance between the churches of Zurich and Geneva and that Bern would also accept some years later.[16] In his correspondence with other churches, he also showed himself flexible about issues of ecclesiastical structure and liturgy, warning other churches not to make a Jerusalem of Geneva and to avoid schism over inessential matters of worship.[17] Direct theological challenges in his own backyard were another matter. The most striking case in point is the Bolsec affair.[18] Jerome Bolsec was a French-born Carmelite who threw off the cowl and fled to the Bernese-controlled Chablais, where he worked as a doctor and came into Geneva from time to time to attend the weekly sessions of biblical instruction and exegesis there known as Congrégations. At one of these gatherings in May 1551 he criticized Calvin's doctrine of predestination, which another minister was expounding that day; for this he was privately reprimanded and corrected. When he repeated and expanded his opinion at a second congrégation five months later, Calvin rebutted him with such vehemence that he was arrested on the spot by a judicial official present and subsequently put on trial for blasphemy at Calvin's and Farel's urging. Bolsec's view of faith as guaranteeing assurance of salvation was not far outside the mainstream of Reformed opinion, and as the Geneva authorities discovered when they asked the leading churches of Protestant Switzerland for their opinion about the gravity of his errors, neither Bern nor Zurich were prepared to condemn his statements. Nonetheless, Geneva's Council sentenced him to perpetual banishment. The punishment could have been death had it not been for Bern's intervention. Bolsec was far from the only evangelical to come to Geneva or its environs to escape persecution, only to fall out with Calvin when it emerged that their views were not identical, and to be obliged to move on.[19]

Calvin's conflict-ridden relations with those who disagreed with him is fundamental to the story of his subsequent image and influence, since no work defamed him more thoroughly and powerfully than the hostile biography that Bolsec wrote about him a quarter century after being banished from Geneva, and since no episode from his life would be more enduringly remembered and more frequently cited to his discredit than the trial and execution of Michael Servetus. Bolsec's 1577 *Life* of Calvin depicted the reformer as a cruel dictator whose father had been a blasphemer and who himself was convicted and branded for the crime of sodomy during his youth, before later establishing dubious relationships with most of Geneva's married women. Translated into Latin, German, Dutch, and Polish, this work went through numerous editions in the sixteenth and seventeenth centuries, and was republished in France as late as 1875.[20] Another of those who first attacked Calvin in print was his erstwhile secretary François Bauduin, who left Geneva after a bitter falling out with the reformer and became a professor of law at Heidelberg and (after returning to Catholicism) Angers. The man who spoke out most strongly against the execution of Servetus, Sebastian Castellio, had lived with Calvin briefly in Strasbourg and headed Geneva's secondary school (*Collège*), before disagreements over questions of biblical interpretation led Calvin to oppose his candidacy for the ministry and Castellio to leave Geneva for Basel.

The Servetus affair was of course the most notorious episode of all in the history of Calvin's relations with his theological opponents. Much ink has been spilled over the question of Calvin's personal implication in the trial and execution of the Spanish doctor. Calvin's modern apologists have repeated that he was only partaking of the errors of his time in believing that the secular authorities had the duty to punish heresy, that he intervened after Servetus's conviction in favor of a more lenient punishment, and that every other state-supported Western European church would have been just as prepared to support the execution of a man whose radical questioning of the Trinity shocked contemporary Christians of all theological orientations. The first claim is exaggerated, as Ernestine van der Wall observes in her contribution. Castellio's protest against Servetus's execution shows that sixteenth-century minds could think otherwise. The second assertion is true but incomplete. After Servetus's condemnation Calvin urged (in vain) that he be given the grace of being strangled before his body was committed to the flames, but prior to that he played a central role in seeing to it that Servetus was brought to trial and convicted. Servetus was, in fact, tried twice, once by a civil tribunal in Vienne under the antiheretical legislation of Henry II, where he was burnt in effigy after escaping from prison, and the second time in Geneva, where he was burnt in the flesh after his condemnation by the Small Council. Guillaume de Trie, who denounced Servetus to the Dominican Matthieu Ory in Vienne, where Servetus was living and practicing medicine under the pseudonym of Michel de Villeneuve, was close to Calvin, who had been in prior correspondence with Servetus, knew his views, and was vigorously opposed to them. Calvin then provided the French tribunal some of the letters between them that were crucial to proving Servetus's guilt. The civil plaintiff against Servetus in the second trial in Geneva was Calvin's secretary, Nicolas de La Fontaine. Calvin himself repeatedly attempted to make Servetus retract. Such exchanges between the two as are still extant show a radical difference of position and a great deal of personal dislike.[21] As for the final claim that all other magisterial reformers or Catholic theologians would have been just as happy to put Servetus to death, this contains the most truth. Unlike in the Bolsec affair, the Swiss cities and their theologians all encouraged the Genevan authorities to show no mercy to Servetus. More people were undoubtedly put to death for their beliefs in other parts of Europe, including Zwingli's Zurich, than in Calvin's Geneva. Yet since Geneva seemed a beacon of hope and refuge for religious dissidents during the 1540s and 1550s, and since Calvin, himself a refugee from persecution, did all in his power to rally international support for freedom of worship for the Reformed in France, to find that he too insisted upon the obligation of magistrates to punish heresy, and that he invoked the government's aid to have silenced or to banish those who parted company from him on theological questions, was particularly disillusioning for those who had previously suffered persecution in Catholic lands and now found Geneva no more welcoming. The protests of Castellio and a few other like-minded dissidents not only meant, as we have already seen, that one of the earliest uses of the term "Calvinist" would be as a synonym for those who favored the execution of religious dissenters. Once Castellio's writings about this affair were republished and translated in the Low Countries between 1578 and 1618, they ensured that this instance of Protestant intolerance would be forever recalled. In the Dutch Republic of the eighteenth century, as van der Wall's chapter shows, and in the Europe of the Enlightenment more generally, the Servetus affair was an aspect of Calvin's biography that few who wrote about him could ignore. In the twentieth century, the Viennese intellectual Stefan Zweig returned to the subject under the shadow of Nazism in his 1936 *Castellio gegen Calvin oder ein Gewissen gegen die Gewalt* (Castellio against Calvin or conscience against force), depicting Calvin as a dictator bent on crushing all forms of free expression, with enough force that church groups planning the Calvin commemoration of 2009 still worried about how to counter the book.[22]

■ CALVIN AGAINST THE CALVINISTS? THE PROBLEM OF PREDESTINATION

If the Servetus affair is not the first thing that most people associate with Calvin, then the doctrine of predestination is. Readers will discover, however, that predestination receives little extended examination in the essays that follow. Is this because the doctrine was not terribly important for Calvin and later generations of Calvinists altered or even betrayed his thinking in emphasizing it so strongly? This difficult and much debated issue speaks so directly to the history of Calvin's image and influence that some remarks about it are necessary here.

The issue, in fact, has two parts. The first concerns the originality of Calvin's views on predestination and the place of it in his thought. Albrecht Ritschl, the great Göttingen theologian of the nineteenth century, was the first to question the importance of predestination for Calvin in 1868.[23] In his wake, leading commentators on Calvin's theology have regularly stressed that, notwithstanding the place that the doctrine came to occupy within Reformed orthodoxy, it was not particularly central to Calvin's thought, much less its central organizing principle. The subject first appears as an independent doctrine in his *Catechism* of 1537. As François Wendel's classic analysis shows, it occupies more and more place in the *Institutes* in the course of successive editions. While his treatment of the topic undergoes many formal changes across the decades, however, the substance of his ideas alters little.[24] Throughout his writings, Calvin links predestination ambiguously either to redemption or providence. Throughout, he puts forward the idea that the church is the people elected by God while arguing at the same time that it is a mixed body, composed of those who will be saved and those who will be damned. While he stresses election to salvation but not to damnation in his controversy with Bolsec, he prefers in the *Institutes* of 1559 to emphasize God's prescience: God elects to salvation those whom he foresees will be true believers, which implies that he also foresees the others as unbelievers and condemns them.[25] In his *Sermon against Bolsec* in 1551, Calvin argues that election precedes faith against Bolsec's assertion to the contrary.[26] In the *Institutes* (3, 19–25; 4, 18–20), he asserts that God foresees who will believe and elects or condemns as a function of this. Either way, no mention appears of God's eternal decree whereby the Almighty dictates from all eternity who will be saved or damned. Even when Calvin's doctrine comes closest to the later, standardized, idea of double predestination, his own formulation remains open ended. Developed in the context of polemic against the Roman Catholic view of good works and free will, as well as in the context of the Bolsec controversy, Calvin's doctrine amounted to stating the pastoral minimum necessary to convince his congregation of the fundamental inequality of their relationship to God, whose ways remained hidden to all human individuals and institutions. When we consider the importance of other topics such as Christology and the Eucharist in his thought, the doctrine of predestination clearly assumes a secondary importance. The ambiguities of his presentation account, at least partially, for the adaptability of his views to the schemas that will be later imposed on them.

Furthermore, Calvin's views on predestination were anything but radically original. They could be viewed simply as a renewal of Augustine's anti-Pelagian position. In essence, they differ little from the views of Bucer, Vermigli, or even the Luther of the 1525 *Bondage of the Will*. Yet in comparison with these latter, Calvin did express himself more forthrightly on the issue. Perhaps more importantly yet, the conflict with Bolsec led him to publish a short work entirely dedicated to the subject. Vermigli's inquiry about the controversy in 1555 also led Beza to reply in the form of his famous table of predestination, the *Tabula praedestinationis*, which presented election and reprobation in diagram form as exactly symmetrical in God's mind, both constituting a part of his eternal decree. As a result of these controversies and of the increasingly prominent place that the doctrine assumed in successive editions of the *Institutes*, and even though Calvin's views on the subject were not terribly original, an emphasis on predestination had come to be one meaning of the word "Calvinist" by the 1550s, as we have already seen.

The second part of the problem concerns the degree of similarity or difference between Calvin's concept of predestination and the views on this subject that came to prevail within Reformed orthodoxy over the course of the next two generations. During the 1960s, Ernst Bizer and Basil Hall argued strongly that "Calvinism" departed sharply from Calvin's own thought during the later sixteenth century, becoming more rigidly doctrinaire, more predestinarian, and less centered on the person of Christ.[27] In Hall's classic formulation of the thesis of "Calvin against the

Calvinists," Theodore Beza was the culprit who first distorted the careful biblical balance of Calvin's thought. Where Calvin had placed his discussion of predestination under the doctrine of salvation, or so Hall argued, Beza returned it to the sections of his works devoted to God and providence, where the medieval scholastics had placed it. Thinking systematically, he deduced and formulated a clear supralapsarian doctrine of double predestination; God's determination of who would be saved and who would be damned was made before Adam's fall. He illustrated this in his table of predestination. A second stage in the distortion of Calvin then came at the end of the sixteenth century, when the hugely influential English theologian William Perkins not only reiterated supralapsarian double predestination but emphasized that all believers were duty bound to find assurance of their election in the movements of their soul and to demonstrate their election outwardly in works of piety; Calvin, by contrast, had always pointed believers toward scripture and the sacraments to reassure them that Christ had died for them. The problem of how one might know if one was among the elect or not came sharply to the fore in English Puritan circles.[28] Sparked by these works, investigation of the relationship between Calvin, Beza, and different forms of seventeenth-century Calvinism became one of the most active fields of investigation in Calvin studies for the next four decades.[29]

The results of this research and debate suggest that Hall's drawing of a sharp distinction between Calvin's and Beza's views on predestination rests on a reading of Calvin that underestimates his hesitation about whether to treat predestination in the context of redemption or divine providence. Furthermore, as we noted, Beza's *Tabula* was an occasional piece, produced in response to Vermigli's request for more information about Calvin's doctrine of predestination following the Bolsec controversy. It appeared in Calvin's lifetime, and so, we may presume, with his assent. Now either Calvin was in agreement with its supralapsarian orientation or the *Tabula* was not intended as a logical demonstration of the supralapsarian doctrine of predestination and so did not show this dogma to be central to Calvin's theology. In fact, as Richard Muller and others have suggested, if it were to be read from the bottom line upward and not, as has been usual (and, we might add, more logical), from the top downward, it cannot be viewed as a proof of supralapsarianism, but as a general statement on predestination along the lines argued by Calvin.[30] It might also be noted that when Lutheran Hanover entered into talks with the Reformed theologians of Brandenburg in quest of religious union during the 1690s, the principal theological negotiators for Hanover, Gottfried Wilhelm Leibniz and Gerard Wolter Molanus, viewed the supralapsarian Reformed understanding of "God's absolute decree" as one of the chief stumbling blocks in the way of union and judged Calvin to be the initiator of this view, on the basis of considerable familiarity with his writings.[31] This shows how early and how firmly the idea that Calvin was the author of predestinarian Calvinism had taken root, even if Leibniz and Molanus also noted that Beza, Girolamo Zanchi, and the acts of the 1586 Lutheran-Reformed Colloquy of Montbéliard, where predestination was a major point of dispute, all gave the doctrine greater prominence.

Yet while the thesis of "Calvin against the Calvinists" underestimates the ambiguities of Calvin's treatment of predestination and overstates the gulf between his views and Beza's, and while "Calvinism" had come to be associated with the forth-right affirmation of predestination by the 1550s as a result of the Bolsec affair and Calvin's increasingly detailed treatment of the subject in successive editions of the *Institutes*, there is no doubt that predestination still became considerably more prominent in theological discussions in the two generations after 1564. One important cause of this was the rise of so-called Protestant scholasticism. Concerned to convey the doctrines encapsulated in the various Reformed confessions of faith during Calvin's lifetime to subsequent generations of pastors in as clear and effective a fashion as possible, professors of theology in Reformed institutions of higher education increased the priority given to systematic theology and returned to the tools of Aristotelian logic. In working out clear, logical presentations of God's divine decrees, they began to discover aspects of the question of predestination that Calvin had not even anticipated, notably that of the sequence in which God had determined Adam's fall and the salvation of the elect. Debates broke out about predestination in several Reformed churches. Those in the Netherlands, sparked by the Leiden theologian Jacob Arminius's critique of Perkins's views on the order and mode of predestination, proved particularly contentious. Ignited in 1603, the controversy was not resolved until fifteen years later, when an international synod at Dordrecht condemned Arminius and defined a position subsequently schematized as "the five points of Calvinism," which were encapsulated still later in the English acrostic TULIP: the Total depravity of human nature, the Unconditional election of the saints, Christ's Limited atonement, Irresistible grace, and the Perseverance of the saints in faith throughout their lifetime.[32] The contemporary English-language dictionary definitions that we encountered earlier that oppose Calvinism to Arminianism and link it to these five doctrines clearly make sense only in the wake of this synod.

While these definitions identify Calvinism with the positions that triumphed at "Dort," it is worth remembering that Arminius himself issued from the Calvin heritage and had studied at the Geneva Academy. He never denied this heritage, while denying the "Calvinist" doctrine of predestination. Furthermore, whatever the subsequent turns the dispute took, there is no doubting that both Arminianism and anti-Arminianism were basically a product of Calvin-inspired Protestantism. But in reality, neither side in the debate was simply repeating what Calvin himself had written. Each was pulling his ideas in one direction or another, using terminology that he had not used to answer questions that he had not asked. To inquire whether Calvin himself taught the five points of Calvinism thus borders on anachronism, since it asks what he thought about questions he did not carefully consider. The same is truer still of the issue of assurance of salvation, which became a matter of detailed examination and debate in England and New England only in the decades after the Synod of Dort, and where, once again, the questions debated were not ones that had preoccupied Calvin. While some aspects of Calvin's treatment of election and providence can be seen in retrospect to anticipate or agree with the more specific doctrines defended by seventeenth-century "Calvinists" regarding either the sequence of the divine decrees or the nature of saving faith and the marks of assurance, and while other aspects of the Genevan reformer's treatment of the pertinent issues are at variance with later "Calvinism," we finally adhere to the conviction of many modern scholars and postulate a gap between the views of Calvin himself and those of the next generations for the simple reason that subsequent debates raised questions and perceived complexities that Calvin himself did not confront. More importantly, we stress that the question of "Calvin against the Calvinists?" illustrates that it can often be misleading to seek, within the varied, generally brief, and occasionally ambiguous or contradictory treatments that Calvin gave many topics, a single essential outlook that represents the "real Calvin," and then to line this up neatly either in agreement with, or in opposition to, later doctrinal formulae. Calvin was not a "Calvinist" any more than Plato was a "Platonist" or Aristotle an "Aristotelian." As Cornelis van der Kooi emphasizes in his essay, the concept of appropriation is particularly helpful in thinking about the influence of a thinker such as Calvin across the centuries, since it implies an active role for those subsequently touched by his writings, who do not simply receive and preserve his ideas, but apply them to their situation and concerns, and in the process often change them.

■ A TEXTUAL HISTORY OF INFLUENCE: ADAPTING AND COMPLEMENTING THE *INSTITUTES*

Not only do the contexts in which later generations read an author change, the very texts that carry a thinker's ideas forward may also be modified. This happened to Calvin's works, most notably to his *Institutes*. Paying more attention to the textual history of this and other comparable works, we suggest, could be another illuminating way of understanding the transmission of his ideas to subsequent generations and the modifications they underwent in the process. In a short study of the early editions of the *Institutes* first published in 1997, Richard Muller argued that the early paratextual apparatus edited by sixteenth- and seventeenth-century editors shows their accurate and sophisticated understanding of Calvin's theology, which modern scholarship would do well to take into account.[33] We should like to view the issue from a rather different angle, that of theological and methodological changes that these early editors imposed on Calvin's *opus*. It is important to bear in mind that Calvin was initially received through the 1559 edition of the *Institutes*, the popularity of which was largely due to its structure and the way it could be adapted to varying theological contexts.[34] Calvin himself qualified the *Institutes* as a collection of *disputationes* and loci communes already in 1539.[35] He intended the *Institutes* to be just that: a collection of doctrinal commonplaces that would save him lengthy digressions in his biblical commentaries. This choice of literary form proved highly successful, so successful that Peter Martyr Vermigli's ideas also came to be cast in the same mold. Vermigli had initially organized his ideas about doctrine differently, in substantial excursuses within his biblical commentaries, under distinct subheadings. He would no doubt have sunk into obscurity had these not been reorganized into the form of loci communes structured in exactly the same fashion as Calvin's *Institutes*.

The initiator of the project to extract loci communes from Vermigli's commentaries was Calvin's successor Theodore Beza, who wrote to Bullinger in early July 1563, only a year after Vermigli's death and during Calvin's lifetime, "Some here think it would be a labor most useful to the churches if someone were to put together in a corpus the loci communes from Martyr's works and have them printed separately."[36] What did Vermigli offer that Calvin did not? Pending further work on this, we suggest an interest on Beza's and Calvin's part in the Florentine's more overtly ethical orientation, combined with a desire on the part of Geneva to present all of Reformed theology in the framework of Calvin's *Institutes*. Vermigli's loci communes supplemented the *Institutes* on ethical matters, on which Calvin was thought to be too brief, and this had the further advantage of showing that the two men basically agreed on the doctrine of predestination. The task of compiling the commonplaces was undertaken by Robert Le Maçon, a member of the French Refugee Church in London, with Beza's help and encouragement. The compilation, which appeared while the vestments controversy was at its height in England, was Le Maçon's sole achievement of any note.[37] No doubt for reasons of diplomacy, Le Maçon did not mention in his preface that the arrangement of Vermigli's *Loci* takes Calvin's *Institutes* as model. This would be done in 1580 by Rudolf Gwalther in the Zurich edition, which also contained a long extract on free will and some of Vermigli's doctrinal letters. When Gwalther mentioned the name of Calvin and his *Institutes* as a model of the loci communes method in his preface to the second expanded edition of Vermigli's *Loci*, he emphasized the importance of locus communis as a unifying factor in works of Reformed theology. He addressed the new edition explicitly to students of theology, giving it the full status of a textbook. He stressed the importance of summarizing the whole of Christian faith under general headings and commended the practice as biblically rooted and confirmed in the Christian tradition. Calvin to him was the highest authority and the model to follow in the matter of loci communes. In short, by 1580, on the initiative of Geneva and with Zurich's full approval, Vermigli's *Loci communes* were being diffused under the Calvin label. Only thus, it was thought, could his ideas exert substantial influence. It is something of a irony that a theologian who is sometimes presented as a different Reformed voice whose importance has been underestimated because of the excess attention given to Calvin only achieved wider diffusion after his ideas were restructured in the mold of Calvin's *Institutes*.

At the same time that Vermigli's observations scattered among his commentaries were being reshaped into loci communes structured like Calvin's *Institutes*, the *Institutes* themselves were being reshaped through the addition of further reading aids such as marginalia highlighting their principal themes and indexes. Translations, digests, and summaries were also made of the work, which had come to be seen by the Reformed world as suitable for all "pious believers" regardless of their intellectual level, from professional theologians to the barely literate.[38] The addition of various types of paratextual aids to the *Institutes* began in Calvin's lifetime. Both the 1559 Latin and the 1560 French editions of the *Institutes* contained Nicolas Colladon's additions to the commonplaces, while those of Augustin Marlorat were first added to the 1562 French edition, which did not contain Colladon's. The first appearance of these subdivisions in print would show that Calvin himself approved of their being added to his work, over and above his own divisions and subdivisions. This addition of marginal guides or indexes to loci communes to the work of an author who was considered an authority on the subject could not be motivated solely by the indexer's wish to bring out Calvin's meaning better. There were other factors at stake.

Nicolas Colladon, Calvin's friend and enfant terrible of the Genevan Company of Pastors, compiled his index of *loci* after the edition had gone out on sale. Despite the fact that Calvin himself requested the index, Robert Estienne was reluctant to publish it, thinking that the ordering of the *Institutes* was sufficiently clear, without the addition of any further paratextual guideposts. He eventually did publish it, however, albeit along with a caveat. Undeterred by Estienne's reluctance, Colladon went on to expand his index slightly at Calvin's request and to translate it into French. This was added to the French edition of the *Institutes*, also after it had come out from the presses of Jean Crespin in 1560. Colladon then continued to expand the indexes, which were added in their full form together with a marginal apparatus in the 1576 Lausanne edition of the *Institutes* by François Le Preux, which also included Marlorat's indexes. This edition, coedited by Colladon, who by then had been teaching at the Academy of Lausanne since 1572, constituted a turning point in the publishing process of the *Institutes*, as the number of guideposts for the reader in the shape of marginal chapter summaries, references, and so on began to crowd out the original structure and content of the book. As Colladon explained to the Bernese theologian Blaise Marcuard in a letter of 1576, his compilation of loci communes, cross-references, and references to other authors had been put together for no reason other than for teaching those who were in his care. The printer François Le Preux wanted to use them to improve on the apparatus of the Genevan editions and satisfy the need expressed by theology students for a fuller apparatus to the *Institutes*.[39] What Colladon's apparatus and his letter to Marcuard show is that the Calvin who was taught in the late sixteenth century was already a heavily adapted Calvin; for the benefit of Lausanne and other students, the initial collection of loci communes that was Calvin's *Institutes* had been cut up into bite-sized pieces, annotated, abridged, and reduced under further commonplace headings.

Colladon also explained to Marcuard that he put in cross-references not just to the works of church fathers and other ancient authors, as they contain "many similar points which are worthy of note," but also to recent authors, especially to Luther "because of pseudo-Lutherans who treat certain dogmas (such as predestination, divine providence and free-will) not just so as to weaken that holy man's pronouncements on them but so as to overthrow them, whereas they glory all the while in his name, considering themselves to be disciples of such a great doctor." He also referenced Erasmus, recuperating him for the cause of the Reformation: "As many are impressed by the authority of Erasmus (and it is indeed great among the learned and those who have been educated in the Humanities), I have also noted certain passages from his letters to Sadolet and Steuchus where he demonstrates that neither auricular confession nor images in churches etc. are in accord with the word of God and that they do not conform to the usage of the earliest, truly apostolic church. This is...advisable to bring...to the attention of those who feel differently." Just as Vermigli gained authority from being put in the *Institutes* framework, so Calvin gained in the power to convince from being presented as part of a wider tradition, composed notably of Luther and Erasmus. Colladon's aim was practical: his candidates for the ministry would be confronted by parishioners who also wondered about the coherence of Reformed doctrines. Showing their agreement with the ideas of Calvin's spiritual predecessors facilitated the teaching and preaching of the Genevan reformer's theology and situated him in continuity with the church fathers and other masters of the European Reformation. This cast Calvin's voice as authoritative within the true universal church and not just an isolated clamor.

Marlorat's indexes served a different, complementary purpose. As we noted, they were added for the first time to the French version of the *Institutes,* which appeared from the presses of Jacques Bourgeois in 1562 only a few months before their author's execution in October that year. Marlorat's preface to his biblical index suggests that this was intended to solve the problem of inadequate knowledge of biblical exegesis among candidates for the ministry. To remedy this, he offers the *Institutes* as an exegetical guide at odds with Calvin's own intentions as expressed in his preface to the reader in the 1539 edition. Whereas Calvin thought that the *Institutes* should be used together with biblical commentaries, Marlorat found the average student's knowledge of basic points of doctrine to be so poor that he needed the *Institutes* as an aid to biblical interpretation. Does this mean that Calvin's commentaries were not doing the job and did not serve the very purpose for which they were intended? According to Marlorat, the problem with commentaries was that they focused on the exact meaning of the text, while presupposing a good knowledge of basic points of doctrine. The *Institutes,* unlike biblical commentaries, contained biblical citations in a doctrinal context, which meant that an inexperienced or unskilled student could use Marlorat's list of biblical passages to see which of them could be used to support or refute a particular doctrine. The other index compiled by Marlorat was simply a subject index in more or less alphabetical order. Colladon's and Marlorat's indexes and marginal guideposts to key themes complemented one another. Those who wished to find out quickly about a topic such as baptism turned to Colladon. Those who were laboring on a text such as the first part of Genesis and did not know what doctrine to refer it to could look it up in Marlorat's index and then follow Calvin's exposition or the exposition Marlorat attributed to him. The two indexes together, as they were printed in the 1576 Lausanne edition, constituted an important pedagogical aid to teaching Calvin in a schematized fashion to the common run of theology students.

Editorial intervention in and around the text of the *Institutes* was not only used to schematize it and make it easier to use; some makers of abridged editions actively also altered contents. The *Institutes* were adapted to Anglican use in Edmund Bunnie's (1540–1618) *Compendium* of the work, which came out in 1576.[40] Bunnie did not share the Genevan confessional stance. Known for his moderation, he viewed the Roman Catholic Church as a true church and respected some of its positions, even while claiming the pope to be the Antichrist. He nonetheless believed that teaching Calvin was essential and that the fourth edition of the *Institutes* was especially valuable for its strict ordering of material under topic headings that other authors, notably Musculus, applied in a more scattered, disorderly fashion. Naturally, the text of the *Institutes* as Bunnie presented it was heavily edited to conform to the positions of the Church of England where these were at variance with Genevan ideas, notably on the subject of ecclesiology.

The *Institutes* were transformed in a different way by Caspar Olevianus and Johannes Piscator of the Herborn Academy. Olevianus, Calvin's former student and the coauthor, with Zacharias Ursinus, of the Heidelberg Catechism, taught briefly at Herborn and died there in 1585. His *Institutionis Christianae Religionis Epitome* was published in Herborn a year later by Corvinus.[41] It set out the *Institutes* so as to make as clear as possible the scope and purpose of the work. Olevianus describes it as having a twofold subject: the knowledge of God, which leads to immortality, and the knowledge of ourselves, which is directly subordinated to the knowledge of God. This is in fact a creedal abridgment of the *Institutes* but one that omits all reference to the work's more specific handling of ecclesiology and other matters and apparently divorces it from its historical context, quite unlike Colladon's apparatus. Olevianus, however, was quite correct and faithful to the structure of the 1559 edition in seeing the latter as following that of the Apostles' Creed. Piscator, a disciple of Olevianus and professor at Herborn from 1584 to 1622, in turn, extracted from Olevianus's *Epitome* a set of *Aphorismi doctrinae christianae*, first published in 1589 and reprinted several times by 1630. While Olevianus's *Epitome* shows a slanting but not a fundamental betrayal of Calvin's scope and purpose, the same cannot be said for Piscator's *Aphorismi*. Piscator gained notoriety as a theologian for his opposition to the doctrine of the active obedience of Christ (the view that in addition to paying for our sins, Christ actively obeyed every article of God's law). He maintained that if the imputation of the active obedience was effective, man would be free from obedience to as well as from the curse of the law. This eventually led to an exchange of letters between 1584 and 1587 with Theodore Beza, who opposed Piscator's view. The full title and disposition of the *Aphorismi* shows it to be an adaptation of Calvin, not just to classroom teaching, but to Piscator's own theology.[42] The text of the *Institutes*, such as it is, is paraphrased almost beyond recognition and the doctrine of justification expounded in the work is Piscator's. The *Aphorismi* came to be widely used far beyond Herborn. Subsequent editions continued to repeat views on the doctrine of Christ's active obedience directly opposed to Calvin's and Beza's. Even more clearly than Bunnie's *Compendium*, this case shows how some of the abridgments and reorganizations of the *Institutes* transformed parts of it beyond recognition. The editions and reworkings of Calvin's *Institutes*, while adding to the work's pedagogical utility and thus its influence, also nudged readers toward a certain reading of Calvin and at times substantially so altered the ideas that they can no longer be said to be his.

Further research into these sorts of textual transformations and the effects they produced might help clarify the complicated afterlife of Calvin's ideas not just in the first generations of Reformed orthodoxy but also in the nineteenth and twentieth centuries. As the contributions of van der Wall, André Encrevé, and David Bebbington show, new editions of Calvin's works became rare during the eighteenth century, only to revive in the nineteenth century, with the fifty-nine volumes of Calvin's complete works for the *Corpus Reformatorum* prepared between 1863 and 1900 by the Strasbourg scholars Guillaume Baum, Eduard Cunitz, and Eduard

Reuss representing the culmination of this revival.[43] This landmark of modern scholarship about the reformer, the edition of reference for scholars ever since, made Calvin's letters, sermons, and lesser treatises available as never before. As Muller has noted, it was also a turning point in the textual history of the *Institutes*, as it omitted the paratextual guides and divisions found in early modern editions; those added to subsequent editions were different from the early modern editions.[44] During the twentieth century, Calvin textual scholarship has confined itself to the preparation of editions of the *Institutes* in different languages, more or less attentive to the alterations made by Calvin at each successive revision, and the publication of sermons and letters discovered subsequent to the preparation of the *Opera Calvini*.[45] Over the same period many theologians, perhaps most notably Abraham Kuyper, Karl Barth, and André Biéler, returned to Calvin for inspiration and offered rereadings of his ideas that affirmed (especially in Biéler's case) that these authors had come to a more authentic understanding of his views on the basis of acquaintance with a wider range of Calvin's texts. One wonders if historians of nineteenth- and twentieth-century Reformed theology might benefit from reflecting about the relationship between the nature of modern rereadings of Calvin, the corpus of his work available when each was offered, and the paratextual apparatus and editorial commentary that accompanied the editions they used.

■ MODERN TIMES AND WIDER SPHERES OF INFLUENCE: CALVIN, DEMOCRACY, AND CAPITALISM

"Lost, then found": does the title of André Encrevé's chapter summarize Calvin's presence within the religious and historical imagination not just of France's Protestant minority between the eighteenth century and the twentieth century but of the better part of international Protestantism? The displacement of orthodoxy by a simpler, moralizing religiosity within most Reformed churches around the turn of the eighteenth century begat the "distant" Calvin emphasized by Ernestine van der Wall in her examination of his place and image within Dutch Protestant circles during the Enlightenment. The chapters of Encrevé and Bebbington, dedicated respectively to French Protestants and British Evangelicals during the nineteenth and twentieth centuries, then reveal a revival of interest in publishing Calvin's works, a growth of historical knowledge about him, and, in at least certain theological circles within both of these movements, new attention to and new appropriations of his writings. The chapter of Cornelis van der Kooi digs down into the thought of the neo-Calvinist movement in the Netherlands that may have done more than any other renewal movement of the late nineteenth century and early twentieth century to raise the banner of Calvinism, while John de Gruchy's chapter reveals how different understandings of Calvin and Calvinism contributed to the making and unmaking of the ideology of apartheid in South Africa. If we stand back from these essays, the image of a wave that receded in the eighteenth century and then advanced again in the nineteenth century and first half of the twentieth century indeed appears to capture the trajectory of Calvin's influence in its very broadest terms.

At the same time, and above all, these essays show how varied both attitudes toward and knowledge about Calvin were within the increasingly differentiated religious and cultural landscape of the nineteenth and twentieth centuries. It emerges that the way in which the reformer was viewed and appropriated was shaped not only by the theological or cultural orientation from which any given individual approached him; nationalism and national identity also played a role. In an age that celebrated heroes, nineteenth-century British Evangelicals were far more likely to glorify their fellow countrymen Knox or Latimer than the foreign Calvin. At the same time, even those of their French Protestant counterparts whose religious outlook was scarcely Calvinist in any meaningful sense of the word, of whom there were many, felt compelled to defend his reputation and to emphasize his accomplishments, simply to give their cause a respectable French pedigree and to respond to the charge spread by conservative Catholic nationalists that Protestantism corrupted the French national genius with alien Germanic ideas. Inherited meanings of the word "Calvinism" also turn out to have played a role. For the better part of the nineteenth century in Britain, the association of Calvinism with a specific outlook on predestination and saving faith meant that the great majority of Evangelicals, anti-Calvinists on these issues, started out with a negative view of Calvin and were little impelled to read him. But as Dutch neo-Calvinism showed how a broad political and religious movement could be rallied under the flag of a different sort of Calvinism in another national context and began to create international organizations, the minority of British Evangelicals who were predestinarian Calvinists gained new inspiration from their example and new alliances through affiliation with their organizations. In the interwar and immediate post–World War II periods, Karl Barth's theology emphasizing the radical sinfulness of man and the total alterity of God, a theology that parted company from Calvin's on certain points but drew inspiration from him and directed readers to see what in his works might speak to the twentieth century, exercised considerable appeal in both France and Britain, leading to an increased attention to Calvin and the appointment of more theologians with a strong interest in his ideas in Protestant theology faculties and seminaries than previously. These last observations prompt a larger methodological remark. The final essays in this volume are all organized within national frameworks. Combining their findings as we have just done here would also seem to suggest the potential interest of a transnational approach to our subject that would highlight the role and influence that the various international Calvinist conferences and associations, as well as the movement of theology students and ideas across borders, had in altering Calvin's image and influence. Readers will also encounter in the final chapters many more findings that inspire wider reflection and suggest avenues for additional research.

What readers will not find in these final chapters, as we have already said, is any examination of Calvin's contribution to modern capitalism or to a political order characterized by commitment to representative democracy and human rights. Harro Höpfl's close analysis of Calvin's own characteristically brief statements about the best form of government and about the duty and limits of obedience to secular authority suggests that Reformed resistance theory departed very quickly from Calvin's formulations of these questions. Heinz Schilling's exploration of

Calvinism's place in the European state system around 1600 shows that the Reformed churches and rulers had an orientation to politics that differentiated them from their Lutheran or Catholic counterparts, but that it was dictated more by the circumstances within which they found themselves than by a specific theological legacy inherited from Calvin. The claims that Calvinism encouraged republican liberty and economic dynamism can both be traced back into the confessional polemics of the early modern era. Both became widely shared commonplaces in the wake of the French and Industrial Revolutions, well before the publication of Max Weber's *The Protestant Ethic and the Spirit of Capitalism* (1904–1905) and Ernst Troeltsch's *The Social Teachings of the Christian Churches* (1911) bestowed a new level of theoretical sophistication, empirical substantiation, and academic legitimacy on them. The Weber thesis in particular would spark such vigorous debate among historians, sociologists, and theologians for much of the twentieth century that still another powerful association with Calvin is the term "capitalism." While both Weber and Troeltsch took care to distinguish between Calvin's own thought and later Calvinism, the prominence acquired by their writings made it impossible for twentieth-century students of Calvin himself to avoid discussing his views on politics and economic ethics and commenting on his contribution to modernity in these realms. Yet after the chapters of Höpfl and Schilling, this book moves away from these themes. Why?

A brief review of the rise and fall of these views may answer this question while also contributing to the *Begriffsgeschichte* of "Calvinism." That Calvinism was a creed of republicanism and sedition was a staple of Catholic and Lutheran attacks in the first century of the Reformation. As Reformed churches proliferated in France around 1561, for instance, alarmed Catholics repeatedly charged that they sought to replace the monarchy with a Swiss-style confederation. In an age when monarchy was the dominant and most admired form of government, this was to denigrate the faith. It was precisely to forestall such accusations that Calvin had insisted as strongly as he did in the *Institutes* on the obligation of obedience to the duly constituted authorities. Subsequent generations of Reformed polemicists sought to rebut the charge by stressing how fervently their churches prayed for the health of their rulers and by turning the accusation of sedition back against their Catholic antagonists by recalling the monarchomach writings of Juan de Mariana and Francisco Suarez and by alleging that papists could never be perfectly loyal subjects of kings so long as the pope claimed to exercise a right of oversight over temporal authority.

What began in the sixteenth century as an accusation that the Reformed sought to deny became by the nineteenth century an association that they were proud to embrace. Just when this change took place has yet to be fully clarified. The Glorious Revolution and the subsequent rise of the Whig interpretation of English history were probably important tipping points. Pioneered in the 1720s by the Huguenot refugee to England Paul Rapin de Thoyras, the Whig view of history cast Albion as the land where the constitutional liberties that had once been the common property of all European peoples best survived the efforts of would-be absolute monarchs to abolish them. It was a vision of history that could be easily enlarged to a broader association between Calvinism and the defense of constitutional liberty by running a red thread from Switzerland and Geneva through the Huguenot monarchomachs and the Dutch Revolt to the British revolutions of the seventeenth century. By Voltaire's time, a link between Calvinism and liberty was sufficiently well established for him to contrast the three major post-Reformation confessions thusly: "Papists are slaves who fought under the banner of their tyrant the Pope. The Lutherans fought for their princes; the Calvinists for the liberty of the people." He also wrote, "Calvin's religion conforms to the republican spirit, even if Calvin himself was tyrannical."[46] After the American and French Revolutions, and as the nineteenth century advanced, the view that each of the three main post-Reformation confessions encouraged a distinctive attitude toward politics came to seem still more plausible, with the advent of democracy in the United States (regularly linked by commentators to the new country's Puritan heritage), the Catholic Church's post-Revolutionary alignment with the forces of hierarchy and conservatism, and German unification under the sway of the kaiser. Leading historians, including François Guizot in France, James Froude in England, and Charles Bancroft in the United States all linked Calvinism and republicanism.[47] The American novelist Harriet Beecher Stowe wrote, "Wherever John Calvin's system of theology has gone, civil liberty has gone with it."[48] F. W. Graf's and Cornelis van der Kooi's contributions to this volume show how theologians and historians developed a similar view in the very different circumstances of nineteenth-century Germany and the Netherlands. By the early twentieth century, the conviction that Calvinism was particularly conducive to liberty was such a point of pride among most Reformed Protestants and so fundamental to Calvinist identity that it was a central theme of the Reformation Monument erected in Geneva by international subscription to mark Calvin's four hundredth birthday.

Just as most Calvinists were convinced by 1909 that their faith carried the torch of constitutional liberty down the path of Western progress, so too they were convinced that it had advanced prosperity and well-being, although just how it had done so was disputed. Again, the view of an association between Calvin, Calvinism, and aggressive profit seeking goes back with a negative spin to the confessional polemics of the Reformation. As Muller's chapter here reveals, Calvin's pioneering approbation of loans for commercial transactions at moderate rates of interest led Catholic controversialists to castigate him as the advocate of usury and Reformed polemicists to defend him. By the second half of the seventeenth century, some Protestant authors were willing to suggest that the Reformed faith might indeed be more conducive to commerce and manufacturing than Catholicism, but for reasons other than a permissive attitude toward usury. In 1671, the English economic author Slingsby Bethel wrote that "a kind of natural unaptness to business" prevailed in Catholic lands, while "amongst the Reformed the greater their zeal, the greater... their inclinations to Trade and Industry." This was because, in his view, a "multitude of lazie Priests and Jesuits" burdened Catholic countries, while the Reformed abhorred idleness and were generally smarter.[49] This was clearly an expression of Protestant anti-Catholic stereotypes, but Catholic political economists of the eighteenth century were also willing to suggest that their religion hampered economic growth because its numerous feast days encouraged idleness.[50] This led to campaigns to reduce the number of holidays and heightened the association between Catholicism and economic backwardness already suggested by the economic decline of Spain and Italy and relative vigor of the Dutch and British economies. The central role of Britain, the United States, and Germany in the first and second industrial revolutions further reinforced the perception that Protestant countries were generally more prosperous, while the antimodernist orientation of the nineteenth-century Catholic Church made many of its spokesmen only too happy to suggest that Protestantism was the faith of untrammeled individualism and capitalist exploitation. Max Weber's often misunderstood contribution to this bundle of associations was thus not to launch the idea that Calvinism encouraged the rise of modern capitalism, something already widely believed when he wrote, but to locate the sources of this process in a Calvinist inner-worldly asceticism driven by the anxiety about election that came to the fore among believers as predestination was increasingly emphasized in the generations after Calvin. In order to convince themselves that they truly possessed saving faith, believers lived the disciplined ethical lives that works of Puritan practical divinity assured them were proof of their election.

In the nearly century-long debate that followed the publication of what soon became a classic of the emerging discipline of sociology, Weber's earliest critics included self-identified Calvinists who did not recognize themselves in this depiction of predestination-stressed believers but had no doubts about the link between Protestantism and prosperity. Émile Doumergue, the great French Calvin scholar, lifelong opponent of Liberal Protestantism, and central figure in rallying international support for the Calvin quadricentennial of 1909, devoted fully forty pages of his massive Calvin biography to a critique of "the school of Heidelberg." He criticized Weber for basing his view of Calvinism disproportionately on English Puritan sources of the seventeenth century that were not representative of the movement as a whole and, above all, for overlooking the basic reason why "Calvin's Calvinism" generated economic well-being:

> It has long been remarked that the Protestant peoples have been at the forefront of modern civilization, and in particular have been the richest peoples. Setting aside all hypotheses and systems to limit ourselves to plain reality, what have we found in Calvin's Calvinism? An ardent faith inspiring a morality built above all on work and simplicity....This morality....suffices amply to explain all Calvinist commercial and economic development.[51]

If, in 1909, it was a central conviction of most Reformed Protestants and of many historians and social scientists of other religions that Calvinism made a special contribution to the growth of modern liberty or capitalism, intensive research into these questions over the course of the twentieth century has gradually led most academic experts to abandon such views. The Whig association of Calvinism and political liberty endured largely intact through World War II. John T. McNeill's *The History and Character of Calvinism*, first published in 1954 and long the standard history of Calvinism in the English-speaking world, still asserted: "Most Calvinists have always associated with their faith in the sovereignty of God a feeling for the cause of human liberty and public justice and a strong preference for representative and responsible government."[52] But over the next five decades both changes in the wider world and advances in historical scholarship called into question the view that each of the three major post-Reformation confessions encouraged a distinctive political orientation. The postwar extension of democratic regimes across Europe meant that stable parliamentary democracies were no longer as disproportionately found in countries where Reformed churches were historically important as they previously had been. The Catholic Church abandoned its previous hostility to liberal theories of religious freedom and the rights of man. The ecumenical movement encouraged religious historians to study church traditions other than their own and to observe what united rather than divided them. A growing body of historical scholarship rediscovered the medieval roots of constitutionalism, the early modern Catholic theories of tyrannicide that seventeenth-century Reformed polemicists had already highlighted, Luther's post-1530 embrace of the possibility of resistance to the emperor, and the later Lutheran resistance theories of the period of the Schmalkaldic War.[53] The consensus today among most historians of the Reformation era is that theories justifying the right of resistance to unjust or unconstitutional authority may have been expressed somewhat differently within each major post-Reformation confessional family, but that they were articulated within all three, and in each case had common roots in late medieval scholastic theology and canon law. Indicative of the shift in understanding that has taken place over the past half century is the recent book of a law professor concerned to emphasize Calvinism's contribution to modern conceptions of human rights that opens with the caveat that its choice of authors and texts is highly selective, since "Calvin's original political ideas were…sufficiently 'protean' and 'provocative' to inspire a wide range of both totalitarian and democratic tendencies."[54]

The sprawling debates around the Weber thesis that engaged sociologists, economic historians, historians of religion, and socially conscious theologians for much of the twentieth century have been traced elsewhere in detail.[55] At the risk of oversimplification, let us just note here that the thesis as Weber formulated it generally received a more skeptical reception among historians than among sociologists, and a more skeptical reception among economic and religious historians of continental Europe than among those who study Great Britain and British North America. André Biéler's 1959 doctoral thesis on *Calvin's Economic and Social Thought* convinced most subsequent historians and theologians that Calvin himself was no apostle of or apologist for modern capitalism in its more exploitative aspects.[56] The view expressed by Doumergue that Calvin's economic and social ethic was superior to the alternatives because of its greater valorization of work and austerity was dealt a serious blow during the 1930s and 1940s by studies of early modern Catholic attitudes about work and time discipline, which showed these to be not very different from those of Reformed Christians.[57] A still more damaging blow came with the abundant work of the past four decades on "confessionalization" that has highlighted the parallel modernizing consequences of the Lutheran, Calvinist, and Catholic Reformations. While empirical attempts to determine whether early modern Protestants or Calvinists enriched themselves in business with greater success than their Catholic neighbors and counterparts generally failed to confirm that they did, most of the leading economic historians of the late twentieth century simply disregarded or minimized the importance of confessional differences in economic behavior.[58] Weberian views still survive among a minority of economic historians, development economists, and public policy intellectuals convinced of the importance of religious and cultural factors in economic development, but it is our view that discussion of these topics is now less germane to Calvin's actual influence across the centuries than it is to the history of scholarship and of modern Protestant identity. This is the context within which F. W. Graf's chapter in this volume treats the subject.

At the close of this introduction, we might finally note that the Reformed tradition was and remains a far less monolithic structure than Lutheranism. This is partly due to the ambivalences and the laconic nature of Calvin's thought, as well as to its intrinsic adaptability to a variety of positions, theological, political, economic, and cultural. This adaptability contributed to its wider international dissemination and further diversification. Furthermore, whereas Lutherans could and did use the Augsburg Confession as their key text, as they do to this day, there was never a single Reformed or Calvinist confession, but rather a multitude of agreements, confessions of faith, and catechisms that acquired more or less authority within different churches and denominations. These united particular communities, but not the global Calvin-oriented community. Despite Calvin's own pan-Protestant orientation, this latter never took any institutional form stronger than that of a loose alliance of distinctive confessions or churches—in the sixteenth century, the Harmony of Confessions, in the twentieth century, the World Alliance of Reformed Churches, recently renamed the World Communion of Reformed Churches. We hope that the essays that follow bring out the salient aspects of Calvin as religious leader that account for this wide dissemination, the nature of his influence in some of the diverse places where this was felt during the five centuries since his birth, and the history of the concept of "Calvinism" and its relation to his actual ideas and influence.

■ Notes

1. Calvin's influence in the United States has just been explored in Thomas J. Davis, ed., *John Calvin's American Legacy* (Oxford: Oxford University Press, 2010).

2. In addition to the volume cited in n. 1, see Thomas J. Davis, "Images of Intolerance: John Calvin in Nineteenth-Century History Textbooks," *Church History* 65 (1996): 234–48; Davis, "Calvin and Calvinism in Nineteenth-Century Fiction and Twentieth-Century Criticism," *CTJ* 33 (1998): 443–56; Irena Backus, *Life Writing in Reformation Europe*: Lives *of Reformers by Friends, Disciples and Foes* (Aldershot: Ashgate, 2008); Bernard Cottret and Olivier Millet, eds., *Jean Calvin et la France*, special issue of *BSHPF* 155 (2009): esp. sections 2, 3; and Johan de Niet, Herman Paul, and Bart Wallet, eds., *Sober, Strict and Scriptural: Collective Memories of John Calvin, 1800–2000* (Leiden: Brill, 2009).

3. See p. 256. The original quotation is from *Calv. Opp.* 12: 730.

4. Uwe Plath, "Zur Entstehungsgeschichte des Wortes 'Calvinist,' " *ARG* 66 (1975): 217–22.

5. Bruce Gordon, *Calvin* (New Haven: Yale University Press, 2009). An annual bibliography of works on Calvin and Calvinism has appeared every year in the November issue of the *CTJ* since Joseph Tylenda first published a bibliography of the literature from the years 1960–70 in volume 6 (1971, 156–93). The bibliography for the years since 1997 is also avail-

able online: http://www.calvin.edu/meeter/bibliography. For the literature prior to 1960, see Alain Dufour, "Bibliographie calvinienne en 1959," *BHR* 21 (1959): 619–42. Two recent guides through the literature are Herman Selderhuis, ed., *The Calvin Handbook* (Grand Rapids: Eerdmans, 2009), and Donald K. McKim, *The Cambridge Companion to John Calvin* (Cambridge: Cambridge University Press, 2004).

6. Florimond de Raemond, *L'histoire de la naissance, progrez et decadence de l'heresie de ce siecle* (Rouen: Estienne Vereul, 1618), 937.

7. John Calvin, *Confessio Genevensium praedicatorum de Trinitate, Calv. Opp. R,* series 2, 3: 123–52, gives the text with a full introduction. See also E. Bähler, "Petrus Caroli und Johannes Calvin: Ein Beitrag zur Geschichte und Kultur der Reformationszeit," *Jahrbuch für Schweizerische Geschichte* 29 (1904): 39–168.

8. See Irena Backus, "Un chapitre oublié de la réception de Calvin en France : La *Vita Calvini* de Jean-Papire Masson," *BSHPF* 55 (2009): 181–207, esp. 199.

9. For Calvin's work in this domain, see most recently John Witte Jr. and Robert M. Kingdon, *Sex, Marriage, and Family in John Calvin's Geneva*, vol. 1, *Courtship, Engagement, and Marriage* (Grand Rapids: Eerdmans, 2005), 12–14, as well as the older studies of Kingdon cited there.

10. Jean-Jacques Rousseau, *Du Contrat Social*, bk. 2, ch. 7. See also J.-C.-L. Sismondi, *Statistique du Département du Léman*, ed. H. O. Pappe, *Mémoires et documents publiés par la Société d'Histoire et d'Archéologie de Genève*, (Geneva: Jullien, 1971), 44: 121: "Calvin cependant est le vrai Législateur de Genève, Calvin dont le génie universel sut fonder et consolider ce rapport entre les moeurs, les loix et les coutumes qui fut à lui seul le garant de la solidité d'une constitution."

11. For the politics of the Reformation during Calvin's time in Geneva, Amédée Roget, *Histoire du peuple de Genève depuis la Réforme jusqu'à l'Escalade*, 7 vols. (Geneva: Jullien, 1870–83) remains unsurpassed. More recent studies of importance include William Monter, *Calvin's Geneva* (New York: Wiley, 1967); William G. Naphy, *Calvin and the Consolidation of the Genevan Reformation* (Manchester: Manchester University Press, 1994); and Christian Grosse, *L'excommunication de Philibert Berthelier* (Geneva: Société d'histoire et d'archéologie, 1995).

12. *Calv. Opp.* 14: 455–56, quoted in Witte and Kingdon, *Sex, Marriage and Family*, 467–68.

13. Michel Roset, *Les chroniques de Genève*, ed. Henri Fazy (Geneva: Georg, 1894), 377, quoted in Monter, *Calvin's Geneva*, 99. According to Naphy, *Calvin and the Consolidation*, 195-96 eight Perrinists were ultimately executed while fifteen others escaped execution by fleeing.

14. When *The Lawes and Statutes of Geneva* were published in London by Rowland Hall in 1562 as a model for the young Elizabethan regime, the dedicatory epistle called Geneva "a citie counted of all godly men singularly well ordered, as well as for good policie as also for the governemente of the Churche…, where sincere religion is wonderfullye advaunced, erroure mightely beaten downe, vertue excedingly maynteyned, [and] vice severelye repressed." On the larger myth of Geneva of which this statement was just one expression, see Alain Dufour, "Le mythe de Genève au temps de Calvin," *Revue suisse d'histoire* 9 (1959): 489–518.

15. The fullest elaboration of this view is W. J. Nijenhuis, *Calvinus Oecumenicus: Calvijn en de eenheid der kerk in het licht van zijn briefwisseling* (The Hague: Nijhoff, 1958).

16. For Calvin's position on the Eucharist in relation to Luther's before and after the *Consensus Tigurinus*, see Wim Janse, "The Sacraments," in Selderhuis, *Calvin Handbook*, 351–55, as well as the literature cited there.

17. *Calv. Opp.* 14: 362–65, quoted in Andrew Pettegree, *Foreign Protestant Communities in Sixteenth-Century London* (Oxford: Clarendon Press, 1986), 72.

18. Treated in detail in Philip C. Holtrop, *The Bolsec Controversy on Predestination from 1551 to 1555: The Statements of Jerome Bolsec, and the Responses of John Calvin, Theodore Beza, and Other Reformed Theologians* (Lewiston, NY: E. Mellen, 1993).

19. Others in this category include François Bauduin, Sebastian Castellio, Charles Du Moulin, Lelio Sozzini, Bernardino Ochino, Valentino Gentile, and Giorgio Biandrata. On them, see most notably Ferdinand Buisson, *Sébastien Castellion, sa vie et son oeuvre, 1515–1563*, 2 vols. (Geneva: Droz, 2010). This reprint of the original edition (Paris: Hachette, 1892) also provides updated bibliographical information, including Delio Cantimori, *Eretici italiani del Cinquecento: Ricerche storiche* (Florence: Sansoni, 1939); Mario Turchetti, *Concordia o tolleranza? François Bauduin (1520–1573) et i "Moyenneurs"* (Geneva: Droz, 1984); and Hans R. Guggisberg, *Sebastian Castellio, 1515–1563: Humanist and Defender of Religious Toleration in a Confessional Age* (Aldershot: Ashgate, 2003), a literature of considerable importance for understanding both Calvin and his modern image.

20. Backus, *Life Writing*, 153–69. Bolsec had returned to the Catholic Church when he wrote his *Life* of Calvin. But Chiara Lastraioli, "D' un texte inconnu de Jérôme Bolsec contre Calvin," *Reformation and Renaissance Review* 10 (2008): 157–74, has recently highlighted that he probably wrote songs insulting Calvin as early as 1555, while still a member of a Reformed church. She further argues on stylistic grounds that he authored the anonymous Paris pamphlet of 1556 *Passevent parisien respondant a Pasquin Romain*, which depicted Calvin as a paragon of arrogance and accused him of having sexual relations with many of Geneva's women. For the view that Bolsec's *Life* drew on a wide body of existing satirical literature, including the *Passevent* (whether by him or another author such as Artus Désiré) see Irena Backus, "What Is a Historical Account? Religious Biography and the Reformation's Break with the Middle Ages," *ARG* 101 (2010), 289–304.

21. For a detailed and accurate account of the two trials, see Marianne Carbonnier Burkard, "Des procès de Servet au procès de Calvin," in *Michel Servet (1511–1553): Hérésie et pluralisme du 16e au 21e siècle*, ed. Valentine Zuber (Paris: Honoré Champion, 2007), 27–52; for exchanges of insults, Irena Backus, "Michel Servet et les pères anté-nicéens," in Zuber, *Michel Servet*, 151–60 and nn. 141–59.

22. Stefan Zweig, *Castellio gegen Calvin oder ein Gewissen gegen die Gewalt* (Vienna: H. Reichner, 1936). This work was reprinted twice in the 1980s and translated into French in 1997.

23. Albrecht Ritschl, "Geschichtliche Studien zur Christlichen Lehre von Gott," *Jahrbücher für Deutsche Theologie* 13 (1868): 108–15.

24. François Wendel, *Calvin*, trans. Philip Mairet (London: Collins, 1963), 263–90. See also a summary treatment by Wilhelm Neuser, "Predestination," in Selderhuis, *Calvin Handbook*, 312–23.

25. *OS* 1: 88–90.

26. *Calv. Opp.* 8: 85–140.

27. Ernst Bizer, *Frühorthodoxie und Rationalismus* (Zurich: EVZ, 1963); Basil Hall, "Calvin against the Calvinists," in Gervase Duffield, ed., *John Calvin* (Appleford: Sutton Courtenay Press, 1966), 19–37.

28. In the tradition of the "Calvin against the Calvinists" school, a study by R. T. Kendall further explored changing understandings of what constituted saving faith from Calvin to the English Puritans in his *Calvin and English Calvinism to 1649* (Oxford: Oxford University Press, 1979), arguing that the "experimental predestinarianism" of English Puritanism derived essentially from Beza, not Calvin.

29. For recent summaries of the debate and the state of this question, see Carl R. Trueman, "Calvin and Reformed Orthodoxy" in Selderhuis, *Calvin Handbook*, 466–74; Richard A. Muller, "Was Calvin a Calvinist? Or did Calvin (or Anyone Else in the Early

Modern Era) Plant the TULIP?," http://www.calvin.edu/meeter/lectures/Richard%20 Muller%20%20Was%20Calvin%20a%20Calvinist.pdf.

30. Richard A. Muller, "The Uses and Abuse of a Document: Beza's *Tabula praedestinationis*, the Bolsec Controversy and the Origins of Reformed Orthodoxy," in *Protestant Scholasticism: Essays in Reassessment*, ed. Carl Trueman and R. Scott Clark (Carlisle: Paternoster Press, 1998), 33–61.

31. See Irena Backus, "Leibniz's Concept of Substance and His Reception of John Calvin's Doctrine of the Eucharist," forthcoming in *The British Journal of the History of Philosophy*, 5 (2011) as well as the sources cited there.

32. David N. Steele and Curtis C. Thomas, *The Five Points of Calvinism* (Phillipsburg, NJ: Presbyterian and Reformed Publishing, 1963) provides a convenient, albeit highly apologetic, encapsulation of the history of this terminology and of the conflicts from which it emerged.

33. Richard A. Muller, "The 'Method and Disposition' of Calvin's *Institutio* from the Perspective of Calvin's Late-Sixteenth-Century Editors," *SCJ* 28/4 (1997): 1203–29, reprinted with some abridgement in *The Unaccommodated Calvin: Studies in the Foundation of a Theological Tradition* (Oxford: Oxford University Press, 2000), 62–78.

34. The section that follows draws on preliminary findings of a wider-ranging study that Backus is currently undertaking on the *Locus communis* in the Reformation.

35. *BC* 2: no. 39/4, 61–64; *Institutio* (1539) (Strasbourg: Wendelin Rihel, 1539), *Epistola ad lectorem*, fol. α1v.; Muller, *The Unaccommodated Calvin*, 62–78, esp. 68–69.

36. *Correspondance de Théodore de Bèze, recueillie par Hippolyte Aubert*, ed. Alain Dufour et al. (Geneva: Droz, 1960–), 4: no. 274, 162.

37. See on this Christoph Strohm, "Petrus Martyr Vermiglis *Loci communes* und Calvins *Institutio Christianae Religionis*," in *Peter Martyr Vermigli: Humanism, Republicanism, Reformation*, ed. Emidio Campi, Frank A. James III, and Peter Opitz (Geneva: Droz, 2002), 77–104.

38. See here Olivier Fatio, "Présence de Calvin à l'époque de l' orthodoxie réformée: Les abrégés de Calvin à la fin du 16e et au 17e siècle," in *Calvinus ecclesiae doctor: Die Referate des Internationalen Kongress für Calvinforschung vom 25. bis 28. September in Amsterdam*, ed. Wilhelm Neuser (Kampen: Kok, 1980), 171–208.

39. Colladon's letter figures as preface to the 1576 Le Preux edition of the *Institutes*, the full title of which shows the complexity of textual transmission of the *Institutes* at the time: *D. Ioannis Caluini vigilantissimi pastoris et fidelissimi doctoris ecclesiae Geneuensis: Institutio christianae religionis ab ipso authore anno 1559 et in libros quatuor digesta certisque distincta capitibus ad aptissimam methodum et tum aucta tam magna accessione vt propemodum opus nouum haberi posset: Cum indice per locos communes opera N. Colladonis tunc contexto: Additi sunt postea duo indices ab Augustino Marlorato collecti anno 1562 vt testatur eius epistola, quorum prior res praecipuas; posterior in ea expositos copiosissime sacrae Scripturae locos continet: Accesserunt autem hac editione breues summae in singularum sectionum margine quoad eius fieri potuit et collationes diuersorum locorum eiusdem Caluini, tum in Institutione, tum in variis commentariis, sed praecipue in opusculis eius compluribus, quaedam etiam annotata tam ex veteribus quam recentioribus scriptoribus: Et haec quidem concinnabat hoc anno N. Collado Sacrarum litterarum professor in schola Lausannensi, qui et huius accessionis rationem reddit epistola ad doctissimum virum Blasium Marcuardum Bernensem Theologum, duabus epistolis subiects in ipso libri initio* (Lausanne: François Le Preux, 1576). For a French translation of the methodological part of the letter, see *BC* 3: no. 76/3, 230–31.

40. On this edition generally, see Muller, *The Unaccommodated Calvin*, 60–68.

41. Caspar Olevianus, *Institutionis christianae religionis Epitome ex Institutione Johannis Calvini excerpta . . .* (Herborn: C. Corvinus, 1586).

42. Johannes Piscator, *Aphorismi doctrinae christianae maximam partem ex Institutione Caluini excerpti seu loci communes theologici per Ioannem Piscatorem: Editio tertia ab authore recognita* (Herborn: C. Corvinus, 1594).

43. For the bibliography of Calvin editions between 1600 and 1850, the best guide remains Alfred Erichson, *Bibliographia Calviniana* (Berlin: Schwetschke, 1900).

44. Muller, *The Unaccommodated Calvin*, 63–64. We note that the later sixteenth- and early seventeenth-century paratextual matter was further edited and added to the *Institutes* as published in *Ioannis Calvini Noviodunensis opera omnia: In novem tomos digesta*, 9 vols. (Amsterdam: Widow of Johann Jacob Schipper, 1667–71). Reservations about some aspects of his doctrine were among the additions and merit further investigation (currently being undertaken by Backus). This was the first "modern" edition of Calvin's complete works, not superseded until the work of Baum, Cunitz, and Reuss.

45. Such as the *Calvini Opera omnia: Editio denuo recognita* (Geneva: Droz, 1992–) and Calvin's manuscript sermons in the series *Supplementa Calviniana* (Neukirchen-Vluyn: Neukirchener Verlag, 1961–).

46. Voltaire, *Dieu et les hommes* in *Complete works of Voltaire*, ed. Theodore Besterman, (Oxford: Voltaire Foundation, 1994), 69: 501; and Voltaire, *Essai sur les moeurs et l'esprit des nations*, ed. René Pomeau, 2 vols. (Paris: Bordas, 1990), 2: 243.

47. François Guizot, *L'histoire de France depuis les temps les plus reculés jusqu'en 1789 racontée à mes petits-enfants*, 5 vols. (Paris: Hachette, 1877), 3: 212; and D. G. Hart, "Implausible: Calvinism and American Politics," in Davis, *Calvin's American Legacy*, 65–77, where Froude, Bancroft, and many others expressing a similar view are cited.

48. Stowe, *Sunny Memories of Foreign Lands*, 2 vols. (Boston: Phillips, Sampson, 1854), 2: 408–9, quoted in Peter J. Thuesen, "Geneva's Crystalline Clarity: Harriet Beecher Stowe and Max Weber on Calvinism and the American Character," in Davis, *Calvin's American Legacy*, 227.

49. Slingsby Bethel, *The Present Interest of England Stated* (London, 1671), 21.

50. Paul Münch, "The Thesis before Weber: An Archeology," in *Weber's Protestant Ethic: Origins, Evidence, Contexts*, ed. Hartmut Lehmann and Guenther Roth (Cambridge: Cambridge University Press, 1993), 55–57, 64–66.

51. Émile Doumergue, *Jean Calvin: Les hommes et les choses de son temps*, 7 vols. (Neuilly-sur-Seine: Editions La Cause, 1899–1927), 5: 658–59.

52. John McNeill, *The History and Character of Calvinism* (Oxford: Oxford University Press, 1954), 425.

53. Some landmarks: Brian Tierney, *Foundations of the Conciliar Theory: The Contribution of the Medieval Canonists from Gratian to the Great Schism* (Cambridge: Cambridge University Press, 1955); Tierney, *Religion, Law and the Growth of Constitutional Thought, 1150–1650* (Cambridge: Cambridge University Press, 1982); Frederic J. Baumgartner, *Radical Reactionaries: The Political Thought of the French Catholic League* (Geneva: Droz, 1975); W. D. J. Cargill Thompson, *The Political Thought of Martin Luther* (Brighton: Harvester, 1984); and Thomas Kaufmann, *Das Ende der Reformation: Magdeburgs "Herrgotts Kanzlei" (1548–1551/2)* (Tübingen: Mohr Siebeck, 2003). Particularly influential in suggesting to historians of the European Reformation that contingent circumstances and not essential differences of outlook determined whatever connections happened to develop in specific times and places between the confessions and their promotion of or opposition to princely absolutism was the case study of the Lutheran city of Lemgo's armed resistance to its Calvinist count's attempt to impose a Reformed church order, Heinz Schilling, *Konfessionskonflikt und Staatsbildung: Eine Fallstudie über das Verhältnis von religiösem und sozialem Wandel in der Frühneuzeit am Beispiel der Grafschaft Lippe* (Gütersloh: Mohn, 1981).

54. John Witte Jr., *The Reformation of Rights: Law, Religion, and Human Rights in Early Modern Calvinism* (Cambridge: Cambridge University Press, 2007), 2. For a slightly more ample treatment of the state of the question of possible links between Calvinism and democracy, see Philip Benedict, *Christ's Churches Purely Reformed: A Social History of Calvinism* (New Haven: Yale University Press, 2002), 536–37.

55. Philippe Besnard, *Protestantisme et capitalisme: La controverse post-weberienne* (Paris: Armand Colin, 1970); Gordon Marshall, *In Search of the Spirit of Capitalism: An Essay on Max Weber's Protestant Ethic Thesis* (New York: Columbia University Press, 1982); and Hartmut Lehmann and Guenther Roth, eds., *Weber's Protestant Ethic: Origins, Evidence, Contexts* (Cambridge: Cambridge University Press, 1993).

56. André Biéler, *La pensée économique et sociale de Calvin* (Geneva: Georg, 1959). After immersing himself in Calvin's writings to prepare this thesis, Biéler went on to articulate a socially progressive vision of Calvinism, to advocate the redistribution of corporate profits to alleviate poverty in the Third World, and to write shorter works on social questions whose influence in the struggle against apartheid in South Africa is highlighted in the chapter by John De Gruchy. A brief biography of him may be found in the 2008 edition of *La pensée économique et sociale* (Geneva: Georg, 2008), xiii–xxiii.

57. H. M. Robertson, *Aspects of the Rise of Capitalism: A Critique of Max Weber and His School* (Cambridge: Cambridge University Press, 1933); and Jean Lejeune, "Religion, morale et capitalisme dans la société liégoise du XVIIe siècle," *Revue Belge de Philologie et d'Histoire* 22 (1943): 109–52.

58. Etienne François, *Protestants et catholiques en Allemagne: Identités et pluralisme: Augsbourg, 1648–1806* (Paris: Albin Michel, 1993); and Philip Benedict, "Faith, Fortune and Social Structure in Seventeenth-Century Montpellier," *Past and Present* 152 (1996): 46–78. Cf. Peter Zschunke, *Konfession und Alltag in Oppenheim: Beiträge zur Geschichte von Bevölkerung und Gesellschaft einer gemischtkonfessionellen Kleinstadt in der Frühen Neuzeit* (Wiesbaden: F. Steiner, 1984), 114–25, 267; Fernand Braudel, *Civilisation matérielle, économie et capitalisme, XVe-XVIIIe siècle* (Paris: Armand Colin, 1979), esp. 2: 505–509; and Jan de Vries and Ad van der Woude, *The First Modern Economy: Success, Failure, and Perseverance of the Dutch Economy, 1500–1815* (Cambridge: Cambridge University Press, 1997), esp.165–72.

1 Calvin

Fifth Latin Doctor of the Church?

DIARMAID MACCULLOCH

Ambrose, Jerome, Augustine, and Gregory: the four Latin Doctors of the Church are a miscellaneous bunch. Three bishops plus one scholar who failed in the eremetical life, which he nevertheless continued to extol: three successful politicians, one pioneer of missionary planning, one writer of hymns, and one inspiration for the Western musical tradition. Plus, of course, in Augustine, one creative thinker of genius, who shaped Western Christianity for good, but who was virtually ignored elsewhere in the Christian world.

These are the men who stare in stern benevolence out of the panels of many a medieval pulpit. All their achievements are reflected in the achievements of John Calvin, with the exception of Jerome's failed effort at being a hermit. Truly Calvin was heir to their inheritance, perhaps the most Augustinian theologian of the sixteenth century, creator of a church that could in its peculiar fashion aspire to be the authentic voice of Catholicity in his time. Protestantism, I would hazard, was not a word that had great appeal to John Calvin; Catholicity would have aroused him a great deal more. Let us explore why Calvin might be placed alongside the four Latin Doctors, if Rome were to erect some equivalent of Geneva's great Reformation Wall in a corner of Vatican City.

Calvin might be said to share one other characteristic with the four Latin Doctors. They were innocent of the discipline invented by the medieval Western church that he so despised: theology. No one had talked much of theology before Peter Abelard wrote the *Theologia christiana* in the 1120s, and by then the Latin Doctors were dead and gone, to be digested into the new theological discipline, to become its raw material. Calvin was at the other end of the medieval factory of theology, recycling ore from the scholastic waste heaps. As a civil lawyer of modishly humanist learning, and with an acute humanist sense of history, he escaped the training in scholastic theology that nurtured most of the early Protestant reformers, from Luther to Zwingli to Bucer to Thomas Cranmer. Among the most well-known movers of the Reformation, Calvin was paralleled in this only by Desiderius Erasmus and by Joachim von Watt, the engaging lay reformer of St. Gallen.

That meant that Calvin found it easy to stand back from the scholastic achievement, and select from it what he wanted, which was not much. Bernard of Clairvaux was one of the few medievals who survived his scrutiny, mainly by being effectively prescholastic in his approach to matters of divinity, and Professor Anthony Lane has helped us see just how selective Calvin could be in using Bernard. Once Calvin was exposed to Bernard's writings, he found material that could be judiciously adapted to back up his existing theological positions. Bernard the devout son of the Roman Church unsurprisingly did not feature, nor would one know from Calvin that Bernard was perhaps the most prominent monk of his age. In any case, Calvin's 41 citations of Bernard hardly match up to no fewer than 1,708 quotations from Augustine of Hippo in Calvin's works.[1]

All in Calvin's teaching was, of course, directed in good humanist fashion *ad fontes,* to the wellsprings, and *ad fontes* meant scripture. In the course of delivering a brisk rhetorical kicking to Dionysius the Areopagite, Calvin provided a robust definition of what he thought theologians should and should not do:

> No one will deny that Dionysius, whoever he was, subtly and skillfully discussed many matters in his *Celestial Hierarchy.* But if anyone examines it more closely, he will find it for the most part nothing but talk. The theologian's task is not to divert the ears with chatter, but to strengthen consciences by teaching things true, sure and profitable....Therefore, bidding farewell to that foolish wisdom, let us examine in the simple teaching of Scripture what the Lord would have us know.[2]

Calvin was here actually borrowing his skepticism on Dionysius from Luther; but he was consistently much more relaxed than Luther about using the pre-Christian heritage on which scholastic theology had drawn when making his own reconstruction of the Catholic faith. Professor Irena Backus has pointed out the way in which Calvin's nontheological humanist intellectual background stayed with him in his exposition of theology. Long after his first publication, his textual commentary on Seneca's *De clementia*, he retained his propensity to use philosophical terms drawn from the Stoics and from Aristotle, and his acquaintance with pre-Christian learning was not in the first place mediated by reading what the Fathers had said about them.[3] As Calvin taught himself theology, there remained some limitations: in all his intense concentration on biblical commentary, he very rarely used Hebrew sources at first hand, and the evidence for his having more than a passing acquaintance with Hebrew may charitably be described as scanty.[4]

Calvin's early saturation in civil law rather than theology left its mark on the *Institutes.* From its earliest published version in 1536, this summary of the Catholic faith has a feature that makes it innovative among the early efforts of the reformers to constitute doctrinal statements: where Luther's *Small Catechism* ends with a catalogue of Christian duties, the 1536 *Institutes* makes a systematic attempt to integrate a discussion of civil government with doctrine, and it does so in notably humanist and frequently nonscriptural terms. Calvin's famous if convoluted statement justifying resistance is not couched in scriptural terms at all, but refers to the institutions of ephors in Sparta, demarchs in Athens, or the tribunes of the people in the Roman Republic.[5]

So the young evangelical academic took a fresh, nonscholastic approach to structuring his thinking on the great questions of Christianity, as he tried to create his own properly scriptural basis for the exposition of the Christian faith. The years 1536–1537 saw a pair of publications from Calvin, following the model made conventional by Luther's *Large* and *Small Catechisms*: they were principally structured by the Ten Commandments, Apostles' Creed, Lord's Prayer, and sacraments.

The shorter *Brève Instruction chrétienne* suffered rapid obscurity; in fact, it was lost until 1877. The larger companion of which it was a digest was to enjoy rather more celebrity. Even in its first version of 1536, the *Institutio* represented one of the most substantial efforts so far to provide a systematic basis for the emerging reform of the Western church.

Of course, the *Institutes* changed much before their final majestic form, so comprehensively rearranged from that first catechetical work, but one constant feature in all editions was the preface. It was dedicated to King Francis I of France, whose subject Calvin was in 1535 but who was long dead by the time that the last editions appeared in 1559 (Latin) and 1560 (French). This might seem strange, in view of the propensity of many humanists to change the dedications of their books to pursue congenial or generous patrons, and in view of the fact that as far as Calvin was concerned, King Francis was neither congenial nor generous. Why retain this passionate appeal to a monarch who was one of the greatest disappointments among many for the reformers of the sixteenth century?

Timing was all in that preface, which was so significantly dated August 1535 (when the preface itself was completed), despite the *Institutes'* actual publication in Basel in 1536. By August 1535, all Europe would have known of the violent end to one of the most traumatic seventeen months in sixteenth-century European history, when in June of that year, the Anabaptist reign in Münster was brought to a violent end. A traitor led the combined forces of the bishop and the emperor through the city defenses and captured its Anabaptist king, John of Leiden, and its leaders were awaiting the exemplary sadism of punishment that affronted authority felt appropriate to the crime of rebellion at the time.

With those events in mind, it was essential for Calvin to show the French king how to distinguish his own loyal evangelical subjects, the true Catholics, from the Anabaptists of Münster. It would be easy for French traditionalists to link the destructive regime of John of Leiden to the radical vandals in France, who in 1528 had vandalized a much-loved image of the Virgin Mary in Paris, and in 1534 had shocked all right-thinking people by disfiguring prominent places with printed attacks on the Mass. Calvin was not that removed from these iconoclastic wretches, and his preface to the king was a plea that he might recognize evangelicals as his friends rather than the self-styled Catholics who persecuted them: "Elijah taught us what we ought to reply to such charges: it is not we who either spread errors abroad or incite tumults; but it is they who contend against God's power."[6]

In 1536 Calvin was not to know that he would claw his way to a position in an alien European city in a fashion that had reminiscences of the rise of John of Leiden, similarly with a certain amount of bloodshed in the process, although more assured and long-term in its outcome. It is instructive to consider the similarities between Anabaptist Münster and the Geneva Calvin helped to remold. In both cases, a prominent European city repudiated its traditional overlord, a territorial bishop, and in the confused aftermath of that rebellion, both cities invited in prominent foreigners to help create a religious Reformation, violently destroying much from the past in the process. In the wake of the charismatic foreign leaders, there streamed from regions far from the city a host of ideologically motivated immigrants. Apart from the crowds of ordinary laypeople who arrived in Geneva, all the ministers in the city were immigrants, mostly French; in fact, astonishingly, between the 1540s and 1594, the Genevan ministry did not include a single native Genevan.[7] Both in Münster and Geneva, this exceptional situation triggered constitutional revolutions, both of whose outlines were to haunt European imaginations for centuries to come. Moreover, when Anabaptists talked of the church, what they said was not that different from some of the things John Calvin was inclined to say about the church. His assertions that discipline and suffering were characteristic of the true church were also Anabaptist themes.

Much of Calvin's subsequent development of his theology was designed to show how different he was from an Anabaptist; hence that preface in the *Institutes*, and hence also that pioneering discussion of civil government, which in its first version trumpeted its support for monarchy a good deal more loudly than in later modifications.[8] Certainly Calvin's place in Geneva contrasted sharply with that of John of Leiden in Münster. Rather than becoming a theocrat, his relation to the city authorities was distinctly reminiscent of that of Bishop Ambrose in Milan in relation to successive Roman emperors: wheedling, threatening, flattering, confronting, all against a background of constant detailed scrutiny of government as a busy pastor, preacher, and teacher.

Calvin's preface to the king of France was nevertheless a piece of self-deception. When preaching in Geneva on Acts 5:29, the crucial text about obeying God rather than man, he performed an unhappy balancing act. He told his listeners that this was a demand for resistance to the deceitful church of Rome, but that Anabaptists "and other fantasists" used it even though they "only wished to govern themselves in accordance with their foolish brains, under the pretence of wishing to obey God."[9] Many of Calvin's followers proved indeed over the next century that they could be as destructive and politically revolutionary as any Anabaptist, not least in the kingdom that Francis bequeathed his successors.

When Calvin returned to scripture to repristinate the Catholic faith, he quickly discovered the pitfalls of returning *ad fontes*: he was not the first or last to find that "the simple teachings of Scripture" might need a little glossing. A crisis came for him only a year after the publication of the *Institutes*, and even though the facts about this affair have been easily available in modern scholarship for more than a century, they have been interestingly little noticed before an excellent piece of textual editing by Dr. Marc Vial.[10] The crisis was triggered by accusations made by Pierre Caroli. Caroli, like Calvin, was a refugee from France and had briefly been his colleague in Geneva before becoming chief minister in Lausanne. Caroli then accused his former French exile associates in Geneva, Calvin, Guillaume Farel, and Pierre Viret, of being Arians. The accusation led to an examination of the case at a synod at Lausanne in May 1537, in which the three accused produced a confession of faith that explicitly condemned not only Arius but his bitter posthumous opponent Macedonius and the contrary views of the earlier father of modalist monarchianism, Sabellius.

So far, so orthodox, but among other rash formulations, the Genevan trio's confession of faith adopted a strategy disastrous in terms of the Catholic and Orthodox traditions: it tried to use purely scriptural language, leaving aside the two terms "Trinity" and "person" as being unscriptural. This was precisely what many radical

European Christians were beginning to do, on the perfectly reasonable scriptural-ist grounds that these crucial terms of developed Christian orthodoxy were not to be found in the Bible. Yet to abandon them was to abandon all trinitarian language after the first essays in Western Latin trinitarian theology by Tertullian, together with the whole inheritance of discussion worked out in the wake of the Council of Nicaea of 325. One historical development from such a strategy was the radical Christianity that looked askance at any theology created in the post-Nicene age, regarding it as tainted by the fateful alliance between the church of the Mediterranean and the Roman Empire. What followed from that attitude was the antitrinitarianism whose mid-sixteenth-century variants stretched from London to Lithuania. This movement fostered the developed Socinianism that in turn we now see as one of the founding elements of the Enlightenment.[11]

Such a future was the rather unexpected nemesis of a scrupulous scripturalism, and it has to be said that in the seventeenth century, many Reformed Protestants helped the process on its way. At Lausanne in 1537, Calvin was forced into a corner, and not merely by his own devotional logic, but by his annoyance at being person-ally hounded by Caroli. This led him into the further rashness at the synod of refusing to sign the Athanasian Creed, an act of extreme folly if he were to be taken seriously as a Catholic Christian. Oswald Myconius, minister of Basel, was among the influential voices expressing his displeasure, in particular in a letter to Heinrich Bullinger of Zürich.[12] The aftermath was a rapid retreat in the form of Calvin's two pamphlets published later that year. They reiterated his commitment to the use of the word "Trinity" and emphasized that a further rash statement of the Genevan ministers' confession, identifying Christ with Jehovah, was only what the great although equally contentious Bishop Cyril of Alexandria had said amid the storms of the Miaphysite controversy.[13] The resulting literary warfare rumbled on for a decade. As late as 1545, it was capable of making Calvin fall ill with worry, and of galvanizing him into writing, under the pseudonym of Nicolas des Gallars, a seventeen-thousand-word attack on Caroli in a few days.[14]

Thereafter Calvin in his career as religious leader was haunted by two urgent polemical necessities, which were also profound questions about his theological identity. First was the need to place himself as far away as possible from the Anabaptists. That meant secondly claiming a position of Catholicity that could look respectably mainstream in terms enunciated by the church of the first five centuries—therefore as far as possible from what the early church had defined as heresies. Let us see how he might achieve this.

One way was through Calvin's rediscovery of the tradition of the church. Very quickly the Protestant reformers had rowed back from their initial confident rejection of church tradition in favor of scripture alone, because Anabaptists had with perfect justice pointed out that scripture alone gave the most dubious foundation possible for something which magisterial Protestants much valued: the practice of infant baptism. That consideration had already affected the doctrinal formulations of Huldrych Zwingli in Zurich in the 1520s, and it can be seen to the full in Calvin's developing discussion of another vexing problem for the Protestant Reformation: where their church had been before Luther. Calvin's initial reaction to that question was to say that for long, there had been no visible church before

Luther. From 1539, however, the *Institutes* asserted baldly that even in the worst times: "The Lord used two means to keep his covenant inviolable. First, he maintained baptism there, a witness to this covenant; consecrated by his own mouth, it retains its force despite the impiety of men. Secondly, by his own providence, he caused other vestiges to remain, that the church might not utterly die."[15] Calvin did not argue the case as to why the sacrament of baptism had survived in such comparative lack of corruption, while the sacrament of Eucharist had been perverted into "the greatest sacrilege"; he simply asserted as an axiom that this was how God had arranged affairs.[16] No matter that the Anabaptists asserted that the historical corruption of baptism was as great as that of the Mass: baptism as commonly practiced on infants became the cornerstone of Calvin's case for the authenticity, the authentic Catholicity, of his reform. This was emphasized by the revisions on the subject of baptism and its efficacy as an instrumental sacrament that Calvin added to the 1543 version of the *Institutes*. They were part of a pattern. Calvin performed an even more radical about-face in 1543 on a ceremonial matter which was emphatically visible: the laying on of hands, especially in ordination. That custom, to which he had emphatically denied sacramental character in 1536, was now described as having a sacramental character. The 1543 version of the *Institutes* might be seen as the moment when the doctrine of the tradition of the church came into its own in Calvin's writings.

Randall Zachman frames his excellent discussion of such shifts in Calvin's theology in terms of "dialogue with Roman Catholics," and he is sound in his instinct that they arose from conflict: Calvin's theology, like that of Augustine of Hippo, thrived on conflict.[17] Nevertheless Zachman may be guiding our gaze in the wrong direction. The year 1543 was when Calvin had to face a challenge from a different variety of radicalism from that of Münster Anabaptists: part of the spectrum of those within the very immigrant community of Geneva itself. Naturally they included independent-minded and articulate people with strong opinions, and one was the Savoyard Sébastien Châteillon (now more usually called Sebastian Castellio). In 1543, Castellio put himself forward for the ministry in Geneva, but he was known to have his own stance on a number of biblical and theological problems, the most irksome of which for Calvin was his refusal to accept that the Song of Songs should really be a "canonical" part of the Bible. Calvin was determined to defend the canonicity of the Song of Songs; his theology was based on the principle that God's revelation of his Word was definitively contained within the Bible, and unlike Martin Luther, he was not prepared to pick and choose where the Word was best expressed within the Bible's covers. The Bible was God's to define, however unpromising the sensuous lyrics of the Song of Songs might seem.

However, this raised the uncomfortable question of how the canonical boundaries of the Bible had been set in the early church, as Calvin readily appreciated, given his humanist sense of historical perspective. At some point the church had made decisions about what should be in the Bible and what should not. Calvin had Castellio's views condemned, but he was forced to talk afresh about the tradition of the church: "our first plea and entreaty was that he should not rashly reject the age-long interpretation of the whole of the Church"—this was only a couple of years before the Council of Trent was to make such age-long interpretation an equal source of divine revelation with the biblical text.[18] For all his talk of pleas and entreaties, once Calvin had won his point with the civil authorities, Castellio was sent packing from Geneva, to add his own acid voice to an increasing chorus assailing Calvin's reputation for posterity.

Once Calvin had seen the importance of tradition to his arguments, he was faced with the dilemma of all Protestants who made the same rediscovery: how to pick and choose among the rich storehouse of tradition thus afforded him. He had been badly bruised by the Caroli affair and its revisiting of the fourth-century conflicts on Incarnation and Trinity: how might he best enunciate his loyalty to Catholic tradition? He might have done what so many had done in the fourth and fifth centuries and emphasized the role of Mary, the Mother of Jesus. Mary was the symbol and the means of Christ's Incarnation, the miracle of Christ's coming in flesh and blood in his earthly life in Palestine. Both Zwingli and Luther had written movingly about Mary because they felt real love and reverence for her, and they saw her as a guarantee of the Incarnation.

Calvin showed nothing of the same spirit of reverence for Mary. His fixed hatred of anything he defined as idolatry made him determined to avoid distraction from the worship of God, so he was suspicious of any attempt to give honor to Mary the mother of God. In the whole of the text of the *Institutes,* so soaked in biblical citations, there is only one passing reference to the *Magnificat,* Mary's biblical song when she learned from the angel Gabriel that she would bear the Christ child. Luther had cheerfully remarked in 1523 that Gabriel's greeting "Hail Mary" was no danger to those of firm faith, and the churches of Zurich continued to recite this biblical salutation in their liturgy until as late as 1563—but already in 1542 Calvin bitterly denounced any use of it as "execrable blasphemy," as he did for the traditional titles of honor for Mary, which Luther was happy to commend.[19] Calvin could not ignore Mary's part in the story of the Incarnation, for Christ was "born of the Virgin Mary" and "was incarnate by the Holy Spirit of the Virgin Mary," but he and his successors believed that when Christians had recited these statements in the Creeds, they should not dwell further on them in case idolatry loomed. It was not surprising, therefore, that Calvin should not warm to Luther's emphasis that Christ's coming in flesh by the Virgin could be experienced in every Eucharistic service.

So although Calvin naturally wanted to proclaim a Catholic doctrine of the Incarnation, he found Mary a problem rather than a reliable ally in this. Instead, he turned to the successive councils of the early church. The climax of these statements was the work of the Council of Chalcedon in 451, with its careful crafting of the "Chalcedonian Definition" on the person and natures of Christ. Christ was one person in two natures inextricably linked: he was God the Son and so fully part of the Divine Trinity, while at the same time he was Jesus the human being, born in Palestine. Chalcedon had a particular significance for magisterial Protestants, who saw it as the last general council of the church to make reliable decisions about doctrine in accordance with the core doctrines proclaimed in scripture—magisterial Protestants were all the more inclined to respect the early councils because the radicals of the Reformation rejected their legacy. In Calvin's case, Chalcedon might almost be seen as an organizing hermeneutic for his developed theology.

The balance of statements within the Chalcedonian Definition, with its emphasis on the indivisibility of the two natures of Christ, gave Calvin a model for that general principle which became very important to him: distinction, but not separation (*distinctio sed non separatio*). It was the perfect model to be used by this theologian so consciously striving for a Catholic balance: it can be seen, for instance, in Calvin's discussion of the church, both visible and invisible, or of election, both general and particular—and above all, in what he says about the Eucharist. Already in 1536, Calvin faithfully reproduced the terms of the Chalcedonian Definition when he came to came to discuss the nature of the Incarnation and also of what it means to be human. But once more, it is the watershed 1543 edition of the *Institutes* in which explicit references to the Council of Chalcedon multiply.[20] And as Professor Backus has made clear, this emphasis on the ecumenical councils and the Fathers generally remained a distinctive feature of Reformed Protestant scholarship during the sixteenth century, far more than among the Lutherans. Perhaps, the Reformed felt more need than Lutherans to justify their position against both Roman Catholicism and Reformation radicalism.[21]

Calvin, against his will, became the champion of a non-Lutheran Reformed axis on the Eucharist. He came to a Reformation already divided with distressing clarity since the Colloquy of Marburg in 1529. It was inevitable that Calvin, with his project to define the boundaries of a reformed Catholicism, devoted much energy to finding a formulation about the Eucharist that would give it due reverence and also avoid saying either too little or too much about it. His first instinct had been to disapprove of Zwingli's ideas, and he continued to think that Zwingli's presentation of the Eucharist lacked an appreciation of the mystery that it embodied, "which plainly neither the mind is able to conceive nor the tongue to express."[22] In his attempt to take a middle way in the controversy in a short treatise in that year of failed ecumenism, 1541, he said that Zwingli and Johannes Oecolampadius "labored more to destroy the evil than to build up the good."[23]

However, although Calvin found Zwingli's discussion of the Eucharist inadequate, he also strongly criticized Luther in his 1541 pamphlet. He deeply disapproved of Luther's insistence on finding the body and blood of Christ physically present in the Eucharistic elements. To understand why, we need to consider some of Calvin's other deeply held beliefs, for more than one consideration drove him to reject Luther's Eucharistic theology. First was Calvin's preoccupation with the dangers of idolatry. Paying undue attention to physical, visible objects obscured the worship of God "in spirit and in truth"—this is a phrase from a passage in the fourth chapter of John's Gospel that scores frequent references in Calvin's *Institutes*.

With the "distinction but not separation" principle in mind, Calvin made a firm distinction between "reality" and "sign," which nevertheless would not separate them. The old church betrayed this principle by confusing reality and sign, attributing to the signs of bread and wine worship, which was only due to the reality behind them. Luther, Calvin believed, had also wrongly attributed to the signs that which was only true of the reality: in particular, when Luther asserted that the physical body and blood of Christ were capable of being everywhere wherever the Eucharist was being celebrated in the world. Calvin devoted a substantial section in the final version of the *Institutes* to ridiculing the Lutheran doctrine of ubiquity.[24] He thought on the other hand that Zwingli had separated sign and reality too much. Calvin was firm against Zwingli by stating his conviction that "in the sacraments the reality is given to us along with the sign."[25]

Typically, Calvin returned to Augustine of Hippo, and like so many reformers, he was grateful for the crisp Augustinian definitions of the sacraments as "a visible sign of a sacred thing" or "a visible form of an invisible grace." But lurking always behind his sacramental discussion is the fifth-century clash over the divine and human natures of Christ, so relevant to that famously distinctive feature of Calvin's thought, the *extra Calvinisticum* on the Trinity.[26] Calvin, who always remained sensitive to Lutheran charges that he was repeating the errors of Nestorius, had already inserted into the 1539 *Institutes* an attack on both Nestorius and his extreme opponent Eutyches, and he characteristically amplified that attack in 1543 with one of his explicit invocations of Chalcedon.[27]

For Calvin, then, the signs of bread and wine become an instrument of God's grace in uniting the believer to Christ: hence Brian Gerrish's characterization of Calvin's views on the symbolism of bread and wine as "symbolic instrumentalism," in contrast to Zwingli's "symbolic memorialism," or Heinrich Bullinger's tactful move away from Zwingli to "symbolic parallelism."[28] Calvin distinguished himself from Luther by emphasizing that God's grace, which unites Eucharistic sign and reality, and which makes that sign an instrument of Christ's presence, is offered not to the whole congregation at a Eucharist, but only to God's elect. The body of Christ is not ubiquitous on earth in the Eucharist, as Luther said, but in heaven at the right hand of the Father. God's grace, brought by the Holy Spirit, lifts elect believers to Christ's presence in heaven.[29] As Calvin himself repeatedly pointed out, the ancient words of the Mass, "Lift up your hearts" (*Sursum corda*), beautifully express this idea, although he was not the first doctor in the Reformed tradition to do so.[30] Already in the 1520s Johannes Oecolampadius had found this a poetic and inspiring way of making clear that the elements of bread and wine were not too closely associated with the body and blood of Christ, and Bullinger was happy to quote the ancient liturgical words as well.[31]

So here was a consciously Chalcedonian and Augustinian construction of Eucharistic theology, which carefully avoided approaching the Incarnation through an emphasis on the role of Mary, and which vigorously rejected Luther's view of bread and wine as objectively Christ's body and blood. Heinrich Bullinger and Calvin gradually recognized that more united them on the Eucharist than divided them, and the result was the *Consensus Tigurinus*: a remarkable piece of theological statesmanship and a tribute to both Calvin's and Bullinger's common sense and ability to be gracious when circumstances cried out for it.[32] If anything is evidence for Calvin as Doctor of the Church, it is this. All too rarely in the sixteenth century did theologians acknowledge that they had substantial differences, but then go on to produce a joint statement both sides could find acceptable. Partisans of both sides could find their favorite expressions or insights carefully laid side by side in the text—the great precedent for such balance was of course the Chalcedonian Definition itself. The achievement of the *Consensus* was to create a broad enough area of agreement on the sacraments for the non-Lutheran Protestant churches of Europe to regard themselves as a single family. This had profound implications for the future direction of the Reformation from the Atlantic Isles to the Carpathian Mountains.

It is hardly necessary to point out that the ultimate symbol of Calvin's Chalcedonian orthodoxy was his destructive relationship with Michael Servetus. Even more surprising than Servetus's eventual fiery death in Geneva was the extraordinary sequence of events by which the Inquisition in Vienne was first supplied with the evidence to condemn Servetus from Calvin's own archive and was then formally approached by the Genevan authorities to provide them with the Inquisition's trial records for a renewed heresy trial. Calvin had also ensured that there had been careful international soundings among Protestants about the sentence; after all, the legality of Geneva burning someone who had merely been passing through the city was not immediately obvious. On the whole, he found a cautious endorsement, with the famous and unofficial exception of Sebastian Castellio. The fact that Geneva chose to emphasize the charge of blasphemy rather than heresy only revealed Protestant squeamishness about the heresy word so often employed against them.[33] The concept of religious error underlying both crimes was common to both halves of the riven Western church.

Domestically, the serious crisis in which Calvin had found himself by 1553 came to a head over the next two years, when his very success at widening his support in the civic elite drove the infuriated opposition to open confrontation. Calvin gleefully seized on this as an attempted coup d'état, and from the time of the 1555 coup, his position in the city was secured. John of Leiden lost Münster, but Calvin won Geneva. And the burning of Servetus strengthened Calvin's position not only in Geneva itself but throughout Europe. It was from this moment that he began widely to be perceived as not one reformer among many, but the major voice in Reformation Protestantism—particularly by Roman Catholics. He had shown his seriousness as the defender of Catholic Christianity: a Latin Doctor indeed.

Of course, it was not simply because of this notorious incident that Calvin may be so styled. The cool, measured Latin and French prose of the *Institutes,* the commentaries, and the surviving sermons are a precise, careful distillation of the Western Christian tradition as it had emerged in the fifth century on the back of Chalcedon and the teachings of Augustine. To that we might add the impact of Genevan psalmody even beyond the boundaries of Reformed Christianity. Calvin may not have created it, but without his creation of Reformed Geneva, its impact would have been far less, and psalmody is a fitting monument to a man who very frequently cast himself in the role of King David the psalmist.[34] This whole legacy is one of the many reasons why historians and theologians should do their best to avoid the terms "Calvinist" and "Calvinism" when discussing the Reformed tradition. Such labels demean what Calvin was trying to do, and also what he achieved, which was to provide a very precise delineation of the tradition of the previous fifteen hundred years that calls itself Catholic. There may be other versions of the picture on offer from Rome, Canterbury, or Wittenberg, but it is impossible to ignore the monument to Western Christianity provided by the Doctor of Geneva.

Yet the term "Fifth Latin Doctor" also has its uses in precisely *limiting* Calvin's place in the Christian story. Calvin looked to the Council of Chalcedon as a significant stage in the church's meditation on its message and purposes. Like most Christians in the Latin West and Orthodox East, he would have seen its role in Christian history in terms of triumph: it synthesized the tradition, provided directions for the future, and offered a climax to the doctrinal work of the previous 150 years. Yet if we stand back from this historiographical tradition, we will see that Chalcedon in fact represented a disaster in Christianity. It split the Christian world three ways, between the imperial Christians who accepted what was (to be frank) a Christological formula cobbled together in an attempt at creating unity, and two other sections of the Christian church who, for contrasting reasons, rejected it: the Miaphysites and the Dyophysites of Africa and Asia. The historical chances of the next few centuries, by giving an accidental boost to Chalcedonian Christianity, shifted the whole Christian story westward toward medieval Europe. That has obscured this greatest of might-have-beens in the Christian story, which might have led to Baghdad becoming the center of gravity in Christianity rather than Rome. If so, the fifth Latin Doctor might have taken a very different place in the Christian story.

■ Notes

1. Anthony N. S. Lane, *Calvin and Bernard of Clairvaux* (Princeton: Princeton Theological Seminary, 1996).

2. John Calvin, *Institutes of the Christian Religion*. 2 vols., ed. John McNeill, trans. Ford Lewis Battles, 1, 14. 4, 164–65 (hereafter Calvin, *Inst.*, McNeill/Battles ed.).

3. Irena Backus, *Historical Method and Confessional Identity in the Era of the Reformation (1378–1615)* (Leiden: Brill, 2003), 71, 79, 86, 99–100.

4. See a judicious treatment of this in Anthony N. S. Lane, *John Calvin: Student of the Church Fathers* (Grand Rapids, MI: Baker Academic, 1999), 226–29.

5. The discussion of leadership for rebellion, which became *Inst.* 4, 20.31 is most usefully studied for its variants in Latin and French and over the various editions of the *Institutes* in Harro Höpfl, ed., *Luther and Calvin on Secular Authority* (Cambridge: Cambridge University Press, 1991), 82–83.

6. John Calvin, *Institutes of the Christian Religion,* 1536 *Edition,* trans. and ed. Ford Lewis Battles (Atlanta: John Knox, 1975), 12. Cf. Preface to Calvin, *Inst.* McNeill/Battles ed., 1: 28–29.

7. In chap. 5, in this book, William Naphy notes one case in which the Genevan magistrates attempted to force the native Genevan, Jean Trolliet, upon the Company of Pastors unsuccessfully.

8. Calvin, *Inst.* 4, 20.8, McNeill/Battles ed., 2: 1493–95. Its variants in Latin and French and over the various editions of the *Institutes* are helpfully laid out in Höpfl, *Luther and Calvin*, 56–57, 84–86.

9. John Calvin, Sermon on Acts 5, *Sermons on the Acts of the Apostles, Supplementa Calviniana* 8, ed. Willem Balke and Wilhelm H.Th. Moehn (Neukirchen-Vluyn: Neukirchner Verlag, 1994), 160–61.

10. John Calvin, *Confessio Genevensium praedicatorum de Trinitate, Calv. Opp. R, series* 2, 3: 123–52, gives the text with a fine introduction. The dispute and the literature that sprang out of it are described in detail in Eduard Bähler, "Petrus Caroli und Johannes Calvin: Ein Beitrag zur Geschichte und Kultur der Reformationszeit," *Jahrbuch für Schweizerische Geschichte* 29 (1904): 39–168, esp. 62–96. This issue is also dealt with briefly in Wulfert de Greef, *The Writings of John Calvin: An Introductory Guide,* 2nd ed. (London: Westminster John Knox Press, 2008), 158–60.

11. On this, see Jonathan Israel, *Radical Enlightenment: Philosophy and the Making of Modernity* 1650–1750 (Oxford: Oxford University Press, 2001).

12. Calvin, *Confessio Genevensium*, 129 and n.

13. Ibid., 151–52.

14. On Calvin's traumas over Caroli in 1545, see Jean-François Gilmont, *John Calvin and the Printed Book* (Kirksville, MS: Truman State University Press, 2005), 1–3.

15. Calvin, *Inst.* 4, 2.11, McNeill/Battles ed., 2: 1052.

16. See a similar assertion about God's continual care to preserve "a hidden seed, that the Church should not be utterly extinguished" in Calvin's last and posthumously published work, *Commentary on Ezekiel*, 2 vols., J. King ed., *Calvin's Commentaries* 23 (Edinburgh: Calvin Translation Society, 1847–50), 2: 165; on the Eucharist as the "greatest sacrilege," see Calvin, *Inst.* 4, 2.9, McNeill/Battles ed., 2: 1050.

17. There is an excellent discussion of this and allied shifts in Calvin's perspective in Randall Zachman, "Revising the Reform: What Calvin Learned from Dialogue with Roman Catholics," in *John Calvin and Roman Catholicism: Critique and Engagement, Then and Now*, ed. Randall Zachman (Grand Rapids, MI: Baker Academic, 2008), 165–91, esp. 186.

18. Pastors' memorandum on Castellio, February 1544, *Calv. Opp.* 29: 673–75; quoted in translation in: *John Calvin: Documents of Modern History*, ed. Mark Greengrass and George R. Potter, trans. George R. Potter (London: Edward Arnold, 1983), 101. For Theodore Beza's echo of this championing of Church tradition in his later attacks on Castellio, see Backus, *Historical Method*, 118–21.

19. "Articles agreed upon by the Faculty of Sacred Theology of Paris with the 'Antidote'" in Henry Beveridge, ed., *Tracts and Treatises on the Reformation of the Church*, 3 vols. (Edinburgh: Oliver and Boyd, 1958), 1: 69–120, here 118–20. This is Calvin's riposte to the 25 Articles put out on March 10, 1542, by the doctors of theology in the University of Paris. On Luther, see Walter Tappolet with Albert Ebneter, *Das Marienlob der Reformatoren: Martin Luther, Johannes Calvin, Huldrych Zwingli, Heinrich Bullinger* (Tübingen: Katzmann, 1962), 126; on Zürich, see Gotfried Locher, *Zwingli's Thought: New Perspectives* (Leiden: E.J. Brill, 1981), 60. For further discussion, see Diarmaid MacCulloch, "Mary and Sixteenth-Century Protestants," in *The Church and Mary*, Studies in Church History 39, ed. R. N. Swanson (Woodbridge: Boydell and Brewer for the Ecclesiastical History Society, 2004), 191–217.

20. For discussion of the incarnation and the nature of humanity, see Calvin, *Institutes of the Christian Religion*, 1536 *Edition*, 52. Compare its development in Calvin, *Inst.* 2, 14.1, McNeill/Battles ed., 1: 482. For explicit references to Chalcedon added in 1543, see Calvin, *Inst.* 2, 14.4; 4, 5.4; 4, 7.2; 4, 7.4; 4, 7.5; 4, 9.11.

21. Backus, *Historical Method*, 196–251.

22. Calvin, *Inst.* 4, 17.7, McNeill/Battles ed., 2: 1367. For his comments on Luther and Zwingli in the 1550s, see Bernard Cottret, *Calvin: A Biography* (Grand Rapids, MI: Eerdmans, 2000), 66.

23. *Short treatise on the Lord's Supper* (1541), quoted in Paul Rorem, "Calvin and Bullinger on the Lord's Supper," *Lutheran Quarterly* 2 (1988): 155–84, 357–89, 156. The English text may conveniently be found in a contemporary translation (misattributed to Miles Coverdale) in *Writings and Translations of Myles Coverdale*, ed. G. Pearson (Cambridge: Parker Society, 1844), 434–66.

24. Calvin, *Inst.* 4, 17.16–31, McNeill/Battles ed., 2: 1379–1403.

25. *Commentary on Isaiah* (published 1551), quoted in Potter and Greengrass, *Calvin*, 36.

26. Calvin, *Inst.* 2, 14.4, McNeill/Battles ed., 1: 486–87. A fine treatment of the question is provided by Heiko Oberman, "The 'Extra' Dimension in the Theology of Calvin," *Journal of Ecclesiastical History* 21 (1970): 43–64, esp. 56–57.

27. Calvin, *Inst.* 4, 14.4, McNeill/Battles ed., 2: 1277.

28. Brian Gerrish, "Sign and Reality: The Lord's Supper in the Reformed Confessions," in his *The Old Protestantism and the New* (Edinburgh: T. and T. Clark, 1982), 118–30.

29. The key discussion here is that developed for the 1559 version of the *Institutes*, Calvin, *Inst.* 4, 17.16–34, McNeill/Battles ed., 2: 1379–1411.

30. Calvin, *Inst.* 4, 17.36, McNeill/Battles ed., 2: 1412; compare other instances from Calvin cited by Zachman, "Revising the Reform," 177–79. See also Christopher Kaiser, "Climbing Jacob's Ladder: John Calvin and the Early Church on our Eucharistic Ascent to Heaven," *Scottish Journal of Theology* 56 (2003): 247–67.

31. See T. Harding, ed., *The Decades of Henry Bullinger,* 4 vols. (Cambridge: Parker Society, 1849–52), 4 (The Fifth Decade), 309. With a not uncharacteristic contrariness, Martin Bucer disapproved of the analogy to *sursum corda*: see D. F. Wright, ed. *Common Places of Martin Bucer* (Appleford: Sutton Courtenay Press, 1972), 79.

32. A fine treatment of the genesis of the *Consensus* is provided in Rorem, "Calvin and Bullinger on the Lord's Supper."

33. Leonard Williams Levy, *Treason against God: A History of the Offense of Blasphemy* (New York: Schocken, 1981), esp. 135–47.

34. On Calvin as David, see Herman Selderhuis, *Calvin's Theology of the Psalms* (Grand Rapids, MI: Eerdmans, 2007). On the impact of Genevan psalmody on northern Europe quite apart from Francophone and Anglophone societies, see Eckhart Grunewald, Henning P. Jürgens, and Jan R. Luth eds., *Der Genfer Psalter und seine Rezeption in Deutschland, der Schweiz und den Niederlanden* 16.-18. *Jahrhundert* (Tübingen: Max Niemeyer, 2004).

2 The Ideal of *Aristocratia Politiae Vicina* in the Calvinist Political Tradition

HARRO M. HÖPFL

This is an examination of aristocracy as an orienting principle in Calvin's own political theory and ecclesiology, which goes on to consider its place in the Calvinist political tradition. I argue that aristocracy is the defining feature of Calvin's duplex regimen, the external order and (humanly speaking) the *movens* of the *politia Christiana*. However, the desiderata and the internal complexities of Calvin's political and ecclesiological thought were ill adapted to the circumstances in which many Calvinists found themselves. Adapting the duplex regimen and finding appropriate ways to argue for it, or approximations of it, necessitated accommodations and compromises. These between them, I suggest, constitute the Calvinist political tradition, which bore progressively less resemblance to anything found in Calvin.

Throughout his public life, Calvin was preoccupied with what evangelicals called the external order of the visible church.[1] Thinking about the subject in terms of the forms of government became inevitable once Luther dismissed the papacy as a "tyranny," denied that monarchical rule over the church had any scriptural authority, and insisted on the freedom and rights of Christian communities.[2] In the conventional political theory of the time, if the church was not a monarchy, it must be an aristocracy or democracy, or some combination, since it was obviously not anarchy.[3] But Calvin could not present his ecclesiology as an inference from this simple logic. He had no prima facie grounds for recourse to philosophical or pragmatic "natural" reasoning about forms of government in this context. However much he valued natural reason, prudence, and learning, their province for him did not extend to theology, and therefore, could not be applied to significant aspects of ecclesiology either.[4] Christ might have ordered the visible church in a way that was "folly in the eyes of the world," just as God's will, revealed in scripture, runs entirely counter to the ordinary sentiments of mankind about tyrannical secular rulers (*Inst.* 4, 20.24–28). Thomists could legitimately argue for ecclesiastical monarchy from the natural principles of order and the lessons of history and prudence, as well as from scripture.[5] Calvin could only allow such reasoning in ecclesiology with regard to adiaphora, but his theology is not in any significant respect adiaphorist.

What is decisive here is that Calvin and his followers construed what they were doing as "the cause of reformation" (as Calvinists termed it), but certainly not as "the Reformation," a much later concept. Reformation meant precisely re-formation: restoring the church and the life of Christians to the original form, pattern, or "face" that Christ and the apostles had instituted. That pattern was deemed to be unambiguously enshrined in scripture, and the first generation of reformers needed no very explicit concept of it. In fact, the 1536/1541 editions of Calvin's *Institutes* still treated discrediting Romanist doctrine and practice as almost the only necessity in ecclesiology. Ecclesiastical reform was regarded as a matter of metaphorically, and often literally, stripping away various obvious abuses, accretions, and deformations (collectively "human traditions") from a church that evangelicals already inhabited, using whatever personnel and methods were readily available.[6] The Genevan reformation was still a typical affair of this kind, complete with popular preaching initiatives and upheavals, set-piece disputations between representatives of the old religion and reformers, an official verdict in favor of reform, an incremental dismantling of the old order, assimilation or expulsion of its personnel, and an (initially very experimental) institutionalization of true "evangelical" worship and order. It was, however, already clear to some of the reformers by the 1530s that what was emerging was churches that had exchanged subordination to "spiritual tyrants" for subordination to secular rulers who might be no better. The reformers' insistence that secular rulers could address only external and not true righteousness and ostensibly could not impose obligations on the conscience did not alter the fact that the ultimate authority over management of churches and the ministry had been handed over to them.[7] In Calvin's lifetime, moreover, the Anabaptist challenge and the increasingly acrimonious disputes among reformers themselves over central evangelical themes demonstrated that the marks of the true church—true preaching and the two sacraments—provided little guidance in determining the external order of a true church.[8] All this and a more and more intellectually confident Romanist opposition, culminating in the conclusion of the Council of Trent in 1563, made articulating a model of a rightly ordered visible church essential.[9]

The orthodox reformers came to recognize that, at a pragmatic level, the survival of evangelical churches depended on the authority of the reformed ministry and some kind of discipline.[10] Establishing or consolidating an evangelical church, however, could not be legitimated simply in pragmatic terms, as one might justify changing secular laws and arrangements to meet changing circumstances, though even that was universally regarded as a delicate and hazardous undertaking.[11] On the contrary, in unguarded moments, Calvin said that "the form which the Apostles instituted" was "the only model of a true Church, and whosoever deviates from it in the smallest degree is in error."[12] How much scope there was for pragmatic adaptation to circumstances, therefore, depended entirely on how specific the ecclesiastical model laid down in scripture was deemed to be and how much weight could justifiably be given to various postapostolic practices, doctrines, and institutions. The latter was essential, given that the inclusive churches of the orthodox reformers were unscriptural. It was, however, also fraught with risk: the gathered congregations of the Anabaptists had no such problem and dissociating the orthodox reformation from them tended to accentuate the legitimacy of postapostolic paradigms, which, in turn, played into the hands of the Romanists.[13]

In his Ecclesiastical Ordinances for Geneva in 1541 and in subsequent versions of the *Institutes* and elsewhere, Calvin elaborated an ecclesiastical model that was very specific indeed.[14] He claimed scriptural precept or example, or inference from scriptural principle, for Geneva's most controversial institutions and practices.[15] The injunction to do "all things decently and in good order" (I Corinthians 14:40) provided his ecclesiological *mot d'ordre*.[16] The Confession de Foy of 1537 had already required all Genevan residents to affirm that "les ordonnances qui sont necessaires a la police exterieure de l'Eglise...nous ne tenons point pour traditions humaines, daultant quelles sont comprinses soubz ce commandement general de sainct Paul qu'il vault que tout se face entre nous decentement et par bon ordre."[17] Discipline became his overarching ecclesiastical concept, even though he never formally made it into the third mark of a true church, as the French (1559), Scottish (1560), and Belgic Confessions (1561) were to do in his own lifetime.[18] For Calvin, ecclesiastical good order and discipline depended, in turn, on an aristocratic form of government, modified by elements of popular participation and monarchy. He never, to my knowledge, explicitly described the true visible church as an aristocracy. That would have been rhetorically inept, one thing Calvin certainly was not. The aristocratic principle is, however, plain enough. So Calvin cites Paul as indicating that there is no monarchy among ministers, much less a universal monarchy, and, according to Jerome, "the churches were governed by the common counsel of presbyters" in scriptural times.[19] Bishops were introduced in the postapostolic church, "lest, as usually happens, out of equality dissensions should arise," but they did not have "dominium over their collegae. Rather they were like a consul in the senate" (*Inst.* 4, 4.2). And "according to Peter bishops and pastors are collegae non domini," just as Paul and Peter were equals (Inst. 4, 6.7). Scripture is seen to demand that an evangelical clerus (Calvin's word, *Inst.* 4, 4.9; 4, 12.1) must be carefully selected (*Inst.* 4, 3.10–12, 14–16; 4, 4.9–10, 14–16); the Ordinances of 1541 and 1561 specified all this in great detail. The clerus has distinctive authority and independence (*Inst.* 4, 11.3), and it governs the Church (*Inst.* 4, 3.8; 4, 4.1). It has *potestas* (*Inst.* 4, 8–10) and *iurisdictio* (*Inst.* 4, 11) over it. A *consistoire* of ministers and elders enforces discipline: "consessum seniorum, qui erat in ecclesia quod in urbe est senatus."[20] This ecclesiastical regimen is corporate, not subject to the authority of any one of its members (*Inst.* 4, 6.4, 4, 11.6). It derives its authority from God, but gets its personnel by election, designation, or some combination of the two, in such a way as to select the best men: for humanists like Calvin a true aristocracy is obviously a humanist aristocracy of virtue, which per se has nothing to do with hereditary nobility.[21]

Calvin was explicit that what he valued about the aristocratic form was that it allowed for mutual correction and restraint, but also for mutual encouragement and support: "discipline" meant all of these things.[22] He always interpreted monarchs as intolerant of any kind of restraint, and, a fortiori, popes, who had become virtually synonymous with tyrants for him. By contrast, "it is safer and more tolerable that the government should be in the hands of several [*plures*], so that they should give each other mutual assistance, teach and admonish one another, and that if one should arrogate to himself more than is just, there should be several others as censors and masters or teachers [*magistri*] to constrain their licence" (*Inst.* 4, 20.8).[23] As for pure "democracy," it was one of Aristotle's corrupt forms, and no reputable authority defended it. The simplification of the Aristotelian pure forms that Calvin adopted in the French 1541 version of the *Institutes* made democracy less objectionable.[24] It now merely denoted a form of government in which "the people" or citizens had some part in legislating and in naming or removing magistrates. The *Institutes* was always careful to insist that the *populus* or *congregatio* had some element of authority. No evangelical could have done less, given the polemical weight evangelicals laid on the etymology of ecclesia and the authority of congregations as demanded by scripture, specifically in the selection (*electio*) of ministers, if only to deny popish tyranny and hierarchy.[25] This was entirely compatible with the modified aristocratic form of ecclesiastical polity that Calvin regarded as scriptural; as noted earlier, aristocracy even tolerated some monarchical modifications. A modified aristocratic form for the church was, after all, adopted by Geneva and Strasbourg.

Calvin claimed scriptural warrant for this "imago of the divine institution" (*Inst.* 4, 6.10), but he freely acknowledged that some aspects of the external order of a godly church were not prescribed by scripture, and he recognized some practices and arrangements of the early and patristic church as paradigmatic (*Inst.* 4, 4.1). One reason was that the scriptural churches had been entirely dissociated from the secular polity and, in this respect, resembled those of the Anabaptist "madmen and barbarians" who, for Calvin, were as much of a menace as papists and "flatterers of princes" (*Inst.* 4, 20.1–2). He, therefore, never restricted himself exclusively to legitimatization by scripture, although he did maintain that all legitimate ecclesial practices were either laid down in scripture, directly inferred from it, or, at least, entirely compatible with its principles. However, he seems to have quite deliberately deployed unscriptural political concepts, arguments, and analogies to describe the true visible church. For pastors, he used terms that had originally designated the relationship of imperial agents to their emperor—(de)legates, representatives, mandatories—or that normally applied to the polity.[26] He described the visible church as a *politia* (*Inst.* 4, 3.6), in which the pastorate exercised a *gubernatio, magistratus, administratio, regimen, potestas, jurisdictio,* and in which the "senate" of elders ("senatu...gravium virorum, qui in primitiva ecclesia constituebantur, ut conformandae publicae disciplinae praeessent," *Inst.* 4, 20.4, added in 1539) were "censors of morals" (*Inst.* 4, 11.6). The early bishops were like the Roman consuls in relation to the senate (*Inst.* 4, 4.2). What is more, he repeatedly used the political analogy that just as "no city or country can survive without a magistracy and a polity, so also the church of God...needs a spiritual polity of its own" (*Inst.* 4, 11.1, from 1543). He carefully added that this in no way impedes or diminishes secular authority, but rather helps and promotes it. From 1536 on, the *Institutes* specifed rites and laws to establish and preserve peace, good order, and discipline, in view of men's habits, vices, and diversity of opinion (*Inst.* 4, 10.27). Calvin's reflection that equality usually leads to disorder (*Inst.* 4, 4.2) plainly owes nothing to scripture and everything to political theory. Scholastics and papists thought this demonstrated the naturalness of hierarchy, with a monarch at its apex. Calvin queried but did not reject the term hierarchy (*Inst.* 4, 4.4; 4,

6.10), but he allowed only "what God himself has outlined [*delineavit*] in his Word," namely "moderators" or "bishops" authorized by scripture and the practice of the early church, who had *auctoritas* but no kind of *imperium*. The Ordinances of 1541 stated explicitly that the only way good order and concord could be preserved in the church without derogating from the supremacy of God's revealed will is through the pastorate's self-government in appointing its members and policing their conduct. In this way, papist hierarchy was excluded, and the aristocratic principle preserved. In sum, for Calvin the *Église bien ordonnée* was a polity with its own regime, personnel, laws, jurisdiction, and power, all of which were authorized by God. It differed from the secular polity only in being self-sufficient. In the perfect polity, wholly adequate to the divine purpose and intent, a duplex regimen is required: a true visible church, complemented by the cooperation of secular authority and coextensive with its jurisdiction.

Nevertheless, Calvin's legitimatization of the secular polity, far from being tailored to meet the requirements of his ecclesiastical model, originally had no connection with it. In the 1536 edition of the *Institutes*, written before he had any responsibility for the Genevan church let alone for an enormous network of churches, Calvin's interest in the topic of "political administration" was confined to insisting on the scope and depth of the Christian's duty of obedience to secular authority. The obvious target of his comments, written just after Münster, was the Anabaptists, and his point was to deny the all too plausible and long-standing papist claim that the new gospel inevitably led to rebellion and insubordination. He, therefore, stressed that the duty of obedience of Romans 13 and 1 Peter 2 was not conditional on the form of government, the ruler's fulfillment of his moral or religious duties, or even (it seems) his having a legitimate claim to office. Calvin refers to Old Testament conquerors (*Inst.* 4, 20.24–28) and explains that the true Christian does not make his obedience to rulers conditional on a scrutiny of titles (*Inst.* 4, 20.28–29). His generic term for rulers was not Luther's "princes" (*Fürsten*) but "magistrates." This was remarkable in that Calvin was a Frenchman, and therefore predisposed to monarchy, and because he had chosen the term before Geneva or even Strasbourg had any significance in his life. But then Melanchthon too used the term; perhaps it was simply a piece of humanist classicizing (like referring to churches as "temples") that later came to assume significance. At any rate, the republican terminology in no way compromised Calvin's insistence that the private Christian must obey kings and tyrants as much as virtuous magistrates. He argued in a thoroughly Lutheran, *zwei Reiche* manner that both the ends and means assigned to the ministry and the magistracy are separate and different.[27] The ministry is charged with the First Table of the Law, or *pietas*, the magistrates, with the Second, or *justitia*. If magistrates trespass on the things that are God's, we must indeed obey God and disobey Caesar, but then must also humbly suffer the consequences or flee (*Inst.* 4, 20.31). Astonishingly, the *Institutes* never mentioned the latter alternative in its "political" chapter. However, if there happen to be popular magistrates established for the purpose,[28] which perhaps includes institutions like the principal assemblies of the European polities,[29] they are entitled, indeed obliged, to defend the people's "liberties" (*Inst.* 4.20.31). But unlike the Lutherans of Magdeburg and Melanchthon,[30] Calvin gave no rationale for this exception, never explained its scope, and cited no authority. He never invoked the defense or advancement of the true religion as a justification for resistance.

The *Institutes* of 1543 already qualified much of Calvin's previous doctrine, and subsequent interpolations, published and unpublished sermons, commentaries, and encyclicals complicated his views even more. In the *Institutes*, he came to insist that God's duplex regimen requires that the church and the secular polity, the pastorate and the magistrates, both advance *humanitas* and *pietas* (*Inst.* 4, 20.2, with an important addition in 1559; see the long section added to 4, 20.9 in 1559). And just as his ecclesiology had made a modified aristocracy a sine qua non of a true pastorate and discipline, so his political doctrine after 1543 explicitly made it the best form for secular government as well, which is hardly surprising since his arguments for an aristocratic ecclesiastical regiment had been largely political in nature in the first place. The first *Institutes* had dismissed discussion of forms of government as irrelevant to Christians and inconclusive in any case (*Inst.* 4.20.8). In his addition to this section in 1543, Calvin not only explicitly discussed the "best state of a commonwealth" but now asserted that, in the abstract, aristocracy is the best form of polity, that God had instituted an "aristocracy bordering on politia" for the exemplary commonwealth of Israel, and that a people that enjoyed such a government was singularly blessed.[31] Using arguments identical to those he used for a collegial ministry (*Inst.* 4, 3.2; 4, 10.27; 4, 20.8), Calvin claimed that several heads are wiser than one and that, although each form of government has its typical defects, a well-tempered aristocracy is, nevertheless, superior to monarchy. In his commentaries and sermons, he developed a more qualified version of his objections to the *princeps legibus solutus* and his low opinion of monarchs generally.[32] But in all subsequent versions of the *Institutes*, Calvin reverted to the 1536 text, reemphasizing political obedience regardless of the form of government or the presence of tyrannical rulers (*Inst.* 4, 20.24–29).

Calvin had made it progressively clearer that although magistrates and ministers may and must use different means (the ministry could not employ the sword),[33] the ends ordained for them were identical, and their duty was to cooperate (*Inst.* 4, 11.3). In 1559, he added "to advance and safeguard the external worship of God, and to defend the sound doctrine and the stability *status*] of the church" to the duties of ensuring civil justice, peace, and tranquility, which he had already assigned the secular magistrate in 1536 (*Inst.* 4, 20.2). He had insisted even then that the business of the polity is to attend both to humanitas and the *publica facies religionis*, repressing idolatry, sacrilege, and blasphemy (*Inst.* 4, 20.3). Ideally, too, both church and polity would be aristocracies, with democratic and monarchical modifications. Geneva was, and was seen by many as, exemplary in both respects. Its ecclesiastical ordinances and catechisms were published for the world to see and emulate, but even its civil ordinances were translated for an English public by Robert Fills in 1562.[34] As it stood, Geneva could only be an exemplar for city-states, but the substantial additions and modifications necessary to adapt its ecclesiastical model to more powerful states (much as Calvin disliked large kingdoms) were already being elaborated in Calvin's own time by Huguenot and Kirk practice.[35] Yet these churches too had a synodical and, thus, plainly aristocratic character. Calvin had provided an abstract ideal of the kind of republic in which a godly church could be fully at home. By contrast, a church whose congregation was not coextensive with the totality of subjects in a commonwealth was for him either an illegitimate sect or a situation to be borne until such time as God was pleased to allow the establishment of the *respublica Christiana*. Ever an implacable opponent of sects and schisms, he forbade separation from even barely evangelical churches (such as the Geneva that had expelled him), quite unlike some of the "puritans" who later invoked his authority.[36] His own theology of political obedience made it impossible for him to do more than merely set down an abstract ideal, for obedience itself barred the way to any attempt to implement the respublica Christiana except through the magistrate.

Taken together, then, Calvin's ecclesiology and his political theory constitute an intricate system of affirmations, qualifications, and denials. The tensions between these various elements are only resolved in his own practice, which made the duplex regimen neither a *zwei Reiche/regimente Lehre* nor a Zwinglian or Lutheran conflation of magistracy/*Oberkeit* and ministry. In his literary presentations, he simultaneously affirmed, qualified, and denied: the separation of church and polity; discipline as a constitutive feature of a true church; the necessity of an aristocratic form for both ministry and magistracy; the role of the laity; and the legitimacy of hierarchy.[37] What is more, he never clarified the relative provinces of scripture and secular reason in either ecclesiastical or political matters, sometimes affirming that scripture ought to be enough for true Christians, at other times insisting on the worth, adequacy, and utility of secular wisdom and prudence for secular purposes, but without answering the question of where ecclesiastical externals are located in the secular-spiritual distinction. He claimed exclusively scriptural authority for decisive components of his political theory, notably the doctrine of obedience and nonresistance and the duplex regimen. At the same time, however, he himself employed secular reason and prudence with respect to both church and polity. Quentin Skinner has described him as a "master of equivocation," although perhaps "circumspection" would be more charitable.[38] Unless circumstances were uniquely favorable, as in Scotland, perfect fidelity to Calvin's paradigm of Reformed ecclesiastical polity, preserving his system of affirmations, qualifications, and denials, without compromising essential aspects of it, proved to be impossible for his followers. The various adaptations and compromises that were made, once embedded, became the Calvinist political tradition. At this point, some reflections on the identity of that tradition seem to be called for.

It would be absurd to deny the existence of the Calvinist tradition, in the sense of a continuum of persons and organizations for whom the work and works of Calvin and various foundational documents have been uniquely authoritative, indeed, a principal component of their intellectual and moral formation. But any more precise characterization of this tradition as a whole is certainly beyond me and would seem to be unattainable. There is no consensus on its foundational doctrines, and no agreement even on Calvin's own place in it. Its self-identification is as the Reformed, not the Calvinist, tradition. It does not have uncontested criteria, custodians of orthodoxy, or an approximation to an apostolic succession, like tradition as the Counter-Reformation understood it.[39] Arguably, it is constituted neither by a set of doctrines nor by any "core" doctrine or system of doctrines, from which the rest are inferred. To focus on doctrine would be to minimize, at the very least, the significance of practice and spirit or ethos. It will also, I imagine, be agreed that the idea of tradition as a process in which the thing being transmitted remains forever unchanged in its transmission can now be relegated to tourist brochures and cookbooks. Those who stand in a tradition are not passive recipients of something handed on to them, like a family heirloom or the custom of wearing somber dress at funerals. A tradition is constituted and reconstituted by its recipients: its *Rezeptionsgeschichte* is a narrative of its identity, which, over any extended period, becomes a conundrum like that of the ship of Theseus. But if the concept of tradition is to do any work, it must at least allow us to specify something distinctive forwarded by those who stand in the tradition. My contention is that it is precisely the transmission and reception of Calvin's system of affirmations, qualifications, and denials relating to aristocracy and the duplex regimen, in both doctrine and practice, that defines the Calvinist political and ecclesiological tradition. And it is precisely the tensions and possibilities within that system that constitute, at once, its strength as well as its weaknesses and limits. Finally, it needs to be emphasized again that this political and ecclesiological tradition in no sense exhausts the Calvinist tradition. On the contrary, as I argue later, this tradition rapidly loses its identity, whereas Calvinist piety, worship, scriptural scholarship, dogmatics, and moral sensibility do not.

The most that can be done here is to concentrate on France and the Netherlands as both exemplifications and exemplars. Orthodox evangelicals had insisted on the duty of political obedience and nonresistance, not least to counter the Anabaptists and persistent Romanist accusations of fomenting rebellion. Calvin's unwillingness to compromise on these duties meant that rulers hostile to reformation could stop evangelical church building in its tracks. When faced with hostile secular authorities (normally princes), the Reformed lacked any justification for political initiatives from below to promote the cause: they were left with a choice between flight, martyrdom, or covert worship, which could not remain covert for long, since Calvin was implacably opposed to even outward conformity with the sacrilegious and blasphemous rites of the papists.[40] Moreover, to ward off separatism and divisions between evangelical churches, Calvin insisted on criteria for a true church that forbade evangelicals to separate from even the most minimally reformed state church, however dominated it might be by secular rulers. Here, even discipline became, in effect, an adiaphoron. If Calvin's prohibition of religio-political activism had been followed religiously (so to speak), it would have been impossible to realize his desideratum of fully reformed, godly churches, coextensive with godly polities. Like evangelicals in general, he took confessionalization of the polity and a political criterion for church membership just as much for granted as papists did. In Geneva, the Confession de Foy was a condition of residence. The only escape clause in Calvin's entire oeuvre permitting political initiatives against hostile rulers was the right of popular magistrates to resist tyranny.

Fidelity to the cause, in sum, demanded acknowledging the authority of the duplex regimen. But unless the circumstances of the faithful were exceptionally favorable, as in Scotland, this was only possible at the expense of marginalizing or ignoring all or any of: the duty of obedience, the aristocratic ideal, the independence of the church, and the ideal of a church "purely reformed." To cope with political circumstances, Reformed political thought came to require motifs, emphases, and concepts that were barely intimated in Calvin's own life and work.

The Calvinist tradition of political thought began near the end of Calvin's own lifetime. His foremost personal and ecclesiastical concern was with *ceux de la religion* in France. From 1555 onward, he actively promoted the formation of churches "under the cross," bodies that were illegal under Henri II and of highly questionable legality thereafter. He did not, however, modify the last versions of the *Institutes* (1559/1560) to sanction what he was encouraging in practice; he did not even send clarificatory encyclicals. Even his reactions to the first National Synod of 1559 and the Conspiracy of Amboise in 1560 were ambiguous, whatever he and Beza may have been doing and saying in secret.[41] From 1560 onward, however, a power struggle at the monarchical apex allowed Huguenot activity to be increasingly public and to include propaganda campaigns. The focus of their polemic was the accusation that the Guise and, by implication (later explicitly), the queen regent Catherine de Medici and Charles IX were guilty not only of monstrous cruelty but also of gross illegality, according to certain "ancient laws" or customs of France, specifically those regulating the succession and political practice in cases where the king who succeeded to the throne was still a minor. Huguenots represented themselves as custodians and defenders of the just rights of French kings against overmighty subjects and cast their resistance to tyranny, particularly on the part of the Guise,[42] as a case of lesser magistrates defending traditional customary rights and liberties and the police of France, which provided for its own defense by the Estates General, parlements (an unreliable resource for Huguenots), and various holders of high office who were officers of the Crown, not merely servants of kings.[43]

The same rhetoric mutatis mutandis prevailed in the Low Countries until well into the 1570s. Here Calvinists, not at all clearly distinguishable from other adherents of Gereformeerde Religion or other "patriots," were until the mid-1560s much more interested in proselytizing, iconoclasm, and establishing Reformed churches than in pamphleteering. Until the late 1570s, public justifications of their activities were often very brief and took the form of appeals, addresses, letters, and appendices to documents regarding church reform.[44] Their political purpose was principally to deny responsibility for unlicensed iconoclasm, to rehearse familiar arguments about the duty of obedience, except where God must be obeyed rather than Caesar, and to trumpet their own exemplary performance of that duty, even to the point of martyrdom. There was, at first, a studied ambiguity about what disobeying Caesar might entail. Despite increasing civil divisions, organized religio-political resistance, and open warfare, culminating in the outright revolt of the Seven Provinces, the rhetoric and themes of the *Publizistik* remained largely unaltered until the late 1570s. The actions of the patriots were represented as the defense of the ancient rights, liberties, and privileges of the towns and provinces of the "dear fatherland" (a useful term, given the new polity's problematic identity) by duly appointed magistrates, not private citizens. William of Orange was presented as a royal appointee, and the terms of the relationship between king and subjects were ostensibly found in the *Joyeuse Entrée/Blijde Inkomst*, which were construed as a kind of treaty—French Huguenots had nothing as definite as this to invoke. Defense of the Fatherland was said to be necessitated, in particular, by the introduction of the "Spanish" Inquisition and by the outrages perpetrated by "foreigners," especially the Duke of Alva and Spanish soldiers, against inoffensive men, women (wives, matrons, maidens), and children, mainly, though not exclusively, those adhering to the true gospel.[45] The antiforeigner, anti-Spanish theme is prominent, even though some foreigners were welcomed by the godly: Orange himself was hardly pure Dutch, and Leicester, still less.[46] The patriots represented themselves as trying to make the king of Spain aware of the outrages committed by his agents without his knowledge, a venerable rhetorical stratagem in resistance to monarchs.[47] In an interesting combination of themes, one pamphlet argued that the king of Spain was the prisoner of the Inquisition, monks, and information from careerists in the Netherlands.[48] Conspiracy theories were not eschewed either: iconoclasm was sometimes represented as an "inside job" perpetrated by priests to blacken the reputation of those of the Religion.[49] One innovative element, also present in Huguenot literature, was some concession to toleration, on the grounds that consciences cannot be forced and that attempting to do so would only produce atheists and encourage illegalities.[50] Given the violently antipapist character of this entire literature and its Calvinist premises, these concessions to tolerance were not entirely credible, though more so than they had been in Huguenot writing from before 1572. Enforcing religious uniformity seems to have been widely unpopular in the Low Countries, even before Alva.

Huguenot literature before 1572 and Dutch literature for much longer was theoretically unambitious and opportunistic, though more competently so than John Knox's *First Blast of the Trumpet Against the Monstrous Regiment of Women* (1558). Knox irrevocably alienated both Elizabeth I (notwithstanding his shameless misrepresentation of his own arguments in his subsequent *Apology* to her) and Mary Stuart by rejecting women in general as rulers, on the basis of natural reason and, much more importantly, a putatively comprehensive veto on women rulers by scripture—a clumsy strategy since all Knox objected to, in fact, was a specific Catholic woman ruler. It is evidence of fidelity in *mentalité* to Calvin that Huguenots vehemently denied any suggestion of rebellion or innovation and did not present advancing the evangelical cause as a justification in itself for resistance, unlike Knox's *First Blast* or Christopher Goodman's *How Superior Powers ought to be Obeyed* of 1558. Both books were published in Geneva, and Goodman claimed that Calvin had approved of his. The ostensibly legal or, in a later terminology, constitutional character of the Huguenot argumentation required no reconsideration of the religious duty of obedience. Unlike the Magdeburg Confession and some Dutch literature before 1581, it did not even complicate matters by invoking the natural right of self-defense, which could raise awkward questions about the relative authority of reason and scripture. Calvin himself had allowed popular magistrates, where they happened to be established, to act against tyrants, presumably on the grounds that rulers were owed obedience not as individuals, but as holders of offices defined by positive law. In this way, his consent could not be interpreted as granting private individuals the right to resist. His followers had no difficulty in locating appropriate "lesser magistrates" where they needed them. The argumentation could, thus, proceed within the limits defined by Calvin's own texts for the time being.

Huguenot literature did not explain (any more than Calvin himself, the Dutch, or Lutherans before them) why such moral significance should attach to *loix*, however supposedly *anciennes*, since they were, after all, merely customary or positive law and neither divine nor scriptural: mere "human traditions." Why should these outweigh the obligatory force and significance in conscience of the obedience demanded by Romans 13 and 1 Peter 2.1–2? And why should the not particularly salubrious high nobility, including the king of Navarre, the religiously unreliable Estates General, or lesser estates and parlements count as "lesser magistrates" entitled to offer resistance to lawful monarchs? "Resistance," moreover, was a euphemism for armed uprisings and acts of aggression or self-defense. How could this kind of activity possibly count as something warranted by the ancient constitutions of France or the joyeuses entrées of Low Country towns and counties subject to the king of Spain? Lutheran legitimatizations of wars between components of the Holy Roman Empire, which always cast the conflicts as "normal" and not civil wars, were one thing. Wars in France and the Low Countries, between neighboring towns and provinces, and between relatives within the same kingdom, were quite another. The form of government being defended or invented was, moreover, certainly not an aristocracy in Calvin's sense. The arguments did legitimate the establishment of a duplex regimen at the local and provincial level, but at the expense of the "obedience, martyrdom, or flight" component of Calvin's system of affirmation, qualification, and denial.

The year 1572 effectively meant the end of the project for an evangelical conversion of the whole of France: the issue now was survival.[51] The themes, theories, concepts, and motifs generated were specifically designed to defend *la Réligion*, without which there would have been no need for them.[52] Huguenots were quite willing to risk life, limb, and property; to engage in organized civil war against legitimate kings; to try to enforce constitutional changes on monarchies from below; and even to contemplate the fragmentation of the kingdom for the sake of the Cause, just as the Reformed in the Spanish Netherlands were prepared to see the dominion dissolved. But Huguenots now had to recognize the need to settle for the regionalization of their church polities and for state-conceded religious toleration, and they were obliged to accommodate their argumentation accordingly. What emerged was far more cogent theoretically, but also much less specifically Calvinist. Its cogency found its limits in the lack of any properly Calvinist concept of a polity without a single, defining religion. In this, at least, Huguenots agreed with their Catholic opponents.[53] So did Dutch Calvinists, but their state religion was never fully inclusive, never unambiguously Calvinist, and was obliged from the beginning to concede toleration, at least politically, as a *faute de mieux*. But then Calvin too had readily conceded all manner of imperfections in the Genevan church and polity and, a fortiori, in the refugee churches throughout Europe, in view of the "infirmity of the times."[54] He never, however, allowed either toleration or "Nicodemism."

There is no space here to do more than highlight and illustrate some specific components and episodes of this theorization.[55] Post-1572 Huguenot and Dutch

Revolt political theory characteristically appeals to communes loci that were not from Calvin or particular to Calvinists, France, the Low Countries, or even Protestants. Some of this literature now aggressively asserted the right to defend the true religion and the duty of godly rulers and magistrates to advance it and eliminate popery. It, therefore, maintained both the spirit and the ambiguities of the duplex regimen, but not its inclusive, "state-church" aspirations, which would demand the allegiance of all those living within a political jurisdiction. However, the predominant character and emphases of this literature marginalized it. Its notable features are:

1. Anti-Machiavellianism: Originally a polemical device directed against Catherine de Medici, it became part of a durable European topos entirely independent of the Calvinist tradition.[56] The most conspicuous work of this genre was obviously Innocent Gentillet's *Anti-Machiavel*,[57] but the theme was also fundamental for the theoretically less ambitious but much racier and more widely translated *Discours merveilleux de la vie, actions et deportements de Catherine de Médicis*,[58] the *Tocsin contre les Massacreurs*,[59] and many other pamphlets, such as *Reveille-Matin* (1574).[60] Gentillet turned Machiavellian material (not all of which came from Machiavelli, notably not the favorite "Machiavellian" maxim *oderint dum metuant*) into a Machiavellian "theory" or, at least, a set of doctrinal propositions; Machiavelli himself had provided neither a theory nor doctrines. One unforeseen consequence of this was that the enemies of the Huguenots were able to conflate this "Machiavellism" with positions they imputed to the *politiques*, who were, if anything, actual or potential allies of the Huguenots, and to link both groups with "reason of state." The response to increasingly sophisticated enunciations of reason of state (for example, Botero's ostensible attack on it) required resources and argumentation that owed nothing to Calvin.[61]

2. Natural law and natural right: If resistance to tyranny was justified as the self-defense of armed communities rather than (as in civil law) of individuals, it required reference to natural law and natural rights, neither of which were significant in Calvin's writing. Many Huguenots were explicit,[62] but most theorists, as humanists or lawyers and as Protestants, preferred to follow Calvin's successor and longtime collaborator Theodore Beza, whose 1574 Du *Droit des magistrats* vaguely invoked justice, equity, and "all laws divine and human," rather than something as explicitly scholastic as natural law. They also left implicit the natural law principle *pacta sunt servanda*, an ideal presupposed by the mutual obligations, contracts, covenants, pacts, and treaties that were central metaphors in resistance literature.[63] The principle was also, at least partly, the rationale of all resistance arguments of the Dutch Revolt from the beginning. The Blijde Inkomst (or Intochte)/Joyeuse Entrée was construed as an exchange of promises (obedience in return for guarantees of the ancient privileges, liberties, and rights of the provinces). The various treaties, agreements, compacts, and pacifications that culminated in the Act of Abjuration in 1581 and its explicit rejection of royal authority and assertion of a certain form of sovereignty for the States General were themselves authorized by something like a pact. Natural right seems also to be implicit in the standard appeals of resistance literature to the rights of the people or their representatives and the cliché

salus populi suprema lex, although it was normally presented in the seemingly straightforward assertions that the "people" already existed and "gave itself a king" and that "there can be a people without a king, but no king without a people."[64] The grant was conditional upon good behavior on the part of the monarch, who was to be policed by some general assembly: no people could be supposed so foolish as to enslave itself voluntarily to a princeps legibus solutus. This was decked out with Ciceronian (but these being Calvinists, not Golden Age) stories about savage solitaries being somehow reduced to civility.[65] The whole farrago was later replaced by a vastly more sophisticated account of association by Johannes Althusius, whose similarity to scholastic accounts is palpable. All this was barely hinted at in Calvin's divine authorization of secular government.

3. Fundamental laws: Running parallel to and sometimes eliding such accounts of primitive beginnings were equally extrascriptural accounts of specific peoples instituting kingship, with specific laws and institutions to police the whole, such as François Hotman provides in the *Franco-Gallia*. Even more common was a more or less extensive *tour d'horizon* of a variety of peoples, which illustrated the same lessons about conditional authority, *mutua obligatio*, and covenants.[66] Given that resistance argument required consent to both the principle that princes were subject to laws and the proposition that laws were alterable and often needed to be altered, it became necessary to distinguish between different kinds of laws, with varying degrees of authority and mutability. Hotman called the most immutable laws *leges regiae*, but Beza and Gentillet, without any fanfare, explicitly distinguished, for the first time, "fundamental laws," which were binding on rulers and could not be unilaterally altered by them, from other kinds of law.[67] The source of these fundamental laws and their relation to natural and divine law (which were equally unalterable and binding on even absolute princes) remained obscure. They, in turn, became crucial to the new "public law,"[68] and to what was much later called "constitutionalism." With the polemical turning of "fundamental law" against the Huguenots by the Ligue,[69] the concept became an absolute commonplace. Pierre Grégoire's celebrated *De republica* of 1596 contributed to making it common European property.

4. Growing eclecticism: Huguenot and Calvinist political thought in general comes to be characterized by an increasing eclecticism, utilizing authorities of all kinds, especially Aristotle and the classics in general, but also scholastics and medieval historians. Argument from first principles of natural reason and natural law; induction from experience, prudence, and history; and the use of scripture as a source of historical exempla rather than doctrine: these together compose the "political science" (*scientia gubernatoria*) of all denominations in the next century.[70] An ironic implication of the resort to ancient laws and the unintended relativization of Roman law by humanists, including Calvinists like Hotman in his 1567 work *Anti-Tribonien*, was the renewed significance of medieval law and medieval (scholastic) commentators, who had assimilated the civil law to the circumstances and laws of their own day with a degree of anachronism that exceeded even that of the humanists. The anciennes loix and the ancient customs and institutions were, after all, one and all medieval. Even if Calvinist and humanist techniques of exegesis in terms of loci communes and *methodus* were not scholastic, this did nothing to

prevent exploitation of scholastic thought, *mos Gallicus* or not. Even scholastic distinctions proved not to be all *argutiae* and *sophismi*. Students of law and jurisprudence, moreover, could not forever resist the attractions of casuistry nor of dialectical argument with its *quaestiones, argumenta pro et contra*, and *responsio*. There were conspicuously large numbers of Calvinists among lawyers, and lawyers among Calvinists.

5. Toleration and legitimism: With the prospect of a Huguenot successor to the French throne and the Catholic League's turning monarchomach arguments against that successor[71], increasing concessions were made to monarchical authority and legitimism, as well as to toleration as a justifiable expedient and sometimes even a principle, as it had been, on occasion, in the Netherlands too.[72] The widespread resonance of Jean Bodin's case for sovereignty (in effect, if not theoretically, a case for absolute monarchy) made the position of monarchomachs more difficult still and eventually demanded an enormous theoretical effort from Calvinists, particularly in the Holy Roman Empire.[73] Circumstances in France demanded appeals to Gallican sentiment, conciliarism, and a shared French identity in the attempt to gain support from moderate Catholics and politiques. For this reason too, political argumentation had to rely principally on religious themes, concepts, and texts that provided common ground with Catholics, with specific emphasis on the political utility of religion, in the generic sense.

By the late 1580s, then, Calvin's endorsement of aristocracy was transmuted into a case for a limited monarchy ("constitutionalism") that was no more specifically Calvinist, aristocratic, or republican than its most favored authority, Claude de Seyssel's *La Monarchie de France* of 1519, with *la police* as a "bridle" on monarchs. The godly in France recognized the need to settle for protected minority status, which, in turn, meant espousing toleration in at least one sense of the word. This ran entirely contrary to Calvin's denominational/confessional ideal and his visceral opposition to allowing the survival, let alone resurgence, of popish abominations. The godly in the new United Provinces did indeed secure the abolition of public popery in 1581, but only at the price of abandoning a substantial part of the Low Countries, which remained as a threat to their existence for decades, and of conceding informal toleration within the United Provinces. Its duplex regimen was a shadow of Geneva, notably in the very limited autonomy of the ministry and the weakness of its discipline, which was neither compulsory nor inclusive, but applied fully only to members of the church and not the substantial number of so-called *liefhebbers*, who attended services and had their children baptized without becoming full members.[74] The political literature of the Calvinist international was, moreover, marked by a comprehensive abandonment of Calvin's propensity for biblicism, in favor of an eclectic use of authorities of all kinds, especially legal and historical argumentation. The integration of the Calvinist academies into the mainstream of the European *Universitätsbetrieb* made this imperative in any case. The upshot of it all was the marginalization of the Calvinist *differentia specifica*: the duplex regimen, the aristocratic principle, and the affirmation, qualification, and even denial of the authority of secular reason. Calvin had certainly employed secular reasoning; he had even played a substantial role in drafting Geneva's civic ordinances. He had also compromised aristocratic principles to deal with sympathetic monarchs. But the authorities, the concepts, the loci communes, and the methods of argument that became the focus of Huguenot political theory had been, at best, an ambiguous presence in his thought, and in many cases were completely absent. Nor was their utility in any way confined to Huguenots. Given the increasing abstraction and sophistication of Huguenot political theory, it could also be used freely in the Dutch Revolt, despite the entirely different trajectory of Reformed religion there. Equally, however, there was now nothing to distinguish such theories from those of their Catholic opponents, apart from the continuing centrality of antipopery rhetoric. This was not because Catholics were borrowing from Huguenots, although a detailed familiarity with the enemy often meant unconscious borrowing and assimilation. Rather, it was usually because both sides were drawing on sources whose value Tridentine Catholics had always maintained, but which Calvinists had needed to rediscover and revalidate. The same was true, up to a point and *secundum quid*, in theology generally, but that is a different story.

■ Notes

1. For this ambivalent terminology, which was made canonical for evangelicals by Luther, see Harro Höpfl, *The Christian Polity of Jean Calvin* (Cambridge: Cambridge University Press 1982), 23, 27–30.

2. Luther referred mostly to "spiritual tyrants," that is, the papacy and its bishops, *WA* 6: 406–15, 287, 300, 321–22; and *WA* 11: 265, 267, 271. He equated this with the clerical exercise of *Herrschaft*. See *Geschichtliche Grundbegriffe*, 8 vols., ed. Otto Brunner, Werner Conze, and Reinhart Koselleck (Stuttgart: Klett Cotta, 1972–89), s.v. "Tyrannis," 6: 665–67. The inference, drawn in *Das eine Christliche Versammlung oder Gemeine Recht und Macht habe*, that the authority of the Church must, therefore, be located in the *Gemein(d)e* fell victim to the *Landesherrliches Kirchenregiment. WA* 11: 408–16.

3. The *fons et origo* is Aristotle's discussion in the *Politics*, 3.5. The simplified distinction between three virtuous, three corrupt, and one mixed form (the latter often not mentioned) had been utterly conventional since at least Aquinas, *Summa Theologica*, I-IIae, qu.105, 1, resp. 5; Thomas Aquinas and Tolomeo de Lucca, *De regimine principum*, chaps. 2–5. Sixteenth-century examples include Claude de Seyssel, *La monarchie de France* (1519), ed. Jacques Poujol (Paris: Librairie d'Argences, 1961), chap 1, 103–4; Philipp Melanchthon, *Commentarii in aliquot Politicos libros Aristotelis* (Wittenberg: Klug, 1530), http://daten. digtale-sammlungen.de/~db/0001 /bsb00015210/ images/, 42–43; Peter Martyr Vermigli. For Vermigli, see Robert Kingdon, *The Political Thought of Peter Martyr Vermigli* (Geneva: Droz, 1980), 641, 897–98 (references are to pages of excerpts from original editions of Vermigli's *Commentary on Romans* 13 and *De magistratu*, as used and cited by Kingdon). Zwingli conflated the civil and ecclesiastical form of government. According to him, when Christ spoke of *tyrannis* in Mt. 20:26 and Luke 22:26, he was not referring to "monarchy or aristocracy, which is [office] offered to one [i.e. a monarch or an aristocracy] who does not have the office of preacher, by popular decision and divine vocation." Ulrich Zwingli, *Kommentar über die wahre und falsche Religion* (1525) in *Huldrych Zwingli Schriften*, 4 vols., ed. and trans. Thomas Brunnschweiler, Samuel Lutz, et al. (Zürich: TVZ, 1995), 3: 393–94. Calvin cited no source in *Inst.* 4, 20.8 (from 1536 onward) for the "tres regiminis formae" distinction. The 1543 edition of the *Institutes* attributed it to the "philosophi," and the French edition of 1541 said simply: "on compte trois especes." Jean Calvin, *Institution de la religion Chrestienne* (1541 ed.), ed. J. Pannier (Paris: Societé les Belles Lettres, 1936), 206–7.

4. *Inst.* 2, 2.15, for example, explicitly acknowledges the value of secular (specifically ancient and heathen) knowledge and wisdom, which encompasses law and civil order but no aspect of divinity or ecclesiology. For Calvin on theological reasoning, see Carl Trueman, "Calvin and Calvinism," in *Cambridge Companion to Calvin*, ed. Donald McKim (Cambridge: Cambridge University Press, 2004), 225–44.

5. A characteristic example is Alfonso Salmeron S.J.'s highly regarded *In Epistolas Pauli Commentarii*, vol. 13 (Cologne: Heirat and Gymnius, 1604), *Epistola ad Romanos* 13, Bk. 1, Disp. 14, "De Monarchia Ecclesiae," esp. 273–74.

6. The first reformers used existing ecclesiastical buildings and apparatus, modified to a greater or lesser degree by iconoclasm. Seeking support from *Landesherren* in some places and from magistrates in others was not a matter of doctrine (which was only developed later and inconsistently) but of circumstances and unquestioned assumptions. For Zwingli, see Bruce Gordon, *The Swiss Reformation* (Manchester: Manchester University Press, 2002), ch. 2.

7. This was quite deliberate in the case of Zwingli. See his *Kommentar über die wahre und falsche Religion* and *Von göttlicher und menschlicher Grechtigkeit, wie die zemen sehind und standind* (1523), *Zwingli's Hauptschriften*, vol. 17, ed. R. Pfister et al. (Zurich: Zwingli Verlag, 1942). It was unintentional in Luther's case: see W. D. J. Cargill Thompson, *The Political Thought of Martin Luther*, ed. Philip Broadhead (Sussex: Harvester Press, 1984), chs. 3–4.

8. Even the elementary distinction between the "invisible" and the "visible" church, "external" or "particular" churches was not established until the 1540s. Zwingli made the distinction in *Kommentar über die wahre und falsche Religion*, 14–15; Bucer did not in his *XVI Articles* of 1535 and neither did the *Belgic Confession*. For Bucer's *XVI Articles*, see François Wendel, *Calvin: The Origins and Development of His Religious Thought*, trans. Philip Mairet (London: Collins, 1963), 151–52. In the *Institutes* of 1543, Calvin distinguished between the universal, visible church and the church that was known to God alone (*Inst.* 4, 1.7), before he turned to the individual visible churches, which were distinguished by *notae* that applied only to them (*Inst.* 4, 1.8). He never noted their *landeskirchlichen* character ("oppidatim et vicatim").

9. Calvin's *Antidote to the Council of Trent* of 1547 was one of the first attacks on the council. Much of it was boiler-plate anti-Romanist abuse. For example, it dealt with Soto (not *the* Soto, but Charles V's confessor and a papal theologian at Trent all the same) by describing him as 'a monk' and noting that his name in French means stupid and fatuous. See John Dillenberger, *John Calvin: Selections from His Writings* (New York: Doubleday, 1971), 132.

10. Amy Nelson Burnett, "Church Discipline and Moral Reformation in the Thought of Martin Bucer," *SCJ* 22 (1991): 439–56.

11. Calvin, for example, commented: "Vrai est que les changements [of 'loix et statuts des ancestres'] seront toujours a craindre, et qu'il les faut fuir le plus qu'on peut...Quant aux lois humaines, l'ancienneté doit estre honoree, qu'on ne change point par folle curiosité." *Sermons sur le Deuteronome*, in *Calv. Opp.* 27: 567, sermon 114. He always followed such expressions with the standard humanist/evangelical qualification about the superior authority of revelation and reason over "ancienneté."

12. *Reply to Sadoleto*, in Dillenberger, *John Calvin*, 62. The *Institutes*, in an antipapist, antihuman traditions context, describes scripture several times as "the perfect rule of life." *Inst.* 4, 10.7–8.

13. The matter is admirably handled by McCulloch, chap. 1, in this book.

14. For the best summary account, see Philip Benedict, *Christ's Churches Purely Reformed: A Social History of Calvinism* (New Haven: Yale University Press, 2002), 93–109.

15. The 1537 Articles had already declared that "les ordonnances par lequelles son eglise est entretenue sont...le plus prest que fere se peult confermee a sa parolle qui est la certayne

reigle de tout gouvernement...mays principalement du gouvernement ecclesiastique." *OS* 1: 370; they specifically claimed scriptural warrant for discipline in the form of excommunication and for the office of elder. *OS* 1: 372–73. For the four orders or offices "instituted by our Lord," see *OS* 1: 255; *OS* 2: 328; *Inst.* 4, 10.27. The official text of the *Ordonnances* freely asserts the scriptural character of Geneva's ecclesiastical order. Höpfl, *Christian Polity*, 90–91. Indirectly, the *Institutes* of 1543 claim the same scriptural warrant for the ministry and elders, using expressions like "according to the institution of Christ" and "ordinance of God." *Inst.* 4, 3.4; 4, 3.6–7; 4, 3.8; 4, 4.1–2.

16. *Inst.* 4, 1.12.

17. *OS* 1: 423–24.

18. Alastair Duke, *Reformation and Revolt in the Low Countries* (London: Hambledon Press, 2003), 212; *Belgic Confession*, Article 29, which states that the third mark for recognizing the true Church is the use of church discipline to correct vices ("la troisième des marques pour connaitre la vraie Eglise [est] si la discipline ecclesiastique est en usage pour corriger les vices"). For English and French versions, see Philip Schaff, ed., *The Creeds of Christendom*, 4 vols., 4th ed. (New York: Harper and Brothers, 1884), 3: 419–20. Calvin's role in the French *Confession de Foy* is unclear: see Brian Armstrong, "*Semper Reformanda*: The Case of the French Reformed Church, 1559–1620," and Glenn Sunshine, "Reformed Theology and the Origins of Synodical Polity: Calvin, Beza and the Gallican Confession," in *Later Calvinism: International Perspectives*, ed. W. Fred Graham (Kirksville, MO: Sixteenth Century Journal, 1994), 125–26, 153–54. Calvin contends, however, that "there are three things on which the welfare [or salvation, *salus*] of the church is founded, namely doctrine, discipline and the sacraments." *Letter to Sadoleto* (1540), 93. In this, he echoes Bucer, who also listed "leer, sacramenten und Christlicher zucht." *Ziegenhainer Zuchtordnung* in *Martin Bucers Deutsche Schriften*, vol. 7, ed. Robert Stupperich (Gütersloh: Gütersloher Verlagshaus, 2006), 260–78, here 265. Calvin's use of the term "discipline" was, at that time, imprecise. See, for example, the *Articuli a Calvino et Farelo propositi* of 1538, where "disciplina" refers to organizing Geneva into parishes and to the "germanus excommunicationis usus," whatever that means. *Calv. Opp.* 10/1: 191.

19. *Inst.* 4, 6.10 (in the 1543 edition onward); 4, 6.8–9; 4, 4.2.

20. *Inst.* 4, 11.6. As Alastair Duke notes, the ecclesiastical character of the *Consistoire*—on which Calvin insisted—is grossly understated by Kingdon's formal-legal description of it as "a committee of the municipal government." Geneva was not a "municipality" anyway but a republic that conducted wars and had *ius vitae et necis*. Alastair Duke, "Perspectives on International Calvinism," in *Calvinism in Europe 1540–1620*, ed. Andrew Pettegree, Alastair Duke, and Gillian Lewis (Cambridge: Cambridge University Press, 1994), 1–20, here 11.

21. Quentin Skinner, *The Foundations of Modern Political Thought*, 2 vols. (Cambridge: Cambridge University Press, 1971, 1978), 1: 236–38.

22. For the extreme care that the *Ordonnances* of 1541 and 1561 devoted to the pastorate's self-discipline, *aedificatio*, and moral authority, see Höpfl, *Christian Polity*, 92–94.

23. The context for these comments, which appear in the 1559 addition, was "regiminis formae."

24. *Institution de la réligion Chrestienne* (1541), 206–7.

25. Zwingli represented the view of all the reformers when he maintained that "ecclesia" meant "congregation." See Zwingli, *Kommentar über die wahre und falsche Religion* (1525), *Zwingli Schriften* 3: 203: "Denn die Kirche ist die Gemeinde, die ganze Versammlung, das ganze Volk, die ganze versammelte Menge." Regarding Calvin, see *Inst.* 4, 5.2: "Iam in eligendo (bishops) totam illud ius populi sublatum est"; see also 4, 3.15; 4, 4.11–13. Such a view was attractive prima facie, given the dependence of all reformers on popular support and rhetoric, in which the verdict of the audience is decisive.

26. Höpfl, *Christian Polity*, 106–7.

27. See *Inst.* 4, 20.1. This sharp distinction between the two aspects of the *duplex regimen* was, however, already qualified by his construal of the repression of idolatry, sacrilege, and blasphemy as magisterial functions in the 1536 edition (4.20.8, later modified still further). Zwingli and Bullinger made no such distinction of ends. See Euan Cameron, *The European Reformation* (Oxford: Clarendon Press, 1991), 153–54; Heinrich Bullinger, *Compendium Christianae Religionis* (Zurich: Froschauer, 1556), 90r–91r. Melanchthon also did not make a distinction between the ends of ministry and magistracy. See Philipp Melanchthon [Justus Menius, pseud.], *De defensione concessa humano generi iure naturae* (Wittenberg, 1547), http://daten.digitale-sammlungen.de/~db/0003/bsb00035543/images/, 50–51, 62, 68, 70 (pagination refers to electronic edition).

28. Skinner notes that Calvin did not say "lesser" or "lower" magistrates, the more conventional terms in Lutheran resistance theory, but we know nothing about Calvin's familiarity, if any, with this aspect of Lutheran thought. Skinner, *Foundations*, 2: 209–10, 230–34. The 1541 French version of the *Institutes* refers to "Magistratz constituez pour la defence du people, pour refrener la trop grande cupidité et licence des Roys." 238–39. This "bridle" metaphor is not Lutheran.

29. Calvin's term did not specify any particular "principal assembly"; the French Estates General had not met since 1506.

30. Melanchthon, *De defensione*. Also see Luther D. Peterson, "Melanchthon on Resisting the Emperor: The *Von der Notwehr Unterrichte* of 1547," in *Regnum, Religio et Ratio: Essays Presented to Robert M. Kingdon*, ed. J. Friedman (Kirksville, MO: Sixteenth Century Journal, 1987). In 1530–31 Luther had himself cautiously endorsed resistance, upon legal advice, in the *Torgau Declaration* and the *Warnung an seine lieben Deutschen*. See David M. Whitford, *Tyranny and Resistance: The Magdeburg Confession and the Lutheran Tradition* (St. Louis, MO: Concordia, 2001), 50–51.

31. For the successive alterations, see Harro Höpfl, *Luther and Calvin on Secular Authority* (Cambridge: Cambridge University Press, 1991), 85–86.

32. For Calvin's view of monarchs, see Höpfl, *Christian Polity*, index s.v. "kings."

33. "Neque enim ius gladii habet ecclesia quo puniat velut coerceat, non imperium ut cogat, non carcerem, non poenas alias quae solent infligi a magistratu." *Inst.* (1543) 4, 11.3. It was a commonplace of evangelical polemic that the Romanist "spiritual tyrants" violated God's law and infringed on the rights of secular rulers by using the sword. For a paradigmatic example, see Martin Luther, *Weltlicher Oberkeit (On Secular Authority)*, in Höpfl, *Luther and Calvin* , s.1, 6. But even without the sword, the consistory was coercive enough. *Inst.* 4, 11.5.

34. Robert Fills, *The Lawes and Statutes of Geneva, as well concerning ecclesiastical Discipline, as civill regiment* (London: Rowland Hall, 1562).

35. See Duke, "Perspectives on International Calvinism," 2–3.

36. Höpfl, *Christian Polity*, 98, 283, n.12. His agreement with Bullinger in the *Consensus Tigurinus*, which did not exactly reflect his view of the sacrament, evidences the same concern.

37. Calvin accepted the legitimacy of post-apostolic episcopacy, even of archbishops and patriarchs (*Inst.* 4, 4.4) since it did not involve *dominium*. At times, he even acknowledged that there had been legitimate (i.e., nonpapist) popes—Gregory, for example (*Inst.* 4, 4. throughout). All this left almost as little mark on the Calvinist tradition as his ideal of weekly communion (*OS* 1: 370) and a nonpapist version of confession. See Höpfl, *Christian Polity*, 99.

38. Skinner, *Foundations* 2: 192.

39. For some pregnant observations on this point, see Carl Trueman, "Calvin and Calvinism," in *Cambridge Companion to Calvin*, ed. Donald McKim (Cambridge: Cambridge University Press, 2004), 225–44.

40. Carlos Eire, *War Against the Idols: The Reformation of Worship from Erasmus to Calvin* (Cambridge, Cambridge University Press, 1986), ch. 7.

41. Philip Benedict, *Christ's Churches Purely Reformed: A Social History of Calvinism* (New Haven: Yale University Press, 2002), 134–35, 142.

42. Notable examples include the c.1560 *L'Histoire du Tumulte d'Amboise* 1560, *Les Estats de France opprimez par la Tyrannie de Guise, Supplication et Remonstrance Addressez au Roy de Navarre et autres Princes du Sang de France*, in *Receuil de pieces fugitives* (n.p.: c.1740), 6–13, 26–34, and 178ff.

43. This account is based on the extensive collection of sources assembled and published anonymously in the 1740s as the *Memoires de Condé* vols. 2–4 ("London and Paris," 1743) and in the briefer *Recueil de pièces fugitives*.

44. Duke, *Reformation and Revolt*, 104–5. For the ephemeral and ad hoc character of much of what was published—atrocity-narratives, martyrologies, and addenda to programmatic writing about church reform, see Martin van Gelderen, *The Political Thought of the Dutch Revolt* (Cambridge: Cambridge University Press, 1992), ch. 3.

45. Van Gelderen, *Political Thought*, 15–25. This is a specifically Dutch theme without a French parallel.

46. Huguenots, of course, also used this antiforeigner theme against Catherine de Medici and her Italian courtiers and, on occasion, even against the Guise, who were from Lorraine and, thus, ostensibly not properly French.

47. E. H. Kossman and A. F. Mellink, *Texts Concerning the Revolt of the Netherlands* (Cambridge: Cambridge University Press, 1974), 60, 68, 84, 87, 104 106, 118. The fullest discussion of this literature is van Gelderen, *Political Thought*, ch. 3. Kossman and Mellink's *Texts Concerning the Revolt* is thin on the period before 1570. Van Gelderen's *Dutch Revolt* begins with 1572. See also the excellent collection of documents mainly on ecclesiastical organization and iconoclasm assembled by Alastair Duke in *Select Documents for the Reformation and Revolt of the Low Countries, 1555–1609*. Available online at http://dutchrevolt.leiden.edu/english/sources/Pages/default.aspx.

48. Kossman and Mellink, *Texts Concerning the Revolt*, 117–18.

49. Ibid., 79–80.

50. Ibid., 56–58.

51. The expansion of Huguenot churches and polities from a handful of secret groups in the early 1550s to a highly organized body of *Églises dressées*, capable of sustaining civil war, with as many as 2 million adherents by 1562 was astonishing. See Diarmaid McCulloch, *The Reformation* (London: Penguin, 2003), 307; Benedict, *Christ's Churches*, 144. It even seemed possible that an independent "national" ecclesiastical council (the boundaries of the "nation" as ever undefined and definable only polemically) might provide a religious settlement exploitable in favor of the true religion. This seems fanciful in retrospect, but hindsight is an exact science.

52. Even the titles make this clear: *Question: Assavoir s'il est loisible aux subjects de se deffendre contre le Magistrat, pour maintenir la Religion vrayment Chrestienne* (1573) in Simon Goulart, *Memoires de la Ligue* (1604), 1578, II, 239ᵛ ff. It is explicitly affirmed in Theodore Beza, *Du droit des magistrats*, ed. Robert Kingdon (Geneva, 1574; Geneva: Droz, 1971) and Philippe Du Plessis-Mornay? [Stephanus Junius Brutus, pseud.] *Vindiciae contra Tyrannos* ("Edinburgh": 1579).

53. On the persistence of this belief among Calvinists in the Holy Roman Empire, see Christoph Strohm, *Calvinismus und Recht* (Tübingen: Mohr Siebeck, 2008), 383.

54. Höpfl, *Christian Polity*, 90.

55. My source for the less accessible primary material is Goulart, *Memoires de la Ligue*. See also Skinner, *Foundations*, vol. 2; Kingdon, "Calvinism and Resistance Theory, 1550–

1580," in *Cambridge History of Political Thought* 1540–1700, ed. J. H. Burns (Cambridge: Cambridge University Press, 1991), 193–218; J. H. M. Salmon, "Catholic Resistance Theory, Ultramontanism, and the Royalist Response, 1580–1620," in ibid., 219–53.

56. Höpfl, *Christian Polity*.

57. Innocent Gentillet, *Anti-Machiavel: Discours sur les moyens de bien gouverner et maintenir un Royaume ou autre principalite...contre Nicolas Machiavel Florentin*, ed. C. E. Rathé (1576; Geneva: Droz, 1968).

58. [Henri Estienne], *Discours merveilleux de la vie, actions & deportemens de Catherine de Medicis Royne mere, Auquel sont recitez les moyens qu'elle a tenu pour usurper le gouvernement du Royaume de France, & ruiner l'estat d'iceluy* (1575).

59. *Le tocsin contre les massacreurs et auteurs des confusions en France* (1579).

60. [Nicolas Barnaud?], *Reveille-Matin des françois et de leurs voisins* (Edinburgh: Jaques James, 1574). The preface to the French translation of the *Vindiciae contra tyrannos*, *De la puissance legitime du Prince sur le Peuple et du people sur le Prince* (1581), makes it out to be an anti-Machiavellian work.

61. Höpfl, "Orthodoxy and Reason of State," *History of Political Thought* 23 (2002): 211–37; Höpfl, *Jesuit Political Thought* (Cambridge: Cambridge University Press, 2004), chs. 5–8.

62. For examples, see Simon Goulart, *Memoires de l'estat de France sous Charles neufiesme*, 2nd ed., 3 vols. ("Meidelbourg," 1576–78), 2: 242-v–243v; 3: 83-r; R. A. Mason and M. S. Smith, eds., *A Dialogue on the Law of Kingship Among the Scots: A Critical Edition and Translation of George Buchanan's de Jure Regni Apud Scotos Dialogus* (Edinburgh, 1579; Aldershot: Ashgate, 2004), 18–19, 26–27, 50–51, 97–98. For the Netherlands, see van Gelderen, *Political Thought*, 121–22, 148–49, 162–63.

63. See *Du droit des magistrats* and, especially, the *Vindiciae contra Tyrannos*.

64. This Huguenot *bon mot* appears in various versions. See *Reveille Matin*, 81; *Droit des magistrats*, s.5; François Hotman, *Franco-Gallia*, ed. R. Giesey, trans. J. H. M. Salmon (1573; Cambridge, Cambridge University Press, 1972), ch. 15; *Vindiciae contra Tyrannos*, passim. For the degree to which this work was well known in the Netherlands, see van Gelderen, *Political Thought*, 154–55, 159–60. For the prominence of the third question of the *Vindiciae* in Dutch justifications of revolt, see Richard Saage, *Herrschaft, Toleranz, Widerstand: Studien zur politischen Theorie der niederländischen und englischen Revolution* (Frankfurt: Suhrkamp, 1981), 36–38.

65. See, for example, *De Jure Regni Apud Scotos Dialogus*, 14–15ff.

66. See Harro Höpfl and Martyn P. Thompson, "The History of Contract as a Motif in Political Thought," *American Historical Review* 84 (1979): 919–44.

67. Beza made this distinction only in the French version of *Du droit des magistrats*; Gentillet, in his *Anti-Machiavel*.

68. The Calvinist contribution to "public law" is elaborated *in extenso* in Strohm, *Calvinismus und Recht*. In Roman law and the medieval and humanist commentary on it, the distinction between "public" and "private" law had been unclear and of little significance.

69. For the devising and diffusion of the concept, see Höpfl, "Fundamental Law and the Constitution in Sixteenth-Century France," in *Die Rolle der Juristen bei der Entstehung des modernen Staates*, ed. Roman Schnur (Berlin: Duncker & Humblot, 1986), 328–56. A *Ligue* pamphlet of 1588 has the title: *Articles pour proposer aux estatz et faire passer en loy fondamentalle du Royaume*, available at http://contentdm.lib.byu.edu/cdm4/document.php?CISOROOT=/FrenchPolPa&CISOPTR=10618.

70. Wolfgang Weber, *Prudentia gubernatoria: Studien zur Herrschaftslehre in der deutschen politischen Wissenschaft des 17. Jahrhunderts* (Tübingen: Niemeyer, 1992) has relevance far beyond the "deutsche politische Wissenschaft," despite its subtitle.

71. Illustrated in *Memoires de la Ligue*, 6 vols. (1602); also see Salmon, "Catholic Resistance Theory."

72. Sometimes religious liberty was described as a natural right. See *Discours contenant le vray entendement de la Pacification de Gand* (1579), cited in van Gelderen, *Political Thought*, 225. More generally, see ibid., 218–59.

73. Strohm, *Calvinismus und Recht*, 396–405.

74. See Duke, *Reformation and Revolt*, ch. 11; van Gelderen, *Political Thought*, 216–17.

3

Calvin the Workaholic

MAX ENGAMMARE

Translated by Calvin Tams

It is a cliché repeated by everyone: Calvin was an untiring worker. But was he really such a workaholic, someone utterly unable to enjoy himself when not at work, or did he consciously cultivate an image as an unflagging worker in keeping with a well-defined humanist model? To answer this question, I will examine both the way in which Calvin used his time and the procedures he put in place to enable himself to produce the staggering mass of sermons, commentaries, books, and letters that form his complete works. After having examined these issues, I will turn to the medical domain since Calvin's health is an important aspect in clarifying his self-fashioning. I will conclude by briefly touching on the significance that Calvin's eschatology had for his working life.

■ CALVIN'S USE OF TIME

The five hundredth anniversary of his birth has brought renewed interest in the way Calvin employed his time. Émile Doumergue opened inquiry into the subject; I along with others have followed his lead.[1] Here, however, I would like to go down a somewhat different path.

In the second version of the *Life of Calvin*, Nicolas Colladon added considerably to Beza's portrait of Calvin and adopted a strictly chronological approach.[2] This included providing information on the exact use of the reformer's time: "For he ordinarily spent all of his time writing or studying; even after his meal he walked around in his room for only a quarter of an hour, or half an hour at the most, if there was somebody keeping him company, and then he returned to his studies."[3] Whereas Bullinger followed Marsilio Ficino in recommending an hour-long postprandial walk outdoors—something that Wolfgang Musculus practiced regularly—Calvin paced in his room for fifteen minutes in order to get a little bit of solitary exercise, only prolonging it to a half hour if a secretary or visitor was with him.[4] He almost invented the treadmill. Colladon continued his defense of Calvin against those "who accused him of extravagance," by pointing out that his "free time" was spent reading or writing books. Physical exercise was kept to a minimum.

Calvin was a man who did not sleep very much and ate very little. He had just one meal a day, a supper which he apparently ate around six in the evening, followed by the walk in his room. In addition, he "sometimes had a little bit of wine and an egg around noon."[5] He got up, like all Genevans, at four in the morning to the sound of the réveille-matin bell. This wake-up call, which seems very early to us, was quite normal then. Martin Bucer also reports getting up when the clock struck four in the morning.[6] Like his contemporaries, Calvin also went to bed early at around nine in the evening, and he liked to work in the morning, in keeping with classical and Renaissance principles (one is reminded again of the precepts of Marsilio Ficino). Going to bed, he practiced the *recapitulatio*, a classical meditative practice adopted by humanists and reformers, which he described in a 1558 sermon: "This is, therefore, what we should observe when we each retire privately, think year by year, month by month, and day by day through all our life, in order to condemn ourselves for having used our time so poorly."[7] Reviewing each past day, but also each month and year, was an ancient practice that we read about in Seneca. He had seen it employed by Quintus Sextius, who declared that he used this examination of his day to combat any ill-tempered thoughts.[8] The recapitulation of the day, a Pythagorean recommendation restored by the Stoics, was also valued by Cicero, who had one of the characters in *De senectute* recall at nightfall the day that had just passed.[9] In the sixteenth century, Bullinger practiced the same technique, and Rabelais and many other readers of classical texts were also aware of it. Gargantua "in the middle of the night...recapitulated briefly with his tutor all that he had read, seen, known, done, and understood over the course of the entire day, in the style of the Pythagoreans."[10] Later in the century, Isaac Casaubon followed the same practice and recorded it in his *Ephemerides*. In Causaubon's case, however, Stoicism was not the most important factor in his daily obsession with accounting for his time.[11] The recapitulatio had become an integral part of Reformed spirituality by that time.

The recapitulatio was not always the final activity of Calvin's night, though, since many witnesses speak about his late night labors. In the first version of the *Life of Calvin*, completed in August 1564, Beza asserted that Calvin "had a body so feeble by nature, so weakened by late nights and an excess of sobriety, and he was, in addition subject to so many illnesses, that everyone who saw him thought that he did not have long to live, and, nevertheless, he never ceased to labor day and night on the work of the lord."[12] Beza associated late nights with a sick body, overwork with illness, and in doing so, he sketched the first outlines in the image of Calvin the workaholic. By contrast, in the preface to his commentary on the Psalms, Calvin never refers to late nights at work. He mentions his reserved nature and how he preferred working alone in his study to attending large gatherings, but he is silent about late nights spent studying.

In the second version of their *Life of Calvin*, Colladon and Beza kept the initial passage of the text drafted in haste by Beza and added a second to it. Here, Beza evoked the "very late nights" that had been "so detrimental to his health."[13] Beza mentioned Calvin's nocturnal labors again in the third Latin version of *Calvini Vita* (1575) and in *Les vrais pourtraits des hommes illustres*. He emphasized the many books that Calvin had written and how the reformer had contracted tuberculosis "because of his late nights and excessive abstinence."[14] Working at night was quite rare in the sixteenth century. Productive mornings that began an hour before sunrise were the norm, although we do know of a few others who wrote at night, including the young Pierre de Ronsard. To what end then did Calvin dedicate these late nights in which he worked without the aid of a secretary or student?

Even though Calvin had a taste for poetry—as he confided to Conrad Hubert in 1557—he did not spend these nights either composing poetry or writing biblical commentaries and polemical treatises.[15] Instead, I suspect that until about 1558 and his long illness in the autumn of 1558 and the spring of 1559, Calvin worked on his *Institutes*, since Colladon thought it worth noting, as if it were exceptional, that Calvin produced the final 1559 version by dictation to his brother Antoine and a servant acting as secretary.[16] By then his health was extremely poor.

During the day Calvin was obliged to preach not only the two Sunday sermons, at eight in the morning and three in the afternoon, but also a daily sermon every other week. This he delivered at seven or eight in the morning, depending on the time of the year—generally at eight in his later years. Because of this demanding schedule, he seems never to have been assigned the "daybreak" sermon, which took place on Monday, Wednesday, and Friday at four or five in the morning during the summer and five or six during the winter.[17] Calvin's sermons lasted about an hour, which he monitored using both the hourglass on the pulpit of Saint Pierre and the church's large clock. Frequent references near the end of his sermons ("as will be declared tomorrow, God willing" or "it is true that this cannot be shown for now") suggest that Calvin was quite attentive to this time limit.[18]

After waking and praying, Calvin frequently had books brought to him in bed "at around five or six."[19] He enjoyed using his bed to read, dictate letters, and write since it allowed him to care for his sensitive stomach and fragile health. When necessary, however, he would leave at dawn. In one case, he came to the bedside of Madame de Normandie at five in the morning.[20] On Friday afternoons, he went to the Congrégation, a meeting of pastors where scriptural topics were discussed. On Thursdays, he went to the meeting of the Consistory, a civil and ecclesiastical body designed to ensure proper doctrine and morals. On Mondays, he met with the Petit Conseil. He also gave theology classes every second week for between two and three hours on Monday, Wednesday, and Friday afternoon.[21] And this is all in addition to the time he spent writing letters, making visits, and composing his many written works. In light of such a busy schedule, one can readily understand the complaint that Pierre Viret tactfully expressed after receiving an especially short missive from Calvin. In a long letter dated February 7, 1545, Viret wrote:

> I waited for a letter from you complaining about how I write so infrequently, but you are so busy that do not even have time to complain. As for me, even though I have much more time [*magis otiosus* (sum)] than you, I, nevertheless, do not want to complain about your long silence. On the contrary, I am surprised that you are still able to send me even three words [*apiculum*][22].

Calvin wittily grasped the rod that had been extended to him: "You see how I still feel no shame about my laziness. Consider it the reason that I save myself the bother of writing."[23] He then went on to enclose copies of letters he had just addressed to Luther and Melanchthon Calvin's chronic shortage of time was so well known in Geneva that a printer who had managed to lay his hands on a series of his sermons for publication—an act for which the reformer had given him some "difficulty"—justified his action by saying that Calvin would never be able to review the surreptitiously obtained works anyway, "given how little free time he has."[24]

I have already echoed the consensus of Calvin scholars that the reformer was a tireless worker.[25] Such a view was held not just by those who, like Beza and Colladon, followed and loved Calvin. In his *Historia sui temporis*, Jean-Auguste de Thou depicts Calvin as a great mind and a marvelously eloquent man who "struggled with a number of illnesses over seven years, and yet was no less assiduous in carrying out his duties and applying himself continually to his writing, before he finally died of asthma in Geneva."[26] Struggling with illness and yet working and writing without respite, while at the same time complaining about it: that is the paradox of the intellectual. The consistent association of the two terms—diligence and illness, diligence in illness—is something worth noting. Does it not epitomize the workaholic as a type? For Calvin, in any case, it obliged him to find techniques to manage an overloaded schedule.

■ MANAGING A CHRONIC SHORTAGE OF TIME

Calvin's correspondence, as I have written elsewhere,[27] is filled with references to his busy schedule and to the procedures he put in place to make the best use of it, procedures that finally enabled him to produce nearly a hundred titles. The first "catalogue of books and writings by Mr. John Calvin," compiled by Theodore Beza in the summer of 1564, already included eighty-one titles, in spite of some omissions (such as his lessons on Ezekiel) and the fact that the *Institutes* was counted as a single entry, notwithstanding its five Latin and four French versions—versions that Calvin was constantly rewriting and supplementing. The total obviously also excluded anonymous texts that have subsequently been attributed to Calvin. Beza's initial list included twelve printed sermon collections and fifteen manuscript series of sermons, nearly a third of Calvin's corpus. His books frequently began as oral productions. Sermons, congrégations, theology lessons, and commentaries nearly all began in spoken form. Together they account for nearly half of Calvin's oeuvre. He implemented an effective system for the transcription of his sermons, seeking out a good scribe in 1546–1547, rejecting a certain Jacques—probably not the French doctor and botanist Jacques Daléchamps, who edited Athenaeus—before finally settling on Denis Raguenier in 1549.[28] The faithful Nicolas Des Gallars wrote up his first Old Testament commentary, that on Isaiah, in 1551. After that, Jean Budé and Charles de Jonvilliers used the notes they took during Calvin's lectures to prepare the text of his lessons on Jeremiah, Ezekiel, and the other prophets. Calvin's use of these helping hands, whom he greatly appreciated, saved him time and increased his output.

As is well known, Calvin preached following the *lectio continua* method, going systematically through a book of the Bible, passage by passage. I have shown elsewhere that Calvin regularly took to the pulpit without preparation, thus committing errors of Hebrew in particular, albeit not invariably. However, I noted that by the time he picked up a new passage the following day, Calvin gave an error-free translation. In my article on this I draw attention to Calvin's modesty, intelligence, and true professional conscience: Calvin worked on his daily sermons over some days, before starting on a new sermon cycle. I also show that Calvin knew biblical

Hebrew well enough to warrant occasional direct recourse to the Hebrew Bible (sometimes obscured by lapses of memory) whereas he ignored rabbinic Hebrew.[29] I continue, nevertheless, to read views, more hagiographical than scholarly, suggesting that Calvin knew biblical and rabbinic Hebrew perfectly and that he prepared impeccable sermons and lectures in it. In swaying the minds of those who hold such views, however, the arguments of Calvin's contemporaries will hopefully carry more weight than my own.

Jean-François Gilmont has drawn attention to a practice described by Jean Crespin in the preface to Calvin's lectures on the twelve minor prophets (1559). To capture his words as they were actually spoken, Calvin's students and secretaries, usually Jean Budé and Charles de Jonviller, recorded his words in tandem:

> Each one of them had his paper as ready as possible, and they each wrote as quickly they could. If one of them missed a word (as sometimes happened, especially when [Calvin] was vehement in his exposition of passages that required it), the others recorded it.... As soon as the lesson was completed, Jonviller gathered the others' papers and put them together with his own, and together they looked at them and conferred diligently with one another. Then they appointed someone else to transcribe everything that they had hurriedly recorded, and then finally they reviewed everything so that the next day they could reread it before the author. When there was sometimes a word missing, he put it in its proper place; or if something seemed unclear, he expressed it again more succinctly. This is how these lectures came to be published.[30]

Jean Crespin had already begun to idealize Calvin's method: "It has to be understood that Calvin never wrote anything (as many others do) or used notes of any kind when he interpreted Holy Scripture publicly. And still less after the class was over or the following day, but over the course of an entire hour he did not cease to expound it without ever writing a single word in his book to aid his memory."[31] Listeners moreover appreciated the spontaneity of Calvin's delivery, making a virtue of this apparent shortcoming. One should not forget that, at the time, a word-for-word reading of a previously prepared text was the most common lecture practice.[32] In the 1557 introductory letter "To Christian Readers," found at the beginning of Calvin's lectures on Hosea, Jean Budé attests to this practice and praises the very different teaching style of his master:

> The style which [Calvin] uses here is simple and unadorned, similar to that which we know he used in his lessons. Not in the manner of many who bring from home their lectures completely prepared and then read them to their listeners just as they are written. So the language used is the kind he used to think and express himself on the spot, directed more to teaching and edifying his listeners than to pleasing their ears. Which is why, unless we are greatly mistaken, he has so vividly captured the intent and true meaning of the Prophet, why it seems nearly impossible to add anything to it. For in dissecting so carefully each detailed point, he also briefly shows the purpose of each teaching, applying it so specifically to this time that no one, however rude or ignorant, could be misled.[33]

Seizing "the intent and true meaning of the prophet" or biblical author, was Calvin's primary hermeneutical principle, according to Budé. He reserved special praise for the *ex abrupto* biblical commentary of Calvin, who was able to think on his feet and express the biblical author's intent with spontaneity and concision. The model is the timely inspiration of the Holy Spirit ἐν αὐτῇ τῇ ὥρᾳ, described in Luke 12:11.

That Calvin not only taught without notes but often lectured with little or no preparation is confirmed by the opening remark of a brief letter he wrote to Farel on June 8, 1554: "I do not have the spare time to write right now, since it is nearly time for the theology lesson, and I still have not had the chance to think about what I am going to say."[34] Despite being so pressed for time, Calvin used these few spare minutes to begin a letter rather than to prepare his lecture. Since the messenger left a bit later than planned, he had time after his class to complete the letter.[35] Clearly, he refused to let the smallest moment go to waste and preferred to start a letter rather than take a long time preparing his theology lecture. It should thus be no surprise that he began his lessons at the Auditoire or appeared before his congregants at the churches of Saint-Pierre or the Madeleine without preparation or having merely reread a page or two of his own commentary on the biblical book he was expounding, as I have shown for his sermons on Genesis.[36]

Returning to Budé's preface of 1557 to Calvin's lectures on Hosea, we read praise for the overworked Calvin, weighed down by his duties and too busy to prepare his lectures:

> For as he was usually overwhelmed with countless tasks and able, at best, to snatch a half hour to contemplate his lectures, he preferred for the benefit and edification of his listeners to draw out and explain simply the true meaning [of a passage], rather than trying to please their ears with a vain display or to seek his own glory with some sort of ostentation.[37]

All of this *angustia temporis* lauded by Budé was in some sense orchestrated by Calvin. He sought the best scribe to record his nonprepared sermons and the best students to reproduce the essentials of his hastily assembled theology lectures, but he also constantly let it be known that his time was limited, that he was responding in a hurry, or that he had not managed to find enough time to polish a lecture before giving it his imprimatur. He even evoked his habitual haste and lifelong quest to squeeze the most from each minute in the farewell address he delivered to Geneva's pastors on April 28, 1564, a month before his death:

> When I first came to this church, there was almost nothing. There was preaching and that was all. On my return from Strasbourg, I wrote the Catechism in haste, for I would never have accepted the ministry if they had not solemnly promised me these two things: to hold to the Catechism and to discipline. As I wrote it, they came to fetch the scraps of paper I was using, no bigger than my hand, and brought them to the printer. Even though Pierre Viret was in town at the time, do you think I ever showed him anything? I never had the leisure, though I thought of doing so if I had had it.[38]

In a hurry to write the Catechism and even to have his text rushed to the printer sheet by sheet, Calvin was not only a busy man, but also a man aware that he was very busy. This sense of haste shows throughout his works. It went hand in hand with his strong but anxious personality.

It is easy to catalogue the expressions related to haste in the letters of Calvin. In August 1563 he began a letter to the Admiral Coligny, one of the political leaders of the Reformed in France: "My lord, I recently wrote you in haste most fearful letters, as I was in great distress."[39] Elsewhere, he responds "hastily"; he asks his correspondent to excuse his "shortage of time"; in letters to Farel and Bullinger he confides that he is "*magis obrutus*,"[40] which might be translated as greatly overworked. His correspondents—Farel, Viret, Bullinger, Vermigli—also use the participle obrutus when speaking of him. In a February 29, 1548, letter to Viret, Calvin mocked a treatise by Vallerand Poullain, the *Traité tresutile du saint sacrament de la Cene* (published in Strasbourg in 1547) and suggested that his friend respond to it, if he had the time and pages to waste.[41] Poullain had looked after the printing of Calvin's commentary on the first letter of Paul to the Corinthians (1546), as well as the index in the fourth edition of the *Institutes* (1550), but like everyone, he was not allowed to diverge from the views of the master. *Tempus perdere* was something Calvin avoided completely, never forgetting the teaching he drove home almost daily from the pulpit. God watched over his children each moment of their lives, and on the day of judgment, they would have to account for every minute.

Calvin was not the only one to write *raptim*, to respond *raptim*, to live *raptim*, but this sense of being in a rush is especially pronounced in him and his work. Examining *L'histoire d'un meurtre execrable*, in which Calvin describes the murder of the Protestant convert Juan Diaz at the hands of his Catholic brother, Alfons, one easily detects the signs of editorial haste. "The narration is so concentrated," according to a modern editor, "that it becomes nearly incomprehensible, in the case of the murder itself for example.... One would say that that it is a text written hastily and on the basis of incomplete information."[42] One year earlier, as part of his battle with Pierre Caroli, the former pastor of Lausanne, Calvin and his secretary withdrew to the Genevan countryside to write the reply to Caroli, which they were able to do in three days, even though it ran to one hundred in-octavo pages.[43] In a letter to Guillaume Farel, Calvin described how he was so keen to take the fight to Caroli that his response seemed to take only a moment: "I was so stirred up when we started that I easily flew through to the end" (ut nullo negotio transvolaverim usque ad metam).[44] In this case Calvin seemed to enjoy the task, but his overloaded schedule always obliged him to do things quickly.

Seneca said that the great remedy for anger was taking the time to slow down (*De ira* 2: 29, 1), but I could show at great length how rarely Calvin took any kind of break, since his fiery nature left him little time or inclination for relaxation. One might note here that the expression "angustiae temporis," a lack of time, can be found already in Cicero. Nevertheless, the notion became increasingly prevalent in the Renaissance, with Erasmus emerging as its standard bearer. Before turning to Erasmus though, I need to touch on one point that is related to the furious pace of Calvin's intellectual and spiritual activity: the reformer's chronically poor health.

■ "THIS GREAT MIND IN A FEEBLE BODY"

Theodore Beza and Nicolas Colladon both chronicled the health woes of the man whom Colladon called a "great mind in a feeble body."[45] Beza listed "quartain fever," "stones, gout, hemorrhoids, tubercular fever, shortness of breath, as well as his regular migraines."[46] Concomitantly, Calvin insisted that God was a doctor: "Here is God, the doctor who heals all our spiritual illnesses." He used the same metaphor in describing the office of Jesus Christ, which was "to heal our spiritual illnesses."[47]

Calvin was also not averse to providing his correspondents news about his health or his various afflictions. With a degree of detail that tests our twenty-first century sensibilities, he wrote to Beza about his diarrhea and described to Renée of France, Duchess of Ferrara, the nature of his health problem, not neglecting to mention his hemorrhoids: "Madame, excuse me for writing to you by the hand of my brother because of my weak state and the pain that I suffer from my various afflictions: shortness of breath, stones, gout, and a stercoral ulcer, which prevent me from doing any exercise, which would be the only thing that might offer the hope of relief."[48] When writing to doctors at the renowned medical faculty of Montpellier in search of a precise diagnosis and treatment plan just three months before his death (and two months after the letter to Renée of France), Calvin naturally spelled out yet more intimate details. This letter also betrays the consternation that his ill health aroused among colleagues and reveals that he was seeking an explanation from the Montpellier doctors about why they had prescribed a certain medicine for him after he had asked his own doctor, Philibert Sarazin, about its purpose and had evidently not been satisfied:[49] "For a long time I have suffered from hemorrhoids and anal ulcers, which resulted from scratching myself with my nails during my sleep, when roundworms made me itch, roundworms from which I am now free. But when the itch returns, my nails start the problem all over again." When he included this letter in his 1575 edition of Calvin's *Epistolae*, Beza naturally suppressed this rather intimate passage as well as other similar passages where Calvin carefully described further symptoms: pulled muscles, hemorrhoids, and stones. He was apparently a cooperative patient, interested in any treatment that might "prolong his life"; he did not want to die. Trust in the physician is a principle found already in Hippocrates and Galen, whom Calvin once cites in the *Institutes* (1, 5. 2). In order to fight off illness, a patient must commit his health and his life to his doctor.

Calvin's temperament made him prone to medical problems. Vehement and quick-tempered, he coped poorly with frustration, contradiction, or obstacles. In 1545, faced with having to write to Pierre Caroli, whom he suspected of stealing some documents, he admitted to Viret that he had become so indignant that he needed return to bed until the next morning.[50] This was not the first time his dealings with Caroli led him to become extremely upset. A few years before, Calvin described to Farel how, disappointed with Bucer's advice that he make peace with Caroli, he had refused, stormed out of the room, returned home, and "only calmed down with sobbing and tears." He added this reproach to Farel: "I was sickened all the more that you were the cause of my ills."[51] Such conflicts could set off the chronic stomach problems and migraines from which Calvin suffered. In October 1546, he wrote to Jacques de Bourgogne, seigneur de Falais: "Yesterday at eight in the evening my migraine struck me so violently that I could only open my mouth with great pain."[52] Calvin's regular correspondence with Falais between 1543 and 1548 broke off suddenly when the nobleman welcomed Calvin's enemy Jerome

Bolsec into his house, something Calvin did not appreciate. The reformer wrote a final letter to Falais in June 1554, explaining his position once again and underscoring his sincerity by sharing his conviction that his own end was near: "And so that you know there is no anger or ill-will, I am writing you now as though I were preparing to appear before the Lord, who has afflicted me once again with a suffering that is like a mirror of death before my eyes. I pray him, my lord, that having pity on me and receiving me in his mercy, he will preserve and guide you by his spirit."[53] We do not know exactly what illness made Calvin fear the worst on this occasion, but it was one of many from which he suffered in the 1550s. A letter from Beza to Bullinger relates that Calvin had an acute attack of tuberculosis on Sunday night, December 24, 1559, during which he coughed up a significant amount of blood. Nevertheless, the next morning he was preaching at Saint-Pierre at eight. He had to interrupt his preaching the next day, however, and did not take the pulpit again until Monday, January 8. Calvin could be quite tough in the face of physical suffering.[54]

Charles Cooke and John Wilkinson, two doctors who have recently taken an interest in Calvin's medical history, agree about the basic elements of his medical problems. He suffered from chronic tuberculosis probably from 1558, although it did not flare up seriously until December 24, 1559. He was afflicted with chronic migraines from his student days onward, and later suffered from digestive problems, kidney stones, and gout. Wilkinson adds pleurisy to the list and, perhaps, malaria (because of Calvin's intermittent fevers). Cooke includes blood poisoning (because of those same fevers), a suggestion which Wilkinson rejects.[55] (Already in the sixteenth century, Montaigne was one of many who used to poke fun at doctors' conflicting diagnoses.[56]) Wilkinson also contends that Calvin's generally weak health was aggravated by trigger factors that included inadequate nutrition, stress, lack of exercise, frequent insomnia, and an enormous workload. One could add to this unhappy portrait the reformer's sometimes difficult character, which caused him to suffer from anxiety and to cope poorly with frustration. In spite of his frequent illnesses, Calvin maintained confidence in his doctors, as the letter to the medical faculty at Montpellier shows.

■ THE ERASMIAN MODEL

In a letter to Cornelius Gerard from July 1489 (?), Erasmus praised the *Elegentiae* of Lorenzo Valla, which he had not yet edited, and lauded "all the activity, all the study, all the sweat" that Valla had expended in refuting the foolishness of barbarians.[57] Intensive labor like this was not only respected, it was admired, envied, and almost glorified as an ideal. Given the appearance in 1516 of Erasmus's *Works of Jerome* and his *Novum Instrumentum*, both colossal and demanding undertakings, one wonders how he found the time in the previous year to write about his work, as he did to Willibald Pirckheimer in a letter from October 16, 1515:

> I am overwhelmed by a double burden, whose double weight would require a Hercules and not an Erasmus. Besides other works of little importance, I am working on Jerome and a New Testament which is now about to be printed....I, who am writing you, am not only

overwhelmed with an incredible amount of work, but they have just told me as I rise from
the table that the messenger is leaving. When the opportunity presents itself to me, and I
hope it will be soon, I will be writing you entire volumes and no longer just letters.[58]

With a striking rhetorical mastery that juxtaposes discussion of work with witty
asides, Erasmus casts himself as the overtaxed intellectual. He was, perhaps, the
first intellectual of the modern era to complain like this about being too busy.
Medieval writers did not raise such cavils, although both Petrarch and Gregory the
Great did complain about their health.[59] Jerome learned languages with exacting
care and translated with great precision, producing a tremendous quantity of work,
but nowhere in his letter to Paulinus of Nola or his Contra Rufinum does he complain about translating the Bible or being overworked.[60] Pirckheimer's response to
Erasmus is not entirely free of irony, noting that in the midst of so much work
Erasmus still found time to think of him ("inter tot negotia tua mei quoque memor
es").[61] At the same time, though, he praises Erasmus, inventing a new beatitude for
him: "Felix tu, qui laboribus istis Deo, sanctis ac mundo aceptior eris" (Blessed are
you, who, by your work, are making yourself more pleasing to God, the saints, and
the world).[62] His mountain of work brought Erasmus the triple approval of God,
the saints in heaven, and men on earth.

Often in poor health, Erasmus consistently complained about his feeble physical
state: "I have taken on [the biblical] translation of St. Jerome with such passion that
it matters little that I am destroying myself with the work."[63] He did not hesitate to
describe his physical ills with a degree of detail that would today qualify him as a
hypochondriac. We see evidence of such a tendency in his poem "De senectute"
and in his Encomium artis medicae.[64] It is not surprising to learn that Erasmus was
convinced that he had contracted the plague between Basel and Louvain in 1518,
although his fears ultimately proved to be unfounded.[65] Petrarch, who once again
proves himself in this regard the first Renaissance man, also complained frequently
and feared death, confiding to Boccaccio, on the day of his sixty-second birthday
that he was afraid he would die during his grand climacteric.[66] In the wake of
Erasmus, countless intellectuals would bemoan both a massive workload that
demanded a Herculean effort and their own failing health. Guillaume Budé is
probably the example that comes closest to Calvin.[67]

In the first edition of his Commentaries on the Greek Language, Budé begins
with a long preface to Francis I, which is well known because it called for the
creation of a trilingual college, very explicitly reminding the king of his promise to
establish such an institution and demanding that he carry it out. Budé begins by
detailing the workload that he has endured: "It has been just over two years, oh
mighty king, that I have pursued this work on the Commentary, constantly looking
after and organizing it, by no means working slowly or only out of habit."[68] He
admits that his students had pushed him to complete the task and that he had hurried to do so, "becoming more attentive and fixed upon the task every day." There
is a surprising intimacy between Budé and the first Valois king, as there would be
later between Ronsard and Charles IX. The man of letters treated the king as a confidant and poured out before him the troubles he faced due to his poor health and
his long and arduous labors:

Nevertheless, even with this great courage, I could not complete what I had undertaken and bring it to its end as I had intended. For my progress with the project was impeded by an illness which the doctors confirmed was rooted in my depths because I had studied with too much determination and perseverance. Certainly, at the start of the work, I could handle my labors easily, so great being my desire to bring it to its just conclusion that it nearly divorced my mind from the feelings of my body. But after the condition—having secretly grown and multiplied—surged up within me when I was least suspecting it, my mistress, Philology, was conquered by the indisposition, which came close to making all the practitioners of letters in our time unhappy. For the force of the illness had caused all the medical men to despair, since they could not readily find anything to combat the sickness. Thus, they gave me two choices: either I put an end to my obsession and this lifestyle—which would cause me great sorrow—or, if I wanted to continue as I had previously, they announced that it would put an end to my life, and they let it be known that they thought this with good reason.[69]

Budé depicts himself as facing a choice between his work and his life, since his doctors had diagnosed a fight to the death between the demands of his body and those of his intellectual burden. He continued his lament, his pain constant, swearing that he would abandon "this manner of living that was so clearly harmful to both my body and domestic life." Almost before our eyes, Budé outlines the modern figure of the overburdened and suffering intellectual, pushing his body beyond its limits. It was a model that Calvin, excellent Hellenist that he was, would have been aware of, for he praised Budé's work in his 1532 commentary on Seneca's *De clementia*.[70] Budé struck a similar tone in the postscript to the commentary, noting that he had worked quickly (διά σπουδῆς) in order to ease the difficulties of young men learning Greek. He then returned to the subject of his failing health:

I, therefore, carried out my labors and completed them with the greatest alacrity, in spite of frequent troubles, without ever stopping—even though my family chastised me, urging me to look after my health—before suddenly being forced to take to my bed and then to abandon my studies completely instead of just lightening my excessive load. For what would I do on the day I realized that I was ruined beyond repair.[71]

The rhetoric is brilliant: passion and a furious pace combine with sickness and physical infirmity to undo the intellectual and break him down under the weight of his superhuman studies. Given the vast scope of his project, Budé called on not just one follower but on many to carry the task forward. What the humanist had accomplished by himself required a team to be brought to completion. It is a scenario that would become a staple of humanist rhetoric. What better way to cast himself as a workaholic, going beyond his physical limits and sacrificing his health for scholarship? Aged sixty-two, Budé goes on to complain about his advanced age, even though he would go on to live another eleven years. A final burst of proud vigor allows him to assert that "nevertheless, it was I who found myself alone putting together the present work" (αὐτὸς ἐπ' ἐμαυτοῦ).[72] Whatever hints of modesty Budé lets slip here and there, like intervals in a musical score, can obviously be taken with a grain of salt. Budé was one of many humanists and reformers who complained about their daunting workload and compromised health.

Returning to Calvin, there is an important exchange of letters between him and Beza during and after the Colloquy of Poissy that sheds more light on the subject. In a letter from October 7, 1561, Calvin begins by relating that he had indeed received the previous missive from Beza, which was important because it had detailed the end of the colloquy. Before touching on any other subject, however, Calvin pours out the details of an attack of gout that had afflicted his right foot.[73] Two days later, in a letter to the Zurich pastor Johann Wolff, Calvin refers to "all my troubles which are not unknown to you," before going on, in nearly the same terms that he had used with Beza, about the sharp pain in his right foot.[74] His gout seems nearly to take on more importance than the Colloquy of Poissy. These great intellectuals, however tough, were not strangers to physical suffering.

■ CONCLUSION

I turn again to my initial question: in what ways was Calvin a workaholic? In fact, there were two aspects to it: on the one hand, Calvin worked a great deal and even put measures in place calculated to increase his productivity; on the other, he could not leave his work alone, limiting himself to a ten-minute walk in his room and complaining constantly. Over the course of the Renaissance, the outlines emerged—only faintly at first with Petrarch and then very clearly with Erasmus, Budé, and a host of others—of a model of the intellectual as a heroic worker, who was paradoxically weak in body; one who complained about his suffering, sometimes approaching hypochondria, and shamelessly revealed his most intimate afflictions to kings and queens. All of this came not so much from the intellectual's desire to present himself as a model of self-sacrifice—though this motivation was certainly not completely absent—as from an exaggerated sense of his qualities as an extraordinary thinker and worker.[75] In describing their physical woes, Erasmus, Budé, and Calvin may well have been trying to overcome their anxiety by speaking about their illness, as if *verba* could maintain the upper hand against *res*. It is certainly hard to imagine that they were looking for advice, since neither kings and queens nor Beza and Bullinger were likely to offer them home remedies.

In a letter from 1516, Erasmus confided to Leo X that age was beginning to weigh him down.[76] Nevertheless, the great humanist died at about age seventy. Budé lived three years longer than this. Beza lived until he was eighty-five, while both Luther and Melanchthon reached their sixty-third year. Even Calvin, who died just weeks before his fifty-fifth birthday, lived quite a long life by sixteenth-century standards. As so often seems to be the case, the old people who complain the most live the longest. The figure of the suffering intellectual, killing himself with his work, was not an invention of the nineteenth century. It was a product of the Renaissance, even though Erasmus, Budé, and Calvin may have had distant antecedents like Petrarch, Gregory the Great, or Jerome.

In another way, though, the Calvin who was constantly in a rush was an astoundingly modern figure, stressing the importance of each minute even before the minute hand of the clock had been invented, shortening his postprandial walk by taking it indoors, using the five minutes before a lecture to begin a letter. He did so because he felt acutely conscious, because he believed and he taught, that God watched over his children every minute of their lives, but that every child of God would also need to account for each minute of his time. Calvin instituted a new temporal connection between man and God, to which we are still indebted today. It is this that distinguishes Calvin from the humanist model of Erasmus and Budé.

The figure of the workaholic needs finally to be linked to a theological conception of time. I would suggest that the typology of the workaholic was made possible by a shift in eschatological thinking. The leading figures of the Renaissance and the Reformation showed few signs of eschatological impatience. They did not call upon or wait for the imminent return of Christ, but they did have a view of eternal life that differed from that of medieval Christianity. For Thomas Aquinas and other medieval people, there was no great pressure to complete one's work on earth because it could always be completed in God's presence after death. Early modern intellectuals were mindful that they would complete nothing in the life beyond, and this made it critical for them to do as much as possible while on earth. Following the example of Erasmus, they became once again like Hercules, carrying out the work of a giant here on earth. Beza would even dub Calvin the "Christian Hercules."[77] One thinks also of the giant Gargantua, a very influential model of the intellectual workaholic, albeit a fictional one. Even as he cleaned his body, the Bible was read to him, and in this "secret place," the "most obscure and difficult points" were explained to him.[78] It is clear that Erasmus wanted to complete his work while on earth since he would not take it up again in heaven. Although there is no textual evidence to prove it, I would dare to suggest that Calvin shared this perspective even though he may have viewed himself ultimately as predestined to ceaseless work by the eternal Divinity.

▪ Notes

1. See my *L'ordre du temps. L'invention de la ponctualité à Genève au XVIe siècle* (Geneva: Droz, 2004), 25–45. Translated by Karin Maag as *On Time, Punctuality, and Discipline in Early Modern Calvinism* (Cambridge: Cambridge University Press, 2010). See the exhibition catalogue, *Une journée dans la vie de Calvin* (Geneva: Musée International de la Réforme, 2009), which contains a number of inaccuracies, but of a relatively minor nature.

2. On this, see Irena Backus, *Life Writing in Reformation Europe. Lives of Reformers by Friends, Disciples and Foes* (Aldershot: Ashgate, 2008), 126–35.

3. "Vie de Calvin," *Calv. Opp.* 21: 113.

4. "Vita Wolfgangi Musculi," in Reinhard Bodenmann, *Wolfgang Musculus (1497–1563): Destin d'un autodidacte lorrain au siècle des Réformes* (Geneva: Droz, 2000), 182.

5. Theodore Beza, "Vie de Calvin," *Calv. Opp.* 21: 34. Nicolas Colladon relates that Calvin only had this frugal sort of meal during the last six months of his life, when he was forced to do so by his doctors: Theodore Beza, "Vie de Calvin," revised and supplemented by Nicolas Colladon, *Calv. Opp.* 21: 109.

6. See the "Formula vivendi" of Martin Bucer, which states at the beginning of point 8: "Audita quarta hora, mane uterque surgat." Martin Bucer and Matthew Parker, *Florilegium Patristicum*, ed. Pierre Fraenkel (Leiden: Brill, 1988), 190.

7. 282nd sermon on Isaiah, 57, 1s, August 10, 1558, Eglise française de Londres, ms. F VIII. 3, fol. 21r.

8. Letters to Lucilius (X) 83, 2s. See Seneca, *De ira* III, 36, 1–3: in Seneca, *Moral Essays*, transl. John W. Basore, London: W. Heinemann, 1928–135. 3 vols. vol. I, *On Anger* III. 36, 1–3: 336–9:" All our senses ought to be trained to endurance. They are naturally long-suffering, if only the mind desists from weakening them. This should be summoned to give an

account of itself every day. Sextius had this habit, and when the day was over and he had retired to his nightly rest, he would put these questions to his soul: 'What bad habit have you cured to- day? What fault have you resisted? In what respect are you better?' Anger will cease and become more controllable if it finds that it must appear before a judge every day. Can anything be more excellent than this practice of thoroughly sifting the whole day? And how delightful the sleep that follows this self- examination - how tranquil it is, how deep and untroubled, when the soul has either praised or admonished itself, and when this secret examiner and critic of self has given report of its own character! I avail myself of this privilege, and every day I plead my cause before the bar of self. When the light has been removed from sight, and my wife, long aware of my habit, has become silent, I scan the whole of my day and retrace all my deeds and words. I conceal nothing from myself, I omit nothing."

9. Cited by Jean Starobinski, "Le cycle des heures et le moment de la vérité" (offprint), 157–68, here 158. The letter from Lucilius to Seneca is cited by Jean Starobinski, "L' ordre du jour," in *Le temps de la réflexion* (Paris: Gallimard, 1983), 101–25, here 104.

10. *Gargantua*, ch. 23, in Rabelais, *Œuvres complètes*, ed. Mireille Huchon (Paris: Gallimard, 1994), 70, 1129 n. 5, which cites Cicero's *De senectute*.

11. Compare Olivier Millet, "Le stoïcisme au quotidien. Le journal de Casaubon," in *Stoïcisme et christianisme à la Renaissance* (Paris: Rue d' Ulm, 2006), 145–62. Millet argues here for Stoicism's greater influence on Casaubon.

12. *Calv. Opp.* 21: 33.

13. *Calv. Opp.* 21: 107 (the first passage), 55 (the second passage).

14. *Les vrais pourtraits des hommes illustres* (Geneva: Jean de Laon, 1581, repr. Geneva: Slatkine, 1986), 122.

15. See my "Plaisir des mots, plaisir des mets. Irdische Freude bei Calvin," in *Calvinus Sincerioris Religionis Vindex*, ed. Brian G. Armstrong and Wilhelm H. Neuser (Kirksville, MO: Truman State University, 1997), 189–208, here 200–201, where I cite what Calvin wrote to Hubert Hubert: "Ad poeticen natura satis eram propensus: sed ea valere jussa, ab annis viginti quinque nihil composui, nisi quod Wormaciæ exemplo Philippi et Sturmi adductus sum, ut carmen illud quod legisti per lusum scriberem." Calvin was referring to the poetry contest Melanchthon organized at Worms in 1541, during the course of which he wrote his *Epinicion*.

16. See the French edition of Calvin's *Institution chrétienne*, ed. Jean-Daniel Benoît, 5 vols. (Paris: Vrin, 1957–63), 1: 10. Colladon relates this in the Latin preface to the 1576 edition of the *Institutes*. On this, see Rodolphe Peter and Jean-François Gilmont, eds., *Bibliotheca Calviniana. Les oeuvres de Jean Calvin publiées au XVIe siècle*, 3 vols. (Geneva: Droz, 1991–2000), 2: 762–63, no. 60/8; 3: 225–32, no. 76/3.

17. *Ordonnances ecclésiastiques de* 1561, *Calv. Opp.* 10: 99–100; Thomas A. Lambert, *Preaching, Praying and Policing the Reform in Sixteenth-Century Geneva* (Ph.D. diss., University of Wisconsin, 1998), 285–91. A forthcoming study by Elsie McKee promises to revise and expand our understanding of this subject.

18. Engammare, *Ordre du temps*, ch. 2.

19. Beza, *Vie de Calvin*, revised and supplemented by Colladon, *Calv. Opp.* 21: 109.

20. Calvin to Mme de Cany, Geneva, April 29, 1549, *Calv. Opp.* 13: 246, no. 1179.

21. Charles Borgeaud, *Histoire de l' Université de Genève: L'Académie de Calvin 1559– 1798* (Geneva: Société Academique de Genève, 1900), 53; T. H. L. Parker, *Calvin's Preaching* (Edinburgh: Westminster John Knox Press, 1992), 62–63. Information about the organization of theology classes comes from the *Leges* of the Academy, founded in 1559.

22. "Exspectabam abs te literas expostulatorias quod tam raro ad te scribam, sed occupatior es quam ut vel expostulare liceat. Ego autem etsi magis otiosus sim quam tu, nolo tamen tecum expostulare de diuturno tuo silentio, imo magis miror quod vel apiculum mittere possis." *Calv. Opp.* 12: 28, no. 612.

23. See letter no. 613, from February 12, *Calv. Opp.* 12: 32. It was written, therefore, five days after Viret's letter, but we do not know when Viret's letter left Lausanne or when Calvin received it. It seems possible to me that Calvin, annoyed by Viret's remark, waited a day or two before responding.

24. *Vingtdeux sermons auxquels est exposé le pseaume centdixneufvieme, contenant pareil nombre de huictains* (Geneva: Jean Girard, 1554), fol. A2r, "L' imprimeur au lecteur."

25. The same could be said of Theodore Beza. See Alain Dufour, "Une œuvre inconnue de Bèze?," *BHR* 22 (1960): 403–5, here 403.

26. *Calv. Opp.* 21: 11.

27. See Engammare, *On Time*, 16–28.

28. See Jean-François Gilmont, *Jean Calvin et le livre imprimé* (Geneva: Droz, 1997), 106–8. In June 1547, Pierre de Maldonade suggested a certain Jacques, identified by Gilmont as Daléchamps (who had entered the University of Montpellier in 1545 and obtained his doctorate in medicine in May or June 1547). It is hard to believe that this young doctor, who indeed passed through Geneva in 1547, could be the one who "recueille bien quelques sentences, mais la substance n'y est pas si entiere" as Calvin wrote to Jacques de Bourgogne June 16, 1547. Jean Calvin, *Lettres à Monsieur et Madame de Falais,* ed. Françoise Bonali-Fiquet (Geneva: Droz, 1991), 154. In Calvin's correspondence during the second half of 1547, Jacques Dallichant was merely a letter carrier between the Seigneur de Falais and Calvin.

29. See Engammare, "Joannes Calvinus trium linguarum peritus? La question de l' hébreu," *BHR* 58 (1996): 35–60; Engammare, "Calvin connaissait-il la Bible? Les citations de l' Écriture dans ses sermons sur la Genèse," *BSHPF* 141 (1995): 163–84. For a concise summary of Calvin's method as uncovered by me, see also Gilmont, *Calvin et le livre imprimé*, 195–97.

30. Jean Calvin, *Leçons et expositions familieres sur les douze petis prophetes* (Lyon: Sebastien Honorati, 1565), fol. [*6]r; *Calv. Opp.* 42: 189–90. See also Gilmont, *Calvin et le livre imprimé*, 82–84, 253.

31. Calvin, *Leçons et expositions familieres* fol. [*6]r; *Calv. Opp.* 42: 189–90.

32. Ann Blair, "Principes et pratiques de la pédagogie humaniste et réformée," contribution to the conference held on the 450th anniversary of the foundation of Geneva's Collège Calvin. I thank Ann Blair for sending me a copy of her essay before publication.

33. Jean Calvin, *Leçons et expositions familieres sur les douze petis prophetes* (Lyon: Sebastien Honorati, 1565), fol. *4v; *Calv. Opp.* 42: 187–88. Gilmont, *Calvin et le livre imprimé*, 82–84.

34. "Nunc scribendi non est otium, quum et lectionis instat hora, et quid dicturus sim, nondum meditari licuit," *Calv. Opp.* 15: 148, no. 1962. It was Jean-François Gilmont who first took note of the hurried state in which Calvin so often found himself. See Gilmont, *Calvin et le livre imprimé*, 57; and Engammare, "Calvin connaissait-il la Bible?," 163–84.

35. *Calv. Opp.* 15: 149.

36. *Sermons de Jean Calvin sur la Genèse, chapitres 1 à 20,4, Supplementa Calviniana* (11/1 and 11/2), ed. M. Engammare (Neukirchen: Neukircher Verlag, 2000), 11/1: xliv–xlvi.

37. *Calv. Opp.* 42: 183–84.

38. *Calv. Opp.* 9: 891, 894.

39. *Calv. Opp.* 20: 128 (italics mine).

40. Calvin to Farel, April 20, 1539, *Calv. Opp.* 10: 337, no. 168: "Non memini hoc toto anno fuisse diem unum quo magis obrutus fuerim variis negotiis"; Calvin to Bullinger, November 8, 1542, *Calv. Opp.* 11: 463, no. 434: "sic per aliquot menses obrutus fui in restituendis rebus penitus dissipatis et collapsis, ut alio converterem animum non liceret."

41. *Calv. Opp.* 12: 663, no. 997: "Tu si tantum operæ et temporis perdere voles, statim animadvertes quæ sint improbanda."

42. Jean Calvin, *Trois libelles anonymes*, ed. Francis Higman and Olivier Millet (Geneva: Droz, 2006), 26.

43. Gilmont, *Calvin et le livre imprimé*, 17–20.

44. *Calv. Opp.* 12: 124, no. 672. Cited and translated in Olivier Millet, "Calvin, la main du maître: questions d'authenticité," in *Il Segretario è come un angelo. Trattati, raccolte epistolari, vite paradigmatiche, ovvero come essere un buon segretario nel Rinascimento*, ed. Rosanna Gorris Camos (Fasano: Schena Editore, 2008), 57.

45. *Calv. Opp.* 21: 106.

46. *Calv. Opp.* 21: 33. What Beza calls *phthysic* fever was, no doubt, tuberculosis.

47. *Calv. Opp.* 41: 551.

48. *Calv. Opp.* 19: 56, no. 3573. See also *Calv. Opp.* 20: 278, no. 4090.

49. *Calv. Opp.* 20: 252–54, no. 4077.

50. *Calv. Opp.* 12: 100, no. 658. See also Gilmont, *Calvin et le livre imprimé*, 18.

51. *Calv. Opp.* 12: 398–99, no. 188, October 8, 1539: "Ubi domum redii, correptus sum mirabili paroxysmo, nec aliud solatii occurrebat quam in gemitu et lacrymis. Eoque magis excruciabar, quod tu mihi istorum malorum causa eras."

52. Calvin, *Lettres à Monsieur et Madame de Falais*, 107, no. 21.

53. Ibid., 207, no. 53.

54. *Sermons de Calvin sur Genèse*, 453, 464.

55. Charles L. Cooke, "Calvin's Illnesses and Their Relation to Christian Vocation," in *John Calvin and the Church: A Prism of Reform*, ed. Timothy George (Louisville: Westminster John Knox Press, 1990), 59–70; John Wilkinson, "The Medical History of John Calvin," *Proceedings of the Royal College of Physicians of Edinburgh* 22 (1992): 368–83.

56. Michel de Montaigne, *Essais* 2. 37, "De la ressemblance des enfans aux peres."

57. *Opus epistolarum Des. Erasmi Roterodami*, ed. P. S. Allen, 12 vols. (Oxford: Oxford University Press, 1906–58), 1: 115, no. 26: "ut Vallam non et magnifice laudet et amet quam maxime; qui tanta industria, tanto studio, tantis sudoribus barbarorum ineptias refellit."

58. "Obruimur hic duplici sarcina, quarum utravis Herculem, non Erasmum requirat. Praeter alia minutiora sustinemus Hieronymum et Novum Testamentum, quod nunc typis excuditur.…Scripsimus haec non solum incredibilibus obruti laboribus, verum etiam a coena subito de tabellionis discessu admoniti.…Ubi dabitur commoditas (dabitur autem, ut spero, breui) totis voluminibus tecum agam, nedum epistolis." *Opus epistolarum Erasmi*, 2: 152, no. 362.

59. The dedicatory letter to Leander, bishop of Seville, before the *Moralia in Job* is instructive. Gregory bemoans his stomach problems, his shortness of breath, and his chronic fever, while his pain prevents him from applying himself to his work ("non modica laboris mei studiis in hoc molestia corporalis obsistit"). Gregory the Great, *Morales sur Job*, ed. Dom Robert Gillet and Dom André de Gaudemaris (Paris: Cerf, 1989), 130–46.

60. See chap. 1 in this book, pp. 33–45.

61. *Opus epistolarum Erasmi*, 2: 174, no. 375.

62. Ibid., 175.

63. See Jean-Pierre Vanden Branden, "Considérations d'Erasme sur la médecine, les médecins, les maladies et la pharmacopée de son temps," *Journal de Pharmacie de Belgique* 58 (2003): 104–6, which describes Erasmus as a "forcené travailleur," who led a "vie laborieuse," engaged in an "impétueuse activité éditoriale." See also Christine Bluard, "Erasme et la médecine," lecture published on the site of the Centre d'étude et d'histoire de la médecine of the Université de Toulouse, available at http://cehm.toulouse.free.fr/fichier/T43.doc.

64. Desiderius Erasmus, *Éloge de la médecine* (Brussels: Maison d'Erasme, 1997); *Carmen de senectute*, LB 4: 755–58.

65. *Opus epistolarum Erasmi*, 3: 392–401.

66. Max Engammare, "Soixante-trois, nombre fossoyeur de Pétrarque à Claude Saumaise: Brève histoire de la grande année climactérique à la Renaissance," *Comptes rendus de l'Académie des Inscriptions et Belles-Lettres* (2010): 279–302.

67. See Olivier Millet, "Calvin als Leidensmann: Berufung, Arbeit, Krankheiten," in *John Calvin: Saint or Sinner?*, ed. Herman Selderhuis (Tübingen: Mohr Siebeck, 2010), 50–65. I thank Olivier Millet for sending me a copy of the text before publication.

68. Luigi-Alberto Sanchi, *Les* commentaires de la langue grecque *de Guillaume Budé: L'œuvre, ses sources, sa préparation* (Geneva: Droz, 2006), 23. The text had been published in Greek, but a French translation was also written for the benefit of the king, who did not know Greek.

69. Ibid., 23–24.

70. In addition to *Calvin's Commentary on Seneca's De clementia*, trans. and ed. Ford Lewis Battles and André Malan Hugo (Leiden: Brill, 1969), see also Michel Magnien, "Portrait de Budé en 'intellectuel': La G. *Budaei viri clarissimi Vita* de Loys Le Roy (1540)," *Renaissance and Reformation* 24 (2000): 31–34; cited in O. Millet, "Calvin als Leidensmann."

71. Sanchi, *Les* commentaires de la langue grecque *de Budé*, 289–93, 295–98.

72. Ibid., 292.

73. "Hodie literas tuas accepi, die scilicet nostro [*leg.*: martis], uberrimas et peræque suaves. Unde cognosces in dolore articulari adhuc me deliciis vacare. Non semper tantum otii fuit, toto enim biduo passus sum accerrimos cruciatus in pede dextro. Coepit morbus mitigari quidem nudiustertius, sed non ita remisit, quin pedem teneat devinctum. Atque ut scias me nihil fingere, odor olei mihi prope est amabilis, quamvis sæpe nauseam citet." See *Correspondance de Bèze*, ed. Hippolyte Aubert, Alain Dufour, and Henri Meylan (Geneva: Droz, 1963), 3: 187, no. 200. Letter cited by Émile Doumergue, *Jean Calvin: Les hommes et les choses de son temps,* 7 vols. (Neuilly-sur-Seine: Editions La Cause, 1899–1927), 7: 250.

74. *Calv. Opp.* 19: 36, no. 3560.

75. See Millet, "Calvin als Leidensmann."

76. *Opus epistolarum Erasmi,* 2: 289–90. In the same letter, Erasmus said that his edition of the New Testament had cost him a great deal of sweat, in spite of his failing health.

77. *Calv. Opp.* 21: 170. This has previously been noted by Millet in "Calvin als Leidensmann."

78. *Gargantua*, ch. 23 in Rabelais, *Œuvres complètes*, 64–70.

4 Calvin's Self-Awareness as Author

OLIVIER MILLET

Translated by Susanna Gebhardt

In the humanist republic of letters, print publication customarily required that its author be endorsed (or at least, recommended) by recognized members of this republic, and that he respect certain conventions and schemas that were a mark of membership, particularly in prefaces and letters of dedication. To present oneself as a citizen of the republic of letters entailed adhering to certain standards of humanist style, showing oneself to respond to certain common values, and being able to contribute to the common good without being locked into academic corporatism, political subjection, or ecclesiastical obedience. Created on a model provided by Erasmus, the republic insisted that an ideal author observe these rules by serving the advancement of *studia humaniora* (humanistic studies). John Calvin initially defined himself in this context, but, on becoming a reformer, he rapidly assumed another ideal of prophetic and apostolic origin, becoming a mouthpiece of the Word of God. I wish to examine the confluence of these two disparate paradigms within the person of Calvin, through the prefatory materials of his printed works.[1] Calvin effectively developed, then refined, his image as an author, actualizing and revolutionizing the humanist model so that it reflected his distinctive awareness of himself as author, while conserving several characteristics of the earlier, humanist model of his youth. I will begin with Calvin's first entry into the world of letters, before showing the form taken by his authorial persona once he became a reformer. I shall conclude by outlining the three principles that founded his literary self-perception once he was able to give his published work his distinctive authorial stamp.

■ CALVIN: THE YOUNG AUTHOR

Calvin's first publications show him to be a circumspect, yet audacious young author. In the preface to *Antapologia* and in the dedication to the commentary of *De clementia*,[2] he prudently presents himself as one aware of his own social insignificance.[3] At the same time, he shows that he has thought about what it means to become an "author." His work abounds in rhetorical caveats that show that he is aware of the risk he takes in having his work published, that is, in moving his ideas and language from the private to the public sphere. To be an author means being a part of a social and cultural network, which he can call on to legitimate the display of his name. In *Antapologia*, Calvin serves as the spokesman for the author, his friend Nicolas Duchemin, asserting that the work with which he associates himself respects the humanist rules of polemic (respect for one's adversary). In *De clementia*, a similar balance is established between inclusion within a network—for example, Calvin's overt mention and inordinate praise of Budé—and the pretense of modesty. Calvin is master of all the customary *topoi* or rhetorical commonplaces: *captatio benevolentiae* (gaining the reader's favorable attention), insistence on the text's status as the first fruits of a young author, and promises of the entertainment and profit that the reader will derive from the work. One is, nonetheless, surprised to note that Calvin was either unwilling to include any prefatory recommendations from other authors or unable to obtain them. His commentary, published at his own expense, contains only his own preface. Indeed, this absence, regardless of reasons, introduces a nuance of audacity, not to say defiance.

As Calvin begins to assert himself in the years thereafter, the early editions of his *Institutes* include advertising elements, probably placed there at the behest of his publishers: subtitles promising great things to the reader in the *Institutes* of 1536 (*BC* 36/1) and of 1539 (*BC* 39/4) and the praise of the renowned Jean Sturm in the edition of 1543 (*BC* 43/5, then 45/5 and 45/6). The Strasbourg humanist commends Calvin the author directly on the title page, rather than in prefatory material inside the book. This conferred on Calvin an indisputable, commercial authority as a writer and theologian. These editorial elements reflect a new balance between caution and self-assertion. Even granting that the advertising material could be present due to the insistence of the publishers, it nevertheless reflects the work's self-recognition and also shows that Calvin's name had not yet become prestigious enough to advertise a text by itself. After 1551, Sturm's praise would no longer be necessary and would disappear.[4] In this early phase of his career as a theologian, Calvin's dedication of his commentary on the Epistle to the Romans (*BC* 40/3) to Simon Grynaeus is also a masterpiece of cautious self-affirmation in the way that it positions the work with reference to the commentaries of Melanchthon, Bucer, and Bullinger on the same book of the Bible. The author insists that his exegetical program complements the methods and results produced by his colleagues. While they are all Protestants, in this preface, the French exegete envisages them chiefly as members of a common Christian republic of letters.

After this initial phase, as Jean-François Gilmont has outlined, Calvin was fully confident of the quality of his works, although this did not prevent him from submitting his work to collaborators.[5] In doing so he complied with the humanist model, formulated in antiquity by Quintilian, of *emendatio*, a phase of composition involving revision and abridgment that ensured that an author did not merely follow his natural inclinations,[6] but appeals to the judgments of others—an appeal that had been recommended since Horace.[7]

Calvin's progression from initial restraint to self-assurance is multifaceted. I shall focus here on two of these facets. The most important of these is onomastic. On the title page of the *Institutes* of 1536 and 1539, Calvin remains the same *Johannes Calvinus Noviodunensis* (John Calvin from Noyon) who appears on the title page of *De clementia*. This medieval and humanist habit of distinguishing oneself through mention of one's place of birth was subsequently abandoned by the reformer in publications linked to his presence or activities in Geneva, signifying the fusion of his identity with the authority of his ecclesiastical office in that city. This new rooting represents a major shift in his self-awareness, given expression in the *Epistle to Sadoleto* (1540), as well as in the preface to his commentary on the Psalms (1557). In the front matter of his books, however, Calvin makes mention of his functions in Geneva only once, at the start of his activity there, on the title page of the *Duae epistolae* of 1537 (*BC* 37/1), where he is said to be "professor of sacred letters in the church of Geneva" (*Sacrarum literarum in Ecclesia Genevensi professoris*). This is a proud assertion of a vocation (part academic, part ecclesiastic) in the very work in which he implores his contemporaries to break with the Roman Church. In his other publications, the name of "Jean Calvin" would suffice, without the need for any other official title. The regular absence of a precise delineation of Calvin's offices in Geneva on title pages after 1537 is significant. While Calvin's internationally renowned moral and intellectual authority derived from his Genevan work, his name alone sufficed.

But even before assuming an institutional office, as early as 1535, the young humanist had already taken a decisive step in his self-assertion with the parody of a privilege signed in his name that appeared in the front of Olivétan's French Bible.[8] In this Latin text, serving as preface and intended for the international public, Calvin substituted his own name for that of the political authorities in the grant of privilege, before going on to explain that the Bible, as Word of God, can and must do without any form of legal authorization, for it is the Book par excellence, deriving its authority from God alone, and must be communicated to all. The name of John Calvin is thus provocatively displayed, despite his relative anonymity.[9] This operation was at once decisive for and emblematic of Calvin's image of himself as author. He denied the relevance of all earthly authority and subsequently spoke, wrote, and published in the name of the only authority that mattered, the word of God. At the same time, he parodically exploited the sociocultural conventions of legal authorization to place his name in public as someone authorizing a publication, an authority of sorts himself, indeed in a sense an "author."

The second facet of Calvin's progressive authorial self-assertion after 1530 is prophetic. Already, the epigraph of the *Duae epistolae* (*BC* 37/1) claims prophetic authority for the author. The title page includes the quotation from 1 Kings 18:21: "How long will you go limping with two different opinions? If the Lord is God, follow him; but if Baal, then follow him." The accusatory preface concludes with this quotation from Ezekiel 33:33: "When this comes—and come it will!—then they shall know that a prophet has been among them."[10] As can be seen from the title pages conveniently reproduced in the *Bibliotheca calviniana*, biblical epigraphs recur frequently in the reformer's works, particularly in certain polemical treaties: *Des scandales* (*BC* 50/9 and 50/12, again in 51/8), *Excuse aux Nicodémites* (*BC* 44/9), *Articles de la Faculté de Paris* (*BC* 44/4, 44/5, 44/6, and 55/1), *Petit traicté* (51/13 and 58/4),[11] *Brieve resolution* (55/3),[12] *Responsio* (*BC* 57/2), and *Response à un cauteleux* (*BC* 61/21). They are also to be found in the *Institutes* of 1539 and 1541, on the title pages of the Latin editions of 1543 and 1545, and on those of the Geneva editions until 1554, where the epigraph is always Habakkuk 1:2: "How long Lord?" In 1539, this *cri de coeur* probably stemmed from the same situation of persecution that led Calvin to preface his *Institutes* with a letter to Francis I. As Rodolphe Peter has observed, however, the quotation did not disappear until Calvin had overcome his enemies in Geneva, suggesting that it also served as an allusion to the difficulties met by the author locally.[13] This type of prefatory quotation evokes the practice of medieval preachers borrowing a verse from the Bible to serve as a programmatic introduction (*prothema*) to their sermons. Calvin, however, appears to adopt this practice only when he prefixes biblical verses as thematic epigraphs to each of his *Four Sermons* of 1552 (*BC* 52/9), for his literary framework is naturally very different from that of a medieval sermon.[14] Similar epigraphs introduce his anti-Nicodemite writings and the *Institutes*. Without a history of the use of epigraphs in Western literature, it is difficult to accurately assess Calvin's originality. Printers' mottos were common on title pages in Calvin's day, but the epigraphs in question are not elements of the printer's motto, and in all probability come from Calvin himself. Their common themes confirm that Calvin saw himself as a prophet or apostle and sought a corresponding authority.

■ CALVIN AS BILINGUAL AUTHOR AND TRANSLATOR

How then did the reformer position himself with reference to humanist literary conventions and publishing practices in his writings in both Latin and French? These were two distinct, if overlapping, cultural worlds. The audience for Latin, better educated and more cultivated, had come to expect more carefully composed texts subject to different methods and a different aesthetic than the French-language public, which gravitated toward simpler texts. Calvin occasionally speaks of this. As Gilmont has gathered and annotated his statements, I do not need to go over that ground in detail.[15] Instead, I shall highlight several points.

Calvin's first printed French text, the Genevan *Instruction*, dates from 1537. Adapted from the first Latin edition of the *Institutes*, it is anonymous, although the corresponding Latin text, the Latin catechism of 1538, is signed "*C. authore.*" The texts and contexts certainly differ, but the difference also signals distinct authorial *personae*, with respective practices and consciousnesses. In 1540 then appeared Calvin's first published work in which his name is the first thing to be found on the title page and in the title, the *Ioannis Calvini Commentarii in epistolam ad Romanos* (John Calvin's commentary on the Epistle to the Romans, *BC* 40/3). To be sure, the prominence now assumed by his name derived in large measure from the practices of the publisher, Wendelin Rihel and from the syntactic possibilities offered by the Latin language.[16] But the prominence now given to Calvin's name should not be minimized. The preface to what is Calvin's first biblical commentary announces his larger agenda of exegetical work to come and affirms his role within the fields of religious reform and biblical hermeneutics.

The *Petit traité de la sainte cène* of 1541 (*BC* 41/4) was Calvin's first French publication written originally in that language. The title page reinforced his status as an author by placing an *M.*, the abbreviation of the title *Maistre*, before his name. *M.* commonly was used on French title pages to characterize a person who, having obtained a university degree, could teach; more generally, *maistre* was a nonspecialized title, indicative of a more general authority and conferring a certain honor upon the author. Many of Calvin's French editions would subsequently carry this honorific title; it is the only such title, with just one exception,[17] that would be added to Calvin's name from this date on. It encapsulates Calvin's authority, or would-be authority, for his French-speaking readers.

The *Petit traité* also includes as prefatory material a ten-line acrostic, the first letters of successive lines spelling out his name.[18] The quatrain spells the forename "JEAN," and the hexastich, the patronymic "CALVIN." This poem is addressed to "young and old," an address used in contemporaneous prologues to plays. Through its formula, typical of vernacular literary style,[19] it assumes an audience made up of the ordinary public, that vast and common multitude, the Christian community listening to a sermon or public address or attending a collective event. This para-text, therefore, speaks to the public according to the conventions of the latter's language, as does the author in his treatise, where he adopts, for the first time, a simplified mode of composition and expression that contrasts with the Latin, humanist eloquence of his prior works. Calvin thus tried to adapt the conventions of the world of vernacular print to his manner of deploying the didactic style derived originally from Latin humanist rhetoric.

Subsequently, with the exception of some minor pamphlets, the reformer addressed the vernacular-reading public in works that were either translated from Latin to French or vice versa. This change of practice led Gilmont to suggest a corresponding shift in Calvin's cultural strategy as a bilingual author.[20] The reformer ceased to address two distinctive types of work to two different publics and became his own translator. However, prior to this shift, in 1542, he published a French "exposition" of the Epistle of Jude (*BC* 42/3), probably adapted from his preaching or teaching. Another simplified work, a common man's version of his Latin commentary on the Epistle to the Romans, followed a year later. Uniquely for his work, he thus produced two biblical commentaries in French, adapted for an unlettered public. Here we find no preface or dedication, signaling that Calvin did not consider them worthy of the standard prefatory apparatus provided by a member of the republic of letters. He wrote these, but he did not seek to link his prestige to them, and the reasons for this would repay further study. It appears that Calvin momentarily envisaged developing his exegetical work in two different linguistic and cultural registers, only to abandon this subsequently for a different strategy, that of the systematic translation of his Latin exegetical work into French to produce a precise, vernacular equivalent of these writings. Nothing is more revealing of this shift than the fact that he subsequently oversaw a complete French translation of his commentary on Romans, which appeared in 1550 (*BC* 50/4).

For the *Institutes*, Calvin had embraced the full translation method as early as 1539–1540. The result was his French edition of 1541.[21] The title page of the first French version underlines the fact that the translation is the author's own work. The *Institutes* are his sole work where Calvin stresses that he is also the translator. Be that as it may, the mention features in all the French editions through that of 1557 (*BC* 57/6). The last French version translated from Latin, appearing in 1560, does not include a mention of Calvin as translator, which reflects, I would suggest, that this was no longer necessary as Calvin's involvement was now generally under-stood. On the other hand, this latest version contains for the first time the same preface as that of the final Latin version of 1559. This shows that, in the eyes of Calvin and his contemporaries, French was taking on a new dignity in religious matters, a dignity that was the product of Calvin's work, both ideological (given his concern to make doctrine accessible to the unlearned) and literary (given his interest in making French an adequate instrument for the translation of a Latin theological work). Although he maintained certain cultural distinctions in his use of both languages until the end of his life and presented his authorial self differently in each, he thus contributed fundamentally to the promotion of the vernacular and to narrowing the gap between the literary and aesthetic qualities of writings published in the two languages. After the turning point of the 1540s, only a few of his pamphlets still bore stylistic traces of a rapidity of composition (or dictation) and familiarity of tone of the sort previously considered appropriate, or at least acceptable, for publication in the vernacular. If Calvin remained a Janus-faced author until his death, his two faces looked a great deal like one another, much to the benefit of the vernacular, and the reformer became the renowned French author that we know today, without abandoning his stature or claims as a Latin author.

For understanding how Calvin situated himself in the republic of letters, the way in which he positioned himself in relation to Philipp Melanchthon is particularly revealing. In the preface to a French translation of Melanchthon's *Loci communes* (Commonplaces) that Calvin probably prepared himself, published in Geneva in 1546 under the title *La Somme de theologie*, he wrote: "If this book was printed in Latin, it would be superfluous for me to make a recommendation: and one might even judge me presumptuous and bold, since the author is as well known amongst men of letters as any one in the world. Since he is renowned for his great learning, he is the one to recommend the books of others."[22] The passage makes explicit the conventions of the republic of letters of the day. Melanchthon needed no recommendation as the senior and internationally renowned scholar and theologian. Calvin took the liberty of doing so only in his capacity of editor (and no doubt translator) of Melanchthon's work. Calvin had already shown his deference to Melanchthon's greater international prominence by dedicating his 1543 Latin *Defensio* (*BC* 43/3) to the German humanist and theologian, as disciples did when addressing a master within the republic of letters. In this dedication he emphasizes his audacity in invoking so great a man but justifies his gesture by invoking the signs of esteem that Melanchthon had shown for him as an author. This dedication to Melanchthon served a tactical purpose in the context of the polemics of the epoch: Calvin was thus showing that Geneva shared Wittenberg's overall goals, while outlining some of the main doctrinal differences in the preface. It also suggests, however, that even after Calvin's conversion and his taking up new ecclesiastical office in Geneva, he continued to respect to some extent the protocols of the humanist office. Furthermore, it helped sophisticated readers identify the rhetoric that Calvin used in this and other treatises as the (atticist) union of simplicity and clarity that Melanchthon was the first to use in didactic works and that I have called "Germanic."[23] This does not mean that Calvin's style was exactly identical to Melanchthon's. Renaissance rhetoric allowed for a measure of difference between an author and his model, a difference that Calvin himself explained and defended elsewhere in defining himself as an author in the grand style.[24] One example of this comes precisely from the preface of the French translation of *Loci communes*:

> I see that the author, being a man of profound knowledge, has not chosen to enter into subtle disputes, nor to treat these matters with as much artifice as he could have easily done, but to lower himself, seeking only edification. This is certainly the manner and style that we all should follow, unless our opponents constrain us by their caviling to depart from this path, so true is it that the greatest simplicity is the greatest virtue in treating Christian doctrine.[25]

Calvin here acknowledges the German humanist as master of his own ideal of simplicity while opening a breach for the vehemence that would be the mark of his own style, forced upon him by the context of dispute in which he found himself. He thus situates himself within the prevailing model of humanist eloquence, that of imitation, without renouncing his individual style, the pledge of his own authenticity.

■ CALVIN THE POLEMICIST

Calvin the polemicist was, indeed, a vehement pamphlet author. At times, to avoid the wrath of the censors, especially those of the French monarchy, he wrote under cover of anonymity, a phenomenon that merits further study.[26] At other times he used a pseudonym. One example is the formal Latin defense against Pierre Caroli of "Guillaume Farel and of his colleagues" published in 1545 under the name of Nicolas Des Gallars, Calvin's secretary and frequent literary collaborator, with no preface or dedication (*BC* 45/10). Caroli, as is well known, accused Calvin and Farel of Arianism for their refusal in 1537 to adopt the Nicene trinitarian theology and for their designation of Christ as "Jehovah." Calvin's correspondence reveals in fact that he wrote the work, albeit with some help from Des Gallars. Neither Calvin nor his first biographers, Colladon and Beza, nor any of the editors of his treatises, either during his lifetime or in the centuries after his death, ever mention this or include the tract among his works. By using the name of his secretary and subsequently succeeding in avoiding public acknowledgment of his authorship, he was able to conceal his personal engagement in a quarrel with a man for whom he felt only scorn. At the same time, he was able to slip a defense of himself into the pamphlet.[27] Both humanist conventions and personal pride explain why Calvin hid behind the name of Des Gallars. Yet the matter is more complex than this. In his private correspondence Calvin makes it clear that he anticipates that some will attribute the work to him. Revealing an awareness of his own style, he indicates that he deliberately wrote certain parts in a different manner from his usual style so that some will think that part of the work was indeed written by Des Gallars, something that was not so difficult to do since Des Gallars was his secretary. But he did not go so far as to attempt to erase all traces of his own authorship. He relies, in fact, on the indulgent complicity of his public, the only one he is concerned about. Finally, because writing under another's name gave him more freedom, he felt particularly inspired, heated (*incalueram*) by the game (*ludebam*) permitted by the adopted mask.[28] Since Quintilian, the term *incalueram* had always had a very definite meaning, denoting a type of literary inspiration—the *calor*—different from the Platonic *furor*, which was closely tied to improvisation and allowed considerable room for both technical skill and individual genius.[29] Calvin seems to have found it the height of both enjoyment and personal individuality to be himself through another. This mimetic engagement is unique in his literary work, and perhaps in all the literature of the sixteenth century.

Calvin's treatise against the Anabaptists (44/7) also makes it clear that he dislikes responding to unworthy adversaries, yet this time he publishes the book under his own name and adds a dedication to the ministers of Neuchâtel. In it he apologizes for having to refute a "booklet" of no value "made by ignorant people,…since I could employ myself, as it seems, in better and more profitable things."[30] In doing so, he is fulfilling his vocation as doctor and pastor, and he defends doing so with justifications borrowed from the Bible, primarily from the prophet Ezekiel, a defense that shows a recognition of the humanist convention that one does not reply to those beneath contempt yet indicates that prophetic duty takes priority. This therefore reflects the Augustinian tradition of adapting classical rhetoric to the demands of Christian education with respect to all, and especially the humble.

■ AUGUSTINE AS LITERARY MODEL

Augustine was a model for Calvin in more than rhetoric; he was also a major reference point for Calvin's understanding of himself as an author. This is evident from Des Gallars's preface to the first collected edition of Calvin's writings, the *Opuscula* of 1552 (*BC* 52/8).[31] For this landmark in the construction of the figure of Calvin the author, Des Gallars collected about twenty titles, most them short treatises, in a perspective that united humanist culture and confessional, Reformed propaganda. Some, originally published in French, now appeared in Latin. The notion of the author was very much at stake here, for the purpose of the collection was to assemble and transmit to posterity the works of a man to whom God had given the power to defend the truth against all attacks upon it. The model of the recovery and editing by a prior generation of humanist scholars of the complete works of church fathers such as Augustine undoubtedly furnished a precedent for collecting Calvin's work in this manner. Calvin, in Des Gallars's view, is one of the major instruments in an era of dramatic struggle between truth and diabolic Roman machinations. His personal calling, his gifts as a writer and theologian, and his significance for the history of the church all call for the erection of such a monument. No doubt these remarks of Des Gallars correspond to Calvin's intentions. By leaving to Des Gallars the task of expressing his own sense of himself as an author, Calvin respected the demands of modesty, while avoiding the need to correct his old texts in light of subsequent developments or discoveries. Des Gallars specifically praises the fact that they are being published unchanged, not only because the texts are worthy of being reissued as is, but also because the time saved allows Calvin to write other, much awaited books.[32]

In Calvin's dissociation from the editing of this book, we see the limits for him of the Augustinian model: unlike the African church father, he never retracts his former teaching and leaves others with the task of writing a literary history of his work, a history of which Des Gallars's preface of 1552 can be seen as the first draft, and which is completed the next year in Claude Baduel's preface to the Latin translation of the *Quatre sermons* (*BC* 53/4), (a text that is, to my knowledge, the first to cast the Calvinist Reformation as the successor of the Lutheran).[33] Calvin's success in getting others to speak on his behalf in this regard would be continued after his death in the 1566 collection of *Petits Traités*, attributed to Theodore Beza, in the 1575 Latin edition of his correspondence, also prepared by Beza, and in the three official biographies of the reformer published from 1564 to 1575.[34] Here again things are said for Calvin that the conventions of his culture would not have permitted him to say himself, as in Beza's defense of Calvin's polemical vehemence in the preface to the *Petits traités*, where Beza explains that in the case of prophets, apostles, and those who bear the burden of disseminating the word of God, God forms their temperament to suit the needs of their mission. Thus, from 1552, Calvin had progressively established a monumentalization of his authorial countenance by delegating the task to his collaborators, whose statements on the subject he undoubtedly approved.

■ ORAL TEACHING AND WRITTEN WORD

Another domain in which we can observe Calvin's awareness of himself as a writer is that of the publications derived from his oral teaching: his sermons in French and his exegetical lessons in Latin. Once again, others do the talking for him, for the volumes in question were edited by others, and the sermons have no dedications.[35] Calvin let manuscript copies of his sermons circulate "to everybody."[36] Despite reservations, he also allowed these works to appear in print in the interest of the edification of a public beyond Geneva, especially in France. Yet the passage into print evidently troubled him, for their canonization implied a rhetorical and literary quality that these works, directly transcribed from oral teaching done without oratorical pretension, lacked in his eyes. His reservations are constantly reiterated from preface to preface, right down to the last collection of sermons published in his lifetime, in 1563 (*BC* 63/22).[37] Their constant reiteration makes it impossible to believe that the texts were wrenched time and again from the unwilling author. They must be understood as serving to justify the publication of texts that fell short of the requirements of humanist eloquence. The same excuses are found in the front of Calvin's published exegetical lessons, for instance on Jeremiah in 1563 (*BC* 63/19). Calvin must have developed this strategy in collusion with his collaborators. The prefaces serve to emphasize that one is going to read what are genuinely Calvin's works and Calvin's words, but that he does not vouchsafe for their style as oratory.

The prefaces in question introduce variations on three central themes. The first compares the public and private arenas. The sermons are presented as having been addressed and adapted to the limited, mediocre Genevan public, not the general public at whom print publication is usually aimed. Calvin himself, in the preface to his lessons on the twelve minor Prophets (*BC* 59/5) juxtaposes his "manner of private teaching" to public education, thereby distinguishing an exegetical lesson from teaching done from the pulpit.[38] The second theme is that these texts convey improvised speech, taken down in shorthand by scribes and published according to the transcripts, without recourse to the rhetorical arts characteristic of a public speaker. A third theme engages the opposition between rhetoric, associated with artifice, and authenticity. Divinely inspired by a method that rejects the art of literary composition, this authenticity implies the guidance of the biblical text, and as such, is superior both in terms of true eloquence and edification.[39] The art of rhetoric is further discredited in a preface by Jacques Roux that opposes Calvin's raw sermons to homilies made "at leisure,"[40] and in another by Conrad Badius, who distinguishes his sermons from the "display of human eloquence" and the "declaiming of some secular harangue."[41] In the same preface, Badius devalues two important aspects of oratory, "gestures...and fine language," the better to highlight the solid core of Calvin's sermons. This third theme also serves the purpose of promoting Calvin as an authority on preaching. The preface to the sermons on Psalm 119 (*BC* 54/13) explicitly states that the published work is being presented with the aim of not only enlightening the absent but also of demonstrating how preaching was done in Geneva. The same theme appears in the preface to the sermons on the Ten Commandments (*BC* 57/10). This demonstration of Calvin's methods was considered to be as important for the far-flung public as the biblical substance of the sermons. The achievement of this goal depends precisely on the absence of formal rhetoric in these improvised homilies, because their published version is ultimately intended to emphasize what is most characteristic of Calvin's preaching, its "efficiency." One preface, by the printer Jean Girard, after noting that he is publishing sermons in the volume "that the author has not written," but merely "spoken once," explains that he gives this warning "to the end that the argument be treated more efficiently, as it should be when readers think themselves to be present."[42] The absence of art and formal rhetoric is also indirectly eloquence: it invites readers to imagine themselves in Geneva, face to face with the reformer, a process facilitated by the authenticity of the testimony of plain speech. The words affect the reader in a way that a revised sermon could not. They encourage emotional and spiritual identification, generating a rhetorical effectiveness more powerful than that created by art. Girard's evocation of the idea of "being present" has a precise rhetorical meaning. Being present is what results from *energèia* (or *hypotyposis*), the rhetorical technique by which true eloquence succeeds in putting an object "before the eyes" (to use the time-honored phrase) of the public. The reader of Calvin's sermons thus has the opportunity to be transported to Geneva, to have direct access to the preaching of a man who takes his inspiration directly from the biblical text, and the force and success of whose preaching in situ we know to have depended on bringing his public into contact not with himself but with the inspiration and force of the scripture. Another preface (*BC* 61/24) adapts this topic. Commenting on the fact that Calvin had not seen the text, it emphasizes the improvised quality of these sermons that will introduce readers to the preacher's words "as the Spirit of God gave him to speak," rather than to homilies written at leisure.[43] The art of improvisation, linked to *calor* in the rhetorical tradition,[44] evokes Luke 12: 11–12: "do not worry about...what you say. When the time comes, the Holy Spirit will instruct you what to say." Both the *sinceritas* of the exegete and his pastoral capacity to accommodate his words to the immediate needs of his Genevan flock are obvious here. Still another preface, this one from 1562, presents his sermons as "simple, familiar, yet full of authority and efficacy."[45] Finally, Calvin himself offers a variant on the same *topos* in the 1563 dedicatory remarks accompanying his lessons on Jeremiah (*BC* 63/19). After excusing the publication of a text taken from notes on improvised lessons intended for a mediocre audience, he says that readers will find in his exegetical method a simplicity that could be a good antidote for excessively ostentatious commentators on holy writ. *Simplicitas* is a token of *sinceritas* in his sermons and exegetical lessons.

In sum, the prefaces to Calvin's sermons and commentaries do not just excuse the publication of unpolished texts in the service of edification. They signal that Calvin's sermons provide a Genevan model of preaching and teaching distinct from the method of commonplaces found in Bullinger's *Decades*, the other widely disseminated model of Reformed preaching of the period. We may assume that Calvin consciously sought to advance his model on the international stage.

■ CALVIN'S THREE PRINCIPLES OF AUTHORIAL SELF-ASSERTION

Calvin's authorial posture thus took its definitive form relatively early in his publishing career. In this final section, I would like to identify three principles that he used to assert his moral and intellectual authority as an author: the principles of sacrifice, coherence, and interaction with the public.

First, Calvin and those around him constantly highlight how he sacrificed his own personal inclinations to the demands of his vocation as churchman, dictated by his reforming agenda and his duties in Geneva. A few telling examples will suffice. The theme of self-sacrifice accompanies the first portraits to illustrate publications of Calvin and thus to further advance his canonization as a writer. These portraits appeared after his death in two works of 1566, a French edition of the *Institutes* (*BC* 66/2) and a *Recueil des opuscules* (*BC* 66/3). Above the portrait, engraved by René Boyvin in 1562, one finds the words *Prompte et Sincere*, extracted from the full motto of the reformer: *Cor meum tibi offero Domine prompte et sincere* (I give you my heart, Lord, promptly and sincerely),[46] a motto linked to his vocation in Geneva, and more precisely to his return to Geneva in 1541.[47] In a similar spirit of self-sacrifice, Calvin liked poetry but renounced it in favor of whole-hearted devotion to works of prose, becoming primarily a commentator and an exegete of the holy scripture. The reformer abandoned his own translation of the Psalms, published in 1539 in *Aulcuns Pseaumes*, in deference to the superior poetic quality of the work of Clément Marot. His only published Latin poem, *Epinicion Christo cantatum* (A song of victory to Christ–originally a hymn sung in ancient Greece to honor the victor of one of the great Hellenic games), found its way into print because the text had been condemned by an inquisitor of Lyon, and Conrad Badius thought that a French translation of this militant pro-Reformation work might be a good way to keep his temporarily idle press turning.[48] From 1556–1557 onward, the Genevan reformer and his collaborators fashioned an image of him as a man of suffering, sacrificing his health, his career as a writer, his personal predilections, and ultimately his life to his work as an interpreter and spokesman of the word of God. The preface to his 1557 commentary on the Psalms (*BC* 57/4) already expressed this image. His biographers would amplify and spread it after his death. Here too Calvin had a humanist model to follow: that of Erasmus and Budé, sacrificing their vigils, health, and tranquility in the advancement of the *studia humaniora*.[49] Erasmus, in particular, adapted the symbol of the labors of Hercules in his adage so as to make it stand for the new type of office of the humanist in the republic of letters.[50] Once again, Calvin transforms this humanist model as a result of his conversion and new prophetic calling, making the *studia biblica* the cause for which he sacrifices so much.[51] Fashioning himself as an evangelical Hercules, Calvin refuses to reduce himself to the models offered by the old humanist culture, instead adapting these models to fit his aims.

Second, Calvin insists recurrently on the internal consistency of his work. We have already seen that he was not one for *retractationes*. Beyond this, he frequently refers his readers or adversaries to his previous works, as if he had already considered and treated every possible question or objection.[52] He did not simply want to avoid having to repeat himself. These references signal his conviction that consistency and clarity were a moral duty for an author. The same concern is also highlighted by the fact the *Institutes* retain the 1535 dedication to King Francis I right down to the final editions published in Calvin's lifetime, long after the death of the monarch and after the circumstances that occasioned the original dedication had dramatically changed. Furthermore, we witness the same interest in consistency when we read the reformer's stock taking of twenty-five years of Calvinist reform and thirty years of persecution in the kingdom in the dedication of his lessons on Daniel from August 1561, during the preparations for the Colloquy of Poissy. In this dedication to the French Protestant churches, he adopts a very personal tone and uses the biblical quotation (Luke 21:19) on which he ends his 1535 dedication of the *Institutes* to Francis I: "Now, even though God with his wonderful power has advanced the restitution of his church further than I would have dared hope, we must still bear in mind and not forget that Christ ordered his disciples to hold firm their souls in patience [cf. Luke 21:19]."[53] This allusion also recurs in other letters addressed to the French churches. Through it, Calvin sends a signal of strength and solidarity to his compatriots. This historical perspective, which also emphasizes the authority of the reformer in his own country, allows him at the end of the same preface to issue a genuine prophecy about the trials awaiting the French Protestants.[54]

Moreover, from 1539–1540, with the publication of his commentary on the Epistle to the Romans and the second edition of his *Institutes*, Calvin planned and then constructed the core of his work as an author around two axes meant to complement one another: biblical commentaries and the doctrinal commonplaces that composed the ever-growing *Institutes*.[55] Through this division, he sought to establish an authoritative method for theology that facilitated the formulation of Christian doctrine, while avoiding dogmatic speculations detached from biblical revelation. Calvin was not a systematic theologian in the modern, technical sense of this term, but he was a systematic author, constructing his work as a coherent whole and insisting on its coherence.

After the master's death, Beza noted in the preface to the posthumous edition of Calvin's sermons on Ezekiel that, had he lived one or two years more, he would have finished commenting on all of the books of the Bible and thus produced "a perfect understanding of the Old and New Testaments."[56] Although Beza seems to suggest that Calvin's exegetical work was unfinished, this is in fact not what he feels. Appearances to the contrary, he does not imply that Calvin should have commented on every single book of the Bible (including those that his master did not, in fact, take up). Rather he suggests that this could have been done, had Calvin lived longer. He thus presents the portrait of an author who sought to be a global interpreter of the entire biblical revelation, probably reflecting Calvin's intention. Here is another form of coherence in Calvin's work, a hermeneutical, rather than chronological or methodological, one: Calvin did not neglect any of what he perceived to be *key instances* of the way God reveals himself in scripture.

Third, Calvin regularly interacts with his reading public. He explains readily that the development of his work responds to the needs of a given audience. Sometimes he addresses negative reactions to a previous work. On other occasions, he seeks to further the edification he believes his readers received from a prior publication. The first was especially typical of polemical exchanges. When Calvin deemed that a previous publication did not have the desired impact, he took up the subject again, using locutions such as "my position is challenged: therefore, I express it once again."[57] These are simple rhetorical devices serving to justify new publications on an old subject and do not merit extended analysis. More interesting is the way in which the Latin translation of the *Traité des reliques* (*BC* 48/4), a work that purports to compile a global catalogue of all the relics known to the author, assumes the agreement of its readers with its gist and aims not at the past but at the future. The translator Des Gallars appeals to readers to help out and complete the catalogue.[58] The irony of the appeal is consistent with that of the treatise, for, needless to say, continuation of the catalogue would be superfluous; what Calvin provides already suffices to demolish claims for the authenticity of relics and to expose the sham of their promoters. Yet this call to complete the catalogue, which Beza and Colladon reiterate in the 1565 and 1575 biographies of the reformer,[59] highlights a theme central to the treatise: that of the infinite proliferation of superstition once given free rein. This form of interaction with readers also serves to associate them more closely with the views of the author. But the most recurrent way in which Calvin expresses a form of interaction with his audience lies in his frequent claims that the excellent reception of one of his works justifies a new augmented edition.[60] He says this about the *Institutes* from its second edition in 1539 (*BC* 39/4) onward, and we have already seen that this was a pivotal moment for his developing sense of himself as an author and of his life's work as a biblical expositor.[61] The unexpected success of his first edition, he asserts in 1539, compels him to produce an even better version. In the preface of the last Latin version of 1559 (*BC* 59/4), subsequently translated and used for the French edition of 1560 (*BC* 60/8), he asserts poetically that he has grown by teaching others, and it is they who have "drawn" out this great text from him. The Latin version is a couplet:

> Quos animus fuerat tenui excusare libello,
> Discendi studio magnum fecere volumen.
> (Those whom I wanted to defend in a small booklet,
> Their zeal for learning made it grow into a mighty tome.)

The French is a quatrain:

> Ceux desquels je voulais l'innocence défendre
> En un simple livret, m'ont si bien su poursuivre
> Par leur zèle fervent, et saint désir d'apprendre,
> Qu'ils ont tiré de moi à la fin ce grand livre.

This might be translated:

> Those whose innocence I wished to defend
> In a simple booklet, have followed me
> With their fervent ardor, and holy wish to learn,
> That they ultimately drew this great book from me.

Just as the intellectual progress of the theologian is linked to his writing, his book accommodates the deepening educational needs of his growing public. The formulation of doctrine and the development of methods for presenting it are thus presented as growing from a dynamic relationship between the author and his public; this is an eminently humanist pedagogic conceit. The author no longer must apologize for appearing in print. His task has now become to maintain an ever richer rapport with his audience, and to respond to his increasing notoriety by producing ever more accomplished work. The audience itself plays an active role in the production of text, as highlighted by the Latin couplet, with its factitive verb: "[the readers], by their wish to learn, have [made] a great book." A similar idea appears in the preface to the commentary of the Psalms (*BC* 57/4), referencing the beginning of Calvin's career in the 1530s, when he modestly began his teaching career with oral lessons to a small group: "Those who had some desire of the pure doctrine gathered around me to learn, even though I was just a beginner myself."[62] His whole career as a doctor of the church, he suggests here, grew out of a mutual relationship between a teacher and his students in which each party was eager to improve.

The examination of the editorial paratext of Calvin's publications thus shows that both continuities and changes marked his understanding and presentation of himself as an author. The elements of permanence derive from his early humanist formation. This made him intensely aware that a work must be delivered to the public only after having been polished and completed according to the highest standards of rhetorical art, for in the public arena the preservation of the speaker's *dignitas*, the demonstration of due respect for the audience, and the persuasion of the latter all depend on an apt eloquence. In this same humanist context, the reference to Melanchthon remains central, at least until the 1550s. Melanchthon's significance lies both in the homage Calvin renders to the German humanist's model of didascalic eloquence, and in Calvin's assertion—via differentiation from the *praeceptor Germaniae*—of his own distinctive identity as an author. Implicit here is a certain justification of his own style of eloquence, perhaps even a suggestion of its superiority to Melanchthon's, for the tasks at hand. A final element of permanence, enduring in a modified form even after his evangelical conversion, lies in the manner in which he embodies the new humanist figure of a man so devoted to his intellectual labors that he sacrifices all to them. His is a biblical office of a prophetic and ecclesiastical type, but it reproduces the same cultural model originally formulated by Erasmus to enhance his own moral stature and that of the learned humanists of the republic of letters.

Changes may also be noted, changes that began with his conversion but then continued through the several turning points we have identified here. If he absorbed from his humanist formation a reticence about allowing unpolished texts to appear in print under his name, the increasing value he placed upon the utility of a text as a criterion for publication, as opposed to other criteria such as the enjoyment the public might find in reading it, made him willing to accede to the publication of texts that would have been judged imperfect according to humanist standards of rhetoric, albeit always with prefatory excuses for doing so. After initially accompanying his publications with commendations from prestigious senior figures, he felt no further need to rely on these from 1551 onward. His vocation, identified with the figure of the prophet as mouthpiece of God's word, became the essential foundation of his authorial authority.[63] From the early 1550s he mobilized a circle of collaborators, who first promoted the monumentalization of his work and then, from the years 1556–1557, fashioned him as a hero completely dedicated to evangelical battle.[64] Finally, if Calvin continued throughout his life to use certain distinct literary conventions, depending on whether he was writing in French or Latin, these differences became blurred or secondary over time, as his writings in both languages increasingly were composed of texts also published in the other language, fused into a single oeuvre with an overarching structural coherence. That oeuvre grew from an ongoing interaction with a public created by the work, a public whose growth in size was part and parcel of the advance of the Calvinist reformation in France and across Europe.

■ Notes

1. This was where authorial intention and the fashioned self-image were expressed directly and systematically in the Renaissance. My examination is greatly indebted to Rodolphe Peter and Jean-François Gilmont, *BC*, the definitive material bibliography of Calvin's works, to which I refer throughout. I adopt Peter's and Gilmont's abbreviation of the title followed by the final two figures of the original year of publication and the number of the work in chronological order within that year (for instance, *BC* 32/1 for Calvin's commentary on *De clementia*) with volume and page number where applicable.

2. *Joannis Calvini Epistolae*, vol. 1 (1530–September 1538), ed. Cornelis Augustijn and Frans Pieter van Stam (Geneva: Droz, 2005) (hereafter: Calvin, *Epistolae*, 1), no. 2, 43–46; no. 8, 60–68.

3. In the dedication of *De clementia*, Calvin qualifies himself as *unus de plebe humuncio*, a "man of nothing, descended from the people." Calvin, *Epistolae*, 1, 61. On this dedication, see Michael L. Monheit, "The Ambition for an Illustrious Name: Humanism, Patronage and Calvin's Doctrine of the Calling," *SCJ* 23/2 (1992): 267–87.

4. This preface appears for the last time in the Latin (*BC* 50/16) and French (*BC* 51/11) versions of 1550 and 1551 respectively, where it is relegated to the verso of the second page.

5. Jean-François Gilmont, *Calvin et le livre imprimé* (Geneva: Droz, 1997), 154.

6. Quintilian, *Institutio oratoria* 10, 4, 1–2.

7. Horace, *Ars poetica*, 5, 292.

8. Calvin, *Epistolae*, 1, no. 20, 107. See also Olivier Millet, *Calvin et la dynamique de la parole: Étude de rhétorique réformée* (Paris: Champion, 1992), 456–57.

9. The preface begins: "Ioannes Calvinus caesaribus, regibus, principibus gentibusque omnibus Christi imperio subditis salutem." Calvin, *Epistolae*, no. 1, 107. In the remainder of this text, Calvin incorporates the *topoi* from his early prefaces of 1531 and 1532, indicating that their import is limited by the biblical text.

10. The biblical text here is taken, where possible, from the Revised Standard Version of the Bible (Oxford: Oxford University Press, 1989).

11. 1 Kings 18:21; the epigraph from *Duae epistolae* of 1537.

12. The recent edition in Jean Calvin, *Œuvres*, ed. Bernard Roussel and Francis Higman (Paris: Gallimard, 2009), does not signal the presence of the epigraph in this (second) French edition.

13. Rodolphe Peter, "Les premiers ouvrages français imprimés à Strasbourg," *Annuaire de la Société des amis du Vieux Strasbourg* 17 (1987): 23–37.

14. See *Calv. Opp.* 8: 369.; John Calvin, *Œuvres françoises*, ed. Paul. L. Jacob (Paris: Librairie Charles Gosselin, 1842), epigraphs drawn successively from Ps. 16:4, Heb. 13:13, Ps. 27:4, and Ps. 27:8.

15. Gilmont, *Calvin et le livre imprimé*, 155–64.

16. See, for instance, the titles of *BC* 42/5 and, by contrast, *BC* 43/3.

17. *BC* 43/7: . . . *per D. Joan. Calvinum*, where D. indicates a doctor, which Calvin was not.

18. See the text in Calvin, *Œuvres*, 833.

19. See also the Calvinist preface to the 1546 French translation of Melanchthon's *Loci communes*: "The great and meek will be able to take good education and use, for they come with a great desire to enjoy." *Calv. Opp.* 9: 847. This is a real topos of vernacular and popular literature.

20. Gilmont, *Calvin et le livre imprimé*, 160–65.

21. For his successive attempts to render a simplified French version from the Latin *Institutio*, see Calvin, *Institution de la religion chrétienne (1541)*, 2 vols, ed. Olivier Millet (Geneva: Droz, 2008), 1: 22–26.

22. *Calv. Opp.* 9: 847.

23. See Millet, *Calvin et la dynamique*, 125, 137.

24. See Jean Lecointe, *L'Idéal et la différence, la perception de la personnalité littéraire à la Renaissance* (Geneva: Droz, 1993); Millet, *Calvin et la dynamique*, 122–25.

25. *Calv. Opp.* 9: 848.

26. See the remarks in the introduction to *Trois libelles anonymes*, ed. Francis Higman and Olivier Millet (Geneva: Droz, 2006), 8–10.

27. Jean Calvin, *Défense de Guillaume Farel et de ses collègues contre les calomnies du théologastre Pierre Caroli par Nicolas Des Gallars (Pro G. Farello et collegis eius adversus Petri Caroli theologastri calumnias defensio Nicolai Galasii) : Avec diverses lettres de Calvin, Caroli, Farel, Viret et autres documents*, ed. Jean-François Gounelle (Paris: Presses Universitaires de France, 1994). See also Viret's letter on this subject to Calvin, no. 660 from July 14, 1545, *Calv. Opp.* 12: 102–3.

28. See the August 1545 letter to Farel on the same subject: *Calv. Opp.* 12: 124. For Calvin's reports about Melanchthon's rhetoric, see Olivier Millet, "Calvin, la main du maître: Questions d'authenticité," in '*Il Segretario è come un angelo': Trattati, raccolte epistolari, vite paradigmatiche ovvero come essere un buon segretario nel Rinascimento*, ed. Rosanna Gorris Camos (Fasano: Schena Editore, 2008), 55–57.

29. On this subject, see Perrine Galand-Hallyn, *Les yeux de l'éloquence: Poétiques humanistes de l'évidence* (Orléans-Caen: Paradigme, 1995).

30. Calvin, *Œuvres françoises*, 624.

31. *Calv. Opp.* 9: x.

32. *Calv. Opp.* 9: xii: *Nam maiora in dies ab ipso exspectamus.*

33. See the text in *Calv. Opp.* 8: 26.

34. On this subject, see Irena Backus, *Life Writing in Reformation Europe: Lives of Reformers by Friends, Disciples and Foes* (Aldershot: Ashgate, 2008), 125–38.

35. See notably the prefaces of *BC* 55/8, 57/3, 57/10, 58/10, and 59/5, as well as the references *infra*; Gilmont, *Calvin et le livre imprimé*, 106–16.

36. John Calvin, *Lettres françaises*, 2 vols., ed. Jules Bonnet (Paris: Meyrueis, 1854), 2: 26 (= *Calv. Opp.* 15: 446, no. 2118, from February 20, 1555).

37. See text of the preface in *BC* 59/5, 717, in which the publishers explain the recording of these texts from the oral word of the master, the establishment of a standardized copy from two shorthand sources, and their revision by the master. Calvin is qualified as "author" only after this explanation. Calvin, in his own dedication of the *Praelectiones* to King Gustav of Sweden, also partly reproduced in *BC* 59/5, 2: 717, recalls a previous edition of 1557, adding that he was not "author of this impression there, so that in another way I am sufficiently distressed and grieved to correct what I write with greater labor and diligence."

38. Preface cited in *BC* 59/5, 2: 717; cf. *BC* 57/3, 2: 623.

39. See, for instance, the preface cited in *BC* 57/3, 2: 624.

40. Preface cited in *BC* 62/21, 2: 952.

41. Preface reproduced in *BC* 62/22, 2: 956.

42. Preface reproduced in *BC* 46/3, 1: 219.

43. Preface cited in *BC* 61/24, 2: 858.

44. On this subject, see Calvin, *Œuvres françoises*, 624.

45. Preface cited in *BC* 62/19, 2: 944.

46. See further H. Maillart-Gosse, "Catalogue des portraits gravés de Calvin," published as appendix 1 to Émile Doumergue, *L'iconographie calvinienne* (Lausanne: G. Bridel, 1909), 226–58.

47. See also the letter to Farel from October 1540, which contains the sentence: "Cor meum velut mactatum Domino in sacrificium offero." *Calv. Opp.* 11: 100, no. 248.

48. *BC* 44/8. See also the critical edition of the Latin and the French text: *Loflied en hekeldicht: De geschiedenis Calvijns enige gedicht: Het epinicion Christo cantatum van 1. Januari, 1541*, ed. Erik de Boer (Haarlem: AcaMedia, 1986).

49. See chap. 3 in this book, pp. 67–83.

50. Erasmus, *Opera omnia* (Amsterdam: Elsevier Press, 1969–), *Adagia*, ed. Silvana Seidel-Menchi, vol. 2: 5, 23–41. On this subject, see my essay "Calvin als Leidensmann," in *Calvin: Saint or Sinner*, ed. Herman Selderhuis (Tübingen: Mohr Siebeck, 2010), 50–65.

51. Note the appearance of this theme at the end of Beza's second (1575) biography of the reformer. *Calv. Opp.* 21: 170.

52. See for instance, the preface to *Acta Synodi tridentinae cum antidoto* (*BC* 47/3), which returns in the *Supplex exhortatio* of 1544 and in the various polemical publications against the Nicodemites.

53. *Calv. Opp.* 18: 620. See the text of the *Institutio* (preface of 1535): "ut in patientia nostra possideamus animas nostras, et manum Domini fortem expectemus."

54. *Calv. Opp.*, 18: 623: "Quod si diutius adhuc dimicandum erit, ut vobis denuncio restare duriores quam putatis pugnas."

55. On this subject, see the preface to the commentary on Romans (*BC* 40/3), *Calv. Opp.* 10: 402, no. 191, and the preface to the *Institutio* of 1539 (*BC* 39/4), *Calv. Opp.* 1: 256. The former defines the adopted method, the latter calls attention to exegetical commentary by referring to the sample of the commentary on Romans. Note also that the preface to the *Institutio* of 1539 ends with a quotation from St. Augustine, with whom Calvin associates his authorial self, who "wrote by advancing, and advanced by writing" (*Ego ex eorum*

numero me esse profiteor, qui scribunt proficiendo et scribendo proficient). On this subject, see Millet, *Calvin et la dynamique*, 548. For Calvinist commonplaces and their role in propagating the doctrines of the Reformation, see Irena Backus, "Loci communes oder 'Hauptsätze': Ein Medium der europäischen Reformation bei Calvin, Vermigli und Bullinger," in *Calvinismus: Die Reformierten in Deutschland und Europa: Eine Ausstellung des Deutschen Historischen Museums Berlin und der Johannes a Lasco Bibliothek Emden*, ed. Ansgar Reiss and Sabine Witt (Dresden: Sandstein, 2009), 97–104.

56. *BC* 65/6, 3: 65.

57. Examples of this include his prefaces to *Epistolae duae* (*BC* 37/1, see *OS* 1: 288); *Quatre sermons, BC* 52/9; esp. in Calvin, *Œuvres françoises*, 211.

58. Text reproduced in *Calv. Opp.* 6: xxv.

59. Text reproduced in "Prolegomena" of *Calv. Opp.* 6: xxvii. See also Backus, *Life Writing*, 134.

60. See the dedication to King Gustav Vasa in the lessons on the twelve prophets (*BC* 59/5, 2: 717), which builds on the success of the lessons on Hosea (*BC* 57/3).

61. See *Calv. Opp.* 1: 256.

62. *Calv. Opp.* 31: 22.

63. On Calvin's understanding of himself as prophet, see Max Engammare, "Calvin: A Prophet without a Prophecy," *Church History* 67 (1998): 643–61.

64. Humanists like Erasmus and Budé also used their followers to this end, intending to keep up their reputation after their death; but Calvin does so in the context of his reforming struggles.

5 Calvin's Church in Geneva

Constructed or Gathered? Local or Foreign?
French or Swiss?

WILLIAM NAPHY

When Calvin returned to Geneva in 1541, he was entrusted with two key tasks. First and foremost, for most historians of Calvin and Calvinism, he was to write the regulations for the Genevan church. This would eventually lead to the Ecclesiastical Ordinances. However, of equal importance, he was responsible for leading the committee to write what would become Geneva's first, postrevolutionary constitution. Significantly, he would also be very closely involved, near the end of his life, with the drafting of the city-state's second constitution.

Traditionally, the constitution has been rather overlooked and, more importantly, the two tasks have been seen as relatively distinct. In fact, I think they must be seen as part of a very closely interconnected project. By 1541, the city had seen the consequences of a very loose, ad hoc approach to structures. The upheavals of 1538–1540 had exposed the structural weaknesses of both the political and ecclesiastical systems. By 1541, the church was more or less in a state of chaos. The sacking of Calvin and Farel along with the subsequent loss of staff with the political changes of 1540 had shown the need for a well-organized and unified ecclesiastical structure working, ideally, in close harmony with Geneva's political leaders. A desire to avoid future clashes with the ministers was a lesson well learned by 1541.

However, the city had also learned the lessons of a political system that was perhaps "too democratic" and too responsive to the city's large and politically active male population. The crises of 1538–1541 had seen the city come into direct diplomatic and political conflict with its main military protector, Bern. This threatened the city-state with isolation, which left it dangerously exposed to its Catholic neighbors. Also, faction had brought Geneva close to civil war. Just as the city needed an ecclesiastical settlement that would harmonize relations between church and state, it needed a constitutional structure that would provide for a balancing of factions and lessen the ability of political dispute to endanger the republic.

It says much about the city's assessment of Calvin in 1541 that this foreigner only recently returned from exile was given so great a role in both tasks. Clearly in the short time he had worked in Geneva, its elite had come to appreciate Calvin's organizational skills as well as his intellect. However, it must also have been apparent that the state and church were not being turned over to a radical. Both tasks involved taking what already existed and developing an integrated and systematic structure that would provide the republic with what it most desperately wanted and needed—stability.

In general, this produced a structure in both cases that relied heavily on preexisting realities. But the task was not simple. The revolution and Reformation in the mid-1530s had delivered to the city a host of powers, responsibilities, territories, and overlapping jurisdictions that were exceedingly complex. The city had inherited—or, more accurately, nationalized—the institutional holdings of the church, as well as the possessions of the bishop, the canons, and leading pro-Savoyards. The city had also taken on judicial, legislative, and ecclesiastical roles that had been previously exercised by a similarly diverse collection of individuals. In most cases, this had led to ad hoc arrangements whereby preexisting political and ecclesiastical structures took on many of these roles and responsibilities. Calvin's job was to take these many disparate threads of power and politics, roles and responsibilities, and weave of them a single, coherent garment in which to clothe the republic.

Before I discuss this in greater detail, it is important to bear in mind a few key points. First, the chief goal was to provide a stable structure both for the church and the state. Stability and harmony were of paramount importance; this required a structure that provided forums in which church and state could meet as well as structures that insured dialogue and compromise replaced posturing and conflict. It was also important that the new structures had claims to legitimacy grounded in realities predating the revolution. That is, the structures should not be radical and ought to relate to what any Genevan would recognize as "Genevan." The city's rulers set up committees, albeit with Calvin taking a leading role, to produce Genevan solutions for this Genevan situation. Also, Calvin was not given carte blanche. He was helping to prepare drafts, not final documents to be accepted by acclamation. Finally, it is important to remember that just as the city's leaders had obviously had enough time to get to know Calvin he must also have learned much about Geneva and its inhabitants. Moreover, it is clear that he too desired a structure that was traditional and stable.

■ STATE

It is worth stressing the role of checks and balances in Genevan political culture. Since the late fourteenth century, the city's traditional political system had been designed to defend the rights of the citizenry against the untrammeled executive and judicial power of the prince-bishop, the canons, and the dukes of Savoy.[1] This system of protection and oversight by elected magistrates was institutionalized and codified by Calvin in the 1542 postrevolution constitution. Thus, the rewording of his draft Ecclesiastical Ordinances—so often viewed as a vague compromise that settled nothing—would not have been vague to the magistrates; rather it was designed to be acceptable both to ministers and magistrates for entirely different reasons.

Although I want to return to the Ordinances later, it is essential to dwell on this second task Calvin undertook upon his return. This role of constitution drafter cannot be overlooked. After the revolution from Savoy and the coup d'état against the city's prince-bishop, the city had been running an ad hoc administrative and judicial system. Although much of the governmental bureaucracy predated the revolution and required few changes, whole swathes of executive and judicial power had previously rested elsewhere, with others. These needed to be redistributed.

While Calvin's constitution was a conservative document, it must be placed in the longer context of the Genevan government. It is true that the constitution was more conservative than the immediate situation it replaced. That is hardly surprising. The document was codifying and regularizing an ad hoc situation, not replacing a preexisting constitutional arrangement. One might just as well stress and overemphasize the relatively conservative nature of the 1787 US Constitution vis-à-vis the nonconstitutional, noncodified situation during the period of the Continental Congress. In reality, all Calvin did was take the documents that had underpinned and structured the prerevolutionary system and rewrite them, reallocating the powers of the prince-bishop, the canons, and the dukes to those local Genevan bodies that had previously existed. A few new offices and officers were created: most notably the city's investigating magistrate (the lieutenant). However, this simply acknowledged the realities of the postrevolutionary settlement.

As with the Ordinances, one is inclined to look at the political constitution and to find areas of vagueness. It is true that the codified version of Geneva's revolutionary settlement was more conservative than the revolutionary reality, but the transfer of executive and judicial power from the hands of bishops, canons, and dukes to those of elected, local magistrates was radical and resulted in an extremely open, quasi-democratic, and responsive system. However, one cannot infer from this that Calvin was some proto-democrat. Geneva's revolution, by its very nature, resulted in a more open and responsive state, and Calvin simply codified that reality in a document that used as its framework and foundation the preexisting structures and systems native and traditional to Geneva and its citizens.

Although a full discussion of the constitution has no place here, it is worth noting some of its salient features. First, it was very participatory indeed. If one accepts a population of about ten thousand for Geneva in the 1540s and assumes that half were women and a half were under the age of twenty-five then one can safely assume that the number of males over the legal age of responsibility was unlikely to be more than about twenty-five hundred. This population in turn was divided into three legal categories: native-born *citoyens*, who could fill offices in the city's higher councils; immigrants to the city, who had been granted the status of *bourgeois* usually in return for a fee and had the right to participate in elections and general assemblies (*conseils généraux*); and resident aliens or *habitants*, who registered with the state and whose ability to rent accommodation or conduct business was controlled. If these last remained in the city but did not acquire rights of bourgeoisie, their status was passed along to their children. As the number of people in this situation grew during the seventeenth century, a fourth legal category emerged, that of *natifs*, native-born inhabitants of the city without political rights. The division of the population among these different categories at the moment when Calvin returned in 1541 is unknown, although it is certain that the ranks of the *habitants* would soon be swollen by the arrival of growing numbers of religious refugees. Good evidence becomes available only after 1625. Between this date and 1675, the combined percentage of those with political rights (i.e., citizens and bourgeois) fluctuated between 40 and 50 percent of the total adult male population.[2] It is thus probable that at least half of the adult male population of Geneva, and probably more, had political rights in the early 1540s. Furthermore, out of these less than two thousand men who were called to the general assemblies of the city, fully two hundred sat in the larger of the city's two governing councils. One thus gets a sense of how strongly the voice of the local adult male population would have been heard. It nonetheless bears stressing that most posts of responsibility were filled from slates provided by the outgoing government. Elections were co-optive and not entirely free. One could not just "stand for office."

It is perhaps worth pausing at this point to have a slightly closer look at the newly formed Genevan "Republic" and its own self-understanding of just what sort of polity it was. As Thomas Maissen has recently shown, the word *republic* was used in Genevan edicts and political debates from the time of independence onward. Calvin himself spoke of "this republic." But the word initially seems to have meant nothing more than "commonwealth." Only in the early seventeenth century did the assertion that Geneva was a republic come to imply that it was a sovereign state in which final authority rested with the body of citizens rather than a monarch.[3] Throughout the sixteenth century, documents produced by the authorities tended to focus more on the *seigneurie* as the focal point of power and "self-consciousness" (if one will).[4] Indeed, one has a very strong sense that later disputes between the (foreign) ministers and magistrates had less to do with the preservation of everyone's rights and more to do with the protection of the privileges and reputation of the *seigneurie*, the magistracy. For example, there was little debate about the ability of the Consistory to excommunicate "normal" Genevans (even citizens), but there was considerable demand for the reservation of that power to the Senate when the possible excommunicant was a senior magistrate.

As Harro Höpfl has highlighted, Calvin's statements about the ideal form of government underwent an extremely significant shift after he entered the maelstrom of Genevan constitution drafting and church-state politics and spent three years in Strasbourg, reflecting on what went wrong the first time around in Geneva and thinking hard about questions of the best form of church and state before returning to the former episcopal city and winning approval for his ecclesiastical ordinances. Where the first editions of the *Institutes* said that private individuals should not even speculate about the best form of government, Calvin modified this statement in the 1543 edition and set forth his own opinion. While all forms of duly constituted authority had their advantages and disadvantages and were to be obeyed, he wrote that "the form that greatly surpasses the others is aristocracy, either pure or modified by popular government."[5] For the rest of his life, he would reiterate this preference for aristocratic or mixed polities and often express in the pulpit sharp criticism about the behavior of power-hungry kings, even while always allowing for the appropriateness of different forms of government in different places and seeking to woo princes who might be sympathetic to his reformation.[6] It would thus be anachronistic to call Calvin either a republican or a democrat in the modern (and uncapitalized) sense of those terms. Yet at the same time, Calvin's Geneva was very democratic in that it involved a considerable fraction of the adult males in politics, a much higher percentage than in, say, Bern at the same time. It was also republican, I think, in consciously seeing itself without nobility (the animosity toward the "pretensions" of French refugees of gentry/noble status is but one example—albeit one intermingled with xenophobia). Finally, it was aristocratic and seigneurial in keeping real power in the hands of a few who carefully guarded their privileges and standing both individually and, perhaps most importantly when dealing with Calvin and his fellow ministers, collectively. To the extent that I would speak of republican sentiment—and I do later—I am focusing on the very strong sense arising from the documents of the self-awareness on the part of most Genevans of their status as "citizens" in a "commonwealth." The *seigneurie* no doubt found this rhetorically useful, and that sense (and reality) of political involvement on the part of the wider citizenry in no way lessened the actual grip on power by the *seigneurie*.

Above all, this co-optive system provided continuity and lessened the risk of wholesale and radical change. With annual elections, the city could not risk the entirety of the magistracy being swept away. At the same time, it was still very participatory in the sheer number of men involved in magisterial activities. This was not without problems; many magistrates would have found themselves funding their magisterial work from their own pockets with little hope of compensation. Being a Genevan magistrate may have been an honor, but it was not for the less well off. Nor was it for those with limited free time. Being a magistrate, especially at the more senior levels, was a major time commitment. While we might marvel at Calvin's ability to produce work, we must spare a thought for a senator with daily meetings who was also an elder with a weekly meeting and perhaps also a serving judge, who was still expected to run his business in order to fund many of his magisterial tasks— and that was before the same senator might be asked to head off to Bern with a diplomatic delegation and, upon his return, be sent off to Lyon on a related mission.

The main structure to this system, though, was a layering of councils in a wider structure of checks and balances. This idea of layered responsibility and oversight as well as checks and balances was an approach that has strong echoes in the system arising from the Ecclesiastical Ordinances. The Senate (of about two dozen individuals) was led by four syndics who could not serve consecutive terms. There were also limitations on the power (i.e., senatorial seats) any single family could hold. For major decisions, the Senate was joined by other councilors to form the Council of Sixty. In major debates, some judicial appeals, and other weighty situations, this Council of Sixty was expanded by yet more elected councilors to constitute the Council of Two Hundred. The General Assembly, *in extremis*, might be called upon and, in any case, passed judgment on the actions of the government in the previous year before electing the new government. Judicial power was somewhat detached from this legislative and executive structure especially in the person of the city's newly created chief investigating magistrate, the lieutenant, and his four assistants, the *auditeurs*. They were elected for a year-long term in November and, thus, provided magisterial continuity in February when the councils were dissolved and reelected.

What has this digression to do with Calvin and the structure of the Genevan church? Much, in that it provides insight into the mind-set of the nascent Genevan

Republic. In its core values, the Genevan political ethos was elective, participatory, co-optive, layered, and circumscribed by rather intricate systems of checks and balances designed to inhibit the accumulation of power by any individual, family group, or, even, the previous year's magistrates. Geneva was not a democracy, but it was a newly independent city-state with almost no landed gentry, no nobility of any consequence, and, perhaps most importantly, no significant and sizeable group of wealthy citizens distinct from the mass of the population.

With that context in mind, one can begin to turn to the ecclesiastical structure. Although there were some minor changes in the draft Ecclesiastical Ordinances relating to procedural matters surrounding the appointment of ministers, the sole bone of contention involved the role of excommunication in social control and the relationship of the church and state in its imposition. In the end, a wording was found that covered up the issue and allowed the document to proceed. Basically, this is the normal way in which the Ordinances are discussed and, from the beginning, there is a stress on its problems. One should never forget the reality, however, that the vast bulk of the church's constitution was accepted by all parties and implemented without dispute.[7] It is that body of structures and systems that now needs some consideration.

■ CONSISTORY

Just as the state system was a complex melding of "republican" responsiveness, co-optive continuity, and layered checks and balances, one sees a similar approach to structures when considering that most Calvinistic of all characteristics of the Genevan church, the elders and the Consistory. Calvin's overriding ecclesiological goal, of course, was to establish a system of church discipline with authority over spiritual affairs that was distinct from temporal government with its duty to uphold public order. His great accomplishment was to succeed in this regard to a greater extent than prior reformers such as Oecolampadius and Bucer, who had sought a similar system in Basel and Strasbourg respectively, only to find that the magistrates were too jealous of their prerogatives to allow much power or autonomy to church boards. In Zurich and Bern, reformed before Geneva, moral discipline was understood to be a civic function. In most subsequent Presbyterian or Reformed ecclesiastical polities that looked to the Genevan model, the consistory was made up of the minister(s) of a given parish or locale and the elders. These elders were elected, to the extent that they were elected, in a co-optive manner that relied heavily on the direction of the clergy and socioeconomically prominent members of the congregation. The local consistories formed part of a pyramidal and hierarchical structure that advanced upward to a presbytery (in effect, diocesan) level and, eventually, to the national synod or general assembly. The terminology changed but the structure was fairly consistent. Briefly, the key points were that the Consistory was a local, parish-like body. The elders were drawn from the congregation by a system that relied on it as the assenting body. Magistrates and governmental authorities were only involved to the extent that they were part of that body. Much greater power was invested in superior bodies that were dominated by the clergy and that may or may not have been responsive (or antagonistic) to the organs of the state.

The Genevan structure was flatter; it was single tiered. It also diverged in other key ways from the later Western European Reformed norm. This divergence serves further to highlight the co-operative and consensual nature of the structures that arose from the two systems developed under Calvin's chairmanship. The Genevan Consistory comprised twelve elders and all the nation-state's ministers, the Company of Pastors. Thus, the Consistory was not solely a parish or local body. It was a national institution. This meant that anyone brought before the Consistory faced on the one hand, a meeting of the national assembly of ministers and, on the other, ranks of senior magistrates. Since these magistrate-elders, especially those from Geneva's highest council, held judicial posts, one would have been intimately and terrifyingly aware that, although consistorial power was limited to admonition and temporary excommunication, many of the elders (wearing other hats) held the powers of life and death. If Calvin was able to take the Genevan church further down the road to independence from what strict Presbyterians would later cast as illegitimate, "Erastian" government oversight of church affairs than the other urban reformers of his and the preceding generation had done, there was still much in the structure that developed in Geneva that was very "Swiss." As will be noted elsewhere, this was not without problems, as it certainly was not a full realization of the "sphere of independence" that Calvin sought for the church.

From the outset, this new ecclesiastical court at the heart of a system of checks and balances harbored within itself the most serious threat to the consensual, even cozy, relationship between the church and state—the power of excommunication. It is essential to realize that this was not simply a struggle between the ministers (i.e., the Company of Pastors) and the magistracy (i.e., the *Petit Conseil*). Instead, it was a disagreement between one institution of the state, the Consistory, and another, the Petit Conseil. I cannot stress this point strongly enough. The Consistory had twelve elected magistrates on it, representing all three councils—this will be discussed in greater detail in a moment. There is every reason to believe that these politicians—and the elders were politicians—saw their presence as a sufficient check on the power of the ministers, who were almost entirely foreign born. Moreover, they represented all three councils, and excommunication was not a judicial punishment (it did not involve a fine, imprisonment, or physical punishment, nor did it alter a person's civic status) meted out by a judicial body—oaths were not sworn before the Consistory (until after 1555). These politicians might quite legitimately have concluded that they were sufficient to rule without appeal. The Petit Conseil, for its part, held that the Consistory was a lower level of the republic's bureaucratic and institutional structure and that appeals were possible depending on the sentence. Thus, admonition and remonstrance were decreed and delivered on the spot by the ministers and magistrates of the Consistory. However, the application of excommunication (rather than its recommendation) was seen very much as the recommendation to the criminal courts for further punishment or fines. That is, it was a matter left finally to the Petit Conseil. After all, it was a punishment with a penalty—the loss of personal honor and reputation via the public humiliation of being excommunicated.

The point I am striving to make is that one cannot consider the struggle about excommunication purely as a clash between the church and its ministers, on the one hand, and the state and its magistrates, on the other. Instead, as I said, it is a question of jurisdiction in the institutional structure of the state between one magisterial body, the Consistory, and another. the Petit Conseil. It cut to the heart of a debate over checks and balances. The Constitution of 1542, written by Calvin and derived from the preexisting political structure, had invested supreme judicial and executive power in the Petit Conseil, the body that had previously been primarily charged with protecting the rights and privileges of the citizenry against the power of the non-Genevan executive and judiciary—largely foreign and largely clerical. The postrevolutionary system made this supreme protector of the people their absolute ruler and judge. Clearly, this was dangerous. Just as fundamentally, the creation of the Consistory intruded an entirely new institution, not dependent on any prerevolutionary structure, into the system. The Consistory was more stable in its membership, had greater access to the populace through regular examination and sermons than any other political body, and represented a wider cross- section of the elite by being drawn from all three councils. Just as the newly expanded role and powers of the Petit Conseil made it a dangerously absolute institution, so the Consistory (wholly apart from the involvement of the ministers) was a potential rival to the Petit Conseil as an alternative focus of political and social power. The presence of well-educated, socially prominent, extremely articulate ministers only strengthened the political position of the Consistory.

■ ELDERS

They key point in grasping the political and magisterial role of the Consistory is to remember always that the elders were not only elected magistrates but were drawn from all three Genevan councils. In theory, two elders were meant to be from the Senate, four from the Council of Sixty, and the remaining six from the Council of Two Hundred. Professor Robert Kingdon has very correctly noted that this was not actually the ratio of seats. As can be seen in table 5.1, the reality saw the role of the Senate increased. An additional senator was placed on the Consistory in the form of one of the city's four presiding syndics. With little variation, the rest of the elders were selected on the basis of three from the Council of Sixty and six (as originally proposed) from the Council of Two Hundred. This represented a diminution of the power of the Council of Sixty. However, this council was, by its nature, nebulous and rarely met except to consider matters upon which the Senate wanted additional advice (in particular, foreign affairs). The *Soixante*, to give the council its Genevan name, was purely an advisory body and not part of the normal executive and legislative system as were the senate (Petit Conseil) and the larger council (the *Deux Cents*). Thus, while having only a limited representation, the Council of Sixty was clearly represented by no fewer than one elder (in 1554, admittedly a confused year) and by as many as five elders (in 1558). The elders were, therefore, a standing committee of the city's triple-tiered structure of councils. The elders were also the only such standing committee.

TABLE 5.1 *Consistorial Membership by Council 1543–1558*

Year	Syndics	Petit Conseil	Soixante	Deux Cents
1543	1	2	2	7
1544	1	2	1	8
1545	1	2	4	5
1546	1	2	4	5
1547	1	2	3	6
1548	1	2	3	6
1549	1	2	3	6
1550[i]	1	2	[3]	[6]
1551	1	2	3	6
1552	1	2	3[ii]	6[iii]
1553[iv]	1	2	1	8
1554	1	2	3[v]	6
1555	1	2	3	6
1556	1	2	3	6
1557	1	2	3	6
1558	1	2	5	4

Source: *Registres du Conseil*, annual lists of magistrates

[i] *The Registres du Conseil* do not preserve a list of members for the *Conseil des Soixante or Conseil des Deux Cents* for 1550. However, the only changes from 1549 to 1551 are the loss (possibly through death) of Jean Donzel (*Deux Cents*, 1549) and the addition of Jean Chautemps (*Deux Cents*, 1551). It is, therefore, reasonable to assume that Chautemps was replacing Donzel as an elder drawn from the *Conseil des Deux Cent*s.

[ii] François Symon is not on the list for the *Conseil des Soixante* in 1552 (or that of any other council). However, he had served as an elder from that council continuously since 1545. One can only assume that his name has been omitted from the list (the alternative, that he was not a councillor, seems improbable).

[iii] Blondin, who served as a representative of the *Deux Cents* from 1543, is not on any council list; neither is Guillaume Chiccand (elder from 1546). Again, their names appear to have been omitted from the *Deux Cents* list for 1552. This supposition is supported by Chiccand's membership on the *Deux Cents* in 1553.

[iv] Claude de la Maisonneuve serves as an elder only in 1553. He does not appear on any council list for the year. His nephew, Jean, ceases to serve on the Soixante that same year (having been first elected to a council, the *Deux Cents*, in 1547). Claude does not appear as a councillor until 1555, when he is in the Deux Cents (he is in the *Soixante* in 1556). It is reasonable to assume, therefore, that he was not in the *Soixante* in 1553 and in the lower council two years later. It is more likely that he was in the *Deux Cents* but not noted in the list.

[v] Pierre Bertillion is not listed in the *Soixante* in 1554, despite having served as an elder from this council since 1545 and reappearing in the *Soixante* in 1555. The logical conclusion is that his name was inadvertently omitted.

The magisterial affiliation of the elders is a significant issue. But the more important point is that elders had to be members of these councils; indeed the correct terminology for their office was *commis*, "delegate." While Calvin and the other ministers proved able to exert some influence on the choice of elders, they had no option but to choose from among the available pool of magistrates. Indeed, the elective nature of the posts is important. The Petit Conseil nominated the elders and discussed the names with the ministers. The resulting slate was then put before the Council of Two Hundred for election or, rather, ratification. While other Calvinistic church structures tended to draw their eldership from prominent members of the congregation, who might be magistrates, largely at the suggestion of the ministers and prominent laymen, the Genevan Consistory had an eldership that was a representative, elected body of magistrates.

Magistrates, who often held judicial as well as executive power, were intimately connected to the socio-religious control exerted on the populace by the Consistory.

To the extent that the elders could and did form a political power base for Calvin and the other ministers, they were more than just a theoretical source of political power. These elders already held political power and were able and willing to exert it on behalf of Calvin's vision of a godly society. Moreover, for a decade after 1545, the same group of magistrates became, in effect, professional elders. In other words, it is almost impossible to speak of the church and state as separate units. In most Calvinistic polities, the consistory is very much a creature of the church albeit with the involvement of socioeconomically and possibly politically prominent elders. In Geneva, the Consistory was as much an expression of state and magisterial power as it was of religious and ministerial authority.

Let us be perfectly clear on this. To have a similar structure in, say, Scotland would have meant a member of the royal family, leading members of the aristocracy, and parliamentarians serving on a single, nationwide body with every single minister. That body would convene and personally interrogate individuals from fishwives to leading members of the royal family. If such a hypothetical and admittedly preposterous body had existed, it would be viewed by historians as an incredible example of close connections, clear consensus, and astonishing cooperation between the church and the state in Presbyterian Scotland. And yet, that degree of intertwining of ecclesiastical and secular power was never even a fond thought in Knox's wildest dreams. It was, however, the reality in Geneva. It also serves as the clearest example of the incredibly interlocking nature of the relationship between the "two swords" in Geneva.

■ COMPANY OF PASTORS

One of the most surprising aspects, though, of the Genevan church is its ministerial personnel, collectively, the Company of Pastors. As a group these men were extremely well qualified, of relatively high social status, often wealthy, and (except for Jacques Bernard) foreign. This latter point is not insignificant. Although it can be seen mainly as a comment on the poverty of suitable candidates in Geneva, this is not the sole interpretation. After all, most areas immediately after the Reformation were dependent on their former Catholic clerics (and managed to survive). Geneva was not. It speaks to the magistrates' enthusiasm for supporting their church with the best quality ministers that any natural enthusiasm they may have felt for local candidates was laid aside. Indeed, except for the attempt to force upon the Company the native Genevan Jean Trolliet, the state seems to have accepted a foreign clergy with relative equanimity. Not surprisingly, those problems that arose between the ministers and their magistracy and populace often grew out of cross-cultural difficulties. Nevertheless, the dangers inherent in hiring so many foreigners, of which the authorities were made increasingly aware, seem never to have deterred them from the practice.[8]

One should not make too much of this but it is worth appreciating it for what it was. The practice of recruiting and hiring foreign ministers was, fundamentally, in the hands of the other ministers, in general, and Calvin, in particular. However, once there, the magistracy consistently chose to support these foreigners when they clashed with locals—even ones of high social and political status. This would seem to evidence a close relationship between the church and state, as well as a clear commitment to maintaining a very high quality of religious provision. It is also here that one must question the attempts to model other church structures on those in Geneva. Few polities would be willing to subordinate national prejudice and latent xenophobia to religious excellence. Even fewer would continue to do so when the effort proved problematic. Moreover, although Calvin seems the sole star in the firmament of Geneva's church, in any other situation, most of his colleagues would have shone almost as brightly on their own. The names of Cop, Des Gallars, and Beza are eclipsed only because of Calvin's presence. However, Geneva did more than support the Company and ensure good preaching. It attracted, hired, and supported some of the most prominent and influential leaders of francophone Protestantism in a purely local parish setting. If one were to try to replicate the Genevan situation elsewhere (as many such as Knox would have), how was this aspect of the Genevan church to be duplicated and which state was likely to consider—let alone undertake—the effort?

Finally, let us not overlook the Company in practice. The entire body of ministers for the nation met weekly. There was no system of hierarchical delegation of power and oversight. There was no need for superintendants or Reformed bishops, synods, or general assemblies. The simple realities of life in a geographically small nation allowed the ministers to function as a single body. Indeed, within the city it is somewhat difficult to see how the city's ministers related to any parish structure. The city itself had a body of ministers and a number of physical places to hear sermons and worship. Moreover, while other national bodies mostly consisted of ministers, they also had prominent lay participation—what they did not have, though, was every minister of the nation. The Company of Pastors was just such a body— the entirety of the nation's clergy meeting every week to consider major international developments along with local issues and to engage in self-evaluation—as a ministerial body. However, Geneva's structural equivalent to a national synod or general assembly, combining clergy and magistrates, was not the Company but the Consistory. To the extent that Geneva had a body like a national synod or general assembly that combined the clergy—as a group—and leading magistrates then, structurally, though not in activity, that body was the Consistory.

■ DEACONS AND THE BOURSE

The diaconate is a more problematic area to discuss. The term "deacon" was not really used. This does not mean that the office did not exist. Instead, the ordinances set forth a clear system for the Genevan diaconate. There were two kinds of deacons; one received and dispensed money, while the other ministered to the poor and ill. The method of selection was the same as for the magisterial delegates to the Consistory, the elders. The Petit Conseil was to select the deacons, then discuss the nominees with the ministers, and finally present the approved slate to the Council of Two Hundred for acceptance. On the surface, this is yet another example of the close co-operation of church and state. The "deacons" nominated, approved, and elected were, in reality, the city's *hospitalier* and his assistants, the *procureurs*. In effect, the Ordinances simply accepted a preexisting office, along with its system of election, as the diaconate. The only alteration was the involvement of the Company of Pastors, whose advice and opinion were sought. This is no small point. When establishing a Genevan diaconate, Calvin drafted the Ordinances very much as he did the republic's civil constitution. He codified and regularized a preexisting situation intruding novelty only when absolutely necessary. Nevertheless, the more significant point is that both the church and the state were able to institutionalize a comprehensive system of poor relief and social welfare, including a general hospital and a plague hospital, with complete equanimity and unanimity. As Kingdon has noted: "In effect Calvin did not create but rather consecrated or sacralized an institution that had already been created in Geneva to handle the problems of the poor and unfortunate."[9] Once again, the church and state worked as one to institute and maintain a unified ecclesiastical and secular system of bureaucracy and authority in Geneva.

■ EDUCATION AND DOCTORS

Perhaps this is the best place to consider the other office of Calvin's ecclesiology: doctors. Although Geneva was not able to realize its and Calvin's ambitions for an institution of higher learning until 1559, one must not overlook the city's keen support for education. Geneva's magistrates had been actively involved in running and funding public education well before the Reformation. In the period thereafter, they repeatedly showed a desire to attract some of the best-qualified educationalists of the francophone world, echoing their enthusiasm for outstanding ministers. One need only mention Mathurin Cordier, Sebastien Castellio, and Louis Enoch, who were employed to work in the state's public system. Later names such as Beza, Hotman, Pierre Charpentier, Lambert Daneau, Jean Diodati, François Turrettini, and Théodore Tronchin all testify to the state's determination to support "doctors" not only in the provision of theology but also law and medicine. The attempts to hire men such as Emmanuel Tremellius only reinforce the image of the state's commitment to education.[10]

Indeed, there seems to have been little cause for conflict in this area. Although Karin Maag, in her excellent work on the subject, has demonstrated that the church and the state could differ on the subject matter to be offered at the Academy, she has also proven that ministers, for example Calvin and Beza, could differ in emphasis on the role of and priorities for higher education.[11] The provision of law is the best example. In fact, the greatest deterrent in attracting, maintaining, and keeping doctors was not any disagreement between the church and state but, rather, money. The simple reality was that the state was unable to provide the wherewithal to realize the educational ambitions that it shared with the ministers. Indeed, experience showed that both the state and the church frequently overextended themselves in attempts to make their dreams real.

Where a conflict existed was in the target audience for the work of the educators. Calvin's *Institutes* stressed that the role of the teacher was "to keep doctrine whole and pure among believers."[12] The Ecclesiastical Ordinances made it clear that the office pertained to the school system for boys and girls and culminated in a *collège*. The office existed and was maintained and supported in a spirit of concord by both the church and the state. Calvin certainly intended that the upper reaches of this educational system would serve not only Geneva but also the French Reformed ministry, but in reality this slightly more expansive vision of education and the doctorate was not incompatible with the interests of the state. In addition, one must note that, as with elders, there was an elective element to the appointment of teachers and, more importantly, that the state was thoroughly involved in the process. The Ecclesiastical Ordinances decreed that candidates were to be examined by ministers in the presence of two members of the Petit Conseil before passing a recommendation to the Council of Two Hundred for ratification by vote.

■ IMMIGRATION AND CHARITY

One final area remains that sheds light on the nature of Geneva's ecclesiastical settlement and the structure Calvin brought into existence in the city. That area is charity. Even here, Calvin simply built on what already existed. It is fortunate that accurate records relating to the care of poor strangers exist for the entire year that ended in October 1539. In the period from October 1538 to October 1539, the city hospital assisted 10,657 poor strangers as they passed through Geneva.[13] This figure does not include those Genevans (estimated at about 5 percent of the total population) who received regular assistance from the hospital.[14] Thus, Geneva, a city of about 10,000 persons, was attempting in a one-year period to support some 500 local poor people on a regular basis and an additional 10,000 strangers.[15] While this caused problems for the city, these were largely the result of limited resources.

Indeed, it is certainly an understatement to suggest that this was merely problematic. Calvin and his fellow ministers (all but one of whom were also French) were dedicated to providing refuge to their compatriots and coreligionists. The initial small trickle of refugees no doubt made it easier to convince many Genevans of the need for charity.[16] Also, when the trickle became a flood in the early 1550s, the ministers had already had nearly a decade in which to preach the virtues of being a haven of refuge for these "pauvres fidèles." Perhaps just as importantly, the group of magistrates who were, in effect, permanent elders on the Consistory seems to have imbibed deeply from this well in that they not only supported the ministers against their fellow magistrates concerned about the growing influence of the refugees but also oversaw the mass enfranchisement of them in 1554–1556, which completely altered Geneva's political balance of power. It would not be fanciful or merely hypothetical to suggest that this key group of magistrates, having served closely with the ministers for a decade were probably less troubled by "foreigners," more appreciative of their value to Geneva, and more convinced of the religious rightness of being a refuge. Without premeditation, the evolving nature of Geneva's institutions, the developing relationship between elder-magistrates and ministers, and the relatively limited early influx of refugees joined to make Geneva initially open to the larger influx. And at the crucial point, these circumstances led key politicians to side with the refugees against their xenophobic peers.

By the close of 1543, when Calvin's new political and ecclesiastical structures were in place, a clear pattern had begun to emerge in the relationship between the city and foreigners. Geneva was willing to assist strangers on their way when it was able to do so. Only when local conditions or the sheer scale of the refugee influx strained its resources did the city take direct action, which was in most cases fairly ineffective. This general compassion extended to minor details as well. For example, the Senate gave Calvin permission to provide a special Eucharist for strangers who had arrived too late in the spring of 1544 to attend the Easter service.[17]

Even when trying to discourage strangers from settling, the city showed compassion. The magistrates ordered that the fines for illegally renting to a foreigner were to be paid directly to the hospital to assist the poor.[18] In an apparent effort to stop the refugee problem at its source, a syndic was sent to one of the French areas hardest hit by persecution during 1545, Mérindol in Provence, with money for the Protestant minister there and his flock.[19] Geneva's enthusiasm to stop the flow of refugees from Provence is understandable when one realizes that over four thousand strangers arrived that year from Mérindol and Cabrières alone.[20] Still, even the poor strangers being expelled were not forgotten. Geneva ordered its guards to provide them with bread for their onward journey.[21]

It is clear that the press of refugees continued to be an enormous strain on Genevan resources and society as, for example, when 500 French poor arrived from Strasbourg in June 1547.[22] By 1551, however, many in the city awoke to a greater danger, the threat presented by allowing so many strangers to settle in Geneva. Obviously, from the point of view of local Genevans, this was an entirely different issue from that posed by the waves of transient poor strangers needing temporary charity (a problem largely solved by the effective establishment of the Bourse Française in the late 1540s).

Geneva was, therefore, very much a city that put into practice its theology of charity to the poor and coreligionists. Over 1,300 people were enrolled as habitants, resident aliens—that is, not just poor passing through—from 1549 to 1555. Admittedly, relatively few remained in Geneva permanently. Still, while the years 1535–1554 had seen an average admission of 23 outsiders to permanent citizenship—naturalization—the period 1555–1557 saw, on average, 119 per year. Thus in the first twenty-year period of the republic's history, around 250 individuals were naturalized, while in the later three-year period over 460 were granted bourgeois rights. Clearly, this was more than simple charity, but it does highlight that Geneva did more than simply usher the poor in one gate and out another. The city was moved by compassion to take to its heart waves of refugees both temporarily and, in some cases, permanently. This charity, I would argue, was one of the most striking features of Calvinism in Geneva.

■ CONCLUSION

What is the point of all this in relation to the workings of the church and state in Geneva? First, it is to stress the unified nature of the relationship. Moreover, it highlights the immense area of overlap between the ecclesiastical and political realms. Finally, and most importantly, the Genevan polity and the Genevan church can be seen as a single, national unit comprising much of the same personnel and the same space. The composite, undifferentiated, and national character of the Consistory is simply the most obvious expression of this. Despite the slightly detached nature of the rural parishes, for the most part, the republic functioned as a single congregation. There is no clear sense that people in the city confined themselves to attending a specific "temple." Rather sermons, catechisms, and even communion were offered to the entire city, as a composite parish, in various locations.

But does this answer the question about what kind of structure or model it was? Whether Calvin's model was more Swiss or Genevan, local or immigrant, is actually a question *mal posée*, as it implies that the Genevan Reformation was, in some way, more a result of multiple factors and impulses than reformations elsewhere. It was not. In that sense, it was not unique. Rather, it might be more useful to ask what made the Genevan model unique. First, it was politicized. At almost every level, not only magistrates but also other elected politicians were involved in the Genevan church structure. This led to a level of activism and involvement by the local population that was unique. Yes, in other Protestant ecclesiologies, magistrates played a role. In France, the Dutch Republic, Scotland, and elsewhere, one could find magistrates serving as elders and deacons. But, in Geneva, they *had* to be magistrates and elected ones at that. Moreover, on the Consistory, these magistrates were organized in a way that ensured that the Consistory was, in effect, a subcommittee of the Genevan council system. The diaconate was, as noted, effectively and solely a department of the elected state.

While surprising in the context of (later) Reformed ecclesiologies that largely looked to the "Genevan model," this would not seem as strange in Protestant Switzerland. Nor was it something that Calvin actually desired. Rather, it dramatically illustrates the extent to which Geneva was at once "Calvinistic" (that is, shaped by Calvin's ideas and goals) but also "local," with a keen interest in the Confederation. This created a tension, which I have discussed elsewhere, between Calvin and his fellow French ministers and many leading Genevans.[23] The orientation of Geneva— its foreign policy, its sense of its own place, and its structural developments—often exposed this tension. Obviously, this exposed Geneva, in general, and its church structure, in particular, to the danger of the "infection of faction." But the answer to the question of what made Geneva unique does not explain what made it such an exemplary model—a model to replicate or try to replicate elsewhere. It does not explain the attractiveness of the Genevan model. What did opponents mean when they labeled Geneva the "Protestant Rome"? What did Knox mean when he said that Geneva was "the most perfect school of Christ that ever was in the earth since the days of the apostles? In other places I confess Christ to be truly preached; but manners and religion so sincerely reformed, I have not yet seen in any other place."[24]

Saying that Geneva was like Rome was more than just a way of saying Calvin was "a bit bossy." It also suggested deference to the place, a respect for its teaching, a willingness to turn to it for advice, an expectation that in some way Geneva was leading. When Knox compared it to Jerusalem he was also saying something that had profound resonance. Jerusalem was full of preachers who had literally been touched by and had touched Christ. The Christian "city-state" within the Jewish city was so imbued with faith that those with needs had them met out of the common charity of all. The congregation was peopled by many upon whom the Holy Spirit had settled at Pentecost.

So what made the model work and what made it attractive? First, there was the presence and ministry of Calvin. Calvin the workaholic did more than just churn out great theological writings. In his "spare time," he also poured himself into a very real and effective personal pastoral ministry in the city. There can have been few people in the city who had not personally benefited (through sermons, Consistory, or congregation) from Calvin's learning and enthusiasm. Moreover, as Knox implied, Calvin had accompanying him, shoulder to shoulder, other ministers who were collectively one of the greatest gatherings of ministerial talent, learning, and skill anywhere in Reformation Europe. Knox and others also beheld a city stirred by charity not only to care for its own but also the tidal wave of religious refugees that poured into Geneva from across Europe in the early 1550s. Yes, there were tensions but I can imagine few Christian (or post-Christian welfare states of today) able or willing to cope—let alone cope gracefully—with a comparable level of immigration in so short a time. Not only did this hospitable charity reflect well on the Genevans—living in a not particularly wealthy city—but it also filled the city with men, women, and children who had abandoned much and often lost more for the sake of their faith.

Obviously, the Genevan Reformation was, it is hardly worth noting, a mix of factors and impulses both internal and external. More importantly, it was powered by a level of political and civic activism and involvement that explains not only many of the problems it faced but also why fishwives felt free to discuss the things of faith—albeit not always with a level of discernment pleasing to the Company. Finally, it was a model worth admiring and emulating because it was—or at least appeared to be—led by true quality sustained by heartfelt charity, strengthened by sacrificial determination. Geneva was a model not because it was local, or international, or even unique; it was a model because it was exhilarating and inspiring.

■ Notes

1. See Émile Rivoire and Victor van Berchem, eds., *Les Sources du droit de canton de Genève*, 4 vols. (Aarau: H. R. Sauerländer, 1927–35), esp. vols. 1–2.

2. Alfred Perrenoud, *La population de Genève du seizième au début du dix-neuvième siècle : Étude démographique* (Geneva: Société d'histoire et d'archéologie, 1979), 182–85, 193.

3. Thomas Maissen, "Vers la République souveraine: Genève et les Confédérés entre le droit public occidental et le droit impérial," *BSHAG*, 29 (1999): 5–8. I am grateful to Philip Benedict for his kind suggestions for revision here and elsewhere.

4. See Robert Oresko, "The Question of the Sovereignty of Geneva after the Treaty of Cateau-Cambrésis," in *Republiken und Republikanismus im Europa der Frühen Neuzeit*, ed. H. G. Koenigsberger (Munich: Oldenbourg, 1988), 77–100.

5. Harro Höpfl, *The Christian Polity of John Calvin* (Cambridge: Cambridge University Press, 1982), 124.

6. Ibid., 152–66.

7. For Calvin's account of this compromise, see his March 14, 1542, letter to Oswald Myconius, *Calv.Opp.* 2: 378–79. Although Calvin presents a valiant resistance to magisterial pressure in defense of a correct ecclesiology, it is worth recalling that Calvin is simply giving his version of events. See William Naphy, "Calvin's Letters: Reflections on their Usefulness in Studying Genevan History," *ARG* 86 (1995): 67–89.

8. For a brief discussion of the ministers, see William Naphy, "The Renovation of the Ministry in Calvin's Geneva," in *The Reformation of the Parishes: The Ministry and the Reformation in Town and Country*, ed. Andrew Pettegree (Manchester: Manchester University Press, 1993), 113–32. On the pre-Reformation clergy who remained in Protestant Geneva, see Gabriella Cahier-Buccelli, "Dans l'ombre de la Réforme: Les membres de l'ancien clergé demeurés à Genève (1536–1558)," *BSHAG* 18 (1989): 367–89.

9. For origin of this quotation see transcripts of discussion on paper by William Naphy, "Church and State in Calvin's Geneva" in *Calvin and the Church*, ed. David Foxgrover (Grand Rapids not, Calvin Studies Society, 2002), 22.

10. See Karin Maag, *Seminary or University? The Genevan Academy and Reformed Higher Education, 1560–1620* (Aldershot: Ashgate, 1995); William Naphy, "The Reformation and the Evolution of Geneva's Schools," in *Reformations Old and New: Essays on the Socio-Economic Impact of Religious Change, c. 1470–1630*, ed. Beat Kümin (Aldershot: Ashgate, 1996), 185–202.

11. Karin Maag, *Seminary or University? The Genevan Academy and Reformed Higher Education.* (Aldershot: Ashgate, 1995).

12. John Calvin, *Institutes of the Christian Religion*, ed. John T. McNeill, trans. F. L. Battles, 2 vols. (Philadelphia: Westminster, 1960), 2: 1057.

13. The city also cared for seventy-two regular pensioners. Bernard Lescaze, *Sauver l'âme, nourrir le corps: De l'Hôpital général à l'Hospice général de Genève, 1535–1985* (Geneva: Hospice géneral, 1985), 24.

14. William Innes, *Social Concern in Calvin's Geneva* (Allison Park, PA: Pickwick, 1983), 132.

15. By 1550, the population of Geneva had risen to between 12,400 and 13,893 but it would balloon to around 21,400 by 1560. See Alfred Perrenoud, *La population de Genève du seizième au début du dix-neuvième siècle: Etude démographique* (Geneva: Société d'histoire et d'archéologie, 1979), 24, 30, 37.

16. The stress caused by this "charity," as well as the legal limitations placed on it (for example, on getting accommodation and doing business), is a recurring theme in William Naphy, *Calvin and the Consolidation of the Genevan Reformation* (Manchester: Manchester University Press, 1994).

17. AEG, Registres du Conseil (henceforward RC) 38, fol. 152v (April 7, 1544).

18. AEG, RC 40, fol. 66v (March 27, 1545).

19. AEG, RC 40, fol. 114 (May 14, 1545). The city sent ten écus. This was not an isolated event; on April 25, 1543, an unspecified amount of money had been sent to aid those who were being persecuted in Metz in Lorraine. AEG, RC 37, fol. 71.

20. Innes, *Social Concern*, 133.

21. AEG, RC 40, fol. 149 (June 15, 1545).

22. AEG, RC 42, fol. 128 (June 3, 1547).

23. For further discussion on this and the local Genevan enthusiasm for the Confederation in particular, see William Naphy, "Genevan Diplomacy and Foreign Policy, c. 1535–1560: Balancing on the Edge of the Confederacy," in *Eidgenössische "Grenzfälle": Mülhausen und Genf/En Marge de la Confédération: Mulhouse et Genève*, ed. W. Kaiser, C. Sieber-Lehmann, and C. Windler (Basel: Schwabe, 2001), 189–219; Naphy, "Genevan National Security and Defence Spending," *War in History* 5/4 (1998): 379–99; and Naphy, "The Usefulness of Calvin's Letters," 67–89.

24. John Knox, letter to Anne Locke, 1556. Quoted here after Carter Lindberg, *The European Reformations* (Chichester : Wiley-Blackwell, 2010), 234.

6 Calvin, the Swiss Reformed Churches, and the European Reformation

EMIDIO CAMPI

The topic of John Calvin, the Swiss Reformed churches, and the European Reformation is not exactly a "commonplace" in Reformation history. While there is a long-standing tradition of studies on "Calvin and Geneva" and on "Calvin and the European Reformation," much remains to be learned about "Calvin and Swiss Reformed Churches."[1] Some years ago, the Amsterdam editors of Calvin's letters drew attention to the subject,[2] and more recently, the American historian Michael W. Bruening has highlighted the significance of religious, social, and political forces in the Pays de Vaud for a complete understanding of the development of Calvin's theology as well as of Calvinism.[3] A carefully formulated sentence in the introduction to Bruening's book makes an excellent starting point for this essay: "By looking at Calvin in the context of Vaud and the Swiss Confederation, we can see him grow from a local city pastor into a regional religious leader and eventually into a figure of staggering international importance."[4]

What then are we to make of the "Swiss Reformed churches" in this context? Are they to be viewed as a distinct factor separate from the more purely theological culture of classical Calvinism? Is there an identifiable sense of continuity stretching from Geneva through the Swiss Confederation to Europe? I am not only persuaded that a more refined understanding of these questions could challenge many of the preconceptions that dominate our view of the European Reformation but also confident that they constitute a welcome reminder of the kind of discoveries that make the study of the origins of the Reformed confession so exciting and fascinating.

What follows is divided into three parts. First, I examine of the crucial events and essential patterns of Calvin's relationship with the three major centers of the Confederation: Bern, Basel, and Zurich. Second, I present some thoughts on the influence and importance of Calvin in the wider context of the European Reformation. Finally, I offer some brief reflections on the thorny problem of Reformed confessionalization.

■ I CALVIN AND THE SWISS REFORMED CHURCHES

Bern

Calvin painted an extremely negative picture of his relationship with Bern in his *Discours d'adieu aux ministres*: "The church [of Bern] has betrayed our church, and they have always feared me more than they have loved me there. . . . They were always afraid that I would trouble them in their doctrine of the Lord's Supper."[5] While this statement of disillusionment was indeed but one side of the coin, Calvin was, in fact, involved in numerous disputes with Bernese officials and theologians. The major problem was that the new Reformed order in Geneva and in the French-speaking territories of the Pays de Vaud was continually threatened by Savoy and France, and, thus, needed Bernese support. Bern, however, had officially adopted the Reformation along Zwinglian lines in 1528 and, therefore, the magistrates there retained complete control over the church. This type of church-state relationship, to which Calvin would so strongly object, had also been established in the Pays de Vaud, under Bernese political and military control prior to his arrival. Consequently, the authorities expected the implementation of their church polity, including their approach to discipline and liturgical practices. In reality, however, Calvin had greater theological influence among Vaudois pastors.[6] The interaction had already been difficult during Calvin's first period of ministry in Geneva with the so-called Caroli Affair.[7] Nevertheless, it seemed that everyone was inclined to let bygones be bygones when Calvin returned to Geneva in 1541. However, the latent confessional antagonism reemerged in 1547 when a serious dispute over the Lord's Supper broke out in the Pays de Vaud between the Calvinist faction, led by Pierre Viret, and the Zwinglian faction, led by André Zébédée. With his controversial treatise *De la vertu et usage du ministère*, which essentially presented the Calvinist understanding of the Lord's Supper and the use of excommunication, Viret had attacked both the role of Bernese magistrates in church affairs and the Zwinglian ministers.[8] The so-called Zébédée Affair,[9] which continued for over a year, illustrates not only how sensitive the Bernese church was to differences of doctrine and practice, owing in large part to a deep awareness of its own Zwinglian tradition. It also provides an illustration of the dilemma facing the Reformed churches in the Confederation: how far they were to strive for union with Calvin?[10] Far from being a detached observer in these events, the Genevan reformer was painfully aware of the great resentment that still persisted against his theology. This may well have convinced him of the necessity of reaching a pan-Helvetic agreement on the Lord's Supper. And yet, even this project, which was later to be known as the *Consensus Tigurinus*, was not enough to eliminate all doubts. Calvin was especially stricken by the fact that the two prominent Bern theologians, Johannes Haller (1523–1575) and Wolfgang Musculus (1497–1563), in compliance with the city council's decision to dismiss the Zurich Agreement, did not sign it, even though they agreed with its content.[11] Nevertheless, despite the feeling that they had been outmaneuvered by Bullinger and Calvin, the Bern church finally adopted the *Consensus* when it was published in 1551.

The doctrine of predestination was another aspect of Calvin's theology that came under the scrutiny of both friends and opponents in Bern. After Jerome Bolsec was arrested in Geneva in October 1551 for his public attacks on Calvin's doctrine of predestination, Bern,[12] alongside Zurich and Basel,[13] urged a measured approach. In late December, Bolsec was banished from the city and moved to Thonon, a safe haven in the Bernese lands, from where he not only continued to voice his criticism but quickly found supporters, such as André Zébédée, united by their hatred of Calvin's teaching. Protest letters from the Genevan ministers complaining that Bolsec and his allies did not even shrink from cursing Calvin as the Antichrist had no effect.[14] The reaction of the magistrates showed Calvin unmistakably what sort of reputation he enjoyed in Bern. They requested that the Genevan Small Council ensure that its clergy end their criticism of Bern and its church.[15] In the ensuing months, the increasingly obvious theological differences between the Bernese and the Genevans led to a ban on sermons in Bern and its territories concerning predestination and the Lord's Supper in accordance with the Genevan rite.[16] The use of Calvin's *Institutes* at the Lausanne Academy was also regarded as "intolerable."[17]

The negative influence of these actions became clear with the approach of negotiations with Bern about the renewal of the treaty of *combourgeoisie* upon which Geneva relied. When February 8, 1556, arrived, Bern was so annoyed by the defeat of the Perrinist party and the victory of Calvin's followers in the elections of November 1555 that its leaders allowed the treaty to expire, thereby leaving Geneva in a vulnerable situation. Protracted negotiations resumed with the help of the Swiss cities but with no results. Bern and Geneva were now divided by both theology and politics. What settled the question was the common threat to their freedom represented by the territorial claims of Duke Emmanuel Philibert of Savoy. On January 9, 1558, Bern and Geneva signed an *alliance perpétuelle* whereby both cities pledged to protect each other. However, after 1555 the "*odium Calvini* was so strong in Bern that he had no influence there at all."[18] In May 1555 Calvin addressed a long letter to the Council of Bern, defending his doctrine of predestination and making no attempt to conceal his deep conviction about the nature of ecclesiastical discipline, which he regarded as a crucial issue in the quarrel with Bern. But he did so with a sense of resignation because he saw no possibility of reconciliation. Indeed, he increasingly turned his attention to France and the religious situation in Europe.[19]

Basel

Calvin's relations with the Basel church were of a completely different nature.[20] His epistolary contacts with the brilliant scholar Simon Grynaeus (1493–1541) are of particular note. Calvin, in fact, dedicated his 1540 *Commentary on the Epistle to the Romans* to Grynaeus in appreciation of their conversations during his first stay in Basel, during which they discussed exegetical questions extensively.[21] Grynaeus's death in 1541 left behind a gap in Calvin's personal ties to Basel, which Oswald Myconius (1488–1552), the antistes of the Basel church, was unable to fill. The debates and events most relevant to our discussion did not, however, occur during Myconius's term of office, but during that of his successor Simon Sulzer. A native of the Bernese Oberland, he had been one of the leaders of the Bern church in the early 1540s, but being sympathetic to Bucer's teaching of the Lord's Supper he was deposed from office in 1548 and asked to leave the city. Sulzer moved to Basel, his wife's native city, where he was appointed professor of theology and within five years became the antistes of the Basel church.[22]

Until the early 1550s, there was a friendly understanding among Calvin, Sulzer, and the Basel establishment that gradually faded away during the "Second

Eucharistic Strife." They endorsed the indictment of Servetus and gave their assent without hesitation to his execution.[23] On the other hand, first in the Bolsec affair and then during the trial of the Spaniard, massive opposition to Calvin began to mount in Basel, supported by humanistic religious refugees at or in the vicinity of the university, whose orthodoxy had always been viewed with doubt by the exponents of the Swiss Reformed churches. The leaders of this so-called Basel faction included Sebastian Castellio (1515–1563) of Savoy, who had fallen out with Calvin in Geneva in 1545, and Celio Secondo Curione (1503–1569) of Piedmont, who came to the Lausanne Academy in 1542 and began his tenure at the University of Basel as a professor of rhetoric in 1546.[24]

After Calvin expressed his point of view in a letter to Sulzer on September 9, 1553,[25] the antistes promised him the support of the Basel church,[26] although he protected Castellio and Curione, who were voicing their opposition to Calvin's theology. In fact, the first of a series of polemical treatises against Calvin promptly appeared in Basel in December 1553: the *Historia de morte Serveti*,[27] which was very likely written by Castellio himself. Calvin, for his part, justified his actions in the *Defensio orthodoxae fidei de sacra trinitate*.[28] Early March 1554 saw the publication of an alternative to Calvin's views in the tiny but epoch-making pamphlet titled *De haereticis, an sint persequendi*. This book had also been chiefly the work of Sebastian Castellio, but it was financed by the wealthy Italian Marchese Bonifacio d' Oria[29] and coauthored by Celio Secondo Curione. It was, in fact, a product of the Basel liberal humanist faction. The pseudonymous authorship did not prevent Calvin from suspecting the Basel circle immediately after its publication.[30] He described the book as "full of unbearable blasphemies,"[31] and its authors as "brazen scribes" who "not only obscure the light of pure doctrine with the fog of heresy, and rob the simple and less educated of their reason through their evil lunacies, but also take the liberty of destroying the entire religion through the unholy freedom of doubt."[32] Moreover, Curione, who privately complained to Bullinger that Calvin was following Bucer on the issue of the Eucharist, overtly opposed Calvin's doctrine of predestination in a treatise of 1554 with the programmatic title *De amplitudine beati regni Dei*.[33]

The brief account of the controversy that broke out between Calvin and Castellio on the persecution of heretics and the freedom of religion shows that the interaction of the Genevan reformer with Basel produced a different kind of opposition than in Bern. In Basel, an academic elite, who had little involvement in the life of the Reformed church and even experienced some disillusionment with the new faith, joined together in a loose coalition aimed at fostering a middle course between the Erasmian tradition of tolerance and the increasingly strident positions expressed by Calvin. Essentially this was possible because Sulzer must have turned a blind eye to the activities of Castellio, Curione, and others, such as the influential Lucchese printer Pietro Perna and the Dutch Anabaptist David Joris.[34] Moreover, the sympathy of the antistes for middle positions or concealment during the second dispute over the Lord's Supper led to a further cooling off of relations between Geneva and Basel.[35] When the Hamburg pastor Joachim Westphal (ca. 1510–1574) attacked the *Consensus Tigurinus* in two polemical treatises, Calvin and Bullinger wanted to reply on behalf of all the Swiss Reformed churches. Sulzer, however, was not willing to openly support the two reformers. He not only condemned Calvin for his excessive partisanship in the strife against Westphal but also argued that the *Consensus Tigurinus* should never have been published in the first place.[36] Calvin had no understanding for Sulzer's ambiguous points of view and summed up his opinion with usual clarity in a letter to Bullinger: "I have always feared that Sulzer would remain cold in order to be able to remain neutral. But I had in fact expected something better or at least less witless."[37]

Zurich

If we are to take the temperature of Calvin's relationship with other Swiss reformed cities, there is no denying that the connection with Zurich represents the crucially defining relation. Calvin traveled to Zurich five times—on three occasions with Farel—in order to discuss political and ecclesiastical affairs. In addition to Heinrich Bullinger, Calvin came to know a great number of Zurich's theologians, including Leo Jud, Rudolf Gwalther, Konrad Pellikan, Theodor Bibliander, Konrad Gessner, and later, Peter Martyr Vermigli, whom Calvin held in particularly high esteem.[38] These contacts soon led to extensive correspondence that reinforced strong personal bonds of sympathy, characterized by an unusually intense exchange of thought on theological, ecclesiastical, and political issues, including the correspondents' literary and personal plans. Judging by the number of letters sent, Calvin's correspondence with Bullinger and others in Zurich was only exceeded by his communication with Farel and Viret,[39] which demonstrates in what high esteem Calvin held his colleagues from Zurich.[40] The frequent concurrent letters exchanged between the Genevan and Zurich City Councils were further evidence of this strong relation.

The results of these epistolary contacts, which have recently been studied in depth, are quite suggestive.[41] They confirm, in the first instance, that the years 1541 to 1549 were affected by three closely related problems relevant to Calvin's relations with the Swiss Confederates: the conflicts with Bern in matters of church polity, the efforts to form an alliance of the Protestant states of the Confederation with France, and the agreement with Zurich on the doctrine of the Lord's Supper.

Calvin's plan was to anchor Geneva in the Confederation, but on his terms. He hoped to attain a theological understanding with Bullinger concerning the Lord's Supper that would make it possible to conclude the conflict with the Bernese church. Moreover, along with the Council of Geneva he sought the help of Zurich in providing stability to the difficult, tumultuous relations with the Bern magistrates. Finally, Calvin expected to persuade the Bernese and the Zurichois to emerge from their isolation and act as part of a central European political force for effecting religious change along Reformed lines. We must remember that with the Schmalkaldic League's defeat and the imposition of the Augsburg Interim, it seemed to many that Lutheranism was dead and that the final hope for the survival of the Reformation lay in the Swiss Confederation. And we should not overlook the fact that the renewal of the Swiss Confederate alliance with King Henry II of France (1519–1559) opened up the possibility of unity among Swiss Protestants, or at the very least, of assisting the Protestants in France, who had come under considerable pressure.

Calvin sought to campaign personally in Zurich for this political master plan and visited Bullinger twice to that end. However, he did not see his hopes fulfilled. Bern and Zurich did not join in alliance with France, and Bern continued to play its role as military protector of Geneva. On the other hand, Bullinger and Calvin were at least able to agree on their understanding of the Lord's Supper, an agreement that both parties, in fact, went on to uphold. This was the result of a long, chiefly private theological dialogue between Calvin and Bullinger from 1547 to 1549. Both reformers spared no effort for this, exchanging ideas about a solution to the problem in numerous letters and meeting in Zurich three times with the assistance of Farel. A compromise made this agreement theologically possible by taking a number of Zwingli's main views into account and through determining the presence of Christ, alongside granting that salvation is the work of the Holy Spirit.[42] The compromise was certainly uneasy and did not prevent Calvin from reverting to his former position on spiritual presence in 1561. However, there is no point in discussing here whether Calvinism prevailed over Zwinglianism or whether Calvin gave up his primary position in order to make this possible. It is far more important to emphasize the future impact of the text. In a lengthy and complex process that culminated with the Synod of Dort, the two streams would merge to form a completely new type of church, the Reformed Church, which solidly opposed Roman Catholicism within Western Christianity together with Lutheranism and other outgrowths of the Reformation.

The second striking feature of the contacts with Zurich is that this "*entente cordiale*" did not exclude differences of opinion on a number of matters. For example, concerning the Bolsec affair and the question of predestination more generally, Bullinger did not hide his disagreement with Calvin, and the discussion became increasingly bitter. Calvin wrote to Farel about Bullinger: "I complained lately of the theologians of Basel, who, as compared with those of Zurich, are worthy of very great praise. I can hardly express to you, my dear Farel, how much I am annoyed by their rudeness. There is less humanity among us than among wild beasts."[43] Even after the dispute was resolved in Calvin's favor and Bolsec was expelled from the city, [44] Calvin was still unable to let things stand as they were. He wrote to Bullinger: "Although you disappointed my expectations, I nevertheless gladly offer you my friendship. Before the others I will maintain silence as if I was entirely satisfied."[45] While the disagreement between Calvin and Bullinger eventually subsided,[46] they continued to maintain differing opinions in regard to predestination.[47] There was, however, no difference of opinion in the much more difficult matter of Michael Servetus. Both Bullinger and the Zurich pastors declared Servetus a heretic and urged the Geneva Council to carry out its duty in the matter.[48] Zurich's position, thus, corresponded with the consensus of the time, which was questioned by only a few outsiders, often individuals like Castellio or Curione who were in danger of persecution themselves.

One final point, of paramount importance in the relationship between Calvin and Bullinger, needs to be mentioned—their common efforts on behalf of religious refugees. The help extended by Geneva and Zurich in the sixteenth century to Reformed Christians under attack in Italy, France, England, Hungary, and Poland derived primarily from Calvin and Bullinger's true empathy and strong commitment to the fate of the persecuted. Just to name a few examples: Calvin's indefatigable efforts on behalf of the Waldensians, whose grave situation of persecution in the Luberon region of Provence in 1545, in Piedmont in 1560, and Calabria in 1561 was (as might be expected) perceived first in Geneva, is quite well documented. Less known, however, is that they then received support and found succor in both Geneva and Zurich.[49] Calvin and Bullinger's support of Reformed Christians in France was even more extensive. Bullinger continually supported Calvin's (and Beza's) unflagging efforts, whether with material and literary assistance or with petitions and common delegations, even though the two friends did not always agree about what type of assistance was appropriate.[50]

To sum up, Calvin's relations with Bern were those most riddled with conflict. In Bern, Calvin's criticism of the liturgical rites and of the state's role in the affairs of the church, combined with the eruption of the predestination polemic in the French-speaking communities, proved immensely threatening to significant sections of the magistracy and clergy. Many were increasingly concerned about peace and order in the Bernese lands and feared losing their own theological tradition; thus they were solidly opposed to central aspects of Calvin's thought and action. The Basel church, influenced by the reserved Simon Sulzer, was essentially well disposed, but Calvin regarded this church as lacking in zeal and courage. The academic elite of the city, under Castellio and Curione, was a stronghold of fierce opposition that attempted with both eloquence and scholarship to provide alternatives to Calvin's theology. Finally, Calvin found in Zurich a true comrade-in-arms, Heinrich Bullinger, who remained loyal to Calvin despite initial reservations, occasional theological differences, and differing positions regarding church polity. The *Consensus Tigurinus*, the founding charter of Reformed Protestantism, remains to this very day an eloquent symbol of the mutual respect and personal friendship between Calvin and Bullinger. This overview of Calvin's relationship with the Swiss Reformed cities of Bern, Basel, and Zurich thus most strongly demonstrates that, as he asserted in his *Discours d'adieu*, Calvin was indeed both "feared and loved" in the Swiss Confederation of his time.

▪ II CALVIN AND THE EUROPEAN REFORMATION

The second part of the chapter presents some thoughts on the influence and importance of Calvin in the wider context of the European Reformation, where he also elicited strong reactions, ranging from enthusiastic admiration to vehement rejection. This is a subject that has been fairly thoroughly explored. I propose to address the question from a somewhat different angle than that of most of the writers who have concerned themselves with analyzing the continental expansion of Calvinism. For rather than addressing the question through a geographical analysis, I will offer a series of observations from a systematic perspective, examining Calvin's relations with the Roman Church, the radical reformers, and the variegated Protestant camp.[51]

The Roman Church

From 1539 to 1541, Calvin was active with other leading reformers and urban politicians in efforts to reach the greatest possible degree of agreement with the

Roman Church. He participated in the religious colloquies held at Frankfurt (1539), Hagenau (1540), and Worms and Regensburg (1541), although judging from his correspondence with Farel and Viret, he was scathing about attempts to compromise on essentials for the sake of an apparent unity.[52] Even in his 1543 treatise *Supplex exhortatio ad Carolum quintum*, Calvin constantly referred to the church, thus giving a glimpse of his view on its catholicity.[53] This work, written at the request of Martin Bucer to clarify the state of the question between the Protestants and Rome, along with his participation in the religious colloquies, earned him the friendship of Melanchthon and esteem among the front ranks of Protestant theologians.[54]

With the beginning of the Council of Trent in 1545 and the subsequent process of confessionalization, the various sides became entrenched, and it proved increasingly obvious that no consensus would be possible. It comes as no surprise, therefore, that this circumstance modified Calvin's view of the Roman Church. His most significant work was the *Acta Synodi Tridentinae cum Antidoto* of 1547, in which he lucidly delineated the theological and ecclesiastical issues dividing Rome and the reformers.[55] Impressed by Calvin's treatise, Bullinger urged him to respond to the "popish" Augsburg Interim, which the Genevan reformer, in his trenchant critique, promptly branded as the "Adultero-German Interim"![56]

The papal church became the opposite of the true church, and it was "better to be separated for the sake of union with Christ than to be united in apostasy."[57] Henceforth, he devoted himself more and more exclusively to the task of restoring the true church of the pure Word of God. One cannot read Calvin's writings from after the late 1540s without being struck by this second strand of his thought. Certainly, much is to be found in book 4 of the *Institutes*, but a great deal can be discovered by looking at various treatises, sermons, letters, and above all, at his commentaries on scripture, which offer some of Calvin's more mature reflections.[58] A good example can be found in his *Commentary on Isaiah*, first published in 1550. Commenting on Isaiah 28–32, in which the prophet foretells the imminent restoration of the church and proclaims that God will still be gracious to his church so as to restore her to integrity, Calvin discerns a parallel with the circumstances of his own day:

> Although, as a result of a near extinction of the light of faith, and a horrendous corruption of the worship of God, the people were deformed, they nevertheless boasted of their royal priesthood—just as we see the Papists shamelessly bragging in a similar way today, although a deadly confusion cries out that the entire form of the Church has perished among them. For this reason the prophet defines what the reformation of the Church will involve.[59]

Isaiah's prediction undoubtedly relates to the pious king Hezekiah and his reign during which the temple was restored to its former splendor. However, restorations such as these, Calvin argued, are not accomplished once and for all. They must be undertaken again and again whenever the church is in a state of collapse. Thus, Hezekiah is depicted as an example for all ages, and, not least in Calvin's estimation, for the church of his own day.[60]

Calvin evidently understood his work as "a part of that restorative process of the church...which was there before him, a restoration of the true order of the church, and not a retreat into some ideal church above and beyond this world."[61] On account of this, he was even prepared to admit that the Roman Church had not been altogether destroyed. It is still, as he wrote in his commentary on 2 Thessalonians 2:4, "The temple of God in which the Pope bears rule, but at the same time profaned by innumerable sacrileges."[62] In a passage of his commentary on Ezekiel, he was again free to acknowledge that, although Rome had failed to reciprocate the faithfulness of God, there will always be "a church among them, but hidden and wonderfully preserved."[63] These are but a few representative examples that illustrate Calvin's approach to the question of the relationship with the Roman Church.

The Radical Reformation

Like most reformers of the day, Calvin confronted the Radical Reformation in its full spectrum of Anabaptists, Unitarians, and Spiritualists of all kinds.[64] In the *Psychopannychia*, one of his earliest works, in the *Brève instruction contre les anabaptistes*, published in 1544, and in *Contre la secte phantastique et furieuse des libertins* from the following year, Calvin offered a detailed discussion of their various doctrines.[65] Above all, he clearly rejected the ethical rigor of those who regarded postbaptismal sin as unforgivable, excluding unworthy church members, and the conception of the church as consisting only of regenerate members who willingly embraced a life of discipleship.[66]

The last critique might come as a surprise, since Calvin also stressed the importance of discipline for the well-ordered Christian life and yearned for a visible community of saints.[67] This is no paradox, but rather the consequence of a very different understanding of discipline. The Anabaptists insisted that discipline was an indispensable mark of the true church. Significantly, Calvin regarded this assertion as a dangerous confusion of the distinction that he carefully maintained between marks and discipline. The marks, which he called the "saving doctrine of Christ," constitute the life of the church, whereas discipline, which he compared to the sinews that hold the body together, sustains the church.[68] Discipline, then, pertained to the external organization, not to the definition of the true church. In this manner, Calvin both upheld the substance of the Anabaptist concern and, at the same time, refined their teaching. For him, in perfect keeping with Augustine's ecclesiology, the church is constituted not by the quality of her members but by the presence of the means of grace. Only the preaching of the Word and the administration of the sacraments give the church her character as the body of Christ; the discipline, however important, is "like a bridle to restrain and tame those who rage against the doctrine of Christ."[69] Besides, the intention of discipline is not to expel imperfect people from the fellowship of believers in order to attain ecclesial holiness, but rather to drive sinners to repentance, to restore communion, and to bring health to the body of Christ, although its daily exercise reveals that this ultimate aim can never be entirely achieved.[70]

Moreover, whereas the Anabaptists viewed the church as a fellowship of saints, the reformer, invoking the authority of Augustine, regarded it as a *corpus permixtum*, composed of both sinners and the redeemed.[71] Quoting the parable of the net, in which all kinds of fish are caught but not separated until they are brought ashore (Matt. 13:47–50), the reformer exhorted patience with sinners, certainly not indulging them, but nevertheless firmly endeavoring to purify the church.[72] Through the preaching of the Word and the exercise of discipline, a constructive path should be found between antinomianism and legalism. Calvin saw it in "the judgment of charity," by which we acknowledge that all members of the church who confess faith have an appropriate behavior and participate in the sacraments.[73] Thus, in the context of a resurgent Catholicism boasting about its external institutional unity and radical sectarianism, suggesting a separatist model of a church consisting of visible saints, Calvin steered a middle course between the ecclesiological extremes of Rome and the Anabaptists.[74]

Building Unity between Protestant Churches

Protestants were one in rejecting the Roman Church, but every attempt to unite the evangelical camp in the sixteenth century came to ruin, ostensibly because of differing understandings of the Lord's Supper. In the Sacramentarian controversy, which began as a dispute between Martin Luther and Huldrych Zwingli, Calvin initially supported the Wittenberg Concord of 1536 as the basis for Protestant unity. However, the cool winds blowing from Wittenberg and Zurich in the mid-forties obliged him to take another path in expressing his own understanding of the reality of Christ's presence in the sacrament.

In his *Petit traicté de la Saincte Cene* (1541),[75] perhaps the most balanced explanation of the Eucharist of the Reformation era, Calvin openly discussed the conflict between Lutherans and Zwinglians and was not afraid to criticize both with a striking independence.[76] According to Calvin, what had remained underexposed in the long-standing dispute were the constitutive function of the Holy Spirit and the understanding of the Lord's Supper as spiritual nourishment for the church.[77]

Significantly, when Luther increased his criticism of the Zwinglians with another violent pamphlet, *Kurzes Bekenntnis vom Abendmahl*, in September 1544,[78] Calvin wrote to Bullinger on November 25, 1544, urging him to be tolerant and make allowances for Luther's temperament.[79] Just as he praised Luther, describing him "as a quite outstanding servant of God," who has "always worked till now to break the rule of the Antichrist and spread the doctrine of salvation," he also appealed to Bullinger's acumen to avoid a controversy that would result in "the general shipwreck of the Church." Calvin was all the more disappointed when in the following months the Zurich pastors replied sharply to Luther with the *Wahrhaffte Bekanntnuss*,[80] and Luther fired back even more rudely. On June 28, 1545, Calvin wrote to Melanchthon, exasperated with both sides and deeply disillusioned by what he saw as Melanchthon's weakness in the whole affair.[81]

The positions eventually moved closer, as we have already seen, with the Zurich Agreement of 1549. By that time, Luther was already dead so he was no longer around to express his opinion about the *Consensus Tigurinus*. There were plenty of Lutheran theologians, however, who criticized the Zurich Agreement. The chief among them was the head pastor of Hamburg, Joachim Westphal, who published two pamphlets, *Farrago* in 1552 and *Recta fides* in 1553, both filled with truculent personal abuse. Calvin became the "cow" (*das Kalbe)* and Bullinger inevitably the "bull" (*der Bulle)*. At the request of Bullinger and in contact with Peter Martyr Vermigli, Calvin answered with an apology titled *Defensio* in 1555,[82] a subsequent *Secunda Defensio* in 1556, and an *Ultima Admonitio* in 1557. Thus, the so-called "Second Supper Strife" increased instead of lessening the conflict between the Swiss and the Lutherans.[83]

Even if the style is typical of sixteenth-century theological polemic, Calvin took a more conciliatory approach in an effort to achieve consensus with the Lutherans. Thus, he insisted, for example, that the English exiles in Wesel remain in the Lutheran Church, despite differences in opinion regarding certain ceremonial matters such as using lighted candles and wafers in the celebration of the Lord's Supper.[84] He prefaced his *Secunda Defensio* with an epistle to the pastors of Saxony dated January 26, 1556, in which he urged them to use their powers for the peace and unity of the church.[85] The debates continued and grew in intensity, yet Calvin continued the dialogue, constantly affirming his agreement with Luther and the Augsburg Confession. In the *Ultima Admonitio* he declared:

> But as long as any hope of pacification appears, it will not be my fault if mutual good-will is not maintained. Though from being unworthily provoked I have been more vehement in this writing than I was inclined to be, still were a time and place appointed for friendly discussion, I declare and promise that I will be ready to attend, and manifest a spirit of lenity which will not retard the desired success of a pious and holy concord. I am not one who delights in intestine dissension.[86]

Calvin repeatedly begged Melanchthon to express his opinion on the "Sacramentarian controversy," but his appeals fell on deaf ears.[87] For years before his death in 1560 the *preceptor Germaniae* was himself the object of enraged attacks by the Gnesio-Lutherans Tilemann Heshusius and Matthias Flacius, the self-appointed guardians of Luther's legacy.[88] Various reconciliatory missions by Theodore Beza to Germany between 1557 and 1559 ended in failure. To the strict Lutherans, the *Consensus Tigurinus* not only revived the ghost of the Luther-Zwingli controversy, but considering the simultaneous spread of Calvinism across Germany, the Zurich Agreement seemed, in their eyes, to prove that the Reformed, having perverted true doctrine, aimed to subvert true religion as well. Thus, they mistrusted Calvin's and Bullinger's bridge-building attempts to establish Protestant unity and even mistreated the "Calvinists."[89] Distressed and, perhaps, with a silent insight, Calvin noted in a letter of 1560 to Rector Matthias Schenck of Augsburg that "Wittenberg has produced, I confess, several pious and courageous personalities. But the majority believe themselves to be faithful imitators of Luther by inflating themselves with pretentious arrogance instead of the openness of mind which this man possessed."[90] The hopes of the early 1540s that the breach with the Lutherans could be healed, and the three Protestant capitals—Wittenberg, Zurich, and Geneva—brought together were definitely dashed.

By contrast, the "Second Supper Strife" established Calvin as the foremost reformer of the second generation. Admired by his supporters and criticized by his opponents, he enjoyed widespread influence throughout Europe and impressed his seal on the most eventful years for the process of confessionalization of the

European continent. In addition, the Geneva church became the model of a resilient form of ecclesiastical organization that, although designed for one city-state, could be adapted to the larger needs of great states, especially in case of hostile political authorities. Indeed, the Calvinist Reformation had an extensive capacity largely denied to Lutheranism, whose spread was mostly confined to German territories and Scandinavia, or to Zwinglianism, which took hardly roots beyond the Swiss Confederation, England excepted.

The effect of this can be seen in Europe in the second half of the sixteenth century. Inevitably, Calvin's greatest influence was in France, the land of his birth. The impetus for the foundation of these new churches emanated from him, but it would be misleading to single him out. Theodore Beza and Pierre Viret were highly regarded and Bullinger was the most widely read non-French reformer in France. Furthermore, while benefitting from the leadership of Genevan-trained ministers and Genevan literature, not least translations of the Bible and the metrical psalms, French Protestants developed their own responses to the political challenges of their homeland. Reduced to its essentials, although Calvin continued to advise caution, the onward march of the Catholic state was opposed in the so-called Wars of Religion (1562–1598) by a Calvinist resistance movement led by Louis Prince of Condé and Admiral Gaspard de Coligny.[91]

The extraordinary series of Protestant rebellions, which led to upheavals in Scotland and the Netherlands, looked to Geneva rather than to earlier forms of the Reformation like Lutheranism and Zwinglianism. In Scotland, where in 1560 a Calvinist reformation was established by an alliance of the reformer John Knox with the noble "Lords of congregation" who had successfully rebelled against the Catholic regent, Mary of Guise, the influence of Geneva was pervasive and included doctrine and liturgy, as well as consistorial discipline.[92] In the Low Countries, Calvin's influence was exerted through the Dutch exile churches gathered in London, Emden, Frankfurt, and Wesel, and Calvinism was able to bring together the disparate forces of the Dutch evangelicalism. Calvin was already dead at the outbreak of the Dutch revolt in 1566, but Calvinists played a significant role in the national uprising against Spain spearheaded by William of Orange. Through their sacrifices, "Calvinism was firmly embedded in the foundations of the free Dutch state."[93]

Calvin's great international stature as reformer is indicated also by his involvement in the English Reformation. Yet his influence was arguably neither unique nor decisive, but built on the earlier efforts of other reformers to reach out to the church and theological leadership of the country. He became aware of events in England while in Strasbourg through Bucer, who had dedicated his commentary on Romans of 1536 to Archbishop Cranmer. Yet already in 1531, the distinguished Basel scholar Simon Grynaeus had established a link with the English church,[94] and 1538 saw the first dedication of a book by a Zurich reformer to an English monarch. The author, Heinrich Bullinger, saw in England the potential for a powerful national Reformed church, and throughout his long life, he cultivated a close relationship to the English church. His dedication of the third and fourth Decades of Sermons to Edward VI, Zurich's hospitality to a group of Marian exiles between 1553 and 1558, and its involvement in the "Vestarian Controversy" during the reign of Elizabeth I illustrate how the ties between Zurich and England deepened as time went on.[95] Very important also were the invitations extended to Martin Bucer, Peter Martyr Vermigli, and John à Lasco to settle in England after the Augsburg Interim, since they helped to educate the generation of theologians that was to shape the future of English Protestantism.

Calvin's involvement in English religious politics began with the accession of Edward VI, and a selection of dedications to eminent persons—a common six-teenth-century practice—exhibits his growing interest in England. He dedicated to the Duke of Somerset, regent to the boy king Edward VI, his commentary on I and 2 Timothy (1548). Edward himself received the dedication of the commentary on James, 1 and 2 Peter, 1 John, and Jude (1551), and of the first edition of the commentary on Isaiah (1551), whereas the second edition (1559) was dedicated to the young queen Elizabeth, who refused it, considering Geneva the source of the execrable ideas expressed by John Knox in his vitriolic tract *The First Blast of the Trumpet Against the Monstrous Regiment of Women*. Although the affair damaged relations between Geneva and England,[96] it is undisputed that Calvin exercised a profound and lasting influence over the English church through the stranger churches in London, both French and Dutch.[97] Furthermore, we are now aware how avidly the English read Calvin during the second half of the sixteenth century. His sermons, biblical commentaries, and the *Institutes* were available in English editions and often reprinted. The number of Calvin's works translated into English far surpassed that of his contemporaries, even Bullinger.[98]

Hungary had strikingly little contact with Calvin. It was Basel that initially played an important role in establishing personal contacts with Hungarian and Transylvanian students through Simon Grynaeus, Oswald Myconius, and Sebastian Münster. Closer connections were established with Zurich from 1549, when Bullinger sent the *Consensus Tigurinus* to Hungary for approval. Then, in 1551, Bullinger helped to secure the Reformed church under the trauma of the Ottoman conquest with his *Epistola ad Ecclesias hungaricas*,[99] and it was he who provided the decisive document of Hungarian Protestantism, namely the *Confessio Helvetica Posterior*. Calvin had considerably more connections with Poland than Hungary, and he made a real cultural impact, particularly among the nobility.[100] The king, Sigismund August II (1548–1572), to whom the reformer dedicated his commentary on Hebrews, was vividly interested in reforming the Polish church. Although he remained a Catholic, with his advisor, Francesco Lismanini (a Graeco-Italian brought up in Poland and confessor to Queen Bona Sforza), he tolerated the formation of Protestant congregations. While Lutheranism took roots in Royal Prussia and Great Poland, the nobles of Little Poland, Ruthenia, and Lithuania embraced Calvinism. Among the important correspondents with Calvin were Prince Nikolaus Radziwill in Lithuania and John à Lasco in Little Poland. A Lasco, after a long period spent in foreign lands, returned to his homeland in 1556 to organize Polish Protestantism into a national church along Geneva lines, a mission cut short by his death in 1560. At the same time, Anabaptism, Unitarianism, and other forms of religious dissidence also found a hospitable reception so that, by the end of the 1550s, the situation in Poland had become extremely confused. Calvin had misgivings about this state of affairs, especially because of the protection afforded to "heretics" like Stancaro, Biandrata, and other antitrinitarians. He issued strong warnings, which, however, found little echo. Disappointed, he reduced his Polish involvement. Vermigli and Bullinger, conversely, kept a busy correspondence with a wide range of leading figures, hoping to combat radicalism.[101]

To balance this brief presentation of Calvin's presence in the European Reformation, it should be added that Bullinger and Peter Martyr Vermigli both remained the other luminaries of the Reformed world. Older studies generally have yielded to the temptation to construct an oversimplified model of Reformed Christianity, which is almost equated with Calvin. This neglects the remarkable Swiss impact on the formation of the Reformed tradition. Recent scholarship has shown that previous views of Calvin's European influence must be largely revised, at least for England,[102] Poland,[103] and Hungary.[104] As late as 1600, the official Church of England was marching to rhythms set, at least partly, in Zurich. And England was not unique in this: the Reformed churches of Hungary and Transylvania were also troubled by tussles between the traditions of Zurich and Geneva. In Poland-Lithuania, the Reformed concerns were, by no means, represented by Calvin alone, and the picture that is starting to emerge reveals Bullinger's and Vermigli's conspicuous theological ability and political competence in dealing with that splintered situation. Furthermore, as new studies indicate, while Geneva did indeed give direction to Reform in France, this should not blind us to the significant role played by the Swiss Reformed churches, and, above all, by Bullinger in supporting their coreligionists.[105]

■ III   REFORMED CONFESSIONALIZATION

Finally, I offer some brief reflections on the thorny problem presented by the thesis of Reformed confessionalization.[106] Over the past twenty-five years, no other theory has played a more prominent role in the historiographical debate about the Reformation. A number of case studies have been used to weigh the merits of the confessionalization approach. Church historians have been reluctant to draw clear boundaries among the confessions, particularly between the Lutheran and the Reformed confessions. They argue that pluralism, and not confessional uniformity, was a fact of life in the second half of the sixteenth century.[107] This pertains above all to Reformed Protestantism. The theological differences between Zurich and Geneva testify eloquently to this and so does the existence of the various confessional formularies of Reformed Protestantism.

I am emphasizing this point because the most common and long-standing approach is to equate Reformed Protestantism with the name of the Genevan reformer. But what exactly was Calvinism? If it is defined according to the criteria of the Synod of Dort of 1618 and the *Consensus Helveticus* of 1675, even Calvin himself, in many respects, cannot be regarded as a Calvinist. Moreover, scholars concerned with the history of Calvinism (e.g., Kingdon, Muller, Benedict) have been unable to force it into a single mold. While his preeminence in the Reformed tradition is unquestionable, a number of historians have begun to realize more recently that the richness of the source materials commonly employed breeds an excessively Geneva-centric approach.[108] Only in the last few years, for example, have we returned to a fully conscious awareness that Bullinger's ecclesiastical politics had at least the same wide-ranging European dimension as those of Calvin, and that the influence of both reformers quickly stretched from the old continent to the New World.[109] But this is by no means the entire picture. Considering the current orientation of the historical literature, in which an increasing amount of attention is given to lesser known founding fathers of the Reformed churches, one must continue to ask: how much of what has been peddled under the label "Calvinism" should really be attributed to the thought of Bucer,[110] Zwingli,[111] Oekolampadius,[112] Farel,[113] Viret,[114] Musculus,[115] à Lasco,[116] or Vermigli?[117] Enormous holes are still gaping in our understanding of Reformed confessionalization. Herein lies a complicated historical problem that must be discussed in the context of the confessionalization theory, with due attention paid to the latest research results. The solution cannot be found in a single succinct formula or as the result of logical deduction or induction, but rather only by groping, seeking, and advancing and finally through the careful perusal of heterogeneous source materials.

It is certain, however, that the linear metaphor of the "founder," the myth of the solitary hero, is historically much too shortsighted, not only with regard to Luther and Lutheranism but also to Calvin and the Reformed world. None of this is intended to diminish Calvin's decisive personal role, nor is it to challenge his preeminent significance for the Reformed tradition. However, the progress of scholarship, which of course deserves further analytical testing, has demonstrated specifically and convincingly that a great deal of what was transmitted is not accurately designated "Calvinism," but rather a more variegated Reformed tradition.

From my point of view, two research considerations ensue. First, Reformation scholarship should not be blinded by the didactically reasonable, but historiographically problematic, nineteenth-century Schleiermacherian tradition of theological subjectivity; rather, it should aspire to emphasize the importance of reciprocal interaction between persons and situations.[118] Second, this implies abandoning the idea that Swiss–Upper Rhine Reformation research and Calvin research properly belong in "separate spheres"—as has often been the case unto this day. This is more than just a methodological point. It is indeed a demanding standard involving important historical connections that are in danger of being hidden away. It is certainly ironic that Calvin's contemporaries understood their strongly bonded affinity better than modern historians.

■ Notes

1. The subject enjoyed a short vogue at the beginning of the twentieth century, on the occasion of the four hundredth anniversary of the reformer's birth. See Wilhelm Kolfhaus, "Der Verkehr Calvins mit Bullinger," *Calvinstudien: Festschrift zum 400. Geburtstage Johann Calvins*, ed. Josef Bohatec (Leipzig: Haupt, 1909), 27–125; Arnold Rüegg, "Die Beziehungen Calvins zu Heinrich Bullinger und der von ihm geleiteten Zürcher Kirche," in *Festschrift der Hochschule Zürich für die Universität Genf*, ed. Arnold Rüegg and Gustav von Schulthess-Rechberg (Zurich: O. Füssli, 1909); and Paul Wernle, *Calvin und Basel bis zum Tod des Myconius 1535–1552* (Basel: Reinhardt, 1909). See also two recent surveys: Bruce Gordon, "Calvin and the Swiss Reformed Churches," in *Calvinism in Europe 1540–1620*, ed. Andrew Pettegree, Alastair Duke, and Gillian Lewis (Cambridge: Cambridge University Press, 1994), 64–81; and Emidio Campi and Christian Moser, "Loved and Feared: Calvin and the

Swiss Confederation," in *Calvin's Impact on Church and Society, 1509–2009*, ed. Martin Ernst Hirzel and Martin Sallmann (Grand Rapids: Eerdmans, 2009), 14–34.

2. Cornelis Augustijn, "Farel und Calvin in Bern 1537–1538," in *Calvin im Kontext der Schweizer Reformation: Historische und theologische Beiträge zur Calvinforschung*, ed. Peter Opitz (Zurich: Theologischer Verlag, 2003), 9–23; and Frans Pieter van Stam, "Das Verhältnis zwischen Bullinger und Calvin während Calvins erstem Aufenthalt in Genf," in Opitz, *Calvin im Kontext*, 25–40.

3. Michael W. Bruening, *Calvinism's First Battleground: Conflict and Reform in the Pays de Vaud* (Dordrecht: Springer, 2005).

4. Ibid., 4.

5. *OS* 2: 404. On the identity of the object of Calvin's criticism, who was not directly named, see *Calvin Studienausgabe*, 10 vols., ed. Eberhard Busch, Matthias Freudenberg, Alasdair Heron, Christian Link, Peter Opitz, Ernst Saxer, and Hans Scholl (Neukirchen: Neukirchener, 1994–2008), 2: 303, n. 13.

6. See Carl Bernhard Hundeshagen, *Die Conflikte des Zwinglianismus, Luthertums und Calvinismus in der Bernischen Landeskirche von 1532–1558* (Bern: Jenni, 1842); Kurt Guggisberg, *Bernische Kirchengeschichte* (Bern: Haupt, 1958), 55–242; Guggisberg, "Calvin und Bern," in *Festgabe Leonhard von Muralt zum siebzigsten Geburtstag Mai 17, 1970, überreicht von Freunden und Schülern*, ed. Martin Haas and René Hauswirth (Zurich: Berichthaus, 1970), 266–85; Amy Nelson Burnett, "The Myth of the Swiss Lutherans," *Zwingliana* 32 (2005): 45–70.

7. Augustijn, "Farel und Calvin in Bern," 10–13.

8. Pierre Viret, *De la vertu et usage du ministere de la parolle de Dieu, et des sacrements, dependans d'icelle, et des differens qui sont en la chrestienté, à cause d'iceux* (Geneva: Jean Girard, 1548).

9. On the Zébédée Affair, see Bruening, *Calvinism's First Battleground*, 183–94; and Bruening, "Pierre Viret and Geneva," *ARG* 99 (2008): 175–97.

10. Bruening, *Calvinism's First Battleground*, 192. The issue here is the presence of Calvin's sympathizers in the Bernese territories and the authorities' determination to hunt them down without tearing the fabric of the new Reformed order. In Bern, for example, they deposed and banished Simon Sulzer and his two ministerial colleagues, Beat Gering and Konrad Schmid, who were favorable to "Lutheran" (i.e., Bucer's and Calvin's) teaching on the Eucharist and were rather isolated from the rest of the local clergy (see n. 22). In Lausanne, by contrast, they did not depose Viret because he had the support of the majority of teachers and pastors, and his dismissal would, in effect, have meant dismantling the Reformation there.

11. See Calvin to Wolfgang Musculus, October 22, 1549, *Calv. Opp.* 13: 433–34, no. 1294; Viret to Calvin, November 4, 1549, *Calv. Opp.*13: 443, no. 1300.

12. The most comprehensive account of the Bolsec affair remains Philip C. Holtrop, *The Bolsec Controversy on Predestination, from 1551 to 1555: The Statements of Jerome Bolsec, and the Responses of John Calvin, Theodore Beza, and other Reformed Theologians* (Lewiston, NY: Edwin Mellen Press, 1993). See also Herman Selderhuis, "L'image de Calvin: Chez Bolsec, Calvin et les autres," *BSHPF* 155 (2009): 281–88. See also *Calv. Opp.* 8: 238–42.

13. *Calv. Opp.* 8: 229–34 (Zurich); *Calv. Opp.* 8: 234–37 (Basel).

14. Genevan ministers to the Bern Council, October 4, 1554, in *Calv. Opp.* 15: 250–52, no. 2020; see also Genevan ministers to the ministers of Bern, October 6, 1554, *Calv. Opp.* 15: 256–58, no. 2023.

15. Bern Council to the Geneva Council, November 17, 1554, *Calv. Opp.* 15: 313–14, no. 2047; see also *Calv. Opp.* 15: 312, no. 2046.

16. Bern Council to the ministers of Vaud, January 26, 1555, *Calv. Opp.* 15: 405, no. 2096; and Bern Council to its baliffs, January 26, 1555, *Calv. Opp.* 15: 406, no. 2097.

17. Bruening, *Calvinism's First Battleground*, 220, n. 35.

18. Ibid., 221. See also William G. Naphy, *Calvin and the Consolidation of the Genevan Reformation: 1541–1557* (Manchester: Manchester University Press, 1994) 208–10; and Wulfert de Greef, *The Writings of John Calvin: An Introductory Guide*, trans. Lyle D. Bierma (Louisville: Westminster John Knox Press, 2008), 42–43.

19. Calvin to Bern Council, May 4, 1555, *Calv. Opp.* 15: 600–604, no. 2199. To put it in the somewhat provocative terms of Heiko A. Oberman: "Calvin was not a city reformer in any of the usual senses of the term. He regarded himself as a soldier stationed in Geneva, but at the same time as an officer directing a European army." Oberman, "Europa Afflicta: The Reformation of the Refugees," *ARG* 83 (1992): 91–111.

20. See Wernle, *Calvin und Basel bis zum Tod*; and Uwe Plath, *Calvin und Basel in den Jahren* 1552–1556 (Zurich: Theologischer Verlag, 1974).

21. John Calvin, *Commentarius in Epistolam Pauli ad Romanos, Calv. Opp. R, series* 2, 13: 3–6. On the dedication to his *Commentary on the Epistle to the Romans*, see Nicole Kuropka, "Calvins Römerbriefwidmung und der consensus piorum," in Opitz, *Calvin im Kontext*, 147–67.

22. On the state of Basel's church at midcentury, see the important monograph by Amy Nelson Burnett, *Teaching the Reformation: Ministers and Their Message in Basel, 1529–1629* (Oxford: Oxford University Press, 2006). On the Bucerian leanings of Simon Sulzer, see Burnett, "Simon Sulzer and the Consequences of the 1563 Strasbourg Consensus in Switzerland," *ARG* 83 (1992): 154–79.

23. On these events see Plath, *Calvin und Basel in den Jahren*.

24. On Castellio, see Hans Rudolf Guggisberg, *Sebastian Castellio, 1515–1563: Humanist und Verteidiger der religiösen Toleranz im konfessionellen Zeitalter* (Göttingen: Vandenhoeck & Ruprecht, 1997), trans. Bruce Gordon as *Sebastian Castellio, 1515–1563: Humanist and Defender of Religious Toleration in a Confessional Age* (Aldershot: Ashgate, 2003); and Stefania Salvadori, *Sebastiano Castellione e la ragione della tolleranza: L'ars dubitandi fra conoscenza umana e veritas divina* (Milan: Mimesis, 2009). Modern literature on Curione is extremely limited. The most recent biography is Markus Kutter, *Celio Secondo Curione, sein Leben und sein Werk (1503–1569)* (Basel: Helbing & Lichtenhahn, 1955). See also Albano Biondi, "Celio Secondo Curione," in *Dizionario Biografico degli Italiani*, vol. 31 (Rome: Istituto della Enciclopedia Italiana, 1985), 443–49.

25. *Calv. Opp.* 14: 614–16, no. 1793.

26. Sulzer to Calvin, September 18, 1553, *Calv. Opp.* 14: 622–23, no. 1801.

27. Plath, *Calvin und Basel in den Jahren*, 88–93.

28. See the title page, *Calv. Opp.* 8: 453: "Defensio orthodoxae fidei de sacra trinitate, contra prodigiosos errores Michaelis Serveti Hispani, ubi ostenditur haereticos iure gladii coercendos esse, et nominatim de homine hoc tarn impio iuste et merito sumptum Genevae fuisse supplicium." The work itself: *Calv. Opp.* 8: 453–644.

29. The most complete study—although one to be used with caution—on this extraordinary figure who has received little attention is Manfred E. Welti, *Giovanni Bernardino Bonifacio, marchese d'Oria, im Exil 1557–1597: Eine Biographie und ein Beitrag zur Geschichte des Philippismus* (Geneva: Droz, 1976).

30. Calvin to Bullinger, March 28, 1554, *Calv. Opp.* 15: 93–96, no. 1935.

31. Calvin to the congregation in Poitiers, February 10, 1555, *Calv. Opp.* 15: 435–46, no. 2118; here 441.

32. *Calv. Opp.* 15: 200.

33. Curione tried to publish the book in Basel, but it was rejected. He found a printer by the name of Dolfino Landolfi in Poschiavo, a municipality in the "Freestate of the Three Leagues" (today the Swiss canton of Grisons/Graubünden), who published the treatise in 1554. See Uwe Plath, "Der Streit um C. S. Curione De amplitudine beati regni Dei im Jahre 1554 in Basel," in *Eresia e Riforma nell'Italia del Cinquecento* (Florence: Newberry Library, 1974), 269–81.

34. On Perna as supplier of heretical works at the origins of Socinianism, see Leandro Perini, *La vita e i tempi di Pietro Perna* (Rome: Edizioni di storia e letteratura, 2002); on Joris in Basel, see Guggisberg, *Sebastian Castellio*, 168–71.

35. See Plath, *Calvin und Basel in den Jahren*, 173–92.

36. Sulzer to Bullinger, March 7, 1555, *Calv. Opp.* 15: 491, no. 2141; Sulzer to Bullinger, March 23, 1555, *Calv. Opp.* 15: 521, no. 2160; Sulzer to Calvin, March 28, 1555, *Calv. Opp.* 15: 531., no. 2168.

37. Calvin to Bullinger, June 5, 1555, *Calv. Opp.* 15: 640–42, no. 2218, here 642.

38. On these lesser known but prominent Zurich scholars, see Hans Ulrich Bächtold, ed., *Schola Tigurina: die Zürcher Hohe Schule und ihre Gelehrten um 1550*, (Zurich: Pano, 1999). Vermigli was particularly close to Calvin on the issue of predestination, which Bibliander opposed. In 1560, this unleashed a controversy over predestination in the Zurich church, whose ministers and professors supported Vermigli over Bibliander. On the relationship between Calvin and Vermigli, see Emidio Campi, "John Calvin and Peter Martyr Vermigli: A Reassessment of their Relationship," in *Calvin und Calvinismus—Europäische Perspektiven*, ed. Irene Dingel and Herman Selderhuis (forthcoming, Mainz: Steiner). On the differences between Bibliander and Vermigli on predestination, see Cornelis P. Venema, *Heinrich Bullinger and the Doctrine of Predestination: Author of "the Other Reformed Tradition"?* (Grand Rapids: Baker Academic, 2002), ch. 4.

39. See Bruening, *Calvinism's First Battleground*, 178.

40. Calvin wrote a total of 115 letters to Bullinger, and Bullinger wrote 162 letters to Calvin between 1538 and 1564.

41. Emidio Campi and Ruedi Reich, eds., *Consensus Tigurinus. Die Einigung zwischen Heinrich Bullinger und Johannes Calvin über das Abendmahl* (Zurich: Theologischer Verlag, 2009), esp. 9–41.

42. The text of the *Consensus Tigurinus* is in *Calv. Opp.* 7: 735–44. A new critical edition of the agreement, including a modern English translation and the preceding correspondence between Bullinger and Calvin is in Campi and Reich, *Consensus Tigurinus*, 125–42. On the literary origin and the theological importance of the *Consensus Tigurinus*, see Ulrich Gäbler, "Das Zustandekommen des Consensus Tigurinus im Jahre 1549," in *ThLZ* 104 (1979): 321–32; and Paul Rorem, *Calvin and Bullinger on the Lord's Supper* (Bramcote: Grove Books, 1989). Most recently Wim Janse has drawn attention to the importance of Calvin's dynamic Eucharistic theology in his "Calvin's Eucharistic Theology: Three Dogma-Historical Observations," in *Calvinus sacrarum literarum interpres: Papers of the International Congress on Calvin Research*, ed. Herman Selderhuis (Göttingen: Vandenhoeck & Ruprecht, 2008), 37–69.

43. Calvin to Farel, December 8, 1551, *Calv. Opp.* 14: 218, no. 1571, esp. 218.

44. Bolsec was expelled, not executed, because the Swiss Reformed churches were not keen to have him executed and because he had the protection of Bern. This shows the delicate course Calvin had to steer so as not to antagonize the confederate churches. See Holtrop, *The Bolsec Controversy*, 451.

45. Calvin to Bullinger, late January 1552, *Calv. Opp.* 14: 251–54, no. 1590, esp. 253.

46. Calvin to Bullinger, March 13, 1552, *Calv. Opp.* 14: 302–5, no. 1612.

47. See Peter Walser, *Die Prädestination bei Heinrich Bullinger im Zusammenhang mit seiner Gotteslehre* (Zurich: Zwingli Verlag, 1957), 168–80; Gottfried W. Locher, "Bullinger

und Calvin: Probleme des Vergleiches ihrer Theologien," in *Heinrich Bullinger, 1504–1575: Gesammelte Aufsätze zum 400. Todestag*, 2 vols., ed. Ulrich Gäbler and Erland Herkenrath (Zurich: Theologischer Verlag,1975) 2: 1–33; Richard Muller, *Christ and the Decree: Christology and Predestination in Reformed Theology from Calvin to Perkins* (Durham, NC: Labyrinth Press, 1986); and Venema, *Bullinger and the Doctrine of Predestination*.

48. *Calv. Opp.* 8: 555–58.

49. See Arturo Pascal, "Le ambascerie dei cantoni e dei principi protestanti di Svizzera e Germania al re di Francia in favore dei Valdesi durante il periodo della dominazione francese in Piemonte (1535–1559)," in *Bollettino Storico-Bibliografico Subalpino* (1913): 80–119, 314–33; (1914): 26–38; Euan Cameron, *The Reformation of the Heretics: The Waldenses of the Alps, 1480–1580* (Oxford: Oxford University Press, 1984), 237–39; Hans Ulrich Bächthold, "Ein Volk auf der Flucht: Die Schweiz als Refugium der Waldenser," *Jahrbuch für Europäische Geschichte* 7 (2006): 23–42; and Albert de Lange, *Calvino, i Valdesi e l'Italia* (Turin: Claudiana, 2009).

50. On Bullinger's influence on France, see the seminal, yet often overlooked, work of André Bouvier, *Henri Bullinger, réformateur et conseiller oecuménique, le successeur de Zwingli, d'après sa correspondance avec les réformés et les humanistes de langue française* (Neuchâtel: Delachaux et Niestlé, 1940), 267–424, esp. 217–20, 247–48, 273–78, and 293–96. The most recent survey is Andreas Mühling, *Heinrich Bullingers europäische Kirchenpolitik* (Bern: Peter Lang, 2001), 187–224; and see Mühling, "Heinrich Bullingers politische Beziehungen nach Frankreich," in *Reformierte Retrospektive: Vorträge der zweiten Emder Tagung zur Geschichte des reformierten Protestantismus, Emder Beiträge zum reformierten Protestantismus*, ed. Harm Klueting and Jan Rohls (Wuppertal: Foedus, 2001), 25–36.

51. See, for example, John T. McNeill, *The History and Character of Calvinism* (New York: Oxford University Press, 1954), which for decades was considered the standard work on the Reformed tradition, and the excellent survey of Philip Benedict, *Christ's Churches Purely Reformed: A Social History of Calvinism* (New Haven: Yale University Press, 2002). For further examples, see Menna Prestwich, ed., *International Calvinism* (Oxford: Clarendon Press, 1985); Andrew Pettegree, "Calvinism in Europe," in Hirzel and Sallmann, *Calvin's Impact on Church and Society*, 35–48; Herman Selderhuis, ed., *The Calvin Handbook* (Grand Rapids: Eerdmans, 2009), 57–125; and Bruce Gordon, *Calvin* (New Haven: Yale University Press, 2009), 250–75 and 304–28.

52. See, for example, *Calv. Opp.* 11: 145–47, 171–73, 174–80, and 262–63. See Wilhelm H. Neuser, "Calvins Beitrag zu den Religionsgesprächen von Hagenau, Worms und Regensburg (1540–1541)," in *Studien zur Geschichte und Theologie der Reformation: Festschrift für Ernst Bizer*, ed. Luise Abramowski and J. F. Gerhard Goeters (Neukirchen-Vluyn: Neukirchener, 1969), 213–37.

53. For the text, see *Calv. Opp.* 6: 453–534. However, replying to the accusation commonly leveled against the reformers that they promoted heresy and created schism in the church, he argued: "It is not enough simply to throw out the name of church, but judgment must be used to ascertain which is the true church, and what is the nature of its unity.... [W] e mean a church which, from incorruptible seed, begets children for immortality, and, when begotten, nourishes them with spiritual food (that seed and food being the word of God), and which, by its ministry, preserves entire the truth which God deposited in its bosom. This mark is in no degree doubtful, in no degree fallacious, and it is the mark which God himself impressed upon his church, that she might be discerned thereby." *Calv. Opp.* 6: 520. See Jan J. Steenkamp, "Calvin's Exhortation to Charles V (1543)," in *Calvinus Sincerioris Religionis Vindex*, ed. Wilhelm H. Neuser and Brian G. Armstrong (Kirksville, MO: Sixteenth Century Journal, 1997), 309–14.

54. See Irena Backus, "Un chapitre oublié de la réception de Calvin en France : La Vita Calvini de Jean-Papire Masson (1583) : Introduction, édition critique et traduction française annotée," in *Jean Calvin et la France*, ed. Bernard Cottret and Olivier Millet, special ed., *BSHPF* 155 (2009): 181–207.

55. For the text, see *Calv. Opp.* 7: 365–506. On Calvin's reactions to the Council of Trent, see Theodore W. Casteel, "Calvin and Trent: Calvin's Reaction to the Council of Trent in the Context of His Conciliar Thought," *HThR* 63 (1970): 91–117.

56. John Calvin, *Interim adultero-germanum, cui adiecta est vera christianae pacificationis, et ecclesiae reformandae ratio (1549)*, *Calv. Opp.* 7: 545–674. Bullinger's letter to Calvin, May 26, 1548, *Calv. Opp.* 12: 705–707, no. 1025.

57. Benjamin Milner, *Calvin's Doctrine of the Church* (Leiden: Brill, 1970), 156.

58. See Milner, *Calvin's Doctrine of the Church*; Lukas Vischer, *Pia conspiratio: Calvin on the Unity of Christ's Church* (Geneva: Centre International Réformé John Knox, 2000); and Eva-Maria Faber, "Mutual Connectedness as a Gift and a Task: On John Calvin's Understanding of the Church," in Hirzel and Sallmann, *Calvin's Impact on Church and Society*, 122–44.

59. *Calv. Opp.* 36: 475–76. See Pete Wilcox, "Calvin as Commentator on the Prophets," in *Calvin and the Bible*, ed. Donald K. McKim (Cambridge: Cambridge University Press, 2006), 107–30, esp. 124–26.

60. Wilcox, "Calvin as Commentator," 126. The other passage frequently commented on—particularly by those scholars who have dealt with the question of ecclesiology—is the exposition of Malachi 2:4. Here Calvin makes an unequivocal statement, remarking that defiance of Roman orders is not defiance of, much less separation from, the (true) church: "When we resist the papal priests, we do not violate God's covenant, that is, it is no departure from the order of the church, which ought ever to remain sacred and inviolable. We do not then, on account of men's vices, subvert the pastoral office and the preaching of the word; but we assail the men themselves, so that true order may be restored. We therefore boldly attempt to subvert the whole of the papacy, with the full confidence that we minimize nothing of true doctrine.... [I]ndeed, the order of the church, the preaching of the truth, and the very dignity of pastors, cannot stand unless the church is purged of its defilements and its filth removed." *Calv. Opp.* 44: 433. For further examples in the context of the minor prophets, see Frederik A.V. Harms, *In God's Custody: The Church, A History of Divine Protection: A Study of John Calvin's Ecclesiology Based on his* Commentary on the Minor Prophets (Göttingen: Vandenhoeck & Ruprecht, 2009), esp. 124–29. See also Michael Jenkins, "Unintended Consequences: Schism and Calvin's Ecclesiology," in *Theology Today* 66 (2009): 217–33.

61. Milner, *Calvin's Doctrine of the Church*, 155.

62. *Calv. Opp.* 52: 199.

63. *Calv. Opp.* 40: 354.

64. See William Balke, *Calvin and the Anabaptist Radicals* (Grand Rapids: Eerdmans, 1981); Bernard Cottret, *Calvin: Biographie* (Paris: Lattes, 1995), 280–86; and Akira Demura, "From Zwingli to Calvin: A Comparative Study of Zwingli's 'Elenchus' and Calvin's 'Briève Instruction,'" in *Die Zürcher Reformation: Ausstrahlungen und Rückwirkungen: Wissenschaftliche Tagung zum hundertjährigen Bestehen des Zwinglivereins (29. Oktober bis 2. November 1997 in Zürich)*, ed. Alfred Schindler and Hans Stickelberger (Bern: Peter Lang, 2001), 87–99.

65. *Psychopannychia* (written in 1534, published in 1544), *Calv. Opp.* 5: 165–232; *Briève instruction pour armer tous bons fideles contre les erreurs des Anabaptistes*, *Calv. Opp.* 7: 45–142; and *Contre la secte phantastique et furieuse des libertins qui se nomment spirituels*, *Calv. Opp.* 7:145–248. For example, he attacked their notion of soul sleep between death and the resurrection. He refuted their objections to infant baptism and the use of oaths, their

negative attitude toward the world, and their conviction that a Christian could not hold the office of magistrate. He countered their claim to possess immediate revelations of the Spirit, which disparaged the importance of the ministry of the Word.

66. Thomas H. L. Parker, *Calvin: An Introduction to his Thought* (London: Chapman, 1995; repr. New York: Continuum, 2002), 132–33. Citation is from the Continuum edition.

67. It is true that in the *Institutes*, before beginning his close dissection of Anabaptist ecclesiology, Calvin noted that we should aim at ethical perfection but added that believing that one could achieve it on earth is a "devilish invention." *Inst.* 4, 1.20.23. As he said epigrammatically in the *Brième instruction contre les anabaptistes*, "Whenever, under the pretext of zeal for perfection, we cannot bear any imperfection either in the body or the members of the church, the devil is inflaming us with pride and seducing us through hypocrisy to abandon the flock of Jesus Christ." *Calv. Opp.* 7: 77.

68. *Inst.* 4, 12.1.

69. *Inst.* 4, 12.1.

70. Milner, *Calvin's Doctrine of the Church*, 179; Demura, "From Zwingli to Calvin," 95–96; Gene Haas, "Calvin, the Church and Ethics," in *Calvin and the Church: Papers Presented at the* 13th *Colloquium of the Calvin Studies Society, May* 24–26, 2001, ed. David Foxgrover (Grand Rapids: CRC Product Services, 2002), 72–91, here 87–88.

71. See, for example, *Inst.* 4, 1.8; Calvin's comments on Ps. 26:5, *Calv. Opp.* 31: 266. See Herman Selderhuis, "Church on Stage: Calvin's Dynamic Ecclesiology," in Foxgrover, *Calvin and the Church*, 46–64, here 51–54.

72. *Inst.* 4, 1.13. Also see his treatment of Matt. 13:47 in the *Harmonia ex tribus Euangelistis composita*, *Calv. Opp.* 45: 376.

73. *Inst.* 4, 1.8.

74. See Calvin's explicit affirmation in *Reply to Sadoleto*: "We are assailed by two sects, which seem to differ most widely from each other. For what similitude is there in appearance between the Pope and the Anabaptists? And yet, that you may see that Satan never transforms himself so cunningly as not in some measure to betray himself, the principal weapon with which they both assail us is the same. For when they boast extravagantly of the Spirit, the tendency certainly is to sink and bury the Word of God, that they may make room for their own falsehoods." *Calv. Opp.* 5: 393.

75. *Traité de la Cene, Calv. Opp.* 5: 433–60; *OS* 1: 503–30.

76. *Traité de la Cene, Calv. Opp.* 5: 458–59; *OS* 1: 527–29.

77. In his irenical desire to bring together the opponents, he presented a proposal that is worth keeping before us: "Nous confessons doncq tous d' une bouche, que en recevant en Foy le Sacrement, selon l' ordonnance du Seigneur, nous sommes vrayment faictz participans de la propre substance du corps et du sang de Iesus Christ. Comment cela se faict, les uns le peuvent mieux desduire et plus clairement exposer que les autres. Tant y a que d' une part il nous fault, pour exclurre toutes phantasies charnelles, eslever les cueurs en hault au ciel, ne pensant pas que le Seigneur Iesus soit abaissé iusque la, de estre enclos soubz quelques elemens corruptibles. D' aultre part, pour ne point amoindrir l' efficace de ce sainct mystere, il nous fault penser que cela se faict par la vertu secrete et miraculeuse de Dieu, et que l' Esprit de Dieu est le lien de ceste participation, pour la quelle cause elle est appellée spirituelle." *Traité de la Cene, Calv. Opp.* 5: 460; *OS* 1: 529–30.

78. *WA* 54: 141–67.

79. *Calv. Opp.* 11: 772–75, no. 586. See Alasdair I. C. Heron, "'Wenn Luther uns mit unserem Bekenntnis annehmen will': Luther und die Abendmahlsfrage in den Briefen Calvins bis 1546," in *Frömmigkeit—Theologie—Frömmigkeitstheologie. Festschrift für Berndt Hamm zum 60. Geburtstag*, ed. Gudrun Litz, Heidrun Munzert, and Roland Liebenberg (Leiden: Brill, 2005), 395–409.

80. *HBBibl* 1: 161–69.

81. *Calv. Opp.* 12: 98–100, no. 657.

82. *Defensio sanae et orthodoxae doctrinae de sacramentis, Calv. Opp.* 9: 15–36. See Calvin's letter to Vermigli, November 27, 1554, *Calv. Opp.* 15: 322–23, no. 2053. Moreover, Calvin did not conceal his own admiration concerning the depth of Vermigli's comprehension of the scriptural and patristic foundations of the Reformed understanding of the Lord's Supper. In his *Dilucida Explicatio sanae doctrinae de vera participatione carnis et sangunis Christi in sacra coena* (1560) against Tilemann Heshusius, he declared without equivocation that nothing could be added to what Peter Martyr had already written. *Calv. Opp.* 9: 457–524, here 490.

83. Although it repeats some older inaccuracies about the *Consensus Tigurinus* (see Campi and Reich, *Consensus Tigurinus*, 287–89), see Ernst Bizer, *Studien zur Geschichte des Abendmahlsstreites im 16. Jahrhundert* (1940; repr. Darmstadt: Wissenschaftliche Buchgesellschaft, 1962), 275–99. See also Joseph N. Tylenda, "The Calvin-Westphal Exchange: The Genesis of Calvin's Treatises against Westphal," in *CTJ* 9 (1974): 182–209.

84. See Calvin's letter to the English-speaking congregation in Wesel on March 13, 1554, *Calv. Opp.* 15: 78–81, no. 1929. A good interpretation of this significant document is found in Wilhem H. Neuser, "Die Aufnahme der Flüchtlinge aus England in Wesel (1553) und ihre Ausweisung trotz der Vermittlung Calvins und Melanchthons," in *Weseler Konvent 1568–1968: Eine Jubiläumsschrift* (Düsseldorf: Presseverband der Evangelischen Kirche im Rheinland, 1968), 28–49.

85. John Calvin, *Secunda Defensio piae et orthodoxae*: "Whatever procedure is proposed towards a union, I am not only inclined to accept it, but I would follow it with joy.... [W]hat, then, do I say about myself? It is rather a case of considering the holy alliance with so many churches which this Westphal is seeking to destroy. Whatever he may babble to the contrary, we may be sure of one thing: that, out of the wretched scattering of the papacy, we have not been joined merely humanly in such a unison of faith. Everywhere we all can and do proclaim the same doctrines of the one God and the true and right way to serve Him, the depravity of human nature, salvation by grace, the way to attain righteousness, the ministry and operation of Christ, repentance and its results, faith founded on the promises of the Gospel which gives us the assurance of salvation, prayer to God, and all other principal points. We also call on the one God our Father, trusting in the same Mediator, the same Spirit of divine adoption is the pledge of our future inheritance, by the same sacrifice Christ has atoned for us all, our hearts all trust in the same righteousness gained for us by Him, we all glory in the same Head. It would therefore be astonishing if Christ whom we extol as our peace, who has made an end of all strife, and has disposed God in heaven to be gracious to us, did not cause us to have as well brotherly love also on earth. Is it not, then, our task to fight every day under the same banner against the tyranny of Antichrist, against the vile distortions of Christianity, and against godless superstition and the desecration of all that is holy? To set at naught such pledges of solidarity and such agreement, clearly brought about, as they have been, by God, and to provoke divisions amongst those who follow the same Captain in the field, is a dismemberment of those who belong to Christ, as heartless as it is godless."*Calv. Opp.* 9: 49–50.

86. John Calvin, *Ultima admonitio ad Ioachimum Westphalum, Calv. Opp.* 9: 250.

87. Lengthy quotations in English translation from the correspondence can be found in R. E. Pot, "*Calvin and Ecumenicity*," http://spindleworks.com/library/pot/calvin_ecumenicity.htm. See Timothy J . Wengert, "'We Will Feast Together in Heaven Forever': The Epistolary Friendship of John Calvin and Philip Melanchthon," in *Melanchthon in Europe: His Work and Influence beyond Wittenberg*, ed. Karin Maag (Grand Rapids: Baker Books, 1999), 19–44.

88. Provoked by *De praesentia corporis Christi in coena Domini contra sacramentarios* (1560), written by the strict Lutheran Tilemann Heshusius (1527–1588), Calvin wrote the treatise *Dilucida explication sanae doctrinae de vera participatione carnis et sangunis Christi in sacra coena* in 1561, *Calv. Opp.* 9: 457–524. On Heshusius, see David Steinmetz, "Calvin and his Lutheran Critics," in *Lutheran Quarterly* 4 (1990): 179–94. On Matthias Flacius, see Oliver K. Olson, *Matthias Flacius and the Survival of Luther's Reform* (Wiesbaden: Harrassowitz, 2002). See also the critical review by Martina Hartmann in *H-Soz-u-Kult*, July 17, 2002, http://hsozkult.geschichte.hu-berlin.de/rezensionen/FNZ-2002-006).

89. Benedict, *Christ's Churches Purely Reformed*, 202–29.

90. *Calv. Opp.* 18: 61–62.

91. It is simply impossible to cite the vast literature. The groundbreaking works are Robert M. Kingdon, *Geneva and the Coming of the Wars of Religion in France: 1555–1563* (Paris: Droz, 1956); and Kingdon, *Geneva and the Consolidation of the French Protestant Movement* (Geneva: Droz, 1967). For useful discussions and recent literature, see Philip Benedict, Silvana Seidel Menchi, and Alain Tallon, eds., *La Réforme en France et en Italie: Contacts, comparaisons et contrastes* (Rome: École française de Rome, 2007).

92. See Ian Hazlett, *The Reformation in Britain and Ireland. An Introduction* (London: T & T Clark, 2003), 113–68.

93. Andrew Pettegree, "Religion and Revolt," in *The Origins and Development of the Dutch Revolt*, ed. Graham Darby (London: Routledge, 2001), 67–83, here 82.

94. Diarmaid MacCulloch, *Thomas Cranmer: A Life* (New Haven: Yale University Press, 1996), 173.

95. Heinrich Bullinger, *De scripturae sanctae authoritate deque episcoporum institutione et functione*, ed. Emidio Campi (Zurich: Theologischer Verlag, 2009). See Carrie Euler, *Couriers of the Gospel: England and Zurich, 1531–1558* (Zurich: Theologischer Verlag, 2006), 61–62, 65.

96. See Beza's September 3, 1566, letter to Bullinger in *The Zurich Letters (Second Series), Comprising the Correspondence of Ceveral English Bishops and Others, with Some of the Helvetian Reformers, during the Early Part of the Reign of Queen Elizabeth* (Cambridge: University Press, 1842), 131: "For as to our Church, I would have you know that it is so hateful to the Queen [Elizabeth], that on this account she has never said a single word in acknowledgement of the gift of my *Annotations*. The reason of her dislike is twofold; one, because we are accounted too severe and precise, which is very displeasing to those who fear reproof; the other is, because formerly, though without our knowledge, during the lifetime of Queen Mary, two books were published here in the English language, one by Master Knox against the *Government of Women*, the other by Master Goodman on the *Rights of the Magistrate*."

97. See Judith Becker, *Gemeindeordnung und Kirchenzucht: Johannes a Lascos Kirchenordnung für London (1555) und die reformierte Konfessionsbildung* (Leiden: Brill, 2007). This well-researched dissertation gives a full picture of the theological developments in the stranger churches, including Calvin's role in them.

98. See Francis Higman, "Calvin's Work in Translation," in Pettegree, Duke, and Lewis, *Calvinism in Europe*, 82–99; Andrew Pettegree, "The Reception of Calvinism in Britain," in Andrew Pettegree, *The French Book and the European Book World* (Leiden: Brill 2007), 275–98.

99. *HBBibl* 1 : 383–85.

100. The literature in Western languages is extremely limited and fairly dated. See Willem Nijenhuis, *Calvinus oecumenicus: Calvijn en de eenheid der Kerk in het licht van zijn briefwis-seling* (The Hague: Nijhoff, 1958); Oscar Bartel, "Calvin und Polen," in *RHPhR* 45 (1965): 93–108; and Ernst Walter Zeeden, *Konfessionsbildung: Studien zur Reformation, Gegenre-formation und katholischen Reform* (Stuttgart: Klett-Cotta, 1985). This is a collection of

articles, which appeared between 1953 and 1980, with those on Calvinism appearing in the 1960s. See also n. 103.

101. See Michael G. Müller, "Protestant Confessionalisation in the Towns of Royal Prussia and the Practice of Religious Toleration in Poland-Lithuania," in *Tolerance and Intolerance in the European Reformation*, ed. Ole Peter Grell and Bob Scribner (Cambridge: Cambridge University Press, 2002), 262–81; and Jan Rohls, "A Lasco und die reformierte Bekenntnisbildung," in *Johannes a Lasco: (1499–1560): Polnischer Baron, Humanist und europäischer Reformator*, ed. Christoph Strohm (Tübingen: Mohr Siebeck, 2000), 101–24. For Calvin's correspondence with Poland, see de Greef, *The Writings of John Calvin*, 167–68, 201–3; for Vermigli's correspondence, see John P. Donnelly, "Christological Currents in Vermigli's Thought," in *Peter Martyr Vermigli and the European Reformations: Semper Reformanda*, ed. Frank A. James (Leiden: Brill, 2004), 177–96, esp. 186–96; for Bullinger's correspondence, see Erich Bryner, " 'Den rechten Glauben bewahren.' Bullingers Anliegen in seinen Briefen an polnischen Theologen 1556 bis 1561," in Schindler and Stickelberger, *Die Zürcher Reformation*, 415–24.

102. Diarmaid MacCulloch, "Heinrich Bullinger and the English-Speaking World," in *Heinrich Bullinger: Life, Thought, Influence*, ed. Emidio Campi and Peter Opitz (Zurich: Theologischer, 2007), 891–934, here 933. On the immense, yet often overlooked, influence of Vermigli in England, see MacCulloch, "Peter Martyr Vermigli and Thomas Cranmer," in *Peter Martyr Vermigli: Humanism, Republicanism, Reformation*, ed. Emidio Campi (Geneva: Droz, 2002), 173–201; and Torrance Kirby, *The Zurich Connection and Tudor Political Theology* (Leiden: Brill, 2007).

103. See Mark Taplin, *The Italian Reformers and the Zurich Church, c. 1540–1620* (Aldershot: Ashgate, 2003), 170–214; Andreas Mühling, "Calvin and Eastern Europe," in *The Calvin Handbook*, ed. Herman Selderhuis (Grand Rapids: Eerdmans, 2009), 97–104; and Erich Bryner, "Die religiöse Toleranz in Siebenbürgen und Polen-Litauen im Kontext der europäischen Kirchengeschichte," in *Bewegung und Beharrung: Aspekte des reformierten Protestantismus, 1520–1650: Festschrift für Emidio Campi*, ed. Christian Moser and Peter Opitz (Leiden: Brill, 2009), 361–81.

104. See Jan Andrea Bernhard's latest contribution: "Konrad Gessner und Ungarn: Kommunikations- und bibliotheksgeschichtliche Erkenntnisse," in Moser and Opitz, *Bewegung und Beharrung*, 159–91.

105. See Mühling, *Heinrich Bullinger europäische Kirchenpolitik*, 187–224; Mühling, "Heinrich Bullingers politische Beziehungen nach Frankreich"; and Fritz Büsser, *Heinrich Bullinger: Leben, Werk und Wirkung*, 2 vols. (Zurich: Theologischer, 2005), 2: 115–43, 185–207.

106. For a good, brief summary in English of the "confessionalization thesis," see Heinz Schilling, "Confessional Europe," in *Handbook of European History* 1400–1600, 2 vols., ed. Thomas A. Brady, Heiko A. Oberman, and James D. Tracy (Leiden: Brill, 1995), 2: 641–81.

107. The concept of confessionalization has been criticized and modified in recent research. See, for example, Heinrich Richard Schmidt, "Sozialdisziplinierung? Ein Plädoyer für das Ende des Etatismus in der Konfessionalisierungsforschung," in *Historische Zeitschrift* 265 (1997): 639–82; Thomas Kaufmann, *Dreissigjähriger Krieg und Westfälischer Friede: Kirchengeschichtliche Studien zur lutherischen Konfessionskultur* (Tübingen: Mohr Siebeck, 1998); Harm Klueting, "Die Reformierten im Deutschland des 16. und 17. Jahrhundert und die Konfessionalisierung-Debatte der deutschen Geschichtswissenschaft seit 1980," in *Profile des reformierten Protestantismus aus vier Jahrhunderten: Vorträge der Ersten Emder Tagung zur Geschichte des reformierten Protestantismus*, ed. Matthias Freudenberg (Wuppertal: Foedus, 1999), 17–47; and Marc R. Forster, *Catholic Revival in the Age of the Baroque: Religious Identity in Southwest Germany*, 1550–1750, (Cambridge: Cambridge University Press, 2001).

108. Richard A. Muller, *The Unaccommodated Calvin: Studies in the Foundation of a Theological Tradition* (New York: Oxford University, 2000), esp. 3–17; and Muller, *After Calvin : Studies in the Development of a Theological Tradition* (New York: Oxford University Press, 2003), esp. 25–102; See also Christoph Strohm, "Methodology in Discussion of 'Calvin and Calvinism,'" in *Calvinus Praeceptor Ecclesiae*, ed. Herman Selderhuis (Geneva: Droz, 2004), 65–105.

109. Mühling, *Heinrich Bullingers europäische Kirchenpolitik*; and Mühling, "Bullingers Bedeutung für die europäische Reformationsgeschichte," in *Evangelische Theologie* 64 (2004): 94–105.

110. See Matthieu Arnold and Berndt Hamm, *Martin Bucer zwischen Luther und Zwingli* (Tübingen: Mohr Siebeck, 2003).

111. See Anthony N. S. Lane, "Was Calvin a Crypto-Zwinglian?" in *Adaptations of Calvinism in Reformation Europe: Essays in Honour of Brian G. Armstrong*, ed. Mack P. Holt (Aldershot: Ashgate, 2007), 21–42.

112. Olaf Kuhr, *Die Macht des Bannes und der Busse: Kirchenzucht und Erneuerung der Kirche bei Johannes Oekolampad (1482–1531)* (Bern: Peter Lang, 1999).

113. The publication of Farel's work will no doubt shed light on Farel's status vis à vis Calvin and within the Reformed confession. See *Guillaume Farel: Traités messins*, ed. Reinhard Bodenmann and Françoise Briegel (Geneva: Droz, 2009).

114. See Bernhard Roussel, "Pierre Viret en France," in *BSHPF* 144 (1998): 803–39; Dominique-Antonio Troilo, *Pierre Viret et l'anabaptisme: Un Réformé face aux dissidents protestants* (Lausanne: Association Pierre Viret, 2007); and Michael W. Bruening, "Pierre Viret and Geneva," in *ARG* 99 (2008): 175–97.

115. Rudolf Dellsperger, Rudolf Freudenberger, and Wolfgang Weber, eds., *Wolfgang Musculus (1497–1563) und die oberdeutsche Reformation* (Berlin: Akademie, 1997); Reinhard Bodenmann, *Wolfgang Musculus (1497–1563): Destin d'un autodidacte lorrain au siècle des Réformes* (Geneva: Droz, 2000); and Reinhardt Henning, "Das Itinerar des Wolfgang Musculus (1536)," *ARG* 97 (2006): 28–82.

116. See Rohls, "A Lasco und die reformierte Bekenntnisbildung"; and Michael S. Springer, *Restoring Christ's Church: John a Lasco and the* Forma ac ratio (Aldershot: Ashgate, 2007).

117. See Kirby, *The Zurich Connection*; Luca Baschera, *Tugend und Rechtfertigung: Peter Martyr Vermiglis Kommentar zur Nikomachischen Ethik im Spannungsfeld von Philosophie und Theologie* (Zurich: Theologischer, 2008); Jason Zuidema, *Peter Martyr Vermigli (1499–1562) and the Outward Instruments of Divine Grace* (Göttingen: Vandenhoeck & Ruprecht, 2008); and Torrance Kirby, Emidio Campi, and Frank James III, eds., *A Companion to Peter Martyr Vermigli* (Leiden: Brill, 2009). See also the unpublished doctoral dissertation by Jordan J. Ballor, "Covenant, Causality and Law in the Theology of Wolfgang Musculus" (University of Zurich, 2011) which clarifies for the first time theological similarities and differences between Calvin, Bullinger, Vermigli and Musculus.

118. "[E]s ist…für die historische Theologie…angemessen…an das Leben vorzüglich wirksamer Einzelner anzuknüpfen;…die Elemente jeder historisch-theologischen Darstellung sind weit mehr biographisch, als historisch." Friedrich Daniel Ernst Schleiermacher, *Kurze Darstellung des theologischen Studiums* (Leipzig, 1910; Darmstadt: Wissenschaftliche Buchgesellschaft, 1993), 96, § 251.

7 Calvin, 1509–2009

HERMAN SELDERHUIS

Translated by Susanna Gebhardt

The overwhelming and unexpected attention that Calvin's five hundredth birthday received does not befit a figure who preferred to remain in the background. Calvin feared posthumous veneration, stating his desire to be buried in anonymity. In specifying that his grave be without a headstone, Calvin no doubt also protected it from desecration, although there is no reason to think that he considered this a possibility. In accordance with his wishes, he was buried in a plain wooden coffin in Plainpalais on Sunday, May 28, 1564, at two o'clock in the afternoon.[1] The exact location remains unidentified to this day.

Calvin did not invite undue attention, nor did he often speak of himself, saying: "I do not like to talk about myself."[2] When he did, it was expressed through his relationship with God: "Who I am, they know; in any case, they must know. I am a man for whom the law of our heavenly Lord goes so to heart that nobody may dissuade me from a conscientious application of this law."[3]

■ BIOGRAPHIES

The question raised by this quotation is whether we really know who Calvin was. There are relatively few biographies of Calvin, and most are largely derivative. In her recent book, Irena Backus has pointed to the fact that for centuries a few early accounts determined the image of Calvin, with little verification of their accuracy.[4] Both the predominantly positive and the predominantly negative views of the reformer emerged quite soon after his death and changed little over the centuries. A biography published in Geneva in 1564, the year of Calvin's death, by his successor Theodore Beza describes Calvin as a great reformer and religious hero. With some effort, Beza found a few negative comments to make regarding Calvin's character. The third edition of this work by Beza in 1575 inspired the publication of Jerome Bolsec's *Life of Calvin* (1577), in which he described his "life, manners, devilish cunning and his physical death, with which he left this world under blasphemy, cursing, vexation, and in extreme despair."[5] Bolsec's stated desire was to show the errors of the Calvinist sect in order to lead many back to the Catholic Church, so he naturally did all he could to portray Calvin as a heretic. This is why he paid much attention to the death of Calvin, given the then widely held belief that heretics could only die amid fear and trembling. Calvin's own behavior on his deathbed, thus, identified him as a heretic. But even in his life Calvin had shown his true colors. Bolsec accused him, among other things, of being a glutton, a heavy drinker, an adulterer, a fornicator, a convicted and branded homosexual, a miser, and a revolutionary; moreover, he was ambitious, arrogant, stubborn, vindictive, cruel, and relentless in hounding his enemies. Bolsec additionally presented a number of deviations from orthodoxy of which Calvin was guilty. Bolsec's work was widely disseminated in the sixteenth century, translated into Latin, German, Dutch, Polish, and French. His image of a merciless Calvin, the man without a heart, the relentless hunter of heretics who persecuted his enemies and imposed a joyless lifestyle upon his followers, prevailed for centuries.

Calvin's name nevertheless has become known worldwide, and Calvinism—even if Calvin protested against this designation—is a movement that has not only contributed to the origin of the modern world but has played a socially and ecclesiastically significant role on all continents down to the present day. Friend and foe alike noted Calvin's five hundredth birthday with books, exhibitions, recordings, concerts, performances, and lectures on all sorts of levels. This all leads to a question that goes beyond the person of Calvin: how could his theology simultaneously be so influential and so heavily criticized, then and now?

■ GENEVA AS A MAGNET

God and Calvin had the same working method. Both worked six days per week, with the only difference being that Calvin needed a couple of hours sleep a day.[6] According to Calvin, God was *non otiosus*. He never did, and could not do, nothing. God was constantly active, creating, selecting, caring, and, particularly since the Pentecost, recruiting new believers. Calvin did likewise. He could not live with the idea of a *deus otiosus*. The prospect of a God who calmly sat in heaven not troubling himself with the world would have made life unbearable for Calvin in the Europe of his day. He longed for stability and found peace in a restless God. He too was always busy. Although the Weber thesis in itself does not correspond to Calvin's theology, Calvin himself did instantiate it, as a *Calvinus non otiosus*. And yet, always in motion, he moved little, seldom leaving Geneva after his definitive return to the city in 1541. In July 1543 he revisited Strasbourg. In May 1545, he toured Bern, Basel, Constance, and Strasbourg to solicit support for the persecuted Waldensians. In September 1546, he visited Neuchâtel, and in January 1547, Zurich, where he returned in 1548 to consult Bullinger, a visit that resulted in the *Consensus Tigurinus*. There were additionally a few brief visits to other Swiss cantons and, in 1556, a trip to Frankfurt; but on average Calvin did not take to the road more than once a year. Yet if Calvin rarely budged from his residence after 1541, he was anything but inactive. Indeed, it would be as misleading to think of him as still or idle as it would be to consider that the image of the God of the Bible, especially the God of the Old Testament, is that of a hard and heartless God. Travel was unnecessary for Calvin because people came to him, and his ideas reached far and wide. That he did not leave his pulpit and desk in Geneva, while he was almost omnipresent in Europe, corresponds to God's work and being, as spoken of in the Bible, or in any case, as perceived by Calvin.

The people who came to Calvin and to Geneva were primarily refugees, particularly from France, but also from other countries. When Calvin arrived in 1536, Geneva had about ten thousand inhabitants. Four years later, this figure had already risen by 20 percent to twelve thousand. In 1560 it climbed to approximately twenty-one thousand.[7] Alongside the French refugees, other nonnative communities emerged with worship in their own language, especially groups of English, Spaniards, and Italians. Students and other visitors also arrived from places such as the Netherlands, Germany, Crete, Malta, and Tunis.

Initially, these groups were accepted by the population *nolens volens*, but the French refugees came to be regarded by many as a potential threat. This changed, however, in 1555 when the political tide turned for Calvin. The configuration of the Petit Conseil after the elections that year was such that the majority of its members supported Calvin. In these changed circumstances, the party that resisted Calvin's program and that had engineered rebellion, reformation, and the independence of Geneva from Savoy by placing it under the protection of Bern disappeared from the scene largely because of internal dissensions. Whereas the number of refugees who received citizenship had averaged less than seven per year from 1548 to 1554, those admitted to the ranks of the bourgeoisie rose to 127 in 1555, and to 144 in 1556.[8] These were almost invariably men who stood behind Calvin and his agenda and who, because of their qualities and intellectual formation, were soon to occupy important positions in the ecclesiastical, political, and social fields. Geneva became the forerunner of a phenomenon that really only emerged fully in nineteenth- and twentieth-century cities experiencing social and political transformation: immigrants began to determine the face of a city, their faith replacing that of the natives. The establishment of an outward-looking and integrated Geneva took place without any intervening phase of a French ghetto. This connects with Calvin's view that the face of the world of his time was changing.[9] His theology, which views our life on this earth as a temporary sojourn, with heaven as our ultimate fatherland, encouraged mobility and a pioneering spirit, not attachment to an earthly fatherland.[10] It also connects with his political insight that the old world had ended, that Europe was divided, and that this division ran not between east and west, north and south, but between Roman and Reformed. Nationality, region, and locality did not matter, only the elected course of the people who had gathered to live in the city. That city could be multicultural, but only if it was monoreligious.

Guillaume Farel was of the view that it was God who had brought people from all over Europe into this "refuge."[11] However, one can also say that they were attracted by the phenomenon of John Calvin. Furthermore, while Farel directed his gaze to the venerable Geneva, Calvin's gaze was directed fixedly outward. Improving the world started in Geneva—that was his plan. Others might then praise Geneva, creating what Alain Dufour has called the "myth of Geneva."[12] Calvin did not find it particularly praiseworthy, but wished to reform it so that he could reach out from it to the rest of the world. In short, Geneva acted as a magnet; Calvin wanted to make it a point of departure.

■ GENEVA AS BASE

If we resort to the traditional military figure of speech applied to Christian endeavor, Calvin sent his soldiers all over the world but remained at home as commander, barely leaving his command post. The Academy, founded in 1559, played an essential role.[13] This institution had an enormous attraction for foreign students, who came from France, the Netherlands, Scotland, Poland, Venice, and the Kingdom of Naples. These were people who, after seeing Calvinist practices implemented in Geneva, were meant to return to their homeland and take up important positions in church and politics.[14] Even before the foundation of the Academy, Geneva's Company of Pastors began sending men out in response to demands for ministers, especially to France. During the years from 1555 to 1562, one was sent to London, one to Antwerp, one to Turin, two to the short-lived French colony in Brazil, ten to Piedmont, and at least 220 to France.[15] Calvin could not meet the need for preachers:

> From all sides they would like to have preachers [from us] and one is aware how with the Papists one strives for benefices. The people want to lay siege to my front door, as if they, as is customary at court, would have to turn to me pleadingly, compete in piety amongst themselves and in such manner as they already had Christ's Kingdom in possession. With pleasure we would satisfy their wishes, but we have no space. For a long time, even the last man was taken from the workshop, anyone who was even marginally trained in literature and theology.[16]

Calvin sent his Christian soldiers into the world, bearing Christ on their banner and armed with God's word. These preachers were not carbon copies of Calvin; nevertheless, they proved to be the type of preacher for whom the pulpit was a battleship, from which the allied Father, Son, and Holy Spirit started their operation of liberation from enemy forces, firing effectively at everything that was, or seemed to be, hostile. Like the Old Testament prophets before them and like Calvin himself, these ministers had to be fearless in rebuking friends and foes. This was part of the mission that Calvin entrusted to them:

> That they may dare boldly to do all things by God's Word; may compel all worldly power, glory, wisdom, and exaltation to yield to and obey his majesty; supported by his power, may command all from highest even to the last; may build up Christ's household and cast down Satan's; may feed the sheep and drive away the wolves; may instruct and exhort the teachable; may accuse, rebuke, and subdue the rebellious and stubborn; may bind and loose; finally, if need be, may launch thunderbolts and lightnings; but do all things in God's Word.[17]

This type of preacher became an international phenomenon, as a central figure of the consistory, and as one who became, beyond the church, part of a trinity, in which the merchant and the civil magistrate were the two other partners.[18] It is not for nothing that Calvinist preachers in the Netherlands were called "dominee" (from *dominus*), instead of pastor or preacher. Calvin's ideas, however, were disseminated more widely than were the men whom he used for closely targeted missionary campaigns. It was much more a migration of ideas than of men that emanated from Calvin, although these ideas were not necessarily bound to his name. This is due to the fact that in Calvinistic thought, migration and transformation are inextricably linked, a point to which I shall return.

■ THE WORD AS SEED

Characteristic of Calvin's theology is his concentration on the Word and the proc-lamation and knowledge of it. His sermons are not doctrinal in character, but nonetheless they retain a doctrinal approach, if doctrine is understood to be teaching directed toward everyday life. The focus on the sermon was reinforced by the almost complete absence of the visual in Calvinism and the Calvinist church. One could only hear and read. It is of great importance for the study of Calvin that his sermons, unlike Luther's, do not raise the question of the relationship between the sinner and the grace of God. For Calvin, the question was not how might I find peace with God? But rather how does God work in this world, and how might I serve him? This means that a listener or a reader of Calvin's sermons occupies himself or herself less with his or her own inner life and more with the life of this world. Here I will not speak of contrast with Luther but rather of continuity bet-ween the two. After Luther had opened the door to heaven, Calvin opened the door to the world. This is not an escape from this world, but far more than that, for it is an active "innerworldly asceticism." It is a worldliness in which *meditatio futu-rae vitae* becomes practice. The sermons were an essential means of communica-tion in the effective development and dissemination of Calvin's ideas. He preached twice every Sunday and every day of the week every second week. That is an average of five sermons weekly. From 1549 onward his sermons were dutifully recorded by Denis Raguenier, whose notes in turn were written out more fully with the help of some employees.[19] Their publication was partially subsidized by the *Bourse française*, a diaconal fund for the support of poor refugees from France.[20] By his own count, Raguenier recorded no less than 2,042 sermons prior to his death in 1560 or 1561. His successors recorded an additional 262 sermons, so in total approximately 2,300 sermons were recorded.[21] Some of these manuscripts were sold as wastepaper through what Bernard Cottret has called "the criminal stupidity of librarians."[22] Not only the spoken but especially the printed sermons spread Calvin's message far beyond Geneva.[23]

Calvin thus set a movement in motion simply by staying at home to write and preach. He led a literary war against Rome and other false teachers for what he believed to be biblical reasons. His pen was his most effective weapon, and it is not surprising that a whole battalion of publishers assembled around him in Geneva, ensuring that between 1551 and 1564 some 500 book titles came forth from the city's presses, of which 160 editions were Calvin's own works. Of these, the majority were dispatched to France. Calvin knew how to gain entrepreneurs to finance and traders to transport and smuggle books into France and elsewhere. Like a general, he managed this publication machine, including the network through which his words reached the people. Among his bestsellers were the *Institutes* and the second *Catechism*. Genevan printers also produced a calendar in which former saints' days were replaced with biblical and historical events of the church.[24]

Perhaps no book was more important than the Psalter, an initiative of Calvin's in which the biblical Psalms were put to rhyme by Clement Marot and Theodore Beza. Following the numerous partial editions that grew ever more complete, the full Psalter was finally finished in 1562, and in a matter of months, no less than

27,400 copies were printed in Geneva. In all, seventeen Geneva, seven Paris, and three Lyon editions are known.

Calvin grasped the power of music and put it to positive use, understanding that a line of a psalm sung etched itself more deeply into the heart and mind than a passage read from the *Institutes*. In the psalmbook, music and language worked together. The Psalter made an important contribution to the self-awareness of Calvin's followers. Calvin laid out the psalms in such a way that his audience, consisting mostly of refugees, was momentarily transported to ancient Israel, where they could recognize the people of God that had migrated from the French-speaking Egypt, on their way to the Promised Land. The identification with the struggling and suffering people of God was strengthened by the fact that only the psalms were sung in church, then confirmed by the fate that met the Huguenots and the Dutch Beggars, so it is no surprise that the psalms were on the lips of Calvinists at the stake in France and the Dutch rebels during their long struggle for independence against the Spanish oppressors, whom they likened to the Philistines.[25] Catholic observers noted how powerfully people were drawn to the Reformed cause by psalm singing and sought to counter this influence with translations of their own.[26]

Calvin's letters too were weapons. He knew that they were, in a sense, public documents that would be read not only by the addressee but also circulated from hand to hand. He was an avid letter writer.[27] According to the latest estimates, he wrote two letters per week between 1530 and 1539, then, once his international prominence had increased, six letters a week for the rest of his life: in all more than eighty-five hundred. He received about the same number of letters.[28] Only a fraction of this massive correspondence has survived, but it is still ample: about thirty-four hundred documents. Most are in Latin, the remainder in French. These letters offer unique material. They reveal how Calvin proceeded as a reformer and strove to encourage the spread of Reformed Protestantism throughout Europe. Thinking strategically like a general, he directed his lawyerly skills of persuasion and his prophetic eloquence toward those who held key positions in church and state. When the former confessor to the Bona Sforza, the Italian wife of King Sigismund I of Poland, passed through Geneva in 1554–1555, Calvin made sure to obtain from him a list of prominent Poles likely to respond favorably to letters from him, then wrote to them. This was the beginning of a significant correspondence with Poland.[29]

Even more important in spreading his message were his publications. By around 1600, ninety editions of Calvin's works were published in England, including fifteen editions of his *Institutes*. The work was part of the standard reading of the theology students at Oxford and Cambridge.[30] His commentaries too sold like hotcakes.[31] In total, Calvin wrote commentaries to every New Testament book except the last two letters of John and the book of Revelation. He was to finish his commentaries on the New Testament 1555 but he began commenting on the Old Testament already in 1549 with his lectures on Isaiah. After 1557, all the works of Calvin were devoted to exegesis of the Old Testament. He published commentaries on the Pentateuch, Isaiah, Psalms, and Joshua. His supporters published his lectures (*praelectiones*) on the rest of the prophetic books of the Old Testament. He was regarded as one of the best exegetes of his time.[32] Apart from the content, his commentaries showed a mastery of expression, both in Latin and French. Thanks to his early education in both humanist letters and the law, he made complex theological matter readily understandable. For many, reading his works was a pleasant activity, even if some of his books were so big that they also inspired the publication of compendia.[33] But the question remains of why Calvin was translated so intensely and widely; and what motivated translators, publishers, and especially buyers. The transfer of ideas presupposes a certain attraction or particular interest on the part of the recipient. What made Calvin so attractive and significant? This question is important because of another feature of the reception of Calvin's thought, namely, that readers and users of his writings adapted the contents to their own uses and circumstances.

■ THE FATHER AND HIS CHILDREN

When Calvin was ridiculed because he had no children, (aside from a child who died immediately after birth and the two children of his dead wife Idelette from her first marriage), he responded by saying he had tens of thousands of children throughout the Christian church.[34] If one talks of Calvin's spiritual children, the point can be raised that, while some of the father may be recognized in the children, they nevertheless embarked on a path that was very much their own. In short, a clear "genetic" link between Calvin and Calvinism exists, but is this also the case regarding the content of his thought?

The spread of Calvinism in the sixteenth century was more than considerable. In 1554, there were about half a million Reformed Protestants. By 1600, there were already ten million. This expansion, which Philip Benedict in his overview calls "nothing short of remarkable" is all the more striking in that it occurred in the face of harsh persecution of Reformed Christians in France, Italy, Spain, and the Low Countries, as well as the political and military pressure to which they were exposed in the Holy Roman Empire.[35] Furthermore, direct contacts between Calvin and areas that became Calvinist were often very limited. Calvin had no direct contact with the Netherlands, only indirect ones: his wife came from the southern Netherlands, he wrote a work against Coornhert,[36] and he presumably was acquainted with the Dutch students studying in Geneva. That was the extent of his contact. In Germany, it was scarcely different, and the Reformed Church in the Palatinate did not even want to be known as Calvinist.[37] The *Institutes* was replaced as a textbook there by the *Loci Communes* of Peter Martyr Vermigli. In other countries, the reception was equally ambivalent, with the exception of France, and even there Huguenot theologians were not unequivocally faithful to Calvin.

Even in later theological developments, the direct connection to Calvin is not always evident and sometimes does not exist. A prime example is the Heidelberg Catechism. None of Calvin's catechisms achieved the status of a standard textbook for Reformed youth comparable to that of this work, written by Zacharias Ursinus, which shows traces of the thought of Melanchthon (of whom Ursinus was the pupil) and other Wittenberg influences. Further examples are given in chapter 9 in this book.[38] Direct appeal to Calvin was quite limited among later

Reformed theologians, and editions of his works, even in translation, became rarer over time.

Does this mean that the impact of Calvin, although broad and intense, was also short-lived, with his children and their descendants straying from their father's ways? To answer this question, two further questions must first be addressed. One: is there anything in Calvin's theology that argues for the necessity of keeping to the letter of it? Two: how did Calvin's theology become so influential in different forms and different parts of the world to this very day? This latter question concerns not only the content of his thought but also its form. It brings me to the second part of my essay.

■ THEOLOGY AS INTERPRETATION

To answer the first question, whether Calvin's followers *had* to remain faithful to his views, it is worth considering to what extent Calvin had his own theology. Did his relatively late rise to prominence as a theologian contribute to his theological force? He was a man of the second generation of reformers, meaning that he knew the writings of his predecessors, at least insofar as they were available in Latin or French (he was not well versed in German), that he could draw upon their views on key theological issues and could observe their reception. On issues like the Eucharistic controversy between Luther and Zwingli, the debate over the freedom of the will between Luther and Erasmus, and the controversies over baptism, the covenant, the value of the Old Testament, and the relationship between church and state that pitted the magisterial reformers against the Anabaptists, Calvin could incorporate the fruits of these discussions into his work and avoid many of the dead ends encountered by his precursors. Calvin also had no formal theological training. His *Institutes* was consequently free from the formal ballast and the reversion to scholastic methods typical of so much theological writing at the time. This was reinforced by the fact that, as a humanist, Calvin sought above all to stick close to the sources and to make his exposition as understandable as possible. His sources include reformers like Luther, Bucer, Zwingli, and Oecolampadius, the church fathers—Augustine features the most prominently—and the previous history of the church, including the councils. The most important source, however, was the Bible. In the successive editions of the *Institutes*, the fruit of Calvin's exegetical study of the scriptures may be seen more and more clearly. One could say that the *Institutes* grew with Calvin's broadening knowledge of the Bible.

■ DOCTRINE

Another part of the explanation for Calvin's abiding theological influence lies in his concept of doctrine, in which teachings and life are interconnected in such a way that his theology produces a *theologia practica* in the original sense of the term: a theology could be received outside the academy. The practical religious character of Calvin's doctrine has ensured its preservation in the church over the centuries, even at times when his works were not used as theological texts to train future ministers.

The term *doctrina* is found on almost every page of Calvin's work. A search for the term in his complete works in the *Corpus Reformatorum* yields ninety-five hundred hits. Yet this by no means demonstrates that Calvin was exceedingly doctrinal.[39] On the contrary, for Calvin the term *doctrina* extended to the sermon, confessions of faith, education, and the content of faith and creed. Calvin also connected pastoral care with doctrina. The imparting of doctrina by the pastorate, like the content of the gospel, served to comfort believers. Doctrina, therefore, was more for the heart than the intellect.[40] Doctrina had to be preached because only then was it beneficial. Hence its connection to the sermon; for Calvin, doctrina and *praedicatio* were almost synonymous.[41] Hence, too, its importance in the training of future preachers. As Calvin made known in the first edition of 1536, the *Institutes* were intended to provide a summary of everything necessary for the "teaching of beatitude."[42] The instructional nature of the concept of doctrina as outlined in the first edition of the *Institutes* is clearly related to his view of the scriptures as a school in which people are taught the knowledge of God.[43] He also spoke of the church as a school, alongside scripture. In both cases, the school existed not to expand intellectual knowledge, but to shape human behavior.[44] Doctrina taught a person how to serve God and where to seek peace for his or her conscience. This understanding of doctrina went back to the humanistic tradition of rhetorical *docere*; it was not targeted at noetic knowledge, but at the formation, education, and instruction of the people. Doctrina offered a mirror in which the image of God was perceived. When we look in the mirror, we see that we are formed in the image of God, regardless of how much we have fallen away from it as a result of original sin.[45] Because doctrina was given this meaning, the term became synonymous with Christian wisdom (*sapientia christiana*).[46] This underlines Calvin's practical focus. Doctrina and *applicatio* are inseparable for him.

■ TRANSFORMATION AND MIGRATION

Calvin spoke of the applicatio of doctrina in general, but the same basically applied to the applicatio of his own doctrine. This is essentially the answer to the second question, of how Calvin's theology in its different forms became so influential and decisive worldwide. Many historians and theologians insisted for some time that Calvin and Calvinism are not to be equated. The once influential thesis of "Calvin against the Calvinists" that argued that his doctrine of election was extensively misrepresented in the post-Reformation Calvinist tradition, with the Canons of Dort constituting an unfortunate high point of this misrepresentation, has now been convincingly relegated to the realm of fables.[47] Nevertheless, some genuine differences remain between Calvin and Calvinists. That Calvin's thought spread not only within churches we now unhesitatingly label as Reformed but also within Lutheran pietism, Methodism, Anglicanism, Baptist churches, and Puritanism has to do with the fact that Calvin's theology included elements that were, in the context of the early modern period, an interesting and attractive option, but which could also be transformed easily and were, therefore, suitable for migration. I will give two examples. First, the enormous impact that Calvin had in England. The number of Calvin editions appearing in the 1580s amid the maturation of the Church of

England under Elizabeth I far exceeded those of other theologians.[48] Comparative evidence is particularly telling. In the Netherlands, nineteen editions of books of Calvin were published in the sixteenth century; in Germany, thirty-two; and in England, ninety-one. Remarkable and typical of Calvin's theology is that it won a following among supporters and opponents of the Elizabethan Settlement.

This brings me to my second example. The French church at Wesel consulted Calvin in 1553, asking how its members should face an environment in which they were forced to adapt to the "Catholic-seeming" Lutheranism enforced by the town council. Calvin suggested that they might adapt quietly. One should not refuse to submit to a church because one did not want to adapt to a few liturgical customs.[49] In liturgical matters, Calvin was flexible, allowing for adjustment, an attitude inherent in his thinking. In a word, Calvin's theology does not require conformity, but allows for adaptation. I should like to demonstrate this briefly from just one or two examples.

■ JUSTIFICATION AND SANCTIFICATION

Prompted by criticism from both Rome and the Anabaptists, Calvin laid great emphasis on the fact that there was no *iustificatio* without *sancificatio*. He went so far as to treat sanctification before justification in the *Institutes*. In line with Calvin's conviction that a human being was on earth to serve God and neighbor, Calvin pleaded both for an active commitment to the fight against sin and for leading a sanctified life. His method of preaching law and gospel, with the law as guideline for living the gospel, his ministry, in the form of home visits and thorough cate-chesis, and his creation of the consistory to oversee church discipline are well known. Perhaps rather less well known is the fact that this combination of justifi-cation and sanctification, which Calvin built on the foundations laid by Luther, Melanchthon, and Erasmus, awoke considerable interest in Europe at a time when many magistrates sought to reform morals and restore Christian values and norms. Church discipline was perceived as a practical means of restoring Europe's morality with the secular goal of preserving social peace, which in turn could promote political and economic stability. But the link between justification and sanctifica-tion was also of interest to individuals. The seemingly modern way in which Calvin connected knowledge of God with self-knowledge, as shown by the opening words of the *Institutes*, was a new and attractive idea in his day.[50] The relationship between the two was intensified by the theology of the covenant, which viewed God and man as distinct parties joined by a contract that entailed mutual rights and obliga-tions. In this manner, the value of the individual as emphasized in humanism and the Renaissance was brought into harmony with divine primacy. With this cove-nant, the connection between justification and sanctification made Calvinist doc-trine even more of theologia practica.

■ CHURCH STRUCTURE

Active involvement of its members characterized the structure of Calvin's church. A member of the congregation did not just hear the word or receive the sacrament but was active in church work and in relaying the message of salvation. Calvin's doctrine of the triple ministry (pastors and teachers, deacons, and elders), which mirrored the threefold office of Christ as prophet, priest, and king, necessitated the inclusion of theologically untrained community members in church ministries, thus strengthening the lay element in the composition of the church.[51]

This principle of collegiality, which is a salient characteristic of the Presbyterian church model, operated not only for the individual believer but also for the synodal grouping of individual churches. This accounts for the conviction of individual Calvinist believers that they should actively participate in politics and the world of learning, and in general maintain a higher profile in society than Lutherans or Catholics. Combined with Calvin's notion of "vocation,"[52] namely, that disciples of Christ could be called anywhere at any time, the principle of collegiality ensured a wide geographical, as well as social and cultural, impact for Calvin's thought.

Also essential was the idea of a church that determined its own organization independently of civil authorities while still respecting the authorities' sovereignty in public matters. This made it a mobile church, and meant that Calvinist ideas on church organization could be easily transposed into different social, political, and indeed cultural contexts, from Groningen to Cape Town, New York to Seoul.

■ RELATIONSHIP BETWEEN CHURCH AND STATE

Calvin's emphasis on individual piety and sanctification, combined with an understanding of the church that allowed it to operate independently of the authorities, in varied political, social, and geographical circumstances, fostered a capacity for and an interest in adapting to changing social and political situations. Closely related here is the issue of the right of resistance to civil authority. Calvin was opposed to the people instigating an uprising. From the first edition onward, his *Institutes* stressed the importance of obeying the established authorities. The prefatory address to King Francis I, which, as Olivier Millet reminds us elsewhere in this volume, continued to appear in successive editions long after the king was dead, was directed to arguing that Christian truth was in no way seditious. To Edward Seymour, Duke of Somerset, he wrote that human beings, renewed in the image of Christ, must not rebel but show by their behavior that Christianity did not foment civil unrest. If one lived quietly and humbly, refusing to lewdly and unscrupulously silence the mockers, one would be rewarded by God for this obedience.[53] Yet after insisting strongly on the duty of obedience, Calvin opened a window to resistance in the *Institutes* by allowing that "if there are now any magistrates of the people appointed to restrain the willfulness of kings," they had a solemn obligation to do so should the king "violently fall upon and assault the lowly common folk."[54] Late in his life, as the growing French Reformed churches faced harsh persecution, he embraced constitutional arguments justifying resistance if those around an underage king did not grant the princes of the blood the authority due to them, and he supported the rising of 1562 led by Louis de Bourbon, prince of Condé, and Gaspard de Coligny.[55] His political thinking was thus capable of reassuring secular rulers that Reformed doctrine did not challenge their authority and of justifying resistance under specified conditions. It could appeal to both princes and people, and inspire both magisterial reformations and the resistance of churches that had initially established themselves in defiance of the magistrates.

■ UNDERSTANDING OF SCIENCE

Calvin's view of creation gave a significant impulse to the development of the natural sciences, which offers an explanation for the high percentage of Calvinists among the members of the Académie Française in the seventeenth century.[56] According to Calvin, science was a gift of God, created for the benefit of mankind.[57] The real source of natural knowledge was the Holy Spirit.[58] Whoever dealt with it acknowledged God, obeyed the call of God, and focused on God's creation. Thus, biology was also theology. This engendered a closer relationship between the spiritual and the natural realms for Calvin than for Luther or the Roman Church. Even Calvin's belief that sin had a devastating effect on nature and thought changed little, since God would not let his gifts be squandered.[59] It has been argued in the past that Calvin's rationalist theology makes him the father of the Enlightenment.[60] This is indeed an untenable assertion, but the cognitive impact of his thinking may have contributed to the attraction and spread of his ideas in a period undergoing major developments in the natural sciences.[61]

The adaptability of Calvin's thought accounts for its worldwide and long-lasting impact while making it clear why it could combine with other systems and other views of reality. Some of Calvin's conceptions of church and society functioned well in a church located in a small city-state like Geneva, but could not function efficiently in a modern nation-state without additional support from other religious, social, political, and cultural frameworks. This is at least part of the reason why it is preferable to speak of Reformed rather than Calvinist theology.

■ Notes

1. *Calv. Opp.* 21: 105–106.
2. "De me non libenter loquor," *Calv. Opp.* 5: 389.
3. *Calv. Opp.* 12: 338.
4. Irena Backus, *Life Writing in Reformation Europe*: Lives *of Reformers by Friends, Disciples and Foes* (Aldershot: Ashgate, 2008).
5. On the three versions of Beza's *Life of Calvin*, see Backus, *Life Writing*, 128–38. Citation from Bolsec in *Histoire de la vie, mœurs, actes, doctrine, constance et mort de Jean Calvin...Recueilly par M. Hierosme Hermes Bolsec* (Paris: G. Mallot, 1577; Lyon: Jean Patrasson, 1577), 140.
6. Herman Selderhuis, *Johannes Calvin—Mensch zwischen Zuversicht und Zweifel* (Gütersloh: Gütersloher, 2009), 193–94.
7. William G. Naphy, *Calvin and the Consolidation of the Genevan Reformation* (Manchester: Manchester University Press, 1994), 121–43.
8. Naphy, *Calvin*, 216.
9. Selderhuis, *Johannes Calvin*, 46–48.
10. *Calv. Opp.* 26: 291; and *Calv. Opp.* 31: 63.

11. *Calv. Opp.* 15: 153.

12. Alain Dufour, "Le mythe de Genève au temps de Calvin," in Alain Dufour, *Histoire politique et psychologie historique* (Geneva: Droz, 1966), 62–90.

13. Karin Maag, *Seminary or University? The Genevan Academy and Reformed Higher Education, 1560–1620* (Aldershot: Ashgate, 1995).

14. *Calv. Opp.* 19: 170.

15. The older counts of Robert M. Kingdon, *Geneva and the Coming of the Wars of Religion in France 1555–1563* (Geneva: Droz, 1956), appendixes 1–3, and E. W. Monter, *Calvin's Geneva* (New York: Wiley, 1967), 135, have now been supplemented by Peter Wilcox, "L' envoi des pasteurs aux Églises de France: Trois listes établies par Colladon (1561–1562)," *BSHPF* 139 (1993): 347–74.

16. *Calv. Opp.* 18: 467.

17. *Inst.* 4, 8. 9.

18. See Gerrit Groenhuis, *De predikanten: De sociale positie van de gereformeerde predikanten in de Republiek der Verenigde Nederlanden voor ± 1700* (Groningen: Wolters-Noordhoff, 1977).

19. Wim Moehn, "Predigten," in *Calvin Handbuch*, ed. Herman J. Selderhuis (Tübingen: Mohr Siebeck, 2008), 172–79; and see chap. 3 here, p. 70.

20. Moehn, "Predigten," 174.

21. Ibid., 174.

22. Bernard Cottret, *Calvin: Eine Biographie* (Stuttgart: Quell, 2005), 292.

23. See *BC* for an overview of editions and translations.

24. See Max Engammare, *L'ordre du temps : L'invention de la ponctualité au XVIe siècle* (Geneva: Droz, 2004).

25. Jan R. Luth, "Calvijn en de muziek," in *Calvijn en de Nederlanden*, ed. Karla Apperloo-Boersma and Herman Selderhuis (Apeldoorn: Instituut voor Reformatieonderzoek, 2009), 182–93.

26. Artus Desiré, *Hymnes en François* (Paris, 1561). See Andrew Pettegree, *Reformation and the Culture of Persuasion* (Cambridge: Cambridge University Press, 2005), 61.

27. C. Augustijn, C. Burger, and F. P. van Stam, "Calvin in the Light of the Early Letters," in *Calvinus praeceptor ecclesiae: Papers of the International Congress on Calvin Research*, ed. Herman Selderhuis (Geneva: Droz, 2004), 139–57; and Augustijn and van Stam, eds., *Ioannis Calvini epistolae*, vol. 1 (Geneva: Librairie Droz, 2005), 11–31.

28. See *Calv. Opp. R, series* 2, 6/1: 27.

29. W. Nijenhuis, *Calvinus Oecumenicus: Calvijnen de eenheid der Kerk in het licht van zijn Briefwisseling* (The Hague: Martinus Nijhoff, 1959), 23.

30. See N. G. Carson, "Calvin's *Institutes* and the English Reformation," in *John Calvin's Institutes: His Opus Magnum, Proceedings of the Second South African Congress for Calvin Research* (Potchefstroom: Institute for Reformational Studies, 1985), 441–66.

31. Donald K. McKim, ed., *Calvin and the Bible* (Oxford: Oxford University Press 2006).

32. David Steinmetz, "John Calvin as an Interpreter of the Bible," in McKim, *Calvin and the Bible*, 282–91, here 291.

33. See Irena Backus, "Loci communes oder 'Hauptsätze': Ein Medium der Europäischen Reformation bei Calvin, Vermigli und Bullinger," in *Calvinismus: Die Reformierten in Deutschland und Europa*, ed. Ansgar Reiss and Sabine Witt (Dresden: Sandstein, 2009), 97–103.

34. *Calv. Opp.* 7: 576.

35. Philip Benedict, *Christ's Churches Purely Reformed: A Social History of Calvinism* (New Haven: Yale University Press, 2002), 281.

36. *Réponse à un certain Holandois, Calv. Opp.* 9: 585–628.

37. Herman Selderhuis, "*Ille Phoenix*: Melanchthon und der Heidelberger Calvinismus 1583–1622," in *Melanchthon und der Calvinismus,* ed. Günter Frank and Herman Selderhuis (Stuttgart-Bad Cannstatt: Frommann-Holzboog, 2005), 45–60.

38. See chap. 9 in this book, pp. 182–201.

39. Bouwsma makes a mistake, for example, when he says that, based on the way that Calvin used the concepts of *evangelium* and doctrina, he understood belief "less as trust in God's promises than as intellectual assent to a body of propositions." William Bouwsma, *John Calvin: A Sixteenth-Century Portrait* (New York: Oxford University Press, 1989), 99.

40. Victor D' Assonville, *Der Begriff "doctrina" bei Johannes Calvin* (Münster: Litt, 2001), 126–28.

41. Reinhold Hedtke, *Erziehung durch die Kirche bei Calvin: Der Unterweisungs- und Erziehungsauftrag der Kirche und seine anthropologischen und theologischen Grundlagen* (Heidelberg: Quelle & Meijer, 1969), 42.

42. "Christianae Religionis Institutio totam fere pietatis summam et quidquid est in doctrina salutis cognitu necessarium complectens, omnibus pietatis studiosis lectu dignissimum opus ac recens editum." *Calv. Opp.* 1: 5.

43. "Est enim Scriptura schola Spiritus sancti, in qua ut nihil praetermissum est scitu et necessarium et utile, sic nihil docetur nisi quod scire conducat." *Inst.* 3, 21.3.

44. Also, the Reformed confessions described the church as teacher and educator: Benno Gassmann, *Ecclesia Reformata: Die Kirche in den reformierten Bekenntnisschriften* (Freiburg: Herder, 1968), 266–68.

45. *Calv. Opp.* 55: 395.

46. *Calv. Opp.* 52: 12.

47. See for an overview of the discussion Paul Helm, *Calvin and the Calvinists* (Edinburgh: Banner of Truth Trust, 1981); also, Richard A. Muller, *Post-Reformation Reformed Dogmatics: The Rise and Development of Reformed Orthodoxy,* ca. 1520 *to ca.* 1725, 4 vols. (Grand Rapids: Baker Academic, 2003).

48. Andrew Pettegree, *The French Book and the European Book World* (Leiden: Brill, 2007), 283–90.

49. *Calv. Opp.* 15: 78–81.

50. See for an analysis of the *Institutes* Richard A. Muller, *The Unaccommodated Calvin: Studies in the Foundation of a Theological Tradition* (New York: Oxford University Press, 2000).

51. Although manuals often speak of Calvin's four-fold ministry, the 1559 edition of the *Institutes* (4, 4.1) clearly divides the ministries into three categories.

52. Josef Bohatec, *Calvins Lehre von Staat und Kirche* (Breslau, 1937; reprint Aalen: Scientia, 1968), 636, 640, and 644.

53. *Calv. Opp.* 13: 65–77.

54. *Inst.* 4, 20.31.

55. W. Nijenhuis, "The Limits of Civil Disobedience in Calvin's Latest Known Sermons: The Development of His Ideas on the Right of Civil Resistance," in W. Nijenhuis, *Ecclesia Reformata: Studies in the Reformation,* vol. 2 (Leiden: Brill, 1994), 73–100; and Philip Benedict, "The Dynamics of Protestant Militancy: France, 1555–1563," in *Reformation, Revolt and Civil War in France and the Netherlands* 1555–1585, ed. Philip Benedict et al. (Amsterdam: Royal Netherlands Academy of Arts and Sciences, 1999), 39–40.

56. R. Hooykaas, *Religion and the Rise of Modern Science* (Edinburgh: Scottish Academic Press, 1972), 98–101.

57. *Calv. Opp.* 34: 304; and *Calv. Opp.* 31: 94.

58. *Calv. Opp.* 34: 577.

59. See Herman J. Selderhuis, *Calvin's Theology of the Psalms* (Grand Rapids: Baker Academic, 2007), 61–88.

60. See Michael D. Bush, "Calvinrezeption im 18. Jahrhundert," in Selderhuis, *Calvin Handbuch*, 474–80.

61. See Hooykaas, *Religion*, 98–160.

8 Calvinism as an Actor in the Early Modern State System around 1600

Struggle for Alliances, Patterns of Eschatological Interpretation, Symbolic Representation

HEINZ SCHILLING

Translated by Irena Backus and Susanna Gebhardt

■ HISTORIOGRAPHICAL INTRODUCTION—CALVINISM AND POLITICS

Social scientists and historians have traditionally noted the inclination of Calvin and Calvinism toward political thought and political action, referring to the influential work of Max Weber and Georg Jellinek.[1] In recent years, however, a revisionist debate has arisen among historians, theologians, and legal scholars who have significantly modified the theses of sociologists of religion about the political or social effects of early modern confessions. This also holds for the contrast set up in the nineteenth century (and only found in popular secondary literature nowadays) between a political, self-determined, and free-spirited Calvinism on the one hand and an apolitical, submissive, and servile Lutheranism on the other hand. Such associations are contradicted by the historical finding that the Protestant doctrine of resistance originated in 1550–1551 with the Lutheran Magdeburg's opposition to the Interim ("Magdeburger Herrgottskanzlei").[2] It is obvious that, far into the seventeenth century, "civic Calvinism" was equivalent to "civic Lutheranism."[3]

If there is still some truth to the earlier stereotypes, these cannot be traced back to the sixteenth and seventeenth centuries, less still back to Luther and Calvin and their theology. It is rather the result of developments of the nineteenth century. This differentiation of epochs is also fundamental for the posthumously published book of the Dutch church historian Heiko A. Oberman, *The Two Reformations: Luther and Calvin: The Old and the New World*, despite its flagrant tilt toward Calvin and Calvinism. When still an adolescent, Oberman, like his family and most of his Dutch compatriots, suffered German occupation and violence during the Second World War. His interpretation therefore is based on the contrast between the Reformed tradition of freedom in the Netherlands and the Lutheran tradition of authoritarian power in Germany. As a Luther specialist, however, Oberman hastens to explain that the sinister character of the political culture of

Germany stems not from the historic Luther and early modern Lutheranism, but from an ahistorical myth of Luther that the Protestant elite of the nineteenth and early twentieth centuries modeled after its own image and interests.[4]

In order to describe the origins of the confessional cultures and their political and social corollaries, it is therefore necessary to do some historical archeology to clear away historiographical and ideological-political layers of interpretation of the nineteenth and early twentieth centuries, in order to expose the situation as it obtained in the epoch of reformation and confessionalization. This has recently been demonstrated exemplarily by Christoph Strohm in his study of "Calvinism and the Law" (*Calvinismus und Recht*). Based on wide source material from writings of the late sixteenth century and early seventeenth century, his work proves that there was no fundamental difference in that period between the Reformed and Lutheran theologians' and lawyers' conception of law and politics.[5] Rather, due to the particular historical and legal circumstances under which the Calvinists had to assert themselves (exclusion from the Peace of Augsburg in the empire, persecution in Catholic Europe), their political profile was defined more sharply. It was a specific feature of the writings of the Calvinist lawyers, argues Strohm, that they linked the confessionalizing currents, typical of the age, with the period's otherwise discreet tendency to secularization. They did this in such a way that the latter "got the upper hand so that the predilection for reason-based systems of law and jurisprudence imposed itself." Thus jurisprudence was able to emerge "as a new leading science [instead of theology] at the [Reformed] universities with all the after-effects of the modernization process of Protestant territories as we know it."[6]

The considerations that follow here take up this revisionist approach, and examine, in a comparison of confessional perspectives, the foreign policy programs, expressed by images and actions, as well as the associated symbolic representations of European Calvinism. Central to this discussion are the four decades around 1600, marking the culmination of confessionalization, as is explained in more detail in my earlier investigations, recently brought together in my history of international relations from 1559 to 1660, *Konfessionalisierung und Staatsinteressen: Internationale Beziehungen, 1559–1660.*[7]

■ THE HISTORICAL CONTEXT

Just like domestic affairs, foreign relations of European states and powers came increasingly under the influence of religion or confessional questions during the sixteenth century. In fact, the emergence of an international system of individual states in early modern Europe was greatly influenced by the alliances of religious, ecclesiastical, and political structures and developments. Erasmus of Rotterdam already drew attention to this at the beginning of the sixteenth century, when he castigated the disintegration of the *christianitas*, observing in *Querela Pacis* that the armies of European rulers fought against each other with Christian symbols: *vexilla crucem habent* (their banners bear the cross); *pugnat crux cum cruce, Christus adversus Christum belligeratur* (the Cross is fighting with the cross, Christ leads the war against Christ).[8] By the end of the century, at the height of confessionalization, religious interests of the early modern confessional churches and political interests of early modern states converged so closely that it is appropriate to speak of a fundamental coexistence of religion and politics depending on particular configurations of circumstances.[9]

It is typical of this formation and transition from the medieval era to modern forms of public and private life[10] that both sides—that is, confessional churches as well as the developing states—were still embryonic. For this reason they underwent decisive processes of change and transformation in parallel with confessional and power conflicts. This resulted in a double movement of integration and exclusion within each state and church; pressure to integrate church and state increased while, on the international level, relations between different states and churches became more and more antagonistic and aggressive. Any analysis of this interaction must take into account that the states of the era were not states in the nineteenth-century sense but still largely unfinished early modern states. They therefore had to rely in many ways on the support of nongovernmental institutions and forces. In international politics, thus, governments and nonstate actors coexisted and, among the nonstate actors, ecclesiastical and religious institutions and individuals assumed great importance.

The specific politics of Calvinism was very much conditioned by the historical circumstances of its establishment in Europe, which is why the Calvinist understanding of political theory and practice is no less important than its theology. Calvinism spread in the form of what came to be called the late Reformation, and imposed its presence on the incipient confessional states, quite unlike the early Lutheran and Zwinglian Reformation in Germany and central Switzerland.[11] With a few exceptions, therefore, Calvinism could not politically conquer entire countries or territories. It had no choice but to establish itself in countries or cities where the Lutheran or Catholic confessionalization had progressed to a greater or lesser extent, and where the authorities sought to maintain the confessional status quo with all the political and legal means of control and repression. Furthermore, state formation had progressed so that the late Calvinist Reformation had to cope with pressures from hostile states to a far greater extent than the early Lutheran or Zwinglian Reformation. The pilgrimage (*peregrinatio*) and exile (*exul*) experience, that is the awareness that a Christian is a stranger in this world, that accompanied this brought in its wake a marked "theology of the refugees" (as Oberman called it[12]) and the corresponding conception of ecclesiology according to which each parish was a fully fledged church, capable of acting in any circumstances without seeking permission from a higher ecclesiastical authority. The same experience generated a profound awareness of the Calvinists as the people of God, which went together with an emphasis on predestination and with a readiness for religious and political resistance.

In political thought and action, both on a domestic and international level, the Calvinists inevitably developed a tendency toward activism, seeking to change the status quo. This was particularly evident in the empire, where, as already mentioned, they were legally excluded from the legal and political security granted by the Peace of Augsburg of 1555. The Calvinists also developed a pronounced internationalism. This was primarily an internationalism of intellectuals, many of them humanists, strengthened by the international nature of education. A network of Reformed universities and colleges emerged, including Heidelberg, Leiden, Geneva, and a number of smaller schools such as Franeker and Hardewijk.[13] These institutions not only offered the possibility of study for members of Calvinist minorities frequently excluded from academic training in their homelands but also created an international network of friendships and aroused sentiments that went beyond those of individual places or nations.

This internationalism of education blended seamlessly with the internationalism of political awareness and action. These were not theological but historical conditions that imbued Calvinism, in terms of domestic and foreign policy, with a confession-specific impulse to political activism. By contrast, Lutheran concepts of politics entailed primarily safeguarding and strengthening legal and territorial integrity. To protect the Reformation, Calvinism, unlike Lutheranism, did not rely on territorial or national alliances or on princes or kings acting in their capacity as *Notbischöfe* (emergency bishops). For the legally and politically deprived Reformed congregations, the priority was the organization of opposition and resistance to non-Reformed rulers through international alliances—first in Europe, and eventually in global contexts.

■ ACTORS, CONCEPTUAL MODELS, AND SYMBOLIC REPRESENTATIONS OF INTERNATIONAL CALVINISM

All this explains why Calvinism inclined toward political action and internationalism. As a response to their specific historical situation, Calvinist theologians and communities developed suitable machinery for self-assertion in a hostile environment. This went for not just their organizations and institutions but also for their intellectual and spiritual outlook. I shall consider these developments more closely for the decades around 1600, a time that was crucial for the emergence of the early modern European state and for the final determination of the European confessional map. Here I am not so much concerned with the events themselves as with the concepts and tools deployed by Calvinists. The following pages deal first with Calvinism as an actor in the international system of political alliances and religious unions; second, with the Calvinist pattern of interpretation of the international power system as an eschatological struggle between Christ and Antichrist; and third, with visualization and symbolic representations of the Calvinistic claims to religious truth and to political power. Finally, I shall say something about the special position of Calvinism in the developmental phase of early modern power systems and the *proprium* of Calvinist policies.

Calvinism as an Actor in the International System—Political Alliances and Religious Unions

Given that confessional loyalties or enmities were a factor in foreign policy in the late sixteenth century, ecclesiastical institutions and their confessionally engaged members served as actors in international affairs.[14] This action included clergy as well as laypeople. Church leaders, such as Luther and Melanchthon, Zwingli, or

Ignatius of Loyola already possessed political influence in the first half of the century, including on foreign policy matters.[15] With the confessionalization of states and the formation of confessional power blocs from midcentury onward, the influence of nonstate actors grew at the end of the sixteenth century, as their confessional networks enabled them to determine policy beyond the borders of individual states. Tridentine Catholicism and Calvinism, in particular, developed a strong internationalism,[16] which rested on formal and informal ecclesiastical actors and networks, including forces of resistance to the state. Around 1600, it was mainly this Catholic or Calvinist internationalism that impelled political confrontation on the international level. This was especially evident in the Dutch Republic, where the humanist, largely nonconfessional merchant elite sought peace and reconciliation, while the rigid Calvinists worked in alliance with the princes of Orange and their allies toward war, as did the militant Catholic *camarilla* at the Habsburg court in Spain.

The informal actors and networks and their specific functions positioned themselves differently in the Protestant sphere than in the hierarchically controlled Catholic institutional and clerical church, with its modern diplomats and government apparatuses. The consequences for the history of international relations, however, were quite similar. Thus, at Protestant courts there were no institutions comparable to the papal nuncio or the confessors of the Catholic princes. But the Protestant governments too remained influenced in their foreign policy decisions by the spiritual advice of their theologians. This is especially true for the theological faculties of state universities, and even more so for court chaplains such as Abraham Scultetus (1566–1625), particularly prominent in the Calvinist Palatinate, and Matthias Hoë von Hoënegg (1580–1645) in Lutheran Saxony.[17] Catholic and Protestant clergy alike served as intergovernmental mediators for their respective governments. Thus in the spring of 1590, an unnamed French Huguenot preacher worked with the English government to implement the political projects of Henry IV of France,[18] while the Spanish exiled pastor Cassiodoro de Reina was active across England as an informer and a spy.[19]

The theological heads of the learned Calvinist international community (in particular Calvin and his successor Theodore Beza in Geneva, but also the antistes of the Zurich church Heinrich Bullinger) conducted an extensive correspondence, which included the governments of virtually all Protestant Europe and was not confined to raising theological, pastoral, or internal problems, but was often mainly concerned with questions of alliances and other political relations across and beyond national borders. We know that Calvin regularly wrote letters to princes and politicians, hoping to consolidate or extend the scope and sphere of Calvinist influence as far afield as the Polish court, to give just one example.[20] In 1572, Beza massively intervened in the negotiations on the Polish royal election, in an attempt to prevent the victory of the Catholic Valois candidate.

Like other Protestant city-states, Geneva could not compete with the national and territorial states in training a professional staff of diplomats and other foreign policy experts. Yet having to maintain a wide network of international relations, the Company of Pastors became a sort of "Ministry of Foreign Affairs," with Calvin and later Beza at its head. Their foreign policy, however, did not always comply with the official policy of the Geneva city council, as shown among other things by the latter's sharp rebuke of Beza for going behind the backs of the magistrates and undertaking diplomatic mediations between French exiles and the French government.[21] A similar situation obtained in Calvinist Emden, where in the decades around 1600, the foreign policy of the city and that part of the provincial diet under its leadership was made by the strict Calvinist city preacher and chairman of the presbytery Menso Alting, together with a narrow circle of like-minded elders and councilors. What is more, theoretical propaganda that legitimized it was initially due to the rector of the Latin school and political theorist Ubbo Emmius, and later to the lawyer Johannes Althusius, both strong Calvinists.[22]

In narrow agreement with these theological leaders whom they visited again and again or whose counsel they sought by letter, such men as the French Huguenot and political theorist François Hotman or the Netherlands Calvinist Philip Marnix van St. Aldegonde developed a true shuttle diplomacy, partially on behalf of the state, partially on behalf of the church. As I shall show in the next part of this essay, they let themselves be led by the awareness of an international threat and a common destiny guiding all Protestants, and, with this in view, they carried out an indefatigable policy of alliances, religious as well as political. Already in the late 1560s, Van St. Aldegonde, the Calvinist mayor of Antwerp and a counselor to William of Orange, urged on Calvinist communities the importance of keeping up a regular network of correspondence *(Korrespondenzenwerk)* with William as the political leader in the struggle against Catholic Spain. It involved message exchange and reports on "what is going on for certain" *(wat daer sekerlijcx omgaet)*, or what the Calvinist churches could report of political relevance from their respective city or region.[23] In contrast with this demand, the 1571 Synod of Emden restricted official correspondence among the churches to ecclesiastical affairs because of the concerns of certain underground churches (such as in Cologne) that political matters in the correspondence could bring them into trouble with the Catholic city magistrate.[24] However, toward the end of the century, in the face of the general impression of an increasing Catholic threat, ecclesiastical correspondence began anew to touch on political matters, so as to coordinate actions of the Calvinist churches with those of the Calvinist states.[25] Thus, the ecclesiastical prestate *Korrespondenzenwerk* or communication network of the Calvinist congregations expanded into a system of intergovernmental alliances. The ecclesiastical internationalism had served, as it were, as a springboard for the political alliance of Calvinist rulers and states. A result of the combined efforts of the correspondence of Calvinist refugee churches and attempts at political alliance by Calvinist princes and powers, the Protestant Union established in the empire in 1608 that played such an important role in the outbreak of the Thirty Years' War had a long history behind it.

The actual alliance politics lay in the hands of politicians. Along with the aforementioned Marnix or Hotman, other examples include Sir Philip Sidney in the 1570s as envoy for Elizabeth I of England and Pieter Cornelisz. Brederode as a special envoy of the Dutch States General at the end of the century. Because such political alliances had to overcome differences of dogma within the Protestant camp between Lutherans and the Reformed, theologians necessarily came to play an important role in the practical implementation of the foreign policy plans of politicians. Thus Philipp Melanchthon had already been questioned in 1559 about the chances of a dogmatic and ecclesiastical political accord between the Protestant churches in Germany, Switzerland, England, France, Poland, and Hungary, which seemed essential if the princes' plans for political alliance were to come to fruition.[26] After the first international convention of Protestant powers, held on English instigation in September 1569 in Erfurt, had failed because of the incompatibility of the Lutheran and Reformed positions, consultations, conventions, or synods on the doctrinal questions that divided Reformed and Lutheran theologians in the countries concerned took place as a rule in parallel with the negotiations of political alliances because *foedera Principum* (treaties of the princes) could not hold without corresponding *synodi Theologorum* (synods of theologians).[27]

Significantly, it was not the Lutheran but the Calvinist powers that repeatedly pushed for new union attempts—at times even with regard to the Antitrinitarians, whose possible inclusion was extremely attractive for England and the Netherlands; were it to prove feasible, the desired Protestant alliance would extend southeast to Hungary and Transylvania, thereby weakening the Counter-Reformation axis between the Habsburgs and Poland.[28] However, the Lutherans and the Reformed Protestants could achieve no consensus. Opinions differed even within the Reformed camp: whereas the Genevan theologians were, in principle, in favor of collaborating with the politicians, the Bernese and the chief theologians of Zurich were against it, because they feared that the confessional question might be used as a political tool.[29]

Beside the chancelleries of the Calvinist magistrates and states, international Calvinism possessed an institutional and organizational framework in the Presbyterian synodal network of Calvinist churches, inferior in no respect to that of the (universal) Catholic Church. Calvinist preachers, of whom quite a few (due to their exile experience) had firsthand knowledge of several European countries, thought and operated across borders. Deacons and presbyters, who were often businessmen presiding over internationally operated commercial or industrial enterprises, took advantage of their business and commercial contacts for the cause of Calvinism. The extensive correspondence and the consistory protocols of the large religious communities in coastal cities like London, Amsterdam, and Emden in the west and Gdansk (Danzig) in the east provide evidence of an exchange of information extending over the whole of Europe. Especially active was the diaspora of religious refugees, thus the Dutch, Walloon, and French but also the Italian Calvinists, which stretched from Britain via the Netherlands and Germany to Scandinavia and the Baltic across the continent. The network of these foreign churches became a base for expansive international activities, intellectual, social and institutional, as well as for the religious shaping of Calvinism. In the foreground stood of course theological and ecclesiastico-political questions, such as the unity of doctrine, which was the object of an active shuttle diplomacy between Emden and London in the 1560s. In addition to this interchurch internationalism, the internationalism of the stranger churches also had a political dimension. Occasionally there was even direct contact with the international activities of states and governments. This is exemplified by the cooperation of the refugee diaspora with William of Orange. William tried to use the refugee churches logistically to serve as an international communication network and to finance warfare—in the same way as Elizabeth of England was to do a little later. William thus employed the leaders of London's refugee church, laypeople as well as theologians, for diplomatic activities at the English court and in other Protestant states, occasionally also for contacts with the Protestant opposition in Catholic countries.

Just as the Counter-Reformation relied on the more recently founded religious orders, especially the Jesuits and their lay organizations among Catholics, so the Protestants relied on their religious exiles, pastors and laypeople, to act against their religious and political opponents with the radicalism and zeal typical of refugees. They were ready to use any means when it came to releasing their native country from the hands of their political and religious enemy, as in the case of Calvinist exiles from the Spanish Netherlands or the Bohemian Protestants later. Where the official representatives of the opposing states still put emphasis on the preservation of peace and hence on negotiations, the leading representatives of the informal exile networks refused, in a practically fundamentalist way, all concessions and headed straight for the military decision.[30]

Calvinist Patterns of Interpretation of the International Power System—An Eschatological Struggle between Christ and the Antichrist

Confessional motives played as important a part in the decisions made by the courts and chancelleries as they did in legitimating political action, including propaganda, and in providing interpretation patterns for intergovernmental alliances and conflicts. Given that the concept of politics included religion in the early modern period, religious and secular matters were closely linked verbally. Confessional rhetoric, semantics, and symbols marked political language already in the late 1560s. This phenomenon increased by leaps and bounds at the height of confessionalization and was to shape for at least a generation the discourse of politicians and diplomats, as well as political thinking, propaganda, preaching, and public speaking. This is particularly true of Calvinism, which, from the late sixteenth century onward, suffered from sudden swings between religious and political successes and abrupt setbacks due to the repeated assaults of the Counter-Reformation, initially concentrated on Western Europe. Following on the early successes of the Calvinists in the Netherlands and in the empire in the late 1560s, they experienced from 1572 onward the "syndrome of threat" (*Bedrohungssyndrom*), starting with the St. Bartholomew's Massacre in Paris[31] and amplified by the Spanish Fury in Naarden in December 1573 and Antwerp in November 1576, which was accompanied by iconography and creation of myths very similar to those used in the context of the St. Bartholomew's Massacre[32] and later by the Armada of 1588.[33] Geneva was at the very center of this "syndrome of threat," which here reached its peak with the "Escalade" of December 1602, when the city was saved at the last minute from the invading troops of Savoy.

In the 1590s, international Calvinism had several reasons for a renewal of optimism. In the empire, this was because of the so-called Second Reformation, when some Lutheran territories, including the ancestral homeland of the Saxon Lutherans, went over to the Reformed religion. In Western Europe the reasons were the accession of Henry IV to the throne of France, and especially the famous "Ten Years" (*Tien jaren*),[34] during which the Dutch troops in the northwest (Dollart region) and in Brabant went from military success to military success against the Spanish army.

This period of hope came to an abrupt halt as bitter setbacks occurred with the early death of Christian I, elector of Saxony, the assassination of the French king, and the Spanish counteroffensive. "We imagined ourselves," noted the Palatine chaplain and later dean at Calvinist Emden, Abraham Scultetus, looking back on this phase, that "the golden age [*aureum saeculum*] ... had dawned. But we were very foolish, for within a year... our golden hopes all went up in smoke."[35] The twelve-year truce, signed by the Netherlands with Spain in 1609, was not sufficient to placate feelings of external threat and the resulting individual and collective fears.

The repressive measures and acts of violence of the political and confessional adversaries of the Calvinist, in particular the Counter-Reformation states, but also some Lutheran ones such as Saxony after the death of Elector Christian, created a heightened awareness of political and cultural dangers for early modern Calvinism, with particular determination and rigid will for self-assertion as corollary. This resulted in tension perceptible until this day between "the siege mentality" and triumphalism, as well as a fundamental rejection of Rome, which surpassed even Luther's rejection of the papacy, not on theological grounds but because of the accentuation of political confrontation. In this specific confessional and political situation, at the peak of international political and military as well as confessional crisis, Calvinism developed three dynamic behavior and interpretation patterns that had a lasting influence on the political power projects and actions of the Calvinist power bloc of that time. First, it developed a distinctive internationalism, which emanated from a clear knowledge of the pan-European interdependence of the religious and cultural, military and political conflicts. Second, it inserted the political events and situations into an apocalyptic worldview, which understood the history of politics and power politics as part of the history of salvation. The world events were interpreted alongside the history of salvation, assigned to two antagonistic blocs. They viewed these events as the end-time struggle between Christ and the Antichrist, represented respectively by the Protestant, especially Calvinist, countries and by Spain, the pope, and their Counter-Reformation allies. Especially in the case of the Dutch and English Calvinists, the interpretation of historical events and the legitimation of their own determined political and military action through the history of salvation was strengthened by their viewing their own nations as God's chosen people. They therefore assigned to themselves a particular role in the protection and defense of the divine salvation plan, against the legions of the armies of the Antichrist. Third, it was Calvinism, with its underlying eschatological convictions, that was most energetic in exercising the right (believed in by all confessions) to intervene in confessional matters, especially in France and the Netherlands.

The political and military struggles between the antagonistic confessional blocs became battles for the right, biblical order of both church and state, going beyond confessional differences. There could be no truce in this struggle between the children of light and children of darkness. Even the most insignificant diplomats and correspondents worked on the principle that "the enemy must always be expected to do his worst" and that "the government is to be disturbed by alarming news"—a principle put into practice notably by Wolfgang Zündelin, the Calvinist observer of the Italian states for Hesse and Saxony.[36] And because the conflict was understood as an expression of the biblical end-time, its outcome had to be decided without delay—after preparation by diplomacy, whose task, the Dutch ambassador Pieter van Brederode noted, was "to unify Christians against the Antichrist, so as to protect them from further betrayal and deception by him and his followers."[37] The scene of this struggle was mainly Europe. However, the strict Calvinist circles, which were represented particularly strongly in the West India Company founded with a view to Central and South American trade, were already looking further afield. The Spanish Antichrist was to be combated overseas; lands and commercial rights were to be snatched from the Spanish, their plans for world domination thwarted, and their resources for a campaign in Europe eliminated.

This apocalyptic encouraged without doubt the international thinking of the Calvinists, but also their actual alliance politics around an axis connecting the Netherlands, the Wetterau counties of the empire, the Palatinate, Bohemia, and the Protestant estates in Austria and Hungary-Transylvania. It found an echo too in the Orthodox Christianity of southeastern Europe, where the patriarch of Constantinople, Kyrillos Lukaris, took up this Calvinist pattern of interpretation and celebrated the success of the Dutch forces in Wesel and Hertogenbosch in 1629 as a sign of God's direct intervention in favor of his cause represented by the Calvinists. He even forged plans for a political and religious bridge between Greek Orthodoxy and western European Calvinism. His confession of Calvinist faith printed in Geneva and translated at once into several western and central European languages sparked immediate debate in the West. None other than Father Joseph, Cardinal Richelieu's confidant, undertook the refutation of Lukaris's confession.[38] The fact that such a remote threat was taken to be a politically realistic danger reflects the confessional internationalism of the epoch, as does the reaction of France, where the Catholic government saw it as a threat to recently won consolidation of domestic and foreign policy.

The eschatological activism described here apparently had no effect on certain regions of the Reformed world. The Reformed cantons of Switzerland adopted neutrality early on. In England, the Calvinist apocalyptic was no less strongly pronounced than on the continent, but only the Puritan section of the English nation took it over as a political plan of action. Although King James I embraced predestination and supported the strict Calvinist Anti-Remonstrants within the church, he tried hard to avoid a confessionalization of English foreign affairs and swung over to the Protestant alliance front only under domestic pressure from the Puritans, and then only reluctantly and temporarily.[39]

Visualization and Symbolic Representations of the Calvinist Claims to Truth and Power

Intimately linked to the conflict and warmongering semantics of the opposing confessional and political blocs was the symbolic representation of their respective claims to truth and power. The visual and symbolic apparatus produced in this context with all its texts, images, rituals, ceremonies, and gestures was not just a series of illustrations but a fully fledged historical actor that decisively influenced the emotional climate as well as the dynamic of the confrontations.[40] Within each society, images functioned so as to promote social and cultural integration. On the international level, they acted so as to validate and confirm hostility and so provided one of the triggers for the great religious and political wars of the late sixteenth and the early seventeenth century.

The power exercised by images and verbal representations around 1600 was the natural outcome of two separate but closely interrelated contexts. First, this power was founded on the tradition depicting Christian religion via symbolic texts and rituals that were formalized and sharpened during the confessional age to become Protestant antidotes to the Catholic *fidei symbola* (symbolizations of faith). The visual and ritual manifestations of the confessional religious symbols or confessions of faith were not only an external symbolization of the claim to truth and power of the respective denomination over villages, towns, territories, or states; they produced this confessional truth and its claim to sovereignty, transmitting and implanting it into the identity of the individual and of society in general. Second, the particular power of images and symbols in the sixteenth and seventeenth centuries was the consequence of the still fragile and exposed political and legal relationships within and between the early modern states. In debates over a European state system and in view of competition between states, not yet subject to the rules of a generally accepted international law, Thomas Hobbes a generation later noted clairvoyantly that "reputation of power is power."[41]

Nothing could better create and secure the "reputation of power" than its symbolic representation by rites and visualizations including the given confessional basis of the given state. In the religious and political wars of the confessional age the representational capacity of religion was amalgamated with that of politics and states. Confessionally oriented religious *representation of the sacred* and early modern political *representation of secular power* flowed together into a massive, violent potential of verbal, visual, ritual, and ceremonial activation of people in two directions—the inward integration and the outward separatism and exclusion which verged on the militant.

The confessional age formed the climax of this interpenetration of religious and political armament within the Christian world resulting, as Erasmus noted already in the early sixteenth century, in a situation in which conflicts between Christian states were fought by opposing armies that relied on Christian symbols, whose imagery already partly belonged to the baroque.[42] Tridentine Catholicism and Lutheranism particularly used not only the church but also the external, to represent their power and their claim via powerful pictures and symbols. I remind you of the great flood of representations of Mary on the Catholic side: the Lepanto-Madonna as *Mary victrix* (Mary of Victory), the battle cry *Santa Maria* at the Battle of White Mountain, and especially the transference of entire countries and dominions to the celestial Virgin by Maximilian of Bavaria, Emperor Ferdinand III, the dukes of Savoy, and even the Republic of Genoa.[43] Let us also recall the predominantly Old Testament–based representations of Lutheran power

Vener. P. Dominicus à IESU Maria Carmel. Difcale.

Was macht ihr Soldaten mit eürem Gefchrey? Macht ſ'fchanden ein einiger himlifcher Man,
Mit hauen, mit Stechen, und Schieffen darbey? Der Chrifti und Mariæ tragt d' Bildnüs vor
All eüren Gewalt, all eüer Getöß, Wo dife Zwey wider Eüch ſtritten und Kriegen,
Als was ihr anSöttlet und trohet uns Böß: Wird Eüch all eüer ünderfangen betrügen.

Abb. 9: Dominicus a Jesu Maria und Herzog Maximilian reiten in die Schlacht.
(Bildnachweis und Bildbeschreibung Anm. 136)

Figure 8.1 Image of Mary at the Battle of the White Mountain. (From Klaus Shreiner, "Maria Victrix" in *Kloster-Stadt-Region: Festschrift für Heinrich Rüthing*, ed. Johannes Altenberend [Bielefeld: Historisches Verein, 2002], 134. By permission of Bayerische Staatsbibliothek, Munich.)

Abb. 6: Siegbringende Wirkungen des geschändeten und von Dominicus a Jesu Maria gefundenen Marienbildes (Bildnachweis Anm. 112)

Figure 8.2 Image of Mary at the Battle of the White Mountain. (From Klaus Schreiner, "Maria Victrix," 123. By permission of Bayerische Staatsbibliothek, Munich.)

representation, especially by the Swedish king Gustav Adolf, who during his intervention in the German religious war ostentatiously assumed the pose of heroes of the Old Testament, such as David or Judas Macchabaeus, divine avenger and savior of the persecuted. His landing on the beach of the isle Usedom was announced to the public in paintings, prints, and pamphlets, with the king kneeling on the beach "with folded hands and his eyes turned to the sky in prayer," as the accompanying text informs us.[44]

Figure 8.3 Emblem of the stranger churches representing a ship
in rough seas. (By permission of Johannes a Lasco Bibliothek,
Emden.)

Iconophobic Calvinism might seem at first glance not up to this visual culture.
And yet, upon closer inspection, symbolic representations can be found within it
too that make it appear no less emotional and dynamic than Lutheranism or Roman
Catholicism with their image worlds. First of all iconoclasm itself can be understood as a form of symbolic action. In the Netherlands and in German territories of
the Second Reformation such as the Rhine Palatinate, Hesse, or Brandenburg, it
trumpeted the onset of Calvinist religious and ecclesiastical renewal. More importantly yet, it represented a claim to power on the international level. Immediately
·after the coronation of Frederick V of the Palatinate as king of Bohemia, his
theological advisor, Abraham Scultetus, ordered a purge of Catholic items of
worship from Prague's St. Vitus Cathedral, from December 21 to 28, 1619, in a
symbolic representation of the triumph of Calvinism and its hold on Bohemia.[45]
The religious adversary immediately seized on this to open up the floodgates of
countersymbolism against the Calvinist heresy as witnessed by the Catholic images
produced after the event. Thus at the crucial moment of the Battle of White
Mountain, when the Protestants threatened to gain the upper hand, the charismatic
Spanish Carmelite monk Dominic Jesus Maria rode valiantly in the line of battle,
leading the Catholic troops with an image of Mary. As figures 8.1 and 8.2 show, the
image that he carried was one that the Calvinists had just desecrated by digging out
Mary's eyes, leaving her unable to see.

Calvinist symbolic actions or representations were not so much characterized
by such triumphalist gestures—which, as in Bohemia, mostly failed—as they were

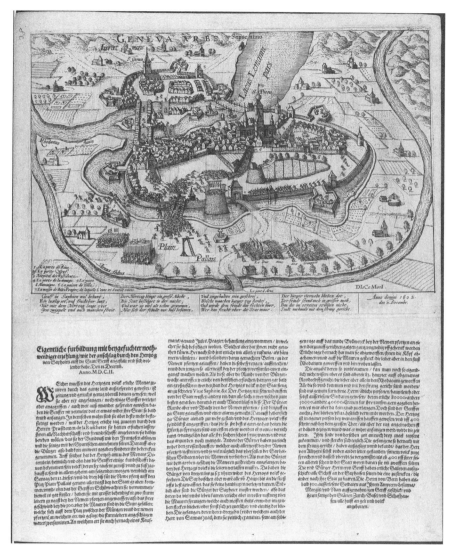

Figure 8.4 Invasion of Geneva by the Savoyard troops, December 1602. (By permission of the Herzog-August-Bibliothek, Wolfenbüttel.)

by images of threats, of being marooned, or of rescue from utmost distress. Figure 8.3, the emblem of the stranger churches representing the ship of the godly amid rough seas and storms, illustrates this well.

Calvinist images are representations of the political dangers and the uncertainty of earthly existence, but also of the unshakable conviction that the knowledge of the threat and the world's depravity compounds the certainty that the Calvinists are God's children. In the midst of political upheaval, rejection, and

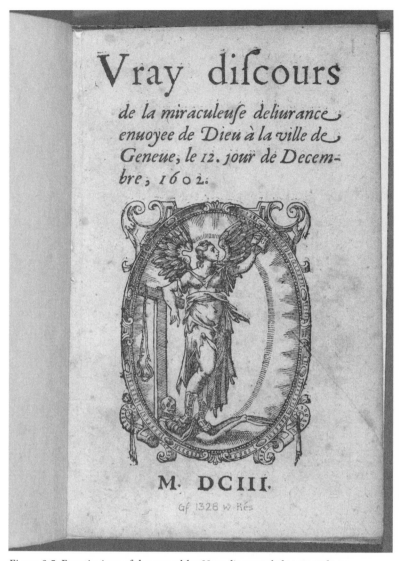

Figure 8.5 Frontispiece of the pamphlet *Vray discours de la miraculeuse deliverance enouyee de Dieu à la ville de Geneve, le 12. jour de Decembre,* 1602. (By permission of the Bibliothèque universitaire de Genève.)

even deadly persecution, the Calvinists know that they are in the hands of God and therefore untouchable—expressed for example by the seal of John à Lasco—a tiny boat steers from a storm into a harbor, while the inscription reads *in portu navigo*: "I navigate in the confines of the port" (that is, in the security of God and the eternal home).

The motif of "strength through weakness," "growth through humiliation," and "triumph through suffering" is especially clear in the context of the Geneva Escalade, the traumatic raid on the night of December 12, 1602, in which the Catholic Savoyard troops managed to scale the walls and penetrate into the Calvinist city-state, only to be repulsed by the rapidly assembled civic militia (fig. 8.4).[46]

The news of this victory was announced in a Genevan pamphlet entitled *True Account of the Miraculous Delivery Granted by God to Geneva the Twelfth Day of December 1602*. Its frontispiece is a meager, crude woodcut showing an angel and the cross triumphing over death (fig. 8.5).[47]

The key message retained was that "God wished to make us henceforth yet more vigilant and to compel us to confess that our preservation and rescue depend on him alone."[48] The pamphlet contrasts the flamboyant representation of saints in the Catholic ritual with the straightforward Calvinist worship of the one true God by picking up on the Savoyard watchword *Our Lady*: "the Savoyard calls on OUR LADY as his watchword. The Genevan soldier calls with fervent desire for the Lord.... All strength comes from the Lord and not from our Lady, as is only right and just."[49]

■ CONCLUSION—CALVINISM AND INTERNATIONAL POLITICS IN 1600

In summing up my arguments the following general conclusions are called for:

First. My examination of the struggles between secular power blocs and confessions around 1600 has shown that it is legitimate to speak of a specific affinity of Calvinism for internationalism and political actions during the political and ideological conflicts that formed the crucible of modern Europe, and especially of the order and organization of the first international state system.

Second. This affinity of Calvinism and political activism was not primarily theologically conditioned. The urge to act in the political sphere arose from the unfavorable historical conditions of the propagation of Calvinism as a late-comer among the early modern confessional churches. Its situation was politically unfavorable because the internal formation of European societies had progressed beyond what it had been at the time of the Lutheran or Zwinglian Reformations in the first half of the century, and it was also ecclesiastically and religiously unfavorable as it coincided with the time in which Tridentine Reform Catholicism had gained strength again and gone on the offensive. In this situation, careful maneuvering and securing of legal positions was not appropriate, as was the case for the Lutherans after they were legally recognized by the Peace of Augsburg. Calvinist politicians and churchmen had to bet on offensive and aggressive political activity aimed at changing the status quo.

Third. In implementing this political activism, Calvinist actors could rely on their specific institutions and networks, concepts, and representations of international politics. This institutional and cultural infrastructure allowed political action even in a constellation where (as in Geneva) the Calvinists were militarily and diplomatically up against superior opponents. It even allowed action where

Calvinists formed a small minority without the support of the princes (as in France and most of the German territories) and had to operate in resistance, or even from the underground.

Fourth. From this propensity to political action resulted relentless efforts to build transconfessional projects and alliances between Lutherans and the Reformed states to confront resurgent Tridentine Catholicism and the Catholic states that supported it. As intervention in the Dutch War of Independence, the French Wars of Religion, and later the Palatinate's attempt to secure Bohemia show, this allegedly defensive political action also included offensive acts of intervention into Catholic territories. Behind such acts stood the *right of intervention in religious matters*, which none of the early modern confessions took as literally as the Calvinists. The tendency toward military intervention on religious grounds could be tamed only in the mid-seventeenth century in the major peace treaties of confession-neutral international law: the Peace of Westphalia, the Peace of the Pyrenees, and the Peace of Oliva. This was "le triomphe de la raison politique" (the triumph of political reason). From then on the principle of state interest and state sovereignty—which excluded any right of intervention especially for religious motives!—became the basis of interior as well as of international affairs. Religion and confession remained a powerful agenda for the rest of early modern Europe but only as part of state interests. The era of intervention by religious reason was over at least until the twentieth century, when secular ideologies again took up the right to intervene into the affairs of neighboring states.

Fifth. The political activism of the Calvinist actors and the eschatological interpretation of the political and military fault lines doubtless accelerated the spiral of historical events that led, after 1600, to the disaster of the Thirty Years' War. Since the eschatological perspective made the political power struggle inevitable, it thrust their representatives into the struggle between Christ and the Antichrist, to fight the decisive combat. Only this eschatological self-understanding and the awareness linked with it of working by God's order and standing on the side of the good made it feasible for the Calvinist action party to challenge the Habsburg world power in Bohemia, in a diplomatically and militarily disadvantageous situation. The same applies to the hasty and reckless iconoclastic movement, which represented this eschatological consciousness symbolically, but was politically unwise. Indeed it cost the cause critical backing within Bohemian society and gave the Catholic opponents a welcome opportunity to score points with anti-Protestant visual propaganda—as is proven by the supposedly battle-determining intervention of the Carmelite monk Jesus Maria.

Sixth. Nevertheless, the extension of the confrontation to constitute the first pan-European state war of modern times is not solely attributable to the Calvinist actors. This was rather an expression of a general transitional crisis that began for Latin Christian Europe at the end of the sixteenth century.[50] This crisis arose on the one hand from the confessional fundamentalism that was to be found not only in the Calvinist world but also in the other camps, among Catholics especially, but also among Lutherans. The resulting inexorable escalation was the price to pay for the dynamism and the accelerated formation of early modern societies under the impact of confessionalization. At the same time the crisis was the result of early modern power-state formation and the resulting competition of separate states for territory, resources, and reputation. The pairing of confessional truth claims and state claims to power is what makes up the fundamental nature of the international crisis of the early seventeenth century.

Seventh. Calvinism was less successful than Lutheranism or Catholicism in developing forceful symbolic representations of its combined truth and power claims—matchless even today is the flamboyant magnificence of Bernini's design of St. Peter's Square as representation of the confessional truth and power of the Roman Catholic Church! But at its core the strategies of Calvinism and Catholicism were not so different. Both main opponents of the era refused any earthly compromise in their common reference to God. Both were characterized by a political internationalism and activism. Both were unwilling to compromise. Both accepted the earthly chaos of a religious war in order to protect their exclusive transcendent truth. The representations of Calvinists as children of God, who are pursued, threatened, strangers in the world, were suitable to guarantee stability and identity in times of defeat for the members of the Reformed Church, and to protect the existence of Calvinism as a minority. The dynamic Calvinist self-assertion through the *Wagenburg* (fortress of wagons) protected by God—which still functioned effectively in South Africa until well into the twentieth century!—was complementary to and contrasted with the more quietist *a-mighty-fortress-is-our-God* representation of Lutheranism.

Eighth. In reality, the balance sheet of Calvinist international politics was negative, for it failed to obtain any long-term military or political success. The expansionist policy of the Palatinate failed. Calvinist Hesse-Kassel could assert itself only under the protection of its Lutheran ally, Sweden. Geneva maintained itself in the long run only with the backing provided time after time and despite all their qualms by the non-Calvinist Swiss confederate states of Bern and Zurich. Nevertheless, one should not underestimate the role that the Calvinist politicians played in the international system around 1600 through their tireless calls for vigilance and inter-Protestant alliance. This was a vital contribution to the creation of the European state order and to the balance of power between Catholic and Protestant forces in Europe as it came to be codified after the "triomphe de la raison politique" in the great European peace treaties of the mid-seventeenth century.

Ninth. An important desideratum for further research is the part played by Calvinist politicians, theologians, lawyers, and political thinkers in the establishment of these treaties, and more generally in the shift from warmongering to "peace-mongering," which came to a breakthrough after the middle of the 1630s. We have to isolate the specific Calvinist contribution to both the establishment of theological conditions for peace and the secular construction of the first European state order realized on the basis of secularized international law. No less necessary to investigate are the important questions of how confessional fundamentalism was overcome, a fundamentalism that, as we have seen, was particularly strong in Calvinist circles at the beginning of the seventeenth century. This implies the investigation of the sources of Calvinism's secularization potential,—a secularization potential that enabled it, alongside other early modern confessions, to not only accept the autonomy of the political sphere achieved in the Peace of Westphalia but to stabilize and develop it further during the following centuries.

■ Notes

1. On this see chap. 12 in this book, pp. 255–66.

2. Thomas Kaufmann, *Das Ende der Reformation: Magdeburgs "Herrgotts Kanzlei" (1548–1551/2)* (Tübingen: Mohr-Siebeck, 2003), with abundant references to the older literature. On Lutheran political theory in general, see Luise Schorn-Schütte's essays, notably "Glaube und weltliche Obrigkeit," in *Religion und Politik,* ed. Manfred Walther (Baden-Baden: Nomos, 2004). She is currently completing a monograph on Lutheran politics.

3. Heinz Schilling, *Civic Calvinism in Northwestern Germany and the Netherlands: Sixteenth to Nineteenth Centuries* (Kirksville, MO: Sixteenth Century Journal, 1991); and Schilling, *Die Stadt in der Frühen Neuzeit* (Munich: Oldenbourg 1993; 2nd ed., 2004).

4. Heiko A. Oberman, *Zwei Reformationen: Luther und Calvin: Alte und Neue Welt* (Berlin: Siedler, 2003), trans. as *The Two Reformations: The Journey from the Last Days to the New World,* ed. and transl. Donald Weinstein (New Haven: Yale University Press, 2003). For historiographical and biographic classification of Oberman's theses, compare Kurt-Victor Selge, "Buchbesprechung," *ARG* 96 (1997): 295–304.

5. Christoph Strohm, *Calvinismus und Recht: Weltanschaulich-konfessionelle Aspekte im Werk reformierter Juristen in der Frühen Neuzeit* (Tübingen: Mohr-Siebeck, 2008).

6. Strohm, *Calvinismus und Recht,* 459.

7. Heinz Schilling, *Konfessionalisierung und Staatsinteressen: Internationale Beziehungen,* 1559–1660 (Paderborn: Schöningh, 2007).

8. *Querela Pacis* in *Erasmus von Rotterdam, Ausgewählte Schriften,* ed. Werner Welzig (Darmstadt: Wissenschaftliche Buchgesellschaft, 1968), 5: 411 and 412.

9. Heinz Schilling, "Gab es um 1600 in Europa einen Konfessionsfundamentalismus? Die Geburt des internationalen Systems in der Krise des konfessionellen Zeitalters," in *Jahrbuch des Historischen Kollegs 2005* (Munich: Oldenbourg, 2006), 69–93; and Heinz Schilling and Elisabeth Müller-Luckner, eds., *Konfessioneller Fundamentalismus: Religion als politischer Faktor im europäischen Mächtesystem um 1600* (Munich: Oldenbourg, 2007).

10. Echoing Reinhard Koselleck's characterization of the late eighteenth century as the "saddle period of modernity" (*Sattelzeit der Moderne*), I have elsewhere called the years around 1600 the "pre-saddle period of modernity": Heinz Schilling, *Aufbruch und Krise: Deutsche Geschichte von 1517 bis 1648* (Berlin: Siedler, 1988), 313.

11. The following material is developed in detail in Heinz Schilling, "Calvin und Calvinismus in europageschichtlicher Perspektive," in *Calvin und Calvinisten—Helvetisches Bekenntnis, Kultur und Politik im Stephansreich vom 16. Jahrhundert bis 1918,* ed. Márta Fata and Anton Schindling (Münster: Aschendorff, forthcoming).

12. See Heiko Oberman , *John Calvin and the Reformation of the Refugees* (Geneva: Droz, 2010).

13. See the chart of Hungarian students in Graeme Murdock, *Calvinism on the Frontier 1600–1660: International Calvinism and the Reformed Church in Hungary and Transylvania* (Oxford: Clarendon Press, 2000), 50.

14. Elaborated in Schilling, *Konfessionalisierung und Staatsinteressen,* 100 and 385.

15. Melanchthon was especially active as a consultant to the princes during the Interim crisis in the empire, 1547–1552.

16. Holger Th. Gräf, *"International Calvinism revisited*; oder europäische Transferleistungen im konfessionellen Zeitalter," in *Das eine Europa und die Vielfalt der Kulturen,* ed.

Thomas Fuchs and Sven Trakulhun (Berlin: Berliner Wissenschaftsverlag, 2003), 137–58; and Aart van Schelven, "Der Generalstab des politischen Calvinismus zu Beginn des Dreißigjährigen Krieges," in *ARG* 36 (1939): 117–41.

17. In general on court preachers see Rudolf von Thadden, *Die brandenburgisch-preußischen Hofprediger* (Berlin: de Gruyter, 1959); for Scultetus, Gustav-Adolf Benrath, ed., *Die Selbstbiographie des Heidelberger Theologen und Hofpredigers Abraham Scultetus (1566–1624)* (Karlsruhe: Evangelischer Presseverband, 1966); for Hoë von Hoënegg, see Hans-Dieter Hertrampf, "Hoë von Hoënegg—sächsischer Oberhofprediger 1613–1645," in *Herbergen der Christenheit, Jahrbuch für Kirchengeschichte*, 1969 (Berlin: Evangelische Verlagsanstalt, 1969), 129–48.

18. Richard B. Wernham , ed., *List and Analysis of State Papers. Foreign Series Elizabeth I, August 1589-December 1596*, 7 vols., (London: Longman, 1964–2000), 1: 309, no. 510.

19. A. Gordon Kinder, "The Protestant Pastor as Intelligencer: Casiodoro de Reina's Letters to Wilhelm IV, Landgrave of Hesse-Cassel (1577–1582)," in *BHR* 58 (1996): 105–18.

20. Ernst Walter Zeeden, *Das Zeitalter der Gegenreformation* (Freiburg: Herder, 1967), 103; and Andreas Mühling, *Heinrich Bullingers europäische Kirchenpolitik* (Bern: Peter Lang, 2001).

21. See Robert M. Kingdon, introduction to *Théodore de Bèze: Du Droit des Magistrats*, ed. Robert M. Kingdon (Geneva: Droz, 1970), xvi; Hippolyte Aubert, Alain Dufour, Béatrice Nicollier, and Hervé Genton, eds., *Correspondance de Théodore de Bèze*, 32 vols. to date (Geneva: Droz, 1960–), 2: 257 ("Projet d' instructions pour les ambassadeurs qui seront délégués auprès d' Henri II," drafted by Calvin September. 1557), 3: 80, 90, and 173 (Beza to Gwalter and Sturm, Calvin to Beza, 1561), and 5: 88 (Beza to Bullinger, 1564); Jan Hendrik Hessels, ed., *Ecclesiae Londino-Bataviae archivum*, 4 vols. (Cambridge: Cambridge University Press, 1887–97), 2: nos. 242, 243, 271 (consistory of the Strangers' Church of London to the bishops of York and London, the archbishop of Canterbury, and the queen, 1589 and 1603); and Ernst Huckenbeck, *Wilhelm Hüls (1598–1659): Ein Beitrag zur rheinischen Kirchengeschichte im 17. Jahrhundert* (Cologne: Rheinland, 1990) (intensive contacts between the president of the Lower Rhine Reformed Church and the Dutch States General).

22. Heinz Schilling, "Die 'Emder Revolution' als europäisches Ereignis," in *Die "Emder Revolution" von 1595, Kolloquium der Ostfriesland-Stiftung am März 17, 1995*, ed. Hajo van Lengen (Aurich: Ostrfiesische Landschaft, 1995), 113–36; Schilling, "Calvinismus und Freiheitsrechte: Die politisch-theologische Pamphletistik der ostfriesisch-groningischen 'Patriotenpartei' und die politische Kultur in Deutschland und in den Niederlanden," *Bijdragen en Mededelingen betreffende de Geschiedenis der Nederlanden* 102 (1987): 403–34; and Schilling, "Johannes Althusius und die Konfessionalisierung der Außenpolitik—oder 'Warum gibt es in der *Politica* keine Theorie der internationalen Beziehungen,' " in *Jurisprudenz, politische Theorie und politische Theologie: Beiträge des Herborner Symposions zum 400. Jahrestag der Politica des Johannes Althusius, 1603–2003*, ed. Frederick S. Carney, Heinz Schilling, and Dieter Wyduckel (Berlin: Duncker und Humblot, 2004), 47–69.

23. That the concrete circumstances and the chronology of the early Dutch church assemblies—in particular that of Wesel—are in dispute (see Owe Boersma, "Vluchtig voorbeeld: De nederlandse, franse en italiaanse vluchtelingenkerken in London, 1568–1585" [PhD diss., Kampen, 1994]) is not pertinent here. Central sources are the Articles of Orange and the response of the Synod of Bedburg, repr. in Hendrik Quirinus Janssen and Johan Justus van Toorenenbergen, eds., *Acten van Classicale en Synodale Vergaderinge der verstrooide Gemeenten in het land van Cleef, Sticht van Keulen en Aken, 1571–1589* (Utrecht: A. van Hoogstraaten, 1882), 5–7. On the Bedburg discussions about ecclesiastical and political content of the "Korrespondenzenwerk," see *400 Jahre Bedburger Synode* (Bedburg:

Eigenverlag der evangelischen Kirchengemeinde, 1971), ed. J. F. G. Goeters, 19; F. G. Venderbosch, *Philipp Marnix*, 93ss (the resistance of the underground congregations of Cologne). See also Heinz Schilling, "Konfessionalisierung und Formierung eines internationalen Systems während der frühen Neuzeit," in *Die Reformation in Deutschland und Europa: Interpretationen und Debatten*, ed. Hans Guggisberg and Gottfried Krodel (Gütersloh: Gütersloher, 1993), 60; and Schilling, "La confessionalisation et le système international," in *L'Europe des traités de Westphalie: Esprit de la diplomatie et diplomatie de l'esprit*, ed. Lucien Bély (Paris: Presses Universitaires de France, 2000), 411–28, here 417.

24. *400 Jahre Bedburger Synode*, 19ss; and Johannes F. Gerhard Goeters, ed., *Die Akten der Synode der Niederländischen Kirchen zu Emden*, (Neukirchen:Vluyn, 1971), 44 § 43.

25. Georg Schmidt, *Der Wetterauer Grafenverein: Organisation und Politik einer Reichskorporation zwischen Reformation und Westfälischem Frieden* (Marburg: Elwert, 1989), 288 and 364.

26. Goeters, *Die Akten der Synoden*, 44 (43 for sociopolitical background).

27. The terms *foedera principum* (treaties of princes) and *synodus theologorum* (synods of theologians) were first used by Melanchthon in *De synodo et foederibus principum* (On the synod and treaties of the princes), December 18, 1559, in *Corpus Reformatorum: Philippi Melanchthonis Opera quae supersunt omnia*, 28 vols., ed. C. G. Brettschneider and H. E. Bindsell (Halle: Schwetschke, 1834–60), 9: 986–90. For the meetings leading to the Formula of Concord, see Irene Dingel, *Concordia controversa: Die öffentliche Diskussion um das lutherische Konkordienwerk am Ende des 16. Jahrhunderts* (Gütersloh: Gütersloher, 1996); and *Theologische Realenzyklopädie*, 36 vols. (Berlin: De Gruyter, 1977–2004), s.v. "Frankfurt," "Naumburg," "Erfurt," "Torgau," "Schmalkalden," "Dessau," and "Jüterborg."

28. See Dingel, *Concordia controversa*; and Mihály Balázs, *Early Transylvanian Antitrinitarianism (1566–1571)* (Baden-Baden: Körner, 1996), 206–11 with nn. 44 and 210.

29. Heinz Schilling, "Die Konfessionalisierung und die Entstehung eines internationalen Systems in Europa," in *Reformation und Recht: Festschrift für Gottfried Seebaß*, ed. Irene Dingel, Volker Leppin, and Christoph Strohm (Gütersloh: Gütersloher, 2002), 127–44, here 134. Another example of the intertwining of religious and political diplomacy is the mission of the French minister Antoine Renault to the Reformed churches and courts in 1603 to 1607 with the aim of discussing the political consequences of the inclusion of a new article identifying the pope as the Antichrist in the confession of faith of the French Reformed churches. See Françoise Chevalier, "L'ambassade d'Antoine Renault auprès des Églises soeurs de Suisse et d'Allemagne (1603–1607)," in *BSHPF* 143 (2001): 579–628.

30. Elaborated in Schilling, *Konfessionalisierung und Staatsinteressen*, ch. B 6, "Dynamisierung und Strukturwandel um 1600," 385–420.

31. Robert M. Kingdon, *Myths about the St. Bartholomew's Day Massacres, 1572–1576* (Cambridge: Harvard University Press, 1988); on the response of the German princes, see Bernard Vogler, "Huguenots et protestants allemands vers 1572," in *Actes du Colloque l'Amiral de Coligny* (Paris: Société de l'Histoire du Protestantisme Français, 1972), 175–89.

32. Note the striking similarity between the famous engraving of the Saint Bartholomew's massacre and an anonymous painting of the Spanish Fury in Antwerp on November 4, 1576, from the last quarter of the sixteenth century: Klaus Bußmann and Heinz Schilling, eds., *1648—Krieg und Frieden in Europa, Europaratsausstellung zum 350. Jahrestag des Westfälischen Friedens*, 3 vols. (Munich: Bruckmann, 1998), 1: 28.

33. Heike Scherneck, "Außenpolitik, Konfession und nationale Identitätsbildung in der Pamphletistik des elisabethanischen England," in *Nationales Bewußtsein und kollektive Identität: Studien zur Entwicklung des kollektiven Bewußtseins in der Neuzeit*, ed. Helmut Berding (Frankfurt: Suhrkamp, 1994), 282–300; and Mia J. Rodriguez-Salgado, ed., *Armada 1588–1988: An International Exhibition to Commemorate the Spanish Armada. Exhibition of*

the National Maritime Museum (Harmondsworth: Penguin Books and National Maritime Museum, 1988). For confessional semantics in general c. 1600, see Uwe Sibeth, "Gesandter einer aufständischen Macht: Die ersten Jahre der Mission von Dr. Pieter Cornelisz. Brederode im Reich (1602–1609)," *Zeitschrift für Historische Forschungen* 30 (2003): 19–52; Matthias Pohlig, "Konfessionskulturelle Deutungsmuster internationaler Konflikte um 1600—Kreuzzug, Antichrist, Tausendjähriges Reich," *ARG* 93 (2002): 278–316; and Schilling, "Calvinismus und Freiheitsrechte."

34. Robert Fruin, *Tien jaren uit den Tachtigjarigen Oorlog 1588–1598* (The Hague: Nijhoff, 1924).

35. Benrath, *Selbstbiographie Scultetus*, 30.

36. Friedrich von Bezold, *Wolfgang Zündelin als protestantischer Zeitungsschreiber und Diplomat in Italien, 1573–1590* (Munich: Sitzungsberichte der philosophisch-philologischen und historischen Classe der k. b. Akademie der Wissenschaften zu München, 1882), 2: 139–74, here 155.

37. Algemeen Rijksarchief, The Hague, MS, Staaten Generaal, Lias Duitsland 6016 1 and 2, correspondance of Pieter Cornelisz. Brederode with the States General, February 14, 1604, fol. hv.

38. For an indispensable treatment of the details of the diplomatic and religious missions of Father Joseph, see Gunnar Hering, *Ökumenisches Patriarchat und europäische Politik, 1620–1638* (Wiesbaden: Steiner, 1968). See also Gustave Fagniez, *Le Père Joseph et Richelieu: 1577–1638*, 2 vols. (Paris: Picard, 1894).

39. For details see Simon L. Adams, "The Protestant Cause: Religious Alliance with the West European Calvinist Communities as a Political Issue in England, 1585–1630" (DPhil diss, Oxford University, 1973); also see Christopher Hill, *Antichrist in Seventeenth-Century England* (Oxford: Oxford University Press, 1971).

40. Horst Bredekamp, "Bild—Akt—Geschichte," in *26. Deutscher Historikertag in Konstanz 2006*, ed. Clemens Wischermann et al. (Constance: UVK, 2007), 289–309, here 309.

41. For citation and its interpretation in the context of the international system, see Schilling, *Konfessionalisierung und Staatsinteressen*, 176.

42. Erasmus, *Querela Pacis*.

43. Robert Oresco, "The Hause of Savoy in Search of a Royal Crown," in *Royal and Republican Sovereignty*, ed. Robert Oresco, G. C. Gibbs, and H. M. Scott (Cambridge: Cambridge University Press, 1997), 272–350.

44. For details, see Heinz Schilling, "La représentation du pouvoir à l' époque de l' émergence d' un système européen d' états souverains," in *La paix des Pyrénées ou le triomphe de la raison politique*, ed. Lucien Bély (Paris, forthcoming).

45. Schilling, *Konfessionalisierung und Staatsinteressen*, 180.

46. Ibid., 260 and 401.

47. However, the copy extant in the University of Geneva Library also contains a foldout with an illustration of the Escalade (shelfmark: Gf 1328 w Rés).

48. *Vray discours de la miraculeuse deliverance enuoyee de Dieu à la ville de Geneve, le 12. jour de Decembre, 1602*, reproduced in facsimile in *C'était en 1602: Genève et l'Escalade, album publié à l'occasion du 400e anniversaire de l'Escalade*, Geneva, new series, 50 (2002): 7–33, here 25.

49. *Vray discours*, 27.

50. Described in more detail in Schilling, *Konfessionalisierung und Staatsinteressen*.

9 Reception and Response

Referencing and Understanding Calvin in Seventeenth-Century Calvinism

RICHARD A. MULLER

The reception of the thought of John Calvin in the works of Reformed theologians of the seventeenth century is a rather complex matter. I leave aside the question of whether or not "Calvinism" is a suitable characterization of the Reformed tradition.[1] Given the character of the tradition itself as fairly broadly defined confessionalism rooted in the work of various reformers in geographically, politically, intellectually, and socially diverse contexts, and given the commonalities between Calvin's own thought and that of significant numbers of predecessors and contemporaries, the actual influence of his doctrinal formulations is particularly difficult to track. Since many of the major concepts and themes found in Calvin's thought were not new ideas and were not given significantly new accents by Calvin, later appearances of the concept or theme in the Reformed tradition cannot be credited directly to Calvin's influence.

In order to assess the response of later Reformed thinkers or "Calvinists" to Calvin and his intellectual contribution to the Reformed tradition, a surer approach is to examine specific patterns of referencing Calvin in the work of various later Reformed thinkers. While recognizing that Calvin's work was received and referenced by later Reformed Protestants in a variety of areas, I have limited the scope of this study to the referencing of Calvin by theologians.[2] I propose to comment on four ways in which Calvin's work was received: (1) the identity of Calvin and the character of his work, (2) referencing Calvin's *Institutes* and *Commentaries*, (3) theological uses of Calvin's work—positive and polemical, and (4) citation and use of Calvin by Herman Witsius and François Turrettini.

■ THE IDENTITY OF CALVIN AND THE CHARACTER OF HIS WORK

Reformed writers of the seventeenth century, however much they respected Calvin's work, remained reluctant to elevate him to high authority and reluctant also to take the name "Calvinist." Responding to the heavy citation of Calvin by Moise Amyraut (1596–1664; professor at the Academy of Saumur) as well as his characterization of the "incomparable Calvin" as the one who, after God, was primarily responsible for the Reformation throughout Europe,[3] Pierre Du Moulin (1568–1658), who served as a minister in Paris and Charenton and as professor in Leiden and Sedan, argued rather pointedly not only that Amyraut had misinterpreted Calvin but also that there was a certain impropriety in citing Calvin as an authority, given that the only suitable authority in doctrinal matters was scripture. Amyraut's usage, in Du Moulin's view, would only serve to justify the accusations of adversaries of the faith who referred to the Reformed Protestants as "Calvinists."[4] Thomas Cartwright (1535–1603), Lady Margaret Professor of Divinity at Cambridge and, after 1574, minister in Antwerp and Middelburg, could complain that his adversary John Whitgift (ca. 1530–1604), professor of divinity at Cambridge and later archbishop of Canterbury, "burdeneth us wyth the authority of Calvin so often."[5] The French theologian and exegete André Rivet (1573–1654), professor at Leiden, although he referenced Calvin's commentaries and defended Calvin against various attacks, also noted pointedly that Calvin was not to be regarded as either the *autor* or the *dux* of "our religion."[6]

In much the same vein, in his *Défense de la Reformation*, the eminent Jean Claude (1619–1687), pastor and professor at Nîmes and Montauban and later pastor at Charenton, commented regarding Luther, Zwingli, and Calvin, that "we do not believe what the reformers said because they said it, but because they proved it; and because those things appeared sufficiently evident in themselves." Therefore, he continued, it is "not on their authority that the Reformation depends."[7] Similarly, in his apologetic history of Calvinism written in response to the Jesuit Louis Maimbourg's polemical history, Pierre Jurieu (1637–1713), professor at Sedan and later Rotterdam, commented that his opponent had endeavored to "make [Calvin] the head of a party, to establish him as a heresiarch, to lay his identity on us, and to call us 'Calvinists' after him."[8] Jurieu continues, echoing the kind of argument we have already seen in Du Moulin and Claude: "All this is without foundation; because it is certain that Calvin was in no way the first reformer, neither of France, nor of Geneva, for the truth that he taught was known before he preached it, and we do not regard him as our head, because we have no other head than Jesus Christ."[9] Jurieu's response evidences several dimensions: on the one hand, he both accepts and denies the label "Calvinist": he recognizes that label has been established but needs to be explained. Those called "Calvinists" by Maimbourg are "the reformers" and what Maimbourg calls "Calvinism" is "the teachings and the worship of the Reformation."[10] As for Calvin himself, Jurieu consistently identifies predecessors, beginning his survey of the Reformation and reformers with Zwingli and Zurich and arriving at Calvin only after a series of chapters in which he notes predecessors of the Reformation like Guillaume Briçonnet and Jacques Lefèvre d'Étaples, defends the life and work of Vermigli, and comments on the distinction made between Zwinglians and Calvinists.

It was crucial to Jurieu's argument that he not identify Calvin as a highly original thinker, but rather as a most profound representative of the truths of scripture taught by earlier reformers. Calvin certainly was "an excellent individual" used by God to further the Reformation but was improperly fastened upon by Maimbourg as his primary target. Nonetheless, Jurieu does offer a very high estimation of Calvin as a theologian over against Maimbourg's comments to the contrary, which were based on Calvin's lack of schooling in things scholastic. Calvin labored to "penetrate the substance of theology," he commented on the text of scripture with a "veracity" that "utterly surpassed all the commentators that had preceded him," and his *Institutes* offered a theology more deeply thought through than ever before![11]

We need remind ourselves it was not by choice that Reformed catholics of the early modern era were called "Calvinists" and that their citations not only of Calvin but also of other reformers were, with very good reason, less numerous than expected by those modern hagiographers of the Reformation who would like to think that Calvin invented a wonderful new theology.[12]

Finally on this issue of the identity of Calvin, one of the more contemporaneously important but historiographically overlooked patterns of reception of the reformers has little to do with the distinctive contents of their thought and much to do with their perceived place in the history of the church and world. Protestant writers of the late sixteenth and early seventeenth centuries understood the transition from the fathers to the scholastics as decline, identified some thinkers— Nicholas of Lyra, John Wyclif, and Jan Hus—who attempted to break free of papal superstition, and then pointed to the providential return of the uncorrupted gospel in Luther, Melanchthon, Zwingli, Bucer, Oecolampadius, Calvin, and others.[13] This historical model could also yield a placement of the reformers in the eschatological battle against the Roman Antichrist. In his reading of the vision of the seven angels and seven last plagues, Thomas Brightman (1562–1607), fellow of Queen's College, Cambridge, a major defender of presbyterian church government, and noted commentator on the Apocalypse, identifies Calvin as well as Melanchthon, Bucer, Vermigli, and Bullinger as "servants of God" literally on the side of the angels, drawing "precepts and instructions" out of vials of God's wrath that "worke the destruction of the enemies of the Church."[14] Here too Calvin is not presented alone, but in the company of other significant formulators of the Reformation.

■ REFERENCING CALVIN: THE *INSTITUTES* AND THE *COMMENTARIES*

The sometimes heard comment that later Calvinist writers, particularly those of the seventeenth century, seldom mentioned Calvin remains one of the sorrier moments in older scholarship on Reformed orthodoxy. The comment is simply untrue; it illustrates, sadly, the tendency of so much of that scholarship to select emblematic documents for dogmatic critique and to avoid a wide reading of the sources. Calvin was, in fact, often cited and much praised by the Reformed theologians of the seventeenth century. The *Institutio christianae religionis* remained on lists of recommended theological works, and Calvin's commentaries were consistently praised and frequently cited—far more, for example, than the works of Emil Brunner or Paul Tillich are cited by theologians of the early twenty-first century.

In the preface to his famed *Institutiones theologicae seu locorum communium christianae religionis* of 1602, Bucanus (Guillaume du Buc, d. 1603), professor of theology at Lausanne from 1591 until his death, recommends three theologians as basic to theological instruction. First comes Melanchthon, whose advice concerning the brevity of theological works Bucanus commends highly. Then grouped together are Wolfgang Musculus (1497–1563) and John Calvin, authors respectively of *Loci communes* and *Institutio christianae religionis*. Bucanus also notes Beza as a significant predecessor.[15] A similar commendation of Calvin's *Institutes* comes from Franz Burman (1632–1679), the follower of Johannes Cocceius and professor at Utrecht. He recommends as basic theological reading a series of doctrinal compendia, including William Ames's *Medulla*, the *Synopsis purioris theologiae* (otherwise known as the *Leiden Synopsis*), Ursinus's *Catechetical Lectures*, and Calvin's *Institutes*, but he specifically identifies Calvin as more important among the reformers than even Vermigli and Musculus.[16] The Leiden professor Lucas Trelcatius Jr. (1573–1607) singled out Calvin, along with Melanchthon and Ursinus, as an example of the analytical method in theology.[17] The Leiden university *Synopsis purioris theologiae* references Calvin and Beza together in its discussion of reprobation, noting without further elaboration that both argued that the will of God is the ultimate cause of all things.[18]

Certainly, throughout the seventeenth century Calvin continued also to be both recommended and defended as a biblical commentator. Rivet noted that among those knowledgeable in such matters, Calvin was considered among the most learned interpreters (*doctissimi interpretes*).[19] Joseph Hall (1574–1656), dean of Worcester, delegate to the Synod of Dort, and later bishop of Exeter, in his comments on the millennium with reference to Daniel 7:27, identified Calvin as an interpreter "whose judgement I so much honour, that I reckon him among the best Interpreters of Scripture, since the Apostles left the earth."[20] Writing in 1654, the widely published English philologist and theologian Edward Leigh (1602–1671) noted that, as a commentator on scripture, "Calvin is not only commended by our Writers, but by the very Papists."[21] Leigh also consistently cites Calvin among "the best interpreters" when he details commentaries on particular books of the Bible.[22] Leigh goes on to cite Thomas Cartwright and Daniel Featley (1582–1645, the noted controversialist, chaplain to Charles I, and rector of Lambeth), echoing Cartwright's estimation that "I would content my self among the new Writers with Mr. Calvin, who performeth best of all others that, which he of himself professeth, that a man in reading his Expositions reapeth the benefit, that for the shortness he useth, he departeth not far from the text itself," and seconding Featley's challenge to "name me one Papist who has preached so often, and wrote so accurately upon the holy Scriptures."[23]

Also from the mid-seventeenth century, Thomas Barlow (1607–1691), the Oxford philosopher and theologian, mentor of John Owen, and later bishop of Lincoln, consistently recommends Calvin as a commentator in his posthumous *De studio theologiae*. Regarding the Pentateuch, Barlow identifies Calvin as "ubi bene, nemo melius"; in identifying commentators on the New Testament, he singles out Beza and Calvin as the two most significant of the modern writers, "inferiour to none."[24] The Puritan minister and theologian Richard Baxter (1615–1691), also identified Calvin as a significant commentator.[25]

In the eighteenth century, a more rationalistic theologian like Johann Christoph Beck (1711–1778), professor of history and later of theology at Basel, could still look back over the history of theological systems, declaim against the philosophical abuses of medieval scholasticism and the excessive reliance on human opinion in past ages, and then point to reformers, notably Luther, Oecolampadius, and Calvin, as reinstituting for the good of the church a "catechetical method" in theology.[26] Beck also notes that Calvin also followed the topical *locus* method begun by Melanchthon and that the *Institutes* was still valued highly in his own time.[27]

■ THEOLOGICAL USES OF CALVIN'S WORK—POSITIVE AND APOLOGETIC

One of the ways in which Calvin's work was used by later writers was through appropriation of his *Institutes*. This could take the form of shortened versions or compendia of the book, or it could involve replicating its pattern of organization in larger theological works. Transmitting Calvin via *loci communes* was also a very good way of making the *Institutes* a functional textbook, an idea that arguably goes back at least to Colladon or even to Calvin himself, given that the *Institutes* could be perceived both as a difficult and as a very adaptable work.[28]

The compendia of the *Institutes*, surveyed in a fine essay by Olivier Fatio,[29] were fairly numerous, particularly in the latter part of the sixteenth century. Notable among these, particularly given the varied backgrounds and roles of their authors, are the compendia by Girolamo Zanchi (1516–1590), theologian, exegete, and professor in Strasbourg and Heidelberg; William Delaune (1530–1610), Huguenot minister, physician, and refugee in England; Theodore Zwinger (1533–1588), antistes of Basel; Caspar Olevianus (1536–1587), professor in Heidelberg and teacher of Johannes Piscator (1546–1625), rector of the Herborn Academy who further abridged Olevianus's *Compendium*; Edmund Bunnie (1540–1619), fellow of Magdalen College Oxford, chaplain to Archbishop Grindal, and rector of Bolton Perry in Yorkshire; and Daniel Colonius (1566–1635), a student of Beza and rector of the Walloon College in Leiden. Several of these works—Zanchi's compendium being perhaps the earliest of the group—were based on the third edition (1543–1545) of the *Institutes*.[30] The works of Bunnie, Olevianus, Piscator, and Delaune were based on the 1559 text.[31] Bunnie and Delaune respected the four-book order of the 1559 edition and lined out the text chapter by chapter. The work of the Herborn theologian Johannes Piscator, by contrast, reflects the order of topics of the 1559 text and begins with a statement of the twofold knowledge of God as creator and redeemer, but it also, presumably because of its brevity, ignores the division into four books and simply lists twenty-eight chapters. It is perhaps of interest that the English version of Piscator's compendium was translated rather freely, with additions or alterations that went beyond Piscator's own interpretive efforts. As a result, it is the one place where Calvin actually does mention the covenant of works![32] Taken together, these compendia indicate not only the importance of Calvin's thought to the next several generations of Reformed theologians but also their interest in digesting it and finding its definitional core.

The shape of the *Institutes* in the majority of editions published during Calvin's lifetime—from 1539 to 1553—was echoed in the organization of Beza's *Quaestionum et responsionum christianarum libellus* (1570–1576), most notably in its placement of predestination and providence together in a single section lodged toward the rear of the work. In the same year that part 2 of Beza's *Quaestionum et responsionum libellus* appeared, Robert Le Maçon published the first edition of the Peter Martyr Vermigli's *Loci communes*. This work, consisting of topical extracts from Vermigli's commentaries and treatises, paid tribute to Calvin's 1559 *Institutes* by largely adopting its four-book organization. Bucanus, whose commendation of Calvin I have already noted, modeled the order of topics in his own *Institutiones* largely on that of Calvin's *Institutio*, with, however, a few modifications, some perhaps drawn from the Le Maçon edition of Vermigli's *Loci communes*.

Calvin's commentaries were, arguably, referenced far more consistently than his *Institutio* in the era of orthodoxy, if only because they loomed so large as a body of biblical interpretation. A good example of this can be found in the late sixteenth-century commentaries of Augustin Marlorat (1506–1562), a Huguenot refugee who wrote the index to the final text of Calvin's *Institutes*. Marlorat's commentaries, which consist of gatherings of quotations from major Protestant commentators on each text, consistently draw on Calvin's commentaries, citing him in the company of Martin Bucer, Erasmus, Wolfgang Musculus, Philipp Melanchthon, Johannes Brenz, Heinrich Bullinger, Konrad Pellikan, and Ulrich Zwingli.[33]

Calvin's views are also often identified as favored readings in the mid-seventeenth century by John Mayer (1583–1664), bachelor and doctor of divinity from Emmanuel College, Cambridge, and rector of Little Wrattling and Raydon, who wrote lengthy annotations on difficult passages in scripture. In the case of Psalm 2, Mayer appears to favor Calvin's reading of the psalm as referring to both David and Christ as distinct from a purely Christological reading.[34] Indeed, throughout the Psalter, Mayer appears to be following Calvin closely, frequently noting Calvin's surveys of various interpretations and either siding with him or acknowledging his interpretation as significant.[35] The authors Mayer references most often are Augustine, Basil the Great, and Henry Ainsworth, leaving Calvin as Mayer's primary Reformation-era point of reference. John Stoughton, fellow of Emmanuel College Cambridge, identifies Calvin, together with Beza, as an interpreter of Paul when noting the alternative translations of 1 Corinthians 2:2, and he returns to Calvin a few pages later, citing him out of Marlorat's compilation and indicating that Paul's "doctrine" is "that the knowledge of Christ Iesus crucified, is sufficient to salvation," before adding that this doctrinal conclusion both "justifies . . . Paul's determination" to preach Christ alone and "warrants Calvin's observation, for the duty both of Preacher and People, as a ground and foundation."[36] Thomas Morton (1564–1659), bishop of Durham, cited Calvin's "excellent contemplation" on the power of God in Christ in the commentary on Colossians 2:15.[37]

By contrast, neither the *Synopsis criticorum* by Matthew Poole (1624–1679; minister of St. Michael-le-Quernes, London) nor the *Critici sacri* by John Pearson (1613–1686; doctor of divinity, King's College, Cambridge; bishop of Chester) used Calvin's commentaries as a source, although Poole does cite contemporaries of Calvin like Sebastian Münster, Paulus Fagius, Sebastian Castellio, and Peter Martyr Vermigli, and Pearson regularly references Sebastian Münster, Paulus Fagius, François Vatable, and Sebastian Castellio.[38] The reason, of course, is clear: both Poole and Pearson were interested in collating textual and philological annotations, not in engaging in theological discourse on the text. Calvin's work, with its largely theological emphasis, did not register as a significant contribution to the establishment of text or to a philological approach to the original languages.

Not all of the Reformed references to Calvin as a commentator belong to these categories of commendation and positive use. Calvin's exegesis also remained a matter of debate and needed to be defended on a series of points. Thomas Cartwright defended Calvin's exegesis against charges of heresy and blasphemy found throughout the Rheims annotations on the New Testament.[39] Similarly, Rivet's referencing of Calvin in his commentaries is largely apologetic. His 1633 commentary on Genesis mentions Calvin six times, in each case defending his reading of a text, whether against the accusations of the Lutherans that Calvin was a Judaizer,[40] or from "calumnies" of Roman exegetes,[41] or attacks on Calvin's trinitarianism by Valentin Gentile, Gilbert Genebrardus, and Cardinal Roberto Bellarmine.[42] The last of these defenses is of interest in that it concerns the first biblical reference to God as Iehovah, at Genesis 2:4, an issue never raised at this point in Calvin's Genesis commentary. Rivet is concerned here to develop the point against Socinus that Iehovah, as the ultimate name of God, is rightly applied to the Trinity, and his reference to Calvin's teaching arises as an extension of this argument. Rivet indicates that Calvin, against these various adversaries, had rightly understood both the *homoousios* of the Son with the Father and the identity of the Son as *authotheos*, namely as *à se vel* per se *Deum*. The defense of Calvin as orthodox on this point remained an issue throughout the era of Reformed orthodoxy.

So, too, the citations found in Rivet's 1634 commentary on Exodus serve to defend both Calvin's doctrine and his abilities as an exegete. In the first reference, Rivet is examining Exodus 1:14, where the Egyptians are said to have made the lives of the Israelites "bitter with hard bondage." He argues that Calvin, in seeing the hand of God here at work, does not make God the author of sin. Indeed, Calvin is in agreement with Augustine: God does not here incite the Egyptians to sin, but rather works his judgments on the Egyptians, preventing their wickedness from prospering.[43] At Exodus 1:18–21, where the Hebrew midwives had been ordered by Pharaoh to kill male offspring and explained their failure to carry out the order on the ground that the Hebrew women delivered rapidly before the midwives arrived, Calvin had been accused of blasphemy (by the Roman Catholic exegete Cornelius à Lapide) for failing to distinguish between lies and virtuous acts, as if God had rewarded lies. Quite the to contrary, Rivet indicates, Calvin taught not that God rewarded mendacity, but piety, mercy, and the fear of God![44] Similarly, Calvin's exegesis of Exodus 6:16 had been impugned by à Lapide: Calvin had identified Moses's mother, Jochebed, as Moses's father's aunt, calling the union incestuous, albeit taking place before the law prohibiting such marriages. The point of the text, in Calvin's view, was to illustrate the sole glory of God, a reading characterized by à Lapide as immodest and ignorant. Rivet explains and defends Calvin's reading of the text, while noting the other options.[45]

Polemical and apologetic citation of Calvin in fact accounts for a large number of the references to Calvin on the part of seventeenth-century writers. Since Bellarmine's disputations against the Reformation, when directed against Reformed theologians, took particular interest in arguing that Calvin had departed from the true faith of the church on a variety of issues, later Reformed writers often defended Calvin's continuity with the great tradition of the Church and with Augustine's teachings in particular. This defense is of particular importance given the major impact that Bellarmine's polemics had on the formation of Reformed orthodoxy, specifically on the Reformed reappropriation of large portions of the tradition in an effort to demonstrate their catholicity. Thus, John Cosin (1594–1672), vice-chancellor of Cambridge University, later bishop of Durham, and a critic of the predestinarianism of Dort, in his writing against Bellarmine on the "catholic" Lord's Supper of the Reformed churches, cites Calvin at length. Calvin's doctrine of a genuine spiritual presence of Christ in the Lord's Supper stands, according to Cosin, both in line with a truly Augustinian understanding of the Eucharist and in direct agreement with all of the major confessions of the Protestant churches.[46]

Richard Field (1561–1616), the learned dean of Gloucester, took up the cudgel on behalf of Calvin in his discussions of free choice, the *limbus patrum*, concupiscence, satisfaction, the authorship of sin, and original sin.[47] Calvin is similarly defended on the issue of free choice by various others, including the St. Andrews and Aberdeen University metaphysician Robert Baron (1593–1639).[48] In the particular case of free choice of the will, Calvin's rather hyperbolic language of the bondage of the will and its inability to do any good (quite in parallel with Luther's *De servo arbitrio*) had to be argued as referring to the specific case of the fallen will in its inability to choose a saving good rather than, as one might read Calvin's unqualified language, as a full doctrine of free choice. Baron pointed out, against Bellarmine, that the issue in debate was not the human power of free choice *in natura sua considerato*, which all human beings can exercise, but rather the limitation of free choice in fallen humanity and the issue of free choice in the instant of conversion.[49]

William Twisse (1578–1646), rector of Newbury and first prolocutor of the Westminster Assembly, devoted a section of his treatise on Sabbath observance to defending Calvin, whose argument for the retention of Sabbath observance against adversaries thought by Twisse to be Anabaptist had been misconstrued. Calvin did not "affix" sanctity in a superstitious manner to a particular day but rather recognized the suitability of replacing the Jewish Sabbath with the Lord's Day and the necessity, not of a superstitious reverence for a particular day, but of the reservation of one day in seven to "the service of God." In framing his defense, Twisse examines a contested passage in the *Institutes* (2, 8.33–34), supplies collateral argumentation from Calvin's commentary on 1 Corinthians, and draws on Antonius Walaeus's similar defense of the point.[50] Twisse's intention here is not so much to use Calvin as an authority but to defend his position and place him on the side of a right understanding of Sabbath observance.

Throughout the seventeenth century, Calvin was also cited on one or the other side of debates that tore at confessional orthodoxy. At several points in the debates at the Synod of Dort, it was recognized that Calvin had not offered resolutions to the problems being raised—as, for example, on the problem of the divine causality in conversion. Similarly, when the issue of *praemotio physica* (God's physical premotion disposing man to act in accordance with his will), drawn from the Dominican counter to the Jesuit *scientia media* ("middle knowledge" of God), was raised in debate, Matthias Martinius (1572–1630) of

Bremen responded to appeals to Calvin's and David Pareus's works for a solution by noting that "neither Calvin nor any of our Divines has yet plainly enough untied that Knot."[51]

In the context of internal debates among Reformed theologians of the era of orthodoxy, Calvin was identified as both infralapsarian and a supralapsarian. It has been observed that, despite the perceptions of a generation or so of historians devoted to the "Calvin against the Calvinists" theory, a late sixteenth-century Reformed writer like the supralapsarian Cambridge professor William Whitaker (1548–1595) did not often appeal to Beza in justification of his approach to predestination but to Calvin—although he did so not to justify a supra- as distinct from an infralapsarian approach but rather to defend predestination against the somewhat synergistic Pierre Baro (1534–1599), the French refugee and Lady Margaret Professor of Divinity at Cambridge, who inclined to believe in cooperation of God's grace and human will in the process of man's salvation and is generally considered as a precursor of Arminianism.[52] Of course, Jacob Arminius (1559–1609), arguing on the opposite side of the debate from Whitaker, saw little difference between Calvin and Beza on predestination, identifying both as cut from the same unpleasantly supralapsarian cloth.[53] John Davenant, Pierre Du Moulin, Francis Turrettini (all infralapsarian), and William Twisse (a supralapsarian) all identified Calvin as infralapsarian in his definitions.[54] Thomas Goodwin (1600–1680), chaplain to Oliver Cromwell's Council of State and president of Magdalen College, Oxford, and himself a supralapsarian, noted Davenant's view of Calvin and commented that although Calvin could be cited as understanding the object of election as the fallen or corrupt mass of humanity, he could also be cited as advocating a supralapsarian object of the decree, and, therefore, could be seen as having "respect" for both later positions.[55] The disagreement arose, perhaps, because, as had been observed at Dort, Calvin himself had not untied that knot.

In the seventeenth-century controversy over hypothetical universalism, Amyraut referred his own doctrines to Calvin with copious quotation and Du Moulin took Amyraut to task for his use of Calvin.[56] In a letter to the Synod of Alençon (1637), Du Moulin had already expressed the worry that use of the term "Calvinism" might seem to indicate that the Reformed churches viewed Calvin "as the Author of a new Religion."[57] A decade later, in his ongoing polemic against Amyraut, Du Moulin returned to the argument and indicated that there was a tactical problem in excessive citation. He warned that Reformed theologians could fall prey to their opponents who accused them of excessive dependence on a single disputed thinker rather than participation in the broader tradition of orthodox Christianity.[58] Writing at length against Amyraut, Du Moulin not only pointed out the danger of using Calvin as an authority for doctrine but also noted that Calvin himself would never have claimed such authority—indeed, he would have been ejected from the pulpit in Geneva had he done so. Du Moulin also contested each of Amyraut's citations of Calvin, noting pointedly that Calvin in no way had supported notions of a conditional or hypothetical decree of universal redemption prior to an absolute decree to save the elect only. Turrettini cited Calvin to the same effect.[59]

Of course Amyraut was hardly alone in his referencing Calvin in favor of a form of hypothetical universalism. Thus, commenting on the proceedings at Dort specifically with regard to the Church of England's confessional stance on the issue of hypothetical universalism, John Overall (1560–1619), then Regius Professor of Theology at Cambridge, commented that Calvin "who was otherwise sufficiently rigid about Predestination" allowed for the "Universality of Christ's Death" in commenting on various biblical texts that others had read in a particularistic way.[60] Davenant expressed a similar opinion.[61] Similarly, in defense of his views on the extent of Christ's redemption, Baxter cited Calvin on 2 Peter 2:1 ("Even denying the Lord that bought them"), Jude 4, Hebrews 6:4–6 and 10:26–29; and 1 Timothy 1:1; 2:3, but consistently placed him in the company of other exegetes, as one major commentator among others.[62] Of course, Calvin was also cited fairly consistently on the other side of the debate. Du Moulin set out to refute Amyraut's most significant citations of Calvin, indicating that Calvin never wrote of a general or conditional decree, nor of "conseils de Dieu frustratoires," nor of an impetration of the remissions of sins without an application.[63]

The previously noted late sixteenth-century debate over ecclesiology between Thomas Cartwright and John Whitgift also involved much citation of Calvin and argument concerning the direction of his thought. In the Salmurian controversies, citation and countercitation of Calvin occurred in the debate between Josue La Place (ca. 1596–1665), professor at Saumur, and Antoine Garissoles (1587–1650), pastor in Puylaurens and later professor at Montauban, over the imputation of Adam's sin to the human race, with both sides claiming precedent in Calvin's theology.[64] There was also frequent citation of Calvin on the part of the English antinomians, who were typically proponents of particular redemption, and countercitation by their opponents.[65] I cannot here settle the question of which readings of Calvin are correct. Perhaps this is yet another knot that he did not untie. What can be said is that his status as a biblical interpreter gave both sides of the debate reason to call on him as a precedent and, in some cases, as an authority, usually with the goal of self-justification in a polemical context rather than as an attempt to understand Calvin's own theology in its detail and nuance.

■ CITATION AND USE OF CALVIN BY WITSIUS AND TURRETTINI

A closer analysis of the citation and use of Calvin's works by theologians of the era of orthodoxy can be provided by examination of Herman Witsius and François Turrettini, two fairly representative thinkers of the era, who both cited Calvin with some frequency. François Turrettini (1623–1687), who studied in Geneva and Leiden before becoming professor of theology in Geneva in 1653, stood as the major representative of theological orthodoxy in Geneva in the latter part of the seventeenth century. Herman Witsius (1636–1708), who served as a professor at Franecker, Utrecht, and Leiden, was an orthodox Reformed exegete and theologian of the Voetian (as distinct from the Cocceian) school of covenantal thought, widely respected in his era.

Turrettini evidences a heavier use of Calvin than Witsius, and some of his usage of "our Calvin" can, perhaps, be traced to civic pride as well as to purely theological considerations. It needs also to be noted that citations are not an adequate index to the reception or influence of a given thinker not only because even lengthy citations of a particular author do not always indicate the actual basis of the argument but also because key formulae and substantial argumentation in both Witsius and Turrettini are often not augmented by citation of predecessors. With those caveats in mind, however, we can draw some conclusions from the number and kind of reference to Calvin found in these writers.

Witsius cited Calvin some twenty times in his *Oeconomia foederum*, referring to him as "our Calvin" and "the judicious Calvin," and speaking highly both of the *Institutes* and of the commentaries.[66] Of course, Witsius cites other theologians and exegetes of the sixteenth century—in fact, twice pairing Vermigli with Calvin and identifying Vermigli as a "most excellent interpreter of Scripture."[67] Vermigli is cited some thirteen times; the "judicious" Musculus, seven; the "venerable" Beza, six; the "very accurate and great" or "learned" Zanchi, five times; and Ames, three times.[68] Most of the citations, whether of Calvin, Vermigli, Beza, or others, are on matters of biblical interpretation, and Calvin is cited almost exclusively as offering exegetical support, including in the case of most of Witsius's citations of the *Institutes*.

By way of example, Witsius references both Calvin and Vermigli, citing them both to support the seventh day of creation as a basis of the Sabbath rule.[69] He views Calvin as most helpful in delineating the differences between the Old and the New Testament.[70] Against William Twisse's reading of Titus 1:2, Witsius pairs Calvin with the Dutch Annotations 1:2 to support his view that the phrase "before the world began" does not necessarily refer to "absolute eternity" but preferably to the duration of the economy of redemption, from the beginning of the promise.[71] There are also several exegetical discussions where other Reformed exegetes— Bucer, Musculus, and Pareus—are cited at length, and Calvin is noted as confirmation of the argument.[72]

What is perhaps of interest here is that Calvin was used to help define exegetical issues in the context of a covenantal theology—a theological model or genre in which Calvin's actual topical influence was relatively minimal and, where it did exist, was largely derivative. Witsius, after all, presented lengthy discussions of the covenant of works and the *pactum salutis*, two topics never touched on by Calvin, and also of the covenant of grace, which Calvin mentioned but never discussed at length. There are no citations of Bullinger or Olevianus in Witsius's *De oeconomia*. His three citations of Ursinus are not related to covenantal issues,[73] while those from Musculus, with the exceptions of the citations concerning the perpetuity of the law and the reference to the Noahic covenant,[74] are not foundational to the definitional structure of Witsius's work. We are left with the conclusion that Witsius's referencing had far more to do with narrowly identified definitions and matters of biblical interpretation than any identification of a broader theological ancestry for his thought. But we are also left with a significant issue concerning the much-debated relationship of Calvin's thought to later covenantal theology. Unlike Bullinger, Calvin did not write any extended treatise on covenant and, given that datum, it can certainly be argued that Bullinger's work gave significant impetus to the development of covenant as a theological *locus* and, ultimately, as an organizational theme in the thought of many later Reformed theologians. From the perspective of Witsius's work, however, Calvin was important for the language of covenant and for the definition of specific issues in ways that Bullinger was not.

Turrettini offered Calvin high praise and referenced Calvin's works with some frequency in his own *Institutio*—in over sixty places, sometimes briefly or only by name, sometimes citing extensively from the commentaries, treatises, or *Institutes*.[75] In contrast, there are roughly twenty-seven references to Beza, sixteen to Vermigli, nine to Zanchi, seven to Bullinger, three to Musculus, and one to Ames.[76] Just to put these citations into perspective, note that Augustine is mentioned more than three hundred times by Turrettini.

A series of references to Calvin in Turrettini's *Institutio* belongs to a category of what might be called traditionary warrants. Thus, for example, Calvin is cited in the company of other Reformed writers who, as a group, ratify Turrettini's views or are defended, as a group, against critics, who were usually Roman polemicists. Thus, Calvin is referenced with Beza "and others,"[77] mentioned with Zwingli, Luther, Vermigli, and Beza,[78] cited with Vermigli on a point of translation,[79] cited with Vermigli and Chamier against an opponent, probably La Place,[80] or cited as in agreement with Bucer and Bullinger on original sin.[81] Turrettini also identifies Calvin's views on the Sabbath as confirmed by Viret, Beza, Vermigli, Bucer, and Zanchi,[82] and cites the reformer with Bucer, Beza, Bullinger, Junius, Piscator, Walaeus, and Gisbertus Voetius on shifting the day to Sunday.[83] There is an interesting reference to Calvin, with Vermigli and Ursinus, on the unity of the covenant of grace against the view of Robert Rollock, Johannes Piscator, and Lucas Trelcatius that the old and new covenants were "diverse in substance."[84] Significantly, it is not Calvin's definition by itself that is taken as definitive, but rather the collective opinion of Calvin, Vermigli, and Ursinus. Calvin is similarly cited with Vermigli, Bullinger, Piscator, and Pareus regarding Rom. 3:25.[85]

Another series of Turrettini's references to Calvin falls into the category of defense against Bellarmine and other Roman polemicists. The question of trinitarian orthodoxy had plagued Calvin since his early reluctance to use the traditional dogmatic language. He had been accused of Arianism by Pierre Caroli and later by Bellarmine, largely on the basis of his identification of the Son as *autotheos*.[86] The issue had been debated between Arminius and his colleagues in Leiden, with Arminius referencing both Calvin and Beza in support of his understanding. Specifically against Bellarmine and Genebrardus, Turrettini asserts that Calvin did not have Arian inclinations,[87] and that his understanding of Christ as *autotheos* had not (improperly) argued that the Son has sonship from himself but had (properly) indicated that the divine essence itself is ungenerated so that, as God, Christ is divine of himself.[88]

Turrettini also defends Calvin against Bellarmine and others, arguing that Calvin never implied that God is the author of sin and that he rightly understood the ways in which God permits evil to occur and uses the wicked as his instruments. In Turrettini's view, Calvin's denials of permission are denials only of an unwilling or "idle permission."[89] Calvin is defended as well against Roman polemicists who identify him as a "patron" of usury.⁹⁰ Calvin also did not ascribe faith to Christ in an improper manner, nor did he claim that Christ despaired on the cross or was damned.⁹¹ Calvin, further, did not reduce faith to understanding, and he rightly and biblically spoke of the invisible church, while fully recognizing that most of the biblical language of *ecclesia* indicates the visible congregations.⁹²

Beyond Turrettini's handful of defenses of Calvin against the accusations of polemicists and his referencing of Calvin as one among several significant reformers, there is a significant series of places in which Turrettini uses Calvin substantively, much as we have seen in Witsius, as a source of exegetical opinion, typically on matters of theological interpretation although occasionally on matters of translation. Thus, Turrettini relies on Calvin's reading of Genesis 3:15, where the seed of the woman is seen to refer preeminently to Christ, but also, through him, to all believers.⁹³ He draws on Calvin's interpretation of 1 Peter 1:18–19 for his view of the Old Testament patriarchs' expectation of Christ.⁹⁴ He also references Calvin on Galatians 3:19 on how Christ is called the mediator.⁹⁵ Calvin is also cited (with Beza) to support reading the reference to God's desire to save "all" in 1 Timothy 2:4–5 as indicating all kinds, and again, to similar effect, regarding the "whole world" in 1 John 2:2.⁹⁶

Numerous and often extensive citations from Calvin's works appear when Turrettini appeals to Calvin to buttress his own views as normative for the Reformed faith. Turrettini cites Calvin, sometimes with others, in the context of internecine controversy for the purpose of definition or argument and for the understanding of particular biblical texts. What is of interest here is that Turrettini deploys Calvin to argue against the views of other Reformed writers who, though they are not heterodox in his view (i.e., not transgressive of confessional boundaries), are nonetheless quite mistaken and must be corrected. Whereas Turrettini typically cites Calvin defensively or apologetically against Roman adversaries, he cites him as a paragon of orthodoxy in the context of intraconfessional disputes. Specifically, he cites Calvin against the supralapsarians, arguing that Calvin was infralapsarian.⁹⁷ He also uses Calvin against an unnamed La Place on the immediate imputation of Adam's sin to his posterity; against an unnamed Piscator and his allies on the imputation of Christ's active obedience to believers; against Amyraut on the limitation of Christ's satisfaction; and against Rollock and others on the substantive identity of the Old Testament form of the covenant with the New Testament form.⁹⁸

The two anti-Amyraldian citations are both exegetical in nature and can be credited, at least in part, to the citation and countercitation of Calvin that had marked the controversy from its inception. The first of these occurs in the context of Turrettini's own discussion of the phrases "ransom for all" and sins of the "whole world" in 1 Timothy 2:4–6. After making his own comments, Turrettini cites first Beza's *Annotationes* to the effect that the "all" of verse 6, *tous pantas*, ought properly to be rendered as *quosvis*, "some." In Turrettini's view, Calvin (who, incidentally, does not go so far as to render "all" as "some") nonetheless confirms Beza's reading in arguing that "the universal particle must always be referred to kinds of men."⁹⁹ In the next citation, Turrettini is likewise arguing over the interpretation of a text, this time 1 John 2:2 with its reference to the "whole world." Here Calvin is the only authority cited, and he is cited at length.[100]

■ CONCLUSION

This study has offered only a partial picture of the understanding of Calvin by Reformed writers during the era of orthodoxy. What emerges, however, from even this brief survey is not the picture of a great founder of an "ism" but of a contributor to a fairly broad tradition who stood respected among a highly significant group of early formulators and codifiers—including thinkers like Bucer, Bullinger, Musculus, Vermigli, and Beza—who were frequently referenced by later generations of Reformed writers. The apologetic comments of Du Moulin, Rivet, Jurieu, and Claude specifically refuse him the status of founder of a religious movement.

If number of citations is an indication of importance, Calvin clearly stood as a significant source of opinion for both Witsius and Turrettini, but he certainly did not stand alone. Indeed, quite a few of the references in Witsius's *De oeconomia foederum* and Turrettini's *Institutio* place Calvin within a group of Reformed writers. And by far the majority of positive references to Calvin in the work of Witsius and Turrettini are related to the theological interpretation of biblical texts. By the way, the majority of the citations of Beza found in Turrettini are from his *Annotationes in Novum Testamentum* and none are drawn from his only recently notorious *Tabula praedestinationis*. Moreover, as my comments on Cartwright, Field, Rivet, Witsius, and Turrettini indicate, Calvin was cited as much by way of apologetic as for his positive doctrine; typically, he is defended against charges of blasphemy and heresy made by Roman polemicists. Indeed, one of the reasons that Calvin was cited more than Bullinger or Vermigli is that he was more frequently the subject of attack.

The evaluation and use of Calvin by various Reformed writers in the seventeenth century reflects a series of churchly and theological concerns. Some of these were related to the writers' self-identification not as "Calvinists" but as members and representatives of what a number of their confessional documents and ecclesiological treatises called the Reformed catholic Church. Some related to perceptions of Calvin's role in the establishment and furtherance of the Reformation. Some rested on estimates of various aspects of his theological work. Some also reflected the fact that appeals to Calvin as a normative thinker were accompanied by certain caveats, most importantly that scripture, not Calvin, was the identified norm of Reformed theology. Calvin was not the source of all of theological arguments that needed elaboration and defense. On a few points of doctrine—notably on issues of free choice and the divine willing of the fall, Calvin had made a series of unfortunate or possibly hyperbolic statements that could not be taken as normative for Reformed teaching. In his characterization of Calvin's *Institutes*, François Wendel commented that "even in Calvin's lifetime its success was immense, and it was never discredited afterwards." This generalization remains uncontested. Wendel went on to conclude that "it was indubitably one of the causes of the very rapid rise of a Calvinist orthodoxy, strictly adherent to the formulas of the *Institutes*, which even the later controversies have only with difficulty managed to modify."[101]

This judgment will need to be qualified: the diversity of later Reformed theology offers evidence that Calvin's definitions were known and typically respected, but not always followed. And even when reflected, his definitions were often modified—sometimes for the sake of defending the Reformed churches against accusations of error. The seventeenth-century Reformed orthodox writers certainly understood Calvin as one among a significant group of predecessors, but as Perry Miller long ago said of the New England Puritans, they "did not think of him as the fountain head of their thought, nor of themselves as members of a faction of which he was the founder."[102]

■ Notes

1. On the broad understanding of "Calvinism," see Philip Benedict, *Christ's Churches Purely Reformed: A Social History of Calvinism* (New Haven: Yale University Press, 2002), xxii–xxiii; John T. McNeill, *The History and Character of Calvinism* (New York: Oxford University Press, 1954), vii–viii; and Perry Miller, *The New England Mind: The Seventeenth Century* (1939; repr. Boston: Beacon Press, 1961), 93–97. My thanks to Irena Backus for careful reading and editorial comment on this essay.

2. Note Aza Goudriaan, "Ulrik Huber (1636–1694) and the Franecker Debate (1686–1687) on Human Reason and the Bible," in *The Reception of Calvin and his Theology in Reformed Orthodoxy*, ed. Andreas Beck and William den Boer (forthcoming from Leiden: Brill), examining the reception and use of Calvin's *Institutes* by a late seventeenth-century jurist.

3. Moyse Amyraut, *Sermon sur les paroles du Prophete Ezechiel, Chap.* 18. *v.* 23, in *Sermons sur divers textes de la sainte ecriture*, 2nd ed. (Saumur: Isaac Desbordes, 1653), 48.

4. Pierre Du Moulin, *Esclaircissement des controverses salmuriennes* (Leiden: Jean Maire, 1648), 231–32: "De l'allegation de Calvin es predications." I owe this citation to Albert Gootjes. This reluctance could be partly due to the negative image of Calvin as a power-hungry tyrant that was conveyed by the reformer's hostile biographies. See Irena Backus, *Life Writing in Reformation Europe: Lives of Reformers by Friends, Disciples and Foes* (Aldershot: Ashgate, 2008), chaps. 4–5.

5. Thomas Cartwright, *A Replye to and answere made of M. Doctor. Whitgifte: Againste the admonition to the Parliament* (n.p., 1575?), 112.

6. Andreas Rivet, *Catholicus Orthodoxus, oppositus catholico papistae* (Leiden: Abraham Commelin, 1630), 5.

7. Jean Claude, *Défense de la Reformation contre le livre intitulé Préjugez légitimes contre les calvinistes*, 4th ed. (Paris: L.-R. Delay, 1844), 210–11.

8. Pierre Jurieu, *Histoire du Calvinisme et celle du Papisme mises en parallèle: Ou apologie pour les Réformateurs, pour la Réformation, et pour les Réformés... contre... Maimbourg*, 3 vols., 2nd ed., based on the Rotterdam printing of 1683 (n. p., 1823), 1: 417.

9. Ibid., 1: 417–18.

10. Ibid., 2: 5.

11. Ibid., 1: 440 (and cf. 1: 441–44).

12. See, for example, Thomas F. Torrance, "Knowledge of God and Speech about Him according to John Calvin," in *Theology in Reconstruction* (Grand Rapids: Eerdmans, 1966), 76.

13. For example, Daniel Tossanus, *A Synopsis or Compendium of the Fathers, or of the most Famous and Ancient Doctors of the Church, as also of the Schoolmen* (London: Daniel Frere, 1635), 85–86.

14. Thomas Brightman, *A Revelation of the Revelation that is the Revelation of St. John opened clearely with a logicall resolution and exposition* (Amsterdam: no publisher, 1615), Rev. 15:7, 520.

15. Gulielmus Bucanus, *Institutiones theologicae, seu locorum communium Christianae religionis, ex Dei verbo, et praestantissimorum theologorum orthodoxo consensu expositorum, analysis* (Geneva, 1602; Bern: Iohannes & Isaias Le Preux, 1605), preface. Also note the translation: *Institutions of the Christian Religion, framed out of God's Word*, trans. R. Hill (London: George Snowden, 1606; 1659). For an estimation of Bucanus's influence, see Richard Tuck, "Power and Authority in Seventeenth-Century England," *Historical Journal* 17/1 (1974): 43–61.

16. Franz Burman, *Consilium de studio theologico feliciter instituendo*, 2.13, 15, as appended to the author's *Synopsis theologiae et speciatim oeconomiae foederum Dei*, 2 parts (Geneva: Ioannes Pictet, 1678).

17. Lucas Trelcatius Jr., *Scholastica et methodica locorum communium institutio* (London: John Bill, 1604), 1: 3.

18. Johannes Polyander, Andreas Rivetus, Antonius Walaeus, Antonius Thysius, *Synopsis purioris theologiae, disputationibus quinquaginta duabus comprehensa ac conscripta* (Leiden, 1626; Leiden: Donner, 1881), 14: 60.

19. Rivet, *Catholicus Orthodoxus*, 116.

20. Joseph Hall, *The Revelation Unrevealed. Concerning the thousand yeares reigne of the saints with Christ on Earth* (London: John Bisse, 1649), 33.

21. Edward Leigh, *A Systeme or Body of Divinity: consisting of ten books wherein the fundamentals and main grounds of religion are opened*, 2nd ed. (London: William Lee, 1662), 1.9, 138.

22. Ibid., 1, 3.41–51; 4.55.

23. Ibid., 1.9, 138, citing Thomas Cartwright, *Letter to Mr. Hildersham*; and Daniel Featley, *Stricturae in Lyndo-Mastigem: or, an answere by way of supplement to the chapters remaining in the booke intitules, A case for the spectacles* (London: Robert Milbourne, 1638), cap. 14 (2nd pagination, 120).

24. Thomas Barlow, *De studio theologiae: or, Directions for the Choice of Books in the Study of Divinity* (Oxford: Leonard Lichfield, 1699), 11, 13.

25. See Richard Baxter, *Gildas Salvianus: the Reformed Pastor*, in *The Practical Works of the Rev. Richard Baxter: with a Life of the Author...by the Rev. William Orme*, 23 vols. (London: James Duncan, 1830), 14: 70.

26. Jakob Christoph Beck, *Fundamenta theologiae naturalis & revelatae* (Basel: Emanuel Thurneysen, 1757), prolegomena, 17 (11).

27. Ibid., 18 (12–13).

28. See Irena Backus, "Loci communes oder 'Hauptsätze': Ein Medium der europäischen Reformation bei Calvin, Vermigli und Bullinger," in *Calvinismus: Die Reformation in Deutschland und Europa: Eine Ausstellung der Deutschen Historischen Museums Berlin und der Johannes a Lasco Bibliothek Emden*, ed. Ansgar Reiss and Sabine Witt (Dresden: Sandstein, 2009), 97–104; and Backus, "*Loci communes* and the Role of Ramism in the Diffusion of Calvin's Reformation," in *Dimensioni e problemi della ricera storica. Rivista del Dipartimento di storia moderna e contemporanea dell'Università degli studi di Roma "La Sapienza"* 2 (2010), 233–48.

29. For a detailed study of the compendia with discussion of their authors, see Olivier Fatio, "Présence de Calvin à l'époque de l'orthodoxie réformée: Les abrégés de Calvin à la fin du 16e et au 17e siècle," in *Calvinus Ecclesiae Doctor*, ed. W. H. Neuser (Kampen: Kok, 1978), 171–207.

30. Jerome Zanchi, *Compendium praecipuorum capitum doctrinae christianae*, in Jerome Zanchi, *Operum theologicorum*, 3 vols. (Geneva: Crespin, 1617–19), vol. 2, part 8.

31. Edmund Bunnie, *Institutio christianae religionis, a Ioanne Calvino conscripta, compendium simul, ac methodi enarratio, per Edmundum Bunnium* (London: Thomas Vautrollerius, 1576; Antwerp: Aegidius Radaeus, 1582), translated as *The Institutions of Christian Religion, written by that reverend father, D. Iohn Calvin, compendiously abridged by Edmund Bunnie* (London: Thomas Dawson, 1578; 1580); William Delaune, *Institutionis christianae religionis a Ioanne Calvino conscriptae, Epitome in qua adversariorum obiectionibus breves ac solidae responsiones annotantur per Gulielmum Launeum* (London: Thomas Vautrollerius, 1583); Delaune, *Editio secunda emendatior: Tabulis etiam & indice multo facilioribus & locupletioribus* (London: Thomas Vautrollerius, 1584), trans. Christopher Fetherstone as *An Abridgement of the Institution of Christian Religion, written by M. Iohn Caluin,* (Edinburgh: n.p., 1585–87); Caspar Olevianus, *Institutionis religionis Christianae epitome ex Institutiones Ioh. Calvini excerpta* (Herborn: Christoph Corvinus, 1586); Johannes Piscator, *Aphorismi doctrinae Christianie maximam partem ex Institutione Calvini excerpti, sive loci communes theologici, brevibus sententiis expositi* (London: Richard Field, 1595; Oxford: I. Lichfield, 1630).

32. Johannes Piscator, *Aphorismes of Christian Religion: or, a verie compendious abridgement of M. I. Calvins Institutions, set forth in short sentences methodologically by M. I. Piscator,* trans. Henry Holland (London: Richard Field and Robert Dexter, 1596), 9.5, 40.On this edition see also Backus, "Loci communes", 244–47.

33. For example, Augustin Marlorat, *A Catholike and ecclesiasticall exposition of the Holy Gospell after S. Matthew, gathered out of all the singular and approved divines* (London: Thomas Marsh, 1570); Marlorat, *A Catholike...exposition of St. Marke and Luke*, 2 parts (London: Thomas Marsh, 1583).

34. John Mayer, *Commentary upon the Old Testament*, (London: Robert and William Leybourn, 1653), Ps. 2:2, 9, 11, 12; 3, 240.

35. Ibid., Ps. 3:2–5; 4:1, 3, 5, 6; 3, 240–42, 244–45.

36. John Stoughton, *Sixe Sermons on I Cor. II.II* (London: Iohn Bellamie, 1640), 10, 16, 18.

37. Thomas Morton, *Ezekiel's Wheels: A Treatise concerning Divine Providence: Very Seasonable for all Ages* (London: Richard Royston, 1653), 120.

38. Matthew Poole, *Synopsis criticorum aliorumque sacrae scripturae interpretum et commentatorum, summo studio et fide adornata,* 5 vols. (London: J. Flesher & T. Roycroft, 1669–76); and John Pearson, *Critici sacri,* 6 vols. (London: James Flesher, 1660)

39. Thomas Cartwright, *A Confutation of the Rhemists translation, glosses, and annotations on the New Testament* (n.p., 1618), e.g., on Matt. 13 (60) and 27 (135), John 1 (211) and 10 (234), and Phil. 2 (499).

40. Andreas Rivet, *Exercitationes CXC in Genesin* (Leiden: Bonaventure & Abraham Elzevir, 1633), 211a, 472b, 701a.

41. Ibid., 242b, 693b.

42. Ibid., 75a.

43. Andreas Rivet, *Commentarii, in librum secundum Mosis, qui Exodus apud Graecos inscribitur* (Leiden: Franciscus Heger, 1634), 19b–20a.

44. Ibid., 32b; cf. Mayer, *Commentary upon the Pentateuch,* Ex. 1:20, 420, who cites Calvin as agreeing with Augustine and Gregory but does not note the controversy.

45. Rivet, *Commentarii, in librum secundum Mosis,* 36b–37a (at Ex. 2:1); cf. Mayer, *Commentary upon the Pentateuch,* Ex. 2:1 (424); cf. Calvin, *Mosis reliqui libri quatuor in formam harmoniae digesti a Ioanne Calvino: Cum eiusdem commentariis,* Ex. 6:15, *Calv. Opp.* 24: 83–4.

46. John Cosin, *The History of Popish Transubstantiation: To which is opposed the catholic doctrin of the holy scripture, the antient fathers and the Reformed churches,* 2nd ed. (London: Henry Brome, 1679), 2.20, 28–29; cf. 5.19, 73–74.

47. Richard Field, *Of the Church, Five Bookes*, 2nd ed. (Oxford: William Turner, 1628), 3, 15 (free choice), 96–98; cf. 281–82, 89; 16 (*limbus patrum*, concupiscence, and satisfaction), 99–101; 23 (God not the author of sin), 117–32; 32 (original sin), 147–49.

48. Robert Baron, *Metaphysica generalis: Accedunt nunc primum quae supererant ex parte speciali: Omnia ad usum theologiae accommodata: Opus postumum, ex museo Antonii Clementii Zirizaei* (Cambridge: John Hayes, 1685), 12, disp. 1, 305.

49. Ibid., 1, 301.

50. William Twisse, *Of the Morality of the Fourth Commandment, as still in force to binde Christians* (London: John Rothwell, 1641), 31–36.

51. Walter Balcanqual to Dudley Carleton, February 23, 1618, in John Hales, *Golden remains of the ever memorable Mr. John Hales of Eaton-Colledge, &c. With additions from the authors own copy, viz., sermons & miscellanies, also letters and expresses concerning the Synod of Dort. From an authentick hand*, 3rd impression (London: George Pawlet, 1688), 484.

52. Peter White, "The Rise of Arminianism Reconsidered," in *Past and Present* 101 (1983), 35, n. 5.

53. Jacob Arminius, *Amica cum Francisco Iunio de praedestinatione per literas habita collatio*, in *Opera theologica* (Leiden: Godefridus Basson, 1629), 459, 466–67.

54. John Davenant, *Animadversions written by the Right Reverend Father in God, John, Lord Bishop of Sarisbury, upon a treatise intituled, Gods love to mankinde* (London: Iohn Partridge, 1641), 21–23; Pierre Du Moulin, *The Anatomy of Arminianisme: or the Opening of the Controversies lately handled in the Low Countries, concerning the Doctrine of Predestination, of the Death of Christ, of the Nature of Grace* (London: Nathaniel Newbery, 1620), ch. 13, 91; Franciscus Turrettinus, *Institutio theologiae elencticae, in qua status controversiae perspicue exponitur, praecipua orthodoxorum argumenta proponuntur et vindicantur, et fontes solutionum aperiuntur*, 3 vols. (Geneva: Samuel de Tournes, 1679–85), 4, 9.30, trans. George Musgrave Giger as *Institutes of Elenctic Theology*, 3 vols., ed. James T. Dennison (Phillipsburg: Presbyterian and Reformed Publishing, 1992–97); Twisse, *Vindiciae gratiae, potestatis, ac providentiae Dei hoc est, ad examen libelli Perkinsiani de praedestinatione modo et ordine, institutum a J. Arminio, responsio scholastica* (Amsterdam: Joannes Jansson, 1632), 1.1, sec. 4, digr. 2, cap. 1, 57–58.

55. Thomas Goodwin, *A Discourse of Election, of the Free and Special Grace of God Manifested Therein* (1682), 2.1, in *The Works of Thomas Goodwin, D.D., sometime president of Magdalene College Oxford*, 12 vols. (Edinburgh: James Nichol, 1861–66), 9: 93.

56. Brian G. Armstrong, *Calvinism and the Amyraut Heresy: Protestant Scholasticism and Humanism in Seventeenth Century France* (Madison: University of Wisconsin Press, 1969), 158.

57. Synod of Alençon, 30, in John Quick, *Synodicon in Gallia Reformata: or, the Acts, Decisions, Decrees, and Canons of those famous National Councils of the Reformed Churches in France*, 2 vols. (London: T. Parkhurst and J. Robinson, 1692), 2: 410.

58. Du Moulin, *Esclaircissement des controverses salmuriennes*, 231–32.

59. Turrettinus, *Institutio theologiae elencticae*, 14, 14.38, 40.

60. John Overall, *Opinion of the Church of England*, in John Ellis, *A Defence of the Thirty Nine Articles of the Church of England*. (London: H. Bonwicke et al., 1700), 133, citing Calvin on Heb. 9:20 and Rom. 5:18.

61. John Davenant, *Touching the Second Article, discussed at the conference at the Hague on the Extent of Redemption*, in Hales, *Golden Remains*, 591.

62. Richard Baxter, *Universal Redemption of Mankind, by the Lord Jesus Christ: stated and cleared by the late learned Mr. Richard Baxter: Whereunto is added a short account of special redemption* (London: for John Salusbury, 1694), 323, 331, 337–38, 369–70.

63. Du Moulin, *Esclaircissement*, 233.

64. As shown by Michael Heyd, "Who Was the More Loyal Calvinist? The Use of Calvin in the La Place-Garissoles Controversy on the Non-Imputation of Adam's Sin" (paper delivered at the conference "Calvin et Son Influence, 1509–2009," Geneva, May 24–27, 2009).

65. As shown by Gert van den Brink, "Herman Witsius (1636–1708) and the English Antinomian Conflict," in Beck and den Boer, *Reception of Calvin*; cf. for example, John Eaton, *The Honey-combe of free justification by Christ alone collected out of the meere authorities of Scripture and common unanimous consent of the faithfull interpreters of Gods mysteries upon the same* (London: R. B., 1642), 2, 3, 20, 21, 29, 38, etc., also citing Luther and Zanchi with frequency.

66. Herman Witsius, *De oeconomia foederum Dei cum hominibus libri quattuor*, 2nd ed. (Leeuwarden: J. Hagenaar, 1677), 1, 7.8, 12; 3, 3.2, 4.19, 8.26, 11.10; 4, 4.24, 34, 48, 50, 52, 6.68, 7.2, 13.33, 34, 44, 13.4, 15, 15.32, 16.50, 27.33.

67. Ibid., 1, 7. 8, 12 (paired with Calvin); 1, 7.16; 3, 14.25; 4, 1.32, 2.6, 3.4, 3.28, 7.5, 7.20, 25, 15.21, 37 (singly or compared with others).

68. Ibid., 1, 6.7; 4, 2.16, 3.4, 4.27, 7i.5, 7.24, 12.34 (Musculus); 1, 8.32, 34; 3, 4.18; 3, 6.6, 8.6, 10.7 (Beza); 1, 2.7, 6.7, 20; 4, 4.4, 27 (Zanchi); 3, 6.11, 11.36, 13.26 (Ames).

69. Ibid., 1, 7.8, 12.

70. Ibid., 3, 3.2, citing Calvin, *Inst.*, 2, 11.4.

71. Ibid., 3, 4.19.

72. Ibid., 3, 8.26; 4, 12.34, 13.4.

73. Ibid., 1, 2.10 (twice); 2, 6.40.

74. Ibid., 4, 4.27, 7.24.

75. Turrettinus, *Institutio theologiae elencticae*, 3, 21.5, 23.8, 17, 26.2, 28.40; 4, 9.30, 17.30, 37; 6, 7.7, 8.5, 8, 10, 11, 13, 14, 9.2; 8, 6.9; 9, 9.17, 21, 40, 41, 42, 10.2; 11, 1.6, 2.31, 8.6, 13.10, 42, 43, 44, 14.12, 19.21; 12, 5.4, 6.30, 7.16, 8.6, 10.18, 11.16; 13, 1.22, 12.5, 14.14, 15, 16.1; 14, 1.13, 13.32, 38, 40; 15, 4.27, 32, 37, 9.5, 14.20; 18, 7.14, 15.12, 29.2, 32.8, 10, 34.20, 43, 48, 50; 19, 26.21, 28.32.

76. Ibid., 2, 5.12, 31, 10.3, 23, 15.7; 4, 9.16, 17.34; 6, 7.7, 8.5, 8, 14; 9, 9.42; 11, 3.10, 12.7, 13.2, 44, 14.12, 16.3; 13, 15.13, 16.1; 14, 1.13, 14.38; 15, 14.20; 18, 15.12, 34.43, 48; 19, 28.8 (Beza); 2, 5.11, 24, 25; 6, 8.5, 8; 9, 9.17, 43; 11, 13.44; 12, 8.6, 10.18; 13, 3.15; 15, 14.14; 18, 10.27, 15.12; 19, 26.21, 28.2 (Vermigli);, 5, 3.7, 14.15; 9, 10.2; 11, 13.44, 16.23, 24.15; 13, 16.1; 18, 34.48; 19, 28.2 (Zanchi); 9, 10.2; 11, 14.12; 12, 10.18; 13, 1.22; 18, 32.7, 34.43, 48 (Bullinger); 2, 7.3; 11, 19.8, 24.15 (Musculus); 11, 14.12 (Ames).

77. Ibid., 6, 7.7.

78. Ibid., 6, 8.5.

79. Ibid., 9, 9.17.

80. Ibid., 9, 9.40.

81. Ibid., 9, 10.2.

82. Ibid., 11, 13.44.

83. Ibid., 11, 14.12.

84. Ibid., 12, 8.6; cf. Calvin, *Inst.* 2, 7.2; the reference to Trelcatius is probably to Lucas Trelcatius Jr., who despite his identification of the Old and New Testament dispensations of the covenant of grace as one in substance also identified a legal aspect of the Mosaic dispensation, subordinate to the evangelical—which would, as with Rollock and Piscator, from Turrettini's perspective too closely presage the Salmurian theology: see Trelcatius, *Scholastica et methodica locorum communium*, book 2 (109–10); and note Richard A. Muller, "Divine Covenants, Absolute and Conditional: John Cameron and the Early Orthodox Development of Reformed Covenant Theology," in *Mid-America Journal of Theology* 17 (2006): 11–56.

85. Turrettinus, *Institutio theologiae elencticae*, 12, 10.18.

86. On the debate with Caroli, see Wulfert De Greef, *The Writings of John Calvin: An Introductory Guide*, trans. Lyle D. Bierma (Louisville: Westminster John Knox Press, 2009), 158–59.

87. Turrettinus, *Institutio theologiae elencticae*, 3, 26.3.

88. Ibid., 3, 28.40, against Bellarmine and Genebrardus.

89. Ibid., 6, 8.8, 10, 11, 13, 14.

90. Ibid., 11, 19.21.

91. Ibid., 13, 12.5, 14.14, 15, against Franciscus Feuardentius, Bellarmine, Genebrardus, Joannes Maldonatus.

92. Ibid., 15, 9.5; 18, 7.14.

93. Ibid., 12, 7.16, citing the commentary and *Inst.* 1, 14.18; 2, 13.

94. Ibid., 12, 11.16.

95. Ibid., 14, 1.13.

96. Ibid., 4, 14.38.

97. Ibid., 4.9.30."

98. Ibid., 9, 9.40 (contra La Place); 14, 13.32 (contra Piscator); 14, 14.38 (contra Amyraut); 12, 8.6 (contra Rollock et al.).

99. Ibid., 14, 14.38, citing Calvin on 1 Tim. 2:4–5.

100. Ibid., 14, 14.40, citing Calvin on 1 John 2:2.

101. François Wendel, *Calvin: The Origins and Development of His Religious Thought*, trans. Philip Mairet (New York: Harper & Row, 1963), 122.

102. Miller, *New England Mind*, 93.

10 The Dutch Enlightenment and the Distant Calvin

ERNESTINE VAN DER WALL

■ THE CULT OF CALVIN: A NINETEENTH-CENTURY INVENTION

What role was assigned to John Calvin in the era of the Enlightenment? How did he function in the battle between traditionalist and enlightened Protestants that characterized so much of the religious history of the eighteenth century? To what extent was Calvin present in the fight for "true" or "authentic" Christianity that marked the eighteenth-century religious debates and which image of the reformer was put forward in this battle? If we choose to focus on Calvin, the author and historical figure, and not on the "ism" associated with his name, the answer to these and similar questions is actually quite simple: generally speaking, it is hard to find John Calvin being considered as a thinker in his own right in the religious and cultural scene of the eighteenth century. This may come as a surprise in view of the status that would be gained by the Genevan reformer over the course of the next century. By 1900, a veritable "cult of Calvin" had come into existence, epitomized by Émile Doumergue's massive biographical volumes and the impressive range of festivities commemorating the four hundredth anniversary of Calvin's birth in 1909.[1] When one looks for commemorative events and publications in the eighteenth and early nineteenth centuries, however, one is surprised to find that there were almost none. Furthermore, not only is Calvin absent, as one might expect, from the thought world of many writers most closely associated with the "party of Enlightenment"; he also is little present in the worlds of traditional Reformed theology, Pietism, and revivalism. Of course, there were some ardent eighteenth-century Calvinists who demonstrated their adherence to him or rather to a form of Calvinism—the names of George Whitefield and Jonathan Edwards immediately spring to mind. But a "cult of Calvin the reformer" as it emerged in the course of the nineteenth century is absent from the previous age. Seemingly, the image of John Calvin as a theologian and scholar in his own right, as well as a private person, was much more a thing of the nineteenth century than of the eighteenth.

■ THE DUTCH ENLIGHTENMENT, CALVIN, AND CALVINISM

Where does that leave the eighteenth century and, in particular, the age of Enlightenment? Here I should like to deal with the question from the perspective of the Dutch Enlightenment. As is well known, the Dutch Republic played a prominent role in the development of the national and international Calvinist tra-dition. The national Synod of Dort of 1618–1619 (which despite its name was strongly international) put an indelible stamp on the elaboration of Calvin's the-ology. Subsequently, subscription to the decrees of the synod was mandatory for all ministers of the nationally subsidized and legally privileged Reformed church throughout the *ancien régime*. That Calvinism was consequently the defining fea-ture of Dutch religion par excellence, and that Calvin was thus the hero of Dutch theology, is the notion that has been cultivated in various circles in the Netherlands since the nineteenth century. Today this image is still popular among scholars, journalists, and others who firmly believe that since the sixteenth century the Netherlands has been a thoroughly Calvinist country. Some Christian politicians wholeheartedly agree with this view, including the Dutch prime minister, J. P. Balkenende, in office in 2009. He had been reared in a neo-Calvinist milieu and was emphatic in showing his attachment to Calvin and Calvinism in the Calvin celebrations of that year.[2]

But who exactly Calvin was and what he stood for is not altogether clear to everybody. While the Dutch are commonly viewed as a truly Calvinistic people—the label "Calvinist" being commonly taken to denote a singularly sober, pessi-mistic, and joy-killing person—the average Dutchman in 2009 hardly seemed aware that once upon a time there was a Protestant reformer whose name had been lent to this popular image. Even a "Calvin glossy," published in the Netherlands in early 2009, did not really seem to help.[3] Nor did it clarify matters to put Calvin on a par with Barack Obama.[4] It requires some mental gymnastics, as well as a particular view of both America's president and the Genevan reformer, to sub-scribe to this opinion. Even latter-day Calvinists seem less than clear about just who Calvin was. In the spring of 2009, a series of debates was organized in the Netherlands that, to judge by their titles, aimed at shedding light on at least four sorts of Calvin: one debate was on "the Catholic Calvin" (appropriately held in the southern Netherlands), a second concerned "the intolerant Calvin," the third dealt with "the brave Calvin," while the last one focused on "the doubting Calvin." Whether the organizers desired to run a contest between these various Calvins is not known but, for whatever it is worth, in view of the age of Enlightenment, one might add yet another Calvin: "the distant Calvin."

The distant Calvin: this designation is indicative of the status of the Genevan reformer in the Dutch Enlightenment. It implies that there is not much to say about "John Calvin and the Enlightenment," if one were to deal only with the Genevan reformer in his capacity as theologian and scholar, that is Calvin *sec*, while leaving aside the theological tradition going under the label of Calvinism. Here, we meet with the knotty problem of the relationship between Calvin, the reformer, on the one hand, and Calvinism, as it developed in the seventeenth and eighteenth centuries in different regions of the globe, on the other. How can one disentangle the two in a manner that does justice to both the reformer and the subsequent theological traditions associated with him? This is not the place to elaborate on this important and complex question. Let us realize, however, that one can hardly avoid dealing with Calvinism or Reformed theology when studying the role of Calvin in later times. Furthermore, if one were to restrict oneself to the topic of "Calvin and the Enlightenment," one would find that there is not much to tell, beyond enumerating the well-known critique of the Genevan reformer by "the party of Enlightenment." As Michael Bush recently noted, "the eighteenth century was a time between two periods of vigorous but quite different Calvin study."[5] This chapter, therefore, deals with both Calvin and Calvinism as they presented themselves in the Dutch Republic in the age of Enlightenment. This shall be illustrated by three case studies.

■ THE ENLIGHTENMENT AND THE SERVETUS AFFAIR

Before turning to "Calvin and the Dutch Enlightenment," let me first make a few general observations. As has been indicated, it seems justified to speak of the distant Calvin in relation to his role as a reformer in his own right in the long eighteenth century, which most historians date from 1688 until 1815 or even beyond. The paucity of secondary literature on the topic of "Calvin and the eighteenth century" confirms this impression. A glance at volumes bearing titles such as "the legacy of John Calvin" or "Calvin's heritage" suffices to reveal that to this day theologians and historians view the legacy of the Genevan reformer as a component of the religious history of the sixteenth and seventeenth centuries, but not of that of the eighteenth century. A handful of Calvinist icons from the period merit recognition—in the Dutch Republic, the names of prominent Calvinists such as Nicolaus Holtius, Alexander Comrie, Petrus Hofstede, Johannes Barueth, and Theodorus van der Groe might be mentioned—but one can hardly avoid the impression that the eighteenth century as such is not among the primary interests of students of Calvinism.[6]

Distant though he may have been, John Calvin was, of course, not absent from the minds of eighteenth-century men and women. A certain ambivalence in their view of him is evident, for example, in the fact that, besides a band of Calvinist admirers, there were also those for whom Calvin was certainly present but in a rather negative fashion, as the forerunner and creator of the persecuting spirit of the orthodox Calvinist preachers of their own day. The growing dislike of religious persecution did much to shape Calvin's image in the era of the Enlightenment, not merely among the party of the Enlightenment but among Calvin's followers also.

For the great figures of the European Enlightenment such as Kant, Voltaire, Rousseau, or Paine, Calvin's image was above all shaped by the dark shadow of the Servetus affair. While some might show some admiration for Calvin's eloquent style and his scholarship, his attitude toward Servetus was rejected out of hand. As is now acknowledged by friends and foes alike, Calvin played an active part in the arrest and trial of the Spanish scholar and was not loath to see him receive the death penalty. He even wrote a tract defending the burning of Servetus. Those who championed freedom of the critical intellect and opposed clerical censorship naturally preferred Servetus to Calvin, not so much because of any theological affinities with Servetus' antitrinitarian theology, but first and foremost because, as they emphatically stated, the idea of burning people at the stake for divergent theological views was beyond their comprehension. They were in no way original in taking this stand. Contemporaries of Calvin had already criticized the burning of heretics, with Sebastian Castellio being the most famous mouthpiece and Jacobo Acontio serving as another striking example.

To Voltaire's mind, Calvin was the epitome of intolerance, a view that colored his treatment of Calvinism too. In the article on dogma in his *Dictionnaire philosophique* (1764), a book that came to be forbidden in various parts of the Netherlands, we read about Calvin being judged by a tribunal of great men. And who are the judges? They are all those who have done good for mankind, such as Confucius, Solon, Socrates, Titus, Antoninus, and Epictetus. Calvin prides himself, in his gross dialect (*patois*), to have kicked the papal idol—although only, Voltaire adds silently, after others had already overthrown this idol. "I have written against painting and sculpture," Calvin defends his case before the lofty tribunal; "I have proven the uselessness of good works, and I have shown that it is diabolical to dance a minuet, so I should be placed next to St. Paul." During his speech, there appears a lighted pile close to Calvin and a dreadful creature emerges, half burned, from the flames, crying "despicable monster, I am Servetus whom due to you has undergone the most cruel death because I disputed with you about the manner in which three persons can form one substance." Thereupon all the judges condemn Calvin to a harsh punishment.[7]

Voltaire set the tone for much of the subsequent freethinking critique of Calvin's attitude, in the Netherlands and elsewhere. The Dutch freethinker Pieter van Woensel echoed the Voltairean view in a short essay on the "history of spiritual persecutions" in his journal, *De Lantaarn voor 1792*.[8] Much later, in 1909, the well-known Dutch freethinker Ferdinand Domela Nieuwenhuis, a former Lutheran minister, published a similarly critical piece on Calvin's behavior toward Servetus, obviously intended to counteract the stream of favorable commemorative publications on Calvin that appeared that year.[9]

We might expect the enlightened party to be highly critical of Calvin's conduct in the Servetus affair, but it is noteworthy that also among Calvinists something of an evolution had taken place in the course of the eighteenth century. Like the party of the Enlightenment, they increasingly tended to distance themselves from Calvin's attitude toward Servetus, though in a more circumspect manner, advancing all sorts of arguments to exculpate their hero. One of the staunchest Calvinists in the republic, the Rotterdam minister and professor Petrus Hofstede, condemned the use of force by the magistrate in religious matters. Citing with approval Dirk Volckertszoon Coornhert and such prominent seventeenth-century Remonstrants as Johannes Uytenbogaert, Étienne de Courcelles, and Gerard Brandt, Hofstede admitted with regret that in the first stage of the Reformation Protestants had sinned against the principle of freedom of conscience due to the confusing circumstances of the day and had defended the killing of heretics. This, however, should be considered as a sad remainder of Roman Catholicism. Only two prominent Protestants had defended the killing of heretics, Calvin and Beza. "What are these two compared to the thousands of Juda?!" he exclaimed. Nonetheless, the cruel sentiment of these theologians might be still present in the eighteenth century. He noted with regret: "I have no other shield to counter this blow than the short statement of the learned Swiss theologian Johann Jakob Zimmerman, who in his book on toleration wrote: 'The Protestant principle of toleration is of basic importance, not the deviations from this principle by some Protestants.'"[10]

Another prominent Calvinist apologist, the Rotterdam minister Jan Scharp, was also critical of Calvin's behavior in the Servetus affair, saying that at times he was very displeased with Calvin having had Servetus burnt at the Genevan stake. The fact was not to be denied; Calvin himself had admitted it, thinking he was doing his duty. But if Calvin was attacked merely for this single case, then Scharp wanted to defend not the act but the man. Why should Calvin be more enlightened than his age? If he were to live in our day, he would have abstained from the act just as we do.[11]

Although Hofstede's and Scharp's argument clearly has an apologetic ring, attributing the mentality of Calvin and Beza to residual Catholicism, later Calvinists often appear to be more on the defensive than their eighteenth-century predecessors. At least that is the impression given by quite a few biographers of Calvin to our own day. One of the favorite arguments to exculpate Calvin is still the one engraved on the Servetus monument erected by Genevan Calvinists in 1903, some 350 years after the execution, which ascribes Calvin's intolerance to the "spirit of the age." Let us recall, however, that Castellio, Acontio, and others were children of that age too, and they apparently were not tempted to succumb to the "errors of their day."

The scholar who, in the age of Enlightenment, made the fullest attempts to deal impartially with Calvin's role in the Servetus affair was the German Lutheran church historian Johann Lorenz von Mosheim. Throughout his life, Mosheim, who is considered to be the first important representative within early modern Western history of a critical approach to the history of church and dogma, was profoundly interested in the history of heresy and heretics and, especially, the history of burned books (his *Bibliotheca Vulcani* project).[12] Mosheim took up the Servetus affair as part of this larger project. Although he wished to present Calvin's part in the affair in as neutral a manner as possible, he made it clear that, in general, his sympathies were not with the Genevan reformer, whom he regarded as a hindrance to the expansion of freedom in the Reformed Church. Nor was Mosheim much taken by Calvin's doctrine of predestination, whose deep mysteries, in his eyes, did little to further peace in the church. He was equally critical of the intricacies of Reformed scholasticism.[13] In his first work on Servetus, the *Historia Michaelis Serveti* of 1727, Mosheim did not refrain from calling Calvin a murderer.[14] He later took back this judgment, however, and said that Calvin's errors were those of his day—the familiar argument of the chorus of Calvin's defenders.[15] Interestingly, funding for the publication of the book came, in part, from the Netherlands, which shows that there must have been some people, or at least someone, who hoped for a rehabilitation of Servetus.[16]

Mosheim's first work about Servetus in 1727, however, was sharply criticized by the Walloon minister of the Hague Armand Boisbeleau de la Chapelle, one of the founders of the *Bibliothèque raisonnée*, who accused Mosheim, as a Lutheran, of cherishing prejudices about Calvin and Calvinism that led him to depict Calvin in a most unfavorable light. Mosheim, taken aback by this accusation as well as other critical comments, wrote to La Chapelle that his was a work of history, not of confessional controversy. La Chapelle was unimpressed and went on with his attempts to prove that the German church historian was far from impartial in his presentation of the material on the Servetus affair. La Chapelle pointed out that the *Historia Michaelis Serveti* was largely based on the *Memoirs of Literature* of the fierce early eighteenth-century anti-Calvinist Michel de la Roche, and he argued that Mosheim provided a historical legitimacy to all sorts of ridiculous and spiteful stories published by Calvin's enemies. La Chapelle agreed with Mosheim that "Calvin sinned in denouncing Servetus to the Syndic of Geneva," but he denied that the reformer had done this "out of malice" or "personal animosity," as Mosheim asserted. Rather, it resulted from ignorance on Calvin's part and was "the unfortunate consequence of the prejudices of his century."[17]

Whether the critical view of the Huguenot minister was shared by other Calvinists in the Dutch Republic at the time is not altogether clear. As we shall see, the Groningen church historian Daniel Gerdes was not amused, either, by Mosheim's treatment of Calvin. Yet as has already been noted, by the latter part of the eighteenth century there were also Calvinists who appeared to side with Mosheim's view rather than with La Chapelle's. Be that as it may, Mosheim's first history about Calvin and Servetus, which soon appeared in a Dutch translation, occasioned the publication of a new edition of a Dutch poem on Servetus by the seventeenth-century Collegiant Joachim Oudaan, which was originally published in 1655. Oudaan "cursed" the idea of having a man killed because of his religious views, treating Servetus as a martyr.[18]

■ THE ENEMY WITHIN

A mere glance at the eighteenth-century developments in the Netherlands discloses that Dutch men and women were increasingly turning from theological doctrines associated with Calvin toward a broader, latitudinarian view on doctrinal matters. I shall pass over the historical and theological factors that contributed to this significant turn of events. Instead I should like to pay attention to a fundamental development that emerged within the Reformed Churches in the seventeenth century. This development is closely linked with the notion of "the enemy within."[19]

To speak of the enemy within is obviously to speak from a particular perspective, marked by a dualist structure composed of friends or enemies. For the Reformed traditionalists of the seventeenth and eighteenth centuries, the enemy within was the growing liberalizing movement that manifested itself among Reformed Protestants. These Protestants were increasingly inclined to turn away from Calvin's tenets and to embrace a more liberal version of Reformed Christianity. Remarkably, then, it was within the Calvinist churches that a movement away from Calvin came into existence. Liberal Protestantism emerged within the official church. Like traditionalism, it can be said to be a product of Reformed Protestantism. The very fact that traditional Protestants saw themselves confronted with an internal movement of liberalization explains the vehemence of the numerous theological and ecclesiastical controversies in early modern and modern Christianity.

Among these liberal currents it was Cocceio-Cartesianism—a particular mix of the theological views of the German-Dutch oriental scholar and theologian Johannes Cocceius and philosophical tenets of the French philosopher René

Descartes—that from 1660 onward laid the foundation for moderate enlightened notions in the Reformed Church. With its emphasis on philology and biblical exegesis unhampered by dogmatics, Cocceianism did much to pave the way for a mitigated form of Calvinism. Likewise the connection of Cocceianism with various Cartesian notions was a major factor in this development.[20]

Another important manifestation of the internal liberalization process was the movement of the neologians that emerged in the course of the eighteenth century and strove to cleanse theology of any dogmatic accretions unacceptable to the enlightened mind.[21] The neologians looked upon themselves as people who continued the Reformation of Calvin and the other major sixteenth-century Protestant reformers. Indeed, they liked to call themselves "the new reformers." Since traditionalist Protestants claimed to be working in the vein of Calvin as well, it is clear that both progressive and traditionalist Protestants traced their genealogy to the sixteenth-century reformers and imagined themselves as the true heirs of the Reformation. This is an indication of the versatility of the label "Reformation" in later times. One may recall that, in the nineteenth century, liberal Christians also liked to present themselves as preserving the true heritage of the Reformation. It goes without saying that liberal believers, like the neologians and their successors, had in mind the formal aspect of the work of the Reformation, viewing the reformers as their models because the latter had dared to question the theological tradition. Traditionalists, on the other hand, went much further in their identification with the sixteenth-century Reformation, praising its representatives for their specific theological insights.

In the eighteenth century, the major discussions in European Protestantism (both Calvinist and Lutheran) revolved around basic theological and ecclesiastical issues that clearly revealed the tensions over orthodox Calvinism, including the issue of subscription to confessional writings, the question of the fundamental and nonfundamental articles of faith, predestination, original sin, atonement, the limits of civil and ecclesiastical toleration, and the extent to which exegesis should be emancipated from dogmatic theology in a quest to return to the gospel preached by Christ and the apostles. The enlightened version of Protestantism was poignantly captured by the Scottish theologian Hugh Blair when he argued: "It is for the sake of man, not of God, that worship and prayers are required; not that God may be rendered more glorious, but that man may be made better."[22] Liberal Swiss Reformed theologians such as Jean-Alphonse Turrettini, Samuel Werenfels, and Jean-Frédéric Osterwald sought a via media between the Reformed orthodoxy of the previous era and the Enlightenment. All three enjoyed great popularity in Calvinist Europe, especially in the Netherlands.[23]

■ THE "CRISIS OF CALVINISM" IN THE EIGHTEENTH-CENTURY DUTCH REPUBLIC

The Dutch Republic was, of course, the country of a flourishing Remonstrant tradition, illustrated by such eminent scholars as Philip van Limborch and Jean le Clerc. It was the hotbed of Cocceio-Cartesianism, the cradle of the Radical Enlightenment of Spinoza and the brothers Koerbagh, and the haven of immigrant

Huguenots, including Pierre Bayle. These currents, each in their own way, contributed to the loosening of rigid Calvinism, particularly Cocceius with his theology of the covenants, his emphasis on the historical dimension of salvation, and his profound philological interest. As noted earlier, the linking of Cocceian views with Cartesians tenets among Cocceius's disciples did much to prepare the soil for the more liberal forms of Reformed theology of the eighteenth century. The Radical Enlightenment also influenced attitudes toward Calvinism, perhaps most importantly by forcing traditionalists who opposed the more extreme positions of the radical wing of the Enlightenment to reflect on their own measure of Calvinism. This could, of course, harden the position of traditionalists, but, consciously or unconsciously, it may also have been instrumental in loosening the strictures of Calvinist theology. To all this was added the intellectual and religious contribution of French Reformed Protestants whose life stories helped to create an atmosphere in which the notion of toleration came to play a formidable role. Each one of these traditions contributed to the eighteenth-century Dutch view of Calvin—to the extent that Calvin was still read at all.

In fact, as the Dutch church historian Simon van der Linde aptly noted in an essay published in 1964, "the number of references to the Genevan reformer by kindred spirits is quite modest" in the eighteenth-century Netherlands.[24] That Calvin was not much read in this period is apparent first of all from the publication history of his works. Although the Netherlands housed Protestant Europe's most active printing centers, not a single complete edition of any of Calvin's Latin works appeared from a Dutch press in the eighteenth century. Readers had to make do with the 1671 Amsterdam edition of the *Opera omnia*, published by the widow J. J. Schipper, unless they were content to use an abridged version of the *Institutes*, published by Joris De Raed in Amsterdam in 1739.[25] As for translations into the vernacular, the only known works are Calvin's *Traité des reliques* and *Contre la secte phantastique des libertins*, both of which appeared in the second decade of the eighteenth century, translated by Carolus Tuinman, a Dutch Reformed minister of Pietist leanings.[26] Unlike Luther's sermons, Calvin's sermons were unavailable in the vernacular in the eighteenth-century Dutch Republic.[27]

Interest in Calvin's life and thought among Reformed theologians and church historians was scarcely more pronounced. The Groningen professor of theology Daniel Gerdes (1698–1765), a conservative divine who belonged to the "serious" Cocceians, authored a critical-historical essay on the *Institutes*, dealing with a first (fictive) edition of the work.[28] Being a great admirer of the Reformation, he wrote a *Historia Reformationis* in which he sketched the Reformation as a European movement comprising various confessions, which was at the time an innovative approach to Reformation history.[29] The work lavished praise on Calvin and took issue with von Mosheim's negative judgment of his role in the Servetus affair. Gerdes was especially taken with Calvin's notions about death and the resurrection of the faithful (in connection with 1 Cor. 15).[30]

The Leiden theologian and church historian Jona Willem te Water (1740–1822) declared Calvin to be the greatest of the reformers. There was no work more eminent than the *Institutio*, he asserted, and Calvin was by far the best example for any dogmatist.[31] In the anonymous *Levensbeschrijving van geleerde mannen*, Calvin was lauded for the work ethos he displayed until his death.[32] Such praise, however, only partially counterbalances the fact that when Calvin was mentioned in Dutch historical and theological studies of the period, it was usually in the same breath with other sixteenth-century reformers.

The only biography of Calvin to appear in Dutch in the eighteenth century was a Dutch translation by the Lutheran pastor George Heinrich (Hendrik) Reiche of the 1794 German biographical work by Johann Friedrich Wilhelm Tischer, entitled *Calvins Leben, Meinungen und Thaten, ein Lesebuch für seine Glaubensgenossen*. The Dutch translation (*Het leven, de gevoelens en bedrijven van Calvyn: Een leesboek voor 't algemeen*) appeared two years later, with a preface by Herman Muntinghe, a middle-of-the-road Calvinist theologian.[33] Muntinghe welcomed this German biography as signaling a diminishment of the tensions between Lutherans and Calvinists that had for so long prevented biographers of both Luther and Calvin from giving a fair judgment of the two great reformers. Fortunately, prejudices were disappearing, the truth was becoming unveiled, and impartiality was getting the upper hand. If any great man had been the victim of profound partiality, it was Calvin, Muntinghe declared. His followers unduly praised their master, while his enemies saw only his faults, forgetting that many of these were inspired by a truly lofty principle, his love for the truth, and that they were often not personal shortcomings but the faults of his age.[34] The learned journal *Vaderlandsche Bibliotheek* also praised Tischer's biography as an impartial story of Calvin's life.[35] The nineteenth-century Mennonite minister and historian Christiaan Sepp wondered why no Dutch author had wished to describe the life of Calvin. Did the memory of his conduct in the Servetus affair stir a conscious antipathy, he asked.[36]

The world of academic theology continued to be constrained by the confessional framework of Dort, since the requirement that all theology professors assent to the decrees of the synod remained in place throughout the century. Still there was no real Calvinist stronghold in the Dutch academic world. The University of Franeker, for example, had its share of broad-minded theologians such as Petrus Conradi, Herman Venema, and Samuel Hendrik Manger, who pleaded for biblical exegesis free from any dogmatic constraint and looked upon the sixteenth-century Reformation as a movement that ushered in a new era of freedom. Venema notably traced his theological views back to Erasmus and George Cassander, Cocceius and Campegius Vitringa, rather than to Calvin.[37] Leiden was also known for academic divines of a latitudinarian mentality, such as Ewald Hollebeek and Jan Jacob Schultens. As for the label "Calvinist," the Leiden liberal theologian Joan van den Honert refused to employ it or to apply it to the Protestant current to which he belonged because he thought it smacked of sectarianism. Among liberally minded divines Van den Honert was not the only one to hold such a view, but in wider circles labeling remained popular. In the Dutch Reformed Church, for example, people until the end of the eighteenth century identified unambiguously with specific theological and ecclesiastical currents within the church (Cocceianism, Voetianism, Pietism, etc.). This sort of labeling continued to play an important role in the calling of ministers. Whenever a vacancy presented itself in a congregation, great care was usually taken to strike a balance between the various currents.

If there were few radical protests against Calvin but also few heartfelt pleas in his favor in the Dutch Republic, this indifferent attitude must be linked to the dominant character of the Dutch Enlightenment in its mainstream Protestant version, which sought to steer a middle course between the Scylla of radical enlightened views (often labeled as Socinian or deist) and the Charybdis of enthusiasm and revivalism. Fear of Socinianism kept Protestant minds engaged well into the eighteenth century. In the mid-1750s, for example, the Dutch translation of a work on the atonement by the English dissenter John Taylor was prohibited by the deputies of Friesland as a "Socinian book."[38] Apparently, when Taylor called it a "dangerous error" to expect "to obtain Mercy and Salvation by a presumptuous, inactive Reliance upon the Blood and Merits of *Christ*; or by the Imputation of his Righteousness to us, instead of obeying, or while we neglect to obey his Commands delivered in the Gospel," the Frisian authorities judged this a threat to public order.[39] But whereas, on the one end of the spectrum, Socinianism remained a negative pole against which orthodoxy defined itself and a charge that could lead to heated discussions and even to censorship, on the other end of the spectrum, "enthusiasm" emerged as an equally dangerous extreme that right-thinking theologians sought to avoid. The so-called Nijkerk revival movement, which created a stir in the Dutch Republic in 1749–1750, elicited negative reactions among liberal Reformed theologians, such as Van den Honert. The minister who played the pivotal role in this revival, Gerardus Kuypers, preferred not to be reminded of this episode later in life when he had transformed himself into a moderately enlightened professor of theology.[40]

While Dutch academic theologians had not yet publicly rejected the Canons of Dort, foreign observers had no doubt that their views had moved away from orthodox Calvinism. The late eighteenth-century German church historian Johann August Christoph von Einem, who continued Mosheim's ecclesiastical history of contemporary church affairs, observed that Dutch Reformed theologians, like the theologians of Geneva, had become Arminians, publicly embracing universalism. To be sure, they had not recanted the Canons of Dort. Their writings nonetheless showed that they were not in favor of the strict predestinarian doctrine proclaimed by the synod and that the number of those who staunchly defended Calvin's system was in steady decline. Indeed, according to Einem, this trend was virtually universal among Reformed churches. The churches of Poland, Hungary, and Transylvania likewise continued to pay lip service to the ancient creeds but had moved away from them. Only in Scotland did the Presbyterians preserve the old teachings. Whatever the status of the creeds in Calvinist countries, ministers of the Calvinist churches did as they liked; "Calvin's system had lost much of its prestige."[41]

■ CASE STUDY 1: "AUTHENTIC" CALVINISM

Just as a monolithic approach to the Enlightenment is inadequate, so too is a monolithic approach to Calvin and Calvinism. Three case studies will show that attitudes toward Calvin and his ideas varied between the more orthodox Reformed Protestants and their liberal and progressive brethren. The first case study concerns the worries expressed by stricter Calvinists in the mid-eighteenth century about the danger of "Amyraldism" or "Salmurianism."

In the 1750s two staunch defenders of Calvin, the Dutch Reformed ministers Nicolaas Holtius and Alexander Comrie, published a famous series of dialogues on toleration, entitled *Examination of the plan concerning toleration, to unite the teachings of the Synod of Dort, established in the year 1619, with the condemned teachings of the Remonstrants* (1753–1759).[42] Toleration had become a major topic in religious and philosophical discussions in the Dutch Republic. Holtius and Comrie felt themselves called to contribute to this ongoing debate out of fear that traditional Dutch Calvinism might not survive the attack on dogmatic Christianity by the so-called party of tolerants, whom they suspected of concocting a devious plan to reconcile the Remonstrants and Contra-Remonstrants, or, in other words, to introduce Pelagianism, in all its evil manifestations, into the Dutch Reformed Church. A prominent member of this "party" was the Leiden-trained theologian Antoni van der Os. Along with the Leiden theologians Jan Jacob Schultens and Joan Alberti, he soon became a main target of Holtius and Comrie.[43]

One look at the title page of the *Examination* suffices to tell the readers that they will be taken back to the national debate of the early seventeenth century between Arminians and Gomarists. Around 1750 this debate was still unfinished; the ideas propagated in the *Examination* are strongly anchored in the seventeenth century. The authors very much like to connect their liberal contemporaries with seventeenth-century representatives of liberal Reformed theology, including Balthasar Bekker, Herman Alexander Röell, Johannes Vlak, and Frederik van Leenhof, whereas they themselves find their major support among seventeenth-century representatives of Reformed theology, such as Franciscus Gomarus, André Rivet, John Owen, and the makers of the Canons of Dort. The title page of the *Examination* mentions a "Society of Adherents of the Dutch Forms of Unity." In the "age of societies," the authors may have thought that such an association should not be lacking. They were rather imaginative in thinking up associations; they also created a fictitious "Old Calvinian Society." With their imagined society of "Adherents of the Dutch Forms of Unity," they wanted to support the "lovers of truth," so that these were not distracted from the pure gospel by the "gratifying" terms of "love" and "tolerance."

The *Examination* is structured as a series of dialogues. The *dramatis personae* are five gentlemen who represent religious currents of the time: Orthodoxus, an orthodox believer; Philalethes, a "lover of truth" (of a traditionalist sort); Pantanechomenus, one who "endures all" (and is a partisan of toleration); Adiaphorus, an "indifferent"; and, finally, Euruodius, an "opener of broad thoroughfares" and partisan of comprehension. Contemporaries would have had little trouble in recognizing these factions or linking the participants in the conversations to specific contemporary names. Indeed, four of the five were understood at the time to represent the following figures: Orthodoxus and Philalethes represented Comrie and Holtius, respectively, and Pantanechomenus and Euruodius were figures for Jan Jacob Schultens and Joan Alberti. To this day, it remains a mystery who Adiaphorus was intended to represent. By opting for the dialogue genre, the authors hoped "to cause as little resentment as possible." Holtius and Comrie cannot see their opponents' actions as anything other than "machinations" by the enlightened party, hiding their true intentions of reconciling the formerly conflicting parties of Remonstrants and Contra-Remonstrants, or even worse, of attempting to convert Reformed Christians to Spinozism and atheism. With this idea of a secret conspiracy, the authors put themselves firmly in the tradition of anti-Enlightenment thought. Again and again, orthodox believers in the eighteenth century detected subterfuge, secret assaults, and hidden agendas behind the writings of the enlightened faction. Pro-Enlightenment thinkers were scarcely less given to conspiracy theories. It is remarkable how much mutual suspicion there was about the other party hatching secret conspiracies.[44]

Every page in the *Examination* reveals a contrasting mode of thinking: old versus new, sad versus cheerful, rigid versus broad-minded, orthodoxy versus latitudinarianism, conflict versus harmony, Dordrecht versus Saumur. The orthodoxy is old, tested, somber, rigid, and roundly supports the "old reformers" and "Dordrecht." The enlightened faction is young; presents new things; is cheerful, civilized, and well mannered; is antischolastic; and favors the "anti-Christian doctrine of the Saumur fathers" and other "newfangled theologians." With ill-concealed distaste, the authors note that in their time people are only interested in what is new. The old tried and trusted Gospels are now to be replaced by a different Holy Writ. However, what masquerades as the "new and greater light" propagated by fashionable thinkers is nothing but their own fantasies. Because they think they have received a greater light than the generations that came before them, they demand that the orthodox jettison their prejudices and distance themselves from the convictions handed down to them by their forefathers. Those ideas, however, were inherited from the most prominent Reformed theologians and synods. In essence, the difference between the two camps, as Comrie and Holtius see it, boils down to a different concept of man's natural powers. The enlightened camp attributes too much to nature, raising free will onto the throne like Dagon and undermining God's free grace. "True" Protestants, however, know that God offers salvation in Christ by his grace freely given.

If ever Calvin came to be identified with Dort and seventeenth-century Reformed orthodoxy, it is in these dialogues. The authors strove to defend Calvin's theology against Remonstrantism and Pelagianism, which they saw especially embodied in Salmurian theology. Calvin himself, however, was hardly mentioned in the many pages of the *Examination*; and when the *Institutio* was quoted at some length (on the doctrine of free grace), the citation was preceded by a quotation from Luther.[45] Amyraldism might look upon itself as Calvinistic, but, in fact, it sapped the bastion of authentic Calvinism. In Comrie and Holtius's view of the rise of Amyraldism, we encounter a typical version of "the enemy within": the true, time-tested doctrine is likened to a besieged city. And it is noteworthy that for these mid-eighteenth-century defenders of orthodoxy, it was no longer Cartesianism, as some fifty years before, that was the dreaded enemy, but the teachings of Moyse Amyraut and the mid-seventeenth-century school of Saumur, whose doctrine of hypothetical universalism smacked dangerously of Arminianism. Here we encounter a strand in eighteenth-century Dutch Reformed thought that had hardly budged from the ideas of early Reformed orthodoxy.

In order to counter this internal hostile force Holtius and Comrie, as noted, created a fictive "Calvinian Society." This "Old Calvinian Society," which was and remained a figment of the imagination, ought to form a barrier against harmful novelties such as those propounded by the professors of Saumur. Its goal was to uphold the three classic forms of unity of Dutch Reformed Protestantism: the Belgic Confession, the Heidelberg Catechism, and the Canons of Dort. The adjective "Calvinian" was closely identified with these confessional writings because they were seen to embody "true" or "authentic" Calvinism.

The notion of "authentic" Calvinism leads us to a broader question that appears to haunt believers of whatever religious faith regarding the true form of their faith. The quest for authenticity tends to be closely associated with a profound interest in the origins of one's faith or persuasion, authenticity being identified with original purity. Every century, of course, has its movements that look for the true, pure form of their faith and assume that they have found it at a given moment in some particular person or current in the past. The eighteenth-century quest for authenticity can be identified with the search for the "essence of Christianity" that became so characteristic of the nineteenth century. Yet in defenders of authentic Calvinism such as Comrie and Holtius, we encounter a paradox. For them, as for many others in the eighteenth century, "true" Calvinism was first and foremost equated with seventeenth-century Dort and the formula it officially embraced. The Dutch, like other European Calvinists, saw Calvin and his theology through the lens of the National Synod of 1618–1619 and the preceding debates between Arminians and Gomarists. So familiar is this that it may prevent us from realizing to what extent "Dort" put an indelible stamp on Calvinism in subsequent centuries, and to what extent discussions of "Calvinism" could be carried on without much reference to Calvin himself.

■ CASE STUDY 2: MODERATELY ENLIGHTENED PROTESTANTISM

The second case study explores a moderately liberal version of Reformed Protestantism, that of the famous Dutch novelist Elizabeth Wolff-Bekker (1738–1804), usually called Betje Wolff. Although the Canons of Dort remained the confessional basis of the Dutch Reformed Church and disciplinary procedures leading to deposition were even initiated against a number of those who broke ranks with them, including Antoni van der Os, the general current of ideas, as we have already seen, was turning away from Reformed orthodoxy. The spread of the idea of toleration bred a profound aversion to religious dogmatism and sectarianism. Some liberal theologians, just like the neologians, thought that Calvin might be regarded as a forerunner of liberal theology in that he had removed the shackles of medieval dogmatism. The main question for many Dutch Calvinists thus became: to what extent was one allowed to deviate from "the fathers of Dort"?

Betje Wolff, a lay theologian of Reformed confessional affiliation, was born into a family of staunch Calvinists and married a Calvinist minister. Gradually, however, she attached herself to the movement of moderately enlightened Protestants who said good-bye to dogmatism and sectarianism and moved away from Calvinism.

She asserted that she did not want to look through "glasses ground by Luther or Calvin." Or, as the protagonist in one of her novels, written together with Aagje Deken, remarks, "Whether I receive the truth from Luther or Calvin, from Saint Paul or Socrates, it does not matter at all, since truth is truth."[46] Her faith was a conscious act, based upon her own investigation: "I do not ask anyone what I should believe; the rule of my faith and life has been written down in the Holy Book; one's own investigation is by far the best thing."[47] It is the duty of Protestants to believe for themselves; each individual alone determines the number and contents of his or her articles of faith. Free investigation is characteristic of the Protestant Church. One cannot rely upon decisions by synods or particular persons since all such judgments are made by fallible men. She wished to return to the "simple faith" of the Bible.

While rejecting dogmatic orthodoxy, Wolff also criticized those whom she depicted as ignorant and arrogant "*esprits forts.*" To convince a friend given to Voltairean skepticism of the value of the Christian faith, she translated the *Life of Jesus* by the Scottish Presbyterian William Craig. More generally, she sought to steer a middle way between dogmatism and freethinking libertinism, pleading for an authentic faith of whatever confession. She belonged to the serious and pious Christians who aspired to a religion with a minimum of dogma in order to prevent religious strife. But this faith was not to be couched in terms and doctrines derived from Calvin and his followers. The quest for religious authenticity was thus shared by orthodox and liberal believers alike, although they differed widely about the contents and form of this true faith.[48]

The historical context of Wolff's religious work was the battle about toleration that had raged in the Netherlands since the 1750s and in which she took an active part during the late 1760s and 1770s. She was a partisan of concord, detesting rigid Calvinist orthodoxy, or what she might call "the Calvinist Inquisition," those orthodox ministers whom she described as "heresy-makers [*ketter-maakers*] who smother the voice of reason." In a satirical piece, she ridiculed the orthodox Calvinist members of the Groningen Consistory who wanted to have a fellow member dismissed because he had danced at the wedding of his daughter.[49] Once again, it was not Calvinism as such that she disliked but the hypocritical, rigid, intolerant version she encountered in her day.

■ CASE STUDY 3: RADICALLY PROGRESSIVE PROTESTANTISM

The third case study concerns a conversion from Calvinism via Remonstrantism to radical progressive religion in the later eighteenth century. Let me state at the outset that this case study cannot be viewed as representative of contemporary developments in the Netherlands. By 1800, the dominant tendency among Reformed divines was one of moderation, embracing the ideal of a middle-of-the-road theology.

There were, however. some Reformed divines who did not share this concern for moderation, expressing · doubts about fundamental Reformed doctrines, including the doctrines of predestination, original sin, and the corruption of human nature. That such doubts could occasionally lead to more radical positions is shown by the case of Paulus van Hemert (1756–1825). Van Hemert resigned from the ministry in 1784 precisely because of such doubts. The Dutch Reformed Consistory, though deploring his deviation from orthodoxy, praised his public acknowledgment of his dissenting views on the grounds that honesty was preferable to the secrecy with which other Reformed ministers tried to disseminate identical sentiments—a clear indication that Van Hemert was not an exception among Dutch Reformed ministers in casting doubt upon traditional doctrines.[50]

According to Van Hemert, the core of all religion was to be found in the ethical principles offered by God to man in the Decalogue and in the life of Jesus.[51] He protested against the view that the church, in the vein of Calvin, should consider Jesus's death as the major issue of his appearance and of world history. Rather Jesus's religion and morality should be the central doctrines. Van Hemert complained that the common heap of Calvinist Christians did not want to hear about Jesus's teaching, but that they were merely interested in the characteristic tenets of Calvin's system, even in those dogmatic notions about which Christians were quarrelling all the time. These Calvinists judged a minister according to his attachment to traditional words, his allegiance to the formularies and expressions of their forefathers, which they regarded as constituting the fundamentals of their faith. Apparently Van Hemert made little or no distinction between Calvin and the "Calvinist" orthodoxy of Dort and considered both of them an entrenched enemy that needed to be overthrown. He believed, however, that the church would flourish only when true Christian virtue and piety were being preached.[52]

Van Hemert was a fervent advocate of the Protestant principle that each believer should judge for himself in religious matters. Those who only repeat the faith of their church do not have any faith at all, he argued. Only free investigation protected believers against unbelief and doubt. Wherever the freedom to think for oneself was limited, religion itself was destroyed. The Utrecht traditionalist divine Gisbertus Bonnet did his best to defend Calvin against Van Hemert, but, as his biographer notes, Bonnet himself appeared to be quite removed from Calvin. For Bonnet, as for Van Hemert, the mysteries of faith did not contain anything contrary to reason. He believed that the decisive norm was to be found in the "eternal truths" of reason. The credibility and veracity of the Bible could be proven with the help of those truths.[53]

It will not come as a surprise to learn that in 1788 Van Hemert became a member of the Remonstrant Brotherhood; only two years later he was appointed professor at the Amsterdam Remonstrant seminary. In his inaugural address on November 24, 1790, he discussed the theory that Christ and his apostles adapted their terms, expressions, and formulations to the understanding of the Jews. In other words, they had expressed themselves in terms understandable for the Jewish people of their day, but much less comprehensible for later generations. This viewpoint was of course a frontal attack on scriptural authority.[54] In 1796, he resigned from the Remonstrant professorship, starting a career as a promotor of Kant's philosophy. At a time when only a handful of people in the Netherlands had heard of Kant, he founded a learned journal on Kantian philosophy. In later years, Calvin and Calvinism disappeared from Van Hemert's view, but his critique of Calvinism and

Calvinists shows that traditional Calvinism was still a force to be reckoned with at the end of the eighteenth century.

■ FROM INDIFFERENTISM TO ENGAGEMENT

These three case studies, each in its own way, illustrate that Calvin was at once present and yet distant in the eighteenth-century Netherlands, that there was a dynamic relationship between the Enlightenment and traditional religion, and that the Enlightenment was no monolithic affair. Throughout the eighteenth century, the focus on Dort and on the confessional creeds, rather than on Calvin himself, made the orthodox Calvinism of Dort the mirror in which the Dutch saw Calvin most clearly reflected. Calvin was little known as a reformer in his own right. "The distant Calvin" was the dominant image of Calvin presented by the eighteenth century.[55] John Calvin as a prominent sixteenth-century reformer is the construction of the nineteenth century, culminating in the commemorative events of 1909. Apparently the scene changed significantly at some point between 1800 and 1900.

When did the change set in? In the Netherlands, the first traces of scholarly as well as theological interest in Calvin the reformer appear in the 1830s. Translations of biographies, articles in periodicals, a new edition of Joris De Raed's eighteenth-century edition of the *Institutio* in 1837: all this and more suggest that it was during this decade that Calvin began to be recovered as a singular theologian. Even in 1835, however, when the Franeker professor Barthold Reinier de Geer published an extensive essay on the moral character of the reformers, the largest part of his essay was devoted to Luther. Next came Melanchthon and Zwingli. Although de Geer's portrait was quite positive about Calvin, both as a theologian and as a man, he was deemed less worthy of attention than either Melanchthon or Zwingli.[56] But Dutch neo-Calvinism was soon to be born. Furthermore, in subsequent generations interest in Calvin was not limited to traditionalist Protestantism. Some liberal theologians also drew inspiration from him and thought themselves to be continuing his work too.[57]

■ TRUE CALVINISM VERSUS REFINED PAGANISM

The basic fight between traditional and liberal Protestants appeared to be about the limits of liberal Calvinism or, in other words, about the limits of Enlightenment. The battle over the boundaries of liberal Calvinism bears testimony to an ongoing pursuit of balance. The clashes also testify to the dynamics between the emerging enlightened tendencies within the Dutch Reformed Church and the traditional Calvinism that looked upon these enlightened tendencies as the enemy within. Traditional Calvinism, however, was less traditional than its adherents thought. Traditionalist theologians tended to formulate their theology at quite some distance from Calvin, although they imagined they were defending "true" Calvinism. The issue of the "enemy within" Dutch Calvinism throughout the long eighteenth century would repay further research

Traditionalists who saw "authentic" Calvinism threatened by the invasion of liberal notions started to talk about a "refined paganism" infecting the church.[58]

The use of this label to designate the internal liberalizing movement is interesting. On the one hand, it pointed back to the pre-Christian era, the stage of civilization in which mankind was steeped in heathenism. On the other hand, the label "refined paganism" set the trend for the future when, by 1900, a binary structure of Christianity became more popular than ever before, with the division between Christians and "pagans," as propagated by such staunch Calvinists as the Dutch theologian and politician Abraham Kuyper and the American Presbyterian John Gresham Machen.

The sentiment of a battle between two fundamentally antagonistic currents within Christianity was also present in the opening address of Edouard Montet, dean of the Genevan Faculty of Theology, who, at the International Council of Liberals and Unitarians convened in Geneva in 1905, maintained that in the domain of religion there were only two options: either a liberal Christianity or a Christianity that remained attached to the chains of tradition and obligatory confessions of faith. Liberal believers had made their choice; what they professed was an evangelical liberal Christianity, what they proclaimed was the liberal religious idea.[59]

Be that as it may, the Dutch Reformed Church had been moving away in the long eighteenth century from orthodox Calvinism as well as from John Calvin himself. It would have been surprised to find that its "distant Calvin" would be transformed into the heroic reformer of the subsequent era.

■ Notes

1. While the emerging "cult of Calvin" had various causes, including the Restoration of the monarchy in England in 1660 (when the English, Scottish and Irish monarchies were all restored under Charles II after the Interregnum that followed the Wars of the Three Kingdoms) as well as the various antirevolutionary movements, not forgetting the upsurge of antimodernist currents in Europe and North America, it may also be viewed in the broader literary-cultural context of the nineteenth-century need of heroism, which was greatly stimulated by Thomas Carlyle's *On Heroes, Hero-Worship and the Heroic in History* (London: James Fraser, 1840). Although Carlyle did not devote a single word to Calvin—his lecture on "The Hero as Priest" singled out Luther and John Knox as "our best Reformers"— his work, nonetheless, sparked a desire to look for heroes. On Calvin and the nineteenth century, see Johan de Niet, Herman Paul, and Bart Wallet, eds., *Sober, Strict, and Scriptural: Collective Memories of John Calvin, 1800–2000* (Leiden: Brill, 2009). This work appeared after this essay had been written.

2. On the Calvinist character of the Dutch, see G. J. Schutte, *Het Calvinistisch Nederland: Mythe en werkelijkheid* (Hilversum: Verloren, 2000).

3. *Calvijn!* (Zoetermeer: Boekencentrum, 2009). On October 30, 2009, in Dordrecht a competition was organized in the field of design and fashion (the "Calvijn Classics Award").

4. See Mirjam van Veen, "Calvijn en Obama lijken op elkaar," *Kerk in Den Haag*, January 2010, 7.

5. Michael D. Bush, "Calvin's Reception in the Eighteenth Century," in *The Calvin Handbook*, ed. Herman Selderhuis (Grand Rapids: Eerdmans, 2009), 479–86, here 479. See also Jörg Engelbrecht, "Aufklärung und Calvinismus in den Niederlanden," in *Ablehnung, Duldung, Anerkennung: Toleranz in den Niederlanden und in Deutschland: Ein historischer und aktueller Vergleich*, ed. Horst Lademacher, Renate Loos, and Simon Groenveld (Münster:

Waxmann, 2005), 295–305, which is one of the few essays to date to deal explicitly with the relationship between Calvinism and the Dutch Enlightenment.

6. See, for example, *The Cambridge Companion to John Calvin*, ed. Donald K. McKim (Cambridge: Cambridge University Press, 2004). Exceptions to this general tendency are the essays by Engelbrecht and Bush (n. 5).

7. Voltaire, *Dictionnaire Philosophique Portatif*, ed. René Pomeau (Paris: Garnier-Flammarion, 1964) s.v. "Dogmes," 168–69. Calvin is being judged, together with Charles, Cardinal de Lorraine of the sixteenth century. On Voltaire's attitude toward Calvin and Calvinism, see Graham Gargett, *Voltaire and Protestantism* (Oxford: Voltaire Foundation, 1980).

8. Amurath-Effendi Hekim Bachi [Pieter van Woensel], *De Lantaarn voor 1792* (Amsterdam: in't Nieuwe Licht, 1792), 131.

9. Ferdinand Domela Nieuwenhuis, *Michaël Servetus: 1511–27 oktober 1553, bij gelegenheid der herdenking van den vierhonderd-jarigen geboortedag (Juli 10, 1509) van Kalvyn* (Hilversum: Storch, 1909).

10. Jan Pieter de Bie, *Het leven en de werken van Petrus Hofstede* (Rotterdam: D. A. Daamen, 1899), 196–97. For Hofstede, see Joris van Eijnatten, *God, Nederland en Oranje: Dutch Calvinism and the Search for the Social Centre* (Kampen: Kok, 1993); Ernestine van der Wall, "Marmontel et la 'querelle socratique' aux Pays-Bas," in *Mémorable Marmontel 1799–1999: Etudes réunies*, ed. Kees Meerhoff and Annie Jourdan (Amsterdam: Rodopi, 1999), 83–96; and Van der Wall, *Socrates in de hemel? Een achttiende-eeuwse polemiek over deugd, verdraagzaamheid en de vaderlandse kerk* (Hilversum: Verloren, 2000). On Servetus and his heritage, see Valentine Zuber, *Les conflits de la tolerance: Michel Servet entre mémoire et histoire* (Paris: Honoré Champion, 2004); and Zuber, ed., *Michel Servet (1511–1553): Hérésie et pluralisme du XVIe au XXIe siècle : Actes du colloque de l'École Pratique des Hautes Études, Décembre 11–13, 2003* (Paris: Honoré Champion, 2007).

11. Jan Scharp, *Godgeleerd-historische verhandeling* (Rotterdam: Johannes Hofhout en zoon, 1793), 82–83, n. b.

12. See E. P. Meijering, *Die Geschichte der christlichen Theologie im Urteil J. L. von Mosheims* (Amsterdam: J. C. Gieben, 1995), 9; Martin Mulsow, "Eine 'Rettung' des Servet und der Ophiten? Der junge Mosheim und die häretische Tradition," in *Johann Lorenz Mosheim (1693–1755): Theologie im Spannungsfeld von Philosophie, Philologie und Geschichte*, ed. Martin Mulsow, Ralph Häfner, Florian Neumann, and Helmut Zedelmaier (Wiesbaden: Harrassowitz, 1997), 45–92; and Joris van Eijnatten, *Liberty and Concord in the United Provinces: Religious Toleration and the Public in the Eighteenth-Century Netherlands* (Leiden: Brill, 2003), 351–55. See also Karl Heussi, *Die Kirchengeschichtschreibung Johann Lorenz von Mosheims* (Gotha: Friedrich Andreas Perthes, 1904); Siegfried Körsgen, "Das Bild der Reformation in der Kirchengeschichtschreibung Johann Lorenz von Mosheims" (PhD diss., University of Tübingen, 1966); and Cornelis Augustijn, "Das Bild der Reformation bei Daniel Gerdes und Johann Lorenz von Mosheim," *NAKG* 64 (1984): 78–90.

13. Meijering, *Die Geschichte der christlichen Theologie*, 320–22.

14. The *Historia Michaelis Serveti* was published under the name of Mosheim's pupil Heinrich von Allvoerden, but, as Mosheim himself declared, the contents of the book and most of its style were his. See Mulsow, "Eine 'Rettung' des Servet und der Ophiten?," 53–54.

15. Meijering, *Die Geschichte der christlichen Theologie*, 371–72; reference to *Neue Nachrichten von dem berühmten spanischen Artzte Michael Serveto, der zu Geneve ist verbrannt worden* (Helmstedt: Christian Friedrich Weygand, 1750; repr. Hildesheim: Georg Olms, 1999), 85. In 1748 Mosheim had published yet another work on Servetus, also written in German, entitled *Andersweitige Versuch einer vollständigen und unpartheyischen Ketzergeschichte* (Helmstedt: Christian Friedrich Weygand, 1748).

16. Mulsow, "Eine 'Rettung' des Servet und der Ophiten?," 55.

17. For La Chapelle's review of the *Historia Michaelis Serveti*, see *Bibliothèque raisonnée* 1/2 (1728) : 366–400; for parts of Mosheim's letter and La Chapelle's continued critical comments, see his "Eclaircissement sur le I. Extrait de l' Histoire de Servet," *Bibliothèque raisonnée* 2/1 (1729) : 88–176, esp. 90–92. See also Mulsow, "Eine 'Rettung' des Servet und der Ophiten?," 49, 54; and Van Eijnatten, *Liberty and Concord*, 352–54. At the time, La Chapelle was very much involved in the so-called beneficial lies controversy, a debate in which he revealed himself not to be free from sentiments of rivalry and even vendetta regarding his opponents. See John Christian Laursen, "The Beneficial Lies Controversy in the Huguenot Netherlands, 1705–1731: An Unpublished Manuscript at the Root of the *cas Saurin*," in *Studies in Voltaire and the Eighteenth Century* 39 (Oxford: Voltaire Foundation, 1994), 67–103, esp. 96.

18. The poem on Servetus appeared in Joachim Oudaan, *Toneelpoëzy* (Amsterdam: Evert Visser and Pieter Visser, ca. 1730). Another edition had appeared in 1712. The Dutch translation of the *Historia Michaelis Serveti* is entitled *Historie van Michael Servetus den Spanjaart, bestaande in een omstandig verhaal van zyn gansche leven, geschreve boeken en ongelukkigen doot*, trans. Wilhelm Otto Reitz (Rotterdam: Jan Daniel Beman, 1729); see Van Eijnatten, *Liberty and Concord*, 353.

19. See Ernestine van der Wall, *The Enemy Within: Religion, Science, and Modernism*, Uhlenbeck Lecture 25 (Wassenaar: NIAS, 2007).

20. See Ernestine van der Wall, "Orthodoxy and Scepticism in the Early Dutch Enlightenment," in *Scepticism and Irreligion in the Seventeenth and Eighteenth Centuries*, ed. R. H. Popkin and A. J. Vanderjagt (Leiden: Brill, 1993), 121–41; Van der Wall, "Cartesianism and Cocceianism: A Natural Alliance?," in *De l'Humanisme aux Lumières, Bayle et le protestantisme: Mélanges en l'honneur d'Elisabeth Labrousse*, ed. Michelle Magdelaine et al. (Oxford: Voltaire Foundation, 1996), 445–55; and Van der Wall, "The Religious Context of the Early Dutch Enlightenment: Moral Religion and Society," in *The Early Dutch Enlightenment, 1650–1750: Selected Papers of a Conference held at the Herzog August Bibliothek, Wolfenbüttel March 22–23, 2001*, ed. Wiep van Bunge (Leiden: Brill, 2003), 39–57.

21. On neology in the Netherlands, see Van Eijnatten, *Liberty and Concord*, esp. 309–79; Ernestine van der Wall, "Religiekritiek en apologetiek in de achttiende eeuw: De dynamiek van een debat," *De Achttiende Eeuw* 32 (2000): 17–36; and Victoria E. Franke, *Een gedeelde wereld? Duitse theologie en filosofie in het Verlichte debat in Nederlandse recensietijdschriften, 1774–1837* (Maarssen: APA-Holland University Press, 2009), esp. 99–114.

22. Hugh Blair, *Sermons*, 5 vols. (Edinburgh: William Creech, W. Strahan and T. Cadell, 1777–1801), 1: 15; quoted by Johannes van den Berg, "Eighteenth Century Dutch Translations of the Works of Some British Latitudinarian and Enlightened Theologians," *NAKG* 59 (1978–79), 197.

23. For Jean-Alphonse Turrettini, see Maria-Cristina Pitassi, "L'apologétique raisonnable de Jean-Alphonse Turrettini," in *Apologétique 1680–1740: Sauvetage ou naufrage de la théologie?*, ed. Maria-Cristina Pitassi (Geneva: Labor et Fides, 1991), 99–118; and Pitassi, "De la controverse anti-romaine à la théologie naturelle: Parcours anti-sceptiques de Jean-Alphonse Turrettini," in *The Return of Scepticism from Hobbes and Descartes to Bayle*, ed. G. Paganini (Leiden: Brill, 2003), 431–77. See also Johannes van den Berg, "The Synod of Dort in the Balance," in *Religious Currents and Cross-Currents: Essays on Early Modern Protestantism and the Protestant Enlightenment*, ed. Jan de Bruijn, Pieter Holtrop, and Ernestine van der Wall (Leiden: Brill, 1999), 1–18.

24. Simon van der Linde, "Calvijn en Nederland," in *Zicht op Calvijn*, ed. Jan van Genderen et al. (Amsterdam: Buijten & Schipperheijn, 1965), 185–219, esp. 208–11. Van der Linde concluded that by 1800 everything seemed to have changed for the better.

25. See Jasper Vree, *Kuyper in de kiem: De precalvinistische periode van Abraham Kuyper 1848–1874* (Hilversum: Verloren, 2006), 23.

26. Carolus Tuinman, *Rommelzoode van allerlei paapsch heiligdom* (Middelburg: Johannes Opsomer, 1712); and Tuinman, *De liegende en bedriegende vrijgeest ontmaskert* (Middelburg: Jacobus Boter, Simon Clement, and Willeboord Eling, 1715), 50. Tuinman was keen to accuse any religious or philosophical innovator of Spinozism, including the Remonstrant professor of Amsterdam Jean Le Clerc, of whom he said: "The God of Spinoza (who is also the God of libertines)…seems to be the Brother of the God of Joh. Clericus of Amsterdam, since they resemble each other like two drops of water." Quoted in C. Louise Thijssen-Schoute, *Nederlands cartesianisme* (Amsterdam: Noord-Hollandse Uitgevers Maatschapij, 1954; repr. Utrecht: HES, 1989), 437, n. 3. One eighteenth-century edition of Calvin's correspondence should also be noted: the 1744 publication of his correspondence with Jacques de Bourgogne, seigneur de Falais: *Lettres de Calvin à Jaque de Bourgogne Seigneur de Falais & de Bredam, & à son épouse Jolande de Brederode* (Amsterdam: J. Wetstein, 1774). See here Vree, *Kuyper in de kiem*, 22–25; and F. P. van Stam, general introduction to *Ioannis Calvini epistolae*, vol. 1, ed. Cornelis Augustijn and F. P. van Stam (Geneva: Droz, 2005–), 11–31.

27. On the meager history of Calvin publications in the eighteenth century, see Bush, "Calvin's Reception in the Eighteenth Century," 480–81.

28. Daniel Gerdes, *De Johannis Calvini Institutione Relig. Christianae Historia litteraria*, in *Scrinium Antiquarium* 2.1 (Groningen: Hajo Spandaw and G. W. Rump, 1750), 451–77; and Klaas Witteveen, *Daniel Gerdes* (Groningen: J. B. Wolters, 1963), 225–27.

29. Daniel Gerdes, *Historia Reformationis sive Annales Evangelii seculo XVI passim per Europam renovati doctrinaeque reformatae* (Groningen: Hajo Spandaw and G. W. Rump, 1744–1752); Witteveen, *Daniel Gerdes*, 198; and Augustijn, "Das Bild der Reformation."

30. Witteveen, *Daniel Gerdes*, 120–21; and Augustijn, "Das Bild der Reformation."

31. Jack de Mooij, *Jona Willem te Water (1740–1822): Historicus en theoloog tussen traditie en Verlichting* (Leiden: Brill, 2008), 100, 209. Te Water, in his history of the Reformation in Zeeland, was happy to see that the Reformed faithful in this province, to a man, clung to Calvin's doctrine, not yielding to any Pelagianism.

32. See *Levensbeschrijving van geleerde mannen* (1733), 768, quoted in Roel A. Bosch, *En nooit meer oude Psalmen zingen: Zingend geloven in een nieuwe tijd: 1760–1810* (Zoetermeer: Meinema, 1996), 149, n. 2.

33. Johann Friedrich Wilhelm Tischer, *Calvins Leben, Meinungen und Thaten, ein Lesebuch für seine Glaubensgenossen* (Leipzig: Voss, 1794), trans. George Hendrik Reiche as *Het leven, de gevoelens en bedrijven van Calvyn: Een leesboek voor't algemeen* (Utrecht: W. van IJzerworst, 1796). In his preface, Tischer related that when he stumbled on Calvin's correspondence, he met a man very different than the one he used to know—not the stubborn and polemical Calvin but a man full of humanity, compassion, and friendship. Tischer then felt obliged to write a new biography of Calvin, as impartially as possible. Reiche also provided Dutch translations of German biographies of Huss, Wycliff, Luther, Melanchthon, and Zwingli.

34. Herman Muntinghe, preface to Tischer, *Het leven, de gevoelens en bedrijven van Calvyn*, vii–xiv. He also praised the "eminent" biography of Luther by Johann Matthias Schröckh, *Abbildung und Lebensbeschreibung Martin Luthers* (Leipzig: Christian Gottlob Hilscher, 1773) trans. as *Levensbeschrijving van Martinus Lutherus* (Amsterdam: Martinus de Bruyn, 1774).

35. *Vaderlandsche Bibliotheek van Wetenschap, Kunst en Smaak* 8/1 (1796): 549–52.

36. Christiaan Sepp, *Bibliotheek van Nederlandsche kerkgeschiedschrijvers: Opgave van hetgeen Nederlanders over de geschiedenis der christelijke kerk geschreven hebben* (Leiden: Brill, 1886), 192.

37. See Johannes van den Berg, "Theology in Franeker and Leiden in the Eighteenth Century," in de Bruijn, Holtrop, and Van der Wall, *Religious Currents and Cross-Currents*, 253–67, here 262, 264.

38. John Taylor, *The Scripture-Doctrine of Atonement Examined* (London: J. Waugh, 1751), trans. as *Verhandeling van het leerstuk der verzoeninge, volgens den inhoudt der Heilige Schrift* (Harlingen: Folkert van der Plaats, 1754). See Van den Berg, "Eighteenth Century Dutch Translations," 194–212, 207–08.

39. Taylor, *The Scripture-Doctrine of Atonement Examined*, 127, quoted by van den Berg, "Eighteenth Century Dutch Translations," 197.

40. Cornelis Huisman, *Geloof in beweging: Gerardus Kuypers, pastor en patriot tussen vroomheid en Verlichting* (Zoetermeer: Boekencentrum, 1996), 98–102; and Doede Nauta, "Gerard Kuypers," in *Opera Minora: Kerkhistorische verhandelingen over Calvijn en de geschiedenis van de kerk in Nederland*, ed. Doede Nauta (Kampen: Kok, 1961), 86–119.

41. Johann August Christoph von Einem, *De oude en hedendaagsche kerklijke geschiedenissen van wijlen den hooggeleerden J.L. Mosheim... vervolgd, uit het Hoogduitsch vertaald* (Utrecht: A. van Paddenburg & W. Holtrop, 1779–81), sect. 2, part 2: 478–81, 591–92.

42. Alexander Comrie and Nicolaus Holtius, *Examen van het Ontwerp van Tolerantie, om de leere in de Dordrechtse Synode anno 1619 vastgesteld met de veroordeelde leere der Remonstranten te verenigen* (Amsterdam: Nicolaas Byl, 1753–59; repr. Houten: Den Hertog, 1993).

43. See Roel A. Bosch, *Het conflict rond Antonius van der Os, Predikant te Zwolle 1748–1755* (Kampen: IJsselakademie 1988); Johannes van den Berg, *Een Leids pleidooi voor verdraagzaamheid: Het optreden van Jan Jacob Schultens in de zaak-Van der Os* (Leiden: Brill, 1976); Van den Berg, "De 'Calviniaanse Sociëteit' en het kerkelijk leven in Nederland omstreeks het midden van de achttiende eeuw," *NAKG* 63 (1983): 205–18; Van Eijnatten, *Liberty and Concord*, 72–73; Ernestine van der Wall, "Toleration and Enlightenment in the Dutch Republic," in *Toleration in Enlightenment Europe*, ed. Ole Pieter Grell and Roy Porter (Cambridge: Cambridge University Press, 2000), 114–32; and Van der Wall, "De Verlichting in Nederland kritisch bekeken: Het 'Examen van Het Ontwerp van Tolerantie (1753-1759),'" *Piëtisme en Verlichting in de achttiende eeuw: Documentatieblad Nadere Reformatie* 27 (2003): 1–17.

44. On the notion of conspiracy, see Gordon Wood, "Conspiracy and the Paranoid Style: Causality and Deceit in the Eighteenth Century," *William and Mary Quarterly* 39 (1982): 401–41.

45. Comrie and Holtius, *Examen van het Ontwerp van Tolerantie*, 185–88.

46. See Ernestine van der Wall, "Religious Pluralism, Toleration, and the Enlightenment: The Dutch Novelists Elisabeth Wolff-Bekker and Agatha Deken," in *La formazione storica della alterità. Studi di storia della tolleranza nell' età moderna offerti a Antonio Rotondo*, 3 vols. ed. Henry Méchoulan, Richard Popkin, Guiseppe Ricuperati, and Luisa Simonutti (Florence: Leo S. Olschki, 2001), 3: 1069–83.

47. Quoted in Nanne van der Zijpp, "Wolff en Deken in de kerkelijke situatie van hun tijd," in *Boeket voor Betje en Aagje: Van en over de schrijfsters Wolff en Deken*, ed. P. Minderaa et al. (Amsterdam: Wereldbibliotheek, 1954), 41–52, here 45.

48. William Craig, *An Essay on the Life of Jesus Christ*, 2nd ed. (Glasgow: Robert & Andrew Foulis, 1769), trans. Elizabeth Wolff-Bekker as *Het leeven van Jezus Christus: Naar de tweede uitgave uit het Engelsch vertaald* (Hoorn: T. Tjallingius, 1770). Also see Wolff-Bekker, *Onveranderlyke Santhorstsche Geloofsbelydenis*, ed. A. J. Hanou (1772; repr. Leiden: Astraea, 2000).

49. On this satirical piece, entitled *De menuet en de domineespruik*, see P. J. Buijnsters, *Wolff & Deken: Een biografie* (The Hague: Martinus Nijhoff, 1984), 119–29.

50. On van Hemert, see Herman Ijsbrand Groenewegen, *Paulus van Hemert als godgeleerde en als wijsgeer* (Amsterdam: Y. Rogge, 1889); Adrianus van den End, *Gisbertus Bonnet: Bijdrage tot de kennis van de geschiedenis der gereformeerde theologie in de achttiende eeuw* (Wageningen: H. Veenman, 1957), esp. 65–85; Simon Vuyk, *De verdraagzame gemeente van vrije christenen: Remonstranten op de bres voor de Bataafse Republiek 1780–1800* (Amsterdam: De Bataafsche Leeuw, 1995), 37–43; and Van Eijnatten, *Liberty and Concord*, 348–49, 468–75. See also the introduction by J. Plat and M. R. Wielema to Paulus van Hemert, *Gezag en grenzen van de menselijke rede*, ed. J. Plat and M. R. Wielema (Baarn: Ambo, 1987).

51. Van Hemert, *Gezag en grenzen*, 16.

52. Groenewegen, *Paulus van Hemert*, 15–18.

53. Van den End, *Gisbertus Bonnet*, 84–85.

54. See also his winning prize essay on the same topic. Published in 1792, it was written in answer to the contest question (*prijsvraag*) of Teylers Godgeleerd Genootschap of 1789.

55. A conclusion echoed by Bush: "The evidence suggests that the eighteenth century understood Calvin poorly, though his name was on many lips." "Calvin's Reception in the Eighteenth Century," 485.

56. B. R. de Geer, *Verhandeling over het zedelijk karakter der voornaamste hervormers in de zestiende eeuw, en den invloed, welke derzelver zedelijke grondbeginsels op hetgene zij ondernomen en verrigt hebben heeft uitgeoefend* (The Hague: J. Thierry and C. Mensing, 1835).

57. The major representative was the Leiden modernist theologian Jan Hendrik Scholten, who saw himself as working in the vein of Calvin when he set forth his religious ideas in his famous two-volume work on the doctrine of the Dutch Reformed Church, *De Leer der Hervormde Kerk* (Leiden: Engels, 1848–50). See also Allard Pierson, *Studien over Johannes Kalvijn (1527–1536)* (Amsterdam: P. N. van Kampen, 1881); and Pierson, *Nieuwe Studien over Johannes Kalvijn (1536–1541)* (Amsterdam: P.N. van Kampen, 1883).

58. See Ernestine van der Wall, *Verlicht christendom of verfijnd heidendom? Jacob van Nuys Klinkenberg (1744–1817) en de Verlichting* (Leiden: Brill, 1994).

59. Edouard Montet, ed., *Actes du IIIme congrès international du christianisme libéral et progressif—Genève 1905* (Geneva: Georg, 1905), 6. See also Montet, "John Calvin and the Reformation Monument at Geneva, Switzerland," in *Freedom and Fellowship in Religion: Proceedings and Papers of the Fourth International Congress of Religious Liberals Held at Boston, U.S.A., September 22–27, 1907*, ed. Charles W. Wendte (Boston: International Council, 1907), 244–54.

11 Lost, Then Found

Calvin in French Protestantism,
1830–1940

ANDRÉ ENCREVÉ

Translated by Calvin Tams

The title I have chosen for this essay may seem overstated since Calvin's name was obviously not unknown to Huguenots at the beginning of the nineteenth century, if only because of the frequent attacks against the reformer by Catholic polemicists.[1] Still, so unfamiliar in 1821 were the outlines of his biography and thought that the principal representative of a liberal current far removed from Calvinist dogma, the pastor Samuel Vincent, felt the need to publish a short article entitled "The Life of John Calvin" in one of the first issues of the journal that he had recently launched to improve the religious knowledge of French pastors, *Les Mélanges de religion, de morale et de critique sacrée*, so that they would have at least a basic knowledge of the reformer's life and thought.[2] "Calvin, the admirable reformer, is still unknown to French Protestants, in an almost unbelievable manner," declared an 1841 article in the *Archives du christianisme*—a journal with a theological orientation directly opposed to that of Samuel Vincent.[3] A century later in 1936, however, pastor Auguste Lecerf, the principal force behind the Calvinist revival in France and founder of the Calvinist Society of France, was officially assigned to teach dogmatics in the Faculty of Protestant Theology in Paris. In 1945, Jean Cadier—soon to be president of the Calvinist Society—was named professor of dogmatics in the Faculty of Protestant Theology in Montpellier. Avid students of Calvin now occupied some of the leading positions in the world of French Protestant theology.

I am going to sketch, therefore, the major outlines of a century that witnessed a kind of return to Calvin or, at least, to a better knowledge of the reformer's thought among French Protestants as a whole, as well as the appearance of a Calvinist movement structured around a society and its publication. Naturally this evolution occurred in the broader context of a return to Calvin's thought in many other countries, including Scotland, the Netherlands, and Switzerland, but space does not permit an extensive exploration of this international context. The return to Calvin developed over two periods, punctuated by the Franco-Prussian War of 1870. And, as curious as it may seem, the politics of French foreign relations played a role in our story.

■ 1830–1870: THE FIRST STEPS TOWARD A REDISCOVERY OF CALVIN

Publications

At the beginning of the nineteenth century, only a few works about Calvin and his thought were available to French Protestants. They could, of course, refer to modern editions of the *Institutes*, either the Latin version published in Berlin in 1834 or the French version of 1560, which was published in Geneva in 1818 with a modernized text, but they certainly did not have access to all of Calvin's works. Not until 1859 would there even be a readily accessible version of the French *Institutes* of 1560.[4] As for works about Calvin, Theodore Beza's *Life of Calvin* was reprinted only in 1842, and it could hardly be called a work of objective scholarship.[5] In theory, readers could also turn to the essay on Calvin in Pierre Bayle's *Historical and Critical Dictionary*, which was, as Hubert Bost has shown, a biting and combative "historical rehabilitation" of the reformer "against [his] detractors who had so long held sway."[6] The article was generally historical in nature, however, and paid little attention to doctrine. By 1830, moreover, it was no longer a work that could be easily found.

This situation was obviously tied to the evolution of Protestant theology. The eighteenth century was hardly friendly toward Calvin and his thought, as exemplified by Geneva's decision in 1725 to abolish the requirement that pastors subscribe to the Second Helvetic Confession. In addition, the persecution of the Huguenots in the eighteenth century had led to the disappearance of a distinctively French tradition in theology, as pastors—forced underground and, after 1726, given only a cursory education at the Seminary of Lausanne—came under the influence of Enlightenment thought and the theology then popular in Switzerland. Consequently, they had little sympathy for the strict and highly structured dogma of Calvin. No French synod officially abolished the obligation of pastors to subscribe to the strongly Calvinist Confession of La Rochelle, but in practice they were no longer required to do. The doctrine of double predestination had also disappeared among them by the beginning of the eighteenth century.

The dominant theology in France, at the time, was quite vague. Sixteenth-century doctrine was not explicitly challenged so much as it was watered down, with emphasis put instead on moral questions. This, for example, is how Jacques Antoine Rabaut-Pomier, a pastor in Paris from 1803 to 1816, describes the Lord's Supper in a preparatory sermon:

> It is a ceremony that sublimely traces, for the disciple of Jesus Christ, a funeral oration of his divine master, which reminds him of what the world too often leads him to forget: the uninterrupted series of virtuous actions, interesting truths, and sanctifying precepts that adorned and made useful his life and, even more, his heroic death, which serves as a model for all those who would like to die well.[7]

Traditional doctrines are politely acknowledged but carefully formulated to allow for a wide range of interpretations, while Christ is presented more as a sage or guide than as a savior. Calvin had become so foreign to French Protestants, in fact, that when Samuel Vincent published an article on predestination in 1822 in the journal he founded, he called Schleiermacher "the most subtle defender of predestination," and mentioned Karl Gottlieb Bretschneider, but did not cite Calvin.[8]

The first biographical works that contributed to a better understanding of Calvin appeared at the beginning of the 1820s. Particularly important was François Guizot's *Calvin*, published in 1822 in the *Musée des protestants célèbres*. As Olivier Millet has shown, Guizot was certainly inspired by Beza's *Life of Calvin* but also greatly influenced by Bretschneider's *Calvin and the Church of Geneva*, a German publication from 1821, which the germanophone Guizot had read in its original language before the French translation of 1822 appeared. Bretschneider's work is interesting because it bestowed on Calvin the status of "religious genius," which, until then, Herder had reserved for Luther.[9] This allowed Guizot to present Calvin as a "genius" in the Herderian sense of the term, for he was able to join together a "synthesizing, doctrinal reformulation of Christian teaching…and a practical implementation of that doctrine by means of ecclesiastical discipline."[10] With these two studies, French readers had a starting point for their rediscovery of Calvin.

The 1830s and 1840s saw a succession of titles, which, though lacking in originality, contained further elements of interest. *The Life and Times of John Calvin: The Great Reformer*, by Paul Emil Henry, the German descendant of Huguenot refugees, was published in Hamburg in four volumes from 1835 to 1844. Although it was never translated into French, it served as the basis for several shorter works that were all highly favorable toward Calvin.[11] There were sections on Calvin in the Genevan André Sayous's work of 1842 , *Literary Studies on French Writers of the Reformation*, which sketched out the reformer's oeuvre and praised his literary style. French Protestants could also turn to the writings of non-Protestant historians like F.A. Mignet, a member of the Académie Française.[12] Several of Calvin's French works, including ten sermons, were published in 1842 by Paul L. Jacob, and a number of Calvin's letters were reprinted in the new edition of A. Ruchat's *History of the Swiss Reformation*, published by Louis Vueillemin in 1835–1838.[13] All of this activity bore fruit, allowing Eugène and Émile Haag to write an important and very well documented essay on Calvin in 1852 for their biographical dictionary of famous French Protestants, *La France protestante*.[14]

It was especially in the 1850s and 1860s, however, that the necessary resources for a better understanding of Calvin appeared in France. Jules Bonnet's many years of research resulted in his 1854 *Lettres françaises*, a collection of 278 of Calvin's missives, including about 170 that were previously unpublished.[15] Several of Calvin's works were published with the aid of the Presbyterian Board of Publication in Philadelphia, including the four-volume *Commentaries of John Calvin on the New Testament* in 1854–1855, the *Institutes*, and the *Commentaries on the Psalms* in 1859.[16] The announcement of the publication of the *Commentaries on the New Testament* led Edouard Reuss—one of the best exegetes of nineteenth-century France—to publish an article in 1853 in the *Revue de théologie et de philosophie chrétienne*, entitled "Calvin as Exegete," in which he maintained that "Calvin was certainly the greatest exegete of the sixteenth century," a verdict that was all the more remarkable because Reuss, who had liberal tendencies himself, was writing in a journal with a decidedly liberal theological bent.[17] A series of articles about

Calvin's life and writing up to 1538 also appeared in the *Revue chrétienne* between 1854 and 1858, written by the Frankfurt pastor Louis Bonnet.[18]

The 1860s saw the publication of a number of resources and books likely tied to the anniversary of Calvin's death in 1864. Especially notable were the appearance of the first volume of the famous *Opera Calvini*, edited by Guillaume Baum, Edouard Cunitz, and Edouard Reuss, which appeared in the *Corpus reformatorum* in 1863, and the first publications of the *Correspondance des réformateurs dans les pays de langue française*, by Aimé-Louis Herminjard.[19] The first five volumes of Jean-Henri Merle d'Aubigné's *Histoire de la Réformation en Europe au temps de Calvin* also came out between 1863 and 1869.[20] Merle d'Aubigné, whose earlier *Histoire de la Réformation du XVIe siècle* (1835–1853) was an apologetically motivated history that covered only the period up to 1531, made few contributions to serious scholarship with his new series, but the criticism with which it was received in both the liberal and evangelical press shows that the works published since the start of the nineteenth century had been effective in raising the expectations and level of knowledge of informed commentators.[21] Whatever their shortcomings, furthermore, Merle d'Aubigné's books brought additional attention to Calvin, as did his shorter publications and his well-attended public lectures.[22] A more scholarly two-volume German biography of Calvin published in 1863 by Ernst Stähelin was not translated into French, and its appearance was barely noted in the French Protestant press.[23] Still, other short works on Calvin appeared around the anniversary of his death in 1864, and while they too offered little that was new, they showed that Calvin and his thought now held much more interest for the Protestant public than had been the case at the beginning of the nineteenth century.[24]

How to Explain the Revived Interest in Calvin

One factor that played an important role until at least 1914 was the desire to respond to anti-Protestant polemicists whose attacks often targeted Calvin. In 1841, for example, Jean-Marie-Vincent Audin wrote a very hostile two-volume *Histoire de la vie, des ouvrages et des doctrines de Jean Calvin*, which had become a best-seller and inspired similar publications.[25] The influence of these works was so great that in his introduction to the *Lettres françaises* of 1854, Jules Bonnet argued that its publication was necessary because:

> the followers of an unfortunately well-known school have an endless supply of curses and outrage for the glorious revolution to which the names Calvin and Luther remain indelibly linked. Never before has the denigration and insult of these heroes of conscience been propagated with more fury, never before have their intentions been so poorly appreciated and their actions so boldly distorted. In opposition to the lies of a party that does not shrink from the most horrible slander, we appeal to the impartial testimony of history.[26]

This passage reminds us that the first half of the nineteenth century also saw the birth of history as a science, and this aroused great hopes among Protestants who saw the nascent discipline as a new way to defend Calvin. Confessional motives remained very important not just in responding to Catholic polemic but also to that of certain agnostics. In 1855, Frédéric Monod felt compelled to respond in this vein to Ernest Renan, who had been sharply critical of Calvin in his review of Bonnet's *Lettres françaises*.[27]

In a religious community, however, doctrinal considerations are often the most important, and one needs to examine the extent to which interest in Calvin can be explained by changes within French Protestant theology. The most significant theological movement in French Protestantism during the first half of the nineteenth century was the Réveil, which at first glance, might be expected to have links to Calvin. The movement, which had a number of British and Swiss supporters, sought to breathe new life into a Huguenot community that had, in its view, become self-satisfied and complacent after surviving persecution, especially in the wake of the Concordat. The movement's remedy was a return to the "pure doctrine" of the sixteenth-century reformers, which had been almost totally effaced during the Enlightenment. Essentially, they believed that ignorance of Reformation teaching and the abandonment of obligatory subscription to the confessions were responsible for the weakness of Christianity in their time. In 1818, Henry Drummond, one of the first British revivalist missionaries to come to Geneva at the end of the Napoleonic Wars, undertook the publication of a new edition of Calvin's *Institutes*. One should not conclude from this, however, that the Réveil was "Calvinist," in the sense of holding to specific elements of his thought. The Réveil, which appeared first in Switzerland and in France after 1815, was largely British in inspiration and it was heavily influenced by Wesleyan Methodism, so much so that at the beginning of the movement in France, its opponents called it "Methodist" in order to suggest that it was foreign to the tradition of Huguenot Protestantism. Wesley, of course, was an Arminian, strongly opposed to the Calvinist doctrine of double predestination. Furthermore, the revival itself was not only characterized by a desire to return to what it called the "pure doctrine" of the Reformation; it was shaped, perhaps even more, by a concern with spirituality. For the revivalists, the profound acceptance of Christianity was, above all, a spiritual experience, the recognition of an emotional bond between the believer and Jesus Christ. Before it was ever grasped by reason or intellect, the truth of the gospel was experienced by the heart. Stemming from British and German Pietism and influenced by early nineteenth-century Romanticism, the revivalist movement actually stood at some remove from the spirituality of the Reformation, even if one can see a certain similarity between its theology of religious experience and the notion of the interior witness of the Holy Spirit that was so important to reformers.

It is difficult to define the theology of the revival in any precise way. Caricaturing it slightly, one might say that revivalists all agreed on the fundamental importance of doctrine, while, at the same, teaching very different doctrines. It is true that they held a number of points in common, which Daniel Robert—the greatest authority on early nineteenth-century French Protestantism—summarized in these terms:

> The heart of man is profoundly corrupt as a result of the sin of Adam. According to divine justice, man deserves only condemnation, but the justice of God has been satisfied by the death of Jesus Christ (fully divine and fully human); believers are those who, trusting in this sacrifice, recognize their misery and, thanks to divine aid (Holy Spirit),

henceforth, perform works in keeping with the divine will (conversion of the heart, rebirth). Just as Christ was resurrected, they too will receive the gift of eternal life; the Scriptures (Old and New Testament, not including the apocryphal books) are the Word of God and contain everything necessary for the Christian. The church is the assembly of believers (little interest in the church as an institution).[28]

This obviously encapsulates the shared foundation of the Protestant Reformation much more than it does any specifically Calvinist doctrine. Revivalists also had a wide range of views regarding specific questions like the nature and limits of biblical inspiration; the proper relationship between church and state; the criteria for church membership; infant baptism; the origin of evil; and, by extension, the limits of human freedom. The majority of revivalist pastors in France were Arminians like Wesley. At most, only a very small number held to the doctrine of double predestination. Indeed Frederic Monod, the only one who did so of whom I am aware, did not even make his views on the issue known publicly; but expressed them only in private letters to his brother, Adolphe, who disagreed with him on the subject.[29] His apparent reticence was likely due to the general rejection of the doctrine by French revivalists—a situation that led to the issue almost never being debated publicly. The movement, thus, stood at a considerable distance from the doctrine of double predestination, which had, for many since the seventeenth century, been seen as the defining mark of Calvinism. Furthermore, most of the questions most actively debated within the movement were ones that had been at the heart of disputes among English Dissenters from the seventeenth century to the nineteenth century but which had not particularly exercised Calvin. Lastly, the great importance that revivalists attributed to individual religious experience—exemplified in the oeuvre of Alexandre Vinet, the best known francophone revivalist—was completely alien to the intellectual world of Calvin and the other major reformers.

The distance between French revivalists and both sixteenth-century thought and specifically Calvinist doctrine was illustrated by the fact that a majority of revivalists had no interest in a return to the Confession of La Rochelle.[30] This led Auguste Lecerf, the most influential French neo-Calvinist of the twentieth century, to conclude in 1932 that the Réveil and Vinet particularly were far from Calvinist:

> The most influential (and also most eminent) thinker of the time, Alexandre Vinet, although clearly evangelical, was against the doctrine of predestination. His individualistic tendencies also prevented him from understanding the doctrine of the covenant of grace in any form recognized by Calvinist traditions. The influence of this personality was, in the end, harmful to what is distinctively Calvinist.[31]

If the Réveil cannot be deemed "Calvinist" in any strict sense, this does not mean that it played no role in the rediscovery of Calvin's life and thought between 1830 and 1870. With its avowed desire to bring about a return to Reformation teaching, its insistence on the importance of doctrine, and its emphasis on the need for Protestant churches to be founded on confessions to which all pastors subscribed, the Réveil inevitably drew attention to the sixteenth century and France's most important reformer. It is certainly no accident that the *Archives du christianisme*, a journal directed by the staunch revivalist Frédéric Monod, published an article in

1841 expressing regret that French Protestants were not making the works of Calvin—especially those still unpublished—more accessible.[32] From this period on, Huguenots all saw the need for a better knowledge of Calvin. Whether they wanted to reclaim him, as the more evangelical components of the Revival did, or wanted instead to stake out an even greater distance from him, as certain liberal theologians did, everyone agreed that Reformed Protestants ought to know his thought far better than they did.

Was the New Interest in Calvin Evident in the Life of the Church?

One indication of renewed interest in Calvin might be found in the "thèses de baccalauréat en théologie" that future pastors wrote at the end of their theological studies. At the time, two Protestant faculties of theology existed in France, one in Strasbourg, which was intended mostly for Lutherans but did have a professor of Reformed dogmatics, and one in Montauban, which was exclusively for Reformed students. In Strasbourg, interest in Calvin came quite late, with only one thesis on him before 1856 (and it actually dealt with both Zwingli and Calvin).[33] A more pronounced interest in Calvin emerged after this, with six theses on the topic between 1857 and 1869, suggesting that professors and students in Strasbourg were abreast of developments in scholarship. In Montauban interest in Calvin came later, and the total number of theses devoted to it was smaller. Even though its theology faculty was reserved for members of the Reformed community and many of its professors were part of the revival movement, Montauban did not see a single thesis on Calvin before 1854. Then, in the period between 1854 and 1870, there were just four theses on the topic, despite the anniversary of 1864 and a flurry of scholarly publications during these years. Clearly, theology students between 1830 and 1870 had only a limited interest in Calvin, and even this only began to emerge after 1850.[34]

Did Protestant publications reserve a more prominent place for Calvin? The *Archives du christianisme au XIXe siècle*, which appeared between 1818 and 1868 and had a fairly eclectic theological orientation until 1824 when its direction was taken over by the revivalist Frédéric Monod, evinced only a limited interest in Calvin, mostly after 1850. Before then, the journal published only two reviews of books on Calvin during the 1820s, a very short review in 1836 of a doctoral thesis in theology on Calvin written at the University of Geneva and the previously cited article of 1841, deploring French Protestants' meager knowledge of Calvin.[35] The situation changed somewhat in the 1850s and 1860s, as the journal responded to trends of the period with reviews of the various editions of Calvin's works and three articles detailing the ceremonies that marked the fourth centenary of his death in 1864.[36] Even so, the final tally was modest. Even a journal influenced by the Réveil that deplored the lack of knowledge about Calvin did relatively little to remedy it.

Analysis of three journals that began to appear in the 1850s and were intended for a more highly educated readership—the *Revue de Strasbourg*, the *Bulletin de la Société de l'Histoire du Protestantisme Français,* and the *Revue chrétienne*—reveals a more mixed picture. The *Revue de Strasbourg* and the *Revue chrétienne*, rivals of sorts since the former was clearly liberal and the latter clearly evangelical, both gave limited space to Calvin, providing hardly any coverage, for example, of the ceremonies commemorating the fourth centenary of his death in 1864. They did publish reviews of the major books on Calvin. Not surprisingly, the *Revue de Strasbourg* used the occasion to criticize what it called Calvin's "need for domination" and his "unspeakable harshness," while the *Revue chrétienne* defended Calvin against those who attacked or "slandered" him.[37] The *Revue* also published several studies of the reformer.[38] But it was the *Bulletin de la Société de l'histoire de protestantisme français* that devoted the most attention to Calvin. The journal's fascination with the reformer was clear from the start; the penultimate issue of its very first volume included a special supplement with the Haag brothers' soon-to-appear article on Calvin, written for *La France protestante*.[39] Evidently, historically minded Huguenots of every theological orientation—the first editor of the journal, Charles Read, was himself a liberal—saw themselves as spiritual descendants of Calvin. Numerous articles examined aspects of his life, and while some were critical of him, all viewed him as absolutely fundamental to French Protestantism.[40] The journal printed previously unpublished Calvin texts as well. Evidently, the greatest interest in Calvin in this period was historical, not theological, in nature, for the *Bulletin*'s in-depth coverage of Calvin was an exception, and the reformer's presence in the Protestant press as a whole remained quite limited.

Within the churches themselves, Calvin's theological influence was also limited. Certainly over time the Réveil gained followers, particularly in the Reformed church officially recognized under the terms of the Concordat of 1802. Under the influence of the revivalists, it moved in a more evangelical direction during the 1840s. As the debate over the confession of faith showed, however, this evangelical influence did not beget resurgence in Calvinist theology. As already noted, the abolition of mandatory subscription to the confession of faith for Genevan ministers in 1725 symbolized the extent to which Protestants there had moved away from the ancestral verities of the cause. It was natural that revivalists—who claimed to represent the thought of the reformers—were interested in bringing back subscription to a confession of faith, something that none of the pastors serving in 1840 had been obliged to do. But when evangelicals in the Reformed church demanded the drafting of a new confession, they sought one updated for the nineteenth century. They were encouraged in this path by the example of the independent churches, a body of independent congregations with revivalist tendencies that emerged in the 1830s and 1840s, using a confession of faith as the basis of their local constitutions. Over time, evangelicals within the officially recognized Reformed church also became more insistent on this, but under the July monarchy the state prevented the meeting of a synod that could adopt a new confessional document. Political events came to the aid of the evangelicals when, in the wake of Revolution of 1848, the Second Republic allowed the churches to meet. French Protestants took advantage of the opportunity to convoke a kind of synod, called a "general assembly."[41] The confession of faith demanded by evangelicals and resisted by liberals was discussed at length. The fact that the churches decided, in the end, not to draft a new confession of faith shows that in 1848 Calvinist ecclesiology had only limited support and that the evangelicals who emerged from the Revival movement were still a minority within the Reformed church of the Concordat.

A significant consequence of these developments was Frédéric Monod's decision to leave the Reformed church. Upset by the synod's refusal to accept an updated confession, Monod founded an independent church, the Union of Evangelical Churches, which was organized on the basis of a confession that he drafted with his theological allies. Yet, as the following passage shows, their confession was far removed both from Calvin's own thought and from that of seventeenth-century Calvinist orthodoxy:

> The Holy Spirit, which the Son has sent on behalf of the Father, regenerates the redeemed who are "elected according to the foreknowledge of God." He lives in them and makes them walk in the knowledge of His word and in the sanctification without which no one will see the Lord. He is granted to all who ask for him. It is by Him that Jesus Christ directs and governs the church, which is his spouse and his body.[42]

As one can see, the confession presented divine election in convoluted terms, spoke of foreknowledge rather than predestination, and preserved ample scope for human freedom. Such a formulation was hardly in keeping with Calvin's thought on the subject. During the 1860s certain liberals, especially the more extreme ones, were harshly critical of Calvin. In 1864, for example, pastor Athanase Coquerel Jr. wrote:

> He [Calvin] created a system that is a masterpiece of logic, but also of absurdity, because it does not take into account important aspects of religious life that should have been given a place in his system. This overly rigid dogmatism ends in a complete absence of morality and religion.... There has perhaps never been a single perfectly consistent Calvinist.[43]

In 1868, pastor Joseph Martin-Paschoud asked: "Do you know when the separation between orthodox and liberal Protestantism began? It began at the foot of the stake of Servetus." He added that Calvin said, "there must be a confession of faith. And with this pretext of reestablishing doctrinal unity in the churches, Calvin established an authoritarian orthodoxy, deflecting or turning back the liberation of the Reformation, and then bowing it under a yoke similar to that of Catholicism."[44] Clearly, Calvin still had committed adversaries among the ranks of Huguenots.

Still by 1870, even if the doctrine of their churches could not be called Calvinist, most Huguenots were happy and proud that France was the birthplace of one of the two great reformers. This offered a small measure of compensation for the fact that France had not become Protestant in the sixteenth century.

■ 1870–1940: A GREATER INTEREST IN CALVIN AND THE EMERGENCE OF A CALVINIST GROUP

Two Examples of Calvinist Renewal

Two examples clearly reveal the growth in historical interest in Calvin and the return to his thought by some French Protestants after 1870. First, with the passage of time, the Reformed Protestants in France became more and more intent on commemorating special events in his life. In 1864, the third centenary of Calvin's death had been duly noted in the Protestant press, but only a small number of articles dealt with it.[45] The most significant events, two lectures by Guillaume de Félice on May 27–28 in the Temple de l'Oratoire and a public meeting organized by the independent churches in the Chapelle Taitbout on May 29, were held in Paris.[46] They were well received but had little impact outside of Parisian Protestantism. And celebrations organized that year in Geneva made only a limited impression on the French Protestant press.[47] By contrast, the fourth centenary of Calvin's birth in 1909 brought together Protestants of all stripes in a "Commission de la fête du centenaire de Calvin," presided over by Paul de Félice, to coordinate joint events beyond the initiatives undertaken by local congregations.[48] The national synods of the three Reformed churches that existed by that date decided to celebrate the occasion with a number of events around Reformation Day but they also organized special services to be held at various times in the local parishes. The Methodist synod also agreed to take part in the celebrations. The Société de l'Histoire du Protestantisme Français commemorated the event by organizing a trip to Noyon, even though the current owner of Calvin's childhood home opposed their wish to place a commemorative plaque on what remained of his house. A number of lectures were also held, most notably in Paris on June 25 at the Temple de l'Oratoire, but in many provincial cities as well.[49] The climax, organized by the Commission de la fête du centenaire, took place November 1 in Paris at the Palais du Trocadéro, where a packed house of more than five thousand listened to speakers evoke the memory of Calvin, often in a decidedly patriotic manner.[50]

Some of the projects of 1909 would no doubt have surprised Calvin. Émile Doumergue (to whom I will return later) commissioned a leather bookmark for use in his massive biography of Calvin, embossed with a portrait of Calvin and the coat of arms and motto of Geneva, and further adorned with silver barrettes bearing Calvin's seal and motto (*prompte et sincere*)—available for purchase at eight to ten francs, with proceeds going to the Monument de la Réformation.[51] According to the liberal journal *Le protestant*, an unidentified but nonetheless "distinguished" composer prepared a cantata with lyrics in French, English, and Dutch.[52]

The French Protestant press also devoted a great deal of attention to festivities held outside the country in 1909, particularly those in Geneva.[53] Where the *Revue chrétienne* had not dedicated a single article to the anniversary of Calvin's death in 1864, it published no less than eight articles on his life and thought in 1909, in addition to a schedule of various commemorative events and reports on many of them.[54] Meanwhile *Foi et vie*, a journal founded in 1898 that generally exhibited little interest in historical subjects, published a lavishly illustrated special edition in October 1909 devoted entirely to Calvin, with articles written by Abel Lefranc, Gabriel Monod, Paul de Félice, Eugène Choisy, Émile Doumergue, Nathanaël Weiss, Charles Gide, and Henri Châtelain.[55]

The desire to celebrate Calvin's memory continued after the First World War. In 1927, on the seventy-fifth anniversary of its founding, the Société de l'Histoire du Protestantisme Français. organized an event at Noyon on July 10, Calvin's birthday, to celebrate the laying of the first stone of the Musée Calvin.[56] The museum was a reconstruction of the house where Calvin was born, which had been damaged by fire in 1557 and then destroyed by the fighting of the First World War. A number of short speeches were pronounced on this occasion, including one by John Viénot, entitled "Calvin: French and Picard Patriot."[57]

In 1935, the Société Calviniste de France and the Société de l'Histoire du Protestantisme Français decided to commemorate the fourth centenary of Calvin's completion of the *Institutes*.[58] To this end, they organized an exhibition at the Bibliothèque nationale entitled "John Calvin and the French Reformation," which was inaugurated in March of that year with the French minister of education in attendance. The two societies also asked the prominent French historian of the sixteenth century Henri Hauser to give a public lecture at the Sorbonne entitled "The Calvinist Economy."[59] From March 13 to 15 the Société Calviniste organized "Journées d'Etudes Calviniennes" in the theological faculty of Paris, the acts of which were published *in extenso* by the *BSHPF*.[60] A large special edition of the *Bulletin* was also devoted to the various events, with similar contributions appearing elsewhere in the Protestant press.[61] Once again, as it had in 1909, *Foi et vie* published a special issue dedicated to Calvin.[62]

Commemorations continued that decade with a celebration in 1938 of the fourth centenary of the founding of the first French Reformed church at Strasbourg. This occasioned the publication of articles in the *BSHPF*, most notably by Eugène Choisy, Henri Strohl, Jacques Pannier, and Théodore Gérold. The Reformed church of Alsace and Lorraine also published a special book for the occasion.[63] With the passage of time, increasingly minor landmarks in Calvin's life were judged worthy of recall.

While commemorations of Calvin multiplied, the adoption of a Declaration of Faith by the Reformed churches of France opened the way for Calvinist teachings to reenter the life of the church. As mentioned earlier, French Protestants took advantage of the loosening of restrictions that accompanied the Second Republic in 1848 in order to convoke a general assembly at which the liberal majority refused to adopt a confession of faith. After the establishment of the Third Republic, they were able in 1872 to hold a national synod that Napoleon III had given them permission to convoke in 1870 but whose gathering had been postponed because of the political upheaval of that year. In contrast to 1848, this synod adopted a Declaration of Faith, to which all new pastors were obliged to subscribe. Certainly, the short declaration (it was not a confession of faith, only a simple declaration) was not Calvinist in any strict sense. Nonetheless, it did assert: "Together with its Fathers and its martyrs, with the Confession of Faith of La Rochelle, and with all the churches of the Reformation in their various confessions [the church] proclaims the sovereign authority of Holy Scripture in matters of faith."[64] The text was adopted only by 60 percent majority, however, as liberals, hostile to the very principle of a confession, refused to accept even a declaration in its stead. The result was a schism in the church between evangelicals, who accepted the decision of the synod, and liberals, who rejected it. Still, this adoption of a declaration was a first step in expanding the influence of Calvinist thought, especially because the document respectfully mentioned the original confession of the French Reformed churches, drafted by Calvin himself.

The 1930s marked the culmination of this evolution, as discussions took place between evangelicals and liberals in the hope of reunifying the Reformed church.

Negotiations were difficult at first, but a breakthrough occurred in October 1934 when liberals accepted the principle of an obligatory confession for pastors.[65] Subsequent discussions went so well that a synod convened in 1938 accepted a revised Declaration of Faith. This document too cited the Confession of La Rochelle, although only after the Apostles' Creed and the Ecumenical Creeds, a modified emphasis that might be interpreted as a concession to the liberal camp.[66]

The fact remains that liberals, who until then had adamantly refused the very principle of any declaration of faith, from that point on not only accepted the principle but also a text that, like the declaration of 1872, referred explicitly to the Confession of La Rochelle.[67] This was an undeniable watershed in the life of French Reformed Protestantism. Clearly, the years from 1870 to 1940 had witnessed a marked growth in the influence of Calvin on French Protestantism. What can explain such a development?

Elements of an Explanation

As strange as it might seem, to understand the evolution sketched here we must turn to the world of international politics. At the end of the Franco-Prussian War of 1870, Germany annexed Alsace and a part of Lorraine and refused to organize a plebiscite to consult the will of the people. This scandalized the French, who saw it as an abuse of power, a violation of justice, and a simple case of theft. French Protestants were particularly shocked because two-thirds of all Germans were Protestant, and the Prussian monarchy that headed the German Empire was avowedly Protestant. Such an abuse of force was, in the eyes of the Huguenots, unworthy of any Christian nation, but especially a Protestant one. It produced a strong reaction against Germany and, indeed, against Germans. Since Luther was German, Huguenots tended to distance themselves from him and sought to demonstrate that the French Reformation had indigenous roots that were actually independent of the German Reformation. This could only lead to a greater emphasis being placed on Calvin.

The rejection of Germany became even stronger after the First World War. A major reason for this was the fact that a significant number of German Protestant theologians had signed a 1914 manifesto granting their complete approval to the actions of their government even after it reneged on its word by violating the neutrality of Belgium, a nation it had agreed to protect according to the terms of the 1831 Treaty of London. Their decision was viewed by Huguenots as a grave moral failure.[68] French Protestant disaffection with all things German became so great that when the Protestant Church of Reims, destroyed by German shelling during the war, was rebuilt, windows were installed representing all of the great reformers except Luther! As I have already noted, during the groundbreaking for the Calvin Museum at Noyon, Jean Viénot saluted Calvin as a "French patriot."

Internal French politics also go some way to explaining the renewed interest in Calvin. The Third Republic was inaugurated in France in 1870, and from 1879 onward it was dominated by anticlerical politicians who worked to secularize French society. This outraged a significant portion of the political right, who tended to be monarchist and viewed France as an inherently Catholic nation. Conversely, a large majority of Protestants, remembering the persecutions that the Roman Catholic Church encouraged the monarchy to pursue, sided with the anticlerical republic, supporting it with their pens and their votes. Their stance provoked a strong current of political anti-Protestantism that produced extremely fierce polemics, especially between 1885 and 1900.[69] Nationalists argued that France was a Catholic nation and that all those who were not Catholic—thus all Protestants— were alien to the spirit of France and were, at the very least, potential traitors in service to Protestant countries like Germany or England. Of course, Protestants defended themselves against these charges and maintained that they were every bit as French as Catholics were, since Protestantism had been an integral part of French culture since the beginning of the Reformation in the sixteenth century. There was no the better way to illustrate this point than to remind opponents that the Reformed were the spiritual descendents of the indisputably French John Calvin. All of this explains why, during the anniversary of 1909, Calvin was cele-brated as a "great Frenchman," a refrain taken up by *Le christianisme au XXe siècle*:

> The remembrance of this solemn occasion, as religious as it is patriotic, will remain deep in the memories and hearts of all those who have the privilege of witnessing it. May it also remain engraved in the conscience and make Parisian Protestants.... proud of the great Frenchman to whom they could on November 1, 1909, render public homage in a government building.[70]

As important as these political elements were, however, theological factors are always most decisive within a church. The changing theological context explains much of the revived interest in the life and thought of Calvin. The clear majority that evangelicals were able to muster at the synod of 1872 resulted largely from the reaction against changes that had occurred within the liberal camp over the decades since 1848. A group of extreme liberals emerged in the 1850s and 1860s who were no longer content to water down traditional doctrine with increasingly vague formulae, as moderate liberals had done since the eighteenth century. Instead they openly challenged traditional doctrine while insisting on their right to remain pastors in the Reformed church. They justified their position by arguing that being a Protestant was not tied to the acceptance of certain points of doctrine gathered together in a declaration of faith, but was defined instead by the free interpretation of scripture. Their attitude shocked, and even outraged, a significant portion of believers and pastors whose view was expressed at a pastoral conference in Paris in 1864: "We regard these denials [those of extreme liberals] as completely destructive to the Christian religion and the Reformed church."[71] This led evangelicals to insist on a declaration of faith that would prevent new pastors from preaching such doc-trines within the church. When they obtained such a declaration in 1872, it repre-sented a step toward a Calvinist ecclesiology. As we have seen, however, liberals—even the moderates among them—refused to enforce the synod's decisions because they did not want to see the exclusion of extreme liberals from the body of pastors.[72] A schism followed, which hardly seemed promising for Calvinism, but over the course of the 1870s, the liberal camp grew weaker, with the majority of the extremists, including Félix Pécaut, Ferdinand Buisson, and Timothée Colani,[73] leaving the church on their own accord. In retrospect, their departure justified the arguments of moderate evangelicals of the 1860s who maintained that their extreme doctrinal presuppositions made it impossible for them to be part of the Reformed church.

Despite the schism that divided the Reformed church after 1879, the general theological climate among the Reformed had come to resemble the situation that prevailed around 1840, with the church being composed mostly of moderate evangelicals and moderate liberals. Evangelical extremists had left the church with Frédéric Monod after the general assembly of 1848, and liberal extremists had departed during the 1870s. This new state of affairs facilitated a move toward Calvinist ideas, since it was only extreme liberals who were fiercely opposed to Calvin. In addition, debate over the Declaration of Faith had drawn attention to important points of doctrine at the very moment when all of French society—shaken by the anticlerical political stance of the republicans and the polemics that stemmed from it—was examining issues of secularism, religious liberty, and the links between religious doctrines and political democracy. This too promoted renewed interest in the religious controversies of the sixteenth century. On the other hand, German developments in exegesis and the history of dogma—especially as practiced by Adolph Harnack—could hardly be ignored in late-nineteenth-century France. These two developments were by no means incompatible with a revived interested in Calvin and, in fact, they contributed to it. After all, Calvin himself had laid out a systematic presentation of Christian doctrine, with a completely original conception of the relationship between church and state. He had also been one of the great exegetes of his time. Finally, the long and complicated doctrinal debates of the previous decades had led many theologians and church leaders to conclude that the issues that had divided evangelicals and liberals since the beginning of the nineteenth century were themselves outdated. If the church was to renew itself, new starting points for debate were needed. This opened the way to a renewed appreciation of certain aspects of Calvin's thought.

The recovery of Calvin took place in two stages. The first occurred in the 1880s and 1890s and was led by Auguste Sabatier. He was probably the most important French Protestant theologian of the nineteenth century, and has been called the "French Schleiermacher" by some.[74] In the context discussed here, Sabatier's significance lay in his riposte to liberals who believed that one could arrive at religious truth by means of historical-critical exegesis, yet opposed the "yoke" of confessions because they were written by men. Sabatier replied that the historical-critical understanding of the Bible was also a man-made yoke. He envisaged a solution for arriving at religious truth that went beyond the use of historical-critical method. Placing himself directly in line with Schleiermacher and Alexandre Vinet and feeling, like Schleiermacher, the same concern to develop a Christian apologetics that would be capable of bridging the gulf between the secular culture of his times and Christianity, he insisted on the fundamental importance of the ethical-religious experience, which he judged to be common to all humans. In this, his thought was reminiscent of Calvin's emphasis on the interior witnessing of the Holy Spirit. At the same time, Sabatier's thought was very much a product of the nineteenth century. More than one reader wondered if his thought left room for the notion of a transcendent God.

Stage 2 came in the 1920s and 1930s, although there had been anticipations of it during the previous decade. Even before 1914, figures like Auguste Lecerf urged a return to Calvin and Calvinist dogmatics in order to free theology from excessive subjectivism and overdependence on emotion. Before the First World War, however, there was only limited interest in Lecerf and no movement coalesced around his ideas. Only in the 1920s and 1930s did an organized neo-Calvinist movement take shape.

Central to its emergence was the First World War—four long years in which the youth of Europe was massacred daily. The war not only killed millions of people; it also destroyed the optimism about progress, human nature, and the merits of Western civilization that had informed nineteenth-century theology. Certain theologians concluded that they could no longer rely on a dogmatics that had been unable to prevent Christians from massacring one another on such a scale. New theological frameworks were needed, ones that distinguished clearly between a powerful and transcendent God and his creatures, whose sinful nature had been brought into sharp relief during the war. Karl Barth's theology offered such a framework. So did Calvin's. It was no accident that Pierre Maury, one of the principal figures in the introduction of Barth's ideas to France, was the son of Léon Maury, a pastor influenced by the Réveil and a historian of the movement, nor that the younger Maury himself was attracted first to neo-Calvinism as a charter member of the Société Calviniste de France before starting to promote Barth's theology.[75] Active in the French army throughout the First World War, he was part of the generation that saw a fundamental need to reexamine the theology that had been powerless to halt such a long and murderous conflict.

It is impossible, within the limits of this essay, to examine the links between Barthianism and neo-Calvinism in the twentieth century in any detail. And no one would characterize Barth as a strict Calvinist since he rejected ideas like predestination and infant baptism. Still, he is relevant to our subject because he insisted on breaking with the basic presuppositions of the nineteenth century, reproaching liberalism for what he called its "humanization of Christianity" and insisting on the total alterity of God.[76] This was all consistent with the respect that Calvin had for the sovereignty of God. However important the differences between Barthianism and Calvinism that remained, there is no gainsaying the degree to which Barthian theology encouraged interest in Calvin.

The Partial Return to Calvin, Step-by-Step

Revived interest in Calvin was nurtured by the continued publication of books and articles on the subject, including many innovative works that appeared during the 1880s and 1890s such as Antoine-Jean Baumgartner's *Calvin hébraïsant et interprète de l'Ancien Testament*, Albert Wattier's *Calvin prédicateur*, and Abel Lefranc's *La Jeunesse de Calvin*.[77] Some of the massive works begun in the 1860s were also continued or completed, notably the *Opera Calvini*, completed in 1900, as well as Herminjard's correspondence of the reformers, which was only interrupted by the editor's death in 1897.[78] These works offered the basic foundation for later scholarship, even if Rodolphe Reuss could still remark in 1899 that the "complete biography of Calvin equal to the level of recent academic research and truly worthy of the French reformer" had yet to appear.[79]

Calvin's own writings also became increasingly available.[80] In addition to a number of his lesser writings, a new edition of the 1560 French version of the *Institutes* appeared in 1888. After Gustave Lanson, a Catholic specialist in sixteenth-century literature, brought attention to the significance of the 1541 edition of the *Institutes* in an article in the *Revue historique* in 1894, its editing was begun.[81] Because of the numerous complications of the task, it did not appear until 1911, but when it did it was the first publication of the work since 1541.[82] The anniversary of 1909 occasioned many works on Calvin, both in France and elsewhere, including the French translation of what was then one of the best Calvin biographies, written by Williston Walker.[83] Republications of Calvin's works after the First World War were quite numerous too, particularly under the aegis of the Calvinist Society, which collaborated in the 1930s with the publishing house "Je Sers," directed by Pierre Maury. From this point on, the major works of Calvin could be easily obtained in France, which had never before been the case.[84]

The Protestant press also showed renewed interest in Calvin during this period, as one can see in the *Revue chrétienne*, then the principal Protestant journal aimed at a broader educated public. It published reviews of books on Calvin, like François Guizot's in 1873 and Gustave Adolphe Hoff's short biography of 1878.[85] It celebrated the appearance of texts by Calvin, paying tribute, for example, to the first twenty years of the publication of the *Opera calvini*.[86] The journal also defended Calvin against the criticism of various authors.[87] In 1896, it followed the lead of other Protestant publications by printing a polemical piece by Auguste Sabatier that countered the attacks on Calvin by Ferdinand Brunetière, the director of the *Revue des deux mondes*.[88] It also published a number of fairly erudite articles, such as Alfred Erichson's essay from 1896, "The Authorship of the *Confession of Sins* Attributed to Calvin."[89] And as we have already seen, the *Revue* gave great attention to Calvin in the anniversary year of 1909.

Interest in Calvin was also apparent in the pages of the *BSHPF*, which did much to refine knowledge about Calvin, especially after Nathanaël Weiss, a connoisseur of sixteenth-century literature, became the journal's editor in 1885. The *Bulletin* worked to resolve scholarly questions, such as the date of the Genevan Catechism's composition or the publication date of the first edition of the *Institutes*.[90] It printed previously unpublished texts by Calvin, like his *Summary of the Books of the Old and New Testament* in 1552.[91] It also kept readers abreast of new books and articles on Calvin. In 1888, it paid a great deal of attention to the innovative book of the non-Protestant scholar Abel Lefranc, *The Youth of Calvin*, actually publishing excerpts of the work that was the first to rebut the accusation that Calvin had been branded for the crime of sodomy, a staple of anti-Calvin polemics ever since Jerome Bolsec first asserted this in the sixteenth century.[92] It also published reviews of most books written on Calvin, in German as well as French.[93] Some of the reviews displayed a high level of erudition in their treatment of the subject.[94] Of course, the *Bulletin* defended Calvin against Catholic polemicists, especially Ferdinand

Brunetière, with whom the journal carried on a heated debate from 1896 to 1901. In the same polemical spirit, near the beginning of the twentieth century and especially in 1908, it followed the example of the rest of the Protestant press and joined the debate over Calvin's responsibility for the burning of Servetus prompted by the erection of statues of Servetus in Annemasse and Paris.[95]

At the same time, the *Bulletin* published articles on specific aspects of Calvin's life and thought that were laudatory, and often indulgent, toward him. Ariste Viguié, the liberal professor of theology at Paris, would write in 1882, for example, that "Calvinist predestination is only a strong means of expressing an intimate feeling of personal and living communion with God and is in no way the fatalistic formula that it would later become."[96] Viguié went on to refute the idea that Calvin was "the incarnation of dogmatism and unyielding logic."[97] He shared none of the fierce hostility that liberals like Athanase Coquerel Jr. had exhibited toward Calvin in the 1860s.

A growing tendency to look not only at the historical aspects of Calvin's life but also at his thought can be found in the *Revue théologique*, the journal published by professors of the Faculty of Protestant Theology at Montauban.[98] Calvin was barely mentioned by either the *Revue de Strasbourg* or the theological supplement of the *Revue chrétienne* (the predecessor of the *Revue théologique*) before 1870, but he became much more visible after that date. This interest increased through the 1880s and 1890s, with frequent reviews and articles analyzing his influence on society or particular aspects of his doctrine, like predestination or the nature of biblical authority.[99] Other publications like *Le christianisme au XIXe siècle* also showed greater interest in Calvin.[100]

Certainly, some liberals like Ferdinand Buisson continued to be extremely critical of Calvin. In his 1892 thesis on Sébastien Castellion, Buisson offered a negative view of the reformer.[101] As an extreme liberal and freethinker, he could hardly appreciate Calvin, even though he had a measure of admiration for him and even compared the *Institutes* to Aquinas's *Summa Theologica*. As P. Cabanel writes:

> The Calvin of Buisson is the Calvin of Castellio (and consequently of Servetus) [...]. With Buisson, we are only invited to see the somber side of Cavin, recognizing the effort he made to make Geneva the protestant Rome, but also calling attention to the harm that came from this imitation of Rome.[102]

Even though he drew attention to the burning of Servetus and the responsibility of Calvin in this affair, Buisson was less hostile to Calvin than many liberals of the 1860s.[103] In his 1894 contribution to Lavisse's *Histoire de France*, he appeared even more sympathetic, expressing admiration for Calvin's work in Geneva.[104] Attitudes had obviously changed a great deal since the diatribes of Martin-Paschoud in 1868.

The list of bachelor's theses defended by students in the theological faculty at Montauban likewise illustrates a very clear growth in interest in Calvin. They were rare before 1870, but twenty-two theses were written on Calvin between 1871 and 1902, with the bulk of them appearing between 1885 and 1900. This was almost certainly related to Émile Doumergue's presence within the faculty of Montauban in these years. A number of theses on Calvin were also defended in Paris, albeit fewer—seven between 1890 and 1904—a number that included those written by Auguste Lecerf and Jacques Pannier, to whom I will return later. By the end of the nineteenth century, therefore, a genuine revival in interest in Calvin is clear. And Doumergue, Lecerf, and Pannier all played a key role in transforming it into a movement after 1914.

Nothing in his early years appeared to destine Émile Doumergue for leadership in the French Calvinist movement. Born in 1844, he studied theology at Montauban where he defended a baccalaureate thesis in 1869 on "Positivism and Independent Morality." His *license* and doctoral thesis examined nineteenth-century apologetics.[105] All this was quite removed from the sixteenth century. His doctrinal views, however, led to his becoming editor-in-chief of the major evangelical journal, *Le christianisme au XIXe siècle*. As a result, he became directly involved in the battles over the synod of 1872 and the refusal of liberals there to accept the Declaration of Faith agreed upon there. In the fierce debates that followed, Doumergue emerged as a spirited defender of the evangelical position. It is possible that the polemics surrounding the Declaration of Faith caused him to reflect on the importance of confessions in the church.

In 1880, Doumergue was named professor of church history in the Faculty of Theology at Montauban, where he would teach for thirty-nine years and gain a reputation for his devotion to his students. In the wake of this appointment, he began to publish articles and give lectures on Calvin in the 1890s, often defending him against his adversaries.[106] His lecture in 1898 for the beginning of the academic year at Montauban, for example, bore the telling title "Calvin: Founder of Modern Liberties."[107] The first volume of his life's work, the massive *John Calvin: The Men and Things of His Time*, appeared in 1899. The work would ultimately stretch to seven in-folio volumes, the last of which appeared in 1927.

Richly detailed and based on original documentation, especially the correspondence of Calvin that Doumergue knew so well, his work also drew on research being carried out then by the Dutch scholars responsible for the Calvinist renewal in the Netherlands.[108] It remains a veritable mine of information to this day. It certainly had methodological weaknesses, as was recognized at the time by Rodolphe Reuss, for instance, whose review for the *BSHPF* criticized Doumergue for losing himself in the details, mixing historical periods, engaging in excessive conjecture, and being far too subjective.[109] The vast and learned work is, in fact, a monument to the glory of Calvin—the last volume is simply titled *The Triumph*—whose quarrels Doumergue adopts as his own and whose life is often described in providential tones.[110] As a fervent patriot, Doumergue was also committed to the indefensible thesis that the French Reformation was completely independent of the German Reformation, which led him to cast Jacques Lefèvre d'Etaples as a thoroughgoing reformer and to speak of "*protestantisme fabrisien.*"[111] Doumergue was clearly carried away by his desire to champion French Protestantism against its foes and exalt the memory of Calvin.

Its methodological shortcomings notwithstanding, this biography had a tremendous impact. Its abundant detail served to make Calvin and his writings far better known, even though its mostly biographical approach allowed for little attention to theological questions. Furthermore, over the nearly thirty years between the appearance of the first and the last volume, Doumergue also took time out to write numerous articles, brochures, and lectures in which he tirelessly defended Calvin and his actions. One example was his campaign for an "expiatory" Servetus monument on Geneva's Plateau de Champel, where the Spanish heretic was burned.[112] Looking ahead to Calvin's four hundredth birthday in 1909, Doumergue launched the idea of countering the damage done to the reformer's modern image by his role in the arrest and trial of Servetus by financing a monument indicating that latter-day Calvinists regretted this action. As Valentine Zuber explains, "since the death of Servetus was one of the principal polemical arguments of anti-protestants, this would be definitively defused if the Calvinists acknowledged the errors of their predecessors and showed their repentance."[113] Doumergue's efforts met with success. The Servetus monument was inaugurated in November 1903 with this carefully conceived inscription: "Respectful and grateful sons of Calvin, our great Reformer, but condemning an error which was of its century, and firmly attached to liberty of conscience according to the true principles of the Reformation and the Gospel, we have erected this expiatory monument."[114] The initiative's success, however, was not complete. It was met with criticism from both liberals, who found the inscription too lenient on Calvin, and those who opposed any questioning, however slight, of Calvin's work.[115]

In Doumergue's wake, others pursued further studies of Calvin. Particularly important was the pastor Jacques Pannier (1869–1945), who became interested in Calvin during his theological studies at the beginning of the 1890s and eventually became a specialist in sixteenth-century French Protestantism.[116] He was an editor of the 1911 edition of the French version of the *Institutes* of 1541, which he subsequently reworked between 1936 and 1939 into a revised and improved edition. His short 1909 book on Calvin's youth was followed by a series of other works on Calvin.[117] He also published numerous articles on Calvin in the *BSHPF* and the *Revue d'histoire et de philosophie religieuse*.[118] Joining the board of the Société de l'Histoire du Protestantisme Français in 1908, he became secretary and librarian of the society in 1923, and then president in 1939. Finally, he played a central role in having the childhood home of Calvin reconstructed and converted into a museum.

Both Doumergue and Pannier had a primarily historical interest in Calvin. For a genuine Calvinist movement to emerge, the theology of the reformer also needed to be revalorized, and it was Auguste Lecerf who took up this task. Born in London in 1872 to agnostic and anticlerical parents who had been obliged to take refuge in England in 1871 after their participation in the Paris Commune, Lecerf converted to Protestantism at the age of seventeen after reading Calvin. He was influenced by Jonathan Edwards, the great American Calvinist who was the major force behind the Great Awakening of 1735, a fact that again underscores the links between revivalism and Calvinism. After theological studies in Paris, he defended a bachelor's thesis in theology in 1895, entitled *The Determinism of Responsibility in the Thought of John Calvin*.[119] More detailed than most bachelor theses, Le Cerf's had a resolutely dogmatic character. He was interested in Calvin's "system," the structure of his thought, as he explained in his introduction:

> If we are committed to Calvin, it is because he was the reformer who most clearly posed the question of the relationship between the bondage of the will and predestination, on the one hand, and between duty and responsibility on the other. And it was he alone who brought a clear and coherent solution to the problem, satisfying the legitimate demands of both the mind and the conscience.[120]

He argued that Calvin's system had shown "that his conception of predestination, conceived as the instrument of absolute justice, necessarily implied responsibility."[121] Lecerf worked for a return to Calvin's thought that would counter the influence of the social sciences on theology (which, in his view, contributed to the humanization of Christianity) and resist the central role given to religious emotion in nineteenth-century theology. He resolutely opposed all subjectivism.

Before 1914, Lecerf's ideas were not widely known since he had published very little. Coming to Paris after the First World War, he began to promote his neo-Calvinist ideas more forcefully, both in articles and in his work as secretary-general of the Protestant Student Association of Paris.[122] While teaching Greek and English in the Paris Faculty of Theology, after 1922 he also gave a free course on Reformed theology that met with great success among both students and the general public because of his clear exposition and his ability to relate Calvinism to the issues of the day. A group of neo-Calvinists, including Pierre Maury and Jean Cadier,[123] eventually took shape, and this allowed Lecerf to found the Calvinist Society of France on December 10, 1926, with Émile Doumergue as honorary president and Jacques Pannier as secretary. Significantly, this was not a society of Calvinist studies, but a "Calvinist" society. Article 2 of its statutes articulated the society's purpose: "It has as goals: 1) to study and promote Calvinism, considered as an element of strength and progress for Christian thought 2) to make known Calvin, his works, and Calvinist religious literature."[124]

From the beginning, the society published a *Bulletin*, which was quite small at first but grew with time. It printed in-depth articles like "Calvin's Doctrine of the Church" in issue 12 and "Calvin and Capitalism" in issue 17. The number of contributors grew steadily, with the addition of names like André Monod, Paul Beuzart, Marcel Cadix, and André Schlemmer. All of this activity made it possible for Henri Clavier to present to the 1935 meeting of the World Presbyterian Alliance a report about France entitled "The Revival of Calvinism."[125]

The success of French neo-Calvinists was apparent from the celebration of "Calvinist" anniversaries. It was also illustrated by the increased presence of Calvin in Protestant journals during the 1920s and 1930s. Not surprisingly, this was especially true of the *BSHPF* under the leadership of Jacques Pannier, who was himself a frequent contributor, but it was also clear in *Foi et vie*, managed during the 1930s by Pierre Maury.[126] Calvin's presence could also be noted in the two journals published by the faculties of Protestant theology at Montpellier and Strasbourg: the *Etudes théologiques et religieuses* (Montpellier) and the *Revue d'histoire et de philosophie religieuse* (Strasbourg).[127] Articles appearing in these journals were mostly historical in nature, but some of them also had a clear theological orientation, revealing again the renewed interest in Calvin's ideas.[128] During these years, Eugène Choisy, Paul Lobstein, Max Dominicé, Henri Clavier, and Marc-Edouard Chenevière also published interesting works on Calvin.[129] The neo-Calvinists' efforts were crowned, of course, by Lecerf's official appointment to teach dogmatics in the Paris theology faculty in December 1936. Quickly promoted to professor after a successful defense of his doctoral thesis in 1938, he saw himself as an interpreter of Calvin's thought and its importance for the contemporary world in particular.[130]

The success of Lecerf and his allies was obviously related to the political and theological conditions of the 1930s. At that time, the ideas of Barth spread rapidly, although it is not clear whether neo-Calvinism encouraged Barthianism or whether the success of Barthianism worked to the benefit of neo-Calvinism. In reality, the two movements—both born out of a fundamental rejection of the presuppositions of nineteenth-century theology—probably cannot be separated. In any case, Barth's resolute opposition to Nazism in 1933–1934 and his insistence at the Synod of Barmen in May 1934 on formulating a confession of faith to serve as the basis for a theological rejection of Nazism had increased his appeal in France. Many Huguenots concluded that a strong affirmation of divine transcendence and the sovereignty of Jesus Christ was the best means to oppose the dictators of the 1930s who sought to establish the transcendence of the state.

In conclusion, can we say that the Calvin who had been lost at the beginning of the nineteenth century was actually found again in 1940? If one understands this as an actual return to all of Calvin's theology by the majority of French Protestants, the answer is no. Yet undeniably, by the end of the 1930s, Huguenots could easily access Calvin's works, they knew his thought much better, and they were aware of what they owed to the reformer. Essentially, they had reached a truce with Calvin. They recognized the limits and the contingency of some of his choices, but this did not prevent a majority of them, at least, from admiring him and considering themselves to be his spiritual children.

Karl Barth—even though he was Swiss—seemed to capture the feeling of most French Protestants in 1946 when he wrote:

> Calvin was never our pope. Calvin could never take the rank of doctor among us, as is the case with Saint Augustine or Saint Thomas in Catholicism.... The true authority of Protestant Christians is the Word, which God himself spoke, which he speaks, and which he will speak eternally by the witness of the Holy Spirit in the writings of the Old and New Testament. Calvin is, for us, a master of the art of listening to this one and only teaching of the church.[131]

■ Notes

1. Michèle Sacquin, *Entre Bossuet et Maurras, l'antiprotestantisme en France de 1814 à 1870* (Paris: École des chartes, 1998). In translating Karl Gottlieb Bretschneider's *Calvin et l'Église de Genève* (Geneva: J.-J. Paschoud, 1822), Guillaume de Félice explained that he did so partly in order to defend the memory of Calvin (iii–iv).

2. Paul-Henri Marron, "Vie de Jean Calvin," *Mélanges de religion, de morale et de critique sacrée* (1821/2): 256–65.

3. *Archives du christianisme au XIXe siècle*, March 13, 1841, 36.

4. John Calvin, *Institution de la religion chrestienne* (Paris: Meyrueis, In 1835). The *Archives du christianisme* noted that, in addition to a two-volume Latin version of the *Institutes*, the Berlin publisher, Eicher, had also just published the seven-volume *Commentaires de Calvin sur le Nouveau Testament* (with a preface by F. Tholuck) and that preparations were being made to make these books readily available in Paris. The journal added: "Nous désirons que...ces facilités engagent un grand nombre de nos théologiens à se procurer ces ouvrages de l'immortel réformateur." December 26, 1835, 191, col. 2. In 1835, Karl Gottlieb Bretschneider had also published in Latin the letters of Calvin housed in the ducal library of Gotha: *Johannis*

Calvini, Theod. Bezeae, Henrici IV regis aliorumque illlius aevi… (Leipzig: F. C. G. Vogelii, 1835). In their essay of 1852 on Calvin for *La France protestante* (see n. 14), the Haag brothers, Eugène and Émile, noted that, for the *Complete Works of Calvin*, there was only an old nine-volume edition published in Geneva in 1671 (this collection was actually published in Amsterdam with the title *Joannis Calvini opera omnia in novem tomos digesta* [Amsterdam: Widow of J.J. Schipper, 1671]). They also mentioned an incomplete edition begun in Hamburg in 1790 by Johann Wilhelm Heinrich Ziegenbein (not in the catalogue of the Bibliothèque nationale de France). The *Traité des reliques* had been republished at the end of the third volume of Jacques Albin Simon Collin de Plancy's *Dictionnaire critique des reliques et des images miraculeuses* (Paris: Guien, 1821).

5. It had been inserted in Paul L. Jacob, *Œuvres françoises de Calvin recueillies pour la première fois, précédées de sa vie par Théodore de Bèze et d'une notice bibliographique* (Paris: Charles Gosselin, 1842). Beza's *Vie de Calvin* was also subsequently been republished and annotated by Alfred Franklin (Paris: Cherbuliez, 1864).

6. Hubert Bost, "Calvin au prisme du *Dictionnaire* de Bayle," in *Calvin et la France*, spec. ed. of *BSHPF* 155 (2009): esp. 262, 245–65. The second edition of Bayle's *Dictionnaire* appeared in 1702.

7. Cited by Daniel Robert, *Les Églises réformées en France 1800–1830* (Paris: Presses Universitaires de France, 1961), 240.

8. Samuel Vincent, "De la prédestination," *Mélanges de religion, de morale et de critique sacrée* (1822/2): 273 n., 278 n.

9. Olivier Millet, "Le Calvin de François Guizot (1822)," in *L'historiographie romantique*, ed. Francis Claudon, André Encrevé, and Laurence Richer (Bordeaux: Editions Bière, 2007), 101–9. Elsewhere, Millet explains that a genius is "une individualité capable de synthétiser et de formuler, par son action et sa pensée, les besoins diffus d'une société et d'une époque, des les rassembler dans une expression cohérente, et de leur permettre ainsi de se réaliser historiquement." "Conclusions et perspectives," *Calvin et la France*, spec. ed. of *BSHPF* 155 (2009): 347. Karl Gottlieb Bretschneider, *Calvin et l'Église de Genève*, transl. by G. de Félice (Geneva: Paschoud), 1822.

10. Millet, "Le Calvin de François Guizot (1822)," 107.

11. See, for example, Félix Bungener, *Calvin, sa vie, son oeuvre, ses écrits* (Paris: Cherbuliez, 1862).

12. André Sayous, *Etudes littéraires sur les écrivains français de la Reformation*, 2 vols., 2nd ed. (Paris: Cherbuliez, 1854); François Auguste Mignet, "Etablissement de la réforme religieuse et constitution du calvinisme à Genève," in *Etudes historiques*, 4th ed. (Paris: Didier, 1877), 255–425. This work was first published in 1843; the relevant lecture on Calvin was delivered in 1834. It is noteworthy that Mignet constructs his picture of Calvin essentially on the basis of works from the sixteenth and seventeenth centuries, especially the 1663 edition of Beza's *Vie de Calvin*, the 1696 essay on Calvin in Bayle's *Dictionnaire*, a Latin edition of Calvin's letters published in Amsterdam in 1667, and the *Histoire de Genève* published in 1680 by Jacob Spon. This shows how few recent French works on Calvin were available in the 1830s.

13. Jacob, *Oeuvres françoises*; Abraham Ruchat, *Histoire de la Réformation de la Suisse où l'on voit tout ce qui s'est passé de remarquable, depuis l'an 1516 jusqu'en l'an 1556 dans les Églises des XIII cantons et États confédérés*, 6 vols. (Geneva: M. M. Bousquet, 1727–28), new ed. published by Louis Vulliemin (Nyon: M. Giral-Prelaz, 1835–38).

14. See Eugène Haag and Émile Haag, *La France protestante ou vie des protestants français qui se sont fait un nom dans l'histoire depuis les premiers temps de la réformation jusqu'à la reconnaissance du principe de la liberté des cultes par l'Assemblée nationale*, 10 vols. (Paris: Cherbuliez, 1846–58), 3: 109–62.

15. Jules Bonnet, *Lettres de Jean Calvin, recueillies pour la première fois et publiées d'après les manuscrits originaux, Lettres françaises*, 2 vols. (Paris: Meyrueis, 1854).

16. John Calvin, *Commentaires de Jehan Calvin sur le Nouveau Testament*, 4 vols. (Paris: Meyrueis, 1854–55); Calvin, *Institution de la religion chrestienne*, 2 vols. (Paris: Meyrueis, 1859); Calvin, *Commentaires de Jehan Calvin sur le livre des Pseaumes*, 2 vols. (Paris: Meyrueis, 1859). All of these publications were subsidized by the Presbyterian Board.

17. Edouard Reuss, "Calvin considéré comme exégète," *Revue de théologie et de philosophie chrétienne* (1853/1): 223–48. He wrote: "Les réformateurs sont trop oubliés. On invoque incessamment leurs noms, leurs doctrines, leur autorité, et on ne lit même pas leurs livres" (225). Founded in 1850, the journal was an organ of extreme liberalism (it was known as the *Revue de Strasbourg* because it was published there, but it had changed its name many times).

18. Louis Bonnet, a series of articles, all entitled: "Études sur Calvin, sa vie, ses écrits, son époque," *Revue chrétienne* (1854): 713–39; (1855): 321–38, 513–29, 723–52; (1856): 321–35, 385–403; (1857): 219–32, 336–52, 471–84 and 705–22; (1858): 347–72.

19. *Calv. Opp.*; Aimé-Louis Herminjard, *Correspondance des réformateurs dans les pays de langue française* (Geneva: H. Georg, 1866).

20. Jean-Henri Merle d'Aubigné, *Histoire de la Réformation en Europe au temps de Calvin*, 8 vols. (Paris: Meyrueis, subsequently Calmann-Lévy, 1863–1878). The work covers only the period up to 1546, the date of Martin Luther's death.

21. See Charles Dardier in *Le lien* (liberal) in 1866: October 13, 20; 1868: June 16, 23, 30; July 25; August 1, 22; September 12, 19, 26; October 3; 1869: February 3, 20; January 22, 1870; February 12, 19, 26; March 19; August 13, 20. See Louis Vueillemin in the *Revue chrétienne* (evangelical) in 1867: 77–94; 1868: 596–615. In his reviews in the *Archives du christianisme au XIXe siècle* (evangelical), Louis Abelous is very critical: "son histoire tourne au panégyrique ou à l'épopée"; 1863: December 10; 1864: June 10; 1866: August 30, qtd. here, 218. See also Louis Rognon, "Essai sur l'*Institution* de Calvin," *Revue chrétienne* (1863): 708–27, which mentions the republication of the *Institutes* in 1859, the first two volumes of Merle d'Aubigné, and the first volume of the *Opera Calvini*.

22. For example: Jean-Henri Merle d'Aubigné, *Caractère du réformateur et de la réformation à Genève, discours* (Geneva: Georg, 1862); Merle d'Aubigné, *Enseignement de Calvin pour les temps actuels* (Geneva: Jullien frères, 1864); Merle d'Aubigné, *Jean Calvin, un des fondateurs des libertés modernes, discours* (Paris: Grassart, 1868).

23. Ernst Stähelin, *Johannes Calvin: Leben und ausgewählte Schriften*, 2 vols. (Elberfeld: Friederichs, 1863). Only *L'Espérance* published a review of the book, July 31, 1863, 253–54. It stated: "La vie de Calvin de Stähelin est un travail consciencieux et original, à notre avis le plus complet qui ait paru sur ce réformateur. (253).

24. Félix Bungener, *Calvin, sa vie, son oeuvre, ses écrits* (Paris: Cherbuliez, 1862); Bungener, *Calvin, quelques pages pour la jeunesse* (Paris: Cherbuliez, 1864); Georges Frédéric Goguel, *Le réformateur de la France et de Genève, Jean Calvin, sa famille, son caractère* (Toulouse: Société des livres religieux, 1863); François Puaux, *Vie de Calvin* (Strasbourg, 1864); Charles Octave Viguet, *Etudes sur le caractère distinctif de Jean Calvin* (Geneva: Bonnant, 1864); Charles Octave Viguet and David Tissot, *Calvin d'après Calvin* (Geneva: Joël Cherbuliez, 1864); M. J. H. Oltramare, F. Coulin, J. L. Tournier, F. Bungener and J. P. Gaberel *Calvin, cinq discours prêchés à Genève le 29 mai. 1864* (Geneva: Joël Cherbuliez, 1864); Guillaume de Félice, *Trois-centième anniversaire de la mort de Calvin* (Paris: Grassart, 1864); Jean-Henri Merle d'Aubigné, *Enseignement de Calvin pour le temps actuel, ou glorifier Christ pensée souveraine du réformateur* (Geneva: Juillien frères, 1864).

25. Jean-Marie-Vincent Audin (1793–1851), a political journalist turned bookseller, converted to Catholicism soon after completing his *Histoire de la Saint-Barthélémy, d'après*

les chroniques, mémoires et manuscrits du XVIe siècle (Paris: Audin, 1826). He went on to write not only a biography of Calvin but also a *Histoire de la vie, des écrits et des doctrines de Martin Luther*, 3 vols. (Paris: Maison, 1841), and a *Histoire de Henri VIII et du schisme d'Angleterre* (Paris: Maison, 1850). All of these works enjoyed considerable success. In 1872, François Puaux dubbed him the "diffamateur en titre du protestantisme." Sacquin, *Entre Bossuet et Maurras*, 346–47. By 1873, his biography of Calvin was in its seventh edition. At the time of the work's original publication, reviews in Protestant journals were sharply critical. See *Le lien*, April 24, 1841, 130–31; May 22, 1841, 164–65.

26. Bonnet, *Lettres françaises*, 1: xviii–xix. For the response of the *BSHPF* to criticism of Calvin, see André Encrevé, "Calvin dans le *Bulletin de la S.H.P.F.* de 1852 à 1902," *BSHPF* 155 (2009): 289–303.

27. See Frédéric Monod, "Les lettres de Calvin et M. E. Renan," *Archives du christianisme au XIXe siècle*, October 27, 1855, 191–92.

28. Robert, *Les Églises réformées*, 374.

29. Ibid., 375, n. 3.

30. There were, of course, exceptions. See the anonymous article "Lettre sur la confession de foi," *Archives du christianisme au XIXe siècle*, January 25, 1840, 9–11, which reminded readers that the Confession of La Rochelle was still in effect and that Reformed Protestants ought to remember that fact. In general though, revivalists demanded the drafting of a new confession adapted for the nineteenth century.

31. Auguste Lecerf, "Les destinées du calvinisme dans le protestantisme français," *Bulletin de la Société calviniste de France* 22 (1932), repr. in *Études calvinistes*, ed. André Schlemmer (Neuchâtel: Delachaux et Niestlé, 1949), 125–33. To be sure, Lecerf's account drew upon his understanding of what constitutes the essence of Calvinism, but examination of Vinet's works also shows that he was not particularly faithful to most of the specifics of Calvin's thought. See also Henri Clavier, *La pensée religieuse de Vinet* (Paris: Fischbacher, 1938), esp. 118–21.

32. Frédéric Monod, "Œuvres, biographies et lettres de Calvin," *Archives du christianisme au XIXe siècle*, March 13, 1841, 36–37. Noting that P. E. Henry, in writing his book, had obtained copies of 334 unpublished letters of Calvin, he commented: "Il paraît que Genève possède en outre plus de 2 000 sermons inédits de Calvin. Combien ne serait-il pas à désirer que ces souvenirs précieux, que les lettres surtout qui sont d'un si grand prix, soient enfin recueillis et publiés avec intelligence et soin, comme l'a fait De Wette pour les lettres de Luther."

33. See Frédéric Lichtenberger, ed., *Encyclopédie des sciences religieuses*, 13 vols. (Paris: Sandoz and Fischbacher, 1877), 13: 251. The thesis in question was written in 1832 by Henri Flach.

34. The following theses were devoted to Calvin in Strasbourg: Louis Sirven, *Étude sur Calvin d'après ses lettres françaises* (1857); C.-F. Donzé, *La sainte cène d'après Calvin* (1857); Camille Corbière, *Théorie de l'Église d'après Calvin* (1858); Jules Thomas, *Histoire de l'Institution chrétienne de Calvin* (1859); Hippolyte Balavoine, *La définition de la justication par la foi selon Calvin* (1864); and Edmond Stern, *La théorie du culte d'après Calvin* (1869). In Montauban: Émile Lys, *Étude sur Calvin considéré comme organisateur de l'Église* (1854); Jean Faure, *Étude sur l'anthropologie de Calvin dans ses rapports avec la rédemption* (1854); Auguste Vesson, *Calvin considéré comme exégète* (1855); and Henry Valès, *De la prédestination calviniste dans ses rapports avec la prédestination paulinienne* (1861).

35. Reviews of John Mackenzie, *Memoirs of the Life and Writings of John Calvin* (1821), 41–52, and of Bretschneider's *Calvin et l'Église de Genève* (1822), 488–93. The thesis reviewed was Jean Gaberel, "Calvin à Genève," July 23, 1836, 122. See also n. 3.

36. Articles on the ceremonies for the Calvin anniversary of 1864 appeared June 20, 1864, 155–56; June 30, 1864, 164–66; August 20, 1864, 210–11; September 10, 1864, 225–26.

37. Reviewing Jean Gaberel, *Histoire de L'Église de Genève depuis le commencement de la Réformation jusqu'en* 1815 (Paris: Cherbuliez, 1862), Jules Steeg wrote: "ce à quoi notre esprit refuse de s'habituer et nous remplit toujours d'une aussi vive douleur, c'est l'âpre acharnement de Calvin contre ceux qui n' admettent pas son enseignement tout entier sur les mystères de la religion et de la théologie. Si la grandeur même de son génie peut servir d'excuse à son besoin de domination, elle fait aussi mieux ressortir et accuse son étroitesse, son intolérance, son inqualifiable dureté." *Nouvelle revue de théologie* (1862): 181. (*Revue de théologie et de philosophie chrétienne.* 1850–57; renamed *Nouvelle revue de théologie*, 1858–62; renamed *Revue de théologie*, 1863–69. all three often referred to under the generic title *Revue de Strasbourg*. For rival perspective see, for example, Eugène Rosseeuw Saint-Hilaire responding to Félix Bungener's *Calvin, Revue chrétienne* (1862): 745–53; and Louis Bonnet responding to Gaberel's book, *Revue chrétienne* (1858): 756–60.

38. See Louis Bonnet's articles cited in nn. 18 and 37; see also the article by Louis Rognon, "Essai sur l'Institution de Calvin," *Revue chrétienne* (1863): 708–27.

39. Eugène Haag and Émile Haag, *Notice sur Calvin, sa vie et ses ouvrages,* (Paris: Cherbuliez, 1853) (article originally published in Haag, *La France protestante* 3: 109–62) Cf., announcement in *BSHPF* 1 (1852–53): 496.

40. For more details, see Encrevé, "Calvin dans le *Bulletin.*"

41. For more details, see André Encrevé, *Protestants français au milieu du XIXe siècle, les réformés de* 1848 *à* 1870 (Geneva: Labor et Fides, 1986), 196–208.

42. Article 2 of the Constitution de l'Union des Églises évangéliques de France, qtd. in *Archives du christianisme au XIXe siècle,* September 8, 1849, 159.

43. Athanase Coquerel Jr., *Le catholicisme et le protestantisme considérés dans leurs origines et leurs développements* (Paris: Michel Lévy, 1864), 38–39.

44. Qtd. in Patrick Cabanel, "Le Calvin de Ferdinand Buisson," *BSHPF* 155 (2009): 273.

45. *Le lien,* June 4, 1864; *Archives du christianisme au XIXe siècle,* May 30, August 20, September 10, 1864; *L'Espérance,* May 6, May 27, June 3, 1864; *Revue chrétienne,* May, June 1864; *L'Espérance,* May 20, 1864. The *BSHPF* published excerpts of a lecture by Jules Bonnet delivered to the Society's general assembly for the third centenary, "Les amitiés de Calvin: I Guillaume Farel—II Pierre Viret," *BSHPF* 13 (1864): 89–96.

46. Guillaume de Félice's lectures were published in *Trois-centième anniversaire de la mort de Calvin* (Paris: Grassart, 1864). For the meeting of the independent churches on May 29, see *Archives du christianisme au XIXe siècle,* May 30, 1864, 130. It must be noted that preparation for the events of 1864 was disturbed by the bitter disputes between evangelicals and liberals following the decision not to renew Athanase Coquerel Jr. as candidate-pastor in Paris. For more on this, see Encrevé, *Protestants français,* 719–40.

47. See especially *Archives du christianisme au XIXe siècle,* April 10, 1864; *L'Espérance,* April 29, June 3, 1864.

48. A commission charged with organizing events had also been named in 1864, but it had been paralyzed by the doctrinal conflict then affecting French Protestantism (see n. 46). See also *Le lien,* June 4, 1864, 222.

49. *Le protestant,* September 18, 1909, 288–89; *Le christianisme au XXe siècle,* November 17, 1909.

50. For more details on these events, see Valentine Zuber, "Les jubilés de Calvin en 1909 à Genève et à Paris," in the soon-to-be-published proceedings of the conference entitled "Giovanni Calvino nel quinto centenario della nascita, Interpretazioni plurali tra dissenso

evangélico e critica cattolica," Florence, March 14–16, 2009, ed. Franco Giacone and Pawel Gajewski (Florence: Olschki).

51. *Le christianisme au XXe siècle*, June 25, 1909, 207.

52. *Le protestant*, February 13, 1909, 53.

53. *Le christianisme au XXe siècle*, July 9, 16, 23, 30, 1909; *Le protestant*, June 26, July 10, 17, 24, 1909; *Revue chrétienne* (1909/1): 579–81; and *BSHPF* 58 (1909): 374–400.

54. These articles in *Revue chrétienne* in 1909/2 included Paul Lobstein, "L'œuvre dogmatique de Calvin," 564–71; Roger Bornand, "Calvin et la cure d'âme," 572–78; John Viénot, "Jean Calvin, l'homme," 613–16; and Charles Lelièvre, "La doctrine de la justification par la foi dans la théologie de Calvin," 699–710 and 767–76. Some of these articles were based on lectures given in 1909.

55. *Foi et vie*, October 16, 1909. Its foreword said: "Nous avons voulu—à propos du IVe centenaire de Calvin—donner un portrait vrai, vivant du Réformateur, qui a été si souvent défiguré. Nous nous sommes adressé aux hommes dont les travaux font autorité" (605).

56. *BSHPF* 76 (1927): 306–89.

57. *BSHPF* 76 (1927): 361–64. Émile Doumergue, Eugène Choisy, and Abel Lefranc were also among the speakers.

58. The book was published in 1536, but the letter to Francis I was dated August 1535. It is, therefore, the completion of the work rather than its publication that was celebrated.

59. *BSHPF* 84 (1935): 227–42. Other lectures delivered on this occasion included: Pierre Maury, "La théologie naturelle d'après Calvin," *BSHPF* 84 (1935): 267–79. In addition, a medal was struck, a concert organized, and steps undertaken to have a street in Paris named after Calvin.

60. Participants included Eugène Choisy, Emeric de Koulifay, Jaques Courvoisier, Henri Strohl, H. H. Kuyper, V. H. Rutgers, Marcel Cadix, Auguste Lecerf, Léon Wencelius, and Albert-Marie Schmidt.

61. *BSHPF* 84 (1935): 57–312. See also *Le christianisme au XXe siècle*, March 7 and 14, 1935, 103, 110, 124; and *Évangile et liberté*, March 6 and 20, 1935, 38–39, 47.

62. *Foi et vie* (1935): 257–342. This included articles by Jacques Pannier, Albert-Marie Schmidt, Pierre Maury, and Auguste Lecerf, as well as selected texts by Calvin.

63. *BSHPF* 86 (1938): 341–81; and *Calvin à Strasbourg:1538–1938: Quatre études publiées à l'occasion du 400e anniversaire de l'arrivée de Calvin à Strasbourg par les soins de la Commission synodale de l'Eglise réformée d'Alsace et de Lorraine* (Geneva: Labor, 1938).

64. Cited in André Encrevé, *L'Expérience et la foi, pensée et vie religieuse des huguenots au XIXe siècle* (Geneva: Labor et Fides, 2001), 90, n. 123.

65. See Jean Baubérot, ed., *Vers l'unité pour quel témoignage, la restauration de l'unité réformée (1933–1938)* (Paris: Les Bergers et les Mages, 1982), 146, n. 50. It is possible that the liberals' view had been influenced by recent events in Germany where, at the instigation of Karl Barth most notably, German Protestants opposed to the Nazis had convoked a synod at Barmen where they adopted a confession of faith.

66. See Encrevé, *L'Expérience et la foi*, 91, n. 123.

67. A small group of evangelicals thought that too many concessions had been made to liberals, especially in the text of the Declaration of Faith of 1938. They refused to join the newly constituted French Reformed Church and set up their own federation, based on the Declaration of Faith of 1872.

68. See Daniel Robert, "Les protestants français et la guerre de 1914–1918," *Francia* 2 (1974): 415–30.

69. See Jean Baubérot and Valentine Zuber, *Une haine oubliée: L'antiprotestantisme avant le "pacte laïque" (1870–1905)* (Paris: Albin Michel, 2000).

70. *Le christianisme au XXe siècle*, November 5, 1909, 368.

71. Qtd. in Encrevé, *Protestants français*, 733.

72. The synod of 1872 stipulated that the Declaration of Faith would be imposed only on new ministers and that no extreme liberal would lose his post, but liberals nevertheless feared that, if they accepted the principle of an obligatory Declaration of Faith, a later synod would drive out liberals who refused to subscribe.

73. Félix Pécaut (1828–1898) studied theology but served only briefly as a pastor before losing his position for his refusal to read the Apostles' Creed from the pulpit. He gained notoriety with the 1859 publication of *Le Christ et la conscience*, a work that denied not only the divinity of Christ but also his moral perfection. His subsequent works sought to define what he called a "Christian theism," which was at ever greater remove from traditional dogmatics. Soon after taking part in the synod of 1872, he ceased participating in church affairs. His views late in life might best be characterized as a sort of spiritual agnosticism. Ferdinand Buisson (1841–1932), who came from an evangelical background, went into exile under the Second Empire and taught philosophy at Neuchâtel, Switzerland, where he sought, with little success, to establish an independent church of a markedly liberal orientation. Returning to his native France after 1870, he became a leading architect of the Third Republic's system of lay primary schools and a religious freethinker. Entering politics after the Dreyfus affair, he championed human rights and the pacifist cause and was awarded the Nobel Peace Prize in 1927. Timothée Colani (1824–1888), who was also raised as an evangelical, became an extreme liberal during his student days in Strasbourg and founded and directed the *Revue de Strasbourg* (cf. note 37), the great organ of liberalism. He took part in the synod of 1872 but soon abandoned theology and ecclesiastical affairs for a career in business and politics.

74. André Encrevé, ed., *Les protestants: Dictionnaire du monde religieux dans la France contemporaine*, vol. 5 (Paris: Beauchesne, 1993), s.v. "Auguste Sabatier," 438. This essay is by François Laplanche.

75. Pierre Maury (1890–1956) was minister in the Reformed Church of Ferney-Voltaire from 1924 to 1929. He was introduced to Barth's theology by Willem Adolph Visser t'Hooft, a leader of the Fédération Universelle des Associations Chrétiennes d'Étudiants in Geneva. He spread Barthian ideas in France through the journal *Foi et vie*, where he was editor in 1928 and director from 1930 to 1940. He was the successor to Auguste Lecerf as professor of dogmatics in the Faculty of Theology in Paris, where he taught from 1943 to 1950. Léon Maury had written a thesis entitled, *Le Réveil religieux dans l'Église réformée à Genève et en France (1810–1850)* (Paris: Fischbacher, 1892).

76. Barth wrote that for Schleiermacher, "l'apologète du christianisme est tout bonnement maître de ce dernier et, tout comme la conscience moderne, il est à même de le considérer en quelque sorte de haut, de le définir selon sa nature, et de l'apprécier selon sa valeur.... A titre d'apologète du christianisme, il a vraiment joué de celui-ci comme un virtuose joue de son violon en produisant des notes et des mélodies qui, si elles ne réjouissaient pas le cœur de ses auditeurs, leur paraissaient du moins acceptables; Schleiermacher ne parle pas en serviteur responsable, mais en véritable virtuose, maître de son affaire." Karl Barth, *La théologie protestante au XIXe siècle*, trans. Lore Jeanneret (Geneva: Labor et Fides, 1969), 250.

77. Antoine-Jean Baumgartner, *Calvin hébraïsant et interprète de l'Ancien Testament* (Paris: Fischbacher, 1889); Albert Wattier, *Calvin prédicateur* (Geneva: Bertoud, 1889); and Abel Lefranc, *La jeunesse de Calvin* (Paris: Fischbacher, 1888).

78. Because of Herminjard's death, the letters published run only until 1544.

79. Rodolphe Reuss, "Une nouvelle vie de Calvin," *BSHPF* 48 (1899): 541. In 1909 Nathanaël Weiss wrote: "jusque dans les dernières années du XIXe siècle on a à peine soupçonné en France l'importance du rôle de Calvin dans le développement religieux, politique et social du monde moderne." *BSHPF* 58 (1909): 265.

80. For example, Jean Calvin, *Le catéchisme français de Calvin publié en 1537, réimprimé pour la première fois avec deux notices*, ed. Albert Rilliet and Théophile Dufour (Geneva: H. Georg, 1878); Calvin, *La vraye façon de reformer l'Église chrestienne et appointer les differens qui sont en icelle* (Anduze: Alfred Castagnier, 1881); and *L'excuse de noble seigneur Jacques de Bourgogne, seigneur de Falais et de Bredam, par Jean Calvin, réimprimée pour la première fois sur l'unique exemplaire de l'édition de Genève de 1548* (Paris: A. Lemerre, 1896).

81. Gustave Lanson, "Institution chrétienne de Calvin. Examen de l'authenticité de la traduction française," *Revue historique* 54 (1894): 61–76; see also *BSHPF* 43 (1894): 106–8.

82. Jean Calvin, *Institution de la religion chrestienne: Texte de la première édition française (1541)*, 2 vols., ed. Abel Lefranc, Henri Châtelain, Jacques Pannier (Paris: Champion, 1911).

83. Williston Walker, *Jean Calvin, l'homme et l'œuvre*, trans. E. Weiss and N. Weiss (Geneva: Jullien, 1909). Other important publications from this year include Eugène Choisy, *Jean Calvin 1509–1564: Sa vie et son oeuvre* (Geneva: J. H. Jeheber, 1909); and Jacques Pannier, *L'Enfance et la jeunesse de Calvin, ses études, sa conversion, ses voyages en France* (Toulouse: Société d'éditions de Toulouse, 1909). A full list of books, articles, and other works published in France and elsewhere on the occasion of Calvin's four-hundredth birthday can be found in *BSHPF* 58 (1909): 264–78, 374–400.

84. Albert-Marie Schmidt, "Esquisse d'une bibliographie calvinienne," *Foi et vie* (1935): 340–42. Specifying that he had included only works that were readily accessible, Schmidt lists nine collections of Calvin's works apart from the *Institutes*, seven of which had been published since 1921. He also refers to twelve monographs on Calvin's life and thought, not including Émile Doumergue's massive work.

85. *Revue chrétienne* (1873): 128; (1878), 647.

86. *Revue chrétienne* (1882): 636–40.

87. See, for example, Frank Puaux's response to Jules Lemaître. (Puaux, "Revue du mois," *Revue chrétienne* (1899/1): 239–40); or Auguste Sabatier's riposte to Émile Faguet. (Sabatier, "Lettre du dimanche," *Revue chrétienne* (1901/1): 442–47).

88. Auguste Sabatier, "Calvin, Pascal, les Jésuites et M. F. Brunetière," *Revue chrétienne* (1896/1): 162–66 (repr. of article in *Journal de Genève*, January 26, 1896). See also *Le protestant*, February 1, 1896, 33–34. Swiss and French Protestants clashed with Brunetière over many years, especially in the wake of a lecture he gave in Geneva at the end of 1901.

89. *Revue chrétienne* (1896/1): 167–79. The journal also published articles about Calvin's life and thought, such as Daniel Ollier, "Le mariage de Calvin" (1892/2): 210–26; Émile Doumergue, "Nérac au temps de Calvin" (1897/1): 10–20; Paul Lobstein, "L'œuvre dogmatique de Calvin" (1909): 564–71; and Léopold Monod, "Le caractère de Calvin d'après ses lettres" (1911/1): 1004–22.

90. Émile Gautier, "Le catéchisme de Genève de J. Calvin, *BSHPF* 43 (1894): 373–78; Nathanaël Weiss," La première édition de l'*Institution* de Calvin, "*BSHPF* 44 (1895): 163–64. In a similar vein, see André Mailhet, "Le voyage de Calvin à Valence, une histoire, une tradition," *Revue chrétienne* 55 (1906): 403–16.

91. *BSHPF* 43 (1894): 465–69.

92. Lefranc, *La jeunesse de Calvin*; see *BSHPF* 37 (1888): 39–52, 92–107, 141–54.

93. For more details see Encrevé, "Calvin dans le *Bulletin*," 299–300. One exception was Paul Lobstein, *Die Ethik Calvin* (Strasbourg: C. F. Schmidt, 1877). There was no review of this book by Lobstein, professor of dogmatics in the Faculty of Theology at Strasbourg, undoubtedly because it was written in German by an Alsatian, shortly after Germany's annexation of Alsace.

94. See, for example, Rodolphe Reuss's critical review of the first volume of Émile Doumergue's massive work on Calvin. (Reuss, "Une nouvelle vie de Calvin", *BSHPF* 48 (1899): 541–60).

95. Nathanäel Weiss, "Calvin Servet, Guillaume de Trie et le tribunal de Vienne," *BSHPF* 57 (1908): 387–404. For the reaction of other Protestant publications to the polemics of 1908, see Émile Doumergue, "Comment on écrit l'histoire," *Foi et vie*, February 1 and 16, 1908, 76–81, 111–15; and Doumergue, "Notes à propos de Servet," *Le christianisme au XXe siècle*, November 27, December 4, 11, 18, 25, 31, 1908; January 8, 15, 1909. On the different Servetus monuments, see Valentine Zuber, *Les conflits de la tolérance: Michel Servet entre mémoire et histoire* (Paris: Champion, 2004).

96. Ariste Viguié, "Les sermons de Calvin sur le livre de Job," *BSHPF* 31 (1882): 548.

97. Ibid.

98. In 1891, it became the *Revue de théologie et des questions religieuses*.

99. Émile Doumergue, "Calvin fondateur des libertés modernes," *Revue de théologie et des questions religieuses* (1898): 685–713; J. Vielles, "Calvin et la prédestination," *Revue de théologie et des questions religieuses* (1897): 101–9; and Jacques Pannier, "L'Autorité de l'Écriture sainte d'après Calvin, son principe, ses preuves, ses conséquences," *Revue de théologie et des questions religieuses*. (1906): 193–211, 367–81.

100. Various articles in *Le christianisme au XIXe siècle* 1–29 (1872–1900).

101. Ferdinand Buisson, *Sébastien Castellion: Sa vie et son œuvre (1515–1563). Études sur les origines du protestantisme libéral français*, 2 vols. (Paris: Hachette, 1892). Buisson's defense of the thesis in 1891 was noted in the *BSHPF* 40 (1891): 448.

102. See Cabanel, "Le Calvin de Buisson," 272.

103. See in this regard Émile Doumergue, "Le bûcher de Servet," *Le christianisme au XIXe siècle*, July 7, 1892, 211–12; Charles Dardier, "Le bûcher de Servet," *Le protestant,* July 23, 1892, 247–48; "Le bûcher de Servet," August 13, 1892, 271–73 (an exchange between Doumergue and Dardier) For Martin-Paschoud see p. 232 and note 44 above.

104. According to Cabanel, Buisson's contribution "présente une analyse assez équilibrée de l'œuvre de Calvin à Genève....Le Réformateur a armé une Église pour les combats redoutables qui l'attendaient et lui a permis de résister aux assauts de Rome et de lui disputer l'empire du monde." Cabanel, "Le Calvin de Buisson," 271. A similar approach is found in the work of the liberal pastor Étienne Giran, *Sébastien Castellion et la Réforme calviniste: Les deux réformes* (pref. Ferdinand Buisson) (Haarlem: J. W. Boissevain, 1914). For Martin-Paschoud see p. 232 and note 44 above.

105. His 1871 thèse de licence was called " *Un chapitre de l'apologétique chrétienne au XIXe siècle* (Toulouse: A. Chauvin et fils, 1871) and his 1872 doctoral thesis *Un nouveau chapitre de l'apologétique chrétienne au XIXe siècle, le sentiment moral* (Paris: Grassart, 1872).

106. In 1894, for example, he published three articles on Calvin: "La confession des péchés est-elle de Calvin," *Le christianisme au XIXe siècle*, March 9, 1894, 71; "Calvin défenseur de l'indépendance genevoise," *Le christianisme au XIXe siècle,* September 14, 1894, 290–91, September 21, 296–97; "Une visite de Calvin à Ferrare," *Le christianisme au XIXe siècle*, October 12, 1894, 320–21, October 26, 335–36.

107. This lecture was published in the *Revue de théologie et des questions religieuses* (1898): 685–713.

108. French Protestants were aware of developments in Dutch theology largely because of the presence of French pastors in the Netherlands serving the "Walloon" congregations there. Among the Dutch authors that Doumergue cites are Abraham Kuyper, Frederick Lodewjik Rutgers, Herman Bavinck, Guilllaume Groen van Prinsterer, R. Furin, Gilles Denjis Jacob Schotel, and B. Bennink Jansonnins.

109. Rodolphe Reuss,, "Une nouvelle vie de Calvin", *BSHPF* 48 (1899): 541–60, esp. 551–52.

110. He writes for example: "Mais ce n'est pas assez; voilà que notre jeune homme rencontre les plus illustres professeurs de droit, l'Estoile qui se trouve encore à Orléans, et Alciat, qui arrive précisément à Bourges .... Cependant la providence n'avait encore accompli

que la moitié de sa tâche. Que serait l'intelligence sans la vie? Et les merveilleuses années d'études sont en même temps de merveilleuses années d'expériences. L'Église a soin de lui révéler toutes ses lacunes, tous ses vices les plus secrets.…Alors, enfin, il est prêt. Déjà il a fait tressaillir son pays au bruit retentissant du discours de Cop. Déjà il s'est gagné partout d'intimes sympathies, par sa propagande secrète et plus efficace. Il peut parler: on peut l'écouter. Et lorsque François Ier, non content de tuer les protestants à coup d'édits, veut les déshonorer à coup de calomnies, lui, Calvin, répond au roi par son *Institution*. Le dialogue, il faut dire le duel, est auguste; et, à contempler les deux adversaires s'avançant l'un vers l'autre, c'est bien de dignité royale que notre imagination est frappée, éblouie. Seulement, il faut dissiper la fausseté des apparences et rétablir la vérité des faits: le roi, vraiment roi, ce n'est pas François Ier, c'est Calvin." Émile Doumergue, *Jean Calvin*, 7 vols. (Lausanne: Bridel, 1899–1927), 1: 514–15.

111. See Daniel Robert, "Patriotisme et image de la Réforme chez les historiens protestants français après 1870," in *Historiographie de la Réforme*, ed. Philippe Joutard (Neuchâtel: Delachaux et Niestlé, 1977), 205–15, here 212. During the First World War, Doumergue enlisted Calvin in the service of France and its allies. See Émile Doumergue, "Calvin et l'Entente," *BSHPF* 66 (1917): 301–12.

112. See Valentine Zuber, *Michel Servet et les conflits de la tolérance. Entre mémoire et histoire* (Paris : Champion, 2004), 640.

113. Ibid., 26.

114. Ibid., 27.

115. Throughout 1903, the liberal Nathanäel Weiss voiced his opposition not to the monument itself, of which he approved, but to the text placed on it. Ibid., 87–107.

116. His baccalaureate thesis, *Le témoignage du Saint Esprit, essai sur l'histoire du dogme dans la théologie réformée* (Paris: Fischbacher, 1893), dealt extensively with Calvin. In 1911, he defended a doctoral thesis entitled *L'Église réformée de Paris sous Henri IV: Rapports de l'Église et de l'état, vie publique et privée des protestants: Leur part dans l'histoire de la capitale, le mouvement des idées, les arts, la société, le commerce* (Paris: Honoré Champion, 1911).

117. Jacques Pannier, *L'Enfance et la jeunesse de Calvin*; Pannier, *Recherches sur l'évolution religieuse de Calvin jusqu'à sa conversion* (Strasbourg: Istra, 1924); Pannier, *Calvin à Strasbourg* (Strasbourg: Istra, 1925); Pannier, *Calvin et l'épiscopat: L'épiscopat élément organique de l'Église dans le calvinisme intégral* (Paris: Alcan, 1927); and Pannier, *Recherches sur la formation intellectuelle de Calvin* (Paris: Alcan, 1931). These works reprinted articles that had appeared in the *Revue d'histoire et de philosophie religieuse*.

118. Jacques Pannier, "Notes sur la géographie calvinienne," *BSHPF* 76 (1928): 281–84; Pannier, "Une première "Institution" française dès 1537?," *Revue d'histoire et de philosophie religieuse* (1928): 513–34; Pannier, "Histoire de la maison de Calvin," *BSHPF* 78 (1930): 401–13; Pannier, "Une famille protestante d'Auteuil et Passy: Les Massicot: Aurait-elle reçu Calvin fugitif en 1533?," *BSHPF* 81 (1933): 353–58; Pannier, "Notes historiques et critiques sur un chapitre de l'"Institution" écrit à Strasbourg (1539), de la vie chrétienne," *Revue d'histoire et de philosophie religieuse* (1934): 206–29; Pannier, "Une étape de Calvin en juillet 1536(?)," *BSHPF* 85 (1937): 174–79; and Pannier, "Une lettre de Calvin en partie inédite (12 mars 1562)," *BSHPF* 85 (1937): 182–86.

119. Auguste Lecerf, *Le déterminisme de la responsabilité dans le système de Calvin* (Paris: Imprimerie Jouve, 1894) [*sic*, actually 1895]. The introduction to this work indicates his debt to Edwards.

120. Ibid., 6.

121. Ibid., 120.

122. See his article "De la nécessité d'une restauration de la dogmatique calviniste," *Revue d'histoire et de philosophie religieuse* (1922): 407–18.

123. Jean Cadier (1898–1981) was a lecturer in practical theology in the Faculty of Protestant Theology in Montpellier from 1936 to 1944, and subsequently professor of dogmatics until 1968. He was president of the Société Calviniste de France for nearly twenty years.

124. *Bulletin de la Société calviniste de France* 1 (1927): 2.

125. The report was published in *Études théologiques et religieuses* (1936): 30–48.

126. In the 1930s, the following articles were published by *Foi et vie*: Albert-Marie Schmidt, "Calvin prédicateur" (1936): 1–11; Noëlle Roger, "L'Académie de Calvin" (1937): 21–33; and Roger Mehl, "Calvin professeur à la Haute École" (1938): 396–404.

127. After the First World War, the Faculty of Protestant Theology at Montauban was moved to Montpellier. The *Études théologiques et religieuses* was founded in 1926 to replace the *Revue de théologie et des questions religieuses*, which had ceased publication in 1915. Significant articles to appear in it include Émile Doumergue, "L'agonie' de Calvin" (1926): 385–401; Henri Clavier, "Calvin commentateur biblique" (1935): 305–46. The *Revue d'histoire et de philosophie religeuse* was founded in 1921 after the return of Alsace to France at the close of the First World War. A French publication, it was intended to contribute to the renewal of the francophone University of Strasbourg. Jacques Pannier published six articles on Calvin in it between 1923 and 1934. See also Robert Will, "La première liturgie de Calvin" (1938): 523–29.

128. See in the *Revue d'histoire et de philosophie religieuse* Jacques Pannier, "Calvin et l'épiscopat" (1926): 305–35, 434–70; Léon Wencelius, "L'idée de joie dans la pensée de Calvin" (1935): 70–109; and Jean-Daniel Benoit, "Calvin et le baptême des enfants" (1937): 457–73. In *Etudes théologiques et religieuse* see Jean Cadier, "La présence réelle dans le calvinisme" (1938): 293–09.

129. Eugène Choisy, *Calvin éducateur des consciences* (Neuilly: Editions de "La Cause," 1926); Paul Lobstein, *Études sur la pensée et l'œuvre de Calvin* (Neuilly: Editions de "La Cause," 1927); Max Dominicé, *L'humanité de Jésus d'après Calvin* (Paris: "Je sers," 1933); Henri Clavier, *Études sur le calvinisme* (Paris: Fischbacher, 1936); and Marc-Edouard Chenevière, *La pensée politique de Calvin* (Geneva: Labor 1938).

130. Lecerf defended his thèse de licence in theology, "De la nature de la connaissance religieuse," in 1931 and his doctoral thesis, "Du fondement et de la spécification de la connaissance religieuse," in 1938. He published them both in his *Introduction à la dogmatique réformée*, 2 vols. (Paris: "Je sers," 1938). He remained professor until his death in 1943.

131. Karl Barth, preface to *Calvin*, ed. Charles Gagnebin (Paris: Egloff, 1948), 9–10.

12 Calvin in the Plural

*The Diversity of Modern Interpretations of Calvinism,
Especially in Germany and the English-Speaking
World*

FRIEDRICH WILHELM GRAF

Translated by Irena Backus and Susanna Gebhardt

A history of the various images of Calvin, as drawn in biographies or general surveys of his theology, is decidedly less gripping than an account of the varied and problematic interpretations of Calvinism. Therefore, my focus is on modern interpretations of Calvinism from 1800 onward. Although many of the patterns of interpretation developed in the discourse on Calvinism in the modern age have been successfully deconstructed by increasingly specialized studies of "confessionalization" in the last forty years,[1] they have retained a lasting intellectual force. In matters of religion and confession, even fiction has a formative social power, for religious ideas shape not only the worldview of religious actors, their cognitive maps and mentalities but also their individual and collective habits.

Two brief preliminary remarks are required. The first concerns the actors in the modern discourse on Calvinism. It is not just theologians and historians of all Christian confessions but also lawyers and economists with historical research interests who have cultivated interpretations of Calvin and Calvinism. They are not merely diligent researchers in academic ivory towers, removed from political reality; they are also concerned with the public dissemination of images of history, and thus with the practice of history and memory politics. The images of history and the confessional interpretations produced by scholars of Calvinism have made a deep impression upon religion and culture and continue to do so. Scholarly interpretations of Calvinism influence the self-perceptions of pious Calvinists and, thereby, contribute to confessional identity construction, to the differentiation between the interior and exterior, the "we" and the "other."

My second preliminary remark concerns growth phases in the history of modern research on Calvin and Calvinism, discursive *Sattelzeit(en)* (saddle-period[s]) as it were, to employ Reinhart Koselleck's term. In Germany, reflections on the specifics of Calvinism as opposed to Lutheranism intensified during the period (beginning in 1830) prior to the German Revolution of March 1848, then again in 1900, and once more since the mid-twentieth century. This scholarly interest in Calvin and Calvinism is, even in the subtlest perceptual differences, an expression of the attempt to find a better understanding of the present. The "cultural dimension" of Calvinism and its productive contribution to the emergence of the modern world is an ever-recurring theme. Studies of Calvinism are a kind of self-conscious discourse on a modernity whose foundations have become uncertain. The image of Calvin or images of very devout Calvinists serve as a medium of self-knowledge, even if only by providing a contrast.

My essay has four parts. The first is about the diverse concepts of Calvinism, the second discusses its religious definitions, the third analyses political Calvinism, and the fourth, economic Calvinism.

▪ CALVINISM IN THE PLURAL; OR, FROM A CONFESSIONAL FIGHTING WORD TO A RELIGIOUS-CULTURAL IDEAL TYPE

The term "Calvinism" has a complex history.[2] Scholarly consensus on its first occurrence has not yet been established. "Calvinism" is first and foremost a polemical designation, a fighting word. It expresses a strong relation to its eponymous founder, Calvin—so strong that through this reference, all his followers become the "same." Some researchers, such as Alastair Duke, argue that the term Calvinist was brought into circulation in 1553 by the circle around Castellio in Basel.[3] In the 1560s, numerous Lutheran and Catholic tracts in Latin, French, and German then expressed criticism of the heretical new doctrines that they attributed to "Calvinists," the *confessio Calvinistica*, and the "erroneous Calvinist teaching." Analogously, "Zwinglians" and "Zwingliani" came under scrutiny. The term "Calvinism" can be traced back to Calvin's letter to Heinrich Bullinger, from June 26, 1548, where, in the negotiations leading up to the *Consensus Tigurinus*, Calvin reported that amid a conflict over Eucharistic doctrine then dividing the Bernese church, "the brothers were ordered to go and be done with their Calvinism and their Buceranism" (iussi sunt fratres abire et facessere cum suo Calvinismo et Buceranismo).[4]

From the mid-1580s, "Calvinism" was used in the confessional polemics of Catholic as well as Lutheran opponents as a fighting word to designate fundamental religious illegitimacy. Lutheran theologians and lawyers often equated Calvinism with papism. In 1602, for example, the Lutheran Dresden chaplain Polycarp Leyser published a treatise entitled "Christianity, Papism and Calvinism" (*Christianismus, Papismus et Calvinismus*).[5] The followers of Calvin initially rejected the term, claiming that it was invented by the devil himself, and it remained controversial until the eighteenth century. If and when it became a self-designation is likewise unclear. In ways that have not yet been investigated, the polemical term "Calvinism" gradually transformed into a typological term for those non-Lutheran churches emerging from the Reformation movement of the sixteenth century that based themselves on Reformed confessional writings such as the Heidelberg Catechism or the Westminster Confession. The denominational pair of Calvinism and Lutheranism was also gradually established in the context of severe conflicts within

Protestantism, although probably at a relatively late stage, no sooner than the nineteenth century.

"Calvinism" is an indispensable confessional term. As an ideal type, it encapsulates the specifics of the third early modern confessional culture beside Lutheranism and Tridentine Catholicism. Already in the nineteenth century, it referred to the sociomoral, ethical, political, and economic forces that had spread, through Calvinism, particularly in western Europe. Moreover, modern religious and political neo-Calvinism can be clearly distinguished from the earlier Calvinism of the "confessional age." Even historians specializing in the history of confessionalization do not know who coined the epochal term "confessional age." The earliest mention of which I know is by Ernst Troeltsch. In his renowned (post-1906) studies on Protestantism, there is a reference to the "confessional age," and the "era of confessionalism and the absolute state."[6] Troeltsch was not only familiar with the concept of "modernization," which, incidentally, appears only twice in the corpus of Max Weber, but also shaped the concept of "the modernization of the Reformation" with reference to "enthusiasts, mystic[s], anabaptist[s], humanist[s]."[7] To put it bluntly, religious modernization had already been discussed in the German language prior to the reception of North American sociological modernization theory, and it was discussed precisely in relation to certain forms of Calvinism.

■ RELIGIOUS CALVINISM; OR, ACTIVE ASCETICISM

In recent years, German scholars of modern history have proposed that the nineteenth century be understood as the "second confessional age."[8] This proposal is exaggerated, but it has the merit of raising awareness of the major role that confessional-political culture wars played in many mixed-confessional societies in nineteenth-century Europe, especially Germany. The new religious and political struggles caught the lasting attention of scholarly interpreters of culture, especially theologians and historians. From the second decade of the nineteenth century onward, confession became a very important issue. This has much to do with the political and, more specifically, the religious-political results of the French Revolution, in the wake of which a decidedly restorative Catholicism blamed Luther's revolution of individual salvation for the disaster of the chaotic, fragmented, and lawless present, and recommended itself as the only reliable guarantor of order. Catholicism and Protestantism became concepts of political struggle, and it was anything but coincidence that the Prussian king Friedrich Wilhelm III prohibited use of the term "Protestantism" in 1817, demanding that his subjects refer to the "evangelical church" instead. Especially in the 1830s and 1840s, Protestant theologians published numerous scholarly writings on doctrinal, ethical, and general religious differences between the two main confessions of the Reformation tradition, invariably marked by the church and political subtext of "union church or confessional church." Participants in the debate included such prominent authors as Max Goebel, Johann Peter Lange, Carl Ullmann, Ferdinand Christian Baur, Alexander Schweizer, and Friedrich and Heinrich Heppe. The old so-called symbolics, a theological discipline that initially amounted to no more than the comparison of confessional writings of the Christian churches, gradually came to cover the whole spectrum of religious life and became known as *Konfessionskunde* ("confession studies"), a discipline of enquiry into the confessionally marked ethos and disposition of the believer.

The most groundbreaking analysis of inter-Protestant confessional differences was written by the brilliant church historian Matthias Schneckenburger (1804–1848). Coming from a background of Württemberg Lutheranism, he taught systematic theology at the new Calvinist University of Bern from 1834 onward and wanted, in view of the massively growing strength of Catholicism, a Protestant Union for Germany. With this end in view, he pursued in-depth work on the differences between Lutherans and Calvinists. His posthumously published 1855 comparison of the the doctrinal concepts "Lutheran" and "Reformed," *Vergleichende Darstellung des lutherischen und reformirten Lehrbegriffs*, is one of the outstanding theological books of the nineteenth century.[9] Employing very subtle religious-psychological terminology, Schneckenburger analyzed Lutheranism and Calvinism so as to construct confessional ideal types that captured the deep antagonism between them. His analysis goes beyond doctrinal differences and those of dogma, engaging in a discussion of fundamental "affective religious diversity, that is to say, a deep, though subtle difference in the most subjective area of piety."[10] According to him, Christianity is not primarily a doctrine, but something lived, and theological dogma is only a secondary conceptual abstraction of religious self-awareness. With concepts derived from Schleiermacher and the idealist theory of subjectivity, Schneckenburger explained that the pious subjectivity of the individual, the "immediate self-consciousness," stood at the center of Reformation protests. Thus, he had to reconstruct the differences between the Protestant confessions as different interpretations of subjectivity. Within the concept of self-consciousness, he differentiated the three elements of mind, will, and soul, and distinguished, within the concept of subjectivity, the elements of self-confidence and spontaneous action. He claimed that the Reformed/Calvinist subject knows itself essentially only as intellect and will, while the Lutheran subject dwells primarily in the deeper unity of these two elements in the soul. In Reformed piety, "the active state before the dormant" prevails, while for Lutherans, "the dormant subjective state of consciousness" dominates.[11]

Schneckenburger's ideal types arguably reflect the religious and political conflicts of his time, and the distinction between active and passive does no more than project modern Protestant confessional conflicts back to the early modern period and its main actors. Schneckenburger's innovative method, however, relies not merely on the learned texts of the theological elites but also on catechisms, prayer books, and religious tracts. Furthermore, he maintains that confessional ideal types uncover religiously and culturally relevant actions even when scholars see them as overly selective and generalizing. The audience of Schneckenburger's lectures consisted mostly of Protestant pastors in Switzerland, who began to view themselves in exactly the way that Schneckenburger taught, that is, as activists obliged to form a union with the Lutherans in order to wage the moral and religious fight with the powers of papism for the sake of the Protestant freedom of the Christian man. In the dominant German Lutheran confessional discourse, Schneckenburger was received with great interest by those who suffered from the "quietism" and "passivity" of Lutheranism, since he put forward a very clear schema in which Calvinism was synonymous with active salvation and Lutheranism with quietism. All the learned research on the early modern processes of confessionalization and the confessional educational milieus of the early nineteenth century would do little to amend this view.

■ POLITICAL CALVINISM; OR, THE IDEA OF FREE, REPUBLICAN CIVIL HUMANISM

In the sixteenth century, defenders of Catholic orthodoxy had repeatedly pointed out that Luther's Christian liberty (*libertas christiana*) undermined the authority of the emperor and the imperial constitution. They viewed the "acatholici" as enemies of the legal system. This forced Lutheran and Reformed theologians and jurists to emphasize their political reliability and to prove that the rediscovery of the evangelical faith was the only true source of binding political order. In the process of confessionalization, theologians and lawyers alike conducted the confessional quarrel as a political dispute over their respective confessions' capacity to maintain public order. The more the crisis that took place after 1570 was perceived as serious, the more they stressed order, sometimes going as far as to reschematize the ordering of knowledge in schemas for new encyclopedias.

In this confessional strife, all sides developed distinct confessional characteristics, which the theoretical discourse of modernization translated into the so-called political exceptionalism of the Germans or their late "journey to the West." An illustration of the tendency to link each confession with a distinct outlook is provided by the pseudonymously published work of the Lutheran Samuel Pufendorf on the state of the German empire "De statu imperii Germanici" (1667). Pufendorf's ruminations on the specifics of the three religions authorized in Germany also covered their political aspects.[12] He argued that the Roman Catholic reproach that Lutherans undermined public order was mistaken and that, in fact, by internalizing religion, the "Lutheran religion" rather strengthened loyalty to civil rulers. To the "Calvinistic religion," Pufendorf attributed an affinity for popular government and republicanism: "People who are knowledgeable have noted long ago that the meaning and specificity of the Calvinist religion is its inclination towards democratic liberty."[13]

The concepts used in confessional polemic had acquired a political coloring as early as the sixteenth century. This continued to be the case in the eighteenth century, despite the strident anticonfessionalism of the Enlightenment and its calls for a human, natural religion of reason. In the violent postrevolutionary debates about the political order of Europe, the question of the elective affinities of confession and political order acquired new political explosiveness. Connections between Christian liberty and civil freedom were often evoked, with special attention being paid to Calvinism. One example will suffice here. On November 15, 1841, Schneckenburger's close friend Carl Bernhard Hundeshagen, a theology professor, gave an official address in Bern entitled "Ueber den Einfluß des Calvinismus auf die Ideen vom Staat und staatsbürgerlicher Freiheit" (Of the influence of Cavinism on the ideas of the state and civic freedom). Hundeshagen (1810–1872), who was sent down from the University of Giessen in 1828 for being a "Burschenschaftler" (member of a German student fraternity fostering the ideals of patriotism as well as strong engagement for freedom, rights, and democracy), wrote a history of religious ideas clearly colored by contemporary political interests. As a constitutional liberal with vehement anti-Catholic prejudices, he wished to show that "the nurture of the entire stock of those civic freedoms with which our era is so concerned in so many ways was originally linked to the Calvinist form of Protestantism and to nothing else."[14] According to Hundeshagen, Calvinist theologians and jurists recognized their own "civic morality,"[15] discovered the "civil state in itself as a being ordained by God [*ordinatio Dei*]," and were particularly aware that "every constitution rests on certain ideal considerations of an ethical nature, and that even the best constitution would degenerate in a most pernicious way unless it encountered compliance with those requirements on the part of rulers and their subjects."[16] It is particularly significant that Hundeshagen used the term "the Calvinist peoples" interchangeably with "west of Europe."[17] He thus embedded the Reformation "in that great European crisis…in which the previously limited monarchy of stem duchies [*Lehnstaaten*] elevated itself to absolute monarchy," analyzing the reasons why "Protestantism in France…had assumed from early on a far more definite political shape than in any other country."[18] The Huguenot state law "laid down" the "notional stockpile" for the later philosophy of constitutional law;[19] it raised "the state into an ideal moral sphere" and thus imposed "its own necessity" on itself, to construe "the rights of all members of the body politic as innate, inalienable and unprescriptible for reasons of moral and rational necessity." Hundeshagen also showed this with reference to religious and political discourse in the Netherlands, Scotland, and England, seeking to prove that the "genesis" of human rights and civil liberties was a "specific product of Calvinism."[20]

In 1868, Hermann Weingarten published his now famous book *Die Revolutionskirchen Englands: Ein Beitrag zur inneren Geschichte der englischen Kirche und der Reformation* (The churches of the English revolutions: a contribution to the spiritual history of the English church and the Reformation).[21] It was followed by Georg Jellinek's no less famous study in 1895, *Die Erklärung der Menschen- und Bürgerrechte* (account of human and civic rights).[22] Both are classics of the political theory of Calvinism, in which certain specific Calvinist *Theologoumena* or theological baggage and concepts of church order are examined for their potential political impact. Both examine synods and parliaments, the concepts of federalism and sovereignty, and the ethical grounds for justification of civil liberties in the image of God (*imago Dei*) doctrine, the doctrine that man is God's noblest creature, his likeness. Jellinek seeks to prove that human and civil rights were not primarily founded by the French Enlightenment or first codified in the French Revolution, but rather in the religiously colored Bill of Rights after the American Revolution. In his major address in 1906 at the Stuttgart *Historikertag* (historians conference), entitled "The Significance of Protestantism for the Rise of the Modern World," Jellinek's friend Ernst Troeltsch would, however, reject all direct deductions of modern freedom from Calvinism. Yet he too operated with the conceptual pairs of "Lutheranism and Calvinism" and "German spirit and western Europe," and he regarded Calvinism as an ethically more radical, logical, politically efficacious, and liberal form of Protestantism, especially because of its moral discipline and "inner-worldly asceticism." Moreover, it was also Troeltsch who gave the young Hans Baron, later one of the great Renaissance scholars, his dissertation topic of "Calvin's view of the state."

Recent research on confessions, in particular, has deconstructed Hundeshagen's work and other similar views of history. Recent findings show that some German princes encouraged Calvinism precisely because they saw that its Old Testament theocratic features strengthened their authority. For the doctrine of the right of resistance, Calvinist ethicists and lawyers harkened back to the Magdeburg Confession of 1550, which came from the pen of Lutheran pastors, who were anything but well behaved and obedient to civil authorities. One can find much more authoritarian, order-oriented fervor in the theologies of prominent neo-Calvinist thinkers of the nineteenth and twentieth centuries.

We also know of the considerable ambiguity of Calvinist theology in terms of politics. *The Puritans in Africa*, the important book by W. A. de Klerk, written in the context of the Dutch Reformed Mission Church in South Africa (Nederduitse Gereformeerde Sendingkerk) used Calvin and early Calvinist orthodoxy to justify the ethos that supported apartheid politics in the church.[23] But the same texts were also employed, by both black and white theologians of liberation, in their explicit appeal to the Theological Declaration of the Synod of Barmen of May 1934, in order to fight against the apartheid regime.

Despite all necessary historical differentiations, the view of history put forward by Hundeshagen and his various successors has a specific orientational function. It expressed the insight that modern universalist notions of liberty—the idea of the human rights of the individual as prior to the state—were developed and motivated not simply by scientific or rationalist thought but also by clearly religious discourse. With all the necessary qualifications, one could say that Lutheranism, with its doctrine of the three estates and its idealization of public welfare, made a significant contribution to the development of particular welfare state ideas, especially in Germany and Scandinavia. In Germany, until the 1950s, it fostered a decidedly antidemocratic and pointedly anti-individualistic social paternalism. Calvinism, however, developed ideals of public order, in which individual freedom, republicanism, civic humanism, and democratic self-government were held in high regard. Indeed, a John Locke could not have reflected on such matters without concepts imported from Geneva.

■ ECONOMIC CALVINISM; OR, FROM WORLDLY ASCETICISM TO THE SPIRIT OF MODERN WESTERN CAPITALISM

Already in the eighteenth century, European scholars debated intensely about possible connections between confession and a country's prosperity. The significant gap between Catholic and Protestant territories provoked debates over whether Protestants' high esteem for work stemming from a specifically Protestant disposition (grounded perhaps in Luther's doctrine of Christian worldly vocation) was the cause of Protestantism's greater wealth, or whether this was due to a Protestant taste for asceticism and renunciation.

This question was raised repeatedly in the nineteenth century. It found its classic formulation in the Heidelbergian intellectual milieu of 1900. Influenced by their mutual friend Jellinek, Max Weber and Ernst Troeltsch, in a complicated "friendship of expertise," worked on the "cultural dimension" of religious ideas, beyond the relatively autonomous cultural sphere of religion.[24]

Here, it is important to take the biographical and political context into account. The debates in the post-"Kulturkampf" (the repressive political movement in German in the 1870s against the Roman Catholic Church) period on the so-called cultural inferiority of German Catholics, who were significantly underrepresented in institutions of higher education, provoked the question of the supposedly specific cultural power of Protestantism and its superior modernization potential. Troeltsch, and Weber more, suffered from the patriarchal-authoritarian political conditions and the lack of civic spirit, for which they blamed the "Prussian master religion," Lutheranism. Thus, their interest was pointedly directed to the coverage of differences of culture and practice between Calvinism and Lutheranism. Weber focused his cultural-historical studies on modern capitalism and its genesis; Troeltsch, on the other hand, looked more generally at the importance of Protestantism for the rise of the modern world.

In 1904–1905, Weber produced his classic essay *The Protestant Ethic and the Spirit of Capitalism*, which appeared in two parts.[25] The debates over the most famous sociological text of the twentieth century have since then filled entire libraries with published reactions, some of which are favorable, and some hostile. Their great number, however, reflects the extraordinary fascination awoken by the Weber thesis, or, as some contemporaries called it, the Troeltsch-Weber thesis. One can praise the *Protestant Ethic* as a case study of the extraordinary impact of religious ideas, but also as a Nietzschean cultural critique of the decline of the free moral individual. Even scholars of Calvinism maintain that Weber traces modern capitalism back to the Puritans, but this is not true. Advised by Troeltsch, Weber familiarized himself with almost all the relevant theological literature.[26]

Renowned scholars of Calvin and Calvinism consider Weber's argument mistaken, merely because he isolated the devout individual from the community of the pious, which was essential to the Puritan lifestyle. Many important books on early modern Calvinism and on Puritanism specifically have appeared since, and many of their authors are no longer familiar with Weber's work. But regardless of the still controversial question of whether Weber's thesis was historically correct, which, methodologically speaking, is impossible to resolve on empirical grounds, his argument has lost none of its fascination. To put it bluntly, his main narrative has become a self-fulfilling prophecy of the advancement of capitalism. Weber has been promoted to the status of a sort of Goethe of social and economic sciences, and people offering seminars on business ethics for global managers need not necessarily have read the *Protestant Ethic* to proclaim such banalities as "no pain, no gain" or to assure their public that no sustainable success is achieved without inner-worldly asceticism. "Saint Max" is gladly worshiped by motivation coaches, who proclaim that the cobbler should not stick to his trade but should instead be flexible and eager to strive for more, namely surplus value. This is a perfect example of scholarly interpretations of religion themselves becoming the shaping forces of religious culture. And even if the Weber thesis demands historical revision, it has still left its imprint on the discourse of capitalism, lending the harsh market economy a kind of religious legitimacy because of its ostensibly religious ancestry. In the United States and in Great Britain, the general public views the open market and capitalism with much more serenity and approval than in Germany, where Catholic social teaching and the Lutheran catechism joined forces in a sort of ecumenical conspiracy to legitimize the corporatist "social market economy."

There are paths that lead from Zurich and Geneva to the United Kingdom of the eighteenth century, to Jeremy Bentham and Adam Smith. The World Alliance of Reformed Churches, a sort of "Internationale" of Reformed churches, has approximately seventy-five million members, which is not that many. Pentecostalism, a late form of John Wesley's Methodism, has meanwhile performed far more successfully and aggressively than any other competitors in the globalized religious markets of the twentieth and twenty-first centuries.

Sociologists of religion interpret such beliefs as "health and wealth religions." In 1990, the Anglican theologian and religious sociologist David Martin showed in his famous book *Tongues of Fire: The Explosion of Protestantism in Latin America* that the strong conversion movement away from the Roman Catholic Church to the Pentecostal congregations can be easily deduced from Troeltsch's, and especially Weber's, patterns of interpretation.[27] The small congregation gives clear and strict moral instructions and fosters a puritanical lifestyle. A moral economy in which strong self-discipline, repression, and asceticism are rewarded is connected with the belief in the active strength of the Holy Spirit. Many Pentecostals give up nicotine and alcohol. They stress family values, resolutely reject openly homosexual lifestyles, and raise their children in a manner that combines strong affectionate bonds with performance pressure. They also invest quite heavily in the education of adolescents and create a visible culture of cleanliness with neatly dressed people, clean houses, and well-maintained yards. Pentecostal churches are attractive, especially in social milieux in which religious belief traditionally does not entail social and moral control.

Most European Christians and especially intellectuals socialized in Protestantism have a hard time understanding a Protestantism that is not characterized by the primacy of the Word, but instead by ecstatic rapture, wild dancing, and spontaneous speaking in tongues. In Ghana, the Pentecostal pastor drives his Mercedes to church and adorns himself in gold jewelry to demonstrate wealth and social advancement. The women wear makeup and invest in fashionable attire and jewelry. Does this still have anything to do with the Puritan self that pursues wealth for reasons diametrically opposed to ostentation? Regardless of all the deep differences, however, certain continuities between Reformed Pietism and "community Christianity" can be detected. Pentecostal religion is determined by a salvation of activism. It claims that man, through active contrition, penance, and conversion, can aspire to an autonomous life—along with a prosperity dividend, so to speak. Successful moral self-discipline is regarded as a sign that the believer is truly inspired by the Holy Spirit. Whereas in classic Calvinism, the theology of sanctification was anchored in predestination or grace, here it is anchored in the Holy Spirit. With regard to religious and moral dispositions, this does not make much of a difference. What, then, does constitute the specifically Calvinist? After five hundred years, can one formulate a concept of Calvinist identity that does justice to the elementary differences of many Calvinist lifeworlds?

Brian Gerrish, one of the grand old men of North American Calvin research, proposes a very narrow, purely theological concept of Calvinism. Calvinism is "the development of Calvin's theology by his spiritual heirs."[28] Thus, the specifics of religious culture, such as the strong emphasis on discipline as a mark of the church (*nota ecclesiae*) in its own right, and especially the older questions about the "cultural dimension" of Calvinist piety, disappear from focus. I, therefore, propose a definition that tries to do justice to both the diversity of the various Calvinisms and their common elements.

Calvin's own insight that the gospel is "not a verbal doctrine, but a life lesson" is such a point of theological convergence. According to Calvin, "this doctrine, if it is to bring us its manifold fruit, must be deeply embedded in our hearts and penetrate our life, yes, it must be worked into us."[29] This particular conduct of life, as stated at the beginning of the *Institutes*, aims at the "knowledge of God and ourselves."[30] Self-knowledge as knowledge of God (*sub specie Dei*), through the hearing of God's Word for the sake of a disciplined, rationalized lifestyle leading to a heightened life experience—this is a central and constitutive element of the decidedly antimagical Calvinist piety, which, with its emphasis on faith in the Word, appears more intellectual than Lutheran or Roman Catholic piety. In terms of theology and practiced piety, Calvinism is the radical Protestant alternative to the Roman Catholic cult of ecclesiastical hierarchy. The inner unity of the diverse Calvinisms can best be defined in opposition to Rome. Calvinism is the new social shape of modern Christianity, which developed an alternative to Tridentine Catholicism with far-reaching consistency and put active salvation into ever-new practices. In its extremely wide variety of manifestations, anti-Roman sentiment remains the determining element of continuity and unity.

Whoever recalls Calvin and Calvinism in major international conferences today can be said to practice memory politics. In a time of newly sharpened religious positions, this might also raise awareness of the fragility of the foundations of the legally ordered coexistence of different believers. Spokespersons for the majority Christian societies in Europe often indulge in explaining to Muslim minorities that politics must be separated from religion. The history of Calvinism also shows the strength of the theocratic temptation to the establishment of a holy way of life, despite Calvin's basic distinction between secular order and religious parish. But the moral arrogance with which many Christians remind Muslims of the functional separation of religion and politics might be one of the late cultural consequences of the Calvinist moral belief in a lifestyle of superior compliance with God's will, while others live in damnation.

■ Notes

1. Heinz Schilling, ed., *Die reformierte Konfessionalisierung in Deutschland: Das Problem der "Zweiten Reformation"* (Gütersloh: Gütersloher Mohn, 1986); Wolfgang Reinhard and Heinz Schilling, eds., *Die katholische Konfessionalisierung* (Gütersloh: Gütersloher, 1995); and Thomas Kaufmann, "Die Konfessionalisierung von Kirche und Gesellschaft: Sammelbericht über eine Forschungsdebatte," *Theologische Literaturzeitung* 121 (1996): 1008–25, 1113–21.

2. For example, see Johann Heinrich Zedler, *Grosses vollständiges Universal-Lexikon*, supplement vol. 4 (1754; repr. Graz: Akademische Druck- u., 1999), s.v. "Calvinisten," col. 1290; see also Friedrich Wilhelm Graf, *Der Protestantismus: Geschichte und Gegenwart* (Munich: Beck, 2006).

3. See Alastair Duke, "Perspectives on International Calvinism," in *Calvinism in Europe, 1540–1620*, ed. Andrew Pettegree, Alastair Duke, and Gillian Lewis (Cambridge: Cambridge University Press, 1994), 1–20, here 4, n. 12.

4. Calvin to Bullinger, June 26, 1548, *Calv. Opp.* 12: 730.

5. Polycarp Leyser, *Christianismus, Papismus et Calvinismus: D. i. drei unterschiedliche Auslegungen des catechismi Luthers* (Dresden: Stöckel, 1602).

6. See Ernst Troeltsch, *Die Bedeutung des Protestantismus für die Entstehung der modernen Welt (1906/1911)*, in Ernst Troeltsch, *Schriften zur Bedeutung des Protestantismus für die moderne Welt (1906–1913)*, ed. Trutz Rendtorff (Berlin: de Gruyter, 2001), 199–316, here 247, 287, 289.

7. This refers to Troeltsch's marginal note in the copy of Paul Gastrow, *Joh. Salomo Semler in seiner Bedeutung für die Theologie mit besonderer Berücksichtigung seines Streites mit G. E. Lessing* (Gießen: Töpelmann, 1905).

8. Olaf Blaschke, ed., *Konfessionen im Konflikt: Deutschland zwischen 1800 und 1970: Ein zweites konfessionelles Zeitalter* (Göttingen: Vandenhoeck & Ruprecht, 2002).

9. Matthias Schneckenburger, *Vergleichende Darstellung des lutherischen und reformirten Lehrbegriffs: Erster Theil*, ed. Eduard Güder (Stuttgart: Metzler, 1855).

10. Ibid., 52.

11. Ibid., 158.

12. Severini Monzambano Veronensis [Samuel Pufendorf], "De statu imperii Germanici ad Laelium fratrem, dominum Trezolani," in *Staatslehre der Frühen Neuzeit*, ed. Notker Hammerstein (Frankfurt: Dt. Klassiker, 1995), 569–931, here 899.

13. Pufendorf, "De statu," 903.

14. Carl Bernhard Hundeshagen, *Calvinismus und staatsbürgerliche Freiheit*, ed. Laure Wyss (Zollikon-Zurich: Evangelischer Verlag, 1946), 38.

15. Ibid., 16.

16. Ibid., 20.

17. Ibid., 21.

18. Ibid., 23.

19. Ibid., 37.

20. Ibid., 38.

21. Hermann Weingarten, *Die Revolutionskirchen Englands: Ein Beitrag zur inneren Geschichte der englischen Kirche und der Reformation* (Leipzig: Breitkopf & Härtel, 1868).

22. Georg Jellinek, *Die Erklärung der Menschen- und Bürgerrechte: Ein Beitrag zur modernen Verfassungsgeschichte* (Leipzig: Duncker & Humblot, 1995).

23. Willem Abraham de Klerk, *The Puritans in Africa: A Story of Afrikanerdom* (London: Collins, 1975).

24. See Friedrich Wilhelm Graf, "Fachmenschenfreundschaft: Bemerkungen zu 'Max Weber und Ernst Troeltsch,'" in *Max Weber und seine Zeitgenossen*, ed. Wolfgang J. Mommsen and Wolfgang Schwentker (Göttingen: Vandenhoek & Ruprecht, 1988), 313–36; and Graf, "Puritanische Sektenfreiheit versus lutherische Volkskirche: Zum Einfluss Georg Jellineks auf religionsdiagnostische Deutungsmuster Max Webers und Ernst Troeltschs," *Zeitschrift für Neuere Theologiegeschichte/Journal for the History of Modern Theology* 9 (2002): 42–69.

25. Max Weber, "Die protestantische Ethik und der Geist des Kapitalismus," in Max Weber, *Gesammelte Aufsätze zur Religionssoziologie*, 9th ed., vol.1 (Tübingen: Mohr, 1988), 1–206.

26. See Friedrich Wilhelm Graf, "The German Theological Sources and Protestant Church Politics," in *Weber's Protestant Ethic: Origins, Evidence, Contexts*, ed. Hartmut Lehmann and Guenther Roth (Cambridge: Cambridge University Press, 1993), 27–49.

27. David Martin, *Tongues of Fire: The Explosion of Protestantism in Latin America* (Oxford: Blackwell, 1990).

28. See Brian A. Gerrish, "Calvinismus," *RGG*[4], 2: 36–39, here 36.

29. See Jean Calvin, *Unterricht in der christlichen Religion: Institutio religionis christianae*, 2 vols. (Moers: Buchh. des Erziehungsvereins, 1938), 3, 6.4.

30. Ibid., 1: 1.

13 Calvin, Modern Calvinism, and Civil Society

The Appropriation of a Heritage, with Particular Reference to the Low Countries

CORNELIS VAN DER KOOI

What is the relationship between Calvin the author and the person, his heritage, and those who considered themselves to be his heirs? Such questions cannot be answered in general terms. This essay will explore the manner in which some of Calvin's heirs in modern times in the Low Countries have appropriated his heritage, focusing on the powerful religious and political movement that developed in the Netherlands in the last third of the nineteenth century known as neo-Calvinism, probably the most important nineteenth-century movement anywhere in the world to self-identify as "Calvinist." Particular attention will be given to the theologian Abraham Kuyper, generally considered to be the founder of this school of thought, which has exercised influence not only in the Netherlands but also in the United States, Canada, Britain, South Africa, and South Korea. After shaping Dutch society and politics in important ways for a century, neo-Calvinism as an all-encompassing life view and worldview has lost its enchantment in the past generation. Nonetheless, its social and public effects remain visible and politically viable. Therefore, I will consider this subject not only as a historical theme; its significance for the present day is equally relevant.

■ SELECTION AND APPROPRIATION OF THE CALVINIST HERITAGE

In thinking about the elements in Calvin's thought about God, man, and the world that took root in later Calvinism and were taken up in Dutch neo-Calvinism in the nineteenth century, the concept of *appropriation* seems particularly useful. With this concept, the role of each new generation is properly highlighted. To speak of "influence" or "reception" is too vague and suggests that those being influenced are simply passive recipients of a clear and fixed message. The word "construction" indicates a preconceived motif on the recipient's part that usually is not present in our relationship to the past. The word "appropriation," however, includes the notion that a human subject or a group plays an active role in receiving, selecting, and forming an image of the past, a set of memories, that in turn shapes its self-image and identity.[1] "Appropriation" implies that something is contributed and that selection is involved. In the specific case of Dutch neo-Calvinism, the way in which Calvin's heritage was received and shaped certainly depended on local circumstances and bears the stamp of its time. More generally, single-cause explanations of specific worldviews or theological motifs that simply label them the product of Calvinistic influence are usually weak and debatable. The context of Scotland was different from that of the Low Countries, and the situation in Korea was different from that in South Africa. Inevitably "Calvinism" became something different in each place.[2]

If I have chosen in this essay to focus on neo-Calvinism as a modern form of selection and appropriation of the Calvinist heritage, this is not because neo-Calvinistic theology in its full breadth still plays a large role in current theological debate, but because of the public aspect of this theology. Significant elements of the social structure of Dutch society are derived from the background in the renewal movement that neo-Calvinism wanted to be. This neo-Calvinism is especially connected to the figures of Abraham Kuyper (1837–1920) and Herman Bavinck (1854–1921). Kuyper, in particular, appealed to Calvinism as the ideology that shaped Dutch society and attempted to demonstrate that the building blocks of the Dutch identity were found in Calvin's heritage, which—to use a favorite image of Kuyper—planted the seed for a modern Christian culture and society. He wanted to convince his liberal contemporaries that Calvinism was not the same as backwardness, with a rejection of science, change, and progress. To the contrary, he argued that modern civic freedoms, such as freedom of conscience, religion, assembly, movement, and the right to vote, were actually derived from the impetus that had its origin in Calvinism. He selected a number of elements from Calvin's thought and from Calvinism and constructed a new form of Calvinism suitable for the demands of the time. The designation neo-Calvinism, first used by his critics,[3] was only later adopted by members of the movement itself and became commonly used. It is similar to neo-Thomism in the Roman Catholicism of the same era in that it attempted to provide an answer to modern questions by reaching back to a more distant past and trying to adapt it to the present. It should be clear that selection and critical appropriation are extremely important in this process. neo-Calvinism is not a simple repetition of a distant and celebrated past; even though it appealed to that past, it was consciously a new creation and bears the marks of its own era.

■ ABRAHAM KUYPER

I cannot at this point provide a full biographical sketch of this many-sided and colorful shaper of Dutch culture but must restrict myself to painting with broad strokes the essential features of his importance.[4] Educated at the University of Leiden, Kuyper began his career as a pastor and academic theologian, but soon sought to reach a wider audience as a journalist. In 1872 he founded the *Standaard*, a daily popular newspaper that created an audience which could be mobilized. Entering politics in 1873, he became a member of Parliament and was the joint founder of the first modern political party in the Netherlands, the Anti-Revolutionary Party (1879). He was one of the main advocates for the foundation of independent, private confessional schools, opposing thus both liberals and orthodox Protestants who identified the nation and public schooling with Protestantism. Interpreting the Dutch nation as being made up of three groups, liberals, Catholics, and Protestants, he broke with the idea of a single Dutch identity. In accordance with this view, he gave the impetus to the founding of the Free University in Amsterdam in 1880. Finally, he was leader in the church secession of 1886 known as the *Doleantie*, which sought to create "free" churches independent of the state-supported public church while remaining bound by the three classic confessions of Dutch Reformed Protestantism, the Belgic Confession of Faith, the Heidelberg Catechism, and the Canons of Dort. If his political career culminated in his being chosen as prime minister, in which position he served from 1901 to 1905, he was above all a "wholesale dealer" in ideas that inspired many contemporaries and irritated many others. Such was the decisive impact of his visionary agitation that the mention of his name creates a feeling of aversion among a segment of Protestant theologians even today. Yet his personal achievements are undeniable landmarks in Dutch history. He shaped a modern version of Calvinism that attempted to meet the conditions and possibilities of a modernizing and differentiating society. The founding of the Free University and the formation of the Anti-Revolutionary Party "stimulated the foundation of a great number of social, educational, and political institutions based on a constitutional expression of Reformed principles," which ended a long period of liberal domination of society and set the pattern for *verzuiling* (pillarization), which characterized Dutch society for most of the twentieth century.[5] In lieu of class loyalty, the division of society along vertical, ideological lines, with Protestants, Catholics, socialists, and liberals each organizing their own social, political, and educational institutions, with minimal governmental interference and in accordance with their own ideological persuasions, came to characterize the social and political structure of the Netherlands.[6]

Kuyper was undoubtedly a child of his times in that he lived during a period in which European society was modernizing and undergoing a process of functional differentiation. Against this backdrop, he took a number of ideas and concepts that he claimed to derive from Calvinism, but were, in fact, based on a strongly selective appropriation of the Calvinistic theological heritage. By waving the banner of the concept of "sphere sovereignty," he not only brought Calvin back to life but also gave his ideas form in institutions appropriate to the growing differentiation of modern society.

■ HEIR OF GROEN VAN PRINSTERER

Kuyper was able to build institutions from his ideas, but he was not the original progenitor of many of them. The Dutch reappropriation of the Calvinistic heritage began earlier in the nineteenth century, against the backdrop of the establishment of the Kingdom of the Netherlands on the drawing boards of the Congress of Vienna, in a restructured nation that was searching for its identity in the aftermath of the French Revolution and the Napoleonic era. In this context, Guillaume Groen van Prinsterer (1801–1876), the spiritual leader of what came to be known as the

Anti-Revolutionary Direction, proposed finding an answer to the French Revolution and its consequences in the Bible: "the gospel against the Revolution." Specifically, he rejected the Revolution's principle of the sovereignty of the people, arguing that the real sovereign from whom all authority is derived is God. If a society no longer acknowledged God as its foundation, the result was uprooting, splintering, greed, and poverty. To heal the flaws of a society that was, at the time, experiencing particularly difficult economic times, a return to the gospel was necessary. With Groen, this ideal of re-Christianizing Dutch society was accompanied by an appeal to Calvin. He found in Calvin an advocate of the idea of the divine origin of all authority. This was important, according to Groen, because sovereignty by the grace of God protects the authority of the government as well as the rights of the people. He was convinced that Calvinism had promoted the formation of constitutional law and civil rights.[7] Anticipating Kuyper, Groen developed a theory of the state in which its authority was limited to a restricted domain. Against those who would make state authority absolute, he argued that in society there are various domains that are independent.[8] God's Word is the guideline and directive for all these domains and, therefore, also for the state. The ideal of the Anti-Revolutionary Direction was a Christian state, but one defined by a greater separation of church and state. Groen wrote: "In my view, political equality for all religious convictions, without exception, is progress....No Caesaropapism, no *ius in sacra*, especially no state religion, only an authority of supervision and a duty of protection. What I want is a Christian state outside the influence of the church."[9]

In holding on to the ideal of a Christian state, yet separating church and state and pushing back the traditional domain of the state, Groen raised some knotty new problems. The realization of a Christian society now became dependent on the degree to which citizens manifested Christian ideals in their political and social consciousness and were willing to mobilize for the realization of a Christian society. And, at this point, his vision contained a built-in tension between ideal and reality, one that would eventually lead to a deep division within the Protestant section of the nation. On the one side stood the ideal of Christendom, the aspiration to build a Christian nation. On the other side stood the hard reality of a society where the vault of heaven receded more and more from view. That tension created countless ecclesiastical, theological, and political conflicts that continue to the present.

A number of Anti-Revolutionary members believed that evangelizing the masses held the key to re-Christianizing Dutch society, but that it was possible to achieve this via the traditional authority structures and institutions, under an oligarchic form of government. Kuyper departed from this conservative direction and sought instead to mobilize the people by empowering them politically. He advocated enlarging and democratizing voting rights in order to place authority in the hands of the common folk, the *kleine luyden*. At the same time, he sought to organize a societal middle field between citizens and government. According to Kuyper, the well-being of a society should not be made to depend on an all-powerful central authority or a privileged elite. As much as possible, the responsibility for family, church, work, schooling, industry, and health care should be placed as close as possible to the people involved, since every believer stands before God and is capable of contributing to a society infused by Christian values.[10] This move was, in fact, a choice for pluralism and a limited role for the government. The structures that this corporate vision of society created are still present in Dutch society today. Like Groen, Kuyper advocated this by an appeal to Calvin. However, he appealed to a completely different element of Calvin's thought than that appropriated by Groen and subsequently by the conservative, Christian-historicist A. F. de Savornin Lohman (1837–1924), the longtime spokesman for the Anti-Revolutionary Party in the Second Chamber of Parliament, legal advisor to the Doleantie, and professor of law at the Free University until Kuyper forced his resignation because of his defense of the established elites and opposition to widening the franchise.

■ CALVINISM: IDEAS UNWOUND IN THE COURSE OF TIME

Throughout his writings and even in the titles of books, such as *Calvinism: The Source and Safeguard of Our Constitutional Freedoms: A Dutch Thought* and, more simply, *Calvinism: Six Lectures*, Kuyper constantly and deliberately spoke about Calvinism—but far less about Calvin. When he did speak of Calvin, he made no secret of the fact that he did not follow the historical Calvin, but merely some of his ideas—ideas, furthermore, that Calvin had expressed as if they were wrapped in swaddling cloths, and which were only unwound over the course of time. The idea of unwinding was very important for Kuyper, especially for his thinking about culture. The historical original does not deserve deference; one does not eat the pit or the seed, but the ripened fruit. Likewise, the historic Calvinism that flowered in later centuries in Puritanism and in the theory of the separation of church and state was more valuable than the Reformation itself. A system must in time grow from a root; time and history are necessary to develop its rudiments, its principle, into full stature. Here Kuyper was deeply influenced by his theology professor at Leiden, J. H. Scholten (1811–1885), who was the first theologian in the Netherlands to speak of principles and the pure development of these principles over time. The shadow of Hegel is obvious. For Calvin, revelation is given in the form of plural *oracula Dei*, more or less closely connected. Scholten and Kuyper, in the warm wind of German idealism, incline toward greater systematic unity and attempt to identify principles from which everything proceeds. Reality, including the reality of faith and society, becomes in their eyes an embracing worldview, a unified system. This was foreign to Calvin but characteristic of Scholten and Kuyper's nineteenth-century Calvinism.

■ THE MOST SIGNIFICANT INGREDIENTS OF KUYPER'S NEO-CALVINISM

What are the most important ingredients of the modernized Calvinism that came to function as Kuyper's public theology? I will first summarize them briefly and then will discuss various sections in historical sequence.

1. Sphere sovereignty: The recognition of God as the only sovereign is related to the distinction between various realms or domains of life. All forms of earthly power and every sphere of life are bound to God's sovereignty.

2. Election: The salvation of the believer does not find its basis in his own faith and merit, or in the mediation of a church, but has its deepest anchoring in God, who elects, calls, and gives new birth in Christ. These moments of calling, election, and new birth give each person his most fundamental identity, exalting his existence and forming a mobilizing strength. They nourish a spirituality that Kuyper himself described as "being near unto God."

3. Sanctification: Because of election and new birth, a person is not tied to sin and total depravity but is directed to the sanctification of life in all its facets. In other words, our earthly existence is not a mistake but a pilgrimage in which Christ in heaven, through the power of the Spirit, binds people to him and carries and supports them in the temporality of this life. This conviction is not confined to personal faith, but is the source of an encompassing life view and worldview.

4. Common grace: With Kuyper the vision of being born again and sanctified goes together with a wider vision of culture. God's grace does not only engender the salvation of individuals through "special grace." A common grace extends throughout the realm of culture. The world in which we live is from God. His purpose is not limited to saving sinners but also includes the salvation of his creation and the indwelling potential of culture. Calvin's theory of common grace is reinterpreted by Kuyper. Not only does humanity belong to God, but so does all of modern life: human communities, scholarship, and technology. The world is God's creation, and he does not desert what his hand has begun. Modern culture and science are a disclosure of God-given potential. Kuyper developed this view in his doctrine of common grace, in which he not only made it possible for the believer to participate in the modern world, but elevated this participation into an issue of obedience to God. History and the modern world may not be left to the devil since they are the battlefield or arena of Christ, in which Christians must be actively involved. By way of conclusion, Kuyper's doctrine of common grace can be regarded as one of the main reasons why neo-Calvinism became attractive and successful in Dutch society. It provided and provides a Christian foundation and inspiration for engaging fully with modern culture.

■ THE VOICE OF SCHLEIERMACHER

Where did the democratizing emphasis in neo-Calvinism come from? In this connection, it is especially interesting to take a look at *Commentatio*, the 1860 text with which Kuyper, as a young theology student, won a prestigious prize from the University of Groningen.[11] The assignment of the competition was to compare the definition of the church provided by Calvin with that of John à Lasco (1499–1560), the reformer who shaped the Reformation in Emden and the Dutch refugee church in London. Strikingly, Kuyper praised à Lasco's understanding of the church as more biblical than Calvin's. A Lasco, in Kuyper's reading, defined the church as a community in which the Holy Spirit lives and the members build each other up through love and reciprocal service. The Spirit of Christ, having poured out a new life principle upon the community, takes possession of its members.[12] From this manner of rendering à Lasco's ideas, another influence on Kuyper's thinking about the church also emerges clearly: Friedrich Schleiermacher, who was in fact the genius behind Kuyper's idea of the church as a society (*societas*) of equals. More than any other thinker of the time, Schleiermacher "drew attention to the social element [*das Gesellige*] in religion and church."[13] From the interplay between equality and difference, the congregation grows and lives as a pluriform community. The conviction that every member of the church could be infused by the Spirit and contribute to the whole led Kuyper to propose already in 1860 not only that the elders of the church should be chosen by the members but also that women, as well as men, could be elders.[14] He preferred the *attemperata democratia* of à Lasco to the aristocratic model of Calvin. The emphasis is on the priesthood of all believers and how this renewed community will bear fruit for the wider national community. A concern with the universal meaning of the Christian faith and a renewed church was already visible in Kuyper's early work.[15]

■ THE LECTURE: THE ORIGIN OF MODERN LIBERTIES

Kuyper's unequivocal choice of Calvinism as an identity came more than a decade after his *Commentatio*, appearing first in his 1874 lecture "Calvinism: the Source and Stronghold of Our Constitutional Liberties."[16] One must read this document against the background of the search for a Dutch identity mentioned earlier, a debate that lasted into the twentieth century. In this debate, a liberal faction located the essence of Dutch identity in humanism, highlighting figures such as Desiderius Erasmus, Dirck Volkertsz. Coornhert, and Johannes Uytenbogaert. This group suggested that the Netherlands was a tolerant country with room for religious minorities and one dominated by an enlightened form of religion. Another group called the "Groninger Direction," theologians strongly influenced by the humanistic ideal of Schleiermacher, situated the key source of Dutch identity in the *devotio moderna* of the late Middle Ages, highlighting figures such as Wessel Gansfort, Geert Grote, and Thomas à Kempis. They sought to suggest that the essence of Dutchness was a national spirituality emphasizing practical piety, care for the sick, education, and service to God and the world—all performed while leading a life of devotion.[17] Kuyper focused his contribution to this debate on the sources of Dutch liberty and constitutional freedoms. He first asked which eighteenth-century revolution—the American or the French—yielded the more effective and enduring results. Answering in favor of the former, he went on to link this to its religious foundations in the Calvinist tradition: "Notice that history shows that the American United States, where the plant of freedom still blooms most effusively, is beholden *not* to the revolution in France, but to Puritan heroic courage."[18] The root of public freedoms lies in man's relationship to God, he argued. The awareness of freedom is born in that relationship. In faith, man binds himself to God, on whom he is dependent without reservation, from whom he receives life, and to whom he owes responsibility. Kuyper described this as the principle of God's sovereignty. All other authority is dependent upon this highest authority and can never be identified with one person. Not only does the principle of God's sovereignty ground the rejection of a class society and the recognition of the equality of all before God, it implies, at the same time, a rejection of the concept of the sovereignty of a people or nation. Following Groen van Prinsterer, Kuyper categorized the French Revolution as a movement arising from unbelief. While basically a spiritual movement, it made the fatal error of rejecting all divine authority, replacing God's sovereignty with the sovereignty of man and founding the doctrine of human rights on this.[19] Kuyper rejected this foundation of human rights because it no longer regarded man as secondary, standing before and depending on God, but as primary and autonomous. In Kuyper's thought, power and authority are never autonomous but are always dependent, relative, and under the critique of God, who is the highest power. Royalty and governments reign by the grace of God, but the right to govern is bound to the office, not to the person. In Kuyper's view, Calvin himself, acting under the influence of events in France, articulated an understanding of the royal succession and the distinction between person and crown that in turn laid the foundation for ideas of the right to drive out tyrants. The ideas that he expressed in germ were further developed by Theodore Beza and François Hotman, each of whom, in his own manner and time, denied the absolute right of royalty and further developed the importance of the lesser magistrates as checks on the abuse of power. The exercise of royal authority had to be conjoined with the power of secondary authorities whose ultimate source was the people themselves.[20]

It is remarkable how strongly Kuyper appeals to the spirituality that is interwoven with Reformed theology in this treatise. He points explicitly to election as a dogma from which proceeds enormous ethical and anthropological power.

> Whoever believes in election knows that he is chosen for something, and therefore has an ethical calling, a calling which, if necessary, must bring the most precious offering, because it is a divine calling. But it is also a calling that will be successful, because God, who is sovereign, is the One who called. And therefore the person does not hesitate, or weigh up the pros and cons, but puts his hand to the plow and keeps working.[21]

Put in modern terms, Kuyper uses the dogma of election as a means of empowerment. It operates as a stimulus and firm trust in our own calling and worth to tackle the things of this life. All are called to be active and to pull their weight. Reformed activism has a theological foundation.

Related to this idea of election was Kuyper's choice of free churches and the members' right to vote. He opposed all clericalism: "A church that confesses election as *cor ecclesiae* cannot be clerical," he wrote, "but must find its strength in the *electi*, that is, in the members of the congregation. From this confession flowed the democratic church principle that later was carried over from the church to the state and engendered the freedoms of the Dutch people, of the England of the Whigs, and of America. Election creates the proud spirit of its citizens and undermines every principle of persecution for one's faith."[22] In many ways, Kuyper was drawing upon the tradition, begun by the Whig historians of the eighteenth century and continued by Guizot and Groen van Prinsterer, that identified the

Reformed tradition—Kuyper calls it "Calvinism"—as the midwife of modern liberty. At the same time, he reinfused it with a spirituality emphasizing the animating power of election within each man and woman. Calvin's contribution to this tradition of liberty under divine sovereignty had been to underscore man's dependence on God and to draw initial attention to the obligation of lesser magistrates to resist tyranny. Later Calvinism further unwound these ideas.

■ CALVINISM AS A LIFE VIEW AND WORLDVIEW

In his 1898 Stone Lectures delivered at Princeton Theological Seminary, Kuyper argued that Calvinism contained *in nuce* a modern, all-encompassing Christian worldview, in which the riches of life, people, science, and culture all came to expression.[23] His concern in these lectures was not the communication of the gospel as such.[24] Rather, against the French Revolution with its anthropocentric perspective and its denial of divine authority, he sought to suggest that Calvinism offered the foundation for a vision of politics and art appropriate to the modern world.[25] This neo-Calvinism shared with neo-Thomism the concern to resist the attempt of liberal thought to confine religion to a limited sphere. It attempted, as Schleiermacher had previously attempted at the beginning of the nineteenth century, to keep Christendom and culture together. Calvinism, it argued, was a worldview and life view that brings all aspects of life under God's sovereignty. This control lays an axe to the root of old hierarchic differences of class and birth:

> If Calvinism places our entire human life immediately before God, then it follows that all men or women, rich or poor, weak or strong, dull or talented, as creatures of God, and as lost sinners, have no claim whatsoever to lord over one another, and that we stand as equals before God, and consequently equal as man to man. Hence we cannot recognize any distinction among men, save such as had been imposed by God himself, in that he placed one authority over another, or enriched one person with more talents than another in order that the man with more talents should serve the man with less, and in serving him serve God. Calvinism condemns not merely all open slavery and systems of caste, but also all covert slavery of women and of the poor; it is opposed to all hierarchy among men; it tolerates no aristocracy save such as is able, either in person or in family, by the grace of God, to exhibit superiority of character or person, and to show that it does not claim this superiority for self-aggrandizement or ambitious pride, but for the sake of spending it in the service of God.[26]

Kuyper's emphasis on equality before God and democracy was a plea against totalitarianism or the domination of a small minority, and, in this regard, his views on the role of the state were aligned with those of liberals like the statesman of the 1848 constitution, Johan Rudolf Thorbecke (1798–1872), whom he greatly admired. In his ideas on the role of religion in the state, however, Kuyper was an antiliberal. Religion must not be pushed back into the personal domain; rather, life convictions and religion must be acknowledged as fundamental for the way people conduct their lives, raise their children, arrange their communities, and think about politics. Religions and life convictions are the source of values, norms, and even art. It is, therefore, not desirable to ban religion from the public domain.

Kuyper's vindication of religion as a source for faith-based institutions had profound implications for Dutch society, since Kuyper pioneered the creation of new institutions shaped by his vision of Calvinism. These came to exercise great influence, and to encourage the pillarization of Dutch society around institutions based on specific world-views.[27]

■ TRACES OF CALVIN?

How much of Calvin himself can be recognized in Kuyper's Calvinism? I will mention several elements. First, that man stands before God in his conscience and religious consciousness and is called by God to a life of obedience and sanctification is a central theme of Calvin's writings. In an environment where Calvin's followers are in the majority, this call to obedience can promote a system in which personal freedom comes under pressure in a "rule of the saints" in which theocratic ideals have no brake because they are those of the majority. But where this majority situation is not present, another dynamic comes to the fore, a critical posture in relation to earthly power and structures of authority. The immediate relation between God and man means that mediating institutions and authority structures do not disappear, but are fundamentally relativized. The early Calvinist criticism of the dogma of transubstantiation is a good illustration. As Christopher Elwood has argued, when the annual, medieval Corpus Christi feasts, with their close symbolic connection between the earthly, royal authority and the host kept in the monstrance, became an object of Calvinistic criticism, that criticism had, as demonstrated by mass iconoclasm, great theological significance in the public realm.[28]

For Calvin, the sacred moves to a different place. Calvin binds man to Christ who reigns at the right hand of the Father. Christ has ascended to heaven; he is not on earth, even though God scatters signs of his glory everywhere in his creation. Contrary to what is often thought, Calvin's universe is not empty. God is not only transcendent, but he shows us in countless mirrors his glory, goodness, and grace through our eyes, through all our senses.[29] The world is a stage for his condescending glory, holiness, and care. But they are mirrors that God himself uses in his freedom. Christ cannot be identified with earthly matter, with earthly power and authority structures. Calvin's spirituality stands and falls with this dialectic of transcendence and condescension.

This dialectic also becomes concrete in the relation of Spirit and Word. The Spirit is bound to the Word, to Christ, but not, as Calvin argues against Sadoleto, to the church.[30] And that interpretation steers the relationship between the subject and the church (and civil government) in a fundamentally different direction. This change of direction becomes concrete in ecclesiology, notably in the doctrine of the office. The offices of prophet, priest, and king do not rest on one person, but are divided over several persons. Those who are appointed to an office do not stand above the church, but are *in* the church, in the body, and Christ is their head. This equality of the members within the body is carried through to all members. In fact, all believers share in the threefold office.[31] It is this radical, critical notion of all earthly authority that gives Calvinism its distinctive combination of an emphasis on loyalty to government with its creation of significant grounds upon which principled revolt and resistance are possible. In essence, Calvin's thought nourishes republican, not royalist institutions.

This change of direction also has consequences for the manner in which responsibility is assumed elsewhere in society: schooling, care for the poor, care for the sick, scholarship. It is this promotion of personal responsibility that is seized upon by Kuyper, becoming a means for mobilizing broad sections of society. The church becomes the school for a responsible and charitable society and the good stewardship of public affairs. Kuyper greeted the striving for securing civic freedoms in a constitution as a great accomplishment. In this way, the absolute power of the state can be reined in and issues of public interest left to the initiative of the citizens as much as possible. The state or the government does not have to regulate everything. Authority does not flow from royalty or a sovereign, but it is bestowed on the lower levels of government that are anchored as firmly as possible in the community to which they are responsible. Striving for a society where righteousness and peace greet each other is not a matter that can be entrusted solely to an all-powerful central government. It is a responsibility that arises from local communities, businesses, or professions. To put it in contemporary terms, there is a *middle field* between national government and the individual citizen. This middle field has direct responsibility for countless matters, such as education, labor, health, elder care, recreation, and (last but not least) the media.

Kuyper thus took further a perspective that Calvin expressed particularly effectively and applied the principles he perceived within the reformer's outlook to the questions of the day—without, however, regularly alluding back to Calvin. Indeed, as he saw it, to cite Calvin too extensively would violate Calvinist principles and be incongruous with the way in which God reveals himself throughout the course of history. "Calvinism came to its fundamental interpretation of an immediate fellowship with God not because Calvin invented it," he wrote, "but because in this immediate fellowship God himself had granted our fathers a privilege of which Calvin was only the first to become clearly conscious."[32] Elsewhere in the same work, he stressed that "Calvinism has never burned its incense upon the altar of genius, it has erected no monument for its heroes, it scarcely calls them by name."[33]

While Kuyper succeeded in creating a variety of intermediate institutions, he failed completely to achieve one of his goals. In his own way, like Groen before him, he attempted to re-Christianize Dutch society. Other Dutch Calvinist political figures such as Johannes Hermanus Gunning Jr. (1829–1905), Philippus Jacobus Hoedemaker (1839–1910), and, in the twentieth century, Arnold Albert van Ruler (1908–1970) also tried to do the same. Their efforts crashed against the reality of advancing dechristianization. Initially, the ideal of sphere sovereignty was that society would again be conquered via the Christian pillar. The intermediate institutions were meant as a means to this end. This failed completely, although Kuyper's followers had greater influence in politics than one might have expected from their small numbers.[34] Kuyper himself remained a proponent of a Christian state in theory, but, under the pressure of the times and the advance of dechristianization, his policies effectively shifted to supporting a neutral state. At his instigation in 1905, article 36 of the Belgic Confession was even changed to delete the passage about the role of the government in maintaining church services and eradicating idolatry and false religion.

■ THE PRESENT SITUATION: PLURALISM

Amid contemporary debates about the identity of Dutch society, the conviction has grown that no one current can convincingly claim to epitomize the nation's identity. The Netherlands has always consisted of a variety of provinces, regions, and linguistic groups—minorities if you will. In such a mixed situation, everyone had to cooperate, especially since the geographic structure of the (literal) lowlands near the sea required people to build dikes, to regulate the water system, and to decide collectively how to maintain and manage these systems. In the reclamation of the Dutch peat areas behind the dunes, farmers worked together with the count. In Friesland, the joint interest in the struggle for regulated water management forced cooperation across wide areas. Since the 1990s, commentators have increasingly invoked what has been called the "polder model" to explain what is said to be a long-standing Dutch distrust of distant and detached authority and preference for cooperative local management. This designation functions, one could say, as a useful myth.[35]

It is clear that it would be difficult to deduce polder culture from Calvinism. The most that one can say is that Calvinism's ideas of personal responsibility toward God and its built-in potential for criticism of all human authority stimulate and give form to a comparable ethos. It is precisely those elements that make neo-Calvinism an attractive export. In a minority situation, this theological grounding for the worth and responsibility of the human person encourages the development of defenses against an over-powerful government or an all-powerful market. In this way, the neo-Calvinistic heritage of Kuyper offers opportunities for a pluralistic society such as the Dutch. Rather than pushing minorities to the edge, it encourages them to enter the public arena and take part in public life. In the field of education, for instance, while accepting that education is financed nearly completely by the state, which demands quality control, it insists that education be organized and implemented on the basis of a worldview or religious foundation. Thus there ought to be schools that offer education from an anthroposophical background, as well as schools with a Protestant, Roman Catholic, or Islamic outlook. The same pluralism should characterize the media. While public regulation distributes licenses for radio and television among associations that must conform to certain stipulations in order to qualify for government financing, these associations are free to express their own worldviews in their programs. For a long time in the eighties and nineties, it was thought that the religious pillarization of society would disappear completely.[36] Indeed, since the 1960s the pillars have gradually become porous, and many hospitals, schools, and newspapers have lost their close association with a single specific worldview. But has pillarization completely disappeared? While the pillars are no longer the closed containers they once were, perhaps, they have become tables around which people gather. In the ongoing debate about immigrant newcomers, the dominant assumption for a long time was that newcomers to Dutch society had to adjust themselves to a modern, liberal identity; there was no room for religion in the public domain. However, the coalition government that ruled the Netherlands from 2007 until 2010 consisting of an orthodox Protestant party, the Christian Democrats (Christen Democratisch Appèl), a fairly radical social and ecological party, the United Christians (Christen-Unie), and the social-democratic Labor Party (Partij van de Arbeid), supported the position that pluralism could contribute more to the cohesion of society than liberal and populist voices that insisted that religion should be banned from the public domain. These diverse parties based their cooperation on a policy that enabled various religious groups to take their identity into the public arena. One should not rule a country by seclusion, but by inclusion. This position would have been hardly thinkable without the neo-Calvinist heritage.

■ Notes

1. See Herman Paul and Bart Wallet, introduction to *Sober, Strict, and Scriptural: Collective Memories of John Calvin, 1800–2000*, ed. Johan de Niet, Herman Paul, and Bart Wallet (Leiden: Brill, 2009), 2–3.

2. An example of this contextual dependence is the manner in which neo-Calvinism in South Africa was used and appropriated in the twentieth century. While the proponents of racial segregation for a time appealed to Kuyper's idea of sphere sovereignty, his Eurocentrism, and his idea of a separate development of non-European peoples, any explanation of the establishment of apartheid ideology must also take into account the struggle of the Afrikaner *boeren* against English colonialism and the *volk* mission theory of the German missiologist Gustav Warneck. In all instances, it is important to ask which elements are appropriated and why. See also R. Vosloo, "Calvin and Anti-Apartheid Memory," in de Niet, Paul, and Wallet, *Sober, Strict, and Scriptural*, 216–43.

3. B. D. Eerdmans, "De theologie van Dr. A. Kuyper," *Theologisch Tijdschrift* 43 (1909): 209–37.

4. For a full biography, see J. Koch, *Abraham Kuyper: Een biografie* (Amsterdam: Boom, 2007); for short English introductions, Peter S. Heslam, *Creating a Christian Worldview: Abraham Kuyper's Lectures on Calvinism* (Grand Rapids: Eerdmans, 1998), 1–84; and James D. Bratt, *Abraham Kuyper: A Centennial Reader* (Grand Rapids: Eerdmans, 1998), 1–16.

5. Heslam, *Creating a Christian Worldview*, 2.

6. For recent overviews, see George Harinck and Lodewijk Winkeler, "De twintigste eeuw," in *Handboek Nederlandse Kerkgeschiedenis*, ed. Herman Selderhuis (Kampen: Kok, 2006), 727–858; and Peter van Rooden, "Long-term Religious Developments in the Netherlands, 1750–2000," in *The Decline of Christendom in Western Europe, 1750–2000*, ed. Hugh McLeod and Werner Ustorf (Cambridge: Cambridge University Press, 2003), 113–29.

7. G. Groen van Prinsterer, *Ongeloof en revolutie: Een reeks van historische voorlezingen*, 3rd ed. (Franeker: Wever, 1976), 44, 107.

8. G. J. Schutte, *Het calvinistisch Nederland* (Hilversum: Verloren, 2000), 130.

9. G. Groen van Prinsterer, *De antirevolutionaire en confessionele partij*, trans. A. J. Dam (Goes: Ooesterbaan & Le Cointre, 1954), 31, originally published as *Le parti antirévolutionaire et confessionel dans l'Eglise Reformee dans Les Pays Bas* (Amsterdam: H. Höveker, 1860), 31. Cited by Schutte, *Het calvinistisch Nederland*, 130.

10. A. Kuyper, *Het Calvinisme: Oorsprong en waarborg van onze constitutionele vrijheden: Een Nederlandse gedachte*, 3rd ed. (Kampen: Kok, 2004), 118: "What we want is to see the church free, by separating her honestly and completely from the state, also financially, and to make the school free from the church, by giving it back to the parents, by

regulation and supervision of the state, because, according to us, the impersonal state cannot provide education. What we want is to strengthen the bond that ties us to the House of Orange, while maintaining the republican status of the people, of which the House of Orange is both symbol and guarantee. We are proponents of decentralization, of organic representation of the people, and of moral colonial politics. We demand greater freedom at the universities, and granting greater independence to the court of justice, if need be, by establishing a jury system."

11. J. Vree and J. Zwaan, eds., *Abraham Kuyper's* Commentatio *(1860): The Young Kuyper about Calvin, a Lasco, and the Church*, vol. 1, *Introduction, Annotations, Bibliography, and Indices*, vol. 2, *Commentatio* (Leiden: Brill, 2005).

12. Ibid., 2: 298.

13. Ibid., 2: 293. See also 1: 50–51.

14. Ibid., 2: 344.

15. Ibid., 2: 363. See also the commentary by Vree and Zwaan in 1: 61.

16. English translation in Bratt, *Abraham Kuyper*, 281–317.

17. The theologians of the Groninger Direction were fervent supporters of the service societies (*Nutsverenigingen*), initiatives that attempted to organize the joint interests and needs of the people in a community. See Joost Kloek and Wijnand Mijnhardt, *1800: Blueprints for a National Community* (Assen: Royal van Gorcum, 2004).

18. Kuyper, *Oorsprong en waarborg*, 91.

19. Ibid., 112.

20. Ibid., 94.

21. Ibid., 105.

22. Ibid., 105.

23. Abraham Kuyper, *Het Calvinisme: Zes Stone-lezingen in oktober 1898 te Princeton (N. J.) gehouden*, 5th ed., ed. George Harinck (Barneveld: Nederlands Dagblad, 2008).

24. See Harinck, in introduction to *Zes Stone-lezingen*, 16.

25. Kuyper's fundamental criticism of the French Revolution as antireligious has given him the reputation of being conservative. See H. W. von der Dunk, *Conservatisme* (Bussem: Fibula-van Dishoeck, 1976), 119–22.

26. Kuyper, *Zes Stone-lezingen*, 37. In quoting from this work, I have relied on the anonymous English translation of the text issued by Eerdmans: *Lectures on Calvinism by Abraham Kuyper* (Grand Rapids: Eerdmans, 1931).

27. Inspired by Olaf Blaschke's thesis that the nineteenth century was a second confessional era, Herman Paul and Johan de Niet have recently suggested that "confessionalization" may be a better term than "pillarization." Paul and de Niet, "*Issus de Calvin*: Collective Memories of John Calvin in Dutch Neo-Calvinism," in *Sober, Strict, and Scriptural*, 73.

28. Christopher Elwood, *The Body Broken: The Calvinist Doctrine of the Eucharist and the Symbolization of Power in Sixteenth-Century France* (Oxford: Oxford University Press, 1999), 22–26.

29. See Cornelis van der Kooi, *As in a Mirror: John Calvin and Karl Barth on Knowing God: A Diptych* (Leiden: Brill, 2005), 77–82.

30. J. Calvin, "Ad Sadoleti Epistolam," *Calv. Opp.* 5: 392–93.

31. *Catechismus Genevensis* (1545), question and answer 34–35, *OS* 2: 113–16.

32. Kuyper, *Zes Stone-lezingen*, 35.

33. Ibid., 34.

34. The Anti-Revolutionary Party never received more than 16 percent of the votes in parliamentary elections, but in coalition with other Christian parties it played a dominant role in the governments of the interwar years. Harinck and Winkeler, "De twintigste eeuw," 738–40.

35. See J. Lendering, *Polderdenken: De wortels van de Nederlandse overlegcultuur* (Amsterdam: Athenaeum-Polak & van Gennep, 2005).

36. For a discussion of the concept of pillarization as a metaphor for modernization, see Janneke Adema, "Verzuiling als metafoor voor modernisering," in Madelon de Keizer and Sophie Tates, *Moderniteit: Modernisme en massacultuur in Nederland, 1914–1940* (Amsterdam: Walburg Pers, 2004), 265–83.

[handwritten notes]

Impact of some ideas

sin   divine grace   prot. 'puritan'

Amer + British literature
(French? Camus?)

Hard work – work ethic – Weber
Image of ____

Scottish poet + Hogg
Hard Core film

staid, stoic, straightlaced
conservative   Knox
total opposite of ZW, Cal, Kuyper
                                Buys

14 Calvin and British Evangelicalism in the Nineteenth and Twentieth Centuries

DAVID BEBBINGTON

The legacy of John Calvin to the Protestants of Great Britain was immense. His version of Reformed theology became virtually universal in the Elizabethan Church of England and remained the norm during the earlier years of the seventeenth century.[1] The Puritans who wished to press further with the task of reformation upheld the same doctrinal scheme, which was codified by the Westminster Assembly during the 1640s. Their heirs who left the established church, either voluntarily or compulsorily, formed Dissenting denominations that were overwhelmingly Calvinist in profession: the Presbyterians, the Independents, and the Baptists.[2] The teaching of Calvin was also warmly embraced in Scotland, where the structures of church life were remodeled much more drastically than in England. By means of its kirk sessions, Presbyterianism created what has been called "a Puritan nation" in early modern Scotland.[3] The people of Britain turned into Calvinists. In Scotland they remained so, all Presbyterian ministers having to profess their allegiance to the theology of the Westminster Assembly down the years into the nineteenth century. In England, on the other hand, the Calvinism of the established church evaporated in the later seventeenth century and the Presbyterian variety faded during the eighteenth. Only the small communities of Independents and Baptists retained their loyalty to Calvin's convictions. The Evangelical Revival of the eighteenth century, however, put the process into reverse. Independents and Baptists grew in numbers, and distinctive Reformed convictions were planted once more in the Church of England. As the nineteenth century wore on and Evangelicals continued to expand, therefore, Protestantism increasingly owed some allegiance to John Calvin. In Evangelical circles, as an Independent divine put it at the tercentenary of Calvin's death in 1864, "it is the spirit of Calvin, more than any other man, which breathes and works."[4]

Nevertheless, for a number of reasons, the extent of the Calvinist commitment of Evangelicals during the nineteenth century needs to be qualified. In the first place, the type of theology upheld by most of the Reformed Protestants differed significantly from the doctrines maintained by Calvin and their Puritan ancestors. The eminent American theologian Jonathan Edwards had introduced a crucial distinction between natural and moral inability. Sinners suffered from no natural inability, imposed on them by their Creator, to believe the gospel; rather they exercised a moral inability, a refusal to repent of their sins, for which they alone were culpable. The Almighty had not created them merely to punish them for their unavoidable failures. This milder form of Calvinism, a species of determinism compatible with human liberty to choose, was the type embraced by most British Evangelicals. Among Baptists, Andrew Fuller was its champion, among the Independents, Edward Williams, and among Scottish Presbyterians, Thomas Chalmers.[5] The exponents of this point of view sat loose to Calvin's writings. A contributor to *The Evangelical Magazine* in March 1809 was typical. "I avow myself," he wrote, "a Calvinist....Do I make the *Institutions* and *Comments* of Calvin the directory of my faith?" The answer was that he certainly did not: the writer merely held the leading doctrines of "that illustrious man."[6] Calvin was still respected: many of the moderate Calvinists, including Andrew Fuller and Edward Williams, subscribed to the first of the nineteenth-century lives of the reformer published in 1809 by John Mackenzie, an Anglican who himself shared the views of Edwards.[7] The theologians of this school nevertheless felt entirely at liberty to diverge from the reformer's teaching. Thus the Independent Alexander Thomson, even when in 1864 celebrating Calvin's achievement, expressed regret at his decree of reprobation.[8] The moderates were denounced by the much smaller number who retained more robust views as "Bastard Calvinists,"[9] but their views came to dominate the Reformed communities. That opened a doctrinal gulf between most Calvinist Evangelicals and John Calvin himself.

There were, second, reasons why members of particular denominations felt distanced from Calvin. The reformer of Geneva suffered in the eyes of an insular people from being a foreigner. Members of the Church of England usually preferred to appeal to the authority of the English reformers of the sixteenth century who were unequivocally their own. On occasion they would defend Calvin, as did the leading Anglican Evangelical Daniel Wilson, later bishop of Calcutta, who in an account of a Continental tour in 1823 described the reformer as a "sober, practical holy writer."[10] In general, however, they regarded themselves as being in continuity with those who had undertaken the reformation of the Church of England in the sixteenth century. In *Light from Old Times* (1891), for instance, Bishop John Charles Ryle, though the most outspokenly Calvinist of Anglican bishops during the nineteenth century, ignored the reformer in favor of such men as Bishops John Hooper, Hugh Latimer, and Nicholas Ridley, the glories of early Protestantism in England.[11] Similarly, in Scotland John Calvin was eclipsed by his disciple John Knox. For a few, such as William Cunningham, the principal of New College, Edinburgh, who loved systematic theology, Calvin was "the man who, next to St. Paul, has done most good to mankind."[12] But for a larger number, Calvin was a remote figure with unappealing characteristics who, unlike Knox, had no direct connection with Scotland. In an assessment of Calvin delivered in a series of lectures in Edinburgh on "The Evangelical Succession" in 1882, J. S. Candlish, a leading figure in the Free Church of Scotland, contrasted the "sternness and determination" of Calvin with the "geniality" of Knox that was reminiscent of the same quality in Luther.[13] To the Dissenters of England and Wales, Calvin was not only foreign but also a champion of the principle that the church was coextensive with the state. Their very existence was predicated on the opposite conviction that religion was a matter for voluntary choice. Hence, as the Independent John Kelly put it in an otherwise appreciative lecture on Calvin, the reformer was guilty of "forcing religious habits on those who were not prepared to receive them."[14] Anglicans, Presbyterians, and Dissenters alike therefore usually lauded their own heroes rather than Calvin.

Some within the Evangelical community, in the third place, actually repudiated Calvin altogether. Methodists, the followers of the eighteenth-century John Wesley, agreed with their founder in rejecting Calvinism in favor of Arminianism. It is true that one independent-minded Wesleyan minister, Samuel Dunn, published a warm account of Calvin's theology in 1837, quoting copiously from his commentaries and sermons, but Dunn was exceptional.[15] W. B. Pope, the greatest of Victorian Methodist theologians, took Calvin's distinguishing points into account in order to refute them at various points in his three-volume *Compendium of Christian Theology* (1880), characterizing divine sovereignty, for example, as "despotic."[16] Others outside the Methodist fold agreed in attacking Calvin. Thus Edward Smyth, an Anglican minister who gloried in being an Arminian, wrote a book in 1809 contrasting the apostle Paul with Calvin, censuring the reformer's "eternal irrevocable decree, assigning to particular men salvation or damnation, antecedent to any foreseen faith or unbelief, good or evil works."[17] Some were more equivocal. Andrew Fairbairn was brought up in the tiny Scottish Evangelical Union that was explicitly anti-Calvinist, but, as the best known theologian of the English Free Churches at the end of the century, he was required to deal evenhandedly with Calvin. His solution, extraordinarily, was to turn Calvin into as much of an Arminian as he dared. Calvin's harsh doctrines were blamed on Augustine, but, according to Fairbairn, "while the system held and awed Calvin's reason it did not yet win his heart."[18] Anglican Evangelicals had found themselves in an even more difficult position over Calvin in the early years of the century because the bishop of Lincoln, George Pretyman Tomline, a pillar of the establishment, argued in a book of 1799 that the Thirty-Nine Articles of the Church of England could not be interpreted in a Calvinist sense, following it up twelve years later with *A Refutation of Calvinism*.[19] The aim of branding Calvinism an alien creed was to drive the Evangelicals out of the church. One Evangelical response was to reaffirm the rightness of Reformed convictions: John Allen, an Anglican schoolmaster, published an edition of Calvin's *Institutes* in 1813 for that reason.[20] Charles Simeon, the judicious leader of the Evangelical section of the clergy, took a different line. Believing there was truth in both Calvinism and Arminianism, but supposing that the Bible rose above such "human systems," Simeon eventually decided in 1822 to try to disarm anti-Evangelical prejudice by publicly disavowing Calvinism altogether.[21] Thereafter, many Anglican Evangelicals regarded themselves not as indebted to Calvin but as simple "Bible Christians." Thus substantial sections of Evangelicalism were outside the Calvinist ranks.

During the nineteenth century, fourth, there was a gradual undermining of Calvinism in circles where it had been upheld. The chief agency was the spread of influences derived from the Enlightenment, with its exaltation of reason and empiricist technique. At first, during the eighteenth and early nineteenth centuries, there was a firm marriage between characteristic ideas of the Enlightenment and the doctrines of the gospel. Both were spreading light and civilization.[22] The ideas of the age of reason were even read back by Evangelicals into the career of Calvin. Thus in 1809 John Mackenzie praised the reformer for being a dispassionate commentator: "Disavowing all authority but that of the Scriptures...his investigations were conducted [in a] spirit of free enquiry."[23] The same temper, however, as the example of Simeon has already illustrated, was unfriendly to inherited doctrinal systems such as Calvinism. "Make your own system," was the advice to candidates for the ministry regularly given by James Acworth, principal of the Baptists' Horton Academy, in the middle years of the century.[24] The effect was to make preachers in denominations with a Reformed tradition, even when wholly Evangelical in outlook, averse to proclaiming distinctive Calvinist doctrine. In Scotland, the United Presbyterians and the Free Church passed Declaratory Acts in 1879 and 1892 allowing divergence from the doctrinal position of the Westminster Assembly so long as there was no departure from the substance of the faith.[25] Gradually more liberal theological opinion was being tolerated, especially among Congregationalists, the new term for Independents. At the first International Congregational Council in 1891, when E. P. Goodwin, a Chicago preacher, called his coreligionists back to a Calvinist profession, there was a sharp reaction from Joseph Parker, the angular minister of the City Temple, where the meetings were being held. He must have his pulpit fumigated, declared Parker. "By this time Calvinism stinketh," he said, "for it hath been dead these two centuries."[26] It was not as lifeless as Parker suggested, but its vitality had been sapped by assumptions stemming from the Enlightenment.

Members of the Protestant denominations, in the fifth place, were propelled further in a liberal theological direction by the newer body of ideas associated with the Romantic cultural revolution. The fresh mood encouraged greater attention to history and so made Calvin and the Puritan inheritance more highly valued, but at the same time fostered a love of the natural, the imaginative, and the personal at the expense of received doctrinal views, especially Calvinism. Thomas Carlyle, the greatest Romantic prose writer of the age, epitomized the shift in sensibility, recommending moral earnestness as a replacement for sterile orthodoxy.[27] The Carlylean theme of heroism is apparent, for instance, in a study of the leaders of the Reformation by John Tulloch, a broad-minded Presbyterian theologian of the University of St. Andrews, first published in 1859 and revised in 1883. He praises "all the moral heroism in Puritanism" but contrasts Calvin unfavorably with Luther because, as an organizer rather than a man of action, he was less heroic. Calvin was like "a Doric column, chaste, grand, and sublime in the very simplicity and inflexibility of its mouldings"; Luther was like "a Gothic dome, with its fertile contrasts and ample space."[28] The taste of the age preferred the Gothic aesthetic, so that Calvin and his system seemed altogether too fixed and confined. In particular, the Romantic shift toward conceptualizing the Almighty as a benevolent Father often led to moral revulsion against Calvinism during the Victorian era. It was vigorously expressed in 1892 by an unusually liberal Baptist minister, Charles Aked. Like Tulloch, he was willing to admire the effects of Calvin's ideas in forging "grand, strong, and heroic servants of the living God," but the content of Calvin's teaching, what Aked called "the doctrine of the gloomy fanatic of Geneva," was no better than "the poison of the rattlesnake and the blood-lust of the tiger."[29] For Aked, original sin and predestination summed up the whole of Calvin's theology, and he hated it. Romantic attitudes, often carrying their exponents beyond the bounds of Evangelical belief, tended to corrode the Calvinist legacy further.

The result of these various factors was that Calvin did not occupy a prominent place in the memory of Evangelicals during the nineteenth century. Perhaps the most significant episode of homage to the reformer was the visit to Geneva in 1816–1817 by Robert Haldane, a doughty Scottish laird who had sponsored widespread itinerant evangelism in his homeland. Drawn by Romantic expectations of the city of Calvin and encountering a small group friendly to Evangelical religion, Haldane expounded there the epistle to the Romans and so sparked off the Réveil in Switzerland.[30] Few of Haldane's contemporaries shared his degree of enthusiasm for Calvin. Between 1800 and the 1830s, there were only six translations of works by the reformer published in Britain. By contrast, in the single decade of the 1840s there were as many as twenty-three.[31] The upsurge of interest was partly a symptom of the rising tide of historical concern associated with Romantic taste, but half the titles were the fruit of a particular venture, the Calvin Translation Society, which was founded in May 1843, the same month as the Disruption split the Church of Scotland.[32] The Evangelicals who left, forming the Free Church of Scotland, supported the publishing scheme because it promised to recruit the memory of the reformer to their cause. Thirteen works of the reformer were issued during the 1850s, ten of them by the Calvin Translation Society. When the society had fulfilled its ambition of publishing translations of most of Calvin's works, however, the demand for new titles fell away. Between 1860 and the end of the century there were only three.[33] At the midcentury peak of interest in the reformer, three biographies of Calvin were published in swift succession. One, a version of the German life by Paul Henry, pastor of the French Reformed congregation in Berlin, was, as its translator observed, marked by "profound admiration for Calvin"; the second, a translation of a Catholic work by Jean Marie Vincent Audin, was an exercise in outright denigration; the third, written by a sober Anglican, Thomas Dyer, provided, according to a reviewer, "a judicious and very readable summary" but claimed originality only for its coverage of Calvin's dealings with the Church of England.[34] No subsequent lives other than popular sketches were published during the century, for no scholar arose to pursue Calvin studies in depth. The Calvin Translation Society represented an isolated peak of interest in the reformer.

Hence there was much less scope for Calvin to mold the political role of Evangelicals than might be imagined. His attitudes that verged on public affairs were more a subject for debate than a spur to action. In one of the most widely circulated presentations of Calvin, the translation of the vivid unfinished account by the Genevan professor of church history J. H. Merle d'Aubigné, Calvin is depicted as a lover of liberty but also as a champion of order.[35] The central question for Evangelicals was whether the element of order had unduly repressed the element of liberty. John Kelly, an Independent advocate of Calvin, spoke for many when he contended that the reformer had exerted a profound influence "in the direction both of spiritual religion and civil liberty."[36] But that assessment was about the long-term effects of Calvinism. When it came to evaluating Calvin himself, there was much more criticism. The reformer had been wrong, declared

Tulloch, to expect the state to suppress vice; Calvin was equally wrong, according to an article in the journal of the interdenominational Evangelical Alliance in 1864, to expect the state to suppress heresy.[37] That observation raised the specter of Servetus. A succession of Unitarians challenged Evangelicals over the years, alleging that Calvin's responsibility for the execution of Servetus on the grounds of his antitrinitarianism revealed the dark implications of orthodoxy.[38] Defenses of Calvin's behavior in the affair varied. It was common to argue that the standards of his age differed from those of the more enlightened nineteenth century, that the policy was a carryover from popish persecution, or that Calvin was taking his virtue of concern for the truth to an unwarranted extreme.[39] One Strict Baptist admirer who wrote a popular biography in 1851 describing Calvin's "glorious doctrines" solved the problem by simply leaving out the execution of Servetus.[40] Others, however, did not wish to excuse the reformer. Henry Stebbing, the translator of Paul Henry's life of Calvin, deplored Henry's efforts at extenuation, and Thomas Dyer agreed.[41] Calvin therefore bore an ambiguous reputation in a land that prided itself on a long history of toleration. The intolerant reformer did not make an attractive political hero.

Calvin also suffered from the burden of association with republicanism. In America, the republican credentials added to his reputation, but in firmly monarchist Britain they did not. Merle d'Aubigné mused that the republican constitution of Geneva might have told against the appeal of his narrative, remarking delphically that his own preference was for monarchy.[42] English Evangelicals were all too aware that they were tainted in the popular mind by association with the Puritans, the Calvinists who had killed King Charles I. This was a particular problem for the Independents, who in the seventeenth century had numbered in their ranks Oliver Cromwell, the military leader of the revolution that had established a republic with himself as lord protector. In the earlier years of the nineteenth century their attitude to Cromwell was extremely reserved. Robert Vaughan, the leading historian among the Independents, treated Cromwell in a book of 1831 as a wily politician, given to "circuitousness and insincerity." Cromwell had injured religious Independency by identifying it with "revolution and republicanism."[43] In this phase, Calvin suffered from guilt by association with his seventeenth-century English disciple. There was, however, a transformation in the reputation of Cromwell in the 1840s. Thomas Carlyle presented the lord protector as an archetypal hero, publishing in 1845 an edition of his letters and speeches that enjoyed enormous sales.[44] In the wake of the altered perception of Cromwell, the Independents began to take pride in his allegiance to their denomination. In a book of 1863, Vaughan praised Cromwell's "signal service" and "transcendent capacity."[45] The lord protector turned into an idol not only of Cromwell's immediate coreligionists but of all the Nonconformists, the newer name in the Victorian period for the Dissenters. John Clifford, the Baptist minister who gave leadership to Nonconformity in public affairs around the close of the century, appealed repeatedly to Cromwell as an inspiration for campaigns in his own day.[46] The chief political Calvinist of the English past had been rehabilitated. It did not follow, however, that the political stock of Calvin himself rose in these years. Because Calvinism as a theological system was in such serious decay, Cromwell's new prestige did not rub off on his theological mentor. At this juncture, Cromwell, not Calvin, was the Nonconformists' political exemplar.

In consequence, nineteenth-century Evangelicals were rarely roused by Calvin or his teaching for the political fray. It has been supposed that the Clapham Sect, the group of largely Anglican Evangelicals led by William Wilberforce who were responsible in the early years of the century for campaigns against the slave trade and other social evils, had Calvinism as its inspiration.[47] That estimate is, however, mistaken. The second most active member of the parliamentary group was William Smith, a Dissenter who adopted Socinian views and so deplored Calvinist theology, and Wilberforce himself recorded that "every year that I live I become more impressed with the unscriptural character of the Calvinistic system."[48] On the other hand, the most outspoken Calvinists, Dissenters such as William Gadsby in Manchester and Joseph Irons in London, were undoubtedly champions of the urban poor in their day, but they drew no connection between their public activities and their distinguishing doctrines, let alone Calvin himself.[49] The Evangelical Nonconformists, who in the second half of the century became the shock troops of liberalism, included large denominations hostile to Calvinism and so, as a body, did not consider appealing to the memory of the reformer. Even Charles Haddon Spurgeon, a doughty Calvinist who was by common consent the greatest preacher of the age, did not make the link. Although the Baptist minister urged support for Liberal policies and candidates,[50] he did not see the Reformed faith as a sanction for participation in public affairs. It was only in Presbyterian Scotland that there were political applications of Calvinism. During the 1830s John Brown, a scholarly minister of the United Secession Church, elaborated his denomination's belief in the separation of church and state. Brown led a campaign for refusal of the annuity tax that was payable in Edinburgh to the established church. Quoting sixteenth- and seventeenth-century texts by Calvinist resistance theorists, he argued that Romans 13 did not require absolute obedience to the authorities. That would be to endorse "slavish principles."[51] The Free Church of Scotland, created in 1843, on the other hand, upheld in its early years the principle of establishment. "The civil magistrate is bound," according to William Cunningham, "to aim at the promotion of religion and the welfare of the church."[52] He saw that axiom as an outworking of Reformed doctrine. Around the middle years of the century, therefore, Scotland did generate Calvinist political perspectives, albeit contradicting each other about whether the state should grant recognition to the church. But an explicitly Reformed view of politics was limited to Scotland and Calvin himself was little, if ever, invoked as its inspiration.

If the memory of Calvin played only a marginal part in public affairs, there was an exception in the area of anti-Catholicism. Militant Protestantism had been bound up with national identity in England and Scotland alike during the sixteenth and seventeenth centuries, and in the eighteenth had been perhaps the strongest factor in uniting the two nations as Great Britain.[53] Hostility to Catholicism began to fade under the influence of the Enlightenment, but it was vigorously revived between the 1830s and the 1850s by circumstances in Catholic Ireland, by the Oxford Movement that seemed to point the Church of England in a Catholic direction, and especially by Evangelicals themselves, hostile to the claims of

Rome.[54] In this revival, the name of Calvin loomed much larger than in other contexts. The evaluation of Calvin by Samuel Dunn in 1837, for example, concludes that to him and his helpers in "the glorious cause of the reformation from Popery, we owe that Scripture light and liberty which we now enjoy."[55] Merle d'Aubigné sustained similar views in the next generation by his vigorous account of the Reformation as a conflict between truth and error with Calvin as "his hero."[56] So did homegrown authors. J. A. Wylie, a lecturer at the Protestant Institute in Edinburgh, published an oft-reprinted three-volume illustrated history of Protestantism in the 1870s that delighted in simple antitheses. Thus he contrasted Calvin's ascendancy in Geneva with the mediaeval authority of Pope Innocent III: "Calvin governed *by* God; Innocent governed *as* God."[57] In 1885 Thomas Lawson, the editor of the monthly magazine *The Protestant Echo*, published a popular life of Calvin designed for young people in which he spent a whole chapter fulminating against priests, the confessional, and absolution as making up "a great fraud."[58] Political Protestantism impinged in major ways on contemporary issues, playing, for instance, a large part in the mobilization of opposition to W. E. Gladstone's proposal of Home Rule for Ireland in 1886.[59] The reputation of Calvin as the great antagonist of the papacy contributed to public affairs.

The events of 1909, marking the quatercentenary of Calvin's birth, form a useful prism through which the developments in the reformer's image over the previous century can be viewed. H. R. Mackintosh, professor of systematic theology at New College, Edinburgh, went in July as a delegate to the international celebrations at Geneva, noting "Calvinistically," as he put it, that "the corruption of human nature came out in the unpardonable length of the speeches."[60] He reported that there was significant support from Britain, with representatives of Scotland, England, and the Welsh Calvinistic Methodists, who took pride in being alone among the world's denominations in calling themselves Calvinistic.[61] Yet in England, the degree of enthusiasm for the occasion was muted. Only the small Presbyterian Church of England organized a public meeting, at which the evident affection for Calvin of the visiting Dutch theologian Herman Bavinck contrasted with the reserve of the English Presbyterian Oswald Dykes, who "did not attempt to portray Calvin as a lovable or a gracious personality," but merely claimed in Carlylean fashion that the reformer's doctrines had "bred up a generation of heroes."[62] There was, it was admitted, "gross ignorance" about Calvin, even in Presbyterian communities.[63] A popular but solid biography published in time for the commemorations by C. H. Irwin illustrates why there was such neglect. Writing from the viewpoint that Calvinism and Arminianism could be reconciled, Irwin, like Dykes, praises the effects rather than the content of Calvin's theology. "His doctrines have their defects," he claims, "but they moulded men."[64] In Scotland, there was rather more effort to remember the reformer, with both local and national events being organized. The General Assemblies of the two main Presbyterian churches, the Church of Scotland and the United Free Church, combined to hold a celebration in St. Giles's Cathedral attended by the lord provost of Edinburgh and the councillors in their robes. It was a grand occasion, but it was as much an excuse to bring the churches together for the first time in "longing for reunion" as an expression of zeal for Calvin. Repeatedly in the commemorations, Calvin was put into the shade by

Knox, who loomed far larger in the Scottish memory.[65] The political significance of the reformer was not wholly forgotten, for the prayers at St. Giles included thanks for what Calvin did "towards establishing civil and religious freedom."[66] But the public role for which he was mostly remembered was expressed in a poem in the magazine of the Church of Scotland that celebrated his triumph over "Romish hate."[67] We may conclude that by the opening of the twentieth century Calvin was only weakly recalled, though more strongly in Scotland than in England. His disciples were more respected than the man himself, his theology seemed superseded, and his political significance, except as a champion against Catholicism, was minimal.

There was one individual, however, who stood apart from the prevailing tone of merely formal acknowledgement of Calvin during the 1909 commemorations. At the English Presbyterians' public meeting, an address by Charles Silvester Horne, the Congregational minister of the central London Whitefield's Tabernacle, "dwelt on the Calvinistic element in the Puritan period of English history."[68] Horne, though forty-four years old, retained the effervescence of youth and put his considerable scholarship into making the Reformed inheritance attractive. Although he was a historian, in the past he had not been an enthusiast for Calvin. Horne's *Popular History of the Free Churches* (1903) mentions the reformer only once, as an influence that retarded the development of church song in England.[69] But Horne had been asked to contribute to *Mansfield College Essays*, a volume that appeared in 1909 to mark the intellectual attainments of former members of the Nonconformist postgraduate college at the University of Oxford, and selected "Calvin in His Letters" as his theme. The writer set himself the task of doing for Calvin what Carlyle had done for Cromwell, restoring his subject's reputation. A nontraditional Calvin emerged, combining "great courtesy, chivalry, and kindliness of spirit." The essayist argued against received opinion that Calvin was on the side of liberty. The tight social discipline of Geneva, according to Horne, was merely a reflection of the practice of mediaeval cities; Calvin was not as extreme as his followers; his letters reveal him as human, flexible, a peacemaker. He was "one of the greatest men, and truest friends of freedom." Furthermore, possessing a "statesmanlike mind," Calvin, though a Christian minister, played a part in public affairs.[70] He had inspired, Horne declared at the public meeting, "an inquisitive, democratic, insubordinate spirit."[71] That clearly appealed to the speaker, who, as a leader of the Brotherhood movement that combined religion with progressive politics, was becoming eager to join the political fray himself. In the following year he was returned to Parliament as a Liberal, the first man to serve in the House of Commons while in pastoral charge.[72] The demands of the two roles proved too great a burden, leading to Horne's early death in 1914, but it is evident that a strongly favorable interpretation of Calvin helped propel this charismatic representative of the Evangelical Free Churches into public life. Silvester Horne was an exceptional figure.

In the earlier years of the twentieth century the attitude to Calvin in British society at large was harshly critical. There were lingering memories of Victorian sages such as J. A. Froude who had pronounced in favor of Calvin's influence over posterity, but the man himself, as Froude had said, was associated "only with gloom and austerity."[73] John Morley, a Liberal politician and man of letters, was unusual in praising Calvin, in his *Oliver Cromwell* (1900), for many of his qualities, yet also highlighted "his unbending will, his pride, his severity" and assumed his theology was a version of fatalism.[74] Ecclesiastical developments did not help. The current within the main churches was running forcefully in a high and broad direction, away from Evangelicalism and toward, in the Church of England, a dominant liberal Catholicism. Churchmen often made pronouncements hostile to Calvin and his teaching. Percy Dearmer, the editor of the two most popular Anglican hymnbooks of the period, asserted in 1924 that Calvinists worshiped a being who was "cruel beyond human words"; C. A. Alington, dean of Durham, published in 1937 an article in a daily newspaper headed "A Doctrine Which Breeds Atheism: Calvin's Travesty of Christianity."[75] Even in Scotland, the sense that Calvin had bequeathed an honorable legacy to the nation was fading. The Scottish literary renaissance around Hugh MacDiarmid regarded Calvinism as a blight on the land. Thus in 1933 Eric Linklater, a prolific author in this circle, declared in a radio broadcast that Scotland was "still crippled by Calvinism."[76] One of the most striking instances of this entrenched anti-Calvinism was an episode during the First World War. In March 1918, during the German offensive in northern France, Maurice Bowra, later to be a celebrated warden of Wadham College, Oxford, but then a callow artillery officer of nineteen, found himself on a hill above Noyon, where the enemy had occupied the cathedral. At first he felt qualms about firing on a historic building, but then he remembered that Noyon was the birthplace of Calvin. He immediately opened fire, feeling that "nothing could be too bad, even after some four centuries, for this enemy of the human race."[77] With this sort of prejudice entrenched in the intellectual elite, twentieth-century defenders of Calvin had an uphill task.

Within Evangelicalism, the earlier twentieth century was marked by a continuation of the earlier trend toward a more liberal theology. Mainstream churches were broadening the bounds of permissible doctrine, welcoming critical study of the Bible and forgetting the terrors of hell. The effects on the appreciation of Calvin were twofold. On the one hand he could be recast in a new image that molded him in accordance with the spirit of the age. Thus Hugh Reyburn, a young Scottish Presbyterian minister who was willing to approach a doctrine of universal salvation, published a full life of Calvin in 1914 that recognized the importance of the *Institutes* but in the end supposed that predestination should be seen only as an expression of evolution. "Darwin," he wrote in his last sentence, "unites with Calvin to guide us."[78] On the other hand, Calvin could be seen as superseded. "The dogmatism of the sixteenth century," declared a female member of the council of the Presbyterian Historical Society of England, "has been largely modified."[79] Hence, she contended, religious questions were approached in a different manner from in Calvin's day. Where such attitudes prevailed, the reformer was largely ignored. Émile Doumergue's seven-volume biography of Calvin, published in French between 1899 and 1927, was not translated into English at all. An essay on Calvin by Doumergue was translated in 1909, but it appeared in New York, not London.[80] When the home of the reformer was rebuilt after the wartime bombardment of Noyon, the United States gave nearly 10,000 francs and France almost 34,000. By contrast, Scotland gave only some 1,330 francs, together with a few pounds, and England gave as little as 140 francs and a handful of pounds.[81] The memory of the reformer was not salient in Britain among the most likely donors, people who had embraced a liberal form of Evangelicalism.

There was, however, a conservative reaction against the growth of theological liberalism, rather as in America there was a fundamentalist backlash against modernism. In Britain, the phenomenon was milder and consequently the polarization was less acute, but it might have been expected that the more conservative would turn to Calvin for inspiration. In general, however, that was not the case. The twin primary theological impulses on the conservative side, the premillennial hope of the imminent return of Jesus to earth and the holiness message of the availability of a higher Christian life, were not conducive to Calvinism. The Keswick movement, which constituted the backbone of conservative Evangelicalism in these years, was the main expression of holiness teaching in Britain and its platforms welcomed the message of the premillennial advent. It is true that Evan Hopkins, the guarding theologian of Keswick, insisted that its teaching must remain compatible with the core of Reformed doctrine, but the central emphasis on sanctification by faith diverged from traditional Calvinist insistence that growth in grace required struggle.[82] A staunch Calvinist attended the Keswick convention in 1930 solely in order to distribute hundreds of pamphlets entitled *Keswick Teaching—Weighed in the Balance and Found Wanting*.[83] Consequently authentic upholders of Reformed teaching often felt isolated. A student in a Welsh theological college reported that "I am looked down upon because I believe and maintain that Calvin was right." Most of his contemporaries, he said, acknowledged that Calvin was a man of God, but they thought the reformer too extreme; some supposed that Calvin taught pagan ideas; and even the strongest fundamentalist in the college would not accept the doctrine of election. His friends gave the student the nickname "Calvin."[84] The prevailing ethos on the conservative wing of Evangelicalism was unfriendly to full-blooded Calvinism.

There was, nevertheless, a small organization in interwar Britain that championed the Calvinist cause, the Sovereign Grace Union. Its beleaguered mentality is brought out by its aims: "to reaffirm the old truths in these days of apostacy [*sic*] and declension" and "to raise a Testimony against Romanism, Ritualism, Rationalism, Arminianism and other evils in religion."[85] The energetic general secretary from the foundation of the union in 1914 to 1931 was Henry Atherton, minister of Grove Chapel, Camberwell, an Independent congregation in south London, but its main support came from Strict Baptists and the most conservative of Anglican churches. Much of its activity consisted in holding lectures up and down the country, often on historical themes. It might be expected that Calvin would figure large in the union's program, but that was not the case. The strong preference was for topics from English history, such as Oliver Cromwell or the Glorious Revolution of 1688. A sixpenny tract on the life of Calvin written by Thomas Lawson, the anti-Catholic biographer of the reformer in the previous century, was on sale by the union in 1918 but soon went out of print and was not reissued.[86] In a 1923 lecture on "The Invincible Reformation," Atherton talked in general terms about Calvin's theological priorities, but the purpose of the speech is apparent from its description as "a stirring Protestant address."[87] The Sovereign Grace Union was one of the network of small organizations that existed during the period to denounce Rome and resist the advance of Anglo-Catholicism in the Church of England. They complained that ritualistic clergy were imitating Roman Catholic practices, such as the reservation of the sacrament, and so undermining the Protestant character of the established church. The threat was as much to national identity as to doctrinal rectitude, and so the reaction often had a political edge. Hence the leaders of the union, including Atherton, were commonly associated with the Orange Order, an organization with Irish roots designed to oppose the public influence of Roman Catholicism.[88] So the union illustrates that Calvinism still had its chief political expression in anti-Catholicism.

In the 1930s, however, the Sovereign Grace Union changed. It became caught up in a Dutch initiative in 1929 to form an International Calvinistic Federation. Atherton responded, leading a tour of the Netherlands that opened his eyes to the possibilities of a Calvinist culture. He was amazed by the numbers flocking to the congregations of the *Gereformeerde* church and by the power of the Calvinist political party founded by Abraham Kuyper. Burgomasters were not ashamed to be called Calvinists and "even on a crowded railway station would not hesitate to speak quite openly of the doctrines of Free Grace."[89] Atherton went on to organize an international Calvinist conference in London in May 1932, with representatives from the Netherlands, Germany, France, Ireland, and South Africa.[90] Several, such as the French Calvin scholar and right-wing activist Auguste Lecerf, were men of weight, and the international federation founded in 1932 was to prove a significant body. Its second conference, held in Amsterdam two years later, attracted the Dutch prime minister, Hendrik Colijn, and the third and fourth, in Geneva in 1936 and Edinburgh in 1938, offered a variety of capable papers. The effects on British Calvinism, as represented by the Sovereign Grace Union, were striking. Calvin himself came into much greater prominence. It was symptomatic that a small Calvin plaque designed in the Netherlands for home display was put on sale.[91] In 1936, the union advertised an edition of Calvin's sermons published in Germany.[92] At the same time, the standard of scholarship in the union rose sharply. Its magazine editor, S. Leigh Hunt, who had once been a candidate for the Catholic priesthood, published perceptive articles on Calvin and Calvinism, eventually acknowledging, in this staunch anti-Catholic periodical, the reformer's honor of the Virgin Mary.[93] Scottish churchmen were drawn in to give solid papers on dogmatics, ecclesiology, and even economics.[94] Calvinism was now seen, in Kuyperian fashion, as a worldview and not just a theology. Kuyper's Stone Lectures of 1898, previously little known in Britain, were circulated.[95] Consequently there was some embryonic formulation of Calvinist political principles, leading, for example, in the magazine to an incidental repudiation of pacifism at the height of its popularity in Britain.[96] In the 1930s, a section of British Calvinism was drawn into the international Calvin revival.

The fullest exponent of the political theory of this phase was Donald Maclean, professor of church history for the Free Church of Scotland and president of the Sovereign Grace Union from 1935.[97] Maclean often represented the Free Church at the general synods of the *Gereformeerde* churches in the Netherlands, developing an admiration for the achievements of their members in public life.[98] In 1927, he was invited to give the first series of Calvin Lectures at the Free University of Amsterdam on aspects of Scottish church history. "Calvin," he contended, "without ever setting foot on Scottish soil, contributed more than any other person to the formation of Scottish character."[99] Maclean set out the political implications of this thesis in a related set of lectures at the Free Church College later in the year. Sovereignty on Calvin's principles, he insisted, derives from the Almighty. The king, therefore, receives authority from above, but the people, who are his equals as priests before God, can challenge his commands whenever he promotes ungodliness or tyranny. In those circumstances, the monarch rather than the people is the revolutionary agent, subverting true principles of civil government. Hence, unlike the French Revolution, the Glorious Revolution of 1688 against a Catholic tyrant in Britain was a legitimate conservative response by the people. Scotland was as opposed as Kuyper's Dutch Anti-Revolutionary Party to "mob rule, violent revolt and uncontrollable anarchy."[100] Eleven years later, in 1938, Maclean elaborated his theme, applying it to contemporary circumstances. The Continent had been torn by irrational revolutions, and the dictators who behaved like the absolutist rulers of seventeenth-century Scotland had to be resisted. The remedy was to be found in the revival of the Reformed faith and its application, on the Dutch model, to all departments of life.[101] As the editor of *The Evangelical Quarterly,* a journal circulating in Reformed circles worldwide, Maclean was already trying to propagate that vision. The Second World War, however, extinguished it. Maclean died before the war was over, and he had no successor as an intellectual intermediary between the Netherlands and his own land. Maclean's was the most remarkable expression of political Calvinism in Britain during the twentieth century.

There was nevertheless a very different instance of the application of Calvinism to public affairs in the interwar years. The two major Presbyterian churches of Scotland wished to merge, but there was a problem because, though they shared allegiance to the same confessional documents, they had different relationships to the state. The Church of Scotland was the established church of the nation, enjoying privileges and responsibilities in areas such as the justice system; the United Free Church, on the other hand, had no such involvement, and some of its members were opposed on principle to the state connection. The resolution of the difficulty was found in an appeal to the principle of "spiritual independence." The notion meant that the church and the state should give recognition and assistance to each other, but that the church should remain immune to state interference within its own bounds. "Spiritual independence" arose chiefly from the debates preceding the Disruption of the nineteenth century, but it was read back into earlier Scottish history, and, to clinch the case, it was attributed to Calvin himself. Thus Alexander Smellie, in an able study of the Reformation in 1925, claimed that Calvin espoused the principle in opposition to the Erastians among the magistrates of Geneva. The reformer's attitude to church and state, according to Smellie, was that "each has its sphere and each is under obligation to Christ."[102] David Cairns, principal of the United Free Church College at Aberdeen, writing in the same year, argued that Calvin endorsed the Old Testament view that nations are responsible to God. The reformer was notably original, however, in drawing from the New Testament the principle of spiritual independence. That perception, according to Cairns, allowed a blending of national religion and ecclesiastical freedom.[103] The "articles declaratory" of a united Scottish church, formulated in 1921 and embodied in legislation in 1929, followed this pattern.[104] The principle of spiritual independence, allegedly derived from Calvin, was incorporated in the constitutional arrangements of Great Britain.

There were comparable efforts to appropriate Calvin for other causes. During the earlier years of the century, some depicted the reformer as a church leader who wanted to relate the Christian faith to social questions. "Calvin," declared a bold English Presbyterian minister in 1930, "was an exponent of what to-day is sometimes called the 'social Gospel.'"[105] In the 1930s, however, when there was a reaction against dwelling on the social implications of the faith, Calvin was represented as an opponent of this approach. In 1938, G. T. Thomson of Edinburgh condemned the social gospel as a handicap to effective Protestantism and saw Calvinism as standing instead for "true doctrine."[106] In a similar way the role of Calvin was a factor in contemporary economic debate. In a scholarly study of Calvinism published just after the opening of the Second World War, Arthur Dakin, president of Bristol Baptist College, argued that the reformer had stood for self-denial, hard work, and private property. Dakin was less sure that Calvin's sanction extended to capitalism, at least in its recent forms.[107] Others were even more wary of making this connection. In the atmosphere of the period, when staple industries were collapsing and the Labour Party was mounting a powerful critique of traditional free enterprise, it seemed unwise to bind Calvinism to the contemporary economic system. When Dean Inge, a right-wing clergyman outside the ranks of Evangelicalism, claimed in 1924 that "John Calvin is the spiritual father of the modern business man," the journal of the Sovereign Grace Union tried to distance the reformer from modern industrial conditions.[108] There was similar reserve over the contention of the German sociologist Max Weber that Calvinism had been responsible for the emergence of capitalism. In 1927, Donald Maclean used the recent researches of the historian R. H. Tawney to show that Weber's case was one-sided.[109] Similarly, the Scottish church historian J. H. S. Burleigh spent the whole of his 1938 paper on "Calvinism and Economics" at the Calvinist congress in Edinburgh arguing that capitalism was older than the Reformation and so Calvinism could not have generated its defects.[110] In an ideological age there was often more effort to secure praise or avoid blame for Calvin than to discover his actual views.

There also developed a powerful association between Calvin and modern liberal democracy. This attitude was shared by all who looked on Calvin with any degree of sympathy. C. H. Irwin ended his biography of 1909 with the rhetorical claim, not based on previous reasoning, that to the nations influenced by it, the reformer's teaching had brought "the priceless boon of civil and religious liberty."[111] The conclusion was the more surprising since Irwin had earlier admitted that Calvin's civil legislation at Geneva had overlooked individual liberty and had spent a chapter wrestling with the perennial problem of the reformer's responsibility for the execution of Servetus.[112] The claim was, therefore, based not on Calvin's life but on his legacy. The common perception of his subsequent influence was summarized in the following year by James Orr, a prolific theologian of the United Free Church, in an article on "Calvinism" in the widely used *Encyclopaedia of Religion and Ethics*, edited by James Hastings. Calvin's system, he declared, "became the soul of Puritanism in England, of Republicanism in Holland, of the Covenanting struggle in Scotland, of democratic institutions in America, identifying itself in every land to which it went with the undying principles of civil freedom."[113] The movements he named had all championed liberty in their nation-building efforts. Calvin himself had to be twisted in the popular memory to fit this paradigm. Thus A. M. Hunter, a young Scottish minister writing in 1920, conceded that Calvin might be aristocratic in sympathies and autocratic in behavior, but he was "democratic in his fundamental convictions."[114] The democratic credentials of Calvinism became a major theme of the twentieth century. Calvinists, according to Dakin in 1940, had been driven by persecution to more explicitly democratic theories, but the seeds had already been sown in their church order, which was based on "the rights of the individual." The legacy of Calvin could, therefore, contribute rights, freedom, and democracy to "the urgent task of creating a truly Christian civilization" after the Second World War.[115] Calvin was almost a recruit to the war effort.

Even before the Second World War, however, the theological climate had begun to change. Two movements in the mainstream British churches shifted thinking toward greater sympathy for Calvin. The first was the electrifying message of Karl Barth about the radical transcendence of God, which was initially articulated in Britain in 1930 by J. E. Daniel, a young Welsh Independent theologian.[116] By 1938, Maclean was able to note that several theological chairs in Scottish universities were occupied by Barthians.[117] The central figure was Thomas Torrance, a professor at Edinburgh only from 1950 but, having personally studied under Barth, already a force in Scottish theology a decade before.[118] Torrance believed that Calvinism had been damaged by hardening into a system, and so he turned attention back to the reformer himself: "In John Calvin the Reformed Church has had a theologian, with magnitude in mind and depth in understanding, second to none in the history of the Christian Church."[119] Torrance took the lead in creating a much warmer Scottish Presbyterian appreciation of Calvin during the later twentieth century. The second movement was a reaction against theological liberalism within Congregationalism that earned the label "Genevan" because of its enthusiasm for Calvin. In December 1936, J. S. Whale, president of Cheshunt College, Cambridge, delivered a lecture on the reformer praising his personal religion, "rooted in faith in divine sovereignty and predestinating grace."[120] In the following month, Nathaniel Micklem, principal of Mansfield College, Oxford, published an article on "The Genevan Inheritance of Protestant Dissent—The Present Need to Affirm It."[121] This was a movement of intellectuals swayed by the Anglican ethos of the ancient English universities. Their assertion was that Calvin was an embodiment of Catholic tradition. Whale's *Christian Doctrine* (1941) called the reformer "the Cyprian of the XVIth century"; Micklem pointed out that the *Institutes* were a commentary on the Apostles' Creed.[122] The next generation of Congregational ministers was deeply swayed by this higher estimate of Calvin. The turn away from a broader theology in circles where liberal Evangelicalism had prevailed meant that in the postwar era Calvin was restored to a place among the great theologians.

The most resolutely Calvinist movement, however, was among conservative Evangelicals. The pivotal figure was Martyn Lloyd-Jones, a Welsh Calvinistic Methodist who, partly under the influence of Donald Maclean, gradually came to adopt an explicitly Reformed theology. From 1938 Lloyd-Jones was assistant and from 1943 the minister at Westminster Chapel, where he exercised a powerful preaching ministry at the heart of London. Although he was aware of Continental forms of Calvinism, attending a 1948 conference in Amsterdam on "Calvin and the Modern Mind,"[123] his own style was molded by the Puritans of England and Wales. Lloyd-Jones praised Calvin as a preacher and arranged for the republication of the *Institutes*,[124] but his ambition was to use Puritan teaching to kindle a fresh revival like the one that had swept Wales in the eighteenth century. Calvinism must not degenerate into dry doctrinal teaching divorced from Christian experience or remote from scripture. "Calvin's main feature," Lloyd-Jones wrote, "is that he bases everything on the Bible."[125] From 1950, the Welshman presided at an annual Puritan Conference at his chapel that grew by the 1960s into a gathering of some 350, mostly of a younger generation.[126] It was the focus of a developing resurgence of Calvinist teaching in British Evangelicalism. There were also an Evangelical Library designed to sow "the seeds of a fresh Awakening to-day,"[127] the *Banner of Truth* magazine founded in 1955 by Iain Murray, Lloyd-Jones's assistant at Westminster Chapel, together with its associated publishing house, the Banner of Truth Trust,[128] and the predominantly Calvinistic Evangelical Movement of Wales, launched in 1948.[129] The organizer of the Puritan conferences was J. I. Packer, a young Anglican who was to become an influential theologian. In 1964, the four hundredth anniversary of Calvin's death, Packer arranged that the papers should be devoted to aspects of the reformer. In a highly accessible account of Calvin's significance for the times, Packer suggested that the integrating concept of his theology was the "Knowledge of God."[130] Packer was to choose "Knowing God" as the title of a subsequent book that was to prove one of the most popular texts in global Evangelicalism.[131] The Calvinistic revival associated with Lloyd-Jones and Packer was one with wide appeal.

The resurgence of Calvinist teaching was initially concerned with churchly issues, but in due course it also became associated with Christian sociopolitical engagement. In the era when conservative Evangelicalism had been dominated by the Keswick message of holiness, withdrawal from the world to preserve the believer's purity had been a common theme. As the Keswick hegemony waned in the 1960s, however, there was a fresh impetus toward involvement with the problems of the world. The seedbed for the change was the Inter-Varsity Fellowship (IVF) of Christian Unions, a network of conservative Evangelical societies in the universities and colleges of Britain. In 1964, one of the most active figures in the IVF, Fred Catherwood, the son-in-law of Martyn Lloyd-Jones, published *The Christian in Industrial Society*, a pioneering discussion of the weekday responsibilities of the contemporary believer. While not directly appealing to Calvin, the book was undergirded by a Reformed theology and showed great respect for the "Protestant ethic."[132] The general secretary of the IVF, Oliver Barclay, who tried to read through the *Institutes* annually, published in 1970 an appeal for Christians to claim the world as God's.[133] The authoritative Evangelical perspective on social questions emerged in 1984 with *Issues Facing Christians Today* by John Stott, the most prominent leader of Evangelical Anglicans in England: "Now we are convinced," he explained, "that God has given us social as well as evangelistic responsibilities in his world."[134] Stott did not parade a Calvinist allegiance, but others were more prepared to avow a Reformed stance. Alan Storkey, a sociologist who in 1969 launched the Shaftesbury Project on the fringe of the IVF in order to encourage Christian social thought and action, was influenced by the Dutch Reformed thinking of Herman Dooyeweerd.[135] There was a Christian Studies Unit dedicated to the propagation of the perspective of Kuyper and Dooyeweerd.[136] Storkey stood several times as a parliamentary candidate for a Christian party, but the influence of these developments on public affairs was generally through more established channels. Catherwood, for instance, became a Member of Parliament and then Member of the European Parliament as a Conservative.[137] But Evangelicals, let alone the Calvinists among them, did not become a significant force in political life. Evangelicalism itself was transformed far more than British politics.

Meanwhile in the later twentieth century, Evangelical scholarship on Calvin showed a broader appreciation of his role. With the relaxation of interconfessional tension in the wake of the Second Vatican Council, Calvin was no longer seen primarily as a standard-bearer of Protestantism. T. H. L. Parker, an Anglican High Church clergyman who had been introduced to the study of Calvin by J. S. Whale,[138] wrote a series of studies on the reformer between 1947 and 1995 including a new standard biography in 1975. Calvin, he contended, was not just a reformer but also a doctor of the universal church.[139] Likewise, in a 1984 article, Paul Helm, an academic philosopher of Reformed convictions, depicted Calvin's mind as strongly formed by late mediaeval theology.[140] The theologian Alister McGrath also insisted in 1987 on Calvin's "remarkable continuity with the leading features of academic Augustinianism characteristic of the late mediaeval period."[141] There no longer seemed a need to stress the break of the Reformation. The old role of Calvin as a sanction for anti-Catholic political campaigning had disappeared. Instead Calvin was depicted more neutrally, by Parker, for instance, as a conservative whose ideas were turned into revolutionary channels.[142] The anti-Catholic Calvin had been deployed in order to reinforce a Protestant national identity, but from the 1960s that too had vanished.[143] Calvin was, therefore, disengaged from his role in molding individuals in the British past. In a biography of Calvin published in 1990, McGrath, with academic detachment, presented the reformer as a major figure in the history of the world. In an extensive discussion of the Weber thesis, McGrath, while inconclusive, leans toward seeing Calvinism as favoring capitalism. There was no longer, after a decade of the ascendancy of free market principles under Margaret Thatcher, any reason to deny the connection for apologetic reasons. But McGrath makes greater claims, considering Calvinism to have promoted artistic creativity and scientific research, as well as human rights: "If any religious movement of the sixteenth century was world-affirming, it was Calvinism."[144] Calvin was no longer seen through the prism of earlier British history, but as a shaper of the whole of Western culture.

By the last years of the twentieth century the legacy of Calvin in British life was relatively small. The chief reason was the decline of the churches over the previous century, a process that accelerated from the 1960s. United Kingdom church membership had fallen from roughly 33 percent of the population in 1900 to a mere 12 percent in 1999.[145] Attendance was even worse, with only some 7.5 percent of the population of England and 11 per cent of the population of Scotland at worship on a given Sunday at the end of the century. Only approximately a third of the attendees in each country were Evangelicals.[146] In England, no survey identified the proportion who were Calvinists, but in Scotland, about a third of the Evangelicals attended congregations that described themselves as "Reformed."[147] Only a tiny proportion, therefore, looked to the tradition stemming from Calvin for their Christian sustenance. Nevertheless, the tradition had not been extinguished. On two occasions, in 1968 and 1983, the Church of Scotland had declined to alter its formal adhesion to the confessional statements of the Westminster Assembly.[148] Some ministers of the Scottish Church, such as James Philip of Holyrood Abbey Church, were distinguished exponents of Reformed teaching.[149] In Wales, the Evangelical Movement guarded its inheritance from Martyn Lloyd-Jones, while in England several smaller denominations such as the Grace Baptists cherished a Calvinist position. In the Church of England, a movement called Reform began in 1993, aiming to make the institutions of the established church more suited to effective evangelism. It was rarely assertive about Calvinism, but its corporate allegiance was to the theological position of J. I. Packer.[150] One of its most vigorous congregations, Jesmond Parish Church in Newcastle-upon-Tyne, was associated with a Christian Institute designed to exert "Christian influence in a secular world" by briefing its supporters nationwide on public issues.[151] Political action, however, was not the aim of any of these Calvinist groupings, which saw defense and propagation of the faith as their priorities. As in earlier periods, the political impact of Calvinism was marginal.

The memory of John Calvin among British Evangelicals was not, therefore, as potent as might be imagined. In the nineteenth century his image was dimmed by a form of moderate Calvinism, by the tendency of British Evangelicals to prefer their own heroes, and by the total repudiation of his thought in many quarters. The advance of theological liberalism arising from the Enlightenment and Romanticism pushed Calvin further into the background. Only around midcentury was there a temporary upsurge of interest in the reformer. His political potential was limited by his reputation for intolerant policies and his identification with republican revolution. Consequently, in general, he did not function as an inspiration for political movements, the one significant exception being the fervent anti-Catholicism that ran through much of British life. In both centuries, it was in Scotland, with its Presbyterian dominance, that Calvin loomed largest, being invoked by the early Free Church of Scotland, by all the Presbyterians in 1909, by Donald Maclean in the interwar years, and by the architects of the Scottish settlement between church and state in 1929. Despite Silvester Horne's advocacy, an aversion to Calvin was widespread during the twentieth century and, in general, neither liberal nor conservative Evangelicals were attracted to him. The Sovereign Grace Union, however, rose from obscurity in the 1920s to become a partner in the international Calvin revival of the 1930s. In these years, Calvin was appropriated for various sociopolitical causes, especially the defense of liberal democracy against dictatorship. The endorsement of Calvin by Barthians and Genevans from the 1930s gave him more favorable treatment, but most crucial was the adoption of his teaching by Martyn Lloyd-Jones, J. I. Packer, and their circle, a recovery that gave rise to a number of sociopolitical ripples in the 1960s and afterward. Scholarship on Calvin no longer saw him as a patron for anti-Catholic campaigns but as a more significant actor on the world stage. Although in a land of declining church attendance Calvin had little salience by the end of the century, there were still groups that, while not regarding him as a political example, firmly upheld his theology. That was the prevailing pattern throughout the period. Calvin was not a major personality, his doctrinal position was shared by some but not all Evangelicals, and he inspired relatively little political activity. The situation was therefore very different from that in the Netherlands, Hungary, or even the United States, where Calvin came to be treated by a section of the population as a political icon.[152] During the 1909 Calvin celebration in London an English Presbyterian leader, Monro Gibson, remarked that many thought of the reformer as "a somewhat unlettered and bigoted Scotsman."[153] The remark, though made in jest, illustrates the distance between most Evangelicals in Britain and an understanding of John Calvin.

■ Notes

1. Patrick Collinson, *The Religion of Protestants: The Church in English Society,* 1559–1625 (Oxford: Clarendon Press, 1982).

2. Michael R. Watts, *The Dissenters from the Reformation to the French Revolution* (Oxford: Clarendon Press, 1978).

3. Margo Todd, *The Culture of Protestantism in Early Modern Scotland* (New Haven: Yale University Press, 2002).

4. Alexander Thomson, *John Calvin: The Man and the Doctrine: A Tercentenary Memorial* (London: Jackson, Walford and Hodder, 1864), 5.

5. David W. Bebbington, "The Reputation of Edwards Abroad," in *The Cambridge Companion to Jonathan Edwards*, ed. Stephen J. Stein (Cambridge: Cambridge University Press, 2007), 246–50.

6. S., "On Names of Religious Distinction," *Evangelical Magazine*, March 1809, 101.

7. John Mackenzie, *Memoirs of the Life and Writings of John Calvin* (London: Williams and Smith, 1809), x, xiii, 246–49.

8. Thomson, *Calvin*, 34.

9. "On Exhortations to Unconverted Sinners," *Evangelical Magazine*, November 1814, 424.

10. Daniel Wilson, *Letters from an Absent Brother*, 2 vols., 3rd ed. (London: G. Wilson), 1: 291, quoted by James Rigney, "John Calvin and English Travellers in Geneva," in *Sober, Strict, and Scriptural: Collective Memories of John Calvin, 1800–2000*, ed. Johan de Niet, Herman Paul, and Bart Wallet (Leiden: Brill, 2009), 329.

11. John C. Ryle, *Light from Old Times* (London: W. Hunt, 1891).

12. Quoted by Jean Henri Merle d'Aubigné, *History of the Reformation in the Time of Calvin*, 8 vols. (London: Longman, Green, Longman, Roberts, & Green, 1863–78), 3: ix.

13. James S. Candlish, "John Calvin," in *The Evangelical Succession: A Course of Lectures Delivered in St. George's Free Church, Edinburgh*, 2nd series (Edinburgh: Macniven & Wallace, 1885), 18.

14. John Kelly, *John Calvin* (Liverpool: R. Smith, n.d.), 24.

15. Samuel Dunn, *Christian Theology: By John Calvin* (London: Tegg and Son, 1837).

16. William B. Pope, *A Compendium of Christian Theology*, 3 vols., 2nd ed. (London: Wesleyan Methodist Book Room, 1880), 2: 352.

17. Edward Smyth, *St. Paul or Calvin; or, A Full Exposition and Elucidation of the Ninth Chapter of His Epistle to the Romans: Whereby the False Glosses of the Calvinists, on That Particular Portion of Scripture, Are Clearly Refuted* (London: W. Baynes, 1809), xxxii.

18. Andrew M. Fairbairn, "Calvin and the Reformed Church," in *The Cambridge Modern History*, vol. 2, ed. Adolphus W. Ward (Cambridge: Cambridge University Press, 1903), 365.

19. Grayson M. Ditchfield, "Sir George Pretyman Tomline," *The Oxford Dictionary of National Biography*, http://www.oxforddnb.com/view/article/27520.

20. John Calvin, *Institutes of the Christian Religion*, 3 vols., trans. John Allen (London: John Walker, 1813), 1: xi.

21. Edward William Carus, ed., *Memoirs of the Life of the Rev. Charles Simeon, M. A.*, 2nd ed. (London: J. Hatchard & Son, 1847), 566.

22. David W. Bebbington, "Revival and Enlightenment in Eighteenth-Century England," in *On Revival: A Critical Examination*, ed. Andrew Walker and Kristin Aune (Carlisle: Paternoster, 2003), 71–85.

23. Mackenzie, *Memoirs*, 178.

24. William Medley, *Rawdon Baptist College: Centenary Memorial* (London: Kingsgate Press, 1904), 26.

25. Alexander C. Cheyne, *The Transforming of the Kirk: Victorian Scotland's Religious Revolution* (Edinburgh: Saint Andrew Press, 1983), ch. 3.

26. *Peace and Truth* [hereafter *P&T*], January 1937, 3.

27. Mark Hopkins, *Nonconformity's Romantic Generation: Evangelical and Liberal Theologies in Victorian England* (Milton Keynes: Paternoster, 2004), esp. 249–50.

28. John Tulloch, *Luther and Other Leaders of the Reformation*, 3rd ed. (Edinburgh: William Blackwood and Sons, 1883), 264, 177, 237.

29. Charles F. Aked, *Calvin and Calvinism* (London: James Clarke, 1891), 18, 11, 7.

30. Timothy C. F. Stunt, *From Awakening to Secession: Radical Evangelicals in Switzerland and Britain, 1815–35* (Edinburgh: T. & T. Clark, 2000), 31–37.

31. Alfred Erichson, ed., *Bibliographia Calviniana*, 3rd impression (Nieuwkoop: B. de Graaf, 1965).

32. Including John Calvin, *Institutes of the Christian Religion*, trans. Henry Beveridge, 3 vols. (Edinburgh: Calvin Translation Society, 1845), 1: ii.

33. These and following statistics based on: Erichson, *Bibliographia Calviniana*, 58-67.

34. Henry Stebbing, trans., preface to *The Life and Times of John Calvin, the Great Reformer*, by Paul Henry (London: Whittaker, 1849), vi; cf. anon. rev., *Quarterly Review*, March 1851, 533; Thomas H. Dyer, *The Life of John Calvin* (London: John Murray, 1850), viii.

35. Merle d'Aubigné, *Reformation*, 1: x–xi.

36. Kelly, *Calvin*, 25.

37. Tulloch, *Luther*, 13; *Evangelical Christendom*, June 1864, 268.

38. Richard Wright, *An Apology for Dr. Michael Servetus* (Wisbech: F. B. Wright, 1806); Edward Tagart, *Sketches of the Lives and Characters of the Leading Reformers of the Sixteenth Century* (London: John Green, 1843), 37; Robert Willis, *Servetus and Calvin: A Study of an Important Epoch in the Early History of the Reformation* (London: Henry S. King, 1877).

39. Mackenzie, *Memoirs*, offers all three: 91, 92, 144.

40. Charles W. Banks, *The Life and Times of John Calvin; with an Earnest Appeal for the Adoption of Open-Air Preaching* (London: Houlston & Stoneman, 1851).

41. Stebbing, preface to Henry, *Life and Times*, vi; Dyer, *Life of John Calvin*, 536.

42. Merle d'Aubigné, *Reformation*, 3: xiv.

43. Robert Vaughan, *Memorials of the Stuart Dynasty*, 2 vols. (London: Houldsworth and Ball, 1831), 2: 263, 260.

44. Blair Worden, "The Victorians and Oliver Cromwell," in *History, Religion and Culture: British Intellectual History, 1750–1950*, ed. Stefan Collini, Richard Whatmore, and Brian Young (Cambridge: Cambridge University Press, 2001), 112–35.

45. Robert Vaughan, *Revolutions in English History*, 3 vols. (London: John W. Parker, 1859–63), 3: 395.

46. David W. Bebbington, *The Nonconformist Conscience: Chapel and Politics, 1870–1914* (London: George Allen & Unwin, 1982), 145.

47. William T. Whitley, *Calvinism and Evangelism in England* (London: Kingsgate Press, 1933), 12.

48. Robert I. Wilberforce and Samuel Wilberforce, *The Life of William Wilberforce*, 5 vols. (London: J. Murray, 1838), 5: 162.

49. Ian J. Shaw, *High Calvinists in Action: Calvinism and the City: Manchester and London, c. 1810–1860* (Oxford: Oxford University Press, 2002).

50. David W. Bebbington, "Spurgeon and the Common Man," *Baptist Review of Theology* 5 (1995): 71–72.

51. John Brown, *The Law of Christ Respecting Civil Obedience, Especially in the Payment of Tribute*, 3rd ed. (London: William Ball, 1839), 51, n., 65, n., 83, n., ix.

52. William Cunningham, *Discussions on Church Principles* (Edinburgh: T. and T. Clark, 1863), 209.

53. Linda Colley, *Britons: Forging the Nation: 1707–1837* (New Haven: Yale University Press, 1992), ch. 1.

54. John R. Wolffe, *The Protestant Crusade in Great Britain, 1829–1860* (Oxford: Clarendon Press, 1991).

55. Dunn, *Christian Theology*, 74.

56. Merle d'Aubigné, *Reformation*, 6: vii.

57. James A. Wylie, *The History of Protestantism*, 3 vols. (London: Cassell, n.d.), 1: 347.

58. Thomas Lawson, *The Life of John Calvin* (London: W. Wileman, 1885), ch. 5.

59. Bebbington, *The Nonconformist Conscience*, 89–93.

60. Hugh R. M[ackintosh], "Calvin's Quatercentenary," *British Weekly*, July 8, 1909, 332.

61. Hugh R. M[ackintosh], "The Geneva Celebrations," *British Weekly*, July 15, 1909, 347, 349.

62. *British Weekly*, May 13, 1909, 129.

63. *Quarterly Register of the Alliance of the Reformed and Presbyterian Churches throughout the World*, May 1909, 224.

64. Clarke H. Irwin, *John Calvin: The Man and his Work*, 2nd ed. (London: Religious Tract Society, 1909), 157.

65. *British Weekly*, July 15, 1909, 347, 349.

66. Lady Frances Balfour, "John Calvin," *British Weekly*, May 27, 1909, 188.

67. Lauchlan MacLean Watt, "Calvin," *Life and Work*, July 1909, 165.

68. *Quarterly Register*, August 1909, 248.

69. Charles Silvester Horne, *A Popular History of the Free Churches* (London: James Clark, 1903), 249.

70. Charles Silvester Horne, "Calvin in His Letters," in R. K. Evans, ed., *Mansfield College Essays* (London: Hodder and Stoughton, 1909), 11, 20, 15.

71. *British Weekly*, May 13, 1909, 129.

72. William B. Selbie, *The Life of Charles Silvester Horne, M. A., M. P.* (London: Hodder and Stoughton, 1920).

73. James A. Froude, *Calvinism* (London: Longmans, Green, 1871), 53.

74. John Morley, *Oliver Cromwell* (London: Macmillan, 1900), 48, 51.

75. Quoted in *P&T*, April 1925, 37; July 1937, 74.

76. Quoted in *P&T*, January 1934, 13.

77. Cecil Maurice Bowra, *Memories: 1898–1939* (London: Weidenfeld and Nicolson, 1966), 83.

78. Hugh Y. Reyburn, *John Calvin: His Life, Letters and Work* (London: Hodder & Stoughton, 1914), 371.

79. Mrs W. W. D. Campbell [M. G. Campbell], "Early English Presbyterianism and the Reformed Church of France," *Journal of the Presbyterian Historical Society of England* 2 (1922): 133.

80. William Park Armstrong, ed., *Calvin and the Reformation: Four Studies by Émile Doumergue, August Lang, Herman Bavinck, Benjamin B. Warfield* (New York: Fleming H. Revell, 1909).

81. "Dons reçus de 1923 à 1929 pour la maison de Calvin et la musée Calvin à Noyon," *BSHPF* (1930): 352. I am grateful to Sébastien Fath for this reference.

82. David W. Bebbington, *Holiness in Nineteenth-Century England* (Carlisle: Paternoster, 2000), ch. 4.

83. *P&T*, October 1930, 74.

84. *P&T*, January 1929, 14.

85. *P&T*, January 1937, x.

86. *P&T*, January 1918, 16.

87. *P&T*, July 1923, 28.

88. *P&T*, January 1928, 9.

89. *P&T*, October 1929, 83–85, quoted at 84.

90. *The Reformed Faith Commonly Called Calvinism: Report of the International Conference held in May, 1932* (London: Sovereign Grace Union, n.d.), 6.

91. *P&T*, October 1931, 67.

92. *P&T*, October 1936, vi.

93. *P&T*, March 1947, 28.

94. For example, at the Edinburgh 1938 conference: Alexander Ross, G. T. Thomson, and J. H. S. Burleigh. *P&T*, July 1938, 100–101.

95. *P&T*, July 1933, 3; April 1929, 39.

96. *P&T*, January 1936, 35.

97. *P&T*, January 1935, 3.

98. George N. M. Collins, *Donald Maclean, D. D.* (Edinburgh: Lindsay, 1944), 73; *Monthly Record of the Free Church of Scotland*, November 1928, 270.

99. Donald Maclean, *Aspects of Scottish Church History* (Edinburgh: T. & T. Clark, 1927), 29.

100. Donald Maclean, "Influence of Calvinism on Scottish Politics," *Monthly Record*, December 1927, 291, 292; March 1929, 64; April 1929, 85, 87. I am grateful to Ken Roxburgh for drawing my attention to this source.

101. Donald M. Maclean, *The Revival of the Reformed Faith* (London: Inter-Varsity Fellowship, 1938), 6, 13–14.

102. Alexander Smellie, *The Reformation in its Literature* (London: Andrew Melrose, 1925), 186.

103. David S. Cairns, *Life and Times of Alexander Robertson MacEwan, D. D.* (London: Hodder & Stoughton, 1925), 167.

104. Douglas Murray, *Freedom to Reform: The "Articles Declaratory" of the Church of Scotland, 1921* (Edinburgh: T. & T. Clark, 1993), 144.

105. F. J. S[mithers] in *Journal of the Presbyterian Church of England* 4 (1930): 183.

106. *P&T*, July 1938, 101.

107. Arthur Dakin, *Calvinism* (London: Duckworth, 1940), 211–12, 223–29.

108. *P&T*, April 1925, 34–35, quoted at 34.

109. Maclean, *Aspects*, 113–14.

110. *P&T*, July 1938, 101.

111. Irwin, *Calvin*, 197.

112. Irwin, *Calvin*, 142, ch. 11.

113. James Orr, "Calvinism," in *Encycolpaedia of Religion and Ethics*, 12 vols., ed. James Hastings (Edinburgh: T. & T. Clark, 1910), 3: 148.

114. Adam M. Hunter, *The Teaching of Calvin: A Modern Interpretation* (Glasgow: Maclehose, Jackson, 1920), 3.

115. Dakin, *Calvinism*, 235–36.

116. Dafydd Densil Morgan, *The Span of the Cross: Christian Religion and Society in Wales*, 1914–2000 (Cardiff: University of Wales Press, 1999), 203–04.

117. Maclean, *Revival*, 9–10.

118. Alister E. McGrath, *T. F. Torrance: An Intellectual Biography* (Edinburgh: T. & T. Clark, 1999).

119. Thomas F. Torrance, *Calvin's Doctrine of Man* (London: Lutterworth Press, 1949), 8.

120. *P&T*, January 1937, 3.

121. Nathaniel Micklem, "The Genevan Inheritance of Protestant Dissent—The Present Need to Affirm It," *Hibbert Journal* 25 (1937): 193–204.

122. Quoted from John S. Whale, *Christian Doctrine (1941)* in P&T, January 1943, 15; Micklem, "Genevan Inheritance," 200.

123. *P&T*, July 1948, 76.

124. David Martyn Lloyd-Jones, *The Puritans: Their Origins and Successors* (Edinburgh: Banner of Truth Trust, 1987), 379; Iain H. Murray, *David Martyn Lloyd-Jones: The Fight of Faith, 1939–1981* (Edinburgh: Banner of Truth Trust, 1990), 194.

125. Martyn Lloyd-Jones, *Knowing the Times: Addresses Delivered on Various Occasions, 1942–1977* (Edinburgh: Banner of Truth Trust, 1989), 35, quoted by Murray, *Lloyd-Jones: Fight of Faith*, 195.

126. *Church of England Newspaper*, January 4, 1963, 3.

127. Geoffrey Williams, "The Revival of Nations: Flames Worth Fanning," *Cylchgrawn Cymdeithas Hanes y Methodistiad Calfinaidd = The Journal of the Historical Society of the Presbyterian Church of Wales* (June 1943): 70.

128. Lloyd-Jones, *Puritans*, ix.

129. Noel Gibbard, *The First Fifty Years: The History of the Evangelical Movement of Wales,* 1948–98 (Bridgend: Bryntirion Press, 2002).

130. James I. Packer, "Calvin: A Servant of the Word," in *Able Ministers of the New Testament: Papers Read at the Puritan and Reformed Studies Conference, December* 1964, (London: The Evangelical Magazine, 1965(?)), 44.

131. James I. Packer, *Knowing God* (London: Hodder and Stoughton, 1973).

132. Henry Frederick R. Catherwood, *The Christian in Industrial Society* (London: Tyndale Press, 1964), 6, appendix.

133. A. N. Triton [Oliver Barclay], *Whose World?* (London: Inter-Varsity Press, 1970).

134. John Stott, *Issues Facing Christians Today* (Basingstoke: Marshalls, 1984), xi.

135. Alan Storkey, *A Christian Social Perspective* (Leicester: Inter-Varsity Press, 1979), 133–34.

136. "CSU Booklist," typescript (n. p., 1984).

137. *The Papers of Sir Frederick Catherwood,* http://janus.lib.cam.ac.uk/db/node .xsp?id=EAD%2FGBR%2F0014%2FCATH.

138. Thomas H. L. Parker, *The Oracles of God: An Introduction to the Preaching of John Calvin* (London: Lutterworth Press, 1947), 11.

139. Thomas H. L. Parker, *John Calvin: A Biography* (London: J. M. Dent & Sons, 1975), vi, xi.

140. Paul Helm, "Calvin and Natural Law," *Scottish Bulletin of Evangelical Theology* 2 (1984): 5–22, subsequently partly incorporated into Helm, *John Calvin's Ideas* (Oxford: Oxford University Press, 2006), esp. vii, 1–9.

141. Alister McGrath, *The Intellectual Origins of the European Reformation* (Oxford: Blackwell, 1987), 107.

142. Parker, *Calvin,* xi.

143. Callum G. Brown, *The Death of Christian Britain: Understanding Secularisation: 1800–1900* (London: Routledge, 2000).

144. Alister E. McGrath, *A Life of John Calvin: A Study in the Shaping of Western Culture* (Oxford: Blackwell, 1990), chs. 11, 12, quoted at 219.

145. Peter Brierley, ed., *UK Christian Handbook Religious Trends No. 2* (London: Christian Research, 1999), 8, 17.

146. Peter Brierley, *The Tide Is Running Out: What the English Church Attendance Survey Reveals* (London: Christian Research, 2000), 27; Peter Brierley, *Turning the Tide: The Challenge Ahead* (London: Christian Research, 2003), 15, 65; Brierley, *Religious Trends,* 12–13.

147. Brierley, *Turning the Tide,* 66.

148. Murray, *Freedom to Reform,* chap. 6.

149. See http://news.scotsman.com/obituaries/James-Philip.5104821.jp, accessed May 19, 2009.

150. See http://www.reform.org.uk/pages/covenant/intro.php, accessed May 19, 2009.

151. Alan Munden, *A Light in a Dark Place: Jesmond Parish Church, Newcastle upon Tyne* (Newcastle upon Tyne: Clayton Publications, 2006), 228–29.

152. De Niet, Paul, and Wallet, introduction to *Sober, Strict and Scriptural,* 11, 14.

153. *British Weekly,* May 13, 1909, 129.

15 Calvin(ism) and Apartheid in South Africa in the Twentieth Century

The Making and Unmaking of a Racial Ideology

JOHN W. DE GRUCHY

Calvin's legacy is always mediated through communities of faith that claim him as their chief reforming ancestor. In South Africa, as elsewhere, that legacy was originally planted by various ecclesial and colonial settler communities, as well as mission societies, coming from different European countries. Although the Dutch part of the Reformed family has been dominant, this diversity of origin has meant that other theological interpretations and historical embodiments of Calvinism have also taken root. But even within the Dutch Reformed Church and its sister churches, Calvinism has found different expressions. In addition to this already complex scenario that has unfolded over almost four centuries, the demography of Calvinism as embodied in various Reformed churches has shifted considerably during the past century. Today it reflects the ethnic diversity that contemporary South Africa represents. All of this has to be kept in mind as we consider the ways in which Calvin(ism) has contributed to the making and unmaking of apartheid. Our subject, then, is complex, defying neat analysis or simple lines of enquiry whether historical, sociological, or theological. Held together by some common threads or family resemblances, Calvinism in South Africa is not a seamless garment but a patchwork quilt roughly woven together and, in some places, badly soiled and in need of repair. There are perhaps as many reasons to decry Calvinism's significance in South African history as there are to regard it as in some ways formative. But one way or another it cannot be ignored when it comes to understanding the making and unmaking of apartheid both as an ideology and as a social reality. In telling the story, I will unpack its paradoxes, indicating its role as providing both theological legitimatization for and critique of apartheid, as promoting both racial segregation and reconciliation, and as serving as both a reactionary force and a prophetic, progressive movement of social transformation.

■ THE PLANTING OF CALVINISM

In 1652, the Dutch East Indies Company established an outpost at the Cape of Good Hope for the purpose of providing a safe haven and source of fresh food for its ships en route to Batavia. As part of this venture the commander of the outpost,

Jan van Riebeeck, was instrumental in planting the established Netherlands Reformed Church in the infant colony. For the next century and a half this infant Dutch colonial church expanded along with the colony. Congregations were established in every town and village as the settlers advanced into the hinterland. Presbyteries and synods followed, and so the Dutch Reformed Church (DRC) at the Cape took root. No other church denomination, confession, or religious faith was allowed public expression, even though there were Catholics and Lutherans as well as Muslims and Jews living in the colony. Even the refugee French Huguenots, who arrived at the Cape in 1688, had to surrender their identity and become subsumed within Dutch settler society and its church. In short, the DRC represented Christendom. Served by ministers trained in Holland, it sought to remain faithful to its confessions, the Belgic and Heidelberg, and to the decrees of the Synod of Dort, which encapsulated the doctrines and spirit of much of Dutch Calvinism. All of this meant that in the formative hundred and fifty years of Christianity in what was to become South Africa, it was embodied and expressed through this particular brand of Calvinism and subject in significant measure to the vagaries of what happened to it in the Netherlands.

But this Calvinism was also mediated by the colonial encounter with indigenous peoples. On the basis that all European settlers who were part of the Reformed faith were Christians from birth by virtue of God's covenant, they represented the new Israel entering a land of promise surrounded by heathendom.[1] This meant that whereas the settlers were God's chosen or elect people, the indigenous peoples were alienated from God. Settler expansion was undoubtedly motivated by economic considerations, chiefly the hunger for land along with a desire to be independent of too much control. But the ideology was provided by readings of the Old Testament that confirmed both the Christendom paradigm and the way in which the colonists experienced and interpreted their hostile environment. What we now refer to as race relations was, thus, initially, determined by religion, and religion meant Dutch Calvinism in the process of reinvention in order to fit the context in which it was taking root.

There was a problem, however, that complicated this neat formula. What was the position of those indigenous people who converted to Christianity, something that increasingly happened as a result of sporadic missionary activity? And what about conversions among the slaves, most of whom had been imported from the East Indies? The Synod of Dort, which was definitive for the Dutch Reformed Church, had decided that slaves who were converted had to be set free. But did this mean that they, thereby, became part of the covenantal community, and if so, what were the social implications? In due course, as the number of converts increased, this led to a weakening of the notion that what separated the ethnic communities was religion; the real reason for keeping apart was social identity, and this was demarcated by racial difference.

This development was critical, but it was based neither on the Reformed confessions nor Calvin's teaching. Calvin had explicitly spoken of the unity of the church as transcending the barriers of *ethnici* and had even declared that Muslims and non-Europeans (he used the word "Barbarians") were the brothers and neighbors of Christians.[2] But it is in this shift from religion as the boundary line between settlers and the indigenous population to race and ethnicity as the demarcation barrier that we discern the beginnings of the shift from Dutch Calvinism as such to what was to become Afrikaner Calvinism. While the official theology of the DRC remained the same, the way in which this was understood was determined by what was happening on the ground rather than by what was being debated in the theological corridors of Leiden. And after a hundred and fifty years of relative isolation from external influence, that ground was in the process of shifting rather dramatically. In the process an alternative brand of Calvinism arrived at the Cape, and Afrikaner Calvinism itself underwent several mutations.

■ AN ALTERNATIVE CALVINISM TAKES ROOT

The waning of Dutch political and mercantile power toward the end of the eighteenth century, and the waxing of British colonial expansion, especially after the defeat of Napoleon, had a decisive impact on the Cape colony. While the Dutch authorities had allowed the Lutherans to build a church in Cape Town in 1780, it was only under governor Jacob Abraham de Mist during the period of Batavian rule (1803–6) between the first (1795–1803) and second British occupations of the Cape, that all restrictions on non-DRC churches and non-Christian religions were lifted. This policy was adopted by the British authorities from 1806 onward. Along with this development several other factors began to play a key role in shaping colonial society, largely as a result of the European Enlightenment, the French Revolution, and the evangelical revivals of the eighteenth century.

The rise of a more liberal theology in the church in Holland had its repercussions at the Cape in an ongoing struggle within the DRC between those adhering strictly to the Reformed confessions and those who were more liberal. The conservatives won the battle, a victory that had long-lasting results on the ethos of the DRC. In this struggle, the conservatives were strengthened and led by several expatriate Scottish ministers who had come to the Cape to serve the DRC after the British took control. As a result the DRC became strongly influenced by evangelical pietism and began to engage in more concerted missionary initiatives among the indigenous population. Thus, Afrikaner Calvinism became not only theologically conservative but also evangelical, pietist, and missionary minded at virtually the same time. The Theological Seminary established in Stellenbosch in 1859 became the center in which this process found its theological home, increasingly isolated from more progressive developments in the Netherlands.

Meanwhile, the evangelical revival in Britain, along with similar movements elsewhere in Europe, led to the birth of the Protestant missionary movement and the arrival of a stream of missionaries at the Cape. Among the first of these missionaries was Dr. Johannes van der Kemp of the London Missionary Society (LMS). A Dutchman by birth, van der Kemp was both a medical doctor and a highly trained theologian and biblical scholar. While open toward people of other Christian traditions, he was a convinced Calvinist, strongly committed to the Reformed faith. Within a few years of his arrival, he married an indigenous woman, thereby demonstrating that his religious convictions did not have racist overtones. Another missionary of the LMS, James Read, not only had similar liberal views but was also the founder of the Calvinist Society in Cape Town in 1804. The superintendent of the LMS in the colony, John Philip, who came several years later, was the leader of the antislavery abolitionist movement and, as such, played a key role in the freeing of the slaves in 1834. All of these missionaries were Calvinist evangelicals and founders of the Congregational Church denomination in South Africa. But because of their views about slavery and race, they were regarded by Afrikaner Calvinists then, and during the years to follow right through to the demise of apartheid, as liberal enemies of both the state and true religion.

During the course of the nineteenth century other Calvinist or Reformed missionary societies established work in southern Africa alongside settler Presbyterian and Congregational congregations: these included the Church of Scotland Mission, the Swiss Mission, and the Paris Evangelical Mission. There were also pockets of Calvinism within other settler denominations that emerged within South Africa, such as the Baptists and the Church of England.[3] All of these expanded both the character and the demography of the Reformed tradition in southern Africa, representing as they did different trajectories within Calvinism and working, as they also did, among different indigenous ethnic communities. The overall result was that by the mid-to-late nineteenth century, the Reformed tradition in South Africa was no longer coterminous with the increasingly monolithic DRC or European settlers. At the same time, most of these other Reformed churches felt less and less able to identify themselves as Calvinist because of the way in which that term had been appropriated within Afrikanerdom, associated as it was with both its nationalist aspirations and its racial attitudes.

■ AFRIKANER NEO-CALVINISM

We must now return to developments in the DRC, and especially events that followed the Great Trek of 1838. This migration into the interior was partly triggered by the freedom of the slaves, something that was regarded by those who trekked as a threat to Afrikaner Calvinist identity. In the process, a new Reformed church was also established beyond the Cape colony, the Nederduitsch Hervormde Kerk, that was adamant that people of color could not be members. But even for those who remained at the Cape, what to do about the increasing number of indigenous converts who attended worship in Dutch Reformed congregations was highly problematic. This was especially the case when it came to the celebration of Holy Communion. Several synods debated the issue, always resolving that the unity of the church, as Calvin and the confessions insisted, took precedence over matters of ethnicity and race.

But finally the synod of 1857 decided that for the sake of those white congregants who could not take communion together with their colored fellow Christians it was permissible to establish separate congregations, even though it was contrary to Calvin's teaching and the confessions. This is now regarded as the action that gave theological justification to what later became known as separate development or apartheid. If the church could develop along segregationist lines, then must that not also be appropriate for society as a whole? What was deemed to be permissible in 1857 soon became policy when separate synods were established in the DRC that prepared the way for independent Reformed denominations, beginning with the Dutch Reformed Mission Church in 1881.[4]

It is not possible within the scope of this essay to trace all the developments that eventually led to the rise of Afrikaner Nationalism and the policy of apartheid and how this was fed by and fed into Afrikaner Calvinism. I can simply recall the significance of the industrial revolution following the discovery of diamonds and gold, the Anglo-Boer war in 1899–1902, the "poor white" problem that resulted, the rise of African resistance to European hegemony, and cultural and political movements within Afrikanerdom itself as it emerged in resistance to English dominance. The latter were firmly, albeit informally, connected to the DRC. The truth is that Afrikaner Calvinism and its support for apartheid were shaped by many nontheological factors. At the same time, it was a Calvinism in search of a theological worldview that would provide legitimacy and direction. And one was at hand in the form of the Dutch theologian and statesman Abraham Kuyper's neo-Calvinism.

The formation of the Gereformeerde Kerken in the Netherlands in 1886, led by Kuyper in reaction to liberalism in the established Netherlands Reformed Church, led to the establishment of the hyper-Calvinist Gereformeerde Kerk, which regarded the DRC as having succumbed to evangelical Pietism and thus departed from true Calvinism. But more significantly, Kuyper's influence eventually spread to the DRC itself. Students for the ministry went to study at the Free University of Amsterdam, where they came under Kuyper's spell and read Calvin through his eyes and that of his colleague Herman Bavinck. In particular, his notion of "sphere sovereignty," which posited that God ruled the world directly in relation to each area of life (politics, culture, education, church, etc.), was used somewhat incorrectly not only to defend the identity of ethnic groups as political, cultural, and religious entities but to do so in a way that led to racial segregation and domination. In this way, a distorted neo-Calvinism gave theological justification to apartheid.[5]

The evangelical pietists within the DRC were no theological or political match for the neo-Calvinist Kuyperians, whose philosophy and theological system appeared to be so systematically constructed on biblical principles. The evangelicals' energy was channeled far more into missionary work, evangelism, and congregational life rather than the cultural and political spheres. The neo-Calvinists, by contrast, through their conferences and publications, such as the influential *Koers in die Krisis*,[6] increasingly won the battle for the theological and intellectual high ground. By the 1930s, Afrikaner Nationalism and Kuyperian neo-Calvinism were so wedded that by the end of the Second World War there was very little that separated Afrikaner nationalism and the DRC. The Afrikaner version of neo-Calvinism's notion of "sphere sovereignty" also provided a theological rationale for the DRC that sought to influence society and politics and yet refrain from speaking prophetically to the state.

Undoubtedly the Dutch Reformed theologian who was most influential in providing a neo-Calvinist apologia for apartheid was F. J. M. Potgieter who, from 1946 to 1977, taught at the Faculty of Theology in Stellenbosch. Potgieter was a student at the Free University of Amsterdam in the late 1930s, where he was strongly influenced by Kuyper and Bavinck, through whose eyes he read and interpreted Calvin.[7] Potgieter not only influenced generations of students for the ministry of the DRC, but he also played a key role in the drafting of synodical documents that provided the theological rationale for apartheid. Highly critical of Karl Barth's doctrine of Holy Scripture, his approach to the biblical text was basically fundamentalist, drawing on the work of very conservative scholars in Holland and North America. Thus, on the basis of a few biblical texts, such as the story of the Tower of Babel, he was able to construct a defense of racial segregation both in church and society. And anything that had even the faintest smell of liberalism, humanism, Roman Catholicism, Marxism, or for that matter, Barthianism came under his polite but severe judgment.

By the 1960s, Calvinism was widely understood, whether on the part of black South Africans, white English-speaking liberal Protestants, or Catholics both Anglican and Roman, as the creed that legitimized apartheid. Indeed, the Anglo-Catholics saw Calvinism and Catholicism as diametrically opposed.[8] Alan Paton, the distinguished author and himself an Anglican layman, put it starkly: "It would almost seem as though Dutch Reformed Calvinist man and Catholic man in South Africa are two different creatures with different and irreconcilable ways of looking at man and the world."[9] This contrasting image prevailed widely and, generally speaking, has still not been corrected, let alone expunged. For the vast majority in South Africa, Calvinism means bad religion, and Calvin, in his own right, is little known except as someone who, it is assumed, taught a perverted racist understanding of Christianity. And yet it is also true, even though it has not reached down into the collective consciousness of South Africans, that theological and church resistance to apartheid, as much earlier to slavery, was also associated with Calvinist and Reformed Christians. This brings us to the role of Calvin and Calvinism in the unmaking of the ideology of apartheid.

■ CALVIN(ISM) AND THE CRITIQUE OF APARTHEID

Long before apartheid became the official policy of the South African government in 1948, there had been Christian opposition to racial segregation. This, as we have seen, can be traced back to the early days of the struggle against slavery by some of the missionaries of the LMS. But what is sometimes overlooked is the role of Christian leaders in the formation of the African National Congress in 1912, several of whom were ministers of churches within the Reformed family, John Dube, a Congregationalist, being the first but not the only one. Dube might have hesitated to call himself a Calvinist given the way in which that term had been abused, but he was a product of the American Board Mission as, too, was Chief Albert Luthuli several decades later. The fact is, whether or not the name of Calvin or the term "Calvinism" was operative, leaders such as these were shaped and formed within that tradition. African leaders may not have been too bothered by the theological niceties that distinguished Calvinists from Arminians, Lutherans, or Anglicans, but those who taught them in the missionary-founded institutions of Lovedale, Tiger Kloof, and Adams College were invariably Calvinist in outlook, albeit of a different stamp to that of Afrikaner Calvinism.

But the Calvinist critique of apartheid was not confined to such voices or institutions. Already in 1952, the DRC professor of missions at Stellenbosch Ben Marais, a colleague of Potgieter, the theological apologist for apartheid, had written a book entitled *Colour: The Unsolved Problem of the West*. Although this was not a direct attack on apartheid, Marais was critical of racial segregation as un-Christian and unjust, as were some DRC missionaries who were daily in contact with African society increasingly feeling the brunt of Afrikaner political power and its policies. A few years later, in 1956, the senior professor of theology at Stellenbosch, Professor B. B. Keet, made a more unequivocal critique of apartheid in *Suid-Afrika-waarheen?* (Whither South Africa?) that sent shock waves through the ranks of the DRC even though it did not immediately achieve the result he had hoped. But these Calvinist voices indicated the emergence of theological dissent against apartheid within the DRC and Afrikanerdom. And the influence of Keet and Marais among some of their students would grow in significance, though for a long period of time not to the same extent as Potgieter's.

It is important at this point to note the influence of Reformed theologians from beyond South Africa who were also becoming critical of apartheid, not least in Holland itself. Theological students from the DRC who did further study in the Netherlands were, at least in certain of the faculties, being introduced to a Calvin that had been largely suppressed in their training, and they were also being introduced to a Karl Barth they had previously known only in largely negative terms. Already in his book *Colour: The Unsolved Problem of the West*, Ben Marais had quoted Barth's categorical rejection of racial segregation whether in church or society based on a questionnaire he had sent to the Swiss theologian. Barth's only comment on South Africa in his *Church Dogmatics* makes the same point.[10]

The conflict over the interpretation of Calvin as represented, on the one hand, by neo-Calvinist Kuyperians like Potgieter and, on the other hand, by B. B. Keet and those around him had much to do with the reception of Karl Barth's theology. This is clear from several of Keet's addresses at Stellenbosch, notably on the occasion of the one hundredth anniversary of the Faculty of Theology in 1959, which also marked the beginning of his retirement.[11] Speaking on the development of theology over the past century, he ended with a plea to his large audience of DRC church leaders and ministers to take Barth more positively and seriously. He alluded to the significance of Barth's theology in the church struggle in Nazi Germany, and especially highlighted Barth's approach to scripture as witness to Jesus Christ as Word of God. In clear opposition to Potgieter, Keet insisted that the Bible is not to be understood in a fundamentalist way but as a witness to Jesus Christ as the Word of God. The subtext to his speech was undoubtedly his conviction that the Bible had been abused within the DRC in its defense of apartheid.

Barth's influence mediated through theologians in Holland, as well as through his own writings and more directly by students who studied in Basel, was a critical factor in enabling some DRC theologians to rediscover Calvin. The numbers were small, but significant. And none was more significant than Beyers Naudé, who was to become the widely acknowledged leader of the church struggle against apartheid. The extent to which Naudé's witness helped to change the image of Calvinism in South Africa can be judged from the words of the Roman Catholic archbishop of Durban, Denis Hurley who, in paying tribute to Naudé, referred to him as a "Catholic Calvinist."

A student of B. B. Keet's at Stellenbosch, Naudé became increasingly aware of the injustices of apartheid during the late 1950s, not least through his exposure to the story of the confessing church in Germany and the contribution made to it by Barth and Dietrich Bonhoeffer. In fact, he like others saw a close parallel between the abuse of Kuyper's notion of the separation of spheres and the Lutheran "orders of creation" theology that the German Christians used to defend their adherence to Nazi ideology. But it was the Sharpeville Massacre in March 1960 that led him, by then a moderator with the DRC, to make a decisive break with his church's support of apartheid.[12] In the process, he established the Christian Institute (CI) in 1963, an ecumenical organization, but one initially aimed at bringing about change in the DRC and providing a platform for dissenting voices within its ranks. That there was growing dissent is evident from various publications at the time such as *Delayed Action!* in 1961. At least in the initial years of the CI, its journal *Pro Veritate* carried articles both on the confessing church in Germany and on Calvin and his relevance for the struggle against injustice in South Africa. This would eventually become an inspiration for many others both within and beyond the various Reformed churches in the country.

André Biéler's important study of *The Social Humanism of Calvin* played an important role in enabling some of us in the 1960s within the circles of the CI to rediscover Calvin's role as a social prophet within his own context. Biéler, in fact, published two further articles at the time in which he spoke directly to us in South Africa, one entitled "True Calvinism" and another his "Letter to Capitalist Christians."[13] Rather than assuming that Calvin was a defender of the social status quo and somehow responsible for the rise of capitalism, we discovered that he was a champion of refugees, the weak, and the poor, and critical of the powerful and the wealthy. We also discovered that his attack on idolatry was not just on images in the church but on the abuse of power by the state. But it also became clear to us that Calvin's understanding of the sovereignty of God meant that every aspect of life was under God's rule and, moreover, contrary to Kuyper, it was the church's responsibility to speak prophetically to the state and to society at large about justice and to do so in ways that were specific and concrete. In this way, Calvin became a source of ideological critique and also a prophet of a society based on justice and the unity of humanity made in the image of God. This was revolutionary stuff, a far cry from the kind of Calvinism to which we were accustomed.

In 1968 Naudé was the moving force behind the drafting of *The Message to the People of South Africa*, a confession of faith that is sometimes likened to the Barmen declaration, although it is significantly different. It was not addressed just to the church but to society as a whole. Its theological critique was explicitly political. It was a categorical rejection of apartheid as a false gospel in contrast to the gospel of Christ—a gospel of reconciliation. Many critics of the *Message*, even some who were opposed to apartheid, thought that it overstepped the boundaries that separate faith and politics. But for Naudé and those who were involved in its drafting as well as the many who gave it their support, the *Message* was a prophetic declaration that the gospel of Christ was not just a message of personal salvation or of relevance to the church but one that had direct implications for political and social life.

Naudé knew that publishing the *Message* and making such a prophetic statement was insufficient in itself. It demanded action, but also more than action. What was required was a comprehensive account of what the "gospel of reconciliation" required concretely in the various spheres of society. Liberation from apartheid was necessary, but more was demanded of Christian witness if the "promised land" was to flourish, just as for Calvin there was more to reforming the church and society than throwing off the shackles of Rome. Geneva had to be reconstructed. With this in mind, Naudé was the inspiration behind Spro-cas, an ecumenical Study Project on Christianity in Apartheid Society, which, during the years 1969–1973, sought to develop alternative policies and structures for South Africa on the basis of biblical principles—the need for transformation, a concern for life, the building of a participatory community, the stewardship of resources, and human worth.[14] The Beyers Naudé Centre for Public Theology at the University of Stellenbosch continues to keep this vision alive, and appropriately so. In this, and many others ways, Calvin's legacy continues to contribute to the humanizing of society through its witness to justice, reconciliation, and peace.

By the late 1970s and into the 1980s, younger voices within the DRC were beginning to speak critically against their church's legitimization of apartheid. In the forefront were those like W. D. Jonker of Stellenbosch, David Bosch of the University of South Africa, and Jaap Durand of the University of the Western Cape, a member of the DR Mission Church.[15] A more trenchant critique was that made by the Presbyterian minister and theologian Douglas Bax, whose book *A Different Gospel* challenged apartheid on the basis of Calvin's theology, the Reformed confessions, and a study of key biblical texts.[16] Although Bax's theological attack on apartheid from a Reformed platform was the most thoroughgoing, perhaps more significant were the voices that were emerging from within the black mission churches of the DRC family. Best known among these was Allan Boesak, whose book *Black and Reformed: Apartheid, Liberation and the Calvinist Tradition* claimed Calvin's legacy in the struggle against apartheid. Drawing on Calvin, Kuyper, Barth, and the Reformed Confessions, Boesak made it clear that the tradition, at its best, was on the side of the poor not the wealthy, the oppressed and not the oppressor.

A critical moment in the church struggle against apartheid came in 1977 when the sixth Assembly of the Lutheran World Federation, held in Dar-es-Salaam, declared that a "status confessionis" existed in South Africa, thereby rejecting any segregation in the life of the church. The notion of a "status confessionis," which Barth and Bonhoeffer had raised in Germany in the 1930s, now became part of the theological language in the wider church struggle. Inter alia, it became the rallying cry of ABRECSA, the Alliance of Black Reformed Christians in South Africa that drew its membership from all the Reformed churches in 1981, and then was affirmed by the World Alliance of Reformed Churches in Ottawa in 1982, and by many of the other Reformed churches in South Africa.[17]

This rallying cry was more than a rhetorical statement; it was a confessional statement, and it became the basis for the Belhar Confession of 1984 approved by the Synod of the DR Mission Church as one of its formal confessions of faith alongside those of the post-Reformation period. For the Belhar Confession not only rejected apartheid as irreconcilable with the gospel, it also made this confession the basis for the unity of the church. This was a highly significant development, not only because the Belhar Confession was the first new confession since the Reformation formally adopted by a Dutch Reformed Church but because it was clearly a confession that, on the basis of Reformed faith, dealt explicitly with a sociopolitical issue, namely, the policy of apartheid. As a result, it now became necessary for the unity of the Reformed family in South Africa to adopt this confession, something that has yet to happen within the white DRC. The influence of Calvin's ecclesiology can be clearly seen in this development. Not only did the Belhar Confession overturn the fateful synodical decision of 1857 that allowed segregation to develop into church policy, but it also bore witness more fundamentally to the doctrine of reconciliation that lies at the heart of the gospel.

■ CALVIN(ISM) AND POSTAPARTHEID SOUTH AFRICA

Calvin's concern to prevent both tyranny and anarchy led him tentatively toward giving his support to the foundations of what we now refer to as constitutional democracy, the cornerstone of the new South Africa. Only in this way can power be constrained and good governance implemented. Such constitutional democracy, while premised on the rule of the majority, is equally premised on the need to uphold certain values. For Calvin, these values were related to the "second use of the law," which governs civil authority. At the heart of these was a commitment to pursue justice and equity, which meant among other things to serve the interests of the poor and the refugee or "stranger in the midst." This is what André Biéler referred to as Calvin's social humanist vision, something far more consonant with social democracy than liberalism, and an economic system that controls as much as possible human greed. Such a vision of society is, in many respects, reflected in the new South African constitution, which is a remarkably progressive document representing what South Africans have struggled for in opposing apartheid as well as what we hope for in terms of the new South Africa.

The unmaking of apartheid will not be complete until a truly constitutional democracy rises in its place and the social and economic injustices of the past have been overcome. If we are true to the legacy of Calvin, those of us in the Reformed family can and must contribute to this project. I say this because there is a distinct temptation among some to withdraw into charismatic piety, focus solely on congregational life, or engage in reactionary politics based yet again on a false reading of Kuyper's doctrine of the sovereignty of God. The present, ongoing attempt to overcome racism and other divisive forces in the life of the church in bearing witness to God's reconciliation remains fundamental to its task in the building of a postapartheid church and society. This is the unity that the church is called to embody in its daily life and witness, and, as such, it is a political witness.

But there is equally the need to struggle against economic injustice and the poverty that results from it. Calvin's legacy also speaks directly to this demand. In addition, his particular concern for the plight of the many refugees who poured across the porous French border seeking a safe haven in Geneva speaks to the challenge facing us, and many other countries, today. In fact, my understanding of Calvin's ministry in Geneva was sharpened by the outbreak of xenophobic violence in some of South Africa's cities in the middle of 2008. There was an uncanny resemblance. And, certainly, the South African constitution insists on respect for ethnic identity and cultural diversity in such a way that all groups, including refugees, should have a sense of belonging and no group should have unbridled power to dominate others. At this point, we see the need to affirm both Calvin, the prophet of social justice, as well as the Calvin that we find, ironically now, in the writings of Abraham Kuyper. The one who insisted that unless nation building takes ethnic diversity and cultural pluralism seriously by being open toward others and inclusive of them, it is simply sowing the seeds for ongoing strife and conflict.[18]

If Barth warns us against the danger of ethnic chauvinism and nationalism, could it be that Kuyper helps us to think theologically constructively about ethnic diversity? The truth is, as Kuyper insisted in his context, unless nation building takes ethnic diversity and cultural pluralism seriously by being open toward them and inclusive of them, it is simply sowing the seeds for ongoing strife and conflict. Both unbridled liberalism and unchecked nationalism are socially destructive, leading either to the tyranny of individual material interests or that of majority group domination or to the anarchy that arises out of resistance either on the part of the poor or alienated minorities. So even as we rejected the abuse of Kuyper's neo-Calvinism in giving legitimacy to apartheid and racial privilege, some are now suggesting that we can learn from him about building a society in which diversity is allowed to enrich rather than divide, to renew rather than destroy.

In sum, reflection on Calvin's legacy mediated through various interpreters and traditions indicates that the tradition we associate with his name has clearly had an ambiguous history in South Africa, as it also had in Geneva itself in the sixteenth century. But there is much in his legacy that has contributed to the struggle for justice, and much that continues to prompt those within the Reformed tradition to contribute to the transformation of society through their witness to the gospel. For it is through the proclamation of the good news of God's reconciliation of the world in Christ, and the way that this is embodied in the life of the church and society, that the core remains of what Calvin and the Reformed tradition is about. This is not only an alternative Calvinism; from a South African perspective, it is authentic Calvinism.

■ Notes

1. Jonathan Neil Gerstner, *The Thousand Generation Covenant: Dutch Reformed Covenant Theology and Group Identity in Colonial South Africa, 1652–1814* (Leiden: Brill, 1991), 259.

2. Sermon on Galatians 6: 9–11, quoted in Eberhard Busch, "A General Overview of the Reception of Calvin's Social and Economic Thought," in *John Calvin Rediscovered*, ed. Edward Dommen and James D. Bratt (Louisville: Westminster John Knox Press, 2007), 75.

3. The Anglican Church in South Africa, officially known as the Church of the Province of South Africa, has been traditionally Anglo-Catholic in orientation, while the separated Church of England in South Africa is conservative, evangelical, and Calvinist.

4. D. G. Cloete and D. J. Smit, eds., *A Moment of Truth: The Confession of the Dutch Reformed Mission Church* (Grand Rapids: Eerdmans, 1982).

5. See George Harink, "Abraham Kuyper, South Africa and Apartheid," *Princeton Seminary Bulletin* 23 (2002): 184–87.

6. H.G. Stoker, F.J.M. Potgieter, and J.D. Vorster, eds., *Koers in die Krisis*, 3 vols. (Stellenbosch: Pro Ecclesia, 1935–41).

7. Potgieter's dissertation, "De Verhouding tussen die teologie en die filosofie by Calvyn" (Free University, Amsterdam, 1939) is mentioned in a footnote in François Wendel, *Calvin* (London: Collins Fontana, 1963), 33, n. 52. See also Hans S. A. Engdahl, *Theology in Conflict: Readings in Afrikaner Theology* (Frankfurt: Peter Lang, 2006).

8. See John W. de Gruchy, "Catholics in a Calvinist Country," in *Catholics in an Apartheid Society*, ed. Andrew Prior (Cape Town: David Philip, 1982), 67–82.

9. Alan Paton, *Apartheid and the Archbishop: The Life and Times of Geoffrey Clayton* (Cape Town: David Philip, 1973), 47.

10. Karl Barth, *Church Dogmatics* IV/1: *The Doctrine of Reconciliation* (Edinburgh: T. & T. Clark, 1961), 703.

11. "Die Onwikkling van die Teologie in 100 Jaar," address delivered at the Moederkerk in Stellenbosch, 1959.

12. Charles Villa-Vicencio and John W. de Gruchy, eds., *Resistance and Hope: South African Essays in Honour of Beyers Naudé* (Cape Town: David Philip, 1985); Colleen Ryan, *Beyers Naudé: Pilgrimage of Faith* (Cape Town: David Philip, 1990); *Many Cultures, One Nation: Festschrift for Beyers Naudé*, ed. Charles Villa-Vicencio and Carl Niehaus (Cape Town: Human & Rousseau, 1995).

13. André Biéler, *The Social Humanism of Calvin* (Richmond: John Knox Press, 1964), originally published in French as *L'humanisme social de Calvin* (Geneva: Labor et Fides, 1961); Biéler, "Calvinism in the Defence of Man," *South African Outlook*, August 1969, 124–25; and Biéler, "Letter to Capitalist Christians," *South African Outlook*, May 1976, 67.

14. See Peter Randall, *A Taste of Power* (Johannesburg: Spro-cas, 1973).

15. F. E. O'Brien Geldenhuys, Nico J. Smith, and Piet Meiring, eds., *Stormkompas* (Cape Town: Tafelberg, 1981); and Adrio König, David J. Bosch, and Willem D. Nicol, eds., *Perspektief Op die Ope Brief* (Cape Town: Human & Rousseau, 1982).

16. Douglas S. Bax, *A Different Gospel: A Critique of the Theology behind Apartheid* (Johannesburg: Presbyterian Church of Southern Africa, 1979).

17. *Apartheid Is a Heresy*, ed. John W. de Gruchy and Charles Villa-Vicencio (Cape Town: David Philip, 1983).

18. Peter S. Heslam, *Creating a Christian Worldview: Abraham Kuyper's Lectures on Calvinism* (Grand Rapids: Eerdmans, 1998), 268–70; and Charles Villa-Vicencio, "Aeolian Harp of Renewal: The Private and the Public in Political Engagement," *Princeton Seminary Bulletin* 26 (2005): 180–98.

He didn't say "I am prophet" but he did say a prophet is a mouthpiece for G's word and insist that he was a mouthpiece for G.

He, like Zwingli, works with a fluid notion of ministry, interchanging prophet + teacher.

■ INDEX

transcendent, God as, 238, 244, 276, 296
transubstantiation, 276
Transylvania, Reformed churches in, 132
Treaty of London (1831), 235
Trelcatius, Lucas, Jr., 185, 193, 200n84
Tremellius, Emmanuel, 113
Tridentine Reformation, 60, 163, 169,
    175–76, 257, 264
trinitarian theology, 41
    antitrinitarianism, 37, 132, 165, 204, 287
    Nicene, 90
    as unscriptural, 36–37
triumphalism, 167, 172
Troeltsch, Ernst, 23, 257, 260, 262, 263
Trolliet, Jean, 43n7, 111
Tronchin, Théodore, 113
true Calvinism, v. refined paganism, 217–18
Tuinman, Carolus, 209, 221n26
TULIP acrostic, 15, 143n108
Tulloch, John, 285, 287
Turrettini, François, 113, 182, 190–95,
    200n84
Turrettini, Jean-Alphonse, 208
Twisse, William, 189–90, 192
*The Two Reformations : Luther and Calvin:
    The Old and the New World*
    (Oberman), 159

Ultima Admonitio (Calvin), 129
underground congregations, resistance by,
    164, 176, 180
Union of Evangelical Churches, 232
Unitarians, 127, 131, 218, 287
United Christians party, 279
United Free Church, 289, 294, 296
United Secession Church, 288
universal salvation, 291
Ursinus, Zacharias, 20, 150,
    185, 193
usury, 24
Uytenbogaert, Johannes, 205, 273

Valla, Lorenzo, 75
van den Honert, Joan, 210–11
van der Kemp, Johannes, 308
van der Linde, Simon, 209
van der Os, Antoni, 212, 214
van Hemert, Paulus, 216
van Ruler, Arnold Albert, 277
Vatable, François, 187

Vaughan, Robert, 287
Venema, Herman, 210
Vermigli, Peter Martyr, 5, 13–14, 16, 73,
    123, 129, 131, 132
    Calvin and, 140n82, 192, 195
    Loci communes (Commonplaces), 17–18,
        150, 187
    predestination and, 136n38
vernacular literary style, 88–89, 209
Vestarian Controversy, 130
Vial, Marc, 36
Viénot, John, 234, 235
Viguié, Ariste, 240
Vincent, Samuel, 224
Vinet, Alexandre, 229, 237
Viret, Pierre, 36, 69, 72–73, 81n23, 123,
    130, 133
    De la vertu et usage du ministère, 120
visible church, 37–38, 46–50, 61n8, 194
Vitringa, Campegius, 210
Vlak, Johannes, 212
Voetianism, 210
Voetius, Gisbertus, 193
Voltaire, 24, 204–5, 215
von Mosheim, Johann Lorenz, 206, 209,
    219n15
Les vrais pourtraits des hommes illustres
    (Beza), 68
*Vray discours de la miraculeuse deliverance
    enouyee de Dieu à la ville de Geneve*,
    174f, 175

Wahrhaffte Bekanntnuss, 128
Walaeus, Antonius, 189, 193
Waldensians, 125, 145
Walker, Williston, 239
Warneck, Gustav, 279n2
Wars of Religion (1562–1598), 130
Watt, Joachim von, 33
Wattier, Albert, 238
Weber, Max, 25–27, 159, 257, 263, 295
    capitalism and, 23, 25, 262
    *The Protestant Ethic and the Spirit of
        Capitalism*, 23, 262
Weingarten, Hermann, 260
Weiss, Nathanaël, 233, 239, 250n79,
    253n114
welfare state, 261
Welsh Calvinistic Methodists, 289, 297
Wendel, François, 12, 195

CO 11:151 – Viret to Cal The magistrate learns
to revere the prophets.

+ April 1541 – CO 11:185–188 Ministers to Cal
Important – they compare Strasb. to Antioch +

CO 11:272 – Sept 1541 – Bucer to Myconius. He
urges Myc. to help Calvin who is being neglected by
many. He then declared they would rather
...in the tomb of the prophets than listen to the prophets
CO 11:343-43 compar. made w/ prophets + pagan

CO 12;12:73-74 Joannes Crispus equates C w/ prophets
CO 12:378 brief mention of false prophets. (for Calvin
CO 12:428(426-29) important ref. to the freedom
of prophecy (de libertate prophetiae) from Simon
Sulzerus to Calvin.